GORAIKŌ

Japan's National Security in an Era of Asymmetric Threats

W. LEE RADCLIFFE

ISBN-13: 978-1499118889
ISBN-10: 1499118880
Library of Congress Control Number: 2014909155
CreateSpace Independent Publishing Platform
North Charleston, South Carolina

To My Father,

for pointing the way

TABLE OF CONTENTS

Section 2: New National Security Structures

• • •

LIST OF ACRONYMS USED IN THIS BOOK

ADCCS	Assistant Deputy Chief Cabinet Secretary
AIP	Air-Independent Propulsion
ARC	Administrative Reform Council
ARPH	Administrative Reform Promotion Headquarters
ASDF	Air Self-Defense Force
ASO	Air Staff Office
ATS	Amphetamine-Type Substances
BADGE	Base Air Defense Ground Environment
C4ISR	Command, Control, Communications, Computers, Intelligence Surveillance, and Reconnaissance
CAP	Combat Air Patrol
CDAA	Circularly Disposed Antenna Array (sometimes called "elephant cages")
CIC	Cabinet Intelligence Council
CIRO	Cabinet Intelligence and Research Office
CIWS	Close-In Weapons System
CONSACM	Cabinet Office for National Security Affairs and Crisis Management
CSAO	Cabinet Security Affairs Office
DA	Defense Agency (also sometimes called the JDA or "Japan Defense Agency")
DPJ	Democratic Party of Japan
DPRK	Democratic People's Republic of Korea (North Korea)
DOD	Department of Defense
DCCS/CM	Deputy Chief Cabinet Secretary for Crisis Management
ERGM	Extended-Range Guided Munition
FTA	Free Trade Agreement
GAKRJ	General Association of Korean Residents in Japan (referred to as the *Chōsen Sōren* in Japanese)
FDL	Fighter Data Link
FDMA	Fire Disaster Management Agency
FIC	Fleet Intelligence Command
FTIO	Foreign Technology Intelligence Office
GSDF	Ground Self-Defense Force
GSO	Ground Staff Office
HUMINT	Human Intelligence

JAXA	Japan Aerospace Exploration Agency
JDA	Japan Defense Agency
JIC	Joint Intelligence Council
JSC	Joint Staff Council
JSP	Japan Socialist Party
JTIDS	Joint Tactical Information Distribution System
KEDO	Korean Peninsula Energy Development Organization
LDP	Liberal Democratic Party
MASINT	Measurement and Signature Intelligence
MDBP	Midterm Defense Buildup Plan
MHI	Mitsubishi Heavy Industries
MIDS	Multifunctional Information Distribution Systems
MOFA	Ministry of Foreign Affairs
MSDF	Maritime Self-Defense Force
MSO	Maritime Staff Office
NASDA	National Space Development Agency
NCCS	New Central Command System
NIS	National Intelligence Service (South Korea)
NLA	National Land Agency
NPA	National Police Agency
NPT	Nuclear Non-Proliferation Treaty
OSINT	Open Source Intelligence
PAC-3	Patriot Advanced Capability-3
PCO	Prefectural Cooperation Office
PLO	Prefectural Liaison Office
PMOR	Prime Minister's Official Residence (referred to as the *Kantei* in Japanese)
PSIA	Public Security Intelligence Agency
RARO II	Remote Aerial Refueling Operator II
RCCS	Regiment Command and Control System
RMA	Revolution in Military Affairs
SDF	Self-Defense Forces
SDP	Social Democratic Party
SIGINT	Signals Intelligence
SM-2/-3	Standard Missile-2/-3
TRDI	Technical Research and Development Institute
VLS	Vertical Launch System
V/STOL	Vertical/Short Take-Off and Landing

• • •

INTRODUCTION

Four Japan Coast Guard patrol ships traveled at high speed toward China's exclusive economic zone in the Sea of Japan, outpacing 15 other coast guard patrol vessels similarly heading west. The four ships pursued what appeared to be a large blue fishing vessel, but its abnormally high speed away from Japanese waters following attempts to hail it suggested the ship was involved in other, shadier activities. It was mid-afternoon in late December 2001, and the waves on the open sea were choppy as a cold wind blew from Siberia and Manchuria over the Korean peninsula towards the Japanese archipelago.

At 1312 that afternoon, the Japan Coast Guard patrol ship *Inasa* ordered the suspicious ship—the *Changyu 3705* or "long-haul fishing vessel 3705"—to stop, but it did not comply. The *Changyu* continued to flee the four patrol ships at a high rate of speed toward Chinese waters.[1]

Until that morning, the Japan Coast Guard and officials at the Prime Minister's new Crisis Management Center were unsure of the vessel's origin. Pictures sent from P-3Cs a day earlier of the vessel mingled with dozens of other Japanese fishing boats were indeterminate.[2] While Japan's Defense Agency had intercepted what it thought were coded messages similar to those used by North Korea, Japanese defense officials had neglected to inform the Japan Coast Guard or the Prime Minister's residence of that crucial but highly compartmented information.[3]

This was the third suspicious ship discovered in and around Japanese waters in a little over two years. While the first two suspicious ships escaped at similarly high speeds, Tokyo had since taken steps to prepare and was determined not to let this one escape.

Previously, the Japan Coast Guard could only fire warning shots at ships it wanted to stop and search.[4] Japanese lawmakers, however, had just passed revisions to the law allowing Japanese maritime units to fire directly on fleeing ships suspected to have committed a serious crime. The revisions also protected crew-members who fire on and injure crew of suspicious ships in the line of duty from criminal liability.[5]

It was a Saturday and the start of the year-end holiday season, therefore many high-ranking officials had already departed Tokyo on vacation. Chief Cabinet Secretary Yasuo Fukuda indicated from his Tokyo residence he would leave response to the situation to those "on the scene." His second-in-charge, Deputy Chief Cabinet Secretary Shinzo Abe—the grandson of a Japanese Prime Minister who would later serve in the post himself—returned from vacation in his hometown in Yamaguchi Prefecture to oversee the situation at the new Crisis Management Center at the Prime Minister's Official Residence, or *kantei*.[6]

Abe would later tell journalists that the *kantei* thought at one point that the ship could indeed be Chinese. The ship was moving slowly westward toward China until approached by the patrol ships, it was by then flying a PRC national flag at its stern, it had a Chinese name, it was painted blue in the style of Chinese fishing boats, and it was equipped with lamps for squid fishing.[7]

By early afternoon, however, it was obvious that the *Changyu* was not involved in any sort of fishing at all. Crew members were observed throwing large black bags overboard, jettisoning cargo they no doubt did not want discovered aboard their boat.[8] It entered China's Exclusive Economic Zone an hour after it was ordered to halt. Japan Coast Guard officials had been in contact with both the Chinese Coastal Defense Control Bureau and the South Korean Maritime Police Agency since that morning, but Japanese officials were increasingly nervous that firing on the

Changyu deep in China's EEZ might cause an international incident. Japan Coast Guard officials gave the order to fire warning shots to halt it for boarding.

Moreover, the Japan Coast Guard had flown two eight-man SSTs—"Special Security Team" special operations units—on a small jet to Kagoshima Airbase, where they were to be flown by helicopter to a large patrol ship and then transported to the scene. But the helicopters available at the Kagoshima Airbase could only carry a few of the men fully outfitted in gear to the waiting patrol ship several hundred kilometers away at a time. The helicopter would have to fly several roundtrips to the patrol ship, taking two to three hours. The teams would not have arrived in time, so the mission was aborted.[9] Had the team arrived in time and attempted to rappel onto the ship, however, their helicopter probably would have been shot out of the sky given the ship's significant arsenal, as Japanese crews chasing the *Changyu* were about to discover.

Six minutes after entering China's EEZ, the patrol ships fired warning shots at the *Changyu* in an effort to halt it for an inspection. The shots prompted a crewmember of the ship to wave a red PRC national flag, an attempted subterfuge to warn off the patrol ships.

The *Inasa* fired another round a minute later when the *Changyu* ignored the halt orders. The patrol ships then fired five warning shots within minutes of each other. In response this time, however, the crew of the *Changyu* retaliated. Two crew members, apparently hiding under a blanket on the deck of the ship, suddenly appeared and opened fire on the patrol ships. The crew of the *Inasa* fired its 20-mm guns at the stern of the ship 11 times—the first shots fired by the Japan Coast Guard directly targeting a suspect ship in the post-war era.[10] The *Changyu* caught fire and stopped briefly two minutes later. The crew of the *Changyu* turned the ship's stern to the wind while several crew members extinguished the fire with fire extinguishers and blankets. "They were well-trained," the *Mizuki*'s

Captain Kazuya Horii would later say.[11] The ship resumed its escape attempt, but it stopped again an hour later.

The patrol ships *Amami* and *Kirishima* carefully came alongside the wounded *Changyu* in an attempt to conduct a boarding operation while the *Inasa* covered their approach 300 meters away. The crew of the *Changyu* began firing at the ships, and the *Inasa* again fired its 20-mm gun in retaliation. Two or three crew of the *Changyu* fired shoulder-launched rocket-propelled grenades at the *Inasa*, and a streak of flames flew overhead milliseconds later. The projectiles just missed.[12] Infrared cameras recording the scene from the *Inasa* would later confirm the rocket attack.[13] Had the SSTs attempted to board the *Changyu* from helicopters hovering overhead, the crew almost certainly would have fired their RPGs or even heavier weapons discovered later to prevent a boarding from taking place.

The *Changyu*, to the surprise of the Japanese crews nearby, quickly began to sink, and it foundered mere minutes later. Evidence would later show that the crew of the *Changyu* scuttled their boat.

The *Inasa*'s captain, Akira Ishimaru, later said his crew fired 186 rounds from its 20mm gun, while a crew member of the *Amami* fired one shot with an automatic rifle. The *Inasa* in turn had been hit by gunfire at least 30 times, while the *Amami*'s bridge was pockmarked with at least 130 bullet holes.[14] The *Kirishima* had about 20 bullet holes in her mast and bridge. Two Japanese crew members were injured by shrapnel in their arms and heads during the exchange of fire and were airlifted to the island of Amami.[15] The JCG immediately began to recover bodies believed to be dead crewmembers. The first recovered body wore a red lifejacket had Korean Hangul characters printed on it.[16]

Nine months later, on September 11, 2002, Japan raised the 100-ton *Changyu* and transported the hull to shore.

Investigators confirmed that the ship was built for speed. The propeller blades were twice the size of normal propellers used on fishing boats, and the ship's keel was V-shaped, characteristic of high-speed boats—similar, in fact, to another vessel suspected of having delivered a large amphetamine shipment to six Japanese men on a fishing boat in the East China Sea.[17] Inside the ship, investigators found an arsenal of heavy weaponry. In addition to the small arms and SA-7 the crew used to shoot at the *Inasa*, investigators found an SA-16 mobile surface-to-air missile launcher, a powerful weapon used to shoot down helicopters and other aircraft by locking onto their heat sources using infrared sensors. A special rail used to support a ZPU-2 anti-air machine gun extended from the end of the bridge to the deckhouse.[18]

In a special launching compartment located in the stern of the ship, investigators found a smaller boat and an underwater scooter. This discovery demonstrated the ship's role in delivering small cargo and perhaps special operatives ashore clandestinely—and retrieving cargo and personnel from shore.[19] Investigators found three smaller craft onboard, including an inflatable, black rubber raft with outboard motor and a cylindrical underwater scooter ideal for launching special operatives ashore undetected. Two similar vehicles had been discovered by Japanese authorities since 1990, indicating previous incursions had taken place undetected.[20]

Tokyo would use the sinking of the *Changyu* as leverage to restart talks with Pyongyang. Talks would lead to the most breathtaking admission in decades: Kim Chong-il himself would admit that North Korea had kidnapped over a dozen Japanese and held them captive for decades.

• • •

Japan's national security posture has changed dramatically in the wake of multiple terrorist incidents and chemical and biological weapons attacks, territorial incursions, and missile and nuclear tests in Asia in the post-Cold War era.

Throughout the Cold War from the late 1940s until the early 1990s, Japan relied on the United States to provide for the bulk of its national security even as it grew to be among the largest economies in the world. Japan developed a limited conventional military capability centered on defending its northern territories from a Soviet invasion and protecting sea lanes until much larger US reinforcements arrived to meet the invading enemy—a strategy called *hoppō jūshi* or "emphasis on the northern areas." Much of Japan's conventional capability was not easily transported beyond its shores, as the country had built over 1,000 tanks and nearly as many howitzers to defend against what was assumed would be an invading Soviet heavy mechanized force on the relatively open plains of its northern island, Hokkaido, into the more mountainous main island of Honshu down to the Kanto plain and Tokyo. Japan maintained only limited transport capabilities and a naval capability to defend sea lines of communication in the Pacific region. Indeed, with most military equipment manufactured in Japan, Tokyo's defense policy primarily served to support the country's industrial base, a win-win for Japanese politicians who could claim to their constituents to be hawkish on national defense while expanding industrial capacity and creating jobs domestically. They could then claim Japan's defense policies were for domestic defense only, citing Article 9 of the country's post-war Constitution in which "the Japanese people forever renounce[d] war as a sovereign right of the nation," to avoid arousing concern among Asian neighbors that Japan was "remilitarizing."

Following the collapse of the Soviet Union in 1991-1992, however, Japan's security environment became much more unpredictable. Japan no longer faced the possibility of a large-scale conventional invasion as during the Cold War. Rather, Japan experienced a series of sudden national security events that were non-conventional and "asymmetric" in nature. The US Department of Defense's (DoD's) *Dictionary of Military and Associated Terms* defines "asymmetric" as "the application of dissimilar strategies, tactics, capabilities, and methods to circumvent or negate an opponent's strengths while exploiting his weaknesses."[21] State and non-state actors that resort to asymmetric courses of action seek to avoid force-on-force conflicts by employing or threatening to employ disruptive or catastrophic capabilities (such as cyber attacks or attacks employing chemical, biological, radiological, or nuclear weapons), or by resorting to irregular warfare or terrorism. And according to the DoD's *Combating Weapons of Mass Destruction*, "many actors seek asymmetric capabilities, like WMD, due to these weapons' ability to drastically alter any imbalance of conventional force. Such asymmetric capability may allow an actor to give them a strategic advantage and to influence public or political will, and coerce the United States or its friends and allies [such as Japan] with the threat of large-scale destruction."[22] Given its geography and population density, Japan was increasingly vulnerable to asymmetric threats in Asia.

Many of the national security events in and around Japan were asymmetric in nature and involved weapons of mass destruction, including the development of and increasingly belligerent threats invoking nuclear weapons, the testing of short- and medium-range missiles that could target increasing portions of Japan (and US forces stationed in the region), and the use of chemical and biological weapons. Other asymmetric events involved the employment of terrorist and guerrilla tactics by both state and non-state actors. And throughout this period Japan remained vulnerable to large-scale natural disasters, an ever-present non-conventional threat to

Japan's security. Because Japan's immature national security establishment and its limited Self Defense Forces were geared solely to defend against a limited conventional invasion primarily from the north, Tokyo was initially unprepared and unable to respond adequately to these new asymmetric challenges, and with each emerging event public calls for reforms grew louder. These post-Cold War national security events thus forced Tokyo to gradually reform its national security structure and its defense forces beginning in the late 1990s, and the process continues to this day.

This book details the major national security events impacting Japanese interests in the post-Cold War era between 1992 and 2006 and their effects on Tokyo's national security structures and defense forces. This era began with the emergence of a North Korea intent on developing nuclear weapons in 1992 and ended with North Korea's nuclear test in October 2006. Tokyo's first major crisis began when Pyongyang announced its intention to abrogate its membership in the Nuclear Non-Proliferation Treaty (NPT) to become a defacto nuclear weapons state in the early 1990s and soon thereafter conducted unannounced tests of short- and medium-range missiles dangerously close to Japanese territory. Unaccustomed to this new threat so close to its shores and paralyzed by political events at home, Tokyo was little prepared to formulate workable policy responses either alone or in tandem with the United States. As the North Korean crisis abated, another domestic national security event suddenly struck Japan's industrial heartland. A powerful earthquake devastated central Japan in the early morning hours on January 17, 1995. While Japan's Self-Defense Forces had conducted many relief missions throughout Japan in previous years and were prepared to respond to this crisis as well, Tokyo was once again preoccupied by political events and did not have access to timely information or to a real-time decision-making structure to manage a prompt and thorough response. Thus Tokyo wasted precious hours as policymakers waited for sufficient information to manage wide-scale relief efforts. The Kobe earthquake created the popular support necessary for Tokyo to begin to examine improvements in the country's crisis response capabilities.

Yet Tokyo had little time for the traditionally plodding, long-term review of national security policy in the aftermath of these two events. In March 1995, two months after the earthquake, a domestic religious cult released chemical weapons in the heart of Tokyo in an attempt to foment revolution and bring down the Japanese government. The cult had also conducted biological- and chemical-weapons attacks on a smaller scale in other areas of Japan that were ultimately unsuccessful, and it had murdered former cult members and their families in addition to targeting senior Japanese officials.

These attacks marked the beginning of a series of terrorist events impacting Japanese interests in the late 1990s. Less than two years after the cult attack, Japan was the target of another major terrorist event when, in December 1996, guerrilla forces in Peru stormed the Japanese Ambassador's residence during a party to celebrate the birthday of Japan's emperor. The resulting stand-off lasted more than four months, during which Tokyo was again powerless to respond. Not far from Japanese shores, in September 1996 and again in 1998 South Korea discovered miniature submarines had secretly transported dozens of North Korean special operations personnel into the country. Coinciding so closely with the seizure of the Japanese Ambassador's residence in Peru and given Japan's geographic proximity to the Korean peninsula, Tokyo was highly concerned that the Japanese homeland might be targeted with similar infiltrations as well. Persistent rumors of North Korean-sponsored kidnappings of Japanese citizens from villages on the Sea of Japan fed those concerns.

These concerns proved well-founded when, in early 1999, the Japan Coast Guard discovered what were believed to be two North Korean ships posing as fishing vessels off the Japanese coast. The disguised ships fled from the area at extremely high speeds when ordered to halt for inspections, and the ships were later thought to have entered a North Korean port. A repeat incident in 2001—described at the outset of this book—led to an exchange of heavy gunfire with Japan Coast Guard ships and, ultimately, the sinking of a disguised North Korean vessel. After Japan raised the ship a year later, Tokyo had conclusive evidence that the vessel was indeed from North Korea. Japanese authorities found heavy machine guns and anti-aircraft weapons on board, code material, and cell phones listing contacts in Japan. Moreover, in September 2002, North Korean leader Kim Chong-il personally admitted to visiting Japanese Prime Minister Koizumi that Pyongyang had indeed kidnapped a dozen Japanese citizens in the 1970s and 1980s. Thus, Japan had incontrovertible proof that North Korean agents had been active in and around Japan for at least thirty years, and as the 2001 sunken vessel indicated, North Korea continued to target Japan actively.

Moreover, regional powers demonstrated an increased willingness to use short- and medium-range missiles and WMD during this time as well. In March 1996, China conducted a series of missile tests and other military drills near Taiwan as an intimidation tactic ahead of Taiwan's first popular presidential election. At least one of the missiles landed near an inhabited Japanese island neighboring Taiwan. Two years later, during the "Summer of WMD" of 1998, India and Pakistan conducted tit-for-tat nuclear weapons tests, Iran conducted a series of missile tests, and North Korea followed by launching its longest-range missile to date, the Taepodong-1. The unannounced missile launch flew over the Japanese archipelago, causing unprecedented concern in Tokyo as North Korea now had a demonstrated capability to launch a ballistic missile that could target any part of the Japanese archipelago. Moreover, Tokyo believed the nuclear and missile tests in Asia were related, as North Korea was strongly suspected of engaging in technology exchanges with both Pakistan and Iran. Further heightening concern in Tokyo and elsewhere, North Korea announced in late 2002 that it had a nuclear weapons capability, and in early 2003 it again announced its intention to withdraw from the NPT. As the United States was increasingly engaged militarily in Afghanistan and in Iraq, North Korea continued to act provocatively, launching cruise missiles and showing signs of preparing for longer-range launches. By the summer of 2006, with North Korea getting little of what it demanded in regional negotiations, it tested another series of short- and medium-range missiles toward Japan, and in October 2006, it tested a nuclear device.

China itself was becoming an increasing concern for Tokyo, as it continued to increase its military budgets at double-digit rates throughout the 1990s and 2000s. Its maritime survey vessels methodically plied the waters around Japan while ignoring Tokyo's multiple requests for clarification of the ships' missions. By the early 2000s, Chinese naval vessels began to appear near Japanese waters as well, and in the most provocative incident to that point, a Chinese submarine passed unannounced through Japanese territorial waters in November 2004 without surfacing and in direct contravention of international maritime conventions. Chinese military commentators began to speak provocatively of Japan as the "first island chain" that blocked Chinese naval access to the Pacific and to the strategically important "second island chain" – Guam, and ultimately Hawaii and the US west coast.

In direct response to all of these events, Tokyo by the late 1990s began to reform its national security and intelligence structures to enable a near-real-time decision-making capability by policymakers. Tokyo took its first step in 1996 with an official examination of the entire government structure including its national security offices housed at the Prime Minister's Official Residence (PMOR). The following year, it established a special position at the PMOR devoted to crisis management, and Tokyo further streamlined and elevated national security decision making at the PMOR following a government-wide reorganization in 2000. By 2002, a completely remodeled PMOR featured a new high-tech "Cabinet Information Collection Center"—the PMOR's 24-hour operations center—and a dedicated Crisis Management Center. Tokyo also began to consolidate and improve its intelligence capabilities with the creation of the Defense Intelligence Headquarters in 1997 and the creation of the Cabinet Satellite Intelligence Center in 2001 in preparation for the launch of Japan's first reconnaissance satellites in 2003. Tokyo further upgraded its intelligence capabilities at the Ministry of Foreign Affairs with the establishment of the Intelligence and Analysis Service and at the National Police Agency with the establishment of the Foreign Affairs and Intelligence Department.

Tokyo began to reform its defense capabilities by 2000 as well, and within two years it stood up the country's first rapid reaction and counter-guerrilla forces focused on defending Japan's southwestern region. This was part of Tokyo's new national security strategy called *ritō bōei* or "remote island defense," a shift from the Cold War-era *hoppō jūshi.* The defense forces began to upgrade its C4ISR capabilities in pursuit of a "revolution in military affairs" in Japan, and in 2004 Tokyo approved the construction of regional missile defense systems. In 2007, Tokyo upgraded its Defense Agency to ministry status, lending the organization more bureaucratic clout and the ability to request its own budgets. Moreover, Tokyo by this time began the first serious discussion of offensive-based weapons to enable a basic preemptive strike capability.

Thus, following over a decade of national security events in the 1990s and early 2000s, Tokyo was at last becoming serious about its national security. With these continuing reforms, Japan is no longer powerless in the face of terrorist events or an incursion of its territorial spaces. Japan is still in the early stages of these reforms, however, and it will continue to improve its intelligence and defense capabilities in cooperation with its staunchest ally, the United States, and in tandem with other emerging allies such as Australia and India. Challenges certainly remain, most notably Japan's shrinking population and its burgeoning national debt. But despite these challenges, and in contrast to the go-go days through the 1980s when the economy was the sole focus, national security has become and will remain a major priority for Tokyo.

The era between 1992 and 2006 represents the *goraikō* or dawn of Japan's 21st century national security policies. *Goraikō* literally means "arrival of light" and is used particularly when watching from Mt. Fuji the first rays of sunlight crest over the horizon. The early- and mid-1990s in Japan represent the moments before dawn when the sky begins to lighten—national security events during that time caused policymakers and defense analysts to acknowledge that the Cold War era had ended and a new era was upon them. The Taepodong launch in 1998 and suspected special operations incursions in the late 1990s were the figurative first rays of light over the horizon, forcing policy makers to recognize the clear and growing asymmetric threats to Japan and to take the first concrete measures to deal with them. The continued maritime incursions, the return of kidnapped Japanese, continued missile tests and ultimately North Korea's test of a nuclear device created increased public support for national security reforms, putting Japan on a sustained path of strengthening its defense and national security structures despite the challenges posed by a rapidly graying society. Dawn has turned to day for Japan and for Asia.

SECTION 1:

History of Threats, 1992-2006

1) Japan's Evolving Threat Environment at the End of the Cold War

The western world experienced dramatic changes between 1989 and 1992. The Berlin Wall fell in November 1989, and East and West Germany were officially reunified a year later on November 9, 1990. The US military ousted Panamanian strongman Manuel Noriega during Operation Just Cause in December 1989, and he was ultimately sentenced to 40 years in prison for drug trafficking in the United States. Six months later, Saddam Hussein's army, the fourth-largest in the world, invaded neighboring Kuwait on August 2, 1990, only to be pushed back to Baghdad by US and coalition forces in the subsequent "Desert Storm" six months later. Shortly thereafter, an attempted coup d'état in Moscow failed in August 1991 as a defiant Russian Federation president, Boris Yeltsin, would not yield to coup leaders. The Soviet Union did not survive the coup, however, and on December 8 Yeltsin and his counterparts in Ukraine and Belarus signed the Belavezha Accords which declared the Union dissolved. Soviet leader Mikhail Gorbachev resigned as president of the USSR on December 25, and the Supreme Soviet dissolved itself the next day. The Soviet Union officially ceased to exist, and the Cold War was over. Former Soviet states Ukraine and Kazakhstan gave up any pretensions of becoming nuclear states when they voluntarily relinquished their Soviet-era nuclear arsenals. South Africa also announced the dismantlement of its nuclear bombs. Israeli and Palestinian officials entered into peace talks at Madrid and Oslo that would become a formal peace agreement in 1993. A new world order—and with it a seemingly more stable security environment—was taking shape.

In East Asia, however, little changed. Two major communist regimes continued their autocratic rule. As Gorbachev released the Soviet grip on Europe, student protests in Beijing's Tiananmen Square that began in mid-April 1989 ended less than two months later when People's Liberation Army soldiers and tanks forcefully drove out the student-protestors on the night of June 3 and early June 4. Hundreds were killed and thousands more were injured. Every year since the 1989 Tiananmen massacre, increases in China's military budgets have outstripped the country's substantial economic growth. The Democratic People's Republic of Korea—North Korea—remained the world's most notable Stalinist regime, where millions would die of starvation in the 1990s even as the country maintained over a million soldiers in uniform. Moreover, while former Soviet states and South Africa gave up their nuclear arsenals and joined the Nuclear Nonproliferation Treaty as non-nuclear states, suspicions deepened concerning North Korea's nuclear ambitions in the late 1980s and early 1990s. North Korea was a major player in the proliferation of missile technologies to other suspect regimes in Iran, Pakistan, and Syria.

There were numerous border disputes in Asia as well, and Communist leaders in Beijing and Pyongyang even claimed the right to rule over their democratizing neighbors, the Republic of China (Taiwan) and the Republic of Korea (South Korea) respectively. As the editorial board member of the business daily *Nihon Keizai Shimbun*, Hisayoshi Ina, summed up in Japan's foreign affairs journal *Gaiko Forum*: "The collapse of the Soviet Union ended the Cold War in Europe, but it did not change the situation on the Korean Peninsula or that over the Taiwan Strait." There still remained a status quo in Asia, Ina noted, as the United States continued to base over 100,000 military personnel mainly in Japan and South Korea in the mid-1990s due to what Ina called a continuing "regional Cold War."[23] Political and security tensions in northeast Asia persisted despite the collapse of the Soviet Union.

Meanwhile, Japan's post-war *Showa* era of economic growth and political stability came to an abrupt end. Foreshadowing the end of the era, Emperor Hirohito collapsed in his palace as he battled intestinal cancer, and following a lengthy hospitalization Hirohito passed away on January 7, 1989 after a 62-year reign. Japan Inc. faced the first in a series of recessions as massive asset bubbles popped that year and the next. The Nikkei 225, a stock index of Japan's most powerful companies, peaked at 38,915.87 on December 29, 1989. By mid-November 2002, the index hit a low of 8,197, a 79% drop in 14 years. From their 1991 peak, average real estate prices in Tokyo had fallen 45% by early 2003.[24] While land prices rose slightly in the Tokyo metropolitan area in 2004, land prices throughout Japan continued their 14-year decline.[25] In politics, Japan's "1955 System"—the continuous rule of the conservative Liberal Democratic Party since 1955—disintegrated when the party lost its majority in the upper house of the Diet in July 1989 and was ultimately swept from power for a time in 1993 following a series of political scandals and corruption allegations, discontent over a new consumption tax, and farmers' retaliation over the liberalization of the agricultural market in the late 1980s and early 1990s. Japan entered a period that would later be called the "lost decade."

As Japan reeled politically and economically, a series of national security events in and around Japan showed how poorly suited the country's Cold War defense structure was for this new era of threats. Japan's defense capabilities until the early 1990s had been designed to counter a possible attack from the Soviet Union, geographically located northwest of Japan. Japan built over a thousand tanks to counter a land invasion from the north and an air-defense network to guard Japanese airspace from Soviet fighters and bombers flying from bases in Siberia as part of a strategy of *hoppō jūshi* or "emphasizing the north." Japanese submarines, meanwhile, patrolled for Soviet attack submarines attempting to clear paths for its ballistic missile submarines from bases in the Far East to the Pacific Ocean, while Japanese destroyers guarded sea lines of communication and minesweepers kept ports and harbors clear of Soviet mines. Japanese forces would defend the Japanese archipelago until US Forces in Japan and elsewhere could join the battle.

As the threat of all-out invasion from the north receded with the collapse of the Soviet Union in the early 1990s, other nonconventional, asymmetric threats to the Japanese archipelago began to emerge. Japan and its leaders were initially little prepared to handle these new national security challenges following decades of reliance on the United States to provide for its national security during the Cold War.

The US Ambassador to Japan at the close of the Cold War, Michael Armacost, succinctly described Japan's inadequate national security structure in a declassified cable written in 1991 following the Gulf War. Armacost wrote: "The GOJ's [Government of Japan's] essentially passive approach to the Gulf War stimulated the already existing debate here [in Tokyo] on Japan's role in the Post-Cold War world, necessary adjustments in the US-Japan relations, and the adequacy of Japan's political and bureaucratic system to handle the new challenges." While "no conclusions were reached," according to Armacost, the Gulf War highlighted "the obstacles to a mature foreign policy" such as "enduring pacifist sentiment and distrust of the Japanese military, the gap between the desire for recognition as a great power and willingness to bear the associated risks and responsibilities, and the inadequacy of

Japan's bureaucratic and parliamentary system in dealing with crisis management." According to Ambassador Armacost, there was at the time a "widespread feeling...that Japan can not simply buy friends with aid, and finance those who are doing the dirty and dangerous work involved in maintaining international stability." Armacost asserted that "Japan's foreign policy formulation and implementation is inadequate" and "[t]he GOJ was caught off-guard by the Gulf Crisis, proved incapable of developing its own analysis of the situation as it evolved, and came up with no policy response other than following the US lead."[26] In short, Japan in the early 1990s was little prepared to develop and implement new policies to meet the emerging asymmetric challenges in a post-Cold War world.

The allied triumph in the Gulf War and the subsequent collapse of the Soviet Union by the end of the year ushered in a new era, but it took Japan a decade of slow, piecemeal changes to adjust to a new international security environment. In the decade following the Gulf War, Japan was bracketed by national security crises that directly affected its national interests in Asia and elsewhere. As each national security crisis highlighted deficiencies in Japan's national security capabilities, Japan slowly overcame the obstacles highlighted by Ambassador Armacost. Reforms did not begin in earnest, however, until after four major national security crises challenged Japanese policymakers in the early- and mid-1990s: North Korea's development of nuclear and missile capabilities, a series of cult attacks using chemical and biological weapons, a major earthquake in the heart of Japan, and a major terrorist hostage incident at the Japanese Ambassador's residence in Lima, Peru. Like the Great Hanshin Earthquake that struck shortly before dawn on January 17, 1995, these national security crises woke Japan's leaders to the need for more comprehensive and timely national security capabilities.

North Korea's Nuclear and Missile Ambitions, pt. 1

The Democratic People's Republic of Korea (DPRK)—North Korea—presented a particular challenge to stability in Asia in the 1990s and 2000s. Following years of suspicious nuclear activity, in March 1993 North Korea declared its intention to withdraw from the Nuclear Non-Proliferation Treaty (NPT). Two months later, at the end of May, it test-fired an intermediate range missile and other short-range missiles towards Japan with no prior notification, demonstrating an improved capability to strike points in Japan—where some 40,000 US troops were stationed—if Pyongyang wished. The threat to the Japanese homeland was increasingly direct and real. In addition and further complicating Tokyo's efforts to establish diplomatic relations with Pyongyang, North Korean agents were suspected of having abducted nearly a dozen Japanese citizens in the 1970s and early 1980s to teach North Korean soldiers proper Japanese and work on North Korean propaganda aimed at Japan. One was a mere 13 years old at the time of her disappearance. While the United States took the lead role in negotiating with the North Korean regime concerning its nuclear policies, Japan's sense of insecurity during this crisis was just as great due to its geographic proximity to the Korean peninsula and long-strained relations with Pyongyang.

North Korea's nuclear program dates to the 1950s. Alexandre Mansourov, a former Soviet official stationed in Pyongyang in the late 1980s, described North Korea's nuclear history in an article in *The Nonproliferation Review.* In 1956, Pyongyang signed two agreements with Moscow to facilitate "joint nuclear research," and in 1959 Moscow agreed to provide a 5-megawatt research reactor. The Soviet Union agreed to host North Korean scientists at the Joint Institute for Nuclear Research at Dubna, and upon their return in the early 1960s, North Korea established its own Nuclear

Research Complex near Yongbyon some 90 kilometers northeast of Pyongyang. In August 1965, the Soviet Union assisted with the construction of a two-megawatt thermal (MWt) research reactor and a critical assembly, which went active two years later and was later expanded to eight MWt using indigenous technology. North Korea entered into an indigenous, rapid expansion phase in the late 1970s, according to Mansourov, when Kim Il-sung authorized a domestic nuclear weapons program and the expansion of facilities for a nuclear weapons program in the Pakch'on area 22 kilometers southeast of Yongbyon. North Korea also opened a uranium mine and a mill to turn uranium ore into yellowcake, a necessary step before the uranium could be used in a nuclear reactor.[27]

In 1980, a US reconnaissance satellite discovered a larger construction site and reactor components at Yongbyon, where North Korea was building a 5 megawatt natural uranium graphite moderated reactor, the ore processing plant and a fuel-rod fabrication plant. The reactor was based on declassified British blueprints of a gas-graphite moderated plant, ideal for producing weapons-grade plutonium out of natural uranium; each irradiated core load could, when reprocessed, produce 30 kilograms of plutonium or enough for about five nuclear warheads.[28] Even before the reactor went critical in 1986, construction began on the first of two larger gas-graphite reactors, which when completed would be capable of producing several times more weapons-grade plutonium. Construction also began the following year on a radiochemical laboratory with a sizeable reprocessing capacity.[29] North Korea's nuclear breakout potential was thus becoming alarmingly clear. As construction proceeded apace on the research reactor in the early 1980s, the United States pressured the Soviet Union to persuade Pyongyang to suspend the facility's construction and join the Nuclear Non-Proliferation Treaty as a non-nuclear state. North Korea demanded—and got—a

Soviet pledge to build four nuclear power plants in return.[30] North Korea subsequently signed the Nuclear Non-Proliferation Treaty in December 1985.

As a signatory to the NPT, North Korea was required to sign a safeguards agreement with the International Atomic Energy Agency (IAEA). The safeguards agreement spelled out inspection procedures to assure the international community that North Korea was using its nuclear infrastructure and nuclear material for peaceful uses only, as required under the NPT. After signing the NPT, North Korea had 18 months to conclude a safeguards agreement with the IAEA. When the deadline passed with no agreement, the IAEA extended the deadline another 18 months without objection. Finally, on May 4, 1992 North Korea submitted its initial report to the IAEA detailing its nuclear-related facilities, after which safeguards inspections were set to begin. All of North Korea's nuclear facilities were subject to periodic IAEA inspections as a non-nuclear member under provisions of the NPT.

The situation on the Korean Peninsula seemed to improve in the final months of 1991 and into 1992. President Bush declared a unilateral removal of all US tactical nuclear weapons from bases outside the United States. In December 1991, Pyongyang and Seoul signed the joint declaration on the denuclearization of the Korean peninsula following South Korean President Roh Tae Wu's announcement that no US nuclear weapons were stationed in South Korea. In January 1992, Seoul and Washington canceled the Team Spirit joint military exercise scheduled for that year. That same month, Under Secretary of State Arnold Kanter held talks with Workers' Party of Korea (WPK) official Kim Yong Sun, the highest-level meeting at that point between the two governments. North Korea then concluded the safeguards agreement with the IAEA in May, opening its nuclear facilities to periodic inspections.[31]

Tokyo, meanwhile, attempted to reestablish relations with Pyongyang in the early 1990s. While Tokyo had established diplomatic relations with Seoul in 1965, it still had no diplomatic relationship with Pyongyang. Japanese-North Korean bilateral relations thawed for a time in 1990, when former Deputy Prime Minister Shin Kanemaru led a Japanese delegation of over two dozen parliamentarians to Pyongyang in September that year. Kanemaru carried with him a personal letter from Prime Minister Toshiki Kaifu. While Kaifu did not issue an apology as such for Japan's colonization of the Korean peninsula in the first half of the 20th century, he cited comments made by his predecessor in expressing regret for the "unfortunate past": "Former Prime Minister Takeshita expressed deep remorse and regret regarding such an unfortunate past period at the Diet in March last year. As Prime Minister, I have periodically made clear that I feel exactly the same way." Kaifu also noted that the issue of compensation "should be dealt with sincerely by the Japanese Government at the time of the normalization of relations." He signed the letter as President of Japan's ruling Liberal Democratic Party (LDP), indicating his statements were based on his position as head of that party, not as head of the Government of Japan.[32] Tokyo could use the issuance of a more official Cabinet or government apology as a bargaining chip in later talks, and the letter represented a trial balloon by Kaifu—backed by his party—to gauge Pyongyang's interest in pursuing talks.

The Kanemaru visit came at a time when a waning Soviet Union and the People's Republic of China were reengaging South Korea diplomatically, thus North Korea was looking to proceed with its own reengagement strategy with neighboring countries such as Japan as well. At the end of the visit Kanemaru, Vice President of the Japan Socialist Party (JSP) Makoto Tanabe, and North Korean leader Kim Il Sung issued a three-party declaration between the ruling Liberal Democratic Party, the Socialist Party of Japan, and the Workers Party of Korea that called for the early establishment of diplomatic relations. Based on this agreement, Japan and North Korea in January 1991 began eight rounds of bilateral normalization talks that lasted until November 1992.

The talks quickly reached an impasse, however, when Japanese delegates requested an investigation into the fate of a Japanese national, Yaeko Taguchi, who was suspected of having been kidnapped by North Korean agents. Taguchi was 22 and the mother of two small children when she went missing on June 30, 1978. Kim Hyon-hui, a North Korean woman arrested in South Korea for traveling on a fake Japanese passport and convicted for her role in bombing Korean Air Lines flight 858 in 1987, had testified that a Japanese abductee named Li Un-hye had taught her Japanese at North Korea's Kim Chong-il Political and Military University. Following Kim's testimony and descriptions of Li, Japanese authorities suspected Li Un-hye was the Korean name of Yaeko Taguchi. This in turn fed suspicions that other Japanese had been abducted. In total, almost a dozen Japanese citizens were feared to have been abducted by North Korean agents in the 1970s and early 1980s, although North Korea's official position during the bilateral talks was that the government had never abducted any Japanese nationals. (The Japanese government ultimately compiled a list of officially recognized abductees in 1997 to use in periodic discussions with North Korea on the issue.) The North Korean delegates walked away from the talks in November 1992 as they refused to discuss the fate of Taguchi, and bilateral ties would remain strained over the abduction issue for more than a decade even as the nuclear and missile proliferation concerns intensified.

Japan was powerless to take a direct role in the North Korean nuclear talks, although the United States coordinated closely with Japan and other allies in the region throughout the nuclear crisis.

Following a tour of Asia in November 1991, US Secretary of State James Baker described the multiple variables facing Japan and the region in a cable to Secretary of Defense Richard Cheney. Declassified in late 2005, the cable provided additional context of the Japanese position concerning the developing crisis on the Korean Peninsula. The South Koreans, according to Baker, wanted to keep Japan as well as Russia out of the "politics" of the issue: "[South Korean] National Security Advisor Kim Chong-whi made it clear that Koreans don't want Japan or the Soviet Union involved in the politics of the peninsula, even though they have a role to play on the nuclear issue." Secretary Baker highlighted continued historical friction in the region: "Japan has important leverage on the North which the South will want to see used effectively; but their own bitter history with the Japanese will inhibit policy coordination." Secretary Baker also noted Japan's hardening stance concerning bilateral relations with the North: "Concerning Japan's negotiations with North Korea to normalize relations, Tokyo's terms have hardened significantly because of the nuclear issue. The new Miyazawa government [Kiichi Miyazawa succeeded Kaifu in late 1991 and served until mid-1993] has moved Tokyo's position close to our own: Normalization and economic aid require not just signing and implementing the IAEA full-scope safeguards agreement, but also foregoing a reprocessing capability. Some Japanese bureaucrats may seek to nibble away at this position, but we should hold them to it. We must continue to work in tandem with Japan on this issue."[33] While Japan possessed potential economic influence on North Korea, it had few options in its bilateral relations with the North particularly after the two-year bilateral talks broke down in November 1992 over the abduction issue. The nuclear talks, at any rate, took precedence over bilateral North Korea-Japan relations and the abduction issue for the time being.

The situation changed dramatically in early 1993. Following IAEA-North Korea discussions in Pyongyang in January 1993, the IAEA requested special inspections of two suspected nuclear sites in February. In an attempt to verify the role of the facilities, IAEA Director General Hans Blix had invoked a special inspection procedure provided for in the Safeguards Agreement. After further IAEA-North Korea consultations, North Korea on February 20 rejected that inspection request, and five days later the IAEA Board of Governors passed a resolution calling for North Korea to accept the special inspections within a month.

Besides the IAEA, intelligence and military officials in a number of countries concluded North Korea probably already possessed a significant amount of weapons-grade plutonium that could be used in a nuclear weapons program. In a public statement, CIA Director James Woolsey indicated that by 1993 North Korea had a sufficient quantity of plutonium to build a nuclear device. By 1995, according to Woolsey, North Korea would have enough plutonium to be able to make five or six warheads.[34] On January 28, 1993, the Russian Intelligence Service made public a list of 16 countries it suspected of having or developing weapons of mass destruction, with North Korea one of the 16. In February, retired general and executive director of the Japanese Research Institute for Peace and Security Katsuichi Tsukamoto said that North Korea was three years from being "nuclear capable." Similarly, Japan's Ministry of Foreign Affairs in March 1993 said in a report that North Korea might possess between 16 and 24 kilograms of weapons-grade plutonium.[35] Indeed, the United States by this time had shared imagery of Yongbyon with Japan's Cabinet Intelligence and Research Office, which Deputy Chief Cabinet Secretary Nobuo Ishihara later called "incredibly detailed," in a September 1996 interview with Japan's *Asahi Shimbun.*

"Even a layman could see the construction" of the suspect facilities, Ishihara told *Asahi*.[36]

On March 12, North Korea in a pique announced its intention to withdraw from the Non-Proliferation Treaty, thus driving the situation to a crisis point. The NPT's article X paragraph 1 declares that "each party" to the NPT "shall give notice of such withdrawal to all other Parties to the Treaty and to the United Nations Security Council three months in advance" of its decision to withdraw from the Treaty. With its announced intent, North Korea had three months before it was no longer bound by the NPT. The IAEA Board of Governors in the meantime called on North Korea to accept the special inspections by March 31 at an emergency board meeting, but following Pyongyang's continued non-compliance, the Board on April 1 referred the North Korea issue to the UN Security Council in line with Article XII.C of the IAEA Statute.

For the first time in its quarter-century history, a signatory nation was declaring its intention to leave the Nuclear Non-Proliferation Treaty. As a signatory of the NPT, North Korea was forbidden from developing or possessing nuclear weapons, but article X represented a special escape clause available to all signatories to the Treaty. No country had invoked this escape clause, however, until now. In three months and one day, North Korea would be free from the provisions of the Nuclear Non-Proliferation Treaty, and many feared that it would remove the irradiated fuel rods from the nuclear reactor at Yongbyon, extract and reprocess the plutonium contained in the rods, and use the plutonium to build five or six nuclear warheads. North Korea could then announce that it was a nuclear-weapons state, perhaps in dramatic and unequivocal fashion by testing a nuclear device. But while North Korea had the right to withdraw from the NPT according to provisions of the NPT itself, no one wanted to see a nuclear North Korea. Thus on May 11—two months after Pyongyang's declared intention to withdraw from the NPT—the UN Security Council passed Resolution 825 calling on Pyongyang to "reaffirm its commitment to the Treaty" and to "honour it non-proliferation obligations under the Treaty and comply with its safeguards agreement with the IAEA."[37] While the Kim regime in May allowed inspectors into Yongbyon to service monitoring equipment in May, its stance remained unchanged.

Equally troubling, North Korean scientists were working to increase the range of the country's missiles. A nuclear device would be useless without a means to deliver it, and a medium- or long-range ballistic missile was the fastest such delivery vehicle. North Korea first acquired short-range Scud-Bs from Egypt in 1981, and successfully test-fired Scud-Bs in 1984. North Korea began pilot production of Scud-Bs in 1985 and then commenced with mass production at facilities near Pyongyang within several years after the Korean Peoples Army had established its first missile unit in 1986. The Scud-B missiles had a range of approximately 500 kilometers, certainly a threat to targets in South Korea such as Seoul but not a threat to US troops stationed at the southern tip of South Korea or in Japan. But a new Scud-C was tested in early 1987, with a greater range than the Scud-B. While most of South Korea was by this time within range of a North Korean missile attack, Japan was out of range throughout the 1980s. The situation began to change when North Korea started development of the longer-range Scud-D in 1989. The Scud-D became known as "Nodong" because it was first fired from a launch pad at No-tong, near Kim Chaek City on North Korea's northeastern coast. The Nodong-1, a single-stage, liquid-fuel ballistic missile, was thought to have a range of 1,000-1,300 kilometers, putting most of Japan and all of South Korea in range of a missile attack from North Korea.[38] North Korea also began developing the medium-range ballistic missile Taepodong in the early 1990s, theoretically placing all of Japan in range of a North Korean missile attack. But North Korean scientists before 1993 had not tested any longer-range missiles to verify their capabilities, and this meant that North Korea did not have an assured medium-range nuclear delivery capability.

North Korea demonstrated progress in extending the range of its missiles at the end of May 1993, two weeks before its withdrawal from the NPT was to be final. On May 29 and 30, North Korea test-launched at least one medium-range Nodong-1 missile and several short-range missiles into the Sea of Japan with no prior notification. According to detailed accounts several weeks after the missile tests, the United States had detected possible missile launch preparations on the northeastern part of the Korean peninsula and notified the Japanese government. The Self-Defense Forces, in turn, dispatched a Maritime Self-Defense Force P-3C patrol plane to the area that captured images of two North Korean ships—a 1,500-ton Najin-class frigate and a 500-ton minesweeper—meandering some 350 kilometers north of Japan's Noto Peninsula. (The minesweeper was reported to have taken the provocative act of pointing one of its machine guns at the P-3C as it flew by.) It was surmised that the frigate was positioned to observe the missile tests down-range while the minesweeper collected the missiles after the tests.[39] The newly developed Nodong-1 was tested at a shorter range of approximately 500 kilometers, but it was launched at a greater elevation than normal indicating it was powerful enough to fly at a range greater than 500 kilometers, thought at the time to be around 1,000 kilometers.[40] The missile landed some 250 kilometers from the Noto Peninsula; with a 1,000-kilometer range, the Nodong-1 could target the eastern half of Japan, but not Tokyo or Okinawa. The missile would need a range of 1,300 kilometers to target all major areas of Japan.[41] While North Korea demonstrated an ability to launch a missile at an increased range, the missile's capability to deliver a nuclear warhead was still very much in doubt. Japanese sources later claimed that the missile broke into pieces after the dummy warhead cracked during reentry.[42] In all, North Korea was reported to have tested a total of four missiles on May 29-30, at least one of which was a Nodong-1 and two or three Scud-Bs or Scud-Cs.[43]

While Tokyo had been closely following launch preparations, the Japanese public was not informed about the tests for almost two weeks. On the afternoon of June 7, Deputy Chief Cabinet Secretary Nobuo Ishihara chaired a meeting of the interagency Joint Intelligence Council (JIC) to discuss issues related to North Korea. Established in 1986, the JIC consisted of senior career officials from the Ministry of Foreign Affairs (MOFA), the Defense Agency (DA), the National Police Agency (NPA), the Public Security Intelligence Agency (PSIA), the Cabinet Intelligence and Research Office (CIRO), and other agencies. The JIC normally met once or twice a month to discuss policy and intelligence matters, but during the North Korean crisis the JIC would meet more often to discuss the situation on the Korean peninsula. Meetings did not last long, usually under an hour, however, and the short duration coupled with their relative infrequency indicated that the JIC served a perfunctory role in interagency national security policy coordination in the early years since its creation. Indeed, the June 7 meeting lasted a mere 30 minutes: DA Deputy Vice Minister Haruno Ueno gave a briefing of the missile launch itself, after which Katsuya Suzuki, head of MOFA's Information Analysis Bureau, reviewed North Korea's foreign policy, as did Yoshio Omori, head of the Cabinet Intelligence and Research Office. Ishihara, the senior career government bureaucrat, requested participants maintain strict secrecy concerning North Korea's missile tests.[44]

Yet four days later, seemingly in a coordinated bid to highlight Japan's vulnerability to a missile attack, Ishihara himself leaked the tests to the media a day after the head of the DA's Policy Bureau, Shigeru Hatakeyama, told a House of Councilors committee meeting that Japan was unable to defend against an attack by North Korea's Nodong-1 missile.[45] Ishihara commuted to work daily via Azamino Station in Midori Ward, Yokohama, where reporters greeted him each morning with questions regarding government policy.[46] Talking with reporters there on June 11, 1993, he remarked to reporters gathered around him: "North Korea has launched missiles in the direction of Japan. There has been talk of Japan providing food aid. But North Korea is this kind of country..." The leak was attributed at the time to an unnamed government source.[47] Prime Minister Kiichi Miyazawa and Chief Cabinet Secretary Kono played down news of the tests, calling the "leak" "only a rumor" without "firm proof."[48] They preferred to keep the test secret so as not to impact the negotiations then taking place in Geneva concerning North Korea's nuclear facilities. Three days later, following increased media scrutiny, the DA on June 14 confirmed missile tests had indeed taken place and provided details of SDF's actions before the launches.[49] But despite whatever failures might have occurred during the tests (such as the disintegration of the dummy warhead upon reentry), their significance was clear. North Korea was building the means to deliver a nuclear device at ever greater distances. Should the missile tests progress along with its nuclear research, North Korea would eventually have the theoretical ability to deliver a domestically produced nuclear warhead on a domestically produced missile to targets in Asia and the Pacific with little warning. *Yomiuri Shimbun* later quoted Ishihara as saying about the leak: "I felt it necessary to make the matter public, in light of alarmingly low public awareness of the North Korean menace. The public urgently needed to be better informed of the potential hazard."[50]

North Korea's missile tests spurred Japan's interest in missile defense, although Japan would take a painfully long ten years to agree to build a system in cooperation with the United States. While Japan had signed a Memorandum of Understanding in 1987 to participate in the US Strategic Defense Initiative (SDI), participation was limited to Japanese private sector research on a so-called western Pacific anti-missile architecture. On May 13, 1993, two weeks before North Korea's missile tests, US Secretary of Defense Les Aspin announced the end of research on the popularly termed "Star Wars" space-based missile defense system and a change in emphasis to theater missile defense (TMD) as the US Department of Defense changed the Strategic Defense Initiative Office to the Ballistic Missile Defense Office (BMDO). The Japanese Government was more interested in TMD precisely because it was not a space-based system, since such a system potentially violated Japan's exclusively peaceful use of space policy. Indeed, the Self-Defense Forces began procuring Patriot missile defense systems for theater defense in 1992. Following the Nodong missile test, in early August 1993 US Undersecretary of Defense for Policy Frank G. Wisner and DA Administrative Vice Minister Shigeru Hatakeyama (who had recently been promoted to the number-two spot at the DA) initiated discussions regarding the possibility of Japan participating in joint development of theater missile defense systems. Undersecretary Wisner suggested the establishment of a working subcommittee composed of US and Japanese defense officials to examine further cooperation in the development of missile defense technologies. Talks continued when John Deutch, the US Under Secretary of Defense for Acquisition and Technology who oversaw the BMDO, visited Japan on September 22-23, and again when Minister of State for

Defense Keisuke Nakanishi visited Washington in late September. Nakanishi and Aspin agreed to establish a bilateral TMD working group, which met fourteen times from December 1993.[51] The US in June 1994 proposed four TMD systems for possible development collaboration, and in September 1994 the Prime Minister's Advisory Group on Defense recommended joint development of TMD.[52] The DA in April 1995 established, based on the fiscal year's budget passed in 1994, a "Ballistic Missile Defense Research Office" that consisted of experts from the DA internal bureaus and uniformed personnel from the Ground, Maritime, and Air Staff Offices to examine the merits of Japan developing a ballistic missile defense system.[53] Thus within a year of North Korea's missile launches, Japan was actively investigating possible cooperation with the United States in developing missile defense systems.

As the first reports of its missile tests were being publicized in Japan and elsewhere, North Korea agreed on June 11, 1993 to suspend its withdrawal from the NPT in a joint US-North Korea statement following talks in New York. The announcement came one day before the end of the three-month period that would have freed North Korea from its nuclear non-proliferation agreements in the NPT. North Korea would later claim that because it merely suspended its withdrawal from the NPT, any later announcement that it was withdrawing from the treaty would require just one day before it was free of the treaty's requirements, not three months. Pyongyang did not consider the NPT three-month clock reset. Talks in Geneva made some progress in July as North Korea agreed to discuss safeguards with the IAEA, while the United States in principle agreed to support the conversion of North Korean reactors to light-water reactors. IAEA inspectors were allowed to visit Yongbyon to service monitoring equipment in August but were not granted full access to the reprocessing plant there.

Japan's internal political situation complicated contingency planning efforts in various ministries and agencies as four prime ministers served at the Prime Minister's Official Residence (PMOR)—commonly called the *Kantei* in Japanese—in the eighteen-month period following North Korea's March 1993 NPT withdrawal declaration.[1] In June 1993, the Japanese Diet (parliament) passed a vote of no-confidence in the Miyazawa cabinet, and a number of the ruling Liberal Democratic Party (LDP) members left the LDP to form a series of new but smaller parties. The LDP thus lost its majority in the lower house of the Diet. The party could not make up for the lost membership and its 223 seats remained below the 256 required for a majority.[54] A seven-party coalition formed to wrest political control of the Prime Minister's Office, electing Morihiro Hosokawa—founder of the reform "Japan New Party"—to replace the LDP's Kiichi Miyazawa as Prime Minister in August 1993. Hosokawa was the first non-LDP prime minister since 1955 and came to the *Kantei* with a reform agenda, yet Hosokawa himself resigned eight months later in April 1994, due to questionable political donations. His successor, Tsutomu Hata, would rule based on a minority coalition for a mere two months, after which the head of the Japan Socialist Party, Tomoichi Murayama, became prime minister, which itself was an extraordinary moment in Japanese politics. As unrelated domestic political issues swept successive premiers from office, day-to-day coordination throughout the North Korean nuclear crisis was thus managed by Nobuo Ishihara, the highest-ranking (and non-elected) government official in Japan.

Ishihara's position was made more difficult as the Japan Socialist Party improved its political prospects in Tokyo during

---

[1] Like the White House in the United States, Japan's *Kantei* or Prime Minister's Official Residence includes not only the office of the Prime Minister but also the policy-making structure and bureaucracy—collectively called the Cabinet Office—that directly supports the Prime Minister's day-to-day governance of Japan.

this time. The JSP, the largest post-war pacifist party with long ties to the communist regimes in the PRC and the DPRK, advocated Japan's unarmed neutrality and had until the early 1990s refused to recognize the constitutionality of the Self-Defense Forces or the US-Japan alliance. The JSP's ultra-pacifist policy positions, historically friendly relations with the DPRK's Workers Party of Korea, and animosity to the US-Japan alliance hindered policy formation on the North Korea issue in 1993-4 and caused the United States to question Japan's seriousness regarding the North Korea nuclear issue. The JSP, for example, opposed legislation that would allow the dispatch of SDF planes abroad to evacuate Japanese citizens from areas of instability (such as South Korea) in the fall of 1993, as the party viewed the dispatch of any SDF units abroad as unconstitutional. (A new faction within the JSP, the "Action New Democracy" faction, supported the bill, however, symbolizing an emerging rift in the party itself between old-school socialists and post-Cold War reformers.) The JSP constantly bickered with its erstwhile coalition members over policy during the 1993-1994 North Korean crisis, hindering substantive Japanese support of US policies on the North Korea issue.

As Tokyo during this time began to plan for contingencies on the Korean peninsula, Ishihara was the senior leadership figure who remained in his position throughout the crisis. While the JIC continued to meet at least monthly throughout the crisis, following the Nodong missile test Ishihara directed government agencies to begin reviewing possible scenarios resulting from the North Korean nuclear crisis. In the summer of 1993, Ishihara first requested Omori's CIRO to compile possible scenarios on the Korean peninsula ranging from the impact of economic sanctions to the outbreak of armed conflict. Besides the legality of supporting possible US military actions against North Korea outside Japanese waters, CIRO highlighted three major scenarios affecting Japan: the evacuation of Japanese nationals from the Korean peninsula; a mass exodus of refugees from the Korean peninsula; and possible North Korean incursions by boat or sabotage of key Japanese defense or power facilities by North Korean agents. (Many officials viewed North Korean sabotage as more likely than a missile attack, because they did not believe North Korea could actually use its missiles to deliver a nuclear payload to targets in Japan.) Of particular concern were Japan's 17 nuclear power plants, 10 of which were situated along the coast on the Sea of Japan.[55]

Following CIRO's study, Ishihara in the fall of 1993 established in secret a special four-member council to coordinate the development of security measures should the Korean Peninsula crisis turn into an armed conflict. The council was made up of officials from Ministry of Foreign Affairs (MOFA), the Defense Agency (DA), and the National Police Agency (NPA), while the Cabinet Security Affairs Office (CSAO) under Tatsufumi Tsuboi operated as the council's secretariat. If hostilities had erupted on the Korean peninsula, the council planned to create a special countermeasures headquarters to be chaired by the Prime Minister to coordinate efforts by the various Japanese ministries and agencies involved in national security, similar to the one created during the Gulf War. The council developed a roster totaling 200 potential support personnel from MOFA, DA, the NPA and other agencies who would work under the auspices of the Cabinet Security Affairs Office during any crisis, while CIRO and the Public Affairs Office would both perform information support roles. The council suggested conducting joint US-Japan sea inspections and sea operations, minesweeping, and logistics support for a US sea blockade of North Korea, and it highlighted the need to secure important facilities such as nuclear power plants. The council also prepared time-limited legislation for immediate introduction into the Diet to support these measures.[56] The existence of the four-member council first came to light when a member of the JSP leaked it to a budget affairs committee at the height of the crisis in May 1994, further eroding trust between career government officials and members of the JSP. Tsuboi, who was present at the time, implied to committee members that the council was actually the JIC.[57] Tsuboi's obfuscation at the committee was an attempt to keep Japanese contingency planning then underway secret. Indeed, with so many politicians and party factions vying for power at the time, career government officials were sometimes reluctant to fully brief their erstwhile political masters precisely because they might leak the information for personal political advantage. The full extent of the council did not surface until two years later, when *Asahi Shimbun* reported on the government's contingency planning during the North Korean nuclear crisis. While nothing came of the contingency planning at the time, the contingency studies completed by the various ministries and agencies in June-July 1994 would form the basis for a study of beefed-up US-Japan security arrangements under the Hashimoto premiership starting in May 1996.[58]

Nuclear talks showed progress in late 1993 when on December 29 North Korea agreed to accept IAEA inspections at the seven declared nuclear sites and a third round of talks. Kim Il-sung spoke positively concerning US-North Korean relations in his 1994 New Year's message, and a week later the party newspaper suggested a solution to the crisis was "in sight."[59] Perhaps because of signs of progress in the talks in late 1993 and into 1994 and due to a possible trade war with the United States, Prime Minister Hosokawa seemingly paid little attention to the North Korea issue. New energy was injected during Prime Minister Hosokawa's Washington summit with President Clinton on February 11, 1994, ostensibly for bilateral economic talks regarding Japan's continued large trade surplus with the United States. (The trade discussions themselves ended without agreement and the Clinton Administration in early March reinstated unilateral trade sanctions to curtail Japanese exports to the US.) But President Clinton also urged Hosokawa to support possible US sanctions proposals against North Korea at the United Nations—a key aspect of sanctions would be a halt in remittances from ethnic Koreans in Japan to their families in North Korea. In response, Hosokawa changed the Japanese position regarding sanctions from "wait until after the IAEA talks" to one in which he allowed that Japan will do "what the law will allow."[60] Hosokawa returned to Tokyo with a new sense of urgency. Yoshio Omori, the director of CIRO, later recalled that Hosokawa told him that President Clinton spoke of a recent White House review of a possible surgical strike on North Korea's nuclear facilities. Hosokawa ordered Omori to prepare all available intelligence on North Korea for his review.[61] Hosokawa also ordered Deputy Chief Cabinet Secretary Nobuo Ishihara to redouble the government's efforts on the issue.[62] However, on the key issue of curtailing remittances sent by ethnic Koreans residing in Japan to family members and others still in North Korea, Hosokawa told a news conference after a morning breakfast with Clinton: "The government [of Japan] has to decide on its actions by taking into consideration the issue of human rights." At a separate news conference, Chief Cabinet Secretary Takemura spoke of the difficulties in tracking the remittances: "The actual situation of remittances of Korean residents in Japan is not clear and thus we do not know what kind of steps there are" to halt them.[63] Tokyo appeared to be dragging its feet on the critical issue of continued money transfers flowing to North Korea.

Despite the positive momentum by March 1994—IAEA inspections and South-North bilateral talks had begun, and the US and South Korea announced suspension of their major yearly joint exercise Team Spirit 1994 as a confidence-building measure—events turned for the worse when IAEA inspectors were refused permission to take swipes from the plutonium production line where seals were found broken on earlier visits. Inspectors, moreover, discovered North Korea had made surprising progress in completing a second reprocessing line for the separation of plutonium from irradiated fuel rods. With this new unsafeguarded line, Pyongyang could potentially produce nuclear material for a weapons program twice as fast if it wished.[64] The IAEA withdrew its inspectors mid-March. On March 19 North Korea representatives walked out of the South-North talks less than an hour after they had begun, after its chief negotiator declared that Seoul would turn into a "sea of fire" if a war broke out on the Korean Peninsula: "Seoul is not far from here. If war breaks out, it will be a sea of fire," Pak Young-su declared.[65] This sudden break-down in discussions led the Clinton administration to begin proposing graduated economic sanctions against North Korea at the United Nations in a bid to compel Pyongyang to allow inspectors to return to suspected sites.[66] IAEA Director General Hans Blix announced days later that although the continuity of safeguards in North Korea had not been broken, his inspection team was unable to conclude whether any nuclear material had been diverted from Yongbyon; the IAEA Board of Governors announced that it could not certify that plutonium was not being diverted to weapons use. The UN Security Council on March 31 thus unanimously passed a presidential statement calling on Pyongyang to allow full inspections to take place.[67] In response North Korea sent a letter on April 19, four days after Kim Il-sung's 82nd birthday, declaring its intention to unload the 8,000 fuel rods containing plutonium from its reactor. While IAEA inspectors could be present, they would not be allowed to verify the location of key rods as they were removed or to measure them, a key IAEA demand in calculating how much plutonium had been extracted in the past. Once removed, the plutonium in the fuel rods could be separated from the waste material and reprocessed, making yet more plutonium available for a possible weapons program.[68]

Just as the crisis was entering its most dangerous phase in the spring and summer of 1994, Japan's internal political situation became almost completely dysfunctional. Hosokawa abruptly declared on April 8 that he was resigning the premiership due to questions surrounding political donations to his campaign. A three-week leadership vacuum ensued as the coalition parties negotiated over two main policy issues in selecting their next prime minister: the imposition of a consumption tax and Japan's support for possible sanctions against North Korea. The Japan Socialist Party in particular opposed sanctions against North Korea. On April 25, talks broke down between coalition party members, and the remaining coalition parties split with the JSP to select Tsutomu Hata as their choice for Prime Minister. Garnering barely enough support in the Diet, Hata was narrowly confirmed three days later. But without JSP support, Hata presided over a minority coalition and was doomed to remain only months in office. Any attempt to pass contentious legislation through the Japanese parliament during this time would have been virtually impossible.

Japan's policy establishment, moreover, strongly debated the halting of remittances from ethnic Koreans residing in Japan to North Korea, a major element of economic sanctions about to be proposed by the United States at the United Nations. Immediately following an early-June US-South Korea-Japan meeting regarding the possibility of enacting sanctions against North Korea, Ishihara presided over a meeting of the JIC on June 6 to discuss Japan's participation in sanctions against North Korea. JIC member agencies produced a list of ten areas where Japan could take action, the most contentious of which was the possibility of halting remittances to North Korea by family members still residing in Japan. Japan had imported Koreans to work in Japan before and during World War II, and some decided to return to the Koreas in a repatriation movement in the 1950s and 1960s, while their families helped to support them by working in Japan. Remittances from Japan to North Korea were estimated at anywhere between $600 million-$1.8 billion each year, and many suspected that Pyongyang took a cut of the remittances. In addition to inter-bank transfers, some ethnic Koreans hand-carried cash to the North via the *Mangyongbong*, a North Korean ship that traveled several times a year between Japan's Niigata Prefecture and North Korean ports such as Wonsan, or by plane through Beijing. A crackdown on remittances would necessitate a search of travelers departing Niigata port and anyone traveling to Beijing with Pyongyang as a declared destination. In addition, Tokyo also worried that an announced halt in remittances would cause an uprising among the 250,000 Koreans still living in Japan, some of whom were still loyal to Pyongyang and were represented by the highly organized General Association of Korean Residents in Japan (GAKRJ or *Chōsen Sōren*).[69] Some JIC members thought that a halt in remittances would be nearly impossible to implement, as family members would find other ways to deliver currency to their families. Some also feared a halt in remittances would exacerbate humanitarian conditions in North Korea that might in turn lead to a mass exodus of North Korean refugees to Japan and elsewhere, creating the situation Japan feared most, short of actual war. The crisis thus presented members of the JIC with a dilemma never before encountered since it was established in 1986, as this was the first time members were forced to make decisions that had repercussions no matter which solution they chose. If Japan did nothing in order to maintain a precarious status quo on the Korean peninsula and within Japan, it would upset the

United States and call into question its support of the alliance, yet if it supported US policies it faced thorny issues of implementation and the possibility of instability or war on the Korean peninsula. As one participant told *Asahi Shimbun* following the meeting, "This is a situation we've never experienced before."[70]

But the JIC could only provide and coordinate policy options—Japan's political leaders held ultimate responsibility in deciding which option to pursue. Yet without the support of the JSP at the time, Prime Minister Hata presided over a minority coalition in the Diet and was essentially a lame-duck prime minister. Diet passage of contentious emergency legislation devised by Japan's various ministries and agencies to respond to a crisis on the Korean peninsula would have been nearly impossible during this time. Diet members could not form a consensus at the time whether or not to support US sanctions or other emergency legislative measures that would have allowed the SDF to evacuate Japanese citizens from the Korean peninsula, for example. And while Prime Minister Hata fully supported US-proposed sanctions in a June 9 phone call with President Clinton,[71] Hata's minority government status and the continued JSP opposition to sanctions rendered full Japanese government support less than certain. Indeed, Hata remained in office less than three weeks after his phone call with Clinton and was replaced by the head of the JSP, the same party that refused to support sanctions against North Korea. Hiroshi Kumagai, the chief cabinet secretary under Hata, later told *Asahi Shimbun* that "I realized we didn't have a legal framework to deal with the situation. I was petrified…Our country would have been thrown into chaos."[72] Nobuo Ishihara later complained in a September 1996 interview with the *Asahi Shimbun*: "We were unable to prepare for anything…Emergency legislation…did not advance much," Ishihara stated, and "we were most afraid that the situation would [deteriorate] all at once."[73]

As the crisis unfolded in late May, US Ambassador to South Korea Jim Laney, former president of Emory University where the Carter Center was located, began to urge former US President Jimmy Carter to help mediate the crisis. Carter had proposed a trilateral presidential summit at the DMZ in 1978, although that proposal faced considerable opposition at the time. After reconfirming recent invitations to visit North Korea, the Carter Center announced the former president's intention to visit North Korea in mid-June.[74] Carter arrived just after Pyongyang again declared on June 13 that it was dropping out of agreements with the IAEA and would no longer allow the international agency to inspect nuclear facilities in North Korea. While there were many contentious issues regarding President Carter's three-day visit, it provided a rare direct channel of communication with the aging Kim Il-sung. Kim agreed to allow IAEA inspectors to remain in North Korea and to a future summit with South Korea's Kim Young Sam. On June 22, North Korea's Kang Sok Ju in a letter to the White House announced the country's freeze on reprocessing the spent fuel and its intention to allow inspections to continue.[75] On June 28, Pyongyang and Seoul announced a South-North Summit would take place between Kim Il-sung and South Korea's President Kim Young Sam the following month. Perhaps because the visit was enough of a face-saving gesture to move from confrontation to conciliation, Carter's visit marked the beginning of the end of this first nuclear crisis.

In Japan, meanwhile, Hata was turned out of the *Kantei* in late June as the JSP negotiated a peculiar political alliance with the LDP and a smaller reform party to form a majority coalition, handing the premiership to JSP leader Tomiichi Murayama in late June 1994. The JSP and the LDP were the strangest of bedfellows, as they had disagreed on practically every policy issue throughout Japan's postwar era. The JSP had been in perpetual opposition since the late 1940s, so Murayama was Japan's first socialist prime minister in 47 years. But with power came a price for the JSP. By forging this political alliance, Murayama and the JSP were forced to revise their pacifist platform, or they risked quickly losing the confidence of their erstwhile LDP junior partner and thus losing the *Kantei*. The United States also viewed the new leadership skeptically. In early June, as JSP members were preparing to visit Pyongyang on June 11, the party continued to assert that it could not support economic sanctions against North Korea without a UN resolution.[76] Signaling a change of party platform less than a month later, President Clinton broached the subject of sanctions and other issues with new Prime Minister Murayama at a July 8 US-Japan summit before the G-7 met in Naples, Italy, and Murayama stressed his support of the US-Japan Security Treaty, the first signal that the JSP was shifting from its traditionally pacifist policies. Days after his return to Japan—and following his recovery from stomach flu the day after his meeting with Clinton in Naples—Murayama began a broad review of JSP national security policy. On July 20 Murayama gave a speech to the Diet in which he stated: "I recognize that the SDF…is constitutional." He also pledged to "uphold" the US-Japan Security Treaty and asserted that Japan's *Hinomaru* national flag and *Kimigayo* national anthem had "taken root deeply among the people and I want to respect their sentiment."[77] These were major policy changes for the JSP. Murayama brought the party's official position more in line with those of its coalition partner, the conservative LDP. The JSP officially confirmed the new policies at an extraordinary party convention in early September, although immediately after the convention Secretary General Wataru Kubo told Asahi Newstar TV that "if we continue to pursue disarmament, the ultimate goal is a Japan that is unarmed."[78] The JSP had recognized the SDF's constitutionality, but it still sought its eventual dissolution.

As these political events were taking place in Tokyo, the SDF and other agencies continued their contingency planning based on the CIRO study in the summer of 1993 and following Ishihara's four-member council planning starting in fall 1993. The planning was also spurred in part by the US as it planned for possible military action against North Korea. The United States wanted to know specifically what support Japan could provide during possible operations over the Korean Peninsula. As part of their own contingency planning, for example, US uniformed officers reportedly surveyed four Japanese Air Self-Defense Force air bases at Chitose, Misawa, Matsushima, and Komatsu for possible use by US AWACS, F-16s, and aerial refuelers.[79] The US wanted to know if Japanese MSDF vessels could help escort and resupply US Navy ships and conduct minesweeping operations near the North Korean coast if a naval blockade or other naval operations were ordered—indeed, a naval blockade in support of sanctions would require a "staggering number of ships" according to one US military officer.[80] Another US official recalled planning that would have required turning Narita International Airport "into a big military staging ground."[81] Japan's assistance was thus critical to the success of any major military operation in the region. In all, according to the *Asahi Shimbun*, the US presented the SDF with a 1,100-point list of various possible support measures in case the US took military action against North Korea.[82] US and Japanese uniformed officers conducted staff exercises role-playing various scenarios for a conflict on the peninsula, while US Air Force General Richard Myers, commander of US Forces in Japan, maintained weekly contact with Japan's highest-ranking military officer.[83] But Japanese policymakers such as Ishihara and senior uniformed SDF officers were unsure about the legality of supporting US military actions outside of Japan under Japanese law and the Constitution since "collective self-defense" was considered illegal. Japan could support US military actions in direct response to an attack on Japan, but not in military operations to defend a third party outside of Japan.

With these operational and legal issues in mind, the SDF's Joint Staff Council (JSC) conducted contingency studies in cooperation with other DA offices that culminated in the "Plan To Cope With the Situation on the Korean Peninsula," compiled in July 1994. Following the secret contingency planning under Ishihara beginning in fall 1993, the JSC recognized that once hostilities began, the government would establish a special countermeasures headquarters chaired by the Prime Minister, who could then order boarding inspections by Self-Defense Forces in the open sea, minesweeping operations, and the creation of emergency legislation to enable SDF logistic support of US sea blockade operations. To address possible requests for SDF support of US operations beyond Japanese territorial possessions, the JSC identified four geographic areas based on distance from areas of military engagement: the "combat zone," the "rear area of a battlefield," the "open sea," and "places in Japan." While an SDF support role in a "combat zone" conflicted with the Constitution and would thus have been impossible, the JSC determined that the SDF could provide support to US forces in Japan. SDF operations in the other two areas were more complicated and were further subdivided into ten subgroups including: escorting US ships or planes; logistical support such as maintenance and supply; and transportation activities. These operations were placed into one of two categories, one in which a political decision (ie, special Diet legislation) was required to implement support, and another in which support was deemed possible without special legislation. The DA then crafted time-limited legislation that would allow for SDF rear-area support of US operations that could be submitted to the Diet if required.[84] SDF officers, moreover, conducted site security surveys of ten nuclear power plants along the Sea of Japan should SDF personnel be ordered to secure the nuclear power plants. The SDF even proposed the placement of antipersonnel minefields on the grounds of the nuclear facilities and infantry and tanks outside the facilities. Based on a request from the US in 1993 to use civilian airports in Japan, JSC officers surveyed civilian airports in Fukuoka, Nagasaki, and Kumamoto Prefectures, and at the ASDF Tsuiki base (in Kumamoto) due to their proximity to the Korean Peninsula.[85] Contingency studies continued even after the crisis ended in late 1994, and recommendations were later adopted in the initial draft of Prime Minister Hashimoto's Far East Emergency study, which began in May 1996 and culminated in the enhanced US-Japan cooperation agreement of 1997.

Perhaps the most provocative Defense Agency study began in early 1994, when Shigeru Hatakeyama ordered a small group from the internal bureaus, the JSC, and the National Institute for Defense Studies (NIDS) to conduct a highly classified study regarding the impact on Japanese security if Japan were in theory to arm itself with nuclear weapons. (Ironically, just as the study group was being assembled, Hatakeyama denied at the Diet on January 31 that Japan was contemplating any change to its nuclear stance following a report in *The Times* that the UK Ministry of Defense thought Japan might abandon its non-nuclear position.[86]) The 31-page study, titled "The Problem of Weapons of Mass Destruction Proliferation" was completed in May 1995 and reportedly found that there were "no merits" to a nuclear Japan. It also stated that a nuclear Japan would damage Japan-US relations because building nuclear weapons would be interpreted as Japanese mistrust of the Japan-US Security Treaty, eroding the Japan-US alliance. The study moreover noted that the international community would be concerned that Japan's nuclear armament would destroy the nuclear nonproliferation regime with the

NPT as the keystone. The costs of nuclear armament would also be prohibitive, the study reportedly concluded.[87] While the study was only theoretical in nature, the study was a further indication of Japan's alarm during the crisis.

A very real concern for Japan was the possibility of a refugee crisis. With North Korea only a few hundred miles away by sea, Tokyo was concerned that any major instability in the country—the collapse of the Kim regime or war on the peninsula—would force tens of thousands to flee to Japan by boat. The Justice Ministry, in charge of immigration, estimated 100,000 North Koreans would attempt to seek refuge in Japan in the event of hostilities on the peninsula. Not only was Tokyo concerned about its ability to process and host such a large number of refugees, it was also concerned that Pyongyang might dispatch a contingent of North Korean special operations forces hiding among the refugees to attack vulnerable points in Japan. On June 13, 1994—the same day Pyongyang again announced its intention to drop out of the IAEA inspection regime altogether—the Cabinet Security Affairs Office completed an eight-page document titled "A Summary of an Analysis of the Situation on the Korean Peninsula," which was classified secret at the time. According to the analysis, a special task force would be created within the Cabinet to handle the refugees, and "if it becomes certain that a large number of refugees would remain in Japan for an extended time, the special unit's powers would be enhanced significantly through legislative measures." The measures would allow the Japan Coast Guard and National Police Agency to cooperate with the Defense Agency to help "separate North Korean agents and terrorists" infiltrating with actual refugees "at every possible stage," including at sea, as refugees landed, at processing points, and in refugee camps. Given the political uncertainty at the time, only after the document was drafted were details briefed to the Prime Minister, who at the time was Tsutomu Hata with only two weeks remaining in office.[88]

Talks began between the US and North Korea on July 8 in Geneva, but on July 9, 1994, North Korea announced the death of its "Great Leader," Kim Il-sung. Given the lack of transparency in North Korea, Japan and other countries questioned the veracity of the announcement. As South Korean intelligence officials had recently reported a clash between Kim senior and his son and putative successor Kim Chong-il, officials in Seoul were initially suspicious of the announcement as well.[89] Japan's Defense Agency immediately ordered the Air and Maritime Self-Defense Forces to launch E2-C, EP-3, and YS-11E planes to fly parallel to the Korean Peninsula to check for any unusual military movements, and the Ground Self-Defense Force monitored North Korean military traffic at its Miho Communications Station. As it monitored the military situation in North Korea, the DA initially suggested four possibilities: Kim's death was natural; Kim was assassinated; a group loyal to Kim Chong-il staged a coup; or an anti-Kim group staged a coup.[90] Kim's death was ultimately declared natural given his age and because the situation on the Korean peninsula remained quiet. Indeed, Yoshio Omori, the head of CIRO at the time of Kim's death, recalled in his memoirs that he was not particularly concerned because there were no reports of military deployments. Omori, moreover, felt that Kim Chong-il was a "smart dictator" who knew how to rule.[91] (As head of intelligence for the Cabinet Office, Omori briefed the prime minister at least once a week and might have relayed this position to Prime Minister Murayama following his return from Naples when he was reviewing his party's pacifist policy stance.) After Kim's death, Pyongyang and Washington agreed to suspend the third round of talks that had begun in Geneva the previous day for several weeks.[92]

Following observance of a mourning period, talks resumed in Geneva August 5-12, during which the United States and North

Korea agreed on basic terms for what would be called the Agreed Framework. An international consortium of countries would build two light-water reactors in North Korea that would operate under full-scope safeguards to meet its energy needs, and in return North Korea would remain a member of the NPT subject to inspections by the IAEA. Talks continued over the next two months, and on October 21, the United States and North Korea signed the Geneva Agreed Framework after North Korea agreed to abide by the provisions of the NPT. To implement the Agreed Framework and manage the construction of the two light-water reactors, the United States, South Korea, Japan, and Russia created a new international organization called the Korean Energy Development Organization or KEDO on March 9, 1995. KEDO would provide 500,000 tons of heavy fuel oil a year for North Korea while the reactors were being built. KEDO would eventually have 13 member countries, with the United States, Japan, and South Korea covering all administrative costs. Japan and South Korea agreed to cover financing and supply of the light-water reactors, while the United States provided heavy fuel oil and the cost of storing North Korea's spent fuel rods.[93]

As the crisis subsided, senior Japanese officials were increasingly critical of Japan's national security structure. In September 1994 Ishihara complained to *Sankei Shimbun* that "fresh intelligence does not reach the *Kantei*." Ishihara also complained that senior intelligence officials seconded to the *Kantei* from other ministries and agencies—notably from MOFA, the DA, and the NPA—work at the *Kantei* for a year or two before returning to their home offices and thus depart just as they begin to understand their duties there. "It would be good to make [the positions] a guaranteed three- or four-year final post," he said, indicating his belief that work at the *Kantei* should be viewed as the pinnacle of one's service in government, not a steppingstone to higher positions elsewhere.[94] Japan's experiences during the North Korean crisis prompted Ishihara to begin a review of the JIC and intelligence functions in general within the cabinet office, which would dovetail with government-wide reform initiatives in the mid-1990s, as discussed later in this book.

Moreover, electoral reforms enacted in late January 1994 helped to stabilize Japan's political system. The reforms replaced Japan's multiseat constituencies with 300 single-seat electoral districts and 200 proportional representation seats (later reduced to 180 seats) in the lower house. Reforms also curbed campaign financing—especially donations from corporations—considered a primary driver of Japan's revolving-door politics in the early 1990s as politician after politician was accused of taking money in return for political favors. The reforms created an electoral environment that served as a foundation for a more stable two-party system in Japan and thus reduced turnover among Prime Ministers. As districts now elected only one representative, far-left parties that lacked credible policies—notably the JSP and the Communist Party—lost significant clout following electoral reform. (The JSP's lack of clear leadership during two major incidents that struck Japan early in 1995, detailed below, certainly did not help its political image.) The parties thus slowly fell out of favor among the electorate. The JSP upper house seat count fell to 38 following elections in July 1995, and following disastrous lower house elections in 1996, the party renamed itself the "Social Democratic Party" in an attempt to reinvent itself. Despite this, SDP members won only 18 seats in the 2000 election and a mere six in the 2003 election. Within a decade, two major parties—the LDP and the Democratic Party of Japan—would vie for political leadership of Japan.

The 1993-1994 North Korean nuclear and missile crisis subsided, yet it was but the first of several North Korean challenges to Asian countries in the post-Cold War era. Less than a year after the Agreed Framework was concluded, North Korea began to deploy operational Nodong-1 missiles while it continued to develop the longer-range Taepodong-1.[95] Despite all the contingency studies during the 1993-1994 crisis, Japan was still little prepared to defend against asymmetric threats from North Korea and elsewhere, either alone or in tandem with the US military. But before Japanese political leaders could digest the events of the past 18 months and review possible reforms, two crises struck at the heart of the Japanese homeland in 1995: an earthquake devastated its industrial heartland, and a fringe religious group led by a messianic leader attacked Tokyo's subway during rush-hour in an attempt to disrupt government and trigger Armageddon.

1995: A Land of Natural Disasters: the Great Hanshin Earthquake

Japan is a land of natural disasters. Thousands of earthquakes, volcanic eruptions, and tsunamis strike in and around Japan each year. Japan is prone to natural disasters because geologically, Japan sits atop four major lithospheric plates—the Eurasian plate, the Philippine plate, the Okhotsk plate, and the Pacific plate. The Philippine and Pacific plates subduct under the Eurasian plate, causing numerous volcanoes to form, while the sudden movements of the plates following a build-up of friction causes earthquakes. The tips of the Eurasian, Philippine, and Okhotsk plates meet to form Mt. Fuji, the majestic volcano at the heart of Japan which has been dormant since its last eruption in 1707. The geographic concentration of these plates makes the Japanese archipelago one of the most seismically and volcanically active areas of the world. Approximately 20 percent of the world's earthquakes that measure 6 or greater in magnitude occur in Japan.[96] According to the comprehensive database on earthquakes maintained by the Japan Meteorological Agency (JMA), an earthquake or tremor struck somewhere in the

Japanese archipelago on average 7.5 times a day from 1992-2005. Japan experienced the fewest number of earthquakes and tremors in 1994—816—during that time period, while the year 2000 was a significantly active year seismically, with an astonishing 17,676 earthquakes and tremors striking Japan that year.[97]

Seismicity of Japan and Kuril Islands: 1990 - 2000

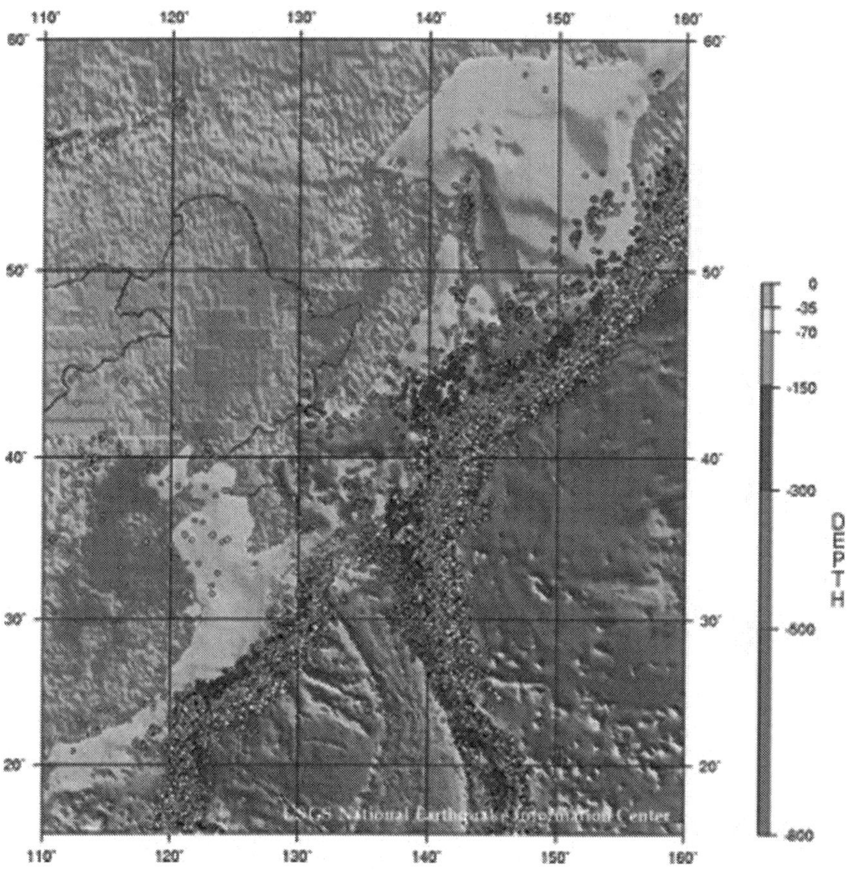

US Geological Survey image of Seismicity of Japan and the Kuril Islands, 1990-2000

While a large majority of these earthquakes are small in size—some not even noticeable to pedestrians on the street—a minority few can cause catastrophic destruction depending on their intensity and location. The JMA measures the intensity of seismic activity on the *shindo* scale of 0-7. Zero and one represent the low end of the scale and are almost imperceptible. A tremor measuring 2 and 3 in seismic intensity will be felt by most people especially in buildings, and hanging objects will sway noticeably. Further up the scale, an earthquake measuring 4 on the scale will wake light sleepers and might cause fright in some. Earthquakes that measure 5 and 6 in intensity cause structural damage. In 1996, the JMA further subdivided earthquakes into "weak" and "strong" categories at the more intense end of the scale to further clarify possible damage caused by these intense earthquakes. Some windowpanes will break and unreinforced concrete-block walls will collapse in the strong-5 range, and roads could suffer damage. The strong-6 earthquakes will cause some non-earthquake-resistant houses and buildings to collapse, and in some cases, these earthquakes will damage walls and pillars of earthquake-resistant houses and buildings. The Big One, the truly catastrophic earthquake, measures 7 in intensity. People are thrown by the shaking, wall tile and windowpanes in many buildings break and reinforced concrete-block walls collapse, even highly earthquake-resistant buildings suffer severe damage and might lean. The ground and roads are considerably distorted by large cracks and fissures and even some changes to topographic features are noticeable, and electricity, gas, and water are cut off over a large area. The last truly Big One to hit Tokyo, the Great Kanto Earthquake, struck in 1923 and killed more than 140,000 people. While modern measuring devices were unavailable at the time, that *shindo* 7 earthquake is thought to have measured 7.9 on the Richter scale. In the 1992-2005 time period, Japan experienced a total of 123 earthquakes in the 5 range and 25 in the 6 range, but only two earthquakes measuring 7 on the *shindo* scale.

At first glance, 1995 seemed an average year for earthquakes. Indeed, almost all 2,006 earthquakes that struck Japan that year measured 5 or less on the *shindo* scale. In contrast, over 17,000 earthquakes struck Japan in 2000, a year of intense seismic activity. There was one exception in 1995, however. An hour before dawn, at 5:46 am on January 17, 1995, sudden movement along the Median Tectonic Fault line in Osaka Bay under Awaji Island created a 20-second earthquake measuring 7 in intensity and 7.3 on the Richter scale (the US Geological Survey measured the quake at 6.9[98]). Later called the *Hanshin Dai-Shinsai* or "Great Hanshin Earthquake," 6,432 people died in the earthquake and resulting fires, while tens of thousands of families were left homeless in densely populated Hanshin area that included the major port cities of Kobe and Osaka in central Japan. Over 200,000 homes were partly or completely destroyed as a result of the earthquake and its aftermath.[99]

The January 1995 earthquake was itself catastrophic in nature, immediately killing almost 4,500 people by one estimate, but the Japanese government's lack of timely response to the natural disaster was roundly criticized as well. While Japanese uniformed and civilian personnel were available in the immediate aftermath of the earthquake, the central government headed by Japan's first socialist prime minister was criticized for its slow recognition of the full scale of the devastation and its plodding efforts to organize an adequate response to it. Indeed, Japan's SDF had years of experience in providing relief following natural disasters of all kinds, having responded to an average of some 800 natural disasters and other events each year since the early 1980s (see graph below). A number of Japanese analysts have examined the response to the Kobe earthquake as a case study of Japan's sclerotic national security system at the time. Kazuhisa Ogawa, a military analyst and former crisis management officer, provided a detailed study of the SDF response that day in several articles he wrote for the monthly *Bungei Shunju.* Toshiyuki Shikata, a retired Ground Self-Defense Force three-star general and consultant to the Governor of Tokyo on disaster response, examined the Hanshin earthquake aftermath in his 1996 book *Kyokutō Yūji* ("Far-East Emergencies"). Iku Aso, an independent journalist and author, wrote a case study of the government's response the Kobe earthquake in his 2001 book *Jōhō Kantei ni Tassezu* ("Intelligence that Does Not Reach the Prime Minister's Official Residence"). Their studies suggested that while local SDF units were available almost immediately after the earthquake struck in the early morning hours and other resources were available in the region including stockpiles of rice and other food, the lack of a seamless, redundant information system coupled with a lack of timely central leadership and coordination among relevant ministries and agencies slowed the government's response.

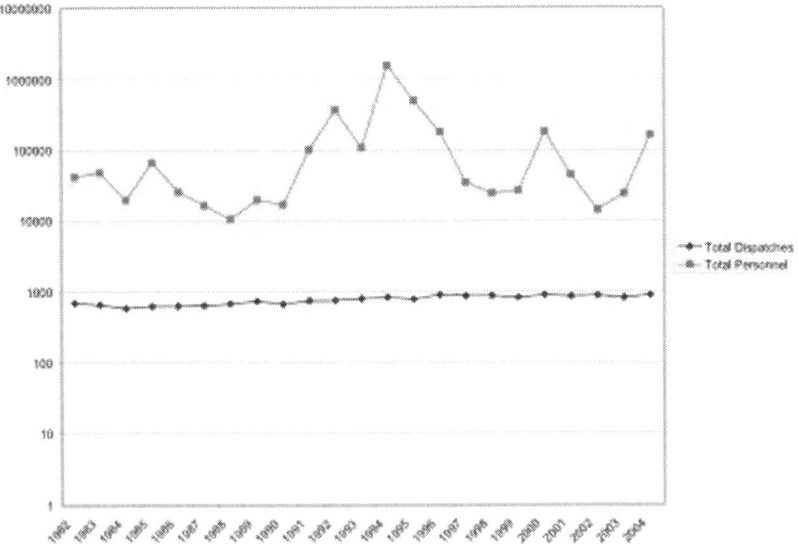

Yearly total of SDF dispatches and personnel to natural disaster areas from 1982-2004. Note: years are denoted as Japan's Fiscal Year, from April 1-March 31, so that

the January 1995 Kobe Earthquake took place during JFY1994 (Bōei Handobukku 2006, pp 314-315).

Colonel Mineharu Yamane, commander of the Middle Army Air Group, was awoken at 5:46 am by the early morning earthquake. Noting the intensity of the earthquake, Yamane, an experienced helicopter pilot with over 4,000 hours of flying time, called the senior duty officer at Yao garrison near Osaka to order the preparation of the over forty helicopters under his command for flight operations in case relief operations were required in one of the 21 prefectures under the Middle Army's jurisdiction. Yamane also ordered air units to assess damage at each of the air squadrons under his command, all part of *dai-isshu hijō kinmu taisei* or level-one emergency service condition. Yamane then provided a situation report by dedicated line to the Middle Army HQ at Itami base, which in turn reported the earthquake to central command in Tokyo. Yamane had by this time turned on the television to find out the magnitude of the earthquake. By 6:05 am, authorities were reporting the quake measured 5 on the *shindo* scale, surely a misreading Yamane thought, as the earthquake felt more powerful than that. Similar preparations were taking place at other Self-Defense Forces (SDF) garrisons, and the SDF had almost 100 helicopters available within hours of the earthquake.[100]

Seismological monitoring facilities controlled by the Japan Meteorological Agency immediately registered the earthquake, but the quake was so powerful that it broke the seismograph at the seismological facility on Awaji Island nearest the epicenter. This delayed the Agency's first report, the 6:05 am reading which Yamane and others saw indicating an earthquake measuring 5 struck near Kyoto. This report relied on data from another facility, however, and thus did not register the intensity as accurately. The

Agency's second report, issued at 6:19 am, stated that a *shindo* 6 earthquake struck near Awaji Island. The third and fourth reports were issued at 6:33 and 6:41. (The JMA ultimately declared the earthquake a magnitude 7.3, while the United States Geological Service ultimately reported the earthquake's magnitude at 6.9.[101]) Each of these reports were sent automatically to the National Land Agency, the Fire Disaster Management Agency (FDMA), and media outlets which in turn reported the earthquake on television and radio. The information was not automatically sent to the National Police Agency, the Defense Agency, or the Prime Minister's Official Residence; Prime Minister Murayama would not learn of the earthquake until over an hour later. The emergency notification system at the time included the PMOR only if a major earthquake struck the Tokyo area, but since this earthquake struck in another region of Japan, information was not automatically reported to the PMOR. Indeed, the PMOR did not have a 24-hour operations center at the time monitoring potential national security events.[102] Thus, the *Kantei* was just waking up to the news later that morning, like the rest of Japan.

Captain Toru Kizaki, the pilot of the first helicopter to survey damage in the area, had arrived to the Yao garrison by bicycle 30 minutes after the earthquake struck. Kizaki was an experienced pilot who participated in a 1993 Hokkaido earthquake response operation and a 1985 rescue operation following the crash of a Japan Airlines B747. Air crews were working with flashlights along the flightline to prepare the olive-drab helicopters as power in the region had been disrupted after the earthquake. The helicopters were already fueled but Kizaki and a crew of two had to warm up the engines in the cold January weather before they could lift off. They were airborne by 7:14 am—less than 90 minutes after the earthquake struck the area. Because of encroaching snow clouds, he and his crew had to fly below the standard 330-meter altitude and at times below 100 meters in altitude. His actions were technically illegal, however, because according to the Air Navigation Act, he was not allowed to fly below an altitude of 300 meters, nor was he allowed to land without permission from local authorities. Yet given the circumstances, he and his crew had to fly low to observe the damage on the ground. As he flew, Kizaki reported by radio extensive damage to sections of the Osaka-Kobe Freeway and about twenty fires in Kobe, but he had to break radio contact each time he flew below 300 meters. Because the only high-performance video equipment in the SDF was located in Tokyo at the time, the crew of the helicopter brought a personal video recorder from home to capture images of the devastation. But the helicopter would have to return to base to send the tape to Tokyo, since neither the helicopter nor the base was equipped with a video transmission capability. Another helicopter took off at 7:30 am to survey the area, and three more took off by 8:30 am.[103]

SDF commanders feared catastrophic fires might ensue, destroying more of the city and killing people trapped in the rubble. This is exactly what happened. By mid-morning, the GSDF helicopters reported extensive damage to fire hydrants, coupled with congested and damaged roads, all of which would hinder firefighting operations. The fires were sure to spread, the pilots realized. Middle Army commanding General Yusa Matsushima and 3rd Division commanding general Teruhisa Asai asked Yamane whether his firefighting helicopters were ready. They were: 15 helicopters were operationally prepared for flight. The local commanders began to plan possible deployments for those 15 helicopters to fight a major fire that broke out in Kobe's Nagata Ward, and to extinguish smaller fires to prevent them from spreading. The helicopters could use a patch of land along Suma Beach Park four minutes from Nagata Ward as a makeshift aerial firefighting landing pad. By early evening, the generals contacted Hyogo Prefecture firefighting authorities to coordinate efforts, but in a bid to protect their bureaucratic turf local authorities replied later that evening that the GSDF was not to proceed with aerial firefighting operations, and that they would contact the GSDF Middle Army headquarters the following morning. The reply was the same the next morning as well: the prefecture would not proceed with aerial firefighting.[104] However, the Kobe fire department had only two helicopters, neither of which was equipped for aerial firefighting. The afternoon of the earthquake, major fire departments in Tokyo, Yokohama, and neighboring prefectures dispatched a total of eight helicopters to the Kobe area and over 1,000 firefighters, but any aerial firefighting capability was reserved for fighting forest fires in the region, because firefighting authorities were afraid that releasing a ton or more of water over a residential area would drown people trapped in the rubble.[105]

In the ensuing ten days following the earthquake, 176 fires destroyed over 658 thousand square meters and completely destroyed Nagata and Hyogo Wards. Over 500 people—8.4% of the total dead—died as a direct result of the fires. For their part, the Kobe City Fire Defense Bureau, which had jurisdiction over the city's firefighting efforts, later cited five reasons for refusing GSDF aerial firefighting assistance: the falling water could cause houses to collapse and could crush or drown victims trapped in the rubble; helicopter rotors could fan the flames; low-flying helicopters would be exposed to dangers such as the rising heat from the flames causing a lack of sufficient oxygen to the engines; the heavy concentration of helicopters in the skies above Kobe would be dangerous; and structural features would render targeting of water difficult.[106]

Prime Minister Tomiichi Murayama first learned of the earthquake at 7:00 am while he was preparing for his day in the *Kōtei* or Prime Minister's Private Residence. He turned on the television to check the latest news. Japan's public broadcaster NHK was reporting that the earthquake measured a magnitude 6, but the station did not have any information about casualties. Murayama changed into his work clothes and at 8:26 headed to the *Kantei* or Prime Minister's Official Residence, adjacent to the *Kōtei*. As various agencies and ministries established *saigai taisaku honbu* or natural disaster task forces in charge of following the situation, at 8:45 am the *Kantei* released a bland statement that the Prime Minister has devoted his "whole energy" to determining the extent of damage and that he will determine a response based on conditions at the site of the earthquake. His morning continued according to schedule, however, as conflicting casualty reports began to arrive at the *Kantei*. The first official information arrived to the *Kantei* from the National Police Agency at 9:50 am: 22 had died in the earthquake, over 200 were injured, and another 230 were believed to be buried under the rubble. At 10:30 am, the FDMA reported what at first glance seemed to be good news: only one person had died, 54 casualties were reported, only a few hundred houses were without water or electricity, and only five highways had collapsed. Yet the FDMA information was old. Despite having dedicated lines of communication with local firefighting authorities, a wireless communications system, and even a satellite communications system, the FDMA information was the least accurate arriving to Tokyo as its satellite comms relay system in Hyogo had been rendered inoperational for over three hours that morning due to a malfunctioning power system, and the Agency's wireless system was similarly out of commission. Thus throughout the morning of the earthquake, the information that reached the Prime Minister through official channels did not cause much alarm. While the television news had been broadcasting images of the destruction throughout the morning,

Prime Minister Murayama reportedly glanced only briefly at the images between his scheduled meetings that morning.[107] Indeed, Chief Cabinet Secretary Igarashi reacted with surprise at a noon news conference when told by a reporter that the death toll had passed 200.

Murayama himself was preoccupied with a political crisis within the JSP, as two dozen Diet representatives were scheduled to meet that morning to officially resign from the party's parliamentary bloc. The "New Democratic League" as they called themselves feared the JSP was being absorbed by the conservative LDP. They wanted to create a right-leaning party to rival the LDP, while a left-leaning group within the JSP supported Murayama. If even 30 members joined the new splinter party, the JSP faced possible collapse since it held only 70 seats in the lower house of the Diet compared with the LDP's 200 seats. The coalition would lose its majority and would be forced to dissolve the lower house of the Diet for new elections.[108] But the group was undeterred, despite the terrible timing. On the morning of the 17th, following shortly after the earthquake, the group met in Tokyo's Nagata-cho district and formally decided to withdrawal from the JSP's parliamentary bloc to prepare for the creation of a new party, and submitted their intention to resign.[109] At noon on the 17th, when asked about the splinter group's decision, Murayama replied angrily: "The Hyogo earthquake is more important than the JSP's problems." Suggesting otherwise, Murayama held a two-hour meeting with the heads of his coalition partners in the early afternoon that day.[110] In subsequent days both the faction and JSP leaders suspended formal decisions until the spring due to the earthquake, which likely extended the JSP-LDP coalition. Murayama would remain in power for another year.

With the political difficulties foremost in his mind and a Diet session scheduled to open later that week, Murayama had initially planned to conduct a press conference addressing the earthquake on the afternoon of the following day, but shortly after 3 pm former Prime Minister Noboru Takeshita and former Chief Cabinet Secretary Masaharu Gotoda strongly suggested that Murayama hold a press conference to show the government is putting every effort into relief operations. (The death toll had reached 500 victims by this time.) Murayama called a press conference at 4 pm, but the *Kantei* still had little information beyond what was being broadcast on television.[111] Chief Cabinet Secretary Igarashi later recognized the information vacuum at the *Kantei*, telling a news conference on January 23: "We could not get adequate information on the seriousness of the quake damage" during those first hours after the earthquake had struck.[112]

The region of Kobe was completely paralyzed following the earthquake. Kobe's main traffic arteries were almost completely destroyed. Nineteen pillars supporting the Hanshin expressway snapped two meters above ground, causing a 600-meter stretch of the elevated highway to fall sideways.[113] The Sanyo Shinkansen Bullet Train line collapsed at ten separate locations between Osaka and Kobe, and one stretch had collapsed onto a separate Hankyu line below. Tunnels collapsed or were otherwise damaged in numerous places in the region. Over 220 pillars supporting one subway tunnel collapsed, while other subway stations were similarly destroyed. Damage to the region's rail network alone totaled some ¥412 billion.[114] Had the earthquake struck during morning rush-hour, the collapsed highways, displaced train tracks, collapsed subway stations, and damaged tunnels would have killed tens of thousands of commuters. The earthquake also damaged all the city's port terminals and cranes. In what had been the sixth-largest port in the world, only seven berths were able to receive limited supplies from ships using their own cranes. By the end of

January, 48 berths were available, but the port would be unable to accept major container shipments for two months. Ships were diverted to ports in Tokyo, Yokohama, and Osaka, as well as South Korea's Pusan port.[115] The city could accept only limited supplies from either sea or land in the days after the earthquake.

Local first responders and health officials faced the monumental task of rescuing and treating earthquake victims. Kobe's 330 paramedics were severely limited during their initial response efforts because of damage to the roads, bridges, and other infrastructure, as well as the magnitude of the destruction. First responders could in many cases hear voices from victims trapped in the rubble calling for help in the hours after the earthquake, but limited manpower and a lack of equipment to remove the heavy rubble safely further slowed rescue efforts. Most of their initial work was limited to extraction by hand of victims from collapsed houses and apartment complexes, many of which were built out of wood. Once extracted, some first responders enlisted the help of private motorists to transport victims to the hospital so that they could continue their search for victims. Because telephone service was down across the region, locals could not call for an ambulance. Thus in many cases, local citizens had to rescue each other from the collapsed buildings and transport them to the hospitals, clinics, or makeshift triage centers at local schools. When an apartment complex housing over 40 Kobe University students collapsed, for example, firefighters were unavailable so local neighbors dug out what survivors they could locate.[116] Kobe paramedics were also hindered in providing advanced care for victims, as only six of the 330 paramedics were trained in Advanced Life Support. Moreover, under normal circumstances prior to giving care the paramedics were trained to seek authorization from a physician, which was in many cases impossible after the Kobe earthquake due to loss of communications.[117] In some cases first responders had to save their own first after some hospitals suffered damage in the earthquake. The top three floors of Kobe's Nishi City hospital collapsed hours after the earthquake, trapping 47 patients and three nurses, for example. While firefighters and SDF personnel had rescued 46 people by that evening, four were still trapped in the rubble. As it was, the entire area including the hospital had lost electricity and doctors were quickly running out of medical supplies. One patient called the scene a "living hell."[118]

In an attempt to secure an undamaged section of town for future relief operations, SDF pilots landed in Oji Recreational Park. At 10 am, Hyogo Governor Kaihara requested GSDF assistance, and with that request the DA established a *saigai taisaku honbu* or "Natural Disaster Countermeasures Office" by 11 am. Some 225 personnel were to be dispatched from Himeji garrison in Hyogo, and the pilots wanted to establish control over the park area as a base of operations as it was the only open space available in Kobe. The main gates had been locked, preventing earthquake victims from entering the park in the hours after the earthquake. The GSDF Middle Army then set to work establishing a relief operations base in Oji Recreational Park. National Land Agency Director-General Ozawa, who had authority over relief operations in the initial days after the earthquake, arrived at Oji late that afternoon for a one-hour helicopter tour of the area. (The death toll had crossed 1,000 victims by the time he arrived.)[119] While scattered teams of SDF personnel in the region had begun rescue operations the day of the earthquake, it was not until 7:05 am the next morning that 293 SDF personnel arrived to begin actual search and rescue operations.[120] They were the first of 2,300 who would be dispatched to the area in the 36 hours following the earthquake for rescue operations.

Severe damage to the region's transportation infrastructure hindered deliveries of supplies and personnel to the region.

Home Affairs Minister Hiromu Nonaka, speaking after a cabinet meeting at 10:50 am, noted that 710 police had been dispatched from the Shikoku, Chugoku, and Kinki regions of Japan but that traffic jams had slowed their arrival to the Kobe area. At 1 pm, the Minister of Transportation requested Japan's three main airlines to provide emergency flight services to the area. By 2:45 that afternoon, 2,200 police officers from around the country had volunteered to assist rescue efforts in Kobe, but transporting them to the area remained a major problem.[121] The ASDF that day provided five C-1 and C-130 transports from Iruma Air Base to begin transporting volunteers and emergency supplies to the region.[122] The ASDF planned to add another 16 transports to the relief effort in the coming days, while the MSDF readied the dispatch of 22 ships and a refueling vessel to transport emergency supplies to the region. (These followed the supply ship *Yura* that had already departed its home port of Kure at 9:40 am the morning of the disaster to deliver emergency food rations to the region.)[123]

DA Director-General Tamazawa had lunch with the Chairman of the US Joint Chiefs of Staff, General Shalikashvili, who was visiting the Prime Minister's Official Residence the day of the earthquake. Shalikashvili offered to send US Forces in Japan to the area to help with disaster relief. The aircraft carrier *USS Independence*, stationed at Yokosuka port near Tokyo, had begun to prepare for possible deployment to Kobe as well, with food and tents readied at the Yokosuka berth to be shipped to Kobe. The *Independence*, moreover, had extensive medical facilities. One technicality ultimately prevented the *Independence*'s deployment to Kobe, however. In 1975, Kobe declared itself a nonnuclear city and required all incoming vessels to certify in writing that they were not carrying nuclear weapons. While the *Independence* certainly was not deploying to Kobe with nuclear arms of any kind, the technicality caused confusion between the national and local governments concerning the legality of the deployment. Kobe Mayor Kazutoshi Sasayama later asserted that the central government had final responsibility to decide whether to allow the *Independence* into the area, but Nobuo Ishihara, the senior central government bureaucrat at the time, blamed the Kobe government's nonnuclear clause for the lack of a dispatch.[124] Japan's Foreign Ministry later cited severe damage to the region's port facilities and difficulty in transporting earthquake victims to and from the *Independence* as reasons for not accepting its deployment to the area.[125] The US also offered aircraft, bulldozers, generators, and rescue dogs to assist rescue efforts; the III Marine Expeditionary Force shipped nearly 60,000 blankets, 62,000 gallons of bottled water, sheeting, and tents to the region.[126] Ultimately, over 60 countries offered aid to Japan, including rescue personnel and dogs from Switzerland and France, relief supplies from Russia, South Korea, and China, 35 dome-shaped houses for temporary shelter from Canada, and 17,000 pair of underwear from Egypt![127] James Lee Witt, the director of the US Federal Emergency Management Agency, also toured the disaster area in early February, but he carefully refrained from answering reporters' pointed questions about what they perceived as the Japanese government's slow response to the quake.[128]

Supplies began to arrive in greater quantities on January 18, but deliveries to victims throughout the region were initially slow. Hyogo Prefecture had requested the delivery of 2,300 tons of rice from Japan's Food Agency on the afternoon after the quake, but the Agency did not begin to prepare delivery of rice from its facilities in Kyoto and Osaka until the next morning, and the Agency officially ordered delivery of 3,000 tons of rice at 11 am. Seven Maritime Self-Defense Force ships departed Kure port at 8 am that morning to deliver emergency food and water to the region, and at 11:40 am an Air Self-Defense Force unit delivered meat, vegetables, and canned goods to the area, but during a 10:40 am press conference DA Director-General Tamazawa was fending off critics who said the DA response was too slow. The Cabinet met again just before 10 am on the 18th and again affirmed that the central government was doing all it could to respond to the crisis. At 1 pm, the SDF dispatched 5,200 uniformed personnel and 65 helicopters to conduct relief operations and deliver food in the region. By 7 pm that evening, 9,500 SDF personnel were in the region and 94 ASDF planes were delivering supplies to the area.[129] Within three days, some 15,000 SDF personnel were assisting with rescue and relief operations in the region. GSDF personnel and other volunteers were making circuits through the damaged areas of the region delivered water, food, and blankets, but the supplies always quickly ran out before their routes were complete. What stores were open those initial days quickly sold out of instant ramen and bottled water.

Notoriously, a Japanese organized crime syndicate began to provide assistance to victims almost immediately after the earthquake. The national headquarters for the *Yamaguchi-Gumi*, one of the three largest *Yakuza* groups in Japan, was located in Kobe's Nada Ward. The *Kumi-cho* or leader of the *Yamaguchi-Gumi*, who at the time was Yoshinori Watanabe, lived in a residential complex next door. The buildings were largely undamaged by the earthquake, and because the group's headquarters had a special stock of supplies in case authorities shut off their water and access to food, Watanabe and his *kumi-in* gangsters began to offer food, water, and powdered milk from their headquarters in Kobe. Watanabe also issued a request to *Yamaguchi-gumi* chapters in other parts of Japan to send supplies to the Kobe headquarters. In the days after the earthquake the group delivered over a thousand *bento* food boxes using their large black vans—notorious for spouting nationalist slogans in the streets of large cities during rallies—and the group also supplied over a thousand blankets and diapers. This form of assistance was virtually uncovered in Japanese media in the days after the earthquake. Most of the initial reports of *Yamaguchi-Gumi* activities came from foreign correspondents and were re-reported after Japanese correspondents read of their activities in the *Guardian*, the *LA Times*, the *New York Times*, and other dailies.[130] Certainly, the *Yamaguchi-gumi* was not the only private organization to deliver relief supplies to the disaster area—the large supermarket chain Daiei re-opened its stores that day despite the regularly scheduled company holiday and arranged emergency shipments from other stores to those in the earthquake-hit area, for example, and the Japan Chain Store Association made similar requests to member stores in the following days. Yet despite the *Yamaguchi-Gumi*'s initial acts of benevolence, however, members soon returned to their criminal ways as they attempted to expropriate the land under destroyed houses from their owners in the weeks after the earthquake.[131]

Even North Korea, which was experiencing drought and famine at home, offered token donations. The North Korean Red Cross Society sent $200,000 to the pro-Pyongyang General Association of Korean Residents in Japan (GAKRJ) to help victims of the earthquake, while North Korean Prime Minister Kang Song-san sent a message of condolence to Prime Minister Murayama on January 18. Prime Minister Murayama took the unprecedented step of cabling Kang on February 3 thanking him for his condolence message, which was the first time a sitting Japanese prime minister wired a message to his North Korean counterpart. A Ministry of Foreign Affairs spokesman had to emphasize that the exchange of messages did not mean Japan recognized North Korea diplomatically and that the messages were exchanged from a humanitarian point of view only. Murayama's response did not refer to the North Korean Red Cross Society's $200,000 offer or Kim Jong-il's condolence message to Han Toksu, leader of the GAKRJ, however.[132]

Given the cold January weather, shelter for survivors was extremely important. By January 26, 599 shelters were housing over 236,000 people in Kobe city.[133] In neighboring Nishinomiya city, 170 locations such as schools and municipal buildings served as temporary shelters for over 40,000 people. Of the 160,000 households there, only 3,000 had running water and sewage. In another neighboring city, Ashiya, 51 temporary shelters were set up, and in Amagasaki city 8,600 people took shelter in public buildings.[134] Rescue workers in the days and weeks after the earthquake became delivery workers, transporting blankets, clean water, and food to shelters across the region as the roads were gradually cleared away and repaired. When Emperor Akihito and Empress Michiko visited the area on January 31, the temperature fell to minus 1.8 degrees C, the lowest that winter, and many of the close to 300,000 homeless remained temporarily housed in unheated gymnasiums, schools, and tents (most municipal gymnasiums and schools in the area do not have central heat, but rather rely on kerosene space heaters in each room for heat).[135] Even as the city rebuilt itself, thousands of residents would still be in temporary shelters on the year anniversary of the earthquake: 48,000 families were still living in city-provided temporary housing a year later, while an estimated 125,000 families were still searching for homes from their temporary accommodations in vacant public apartments.[136]

The Japanese public was greatly dissatisfied with the government's response to the earthquake and thus strongly supported an improved crisis-management capability. In a *Nihon Keizai Shimbun* poll following the earthquake in late January, only 5% of those polled were satisfied with the Japanese government's response to the Kobe earthquake. In addition, 87.6% of respondents wanted the Japanese government to enhance its crisis management capability.[137] Murayama's approval ratings fell to 36% following the earthquake, five percentage points lower than a previous poll in November, according to the *Nihon Keizai Shimbun* poll.[138] Sensing a weakness in his party's erstwhile coalition partner, former Prime Minister and LDP heavyweight Nakasone obliquely criticized Murayama and the JSP for what he claimed was an historical ignorance regarding the SDF's response capabilities in an interview with the magazine *Aera*: "Prime Minister [Murayama] has had hardly any contact with the Self-Defense Forces because he is the chairman of the JSP and he does not know the functions of the SDF very well" and therefore "he was not ready for a disaster." Nakasone was of course referring to the JSP's post-war policy of unarmed neutrality and support for the disbandment of the SDF, which the party had only recently renounced. "The JSP's awareness of defense and disasters is different from that of the Liberal Democratic Party," Nakasone asserted. (Ever the political opportunist, Nakasone then took credit for establishing a disaster response capability in the SDF while he was head of the DA in 1971.)[139] Nakasone's comments and the Japanese electorate's new-found emphasis on "crisis management" underscored the new political reality facing any politician aspiring to become prime minister. Japan's national security was now a major political issue. All future prime ministers and major political parties, moreover, would have to understand Japan's national security structure in order to respond quickly and decisively to any security challenge emerging from within Japan or in areas surrounding Japan, to avoid the criticism faced by the Murayama cabinet in the aftermath of the Great Hanshin earthquake.

In the short term, the need for a 24-hour information fusion center at the *Kantei* emerged as a primary policy goal. As Deputy Chief Cabinet Secretary Teijiro Furukawa later described in his memoirs: "Accurate information did not reach the *Kantei.* The urgent task became how to establish a crisis management system." First on the list of action items was "the equipping of a 24-hour information collection system at the *Kantei.*"[140] Thus, in addition to securing a supplemental budget of ¥2.7 trillion to support reconstruction efforts in the region, days after the earthquake Murayama proposed establishing a 24-hour information collection center at the *Kantei* to inform future prime ministers on a timely basis of disasters and other immediate security concerns. As envisioned, the new center would coordinate information with the National Police Agency, fire departments, and the Self-Defense Forces, and would immediately inform the prime minister, cabinet members, and other concerned officials of a major natural disaster—which was the former duty of the National Land Agency. The center would be placed under the control of the Cabinet Intelligence and Research Office, indicating the center would be plugged into the intelligence structure as well. (While he supported the creation of a 24-hour operations center, CIRO chief Yoshio Omori initially strongly opposed CIRO overseeing the center because he viewed natural disaster information monitoring as fundamentally different from intelligence collection and dissemination. He eventually relented, however.[141]) The Defense Agency also proposed expanding its satellite communications system to transmit pictures of disaster areas directly to the center, although later incidents suggested this capability was not implemented initially.[142] The satellite transmission capability—or lack thereof—would be a recurring issue during later national security events in Japan. An interim center was operating by April 1995, although the main facility would not be ready until major renovations of the Prime Minister's Official Residence were completed in 2004.

It is impossible to know how many lives could have been saved under ideal response conditions. According to former GSDF General Toshiyuki Shikata, approximately 4,500 people died as a direct result of the earthquake. Another 1,000 died in the subsequent fire, pinned under rubble, or because of untimely medical treatment. Another 800 died in the days and weeks after the earthquake due to quake-related injuries.[143] Multiple problems hindered a more coordinated, national response effort. First, the central government did not have access to near real-time, redundant lines of communication, which led to a lack of independent, on-the-ground sources of information besides what was broadcast on the local Tokyo news. Secondly, a disconnect between national capabilities and local government officials' understanding of how to request and incorporate those capabilities while coordinating local response to a major disaster led to significant delays. It was certainly true that the *Kantei* lacked a robust crisis management office devoted to coordinating nationwide relief efforts, but the situation was further exacerbated by the central government's surprisingly strict adherence to bureaucratic rules and regulations that hindered the relief process. While Shikata and others did not state so outright, the implication of their analyses were clear. Tokyo should have understood the magnitude of the situation more quickly, it should have ordered the dispatch of rescue units to the region as quickly as possible based on a thorough acquaintance of Japan's national capabilities, and the central government should have worked more closely with local authorities. But before Japan could digest lessons learned from the Hanshin earthquake, a terrorist act focused the world's attention on a strange millenarian cult with aspirations to destroy and remake the world, starting with a major attack targeting the Japanese central government in Tokyo.

A Cult's Armageddon

On the morning of March 20, 1995, at shortly before 8 am, five men boarded five different subway trains at opposite ends of the major Marunouchi, Chiyoda, and Hibiya lines in Tokyo. The men carried with them liquid-filled plastic bags obscured by newspapers and umbrellas. To hide their identities they wore sunglasses and masks commonly worn by people with colds. The trains intersected in the center of Tokyo at Kasumigaseki station, with the trains all scheduled to arrive within a few minutes of each other shortly after 8 am. This station served the Tokyo central district of Kasumigaseki, the heart of Japan's central government. Within a short walking distance from the Kasumigaseki entrance were the National Policy Agency, Tokyo Metropolitan Police Headquarters, Ministry of Foreign Affairs, the Ministry of Finance, and several other major government office buildings. The men planned to kill central government workers—especially police employees—as the workers commuted to their offices near the Kasumigaseki station in an effort to create chaos within the central government.

During the prior week, Shoko Asahara, the head of the Japanese religious cult "Aum Shinrikyo," met repeatedly with his chief weapons scientists Hideo Murai, Kiyohide Hayakawa, and Tomomitsu Niimi, to discuss plans for an attack. Asahara had learned from an informant that officials at the National Police Agency had decided to raid Aum Shinrikyo facilities by March 22, and he wanted to divert their attention as he prepared for November that year, when he had predicted true Armageddon would begin. Murai, the group's "Minister of Science and Technology," devised the plan to spread deadly poison gas in the subway and ordered Masami Tsuchiya, his chief chemical weapons technician, to manufacture the substance. Murai chose trusted Aum adherents, divided into five teams, to carry the packages onto the subway trains.

On the evening of the 19th, Aum's "Minister of Intelligence," Yoshihiro Inoue, led the five riders on a reconnaissance run on the same Tokyo subway lines they would target the following day. They then returned to Aum's main Kamikuishiki complex at the base of Mt. Fuji early that morning. There, following prayer in front of a large statue of Shiva, the Hindu god of destruction and creation, Murai gave umbrellas and plastic bags to the men. They practiced poking the bags with the specially sharpened tips of the umbrellas so that the liquid flowed freely. (One cultist, 30-year-old Kenichi Hirose, poked so hard in training that he broke the tip of his umbrella![144]) Murai then gave the group the actual gas-filled bags—square plastic packs, normally used for intravenous drips but this time filled with a deadly liquid: Nakagawa and biochemist Seiichi Endo had already filled the bags with six litters of chemical precursors that would form sarin gas when released.[145] Murai also gave the group sarin antidote, in case they too were affected by the gas before delivery was complete. The group left again for Tokyo at 6 am.[146] The teams stopped on the way to their target subway stations to buy newspapers to cover the odd-looking bags of liquid—perhaps in an attempt to tie other groups to the attack, one team bought two newspapers for archrival organizations: the Japan Communist Party's *Akahata* or "Red Flag" and the Buddhist group Soka Gakkai's *Seikyo Shimbun* or "Sacred Teaching Newspaper."[147] The teams arrived at their pre-planned departure stations, boarded their respective subway trains, placed the plastic bags on the floor of the subway cars concealed under the newspapers, and as the trains pulled into their next stations on the way to Kasumigaseki, they pierced the bags with the tip of the umbrella so that the sarin gas mix would spread in each car. They then departed the train and were picked up in front of the station. The delivery took only a few minutes.

The sarin evaporated quickly, turning to an odorless and colorless gas that when inhaled caused loss of bodily functions, vomiting, defecation, twitching, loss of consciousness, and death. The dissemination method was crude, however. After puncturing, the unevenly mixed liquid did not evaporate well and produced relatively little gas, sparing many potential victims. Stories of survivors from that day, detailed in Japanese media and later collected by the famed Japanese novelist Haruki Murakami, illustrated the initial confusion among the passengers and subway workers immediately after the attack: station attendants cleaned up the bags perfunctorily and without wearing any protection except for white gloves; many passengers remained on the trains despite the strange odors and noticeable and worsening symptoms. One man recalled seeing attendants carry the punctured bags out of the Chiyoda line car in a box, liquid spilling from the sides, while another attendant mopped the platform with the newspapers that had covered the bags. After the attendants were done, the passengers stayed on the train to the next station, everyone coughing.[148] Another man recalled how a passenger near the sarin-oozing bags on the Marunouchi line train vomited—but the syrupy sweet smell (others would describe paint thinner or creosote-like smells) emanating from the bags was not at all repellent and passengers remained on the subway car through another three stations despite their severe coughs, itchy eyes, and the vomit. Passengers simply put handkerchiefs to their mouths and opened windows, as did passengers on the other subway trains. Attendants picked up the bags at the fourth station and gave the area a quick wipe down before the train departed again.[149] The sarin placed on the Hibiya line train, however, was fast acting and more potent, with people feeling the effects within two stops and collapsing by the third, although the train continued to Kasumigaseki station before it was taken out of service.[150] Another passenger recalled that "people were dropping like flies" on the Hibiya line train coming from the other direction, and he and other passengers formed relay teams to get the victims up the stairs to the surface, and stopped traffic for rides to the hospital.[151] Hospitals were inundated with real victims and those with phantom symptoms; some were asked to return the next day. In all, 12 people died in the brazen attack and thousands more were injured.

• • •

Chizuo Matsumoto, the founder and leader of Aum Shinrikyo, was born the fourth son of seven children in rural Kyushu in 1955. He suffered from infantile glaucoma and was completely blind in one eye and partially blind in the other. Because of his condition, he was ostracized and bullied as a young boy at school. His parents, who lived in poverty as weavers of traditional Japanese *Tatami* mats, enrolled him at the government-supported Kumamoto Prefectural School for the Blind because of his condition and the difficulties he faced at public schools. Unlike most of the other children there, however, Matsumoto still had partial sight in his right eye and he quickly learned to use this to his advantage. He grew bigger than the rest of the children and with his sight partially intact, he became the bully at the school. He campaigned several times for student-body president in grade school but was not popular and failed to get elected. He continued to believe he would be someone important someday, however, and developed delusions of becoming prime minister.[152]

Matsumoto moved to Tokyo in his early 20s to study for the prestigious Tokyo University entrance exams with aspirations of one day running for political office. Failing the exams, however, he returned to his village for a time and was arrested for assault.

With nothing more for him in his childhood village, he returned again to Tokyo, met a young college student, and married her within a few months. The family of his new wife, Tomoko, gave Matsumoto start-up money for an acupuncture clinic, which quickly flourished because of his skills selling dubious herbal remedies, acupuncture treatments, and high-priced yoga exercises to an increasingly affluent Tokyo middle class. One so-called cure turned out to be tangerine peel soaked in alcohol. Matsumoto was arrested and fined in 1982 for selling fake medicines. Matsumoto in the early 1980s became deeply interested in religious sects, and he began a thousand-day training exercise to join Agonshyu, a strict religious group drawing from aspects of Buddhist teachings. Complaining of the training, however, Matsumoto quit Agonshyu to start his own spiritual organization in February 1984. Officially called Aum Incorporated (drawing from the "om" meditation chant), the group informally referred to itself as the *Aum Shinsen no Kai*—Aum Association of Mountain Wizards. It had 15 members and made money selling "health drinks" and teaching yoga. Sporting a scraggly beard by this time and the droopy eyes from partial blindness, Asahara adopted the pretense of a guru. Asahara claimed to be able to levitate in meditation, and he even distributed photos of himself in a full-lotus position hovering over the floor. The photo was of course a gimmick. Asahara sat in his Shibuya condo with his legs crossed in a full-lotus position, hands on his knees, and begin to hop up and down while a loyal female adherent took multiple photos until one captured Asahara perfectly at the apex of a hop. The photo was published in the popular occult magazine "Twilight Zone," however, and served to establish his guru status. He used the proceeds from the hundreds of new students to open more yoga schools. In the summer of 1986, Matsumoto began to claim that he was the only enlightened man in Japan.[153]

In July 1987, following what he called a religious experience in the Himalayas, Matsumoto decided to change the name of the group to Aum Shinrikyo or Aum "Supreme Truth," and he changed his name to Shoko Asahara. His philosophies were an amalgamation of many different beliefs, taking parts from Buddhism, Hinduism, Astrology, and from the Christian teaching of Armageddon and the teachings of Nostradamus. He published books including *How to Develop Your Spiritual Powers* and *Psychic Power: A Secret Curriculum,* and claimed to be able to teach students how to read minds, levitate, and see the future. His students claimed to have experienced out-of-body experiences and the healing of diseases after Asahara's expensive *shaktipat* laying-of-the-hands sessions—for $500 a session. A liter of Asahara's bath water cost $1,000, and a vial of Asahara's blood cost $10,000; drinking of each had spiritual benefits for its imbiber, he claimed.[154] The Aum Publishing Company churned out books, *manga,* magazines, pamphlets, videotapes, and other religious objects (such as a life-size head of Shoko Asahara himself, found during police raids following the subway attack).

As early as 1987, Asahara began to preach that as spiritual leader he may order violent acts to be carried out by his disciples, and the recipients of the violent acts will benefit karmically.[155] *Poa,* practiced in esoteric Buddhism when one is dying, refers to a "transference of consciousness" from this life to a higher plane after death. It is practiced in hopes of guiding the spirit or consciousness to a better next life.[156] Asahara warped the practice of *poa* to justify murder as a means of providing an improved birth after the victim's life had ended in this existence. During one sermon in January 1987, Asahara told his students: "In my previous existence, I myself have killed someone at my guru's order. When your guru orders you to take someone's life, it's an indication that that person's time is already up. In other words, you are killing that person exactly at the right time and thereby letting that person have his *poa*."[157] Thus, when Asahara ordered his followers to *poa*, it was an order to kill.

Using *poa*, the cult first turned murderous in early 1989. Aum member Shuji Taguchi had witnessed an "accidental" death of another member while conducting a particularly austere training regimen, during with the member was hung upside down and repeatedly immersed into cold water. After the individual died during this practice, his body was burned and his remains thrown in a lake near the compound to hide the death. Distraught, Taguchi wanted to leave Aum, but Asahara wanted to prevent leaks of the death to protect the group during its application for religious status with the central government. Asahara had Taguchi confined to a small cell in February 1989 and when Taguchi would not recant his desire to leave the group, he ordered Taguchi "*poa*'d." Four senior leaders—Hayakawa, Niimi, Kazuaki Okazaki, and Hideo Murai—entered the cell where Taguchi lay, hands and feet bound. They strangled him with a rope, killing him. Hayakawa testified at his trial of the killing: "Because I believed in the spiritual side of defendant Asahara at that time, I thought the murder was a '*poa*' and did it out of mercy so that he would not have to fall to hell for disobeying the guru."[158] In November that year, Hayakawa conspired with Asahara and other members to murder a civil rights lawyer named Tsutsumi Sakamoto, his wife Satoko, and their one-year-old son Tatsuhiko at their home in Yokohama. Sakamoto was the attorney for an association of family members who were trying to rescue their relatives from the cult called the Society of the Victims of Aum Shinrikyo, and the Tokyo Broadcasting System was about to broadcast interviews with Sakamoto and the chairman of the Society. Despite suspicions of Aum's involvement in the Sakamoto murder, the Society remained active in trying to increase awareness of Aum activities even as police were slow to investigate.

Asahara was increasingly obsessed with Apocalypse and the end of the world. In 1989, Asahara published a *manga* or comic book called "The Day of Perishing," in which Asahara claimed to decode the Book of Revelation to "start Aum's salvation work": Armageddon is inevitable, Asahara declared.[159] Asahara told his students that the world would end in 2003 in a nuclear holocaust, and only the spiritually pure—those who had reached enlightenment through the teachings of Aum—were destined to survive. He based this claim on his 1988 book *Mahayana Sutra: Yoga Sutra of Mahayana Buddhism*, in which Asahara described the creation of Shambhala or paradise in Japan under his rule, where state and religion would be unified in his "Lotus Villages." "[T]his plan would bring us a peaceful world without conflicts, a peaceful space where no one betrays other people, and a quiet space filled with true love," he wrote. The 1990-1991 Gulf War served to reinforce Asahara's prophecies of Armageddon, if for a short time. He wrote *The Truth of the Annihilation of Mankind* and *Nostradamus: The Great Secret Prophecy* in 1991 to exploit the war as a sign of the coming end of the world.[160] As criticism of Aum's activities mounted in the early 1990s, Asahara later moved the date of Armageddon forward. By 1993, Asahara proclaimed that Armageddon would occur in November 1997. By this time, Aum under Asahara's command was taking active steps to prepare for Armageddon.

In April 1989, while the government continued to delay a decision regarding the group's application for religious status, Asahara and 200 followers went to the Tokyo metropolitan government building as part of a campaign to win official recognition as a religion. Some followers called the vice governor and other officials. The pressure tactics worked. Unaware of the group's recent murders, the government legally recognized Aum Shinrikyo as a religious organization in August 1989. The recognition was an important protection for the group as according to the Japanese Religious Corporation Law at the time authorities were not permitted to investigate its "religious activities or doctrine."[161] Recognition also granted special tax privileges, thus sheltering the group's rapidly increasing revenue.

That same month, Aum purchased a tract of land at the base of Mt. Fuji, which became the cult's main base of operations in constructing the "Aum Empire." They began construction on Satian No. 2 in December, and a short time later built Satian No. 3 and Satian No. 5, their reception area and printing press facilities for the Aum Publishing Company. ("Satian" derives from the Sanskrit word for "truth.") In 1991, they bought additional land and built Satian No. 8, which housed a computer assembly line, and Satian No. 10 where Aum's main worship hall was located. They also built Satian No. 6, Aum's dormitory (Asahara and his immediate family lived in an expansive area on the first floor of Satian No. 6). Eventually, 873 renunciants would reside full-time at the Aum compound, making up half the population of the local village's 1,700 residents.[162]

Asahara formed his own political party, the Shinri ("Supreme Truth") Party, and he and 24 Shinri Party candidates ran in the February 1990 Diet elections. Not only did all 25 candidates lose, they received fewer than 2,000 votes, fewer even than Aum's professed 5,000-plus membership.

It was around this time that senior Aum scientists began to experiment with weapons of mass destruction. A small group of senior members traveled to several locations in Hokkaido including Kunashiri Island and along the banks of Lake Akan and Tokachi River to collect soil samples containing *Clostridium botulinum* bacterium. The bacterium produces botulin toxin, tiny amounts of which could kill tens of thousands of people if inhaled. Biochemist Seiichi Endo and physician Tomomasa Nakagawa led the group, which also included Hayakawa and Niimi. They returned to culture the samples as Hayakawa prepared a "seminar" on the remote Ishigaki Island to isolate other Aum adherents from the attack.[163] A former cultist described the production process to *Yomiuri Shimbun* shortly after the Tokyo gas attack. At Asahara's request, the unnamed member joined a group of five people to prepare the substance in a large prefabricated building at the Aum's new headquarters complex at Kamikuishiki village. They dressed in orange chemical protection suits with oxygen tanks attached when they entered the room, where four stainless steel tanks were used to culture the botulin toxin. They poured a brown, viscous substance from a pump connected to one of the tanks onto a stainless tray. The group then dried the brown substance into a hardened mass, and once dried they milled it into a fine powder. They then dissolved the powder in a liquid solution, and disseminated the solution from sprayers and a fan in vehicles through the streets of Tokyo and elsewhere.[164] The first attacks took place in April 1990, when the group attempted to release the substance from Aum trucks in central Tokyo, while another attempt soon after targeted the US naval base in Yokosuka. The group's last attempt targeted Narita Airport. Each of these initial attempts to disseminate biological weapons ended in complete failure, however.[165] But Asahara and his Aum scientists were not deterred by their initial failures.

While he was building the Aum compound at Kamikuishiki village, Asahara divided the cult into separate "ministries" to prepare to govern following Armageddon—and to arm itself. The various ministries and agencies were headed by highly intelligent individuals with advanced scientific degrees. Hideo Murai, a physicist, was appointed "Minister of Science and Technology" and oversaw the chemical and biological weapons programs. He was assisted by Seiichi Endo, a former veterinarian and graduate student studying virology who joined Aum in 1989 and became "Minister of Health" in charge of developing biological weapons and genetic experiments, and Masami Tsuchiya, Aum's top chemist with a master's degree in organic chemistry, in charge of developing chemical weapons. Kiyohide Hayakawa was appointed "Construction Minister" based on his training in architecture and engineering. Hayakawa built the facilities in which the weapons of mass destruction and other conventional weapons were produced and stored. Ikuo Hayashi, a cardiac surgeon, joined Aum in 1988 and was appointed Aum's "Minister of Healing." Asahara's personal physician, Tomomasa Nakagawa, also joined in 1988 and headed the group's "Imperial Household Agency" (named for the *Kunaichō* or Imperial Household Agency that managed the Emperor of Japan's day-to-day operations; as the head of the "Imperial Household Agency" and of Aum Shinrikyo, Asahara viewed himself as emperor). Yoshihiro Inoue was perhaps the least educated and certainly the youngest of the senior leaders, having joined Aum while in high school and becoming a renunciant in 1988 at the age of 18. Inoue became "Minister of Intelligence" and was deeply involved in the group's kidnappings and killings. Tomomitsu Niimi became Aum's "Minister of Home Affairs," and Tetsuya Kibe became the Director General of Aum's "Defense Agency." Fumihiro Joyu had worked for Japan's National Space Development Agency before joining Aum in 1989. The youthful and charismatic Joyu became "Minister of Foreign Affairs" and helped to establish Aum in Russia.[166]

Asahara began to expand the cult abroad. By the mid-1990s, Aum would have offices in the United States, Germany, Sri Lanka, Australia, Russia, and elsewhere.[167] Russia was an especially fertile target as the country was experiencing major political upheaval in 1990-1991. A newly established Russia-Japan University served as an unexpected initial link for Asahara to Russia. The idea for a Russia-Japan nongovernmental organization was first raised during a 1990 meeting between Mikhail Gorbachev and Japan's Minister of Foreign Affairs, Shintaro Abe.[168] The University was set up in January 1991, and the decree officially establishing a Russia-Japan University was signed by Russian Federation President Boris Yeltsin on November 13, 1991. The decree stipulated that the University would occupy a posh private residence at No. 14 Petrovka Street.[169] On November 21, the Russian Ministry of Justice registered the Russia-Japan Fund, which was quickly organized into the Russia-Japan University. Oleg Ivanovich Lobov, serving at the time as head of the President's council of experts, was a main supporter of the Russia-Japan University and became its first president. (Lobov would later serve as chairman of Russia's Security Council.) Once the University was established, Lobov and other founders—consisting of former Soviet bureaucrats from the defunct State Planning Committee and the Ministry of Foreign Trade—attempted to find Japanese partners to help fund operations, and even discussed possible deals with Japanese investors during a February 1992 trip to Japan where he met then-Minister of International Trade and Industry Kozo Watanabe and executives of private-sector corporations. Lobov and his partners first approached the Nissho Iwai Corporation, which noted some interested in Japanese business circles but required a corresponding Russian match to any Japanese contribution. The University was not in a position to match funding, so the initial venture led nowhere.[170] Enter Asahara. Actively seeking to expand his operations abroad, Asahara did not require a corresponding contribution or long negotiations. He wanted access to Russia. Accounts differed as to how Lobov and Asahara met, with one account claiming that the two were introduced by a sitting member of the Japanese Diet at a Tokyo hotel, while another account said that Hayakawa visited Russia in November 1991 and again in January 1992 to establish contacts there and ultimately to arrange a meeting between Lobov and Asahara.[171] Whichever account is accurate, Asahara offered funding, and in exchange he gained use of No. 14 Petrovka Street free of charge.[172] (The building housing the Russia-Japan University at No. 14 Petrovka Street mysteriously burned to the ground the day after the March 20 sarin gas attack, however.[173] Lobov quickly distanced himself from Asahara and Aum after the 1995 subway attack, asserting he did not know about the group's plans.)

Aum used the Russia-Japan University as a staging ground to expand its presence in Russia. In March 1992, Aum chartered two planes to fly Asahara and 300 Aum adherents to Moscow for a well-publicized Moscow performance at a Kremlin palace, and he also delivered a lecture at Moscow State University. The cash-flush Asahara met with then-Vice President Rutskoy, Parliament Speaker Khasbulatov, and again with Lobov. The meetings were quite successful, and the group quickly received official registration and permission to build a network of Aum facilities in Russia beginning with a branch at the Russia-Japan University.[174] (Still, even by the time of the 1995 subway attacks three years later, the University had no students or teaching staff despite the publicity and reports that Asahara had donated $1 million to the University.[175]) Asahara dispatched Fumihiro Joyu, the group's Minister of Foreign Affairs, to Moscow to be the "face" of Aum and expand the group's presence throughout Russia. At a price of $800,000 a year, Aum bought an hour of daily broadcast time on Mayak Radio, one of Russia's largest radio stations. In December 1992, Joyu established a "Lotus Village" later called Yeltsy in the suburbs of Moscow with a training hall, hospital, school, apartments, security teams, a pasta factory and a clothing store. Aum also followed a technique it used successfully in Japan to recruit young, intelligent students: it opened yoga clubs at Russian universities.[176] Aum would soon operate at least seven branches in Moscow and eleven branches elsewhere in Russia.[177]

Asahara himself visited Russia with a number of followers again in the spring of 1993, and this time his visit included a stop at Kantemirovskiy base on the outskirts of Moscow, home of the division that later helped quell the armed uprising aimed at toppling Russian President Yeltsin in October 1993. Asahara met with a number of Russian military officials there for talks, and was allowed to hold a Kalashnikov automatic rifle. (Russian diplomats, seeking to downplay Asahara's access, later noted that anyone with money could gain access to military bases in Russia at the time).[178] Between 1993 and the cult's subway attack in March 1995, Aum sent small groups of followers to Russia to train at the Tamanskaya and Kantemirovskaya divisions. By most accounts, Asahara had more followers in Russia than in Japan. By the time of the sarin gas attack in March 1995, some 35,000 followers attended Aum services throughout Russia. Indeed, as explored later, Aum's influence in Russia continued well beyond the 1995 sarin gas attack.

Aum was also expanding its business activities both at home and abroad, including noodle shops, lunch vendors, and entertainment clubs. Aum's personal computer and software operations provided the most funds, however. Managed by Yasuo Hiramatsu, who dropped out of Osaka Prefectural College in 1989 to work full-time for the cult, Aum's personal computer business became a ¥7 billion-a-year operation. Called "Maha Posya," the company procured parts from Taiwan and South Korea to be assembled by cult members into computers. Aum required adherents to work at "Maha Posya" affiliates and outlets as part of their spiritual training, moreover, keeping their pay extremely low. Once the computers were assembled, "Maha Posya" then sold the computers at outlets in Akihabara, a section of Tokyo famous for stores that sell hi-tech gadgets, and in Nagoya at deep-discount prices. The company was also accused of illegally copying and selling software such as "Lotus 1-2-3" without paying for the copyrights, thus keeping prices down.[179] Maha Posya's procurement activities abroad went hand-in-hand with Asahara's overseas expansion: Asahara, his family, and Niimi visited Taiwan in early 1993, where Hiramatsu was preparing to establish a personal computer company called "Japanese Daifanrong, Ltd." According to one account of Aum activities in Taiwan, a Taiwanese police official asserted that Aum contributed some ¥300 million to independence movements in Taiwan. The group reportedly planned to foment turmoil or a coup in Taiwan by 1997, which they believed would cause mainland China to intervene. China's intervention would cause the United States to become involved, leading to a US-China war and World War III.[180]

Aum Shinrikyo at this time began to prepare actively for Armageddon. In 1993, Asahara published two more books describing Armageddon. In his first book that year, *Shivering Predictions by Shoko Asahara,* Asahara predicted a "series of violent phenomena" between 1993 and 2000, and between 1996 and January 1998 "Japan will turn into a wasteland as a result of a nuclear weapons attack" from a US-led alliance and "only one-tenth of the population" would survive. He declared in his *Second Set of Predictions by Shoko Asahara*: "I am certain that in 1997, Armageddon will break out."[181]

In the meantime, following a series of failures weaponizing biological weapons in the early 1990s, senior Aum scientists expanded their efforts to include chemical and conventional weapons in 1993. Aum expanded its weapons research into four areas: CW, BW, conventional weapons, and drugs. Hideo Murai headed the entire weaponization effort, while Endo continued BW research together with amphetamine development and Tsuchiya commenced CW research. Hayakawa was in charge of acquiring and building conventional weapons.[182] As Aum's Construction Minister, Hayakawa was also charged with building weapons facilities including the notorious Satian No. 7 in Kamikuishiki village. Satian No. 7 was a three-story building that housed the chemical plant that produced quantities of sarin gas, some of which was used in the March subway attack. Hayakawa began construction in the spring of 1993 and eventually spent ¥1 billion on the facility. (He claimed at his trial that he did not know the purpose of the facility, saying that had he known the facility would be used to produce and store chemical weapons, he would not have used "such cheap materials" in its construction.)[183] Upon completion of the building, Tsuchiya then began to research the production of chemical weapons, and ultimately succeeded in producing 600 grams of sarin in 1993. The following year he produced up to 30 kilograms of sarin and later small amounts of VX gas. At the same time, Aum purchased a 500,000 acre sheep ranch in Australia, and in April 1994 a group of Aum scientists visited the ranch to investigate the possibility of mining uranium there. Indicating Aum was unsuccessful in finding uranium, the ranch was sold at a loss three months later, but in May 1995 Australian authorities found traces of sarin gas on the carcasses of 24 dead sheep there.[184] By the time of the sarin gas attack, the group had laboratories in Satian No. 7 to test botulin toxin and sarin, a botulin toxin plant at Aum's facility in Kyushu, and a special lab and manufacturing facility for anthrax spores at the group's facility on the top floor of an eight-story building in Tokyo.[185]

Hayakawa traveled throughout Russia looking for weapons-related training and equipment. He visited Russia 21 times between early 1992 and 1995 for a total of 180 days (Joyu meanwhile was busy in Russia managing organizational matters to expand Aum's presence there).[186] Hayakawa led small groups to train on a variety of weapons with the Kantemir and Taman divisions in Russia. Hayakawa also visited scientific institutions such as the Gas Hydrodynamics Scientific Research Institute to investigate software modeling the explosion and dissemination of various noxious gases. Together with Murai, he visited the Kovrovskiy Plant, famous for manufacturing automatic weapons, to buy a large machine gun, claiming they wanted to use it as a model to manufacture small toy guns in Japan.[187] (Police later discovered an Aum plan to build 1,000 automatic rifles domestically in Japan.) In 1993, Hayakawa was put in charge of procuring a large helicopter in Russia. Two other cultists, including Tetsuya Kibe, Aum's Minister of Defense, attended flight training at the Chekhov Base near Moscow.[188] Hayakawa found a helicopter and concluded an informal contract with a seller in Russia, but after returning to Japan to gain final approval for the purchase, the seller dropped out of the deal and Hayakawa was forced to find another helicopter. Hayakawa found another one—a Mil Mi-17—that cost ¥60 million. Reportedly, a company in Vienna with ties to the Russian mafia brokered the purchase, shipped it from Azerbaijan through Slovakia and Austria to the Netherlands, and from there to Yokohama.[189] Aum did not have the infrastructure necessary such as a maintenance facility or a heliport to support helicopter operations because they cost much more than anticipated, so the helicopter sat in storage when it arrived at the Yokohama port. Though it finally found its way to Aum headquarters, the Mi-17 would never fly in Japan. The group then began to experiment with remote-control helicopters, but the operators crashed the small helicopter into a tree within a few seconds after it lifted into the air.[190]

The group conducted its first successful chemical weapons attack on June 27, 1994. Partly as a test of sarin gas, the group chose to target a panel of judges presiding over an Aum-related land dispute. Aum Shinrikyo had attempted to purchase land using a dummy corporation but was facing legal challenges from locals opposed to their purchase. While Aum won the right in court to purchase the land, the landowner attempted to back out of the sale when he found out Aum was the prospective buyer, causing a further legal battle. When it appeared that the landowner would win the case, Endo later testified, Aum leaders including Asahara, Endo, Murai, and Tomomasa Nakagawa planned the sarin attack at an Aum-owned restaurant in Tokyo.[191] With the main judge dead of mysterious circumstances, they reasoned, the replacement judge would be more amenable to Aum's position. The attackers went initially to the Nagano District Court, but the session had ended early and the judges were no longer there. They then went to the parking lot near the judges' residences and began to spray the gas from a vaporizer and fan in a van. In their haste to escape quickly, however, they neglected to shut off the spraying device as they drove through the residential suburb.[192] They sprayed throughout the neighborhood, killing seven residents and injuring scores more; dogs, cats and other wildlife died. The judges survived, however. Of the twelve Aum cultists suspected to have been involved in the "*Matsumoto jiken*" as the incident was called, eleven were also indicted on charges of murder and attempted murder in the March 1995 sarin gas attack.[193]

Aum's attacks using chemical weapons continued on a smaller scale in 1994. On December 2, members of the group sprayed VX gas on Noboru Mizuno, an elderly parking lot operator who had helped to protect the family of an Aum member who wanted to leave the cult. (Mizuno was hospitalized for a month after the attack.) Again on December 12, cultists killed Tadahito Hamaguchi using VX gas—they suspected Hamaguchi of spying on the cult. The cultists staged another VX attack in January 1995 targeting another individual who survived the attack. In all, Aum Shinrikyo attempted more than 20 attacks using chemical or biological weapons, beginning with the attempted botulin toxin attacks in the spring of 1990. The group attempted to use the toxin again in June 1993, followed by four attempts to use anthrax in June-July 1993 in Tokyo. They dispersed sarin in multiple areas of Japan in late 1993 and in 1994, and they used VX and botulin toxin in assassination attempts in late 1994 and in 1995 before the attack using sarin gas on the Tokyo subway in March 1995. There were two further attempts to use hydrogen cyanide in May and July 1995, which injured four people.[194]

What was potentially Aum's most deadly BW effort received surprisingly little coverage in Japan. Few Japanese outlets picked up AP's initial reporting in May 1995 that Aum cultists went to Zaire in October 1992 to obtain the deadly Ebola virus. The story resurfaced in a few outlets following the Senate Government Affairs Permanent Subcommittee on Investigations report on Aum Shinrikyo issued in late October 1995.[195] While the Senate report asserted that staff had "confirmed from Aum documents that in October of 1992 Asahara and 40 followers traveled to Zaire for 'medical assistance' to that country,"[196] one Aum watcher and television commentator called the report "irresponsible" because there was no evidence backing up the claims.[197] While Aum would certainly have been interested in Ebola, this particular BW effort garnered few headlines in Japan.

In mid-1994, a malfunction in some of the equipment at Satian No. 7 caused a chemical leak, sickening some Aum followers and arousing further suspicion in the local community—Ikuo Hayashi later told police that he treated fellow Aum members when gas leaked as the group began operating the sarin gas manufacturing plant at Satian No. 7.[198] Locals complained of the smell to the police, who noticed that some foliage in the area was dying. The NPA scientific lab determined months later that soil samples contained traces of a sarin precursor.[199] *Yomiuri Shimbun* reported on January 1, 1995 that authorities had discovered traces of sarin gas precursors in soil samples collected from Kamikuishiki village in Yamanashi Prefecture, but the paper did not mention Aum by name. Since Aum adherents made up half of the village's residents and there were rumors that Aum was involved in the Matsumoto attack six months earlier, readers understood that *Yomiuri* was referring to Aum Shinrikyo given the increasing scrutiny of the group.

In response to the reporting, Aum declared on January 4 that *it* was the target of a sarin gas attack by a rival organization. Taking advantage of the devastating earthquake that struck the Kobe region later in January, Asahara published a new book in early March 1995, *Disaster is Approaching the Land of the Rising Sun*, claiming that another disaster would soon follow.[200] Internally, fearful that the Japanese government would shut his operations down, Asahara proclaimed the day of Armageddon was sooner than he had originally predicted. In preparation for a final Armageddon to be initiated in November 1995 with the dispersal of sarin gas from helicopters Asahara ordered Murai to produce sarin gas in mass quantities.[201] Cult leaders learned from Aum adherents in the government that the police were preparing to raid Aum facilities by late March, and they thus hastily arranged the subway attacks targeting government workers commuting to central government offices.

The first phone call to emergency 119 was placed at 8:18 am. A station worker at Tsukichi Station on the Hibiya line said that a strange smell had caused many passengers to collapse on the platform of his station. Following so closely after the Kobe earthquake, Prime Minister Murayama's aides were quick to inform him of the attack. Murayama received the first report of the attack shortly after 8:30, and he immediately discussed the situation with

Chief Cabinet Secretary Igarashi, although they could do little more than watch as paramedics, police, and chemical specialists continued response efforts. The Ground Self Defense Force's Staff Office dispatched two chemical specialists to the National Police Agency HQ at a little before 9 am, and at 9:30 the NPA requested that SDF doctors and nurses visit hospitals where victims were being sent to help determine the exact cause of their ailments. The SDF as a precautionary measure placed GSDF chemical units on alert throughout Japan in case of another attack. Before chemical units were dispatched to the scene, however, GSDF commanders wanted Tokyo Governor Shunichi Suzuki's official request for the dispatch of GSDF units before driving through downtown Tokyo in armored vehicles to avoid any undue alarm. Suzuki officially requested dispatch of the GSDF units at 12:50 that afternoon, although he had to request a dispatch based on a "natural disaster" as the law at the time did not address responses in cases of terrorism. The GSDF sent the 1st Division's chemical unit from Neruma Ward and the 101st Chemical Protection Regiment from neighboring Saitama Prefecture to decontaminate the stations.[202] Only GSDF chemical units were capable of decontaminating the stations.

Two days after the attack, the Tokyo Metropolitan Police and the National Police Agency began a series of raids at 25 Aum facilities. Authorities found a virtual arsenal of conventional weapons, amphetamines, and supplies to begin production of large quantities of CW. Although Asahara had ordered its removal prior to the March 22 raid, police found the remnants of the large chemical factory in Satian No. 7 concealed behind a large Buddha relief sculpture. In the three-story production area a main computer controlled the mixing process in multiple tanks, while a side facility on the second floor served as a special testing room. A main control room was found on the second floor, and tanks were hidden under a false-bottom floor in another room. When operational, chemical experts calculated the facility would have been capable of producing over ten liters of sarin at a time.[203] Police found over 30 chemical precursors in over 1,200 drums for the manufacture of CW and conventional weapons, including sarin gas precursors phosphorous trichloride, methyl iodide, sodium fluoride, and isopropyl alcohol, glycerin for the manufacture of dynamite, aluminum trichloride, and 2-PAM chloride for treatment of exposure to nerve agents.[204] Police also found raw pesticide and fertilizer materials, which could also be used in the production of chemical weapons.

In Satian No. 6, Aum's dormitory, authorities found scores of cans containing liquid peptone, a common medium for culturing biological samples, and in a prefabricated shack immediately behind Satian No. 10—Aum's main worship hall—authorities found incubators, an electron microscope, and manuals detailing the production of biological weapons. No botulin toxin was found, however.[205] Police discovered ten atomizers built to spray botulin bacteria. Powered by a 12-volt battery, an ultrasound device vaporized water contained in a vinyl chloride tube and was then blown into the air by a fan with the bacteria, small enough to be inhaled. The devices were the same as those found in a failed botulin toxin attack at Kasumigaseki station on March 15.[206] Satian No. 10 also served as a nursery, where 27 boys and 26 girls were found.[207] Authorities also discovered plans for a 1,700 meter-square BW research center that Aum was preparing to build in Naganohara town, Gunma Prefecture. The four-story facility was to have a cleanroom and an area for production of biological agents. Indeed, construction on the building had begun in February, and it was scheduled to be completed by May.[208] Authorities found two automatic rifles in a pillar in Satian No. 2, which had been presented to Asahara in January 1995 as trial products ahead of a planned large-scale manufacturing of 1,000 riffles and 1,000,000 bullets.[209] Police found computer-assisted machining tools procured in January 1994 by Hideo Murai and a manual describing a five-stage manufacturing process for the rifles. The rifles were to be mass-produced at three Aum facilities, including at Satian No. 10 and at a new "Seiryu Temple" in neighboring Tomizawa village.[210] Also in Satian No. 2, police found 15 small one *tatami*-mat rooms with pad locks on the outside of the doors. Windowless and with a large portrait of Asahara, Aum leaders said the rooms were for meditation. Police believed Aum held hostage those who wanted to leave the group in the rooms.[211]

Arrests began in April and May, and eventually nearly 200 Aum cultists would be indicted for their roles in the CBW attacks. Perhaps the most revelatory arrest came when the Tokyo Metropolitan Police arrested Aum's Defense Minister Tetsuya Kibe on April 6, on the innocuous charge of trespassing in an underground parking lot of a Tokyo condominium. In Kibe's car, hidden with components from an AK-47, police discovered what quickly became known as the "Hayakawa Notebook," a description of Aum's coup d'état plans. Most of the notes dated to 1994, and Hayakawa declared at one point: "We have no choice but to fight now." The notebook contained references to explosives TNT, RDX, HMX, PENT. Other sections described training with AK-47s, presumably in Russia, rides in armored vehicles, and the need to purchase "sniper rifles." It included an explanation of how to handle an artillery system, complete with diagrams, and referenced prices for a T-72 tank: "Used, $200,000-300,000." He noted a Russian city that had a "weapons market," described the need to establish an armory for the purchase of a large quantity of arms, and outlined the establishment of small armed units. He wondered: "Could they be imported into Japan?" Hayakawa noted that he and others had contacted helicopter rental companies in

Japan and also hoped to purchase helicopters. Hayakawa showed a keen interest in non-conventional weapons. In addition to notes on the sarin production process, he included a design for a chemical plant and the description of a "bacteria alarm steel case" and "portable laboratory" for biological weapons research. In a separate section, he noted mysteriously that "uranium is omitted in geological map," and he asked, "How much is a nuclear missile warhead?" The notebook ends with the apocalyptic notation: "1995 November War."[212] The March attacks were thus only the beginning of Aum's terrorist plans, as cult leaders planned more attacks later in the year.

Lobov, for his part, denied complicity in providing Aum Shinrikyo members weapons or information for their attack. When one unnamed senior Aum leader told police that the group had given Lobov $100,000 in France for access to classified military information such as plans for Sarin gas production, Lobov denied the allegations.[213] Russian investigators, for their part, said they attempted to get more information about the allegations but their Japanese counterparts were reluctant to provide further information.[214] The Japanese government did not pursue the alleged Lobov role, and Russian authorities let the matter drop quietly.

Police later learned that Intelligence Minister Inoue had successfully infiltrated Japan's Self-Defense Forces by recruiting active uniformed service members. Inoue received from a first lieutenant in the antitank helicopter corps a textbook on protection against CW used by GSDF cadets.[215] Inoue directed a group of sergeants from an elite paratroop unit near Tokyo to conduct a number of robberies to gain what Aum leaders considered sensitive weapons technologies; Mitsubishi Heavy Industries, as Japan's largest defense contractor, was a prime target. One member, Tatsuya Toyama, a former GSDF sergeant and an Aum follower, was arrested on charges that he and four other Aum members broke into Mitsubishi Heavy Industries' Research and Development Center in Hiroshima Prefecture on the night of December 28, 1994, with the help of an employee at the center. The sergeant later told police that they entered the center to get laser equipment on the order of the "intelligence minister" Yoshihiro Inoue. Inoue and Hayakawa planned to use the lasers on tank turrets to aim their main guns, according to police.[216] In another instance, a GSDF officer was charged with breaking into a chemical company factory in Aichi Prefecture to steal research data on gunpowder and rocket fuel with the help of a company insider who was also an Aum member. The data eventually ended up in Aum's Nagoya branch. Another sergeant with Toyama's paratroop unit and Aum member, Takahisa Shirai, was dismissed from the GSDF for his alleged involvement in a staged firebomb attack on Aum's Tokyo headquarters March 19 in an attempt to confuse the police probe into Aum Shinrikyo. Indeed, during planning for the November 1995 attacks, Inoue suggested in written notes that Aum would activate 50 SDF members together with 200 other subversives for guerrilla operations.[217] Inoue's notes suggested at least some of the SDF cultists might have been willing and active participants if Aum Shinrikyo had gone forward with its planned November 1995 attacks.

Aum's Continued Influence

The March 20 Sarin gas attack was not Aum's last. Police methodically (though some would say slowly) investigated Aum's various facilities and searched for perpetrators of various crimes and other attacks attributed to Aum, but on March 30, National Police Agency Director General Kunimitsu was shot and seriously wounded by an unknown assailant. On April 4 and again on April

11, people complained of odors near a suspected Aum hideout in Shinjuku and on the Keihin Kyuko line in Yokohama. On April 19, mysterious fumes on the Yokohama rail system caused 500 people to seek medical treatment, and two days later 27 people were overcome by fumes in a store near the Yokohama station. On May 5, Inoue and other Aum adherents placed two bags of hydrogen cyanide gas in the men's restroom in the Shinjuku subway station in Tokyo, while more bags of the poison were discovered in the women's restroom on the Hibiya Line's Kayaba-Cho station in Tokyo two months later. On May 16, a parcel bomb wounded an aide at the Tokyo Governor's office.[218] Asahara had ordered at least some of these attacks from his hideout in Satian No. 6, hoping to cause havoc in Japan and instigate a coup d'état. Asahara himself was finally arrested on May 16, found after a tip led the authorities to his small hideout above a corridor in Satian No. 6—he could barely stand on his own when police pulled him out of his hovel, and he had to be supported on the shoulders of several police officers as he was led away from the building.[219]

A more serious incident took place that summer. Just before noon on June 21, 1995, Fumio Kutsumi, a 53-year-old bank employee on medical leave, commandeered All Nippon Airways flight 857 from Tokyo as it flew over Yamagata Prefecture. Kutsumi, seated on the second level of the double-decker Boeing 747, approached flight attendant Mikiko Watanabe with a plastic bag full of a clear liquid and a screwdriver in the other hand. The six-piece screwdriver set included multiple driver types that could be attached to the yellow handle—easily carried through airport security in this pre-9/11 environment—and Kutsumi had attached the x-shaped Phillips head driver attachment after take-off.[220] "Be quiet, look at this. This is for *Sonshi*," he told the flight attendant using the cult's honorary name for Asahara. He gestured as if he would puncture the plastic bag. With the sarin gas attack fresh on her mind, Watanabe knew exactly what Kutsumi was threatening to do. Kutsumi also showed her another bag that he said contained plastic explosives and declared he would blow up the plane if the crew did not do what he ordered. He refused to talk with the pilot, however, and ordered Watanabe to transmit his demands to the pilot from an intercom in the upper deck galley. If the pilot attempted to the leave the cockpit, Kutsumi made a veiled threat that he could not guarantee the lives of the passengers.[221] The flight was almost completely full, with 364 passengers and crew on board.

This was the first hijacking of a Japanese commercial flight since the 1970s. Flight 857 landed in Hakodate, a major city on the northern island of Hokkaido, where Kutsumi made his demands. He wanted the Boeing 747 refueled for a return flight to Tokyo, and he wanted Shoko Asahara delivered to the plane. In Tokyo, the few remaining Aum leaders who were free quickly denied his connection to the cult, saying the group had no one registered under Kutsumi's name.[222] In the meantime, passengers on board the plane began to call emergency 119 from their cell phones to detail Kutsumi's appearance, his actions, and his weapons.[223] By evening, police knew that Kutsumi was likely the only hijacker on board and that he probably was not closely affiliated with Aum Shinrikyo, but rather that he had spent almost a year on medical leave from his job and was most likely mentally unstable. His threat to release Sarin gas from the plastic bag was probably a copy-cat attempt following the Aum Sarin gas attacks in March.

After over 15 hours in the standoff and with dawn quickly approaching, the police decided to act. At 3:30 am on the 22nd, police dressed in ANA uniforms quickly approached the plane with ladders. One group placed a ladder at the nose wheel, climbed up, and began to open the 50-centimeter panel to the "MEC" or main electrical compartment where the plane's "black box" is stored. Police then climbed up a small ladder to attempt an entry from there, although little came of this attempt. Others placed ladders at the three main doors on the left side of the plane. Watanabe, the only flight attendant who was not bound as Kutsumi had been using her to relay messages to the cockpit, thought she heard noises, and quickly realized that the police might be trying to force their way into the plane. (Indeed, the police movements around the plane were being broadcast live on television. Had Kutsumi been working with others, they could have warned him of the impending attempt to storm the plane.) Watanabe watched Kutsumi for a moment of distraction. An ambulance with its siren blaring was sent to the front of the plane in an attempt to distract Kutsumi's attention, and then police swarmed the plane from the sides. Just as police forced open the doors to the main cabin at 3:42 am, a startled Kutsumi put the bag down on the seat as he looked around. Watanabe quickly grabbed the bag and ran to an approaching officer, warning him about the bag and its possible contents. Other police, meanwhile, shouted for everyone to get down as they came toward Kutsumi, who brandished his screwdriver. They easily subdued him and carried him out of the plane, his face bloodied. Seven passengers were taken to the hospital mainly due to shock, but one young woman suffered a one-centimeter stab wound in her shoulder. While personnel from the still highly classified NPA units called "Special Assault Teams" took part in the mission, they allowed Hokkaido tactical units to actually storm the plane.[224] The liquid was benign, as the police expected; the plastic explosives were actually balls of green clay. Kutsumi later told police that he was suicidal because of financial hardships during his nearly yearlong absence from work (although he was receiving roughly $7,000 a month in insurance and other payments!), and that he wanted to kill Asahara before he committed suicide.[225] Whatever his motive or mental state at the time, Kutsumi was sentenced to a 15-year prison term two years later.

Still more seriously, a coordinated plot to free Asahara from jail unfolded in late 1999. A small group of young Aum Shinrikyo adherents in Russia, led by Aum adherent Dmitry Sigachev, plotted the rescue of Shoko Asahara in the summer of 2000. The group did not know each other until 1996, when Sigachev began to search for other believers by creating his own website after the cult was banned in Russia. He then met Boris Tupeiko, Dmitry Volonov, and Alexandr Shevchenko, who would form the core of his group to rescue Asahara from his jail cell in Tokyo. Sigachev also sent an email to leaders of Aum Shinrikyo in Japan—which in early 2000 had changed its name to Aleph—asking for assistance in establishing a spiritual center in Moscow, and (despite the ban) got it. He traveled to Vienna, Austria where he received $30,000, and then to Bali, Indonesia where he received a further $90,000 from Aum affiliated members. (Although they admitted to providing funds to Sigachev in 1999, Aum leaders later denied any complicity in planning the rescue attempt.) The four used the money to obtain small arms, explosives, and communications equipment on the black market in Moscow. The four then moved to Vladivostok to begin preparations for the rescue. Other Russian followers traveled to the city as well. Alexei Yurchuk said he could handle the explosives and detonators; another volunteered to transport weapons and explosives; yet another would locate a hide-out in a neighboring village of Slavyanka for Asahara after the operation. They trained at a gym and learned to pilot a boat for their exfiltration out of Japan. Sigachev traveled to Japan in March 2000 to scope out possible targets, such as the prison where Asahara was kept, the Imperial Palace, the Diet building, and other government ministries. He gave up the idea of bombing the government offices and the Imperial Palace because of the security, but he thought security was lax at the prison when he cased the area after midnight. Sigachev also planned to plant bombs at several public places in Tokyo, Aomori, and Sapporo as distractions. Moreover, Japan was scheduled to host the G-8 in Okinawa in July 2000, a perfect time to attract attention to his cause, Sigachev thought. While other Aum followers tried to convince him to call off the attack— "the Master has said in court that prison is the most appropriate place to meditate," they reportedly told Sigachev—he would not listen. Sigachev returned to Vladivostok to complete preparations for the rescue, which included translating phrases into Japanese such as "I will kill you if you resist!" The group planned to demand $10 million in a threatening email to Prime Minister Mori before escaping from Japan by boat to Vladivostok with Asahara and Niimi, another senior leader at the jail.[226]

Sigachev was arrested when he arrived at Niigata airport in June to make final preparations; his followers were arrested soon after, and the plot was exposed. Russia's Federal Security Service found weapons, explosives, and planning material at their apartment.[227] The Vladivostok District Court in January 2002 sentenced Sigachev to eight years in prison for his role as ringleader of the plot. Two of his comrades were sentenced to lesser jail sentences, while one other received a suspended sentence.[228] Immediately prior to the sentencing at a press conference on December 16, 2001, Aleph's new leader, Fumihiro Joyu (who was released from prison on December 29, 1999 and assumed a leadership role in early 2000), denied involvement in the plot. Joyu did admit, however, that Aleph, gave ¥12 million to the Russian follower in the latter half of 1999 for investment purposes in Russia, but Joyu said that the funds were misused in purchasing weapons. Aleph members attempted to talk the group into giving up the plan after being alerted by fellow members in Russia in March 2000, but according to Joyu they failed and subsequently reported the plan to the Japanese police.[229]

Potentially the most damaging incident for the Japanese government was discovered in 2000. Aleph had in February 1998 reconstituted its computer and software operations and was involved in some 210 computer development contracts with over 190 government and private-sector offices including the Defense Agency and the Ministry of Posts and Telecommunications, and large companies such as NTT, Sumitomo Bank, and Kyodo News. The group provided its services as small subcontractors. The government and large businesses contracted out computer and software operations to large, well-known companies, and those companies in turn employed dozens of smaller subcontractors, which in turn hired other even smaller companies or free-lance engineers and developers, often without the knowledge of the originating agency or business.[230] These contracts gave Aum-affiliated workers access to potentially sensitive and even classified data on personnel, systems, and operations. One Aum-affiliated individual worked on the internet communications system used by the Ground Self-Defense Force and on software development for a project related to the Maritime Self-Defense Force's maritime operations command and control system. Following this discovery, the Defense Agency began adding a special clause to contracts for projects classified *hi*—"confidential"—or higher (*gokuhi* is "secret" and *kimitsu* is "top secret") that requires a contractor to submit a list of all the companies to be employed as subcontractors.[231]

Of the 189 former Aum adherents indicted for their roles in various Aum-related crimes, thirteen Aum members were sentenced to death, including Seiichi Endo, Tomomasa Nakagawa, Yoshihiro Inoue, Kiyohide Hayakawa, and Masami Tsuchiya. Hideo Murai was stabbed to death by a member of the *Yamaguchi-Gumi* in April 1995 in front of Aum's Tokyo headquarters. On

February 27, 2004, following a marathon trial that lasted seven years and ten months, the Tokyo District Court found Shoko Asahara guilty of murder and attempted murder and sentenced him to death. Presiding Judge Shoji Ogawa declared at the sentencing: "We cannot help but say that the motivation and purpose of the crimes are too shameless and ridiculous. They were heinous and grievous offenses."[232] Asahara remains on deathrow, but given the bizarre plots following his arrest in May 1995, the Japanese authorities will surely be on alert for further retaliation when Matsumoto is finally put to death.

Missile Tests Across the Taiwan Strait

The mid-1990s was a volatile time in Asia, as China and France conducted a series of nuclear tests in Asia and as China and Taiwan held a series of missile tests and conventional military exercises with specific political agendas. China's missile tests were considered particularly provocative, as they were conducted on the eve of Taiwan's first-ever popular presidential elections held on March 23, 1996. Yet the tests and military exercises also impacted Japan's security, given Japan's proximity to the test areas. With tensions rising in areas south and west of Japan in the mid-1990s, Japanese leaders began to shift their focus from the Cold War-era strategic emphasis on the north and the defense of Hokkaido to the southwestern areas of the long Japanese archipelago during this time.

On May 15, 1995, China conducted the first of two nuclear tests that year at its nuclear test site in Lop Nor in western Xinjiang Province. The test was thought to have measured nearly 100 kilotons based on readings at the Australian Seismological Centre in Canberra.[233] The next test took place on August 17, and China promised to conduct more tests before the end of 1996.[234] Aside from efforts to modernize its nuclear force, which had been clearly underway since the mid-1980s, the tests themselves were in preparation for possible future accession to the Comprehensive Test Ban Treaty (CTBT), which was finally adopted by the United Nations General Assembly in September 1996. China had not abided by the informal moratorium on nuclear tests observed by the United States, the United Kingdom, and Russia since September 1992, but rather had conducted tests in October 1993, and in June and October 1994, despite complaints by Japan and other countries. (Japan as a matter of policy protested when *any* nuclear weapons state conducted a test of a nuclear explosive device).

A month prior to China's May 15 nuclear test, Japanese Foreign Minister Yohei Kono specifically called on China to join the test moratorium in a speech at the Nuclear Non-Proliferation Treaty (NPT) extension conference then underway at the United Nations in New York.[235] Prime Minister Murayama visited China the week before the May test and reportedly requested Chinese Premier Li Peng to cease testing. After Japan's Meteorological Agency confirmed the test, Chief Cabinet Secretary Kozo Igarashi called the test "quite regrettable," and Vice Foreign Minister Kunihiko Saito issued an official protest to China's charges d'affaires in Tokyo, Wu Dawei. Saito also warned that the Japanese public might not support continued Japanese economic aid to China, coming so closely after Japan agreed in December 1994 to provide China with ¥580 billion in loans. Wu in response said that China had been exercising restraint in conducting the tests and that China supported the total abolishment of nuclear weapons.[236] Japan later announced a freeze in yen grants-in-aid, but at several billion yen per year aid grants to China were far lower than yen loans, which averaged over ¥100 billion per year.[237] Yen loans to China would continue. Nevertheless, Beijing chose a politically sensitive time to conduct a nuclear test, as it came a mere four days following international agreement to extend the NPT indefinitely, with final CTBT negotiations underway in Geneva, and against direct requests from a major aid donor and trade partner, Japan. The August 17 test was similarly a sensitive time for Japan, taking place days after the 50th anniversary of the nuclear bombings of Hiroshima and Nagasaki, which Prime Minister Murayama again called "extremely regrettable."[238] China conducted two more tests, in June and July 1996, after which Beijing finally declared that it would abide by the CTBT once the treaty was completed later that year. China's continued testing despite Japan's protests demonstrated the limits of Japan's "soft power," in this case threats to withhold monetary aid.

Little noticed during the reaction to the May 15 nuclear test, Beijing also announced the closure its first and oldest nuclear weapon manufacturing plant in Qinghai Province that had been in operation since 1987. This announcement signified China had completed its transition from manufacturing first-generation nuclear weapons (in Qinghai) to second-generation nuclear weapons, according to Shigeo Hiramatsu, professor at Kyorin University and an expert on China's military. Development of second-generation nuclear weapons began in the mid-1980s, according to Hiramatsu, and the current round of nuclear tests in the mid-1990s were necessary for China to further reduce the size of its nuclear warheads to allow a single missile to carry multiple warheads, giving China a "multiple independently targeted reentry vehicle" (MIRV) capability.[239] Hand-in-hand with the nuclear tests, China also tested a series of long-range and short-range ballistic missiles in the summer of 1995, beginning on May 29 with an estimated 8,000-kilometer test of the new Dongfeng 31 Inter-Continental Ballistic Missile (ICBM). According to information obtained by the DA shortly after the test, the Dongfeng 31 ("East Wind 31") employed a solid-fuel propellant and had a range in excess of 8,000 kilometers and could be fired from a mobile launcher, enhancing survivability. China was also developing the Julang-2 ("Great Wave-2") submarine-launched ballistic missile, based on the Dongfeng 31, and a 12,000-kilometer Dongfeng 41.[240]

France also conducted a series of six nuclear tests in French Polynesia's Mururoa Atoll in the western Pacific from September 1995 to January 1996. Following so closely after China's tests, France's tests in the Pacific aroused such opposition in Japan that then-Finance Minister Masayoshi Takemura joined a protest rally in Tahiti when the testing began in September.[241] Foreign Minister Kono and others repeatedly protested the tests, and the LDP sent six lawmakers to France to express their concerns about the tests as well. Yet despite the protests France completed the tests to its satisfaction, with Jacques Bouchard, director of military applications at the Atomic Energy Commissariat, telling *Le Figaro*: "The objectives were achieved. It was an indisputable technical success." The tests certified the new TN75 warhead to be affixed to missiles on *Triomphant*-class submarines. The tests also gave French scientists valuable data that would allow nuclear simulations to replace actual tests in the future, "giving us the capacity to renew our current stock in 15 or 20 years without the need for further tests," according to Bouchard.[242] Following the tests France announced its intention to dismantle the site—where it had conducted 181 nuclear tests and at the Fangataufa Atoll between 1966 and 1996—as French officials planned to halt testing and join the CTBT.[243] The continued tests despite Japan's official protestations again demonstrated the limits of Japan's diplomatic influence.

Even as nuclear tests continued in Asia, tensions between the People's Republic of China and the Republic of China—China and Taiwan—increased dramatically in the summer of 1995 as Taiwan's president, Lee Tung-hui, was granted a visa to visit his alma mater in the United States, Cornell University, in June that year. Moreover, on July 20, Taiwan's Legislative Yuan passed reform legislation that institutionalized the direct election of the president on Taiwan. With the island's first-ever direct presidential election scheduled for March 23, 1996, campaigning began for the presidential elections as well as for legislative elections scheduled for early December.

For its part, China's Central Military Commission conducted the first of a series of week-long missile tests on July 21—the day after the Legislative Yuan approved direct presidential elections.[244] China test-fired four Dongfeng 15s and two Dongfeng 21s into the East China Sea the week of July 21-26. The Dongfeng 15, with a range of 500 kilometers, and the Dong Feng 21, an intermediate-range ballistic missile, splashed down in seas north of Taiwan and west of Japan.[245] The Chinese press came out with numerous articles that summer claiming, for example, that Lee's Cornell speech advocated "splitting the motherland" and that Lee supported "the right to be externally independent."[246] To drive home its displeasure, China conducted more exercises in mid-August. The Central Military Commission then planned and conducted exercises simulating an invasion off Dongshan Island in southern Fujian Province in late November, ahead of Taiwan's legislative elections on December 2. Immediately after those elections, China announced a new media campaign ahead of Taiwan's presidential elections invoking its own "slogan": "a vote for Lee Teng-hui is a vote for war."[247] Chinese military authorities also announced that they planned to conduct further military exercises dubbed "Operation Kinmen" and a series of missile tests in the East China Sea during the two-week run up to Taiwan's presidential election. The multiple air, land, sea and missile exercises would simulate an invasion of Taiwan's Kinmen Island. One Chinese military source was quoted in the *Eastern Express* as asserting: "Since Taiwan troops on Kinmen have prepared for an invasion for the past 50 years the exercises will aim at overwhelming firepower as well as extreme speed."[248] Beijing also protested Vice President Li Yuan-zu's two transit stopovers in California on route to attend the inauguration of Guatemalan President-Elect Alvaro Arzu on January 14, 1996. Circulars reportedly issued by the People's Liberation Army said the transit through the United States demonstrated the "splittist tendencies of the Lee Teng-hui clique."[249]

China conducted three major military exercises in March 1996, beginning with missile tests the week of March 8-15 with impact zones near the Taiwanese ports of Kaohsiung and Keelung. On March 12-20, China conducted joint naval and air exercises near Tungshan (along the southern Fujian coast) and Nanyueh Islands (off the northern Guangdong coast). Lastly, China held joint land, sea, and air exercises near Pingtan Island, the closest point in the PRC across the Taiwan Strait from Taiwan, on March 18-25. Given the time period of the final exercises—they continued during the actual elections on March 23—and proximity to Taiwan, the exercises were clearly aimed at influencing Taiwanese voters from supporting Lee. Government-sponsored editorials in Xinhua, China's *People's Daily*, and the *Liberation Army Daily* at the beginning of the military exercises on March 8 and 9 declared Beijing's official position in the strongest of terms: "So long as the splittist activities do not stop for a single day, our anti-splittism struggle will not stop for a single day." "The real danger" facing Taiwan "is allowing Lee's attempts to continue with the 'Taiwan independence' stance unchecked, so jeopardizing the efforts to reunify the motherland," the editorials declared.[250]

Yet the exercises directly impacted the two states' closest neighbor in the region as well: Japan. Taiwan had conducted military firing practices in designated areas of the East China Sea 30 kilometers west of Japan's Yonaguni– Japan's western-most inhabited island with just under 2,000 inhabitants—almost every month since July 1994, and each time local Taiwanese and Japanese fishermen had to avoid the area for ten days as exercises commenced on the 4th of each month. Taiwan held its monthly exercise as planned on March 4-10, 1996, partially coinciding with China's exercises. However, the Japanese Ministry of Foreign Affairs complained that Beijing had not contacted Tokyo directly about the exercises and that the Japanese government had learned of the planned exercises only through an announcement by China's Xinhua news agency two days before China's missile tests were scheduled to begin. The paucity of official information complicated the Japan Coast Guard's efforts to issue a timely warning to shipping in the region prior to the exercises. Local fishermen complained that they expected losses due to a drop in their catch to reach ¥20-30 million because of the exercises.[251] Japan Asia Airway, a subsidiary of Japan Airlines, changed the flight paths of its planes servicing the Naha-Taipei route because of the exercises, although the six-day-a-week Naha-Taipei route would be lengthened only by around ten minutes, the company said.[252] The announcements highlighted the maritime and air traffic in the region, however.

The proximity of the splash zones to inhabited Japanese islands (not to mention their proximity to Taiwanese ports) concerned Japan as well. China had designated two splash zones for its March 8-15 missile tests, one of which was located between Taiwan and several Okinawan islands. It was approximately 60 kilometers northwest of Yonaguni Island. While part of Okinawa Prefecture, Yonaguni is only 100 kilometers from Taiwan and is closer to Taipei than the Okinawa Prefectural capital of Naha 400 kilometers in the other direction. Yonaguni is also just south of the uninhabited Senkaku islets—what the Chinese call the Diaoyutai—and disputed fishing waters in the region: ground zero for territorial disputes between Japanese, Chinese, and Taiwanese fishermen and politicians.[253] Thus, an errant missile could easily cause damage or inflict casualties should it fly off-course and hit an inhabited area on Yonaguni Island or even on Taiwan itself. The tests could, moreover, later serve as precedent for strengthened claims over the waters in the region, another concern for Tokyo.

More worrisome, the Government of Japan could not detect either China's or Taiwan's missile tests. After the missile tests began, Okinawa Governor Masahide Ota claimed that one of China's first missiles hit in waters "a little more than 60 kilometers from Yonaguni Island" on March 8 and called on the Japanese Government to take "appropriate" action against China.[254] But Ota was not in a position to know exactly how far the missile's impact was from Yonaguni, as even Japan's central government could not confirm the missile launches. Although the Self-Defense Forces used "every possible means" to detect the launch and trajectory of China's ballistic missiles in the words of Tetsuya Nishimoto, the DA's Joint Staff Council Chairman, the SDF "failed to detect the launches." The SDF radar network in the area was built to detect airplanes, jetfighters, and bombers, but it was unable to detect ballistic missiles. SDF aircraft similarly could not detect any missile launches. Another unnamed defense official told *Yomiuri Shimbun*: "Japan has no means to confirm a launch, even if a Chinese missile flies off track and drops into Japanese territorial waters."[255]

The United States had assets in the region observing the exercises—it flew an RC-135S surveillance plane from Okinawa's Kadena Air Force Base starting on March 7, for example.[256] The United States had also dispatched the *USS Independence* carrier battle group to monitor the exercises. The Independence, stationed at Yokosuka Naval Base just south of Tokyo, was the US Navy's only forward deployed aircraft carrier in the world. As part of the carrier battle group, the *USS Bunker Hill*, an Aegis destroyer, observed the missile tests in addition to the RC-135S. Moreover, Washington dispatched the *USS Nimitz* carrier battle group at high speed from the Arabian Gulf. The carrier battle group joined the *Independence* just before the presidential elections in Taiwan on March 23. Japan, in contrast, was blind in its own waters. Tokyo was unable to confirm independently the impact zone of any missile or whether a Chinese (or Taiwanese) missile had flown off-course and hit Japanese territorial waters. Tokyo was able to rely on its ally during this crisis, but Japanese policy makers suddenly began to wonder, what if during future crises Washington was unable to dispatch assets to the region as they were already engaged in operations in the Arabian Gulf? What if the *Independence* had been chasing Chinese submarines or other naval assets near Guam and the US could not dispatch units to that particular area in a timely fashion? With the United States engaged in so many contingencies in the world, and with China's military capabilities rapidly expanding, Japan might one day have to provide its own naval deterrent in waters near its southwestern islands. Since the days following the end of the Cold War, Tokyo suddenly realized it was completely blind in its southwestern territory and it was therefore almost totally defenseless. This was, moreover, an area closest to a possible future conflict. And China would grow even more provocative in the region in the decade ahead, as its military budgets grew by double digits in every single year since the fall of the Berlin Wall.

Xinhua called the live-fire exercises "highly successful" as they "demonstrated the country's powerful might in launching air and sea attacks." "We will never allow even an inch of our territory to be split off from the motherland," the official Xinhua news agency declared.[257] Despite the tests—or perhaps because of the PRC's continued belligerency—Taiwanese voters supported Lee in the presidential elections on March 23, 1996. Lee Teng-Hui, head of the KMT, became the Republic of China's first directly elected president, winning 54% of the vote.

• • •

Besides the general threat of instability in Asia, Japan fears Chinese use of military force against Taiwan for other reasons. Tactically, the Defense Agency fears that China might use actions against Taiwan as a *fait accompli* to seize control of disputed outlying islands such as the Senkakus, or even of Japanese islands such as Yonaguni or Ishigaki, during operations against Taiwan. Reflecting this concern, "confidential" DA documents were leaked in 2004 indicating Japan had prepared contingency plans to deploy up to 7,200 troops to protect radar sites and airports on Yonaguni and neighboring Ishigaki and Miyako islands in case China attempted to invade Taiwan militarily.[258] Seizure of disputed maritime areas or even outlying Japanese islands would serve multiple purposes. As China further encircled Taiwan, it would reassert control over Chinese-claimed areas near Taiwan and disrupt Japanese and US access to areas closest to Taiwan.

Strategically, Japan's Nansei island chain forms a long island barrier separating Chinese naval bases near Beijing and Shanghai from the Pacific Ocean. Chinese vessels must pass through this island chain to get to the Pacific Ocean, or they must pass through the Tsushima Strait to the North or through the Taiwan Strait to the south to sail to the Pacific. The Nansei island chain and Taiwan—what the Chinese military calls the "first island chain"—thus form a fence separating China from the Pacific Ocean. Control of Taiwan—and islands northeast of Taiwan—would give China greater uninterrupted access to the Pacific. Control of waters around Taiwan would also give China greater control over key direct shipping lanes from the Middle East and Iran, South and Southeast Asia to Japan through the Bashi Channel and the Luzon Strait. Because Japan imports up to 90% of its energy supplies from the Middle East and Iran, China would potentially have a stranglehold over a major shipping route to Japan if it took control of waters around Taiwan—or Taiwan itself.[259] Thus, if China controls Taiwan, it increases its influence over the South China Sea, and China could therefore control the most direct shipping lanes from Japan to the Malacca Strait and on to the Middle East and Europe. It also opens up less fettered, direct access to the Pacific Ocean.

China's growing military presence in the region was becoming increasingly noticeable in other ways as well. In 1997, the number of scramble operations conducted by the Air Self-Defense Force in Japan's southwestern airzone topped those in its northern airzone for the first time in 30 years. The ASDF's Western Air Defense Force—which protects the southwestern islands around Kyushu, parts of Shikoku, and the southern region of Honshu—and Southwestern Composite Air Division in Okinawa, each scrambled 54 times compared with a total of 39 scrambles by the Northern Air Defense Force.[260] As air operations eased in the north, they increased in the southwest even as North Korea continued to upgrade its missile capabilities. Japan by the mid-1990s faced potential security challenges on multiple fronts.

The multiple missile tests in 1993, 1995 and 1996 further emphasized Japan's need to improve ISR (intelligence, surveillance, and response) and capabilities to counter the ballistic missile threat in the region. Japan's neighbors demonstrated a surprising willingness to use ballistic missile threats and exercises to gain political advantage. To this end, Japan earmarked ¥440 million in its FY1996 budget to continue its study on possible cooperation with the United States on ballistic missile defense.[261] Within two years of the tests, the United States began to provide Japan with ballistic missile early warning intelligence of possible North Korean, Chinese, and Russian missile launches collected by US reconnaissance satellites and intelligence agencies.[262] Yet senior Japanese policy makers were not content to rely solely on their ally the United States. As will be discussed later, Japanese politicians were also seriously examining the possibility of building and launching Japanese reconnaissance satellites and a sophisticated radar system even as a major restructuring of the intelligence organization at the Defense Agency was underway.

Indeed, in addition to China, North Korea was developing intermediate-range missiles in the late 1990s. In October 1996, North Korea readied a Nodong-1 on a launch pad and sent patrol boats to a possible impact area in the Sea of Japan, although no launch followed these activities. In May 1997, a US military source said that following analyses of the size of the missile's engine and fuel capacity the intelligence community now believed the maximum range of the Nodong-1 was 1,300 kilometers, not the previously estimated 1,000 km. The new range put all of Japan into range of the missile, including Tokyo and the main islands of Okinawa. There were signs, moreover, that North Korea was beginning to deploy missile batteries in northeast coastal areas, away from the border with South Korea and closer to the Japanese archipelago.[263] Defense Agency chief Kyuma downplayed reports of the Nodong's increased range, however, saying his Agency could not verify them, and some in the DA believed the report was politically motivated to gain Japan's cooperation in the US missile defense plans.[264] (The latter complaint indicated some doubt on the part of Japan that missile defense was technically feasible.) In September, defense sources in Tokyo said that North Korea had deployed Nodong-1 missiles on movable launchers, although they stated it was highly possible the North installed the missiles before the Nodong-1 development was completed, calling the missiles' readiness into question. Given the reports, the US military kept RC-135 reconnaissance planes on alert at the Misawa Air Base in Aomori Prefecture throughout the summer.[265]

In reaction to the continued missile threats in Asia, Japan's Maritime Self-Defense Force announced it was deploying the *Chokai*, an Aegis destroyer capable of tracking multiple missile targets, to its Sasebo base in southwestern Japan near Nagasaki. The *Chokai* joined the *Kongo*, Japan's first Aegis destroyer, bringing the number of missile-tracking destroyers stationed out of Sasebo to two. The *Myoko* Aegis destroyer was already deployed at the MSDF's Maizuru base on the Sea of Japan.[266] Japan could now keep an Aegis destroyer on station in the Sea of Japan on a long-term, continual basis to track potential missile launches from North Korea. A fourth Aegis destroyer, the *Kirishima*, was deployed at Yokosuka and could be deployed quickly to a contingency in the Pacific or elsewhere. And Japan would begin the construction of the first of four more Aegis destroyers later in the decade, a sign of Japan's growing concern over the threat of ballistic missiles in the region.

A major hostage crisis in late 1996 showed that Japan could still fall victim to terrorism, however, drawing Tokyo's attention away from the missile threat for a time.

1996-1997: Hostage Crisis in Peru

The Aum Shinrikyo cult's chemical and biological weapons attacks were not the only attacks sponsored by a rogue group against Japan in the 1990s. Proving that terrorists can strike at a country's national security interests anywhere in the world without warning, on December 17, 1996, another terrorist incident shocked Tokyo on a completely new and unexpected front. That evening, Japan's Ambassador to Peru, Morihisa Aoki, sponsored a reception at his official residence to mark Emperor Akihito's 63rd birthday. Located in Lima's upscale residential area of San Isidro, hundreds of guests attended the reception at the residence including Peruvian government ministers and high-ranking security personnel, over a dozen ambassadors from other countries, and various members of the diplomatic corps. Even Peruvian President Alberto Fujimori's mother and sister, Rosa and Juana Fujimori, and his younger brother Pedro were present at the reception, and there were reports that President Fujimori himself was to attend the reception as well.[267] Explosions and violence quickly marred the celebration, however. At just before 8:15 pm that evening, rebels blew a hole in the residence's wall and stormed out of a van disguised as an ambulance near the premises. The rebel leader, Nestor Cerpa Cartolini, was disguised as a doctor.[268] Inside the residence, other rebels disguised as employees of a flower shop assisted their comrades' violent entry into the residence.[269] The sudden sounds of explosions and gunfire instigated many of the high-ranking diplomats, military and police officers, and other dignitaries to immediately tear off their insignia and discard their credentials to lower their profiles, knowing the hostage takers would prize them above others. A 40-minute gunfight with the police ensued, and El Arabe, the second in command of the rebels, seized Ambassador Aoki to tell the police through a bullhorn to stop shooting.[270] The mayor of Miraflores, Fernando Andrade, later described on Panamerican TV what happened after the rebels blew through the wall: "We hit the floor, and then...they led us into the inside rooms," following which "[t]hey ordered the diplomats upstairs and identified them by rank and workplace before leading them to different rooms." At that point, Andrade escaped through a window. Andrade added that the rebels wore "red and black uniforms that identify them as members of the MRTA," the Spanish acronym for the Tupac Amaru Revolutionary Movement, a guerrilla group active in Peru at the time.[271]

The MRTA rebels almost immediately released 80 women after taking control of the residence, but over 400 hostages remained including many high-ranking individuals: the ambassadors from Brazil, Bolivia, Cuba, Malaysia, South Korea, and Japan were held inside, as were Peru's Foreign and Agriculture Ministers, the President of Peru's Congress, and dozens of Japanese executives and diplomats.[272] Peruvian security forces immediately surrounded the residence and called on the hostage-takers to surrender. They also cut off power and water supplies to the residence; the air conditioning and fans were cut off, creating stifling-hot conditions inside the residence. The MRTA rebels, for their part, demanded the release of top leaders and hundreds of their followers who were conducting a hunger strike in Peruvian jails. As the hostage crisis continued the following week, the rebel leader, Cerpa, engaged his hostages in long discussions about the poor conditions in which some Peruvians live. One hostage released several days later said that Cerpa talked for hours with groups of hostages about poverty in Peru and the MRTA's ideology. "They appeared to be considerably intellectual," the released hostage was quoted as saying.[273] Cerpa was apparently gaining some sympathy in the residence in the days after its seizure.

According to documents seized days after the seizure of the residence, over a dozen members of the MRTA had trained for six months ahead of the operation in the Peruvian jungle with a stated goal to "take power and establish socialism in Peru and to destroy the repressive machinery of the ruling classes."[274] Some of the released hostages later said that based on their accents, some of their captors were from the Huallaga jungle region—an MRTA stronghold.[275] The hostage situation at the Ambassador's residence was the first assault on Japanese citizens in the country since July 1991, when members of the Shinning Path, another Peruvian leftist guerrilla group, shot and killed three Japanese engineers who had been dispatched to that country by the government-sponsored Japan International Cooperation Agency. Fujimori later claimed that Peru's National Intelligence Service knew about plans to seize the residence since November and had alerted the National Police Director, who in turn instructed his police to be on alert. The police, however, thought the MRTA was incapable of conducting such an attack given recent counter-terrorism successes. Even Fujimori had played up his administration's successes in the fight against terrorism, declaring at a press conference following his reelection as president more than a year prior to the hostage incident in April 1995: "Terrorism is virtually dead. Peru is today one of the safest countries in Latin America."[276] The Peruvian police authorities thus did not take the threat seriously.[277]

It was 11:30 am in Japan when news of the hostage situation reached the Prime Minister's Official Residence (PMOR or *Kantei*). Prime Minister Hashimoto, who had taken over from Murayama as prime minister in January 1996, was in a cabinet meeting when he was informed of the situation. He left the meeting upon learning of the hostage crisis to establish special operations centers at the *Kantei*'s Cabinet Security Affairs Office and in the Ministry of Foreign Affairs. He then called Peru's President Alberto Fujimori at 2:45 that afternoon, the first of many in the coming months. (Ironically, Fujimori was the son of Japanese immigrants who emigrated to Peru from the southwestern prefecture of Kumamoto. Fujimori would use his Japanese ancestry four years later to request asylum in Japan to escape a scandal in the country he once ruled.) Hashimoto then held a press conference to discuss initial government measures, including the dispatch of Foreign Minister Yukihiko Ikeda and other MOFA officials to Lima. Little information was available from Lima since most Japanese diplomats in the area were still held hostage. Hashimoto also ordered National Police Agency Director General Takatsugu Kunimatsu (the same one targeted by Aum Shinrikyo cultists in 1995) to dispatch a medical team from the NPA in case of casualties.[278] That evening, Hashimoto twice visited MOFA's operations room in the basement of the new Foreign Ministry building in Kasumigaseki to check on the latest information. Hashimoto did not return to his personal residence until shortly before 1 am the next morning.[279]

The following day Hashimoto established a 13-member senior team to coordinate the Japanese government's response to the hostage crisis. Foreign Minister Ikeda, Chief Cabinet Secretary Seiroku Kajiyama, and Home Affairs Minister Katsuhiko Shirakawa in his capacity as chairman of the National Public Safety Commission were named to the senior crisis team. Others were named to the team with tenuous connections to the hostage crisis. Minister of Education Takashi Kosugi was named to the team, for example, because a Japanese teacher was believed held hostage. Defense Agency Director-General Kyuma was notably absent, despite the use of DA aircraft to transport high-ranking government officials to and from Peru. (Director-General Kyuma and Telecommunications Minister Hisao Horinouchi were added to the team a week later on December 23.) Other members included two deputy chief cabinet secretaries, the state foreign secretary, and the head of the National Police Agency.[280]

As this group met to discuss Japan's options in the initial days of the crisis, Hashimoto visited MOFA's operations room multiple times a day to be briefed on the latest information concerning the situation. If anything, he wanted to give the perception that he was taking personal charge of this most recent crisis, given the whithering criticism of his predecessors and the central government following the Kobe earthquake and the slow investigations into the Aum cult attacks. Due to the time difference between Tokyo and Lima and Hashimoto's insistence on personally visiting MOFA's operations center, he reportedly got little sleep; he was able to take a brief nap the afternoon of December 23 after already visiting MOFA twice that day, for example, and he would visit two more times before holding a midnight press conference to discuss the status of the hostages.[281] In contrast, he visited the newly established Cabinet Information Collection Center (CICC) at the *Kantei*—a much closer location—only once in the initial days of the crisis, raising initial questions about the efficacy of the CICC.[282] Not only was the CICC relatively new, having been established in May 1996, but it was also located in a cramped room in an adjacent annex building next to the actual *Kantei*. When a crisis actually occurred, the center's staff borrowed a near-by room normally used by the cameramen attached to the Prime Minister's Residence as a Crisis Management Center (CMC). However, operations personnel found that the temporary quarters did not permit them to do their work properly given its make-shift status. It was not until March 1997 that a control room was finally provided to the CICC to properly handle the crisis.[283] But in the interim, Hashimoto was determined to show he was taking a leadership role in handling the hostage crisis, avoiding the mistakes made by his recent predecessors during the North Korea nuclear crisis, the Kobe earthquake, and the Aum Shinrikyo CBW attacks.

The Japanese government did not dispatch any counter-terrorist units to the region to take part in any possible hostage rescue attempt in the early days of the crisis. Called "Special Assault Teams" or SATs, hostage rescue units first gained pubic attention when they were involved in retaking the hijacked plane in Hokkaido in June 1995. Following this success, in April the following year the Japanese government officially recognized their existence and expanded the SATs to ten teams for a total of 200 members. Kunimatsu, who as Director General of the National Police Agency oversaw the SATs, said in a press interview shortly after the hostage crisis began that it was "still too early" to consider an SAT dispatch to Lima and, moreover, Japan had not received a request from the Fujimori government for such a dispatch. While the NPA was also in charge of managing security at Japanese diplomatic missions, there were questions about the legality of dispatching such a team to areas outside of Japan.[284] Japan ultimately took the position that Peru bore primary responsibility for dealing with the hostage situation, citing the 1961 Vienna Treaty on Diplomatic Affairs as declaring the host country responsible for the protection of foreign diplomatic establishments.[285] The strong-willed Fujimori at any rate took charge of the hostage situation from the outset and showed little interest in allowing Japanese units to join the hostage response efforts in any meaningful way. Thus it was Japan's basic policy that Peru was responsible for ensuring the safety of the hostages: Fujimori did not request Japanese help in preparing for a hostage rescue operation, and Japan evidently did not press for a substantive role.

In Lima, Japan's Ambassador to Mexico, Terusuke Terada, established MOFA's day-to-day operations center when he arrived in Lima on December 19. Terada subsequently replaced Foreign Minister Ikeda as the senior Japanese official on the scene in Lima when Ikeda returned to Tokyo on December 23. A career diplomat and fluent in Spanish, Terada had many contacts in the region, having served as the Director General of MOFA's Central and South American Affairs bureau in the early 1990s. Terada met Fujimori prior to the hostage crisis in 1992, and he was reportedly on good terms with the Peruvian president and could call him directly when necessary during the hostage crisis.[286] By Christmas day, the National Police Agency dispatched five counter-terrorism specialists to join Terada's MOFA team in Lima as advisors.[287]

The Fujimori government, for its part, almost immediately began to plan to retake the residence by force if necessary. By December 20, Peruvian security forces had built a model of the residence at Ancon naval infantry base outside Lima where they conducted practice night assaults. According to early plans, Peruvian forces surrounding the building would conduct psychological operations before any assault would begin. Once the order was issued, some 100 elite commandos backed up by snipers and over 1,000 police officers surrounding the area would attempt to retake the residence, most likely at night. Assault planners assured reporters that all hostage takers would be "eliminated," while planners expected casualties among the hostages would be limited to 10% or less.[288] The extensive briefings the Fujimori government provided reporters about the planned assault were more likely part of a psychological operations campaign directed at the hostage takers—who were surely monitoring the media closely—meant to demoralize and distract from the real preparations to storm the residence through other means.

Over the next ten days, interspersed with sporadic explosions and gunfire, the rebels released groups of hostages in batches. The largest group, 225 hostages, was released on December 23 in what the hostage-takers called a "Christmas gesture," and the Uruguayan Ambassador to Peru was released on Christmas Eve. Fujimori and Hashimoto both complained that the Uruguayan Ambassador's release was a quid-pro-quo for Uruguay's earlier release of two Peruvian rebels and would thus be seen as a capitulation to the MRTA's demands. This in turn might embolden the rebels and endanger the negotiations. Hashimoto also denied various rumors that MRTA rebels had asked for upwards of $100 million for the release of Japanese company executives. "We have not even been sounded out" about a ransom, Hashimoto told reporters, "so we cannot even refuse."[289]

The hostages during this time began to receive basic supplies such as food and water and even mail delivered to them by the Red Cross, the sole intermediary during the initial phase of the hostage stand-off.[290] Rosa and Juana Fujimori, the mother and sister of the president, had earlier been released, and Juana personally delivered dozens of turkeys to the residence to serve as a Christmas lunch there. Twenty more hostages including ambassadors from the Dominican Republic and Malaysia were released on December 28. With the release of this group, the MRTA issued a communiqué charging the Peruvian government of terrorism, in line with their long-established propaganda efforts: "We ask that it be clarified…who were the ones who used terror indiscriminately against innocent civilians," and further asked rhetorically: "Who carried out massive massacres among the civilian population?" The MRTA rebels called on Peruvians to witness "the situation in the jails and the drama through which the relatives or our imprisoned comrades have lived."[291] By early January, only 74 hostages remained in the residence.

The hostage situation had stabilized by late December to the point that Hashimoto was able to resume preparations for a major tour of five member countries of the Association of South East

Asian Nations (ASEAN). His January trip culminated in a major speech in Singapore on January 14, 1997, which was billed even before he began his tour as the "Hashimoto Doctrine." Hashimoto declared terrorism, the environment, food and energy shortages, population, and drugs to be the major security issues in the 21st century, and he thus suggested expanding Japan-ASEAN ties to the security realm beyond the purely economic relations that characterized the post-war era. The speech reflected Hashimoto's and Japan's increasing willingness to embrace security-related themes in the region, especially in light of the various national security crises the Japanese government had experienced over the past four years. Upon his return, Hashimoto again engaged the hostage crisis and prepared for a summit with Fujimori in Toronto on February 1, but he reduced the frequencies of his visits to MOFA's operations center. (By the time of Hashimoto's return from his tour of Southeast Asia, the information collection center at the PMOR most likely had been improved to allow for briefings there.) Both before and after his trip to Southeast Asia, Hashimoto prepared the Japanese public for the possibility of a prolonged hostage situation, declaring: "I am not optimistic."[292] It became Hashimoto's constant refrain during the first months of the crisis.

Fearing similar hostage scenarios in neighboring countries and elsewhere, Japan allocated emergency funds for improving security at its diplomatic missions abroad. Foreign Minister Ikeda announced on December 24 a special ¥620 million fund to improve security at ten high-risk Japanese diplomatic missions, mainly in Latin America and Asia. Moreover, 59 Japanese missions would gain additional security guards.[293] By January 17, the Japanese government increased the fund to ¥2 billion to supply bomb and metal detectors and to reinforce walls at high-risk missions.[294] In addition, the National Police Agency received ¥1.08 billion for

SAT facility improvements in FY1997, as Japan prepared to host the 1998 Winter Olympic Games in Nagano Prefecture, apparently a direct result of the hostage stand-off since the Japanese government had not allocated any money for facilities prior to the hostage situation.[295]

In mid-January, the Peruvian government designated Archbishop Juan Luis Cipriani to conduct talks with the MRTA hostage-takers. Cipriani offered mass on Sundays and delivered medical and other supplies to the residence throughout the crisis, and acted as a conduit for exchanging information between the government and the rebels. The Peruvian government, through Cipriani, proposed three points to the MRTA before beginning official talks: setting up a "commission of guarantors" to mediate talks, deciding on a negotiating site, and establishing an agenda of issues to be discussed. Cartolini, leader of the hostage takers, called on the Peruvian government to allow families and representatives of the International Red Cross to visit MRTA rebels in jail, and he continued to demand the release of his fellow MRTA rebels from Peruvian jails, which the Fujimori government refused.[296] Negotiations then proceeded as to who was an acceptable member of a "guarantors commission," with the MRTA demanding the inclusion of representatives from Guatemala (which had on December 29 signed an agreement with the MRTA ending the 36-year civil war) or representatives from a European country.[297] The government and the rebels would haggle over specifics until January 18, when the MRTA accepted Canada as a member of the commission. The hostage takers, meanwhile, released two hostages in mid-January citing health reasons, but the hostage takers probably did not realize exactly who they were releasing: one was Valencia Hirano, leader of the Delta Special Forces unit of the police counterterrorist unit Dincote, while the other released hostage was a senior police officer.[298] Detailed debriefings from these individuals surely added to the intelligence being collected on the hostage takers inside the residence, where seventy-two hostages remained.

Peruvian troops meanwhile increased their psychological operations against the hostage takers. They hurled sticks, stones, bottles, and batteries at the residence and conducted other provocative maneuvers in armored vehicles toward the residence before quickly withdrawing. Helicopters also buzzed the residence. In retaliation, the MRTA rebels fired shots into the air from time to time. Japan protested the actions, saying they were not conducive to a "peaceful solution." Fujimori also strengthened the police presence around the compound, and reporters were removed from the rooftops of buildings within sight of the residence.[299] Initially ignoring Hashimoto's complaints, troops boarded up one of the doors to the residence without notice shortly after 5 am on January 23,[300] and later that same day twenty heavily armed members of the Lima police's special tactical operations unit deployed along a wall next to the residence guarded by two armored vehicles.[301] The unit was joined the next evening by members of the National Special Operations Directorate (DINOES) during mock attack exercises throughout the night outside the residence. The International Committee of the Red Cross suspended delivery of food and water to the residence for several hours in protest (and to protect their own people from any potential crossfire), but they resumed delivery hours later.[302] The operations then ceased for a time as Fujimori prepared for talks with Hashimoto at the end of the month.

On January 29, the guarantors commission was expanded to include Japan's representative during the hostage crisis, Terada, as an observer, immediately prior to a bilateral meeting between Hashimoto and Fujimori in Toronto, Canada.[303] At their talks in Toronto, the two leaders issued a nine-point declaration pledging "to increase efforts to solve" the hostage standoff "in a peaceful manner" and to start "preliminary conversations" with the MRTA rebels, while Hashimoto "expressed his full confidence in the handling of the takeover... and assured that his government will continue to offer its complete support to this effort."[304] Fujimori reportedly also promised to advise Hashimoto in advance of any attempt to retake the residence by force.[305] Following his meetings in Toronto, Fujimori traveled to Washington to confer with President Clinton and then returned to Peru.

Following Fujimori's return, talks on February 8 at a neighboring residence.[306] On February 10, however, police resumed their psychological operations against the rebels by playing loud music outside the residence—few at the time knew that the loud music was intended to drown out the sounds of miners digging tunnels below the residence. Police had also discovered that a Japanese reporter working for TV Asahi left behind a communications device when he entered the residence without permission on January 7. The reporter was later kicked out of the country, but his TV Asahi colleagues interviewed Cartolini and a dozen hostages using the device until it was discovered in mid-February. TV Asahi did not publicize the interviews, but rather passed messages to family members of the hostages in Japan. The network also reported the conversations to the Prime Minister's Official Residence, giving the PMOR additional insight into the situation inside the ambassador's residence.[307] TV Asahi's communications device was not the only one secretly smuggled into the residence, however, as Peruvian intelligence was by this point also conducting surveillance on the compound from a variety of sources. Indeed, talks broke down on March 6 with the rebels accusing the government of digging tunnels under the residence.

The hostage takers increasingly suspected Peruvian preparations to retake the residence as they increasingly heard digging beneath the building. Cartolini personally directed his teams to various defensive points throughout the residence during nighttime defensive exercises, and they kept many of the high-value hostages locked away in a windowless, booby-trapped room on the second floor.[308] The rebels also practiced throwing grenades into rooms where the hostages were kept.[309] Following the Peruvian counter-terrorist and other psychological operations late at night and during the pre-dawn hours, the rebels expected any government assault to take place under the cover of darkness. This expectation would prove fatally wrong, however.

The Peruvian authorities, meanwhile, slowly and methodically prepared for the retaking of the residence by force if necessary. In mid-April, Peruvian intelligence inserted tiny listening and communications devices in everyday items such as a thermos and a guitar, and intelligence officers posing as doctors delivered them to the hostages. When they were able to communicate, the hostages who knew about the devices would open a curtain to signal that no guards were around.[310] Professional miners, meanwhile, dug tunnels from neighboring houses taken over by the Peruvian National Intelligence Service to areas under the Ambassador's residence as Peruvian hostage rescue teams trained in the mock-up of the Ambassador's residence built at Ancon naval infantry base. The hostage takers drew lines along the floor where they thought the tunnels might be. The tunnels, about 3 meters below the residence, had a ventilation and lighting system, and President Fujimori would later describe them as "really sufficiently comfortable to be there several days." From these tunnels, intelligence officers snaked fiber-optic cameras through small holes to monitor various rooms in the residence.[311] Eventually, Peruvian intelligence was able to monitor every room in the residence. Apparently expecting an assault at night, the rebels grew too complacent during daylight hours. Despite knowing of the tunnels below, they had for weeks played a daily afternoon four-on-four game of *fulbito*—mini-football—in the spacious first floor living room, leaving their weapons and grenades in the corner and many of the hostages upstairs.[312]

Indeed, Archbishop Cipriani suspected impatience on the part of Peruvian authorities and sent a letter to Prime Minister Hashimoto on April 20 requesting the Japanese government apply pressure on Peru to achieve a "bloodless" solution to the crisis. Fujimori's popularity was falling precipitously because of recent allegations that Army Intelligence Service officers had tortured and murdered hundreds of rebels. A recent Brazilian report, moreover, claimed that Vladimiro Montesinos, head of the Servicio de Inteligencia Nacional (SIN) and intelligence advisor to Fujimori, had been cooperating with drug traffickers since the late 1970s. Fujimori's support rate had dropped 10% in one week in mid-April, while 70% of those polled in a local survey wanted Montesinos to resign his post due to the allegations.[313] Suspecting that preparations for the possible use of force were complete and given Fujimori's domestic problems, Cipriani worried that Fujimori was ready to retake the residence by force. Residents in neighboring districts, meanwhile, were reporting increased movements of troops and armored vehicles, yet another sign that Fujimori might be preparing to retake the residence.[314]

Cipriani's suspicions proved well-founded. Fujimori had ordered his men into the tunnels on April 20 to await his order to storm the residence. An opportunity to rescue the hostages came on the afternoon of April 22. Just after 3:00 pm, Fujimori received a call from his intelligence service informing him that they knew the locations of each of the terrorists, with eight of the fourteen hostage takers including their leader Nestor Cerpa Cartolini playing a game of *fulbito* on the main level of the residence. Fujimori gave the command to commence "Operation Chavin de Hauntar," named after the labyrinth of tunnels under the ancient capital of Chavin along Peru's northern highlands. A pre-designated signal was sent to a hostage inside via the communications device smuggled into the residence days before. The hostage in turn relayed orders to his fellow hostages, several of whom asked to use the restroom to distract the guards. When the last guard disappeared from sight, other hostages in the second-floor master bedroom opened a large bullet-proof metal door to a balcony, giving unobstructed access to the room from outside. The others were ordered to get down ahead of the coming assault.[315]

At 3:20 pm, hostage rescue teams in multiple tunnels blew open holes in the floor of the residence and streamed into the ground floor of the building. At the same time, separate units entered through a breach in the main door, holes blown in the building's exterior walls, and another through the back garden. The explosions killed several of the hostage takers who had just started playing *fulbito*, and the rest, including their leader Cerpa Cartolini, ran up the stairs to rooms where the hostages were kept on the upper floor. They had trained daily to go directly to the hostages to use as shields in case the Peruvian authorities breached the residence. The fire and the explosions cloaked the corridors in a smoky haze, and the hostage takers did not know the commandoes had already taken control of the upper level. Six more were killed on their way up the stairs. A senior member of the hostage rescue team, Commander Juan Valer Sandoval, was assigned to personally protect Peru's Foreign Minister, Francisco Tudela, but as Sandoval led Tudela to an exit one of the rebels fired repeatedly in their direction, hitting Sandoval several times. Tudela escaped with a wound to the ankle, but Sandoval died in the residence. Separately, Lieutenant Raul Jimenez Salazar entered the room where Cartolini and his men were known to stay. Salazar was killed by one of the rebels in the room, but Salazar's men quickly eliminated the remaining hostage takers there. The hostages, meanwhile, were led on their hands and knees in a line down an exterior stairwell from the second-floor balcony. In all, some 140 Peruvian troops stormed the residence, freeing the remaining 72 hostages alive. Only two members of the hostage rescue teams, Sandoval and Salazar, died during the rescue attempt.[316] All 24 Japanese nationals including Ambassador Aoki were rescued safely. Operation "Chavin de Huantar" was a success.

Not everyone was so lucky, however. Peruvian Supreme Court Judge Carlos Giusti Acuna was wounded in the raid and suffered a heart attack on the way to a local hospital soon after the hostage rescue. He was declared dead when he arrived at the hospital. All 14 MRTA guerrillas were killed in the operation. Whether the 14 guerrillas were executed during the raid remained unanswered. After the rescue operation there were charges that the hostage rescue team purposely killed all the hostage takers as immediate retaliation for their actions. Unconfirmed reports circulated that three younger hostage-takers were gunned down even as they attempted to surrender to the commandoes.[317] General Hector John Caro, the former chief of Peru's National Counterterrorism Directorate, immediately defended the commandos' actions as the rebels "were armed to the teeth," words many Peruvian counter-terrorism officials and Fujimori himself repeated frequently after the rescue.[318] Hidetaka Ogura, a Japanese diplomat who was one of the 72 hostages freed from the residence, continued to claim for years after the rescue operation that several of the hostage takers were gunned down in "extrajudicial executions" after they had attempted to surrender.[319] Indeed, ten officers who took part in the Operation Chavin de Huantar were detained in 2002 during an investigation by the Peruvian Attorney General's Office into the deaths of the 14 hostage takers.[320] The Supreme Council for Military Justice eventually cleared all 142 commandos that participated in the operation of extrajudicial killings in April 2004, however.

The Japanese government was not notified of the operation prior to the hostage rescue effort. Hashimoto explained that after he thanked Fujimori by phone several hours after the operation, "[t]he president was extremely gracious as he explained that the extremely subtle timing of the operation did not allow for prior contact and asked for my understanding in that regard." Hashimoto in turn defended Fujimori's actions, saying: "[H]ad I been in his position, I might have done the same, and although I did tell him that it was regrettable that he was not able to inform me ahead of time, I also told him that I fully understood."[321] Given the overwhelming success of the operation and the fact that all 24 Japanese hostages were rescued alive, the successful hostage rescue enjoyed enormous support in Japan. In a survey conducted on April 24 two days after the operation, over 85% of respondents said they felt the rescue was "appropriate." Just under 82% of respondents felt a lack of prior notification "could not be helped." A much lower 42% of those surveyed expressed support for the Hashimoto Cabinet, however, showing that Hashimoto did not gain politically from the rescue half a world away.[322] After dispatching Foreign Minister Ikeda to Lima to retrieve the hostages, Hashimoto personally visited the Japanese Ambassador's residence in Lima the following month and again thanked President Fujimori for Peru's assistance in freeing all the Japanese hostages. "Thanks to many Peruvian people we could stick to the policy of not yielding to terrorism," he was quoted as saying. "I would like to make it clear that Japan is a country that does not yield to terrorism, but fights it."[323] At a ceremony at Peru's Government Palace, the prime minister pinned the Order of the Rising Sun on Colonel Sandoval's widow and on Capt Salazar's father, relatives of the two Peruvian soldiers slain in the hostage rescue operation.[324]

In return, Fujimori presented Ambassador Aoki with the Grand Cross of the Sun of Peru for "bravery and courage" during the hostage crisis.[325]

Fujimori returned the ambassador's residence to Ikeda and Ambassador Aoki—still in a wheelchair following the hostage rescue—on April 25.[326] The Japanese ambassador's residence was demolished shortly thereafter, and a replacement was built in a more secure location. Ambassador Yoshizo Konishi, who became the new Ambassador to Peru in August 1997, decided not to hold receptions honoring the emperor's birthday in 1997 and 1998 citing security reasons. The first big banquet took place two and a half years later, in May 1999, to celebrate 100 years of Japanese immigration to Peru. It was held at a local Lima hotel.[327]

The memory of the hostage crisis lingered a year later. Hashimoto vowed to fight terrorism, declaring on the one-year anniversary: "We must not allow any recurrence, and will never give in to terrorists."[328] Chief Cabinet Secretary Kanezo Muraoka further declared at a news conference: "We will do our utmost to secure the safety of Japanese nationals abroad, prevent terrorism and strengthen defense of diplomatic missions abroad with much stronger sense of crisis management." Muraoka said at the press conference that in the past year the government standardized defense manuals for overseas missions to follow in preparing for big events and installed metal and bomb detectors and raised the number of local guards at Japanese embassies and consulates.[329] But others criticized the government for not having a wider-reaching crisis management system in place. The former ambassador to Peru, Morihisa Aoki, continued to criticize the government's lack of response capability, complaining: "How can Japan not have a crisis-management system in place, and still call itself an advanced nation?"[330] These would be prophetic sentiments, as Japan's national security structure would be tested yet again over the summer of 1998.

2) Submarines and Special Ops Vessels, Missiles and Nuclear Tests: Asymmetric Threats Intensify

North Korea remained at once a peculiar and specific threat to the Asian region's security in the late 1990s and early 2000s. Despite being the poorest country in the world where millions of its citizens were dying of famine, the Kim regime continued to maintain over one million soldiers in uniform and close to 100,000 special operations personnel. Following the 1993-1994 nuclear crisis, North Korea resumed its belligerent actions targeting its neighbors by infiltrating elite special operations teams into South Korea on multiple occasions in 1996 and again in 1998. North Korea targeted the Japanese homeland as well. Two North Korean spy boats were caught in waters near Japan in 1999, and in December 2001, the Japan Coast Guard took the unprecedented step of shooting at and sinking an escaping special operations craft disguised to look like a Chinese fishing boat.

Moreover, North Korea tested a new, longer-range missile in August 1998 that overflew Japan, causing deep concern in Tokyo since the entire Japanese archipelago was now demonstrably within range of North Korean missiles. As will be detailed later in this book, the event coupled with the spy boat incidents served as a turning point in Japan's national security policy. It reinforced the need for immediate reform of Japan's national security structure, and it was cited by Tokyo as a primary reason for building and launching multiple reconnaissance satellites and a missile defense system. It also created the impetus for Tokyo to begin a review of its national defense policies in 2001. By 2002, North Korea had admitted to kidnapping and holding Japanese citizens over the past four decades, and separately it admitted to running a parallel and hitherto undisclosed uranium enrichment program. Because of these highly provocative actions, Tokyo grew increasingly concerned that Pyongyang threatened the safety of Japan, and it began to plan and build the intelligence and defense forces necessary to meet this threat.

1996-1998: North Korea's Midget Submarines and Special Ops Units

At 1:35 am on September 18, 1996, taxi driver Yi Chin-kyu was driving along a seaside road nine kilometers south of Kangnung city in South Korea when he spotted something strange along the coast. A small vessel of some sort had been beached along the shore several kilometers from the road, and a group of men appeared to be working around the vessel smoking cigarettes. The taxi driver contacted South Korean police, who sent a team to investigate. They quickly discovered that a North Korean *Sang-o* "Shark" class submarine had washed ashore.[331] While the mere presence of a North Korean submarine used for conducting clandestine operations found beached along the South Korean coast was alarming enough, even more so was the location. A South Korean Air Force Base was located nearby. The submarine had most likely attempted to infiltrate or exfiltrate North Korean special forces operatives targeting the airbase.

That same day, two villagers had noticed a stranger wearing blue jeans and canvas shoes with a 38-caliber revolver at his side, clearly out of place in Kangnung. They alerted the police, who detained him and turned the man over to the South Korean military that evening.[332] The man's name was Yi Kwang-su, 31, one of the sub's crewmembers. After a massive search of the area, South Korean authorities found the remains of eleven crewmembers dead of self-inflicted wounds.[333] During his initial interrogation, Yi initially claimed that his team's submarine, with a total of twenty operatives belonging to the Reconnaissance Bureau of the North's Peoples Armed Forces Ministry, developed engine trouble and drifted until it ran aground near Kangnung.[334] During subsequent interrogations Yi later claimed that the sub had infiltrated three North Korean operatives near the Kangnung shores and returned to retrieve them when it ran aground. Yi also increased the number of North Koreans involved in the operation to 26, including five dispatched operatives.[335] He also claimed to have visited the Kangnung area on a previous mission to gather intelligence on civil defense facilities and road networks on the east coast of South Korea.[336] Despite the changes in his stories, the grounded submarine and the nearly dozen dead bodies clearly demonstrated that North Korea was actively infiltrating special operations forces into South Korea—and that over a dozen highly trained operatives were still in the area.

The South Korean authorities began a massive manhunt for the remaining North Korean infiltrators. The Ministry of National Defense mobilized 40,000 soldiers and reservists for the search, supported by Air Force and Naval units, and it imposed a curfew in the area.[337] Four days after discovering the submarine, a South Korean unit found two guerrillas in a valley of Mt. Chilsong, and a firefight immediately ensued; two Korean soldiers were killed and two others were wounded.[338] Six days later, a search party discovered three armed North Korean operatives near Mt. Chilsong and exchanged gunfire, killing one. Complicating matters, the dead North Korean was wearing a South Korean uniform and carrying an M-16 rifle.[339] The fear that other North Koreans were disguised in South Korean uniforms in turn led to a case of friendly fire two days later, when members of a South Korean unit shot and killed a fellow soldier mistaken for one of the North Korean operatives.[340] Several of the North Korean agents managed to elude search parties for almost two months. On November 5 two North Koreans were discovered and later killed in the ensuing gun battle.

One of the slain operatives maintained a diary of his team's operations in the area. It showed that he succeeded in infiltrating the Kangnung coast on the night of September 15, but that the submarine went aground on September 18 while it was departing following the infiltration mission. The crew attempted to blow up the submarine with dynamite, but they were unsuccessful. (This entry was corroborated as investigators found fire scorch marks inside the submarine.) The diary also noted the number of "enemy" killed as he and his partner attempted to elude capture, including two soldiers and three civilians.[341] By November 7, with 25 of the 26 commandos dead or captured, South Korea's Joint Chiefs of Staff decided to return mobilized soldiers to their respective units following the nearly two-month search operation. Only one North Korean commando was believed to be at large.[342] In December, the South Korean government awarded cash prizes to those who discovered and reported the operatives: Yi Chin-kyu, the cab driver who discovered the submarine, received ₩94.5 million (over $110,000 at the time), and Hong Sa-tok and Chong Sun-cha, the villagers who called the police after they saw Yi Kwang-su, received ₩70 million. Others received between ₩10-20 million for assisting in the discovery of other North Korean infiltrators.[343]

Yi testified in late October that he belonged to the 22nd Squadron of the North Korean Ministry of People's Armed Forces Reconnaissance Bureau, whose "basic tasks are to reconnoiter and destroy South Korean military bases, disrupt the rear, kidnap and assassinate prominent figures," Yi stated in the video-tapped testimony.[344] Yi also testified separately that the *Sang-o* had previously infiltrated South Korean waters at least four times in the 1990s, and that half of the sub's 26 crew had infiltrated into South Korea proper at least once in the past, indicating that North Korean special operations forces had extensive and recent experience operating clandestinely on South Korean territory. The *Sang-o,* with a displacement of 325 tons and a length of 34 meters, was a mini-submarine that could carry up to four torpedoes or sea mines and was used by North Korea for reconnaissance along the coast and in shallow ports and harbors. According to Yi, North Korea began to infiltrate South Korean waters using small submarines in 1974. Infiltrations continued until South Korea increased its security posture following the bombing of the Aung San mausoleum in Rangoon in 1983, when North Korean commandos killed four South Korean cabinet members. North Korea resumed its submarine infiltrations into South Korea in the 1990s, however. Indeed, according to Yi, North Korea had established four submarine bases to support its anti-South Korean operations under the direct control of the Reconnaissance Bureau: Nampo base in South Pyongan Province on the west coast; Simpo base in South Hamgyong Province, on the east coast; Taejo base in South Hamgyong Province; and Chaho base in South Hamgyong Province.[345]

Three of the submarine bases were thus on North Korea's east coast, in easy striking distance of both South Korea and Japan's west coast. Whether Yi had misled his captors as to the exact numbers of North Korean operatives or the locations of submarine bases, it was clear that North Korea was actively conducting infiltration operations targeting South Korea. Given its proximity, Japan watched events warily as well. Shunji Taoka, a Japanese military affairs journalist writing in the popular weekly *Aera,* noted that in the twenty years prior to the *Sang-o* submarine discovery near Kangnung, there were over ten incidents in which North Korean ships were discovered near the South Korean coast or were sunk by South Korean forces, although only a few of the infiltrators were found. Taoka, illustrating the proximity of North Korea to Japan, also noted that if the submarine had the same submerged cruising characteristics as Japan's World War II-era *Ha-201* mini-submarine, the *Sang-o* could "very easily" make a 1,400-kilometer round-trip to points on Japan's west coast.[346]

Yet, North Korean clandestine naval incursions continued despite the wide publicity garnered by the Kangnung incident in South Korea and a change in South Korean leadership to a dovish one that espoused a rapprochement with the North. The reformist Kim Dae-jung was elected president in February 1998, and he quickly introduced a "Sunshine Policy" to improve relations with North Korea through cooperative business ventures, reunions of families divided by the DMZ, and the provision of humanitarian assistance with no strings attached. (Kim Dae-jung won the Nobel Peace Prize in 2000 "for peace and reconciliation with North Korea".) North Korea's policies did not change, however.

On Monday June 22, 1998, two South Korean fishermen on the *Tongil* saw what appeared to be a small vessel caught in their fishing net. The fishermen watched as three individuals tried to remove the netting, but they were unsuccessful and disappeared into the vessel.[347] The two ships were 11.5 nautical miles east of the Sokch'o coast within South Korea's territorial waters. The captain of the South Korean ship, Kim In-yong, reported the suspicious vessel to the First Fleet Command via fishery radio communications. The South Korean military went on alert, and the First Fleet Command dispatched a patrol ship, high-speed naval vessels and helicopters to the area, in close liaison with the US military. After locating the ensnared vessel and identifying it as a probable submarine, the South Korean Navy took control of the net in which it was snagged. A Navy diver confirmed initial suspicions: the large tangled object was a *Yugo*-class North Korean midget submarine, smaller even than the *Sang-o* mini-submarine discovered less than two years ago. The following day, South Korea's Joint Chiefs of Staff called the incident "a clear intrusion into our waters" and "a military provocation."[348]

Crewmembers were thought to be still alive inside when the South Korean Navy arrived to tow the submarine, but there were no responses during efforts to communicate with those inside. As the Navy towed it, the submarine sank less than 2 kilometers from Tonghae Naval Base in relatively shallow, 34-meter-deep waters. The South Korean Navy later raised and towed the submarine the final 1.8 kilometers to Tonghae Naval Base.[349] Meanwhile, in an attempt to deny the submarine was conducting an infiltration operation in South Korean waters, North Korea claimed that the submarine began experiencing "troubles in a nautical observation instrument, oil pressure system and submerging and surfacing equipment" while conducting training in North Korean waters on June 20, causing the sub to go "astray."[350] South Korea's Joint Chiefs of Staff again called it "clearly an infiltration," noting that the tide was flowing eastward then, making it difficult for it to have drifted south.[351]

Yi Kwang-su, the former North Korean operative who was captured alive during the 1996 Kangnung submarine infiltration incident, assisted South Korea's 15-member team of experts examining the submarine. Following his suggestion that the main hatch to the submarine's interior could be rigged with explosives, the team used oxyacetylene torches to cut through the stern of the submarine. The team then used an endoscope to check for explosives or other booby-traps, and once the submarine was declared safe the team again used oxyacetylene torches to cut through the main hatch to gain entrance. Inside the 70-ton *Yugo*-class submarine, investigators found two AK rifles, one RPG launching tube, two machine guns, two Czech-made pistols, and two hand grenades, six oxygen breathing apparatuses, three pairs of flippers, and three pairs of diving shoes. According to Pak Sung-ch'un, chief of the joint investigation team, a total of nine North Koreans were aboard the submarine: six crewmen and three "undercover agents," in Pak's words. By the time they were discovered, however, they were dead, five with gunshot wounds to various parts of their bodies indicating homicide, and four with gunshot wounds to the head indicating suicide. There were indications that the crew had initially tried to escape, as investigators found diving equipment between the inner and outer hatches.[352] A tenth body wearing diving gear and ammunition washed ashore at Tonghae City three weeks later on July 12. Although the Ministry of National Defense had again mobilized tens of thousands of soldiers to search for other possible infiltrators, they found nothing besides the one dead body.[353]

During an extensive search of the sub, investigators found a logbook indicating its port of origin: Wonsan, North Korea. In addition, a private memo listed the crew and their ranks.[354] With the log book and other corroborating evidence, investigators confirmed that the crew belonged to the Wonsan Liaison Office under the Operations Department of the Workers Party of Korea. Similar to the Reconnaissance Bureau, which oversaw the submarine infiltration mission in September 1996, operatives of the WPK Operations Department were implicated in conducting infiltration operations along South Korea's east coast and possibly Japan.[355] During a nationally televised press conference on June 26, Lieutenant General Chong Yong-chin, director of the Operations Department of South Korea's Joint Chiefs of Staff, declared: "Considering the crew, their uniforms, and the weapons that have been confirmed up to this point, this incident is clearly an infiltration operation by North Korean special agents."[356]

Thus, yet another North Korean organ was caught conducting a clandestine operation targeting South Korea. This incident further corroborated Yi's 1996 testimony that North Korea had conducted multiple infiltrations since the early 1990s, and many were left wondering how many operations went undetected.

It should be noted that, although the WPK Operations Department and the MAPF Reconnaissance Bureau were technically in different organizations—the Operations Department fell under the North Korea's WPK Secretariat and the Reconnaissance Bureau fell under the National Defense Commission—they and three other clandestine organizations fell under the direct control of a high-ranking secretary belonging to the Workers Party Central Committee. Kim Chung-nin, a close confidant of Kim Il-sung until his death in 1994, originally oversaw the five organizations, and he was later replaced by Kim Yong-sun. The three other organizations were the Social and Cultural Department, the United Front Department, and the External Information Research Department.[357] These organizations, falling as they did under the direct control of one high-ranking WPK secretary, also illustrated the close link between open friendship societies and clandestine operation organizations. The Social and Cultural Department, for example, oversaw the pro-Pyongyang General Association of Korean Residents in Japan (GAKRJ) at the time of the infiltrations.[358] Since the Social and Cultural Department, the Operations Department, and the MPAF Reconnaissance Bureau all fall under one man, sharing of resources and intelligence on both South Korea and Japan during any operation would be quite seamless.

Further ignoring the provocation caused by these highly publicized incidents, North Korea attempted several more infiltrations in November and December the same year. The South Korean military discovered a North Korean boat in the West Sea near the coast of Kanghwa-Do on November 20, but failed to catch or sink it. A month later, the South Korean Navy discovered yet another North Korean boat in South Korean waters. Discovered about two kilometers from the coast of Yosu by Army infrared surveillance, the boat was finally sunk early in the morning on December 18 following a seven-hour chase.[359] The boat was an improved version of a 12.8-meter-long, 10-ton semi-submersible used for infiltrating operatives into and out of coastal areas that could dive three meters below the surface using an improved snorkeling system. It could carry up to eight people, including four crewmen, two guides, and two operatives.[360] In each of these incidents, South Korean military officials coordinated closely with US Forces Korea. Strangely, on December 25, days after the semi-submersible boat was sunk off the South Korean coast, a local resident of Takahama city in Japan's Fukui Prefecture discovered three bodies tied by rope to a large log. Much of their flesh was gone, but they wore military uniforms with star-shaped badges, common in North Korea. Although Takahama was 700 kilometers from the area where the semi-submersible was discovered off the South Korean coast, officials speculated that the three might have been aboard the same vessel before it sank.[361] South Korea's Joint Chiefs of Staff said that the bodies were most likely those of citizens trying to escape from North Korea and were probably not related to the semi-submersible incident, however.[362]

While these operations targeted South Korea, they concerned Japan as well given the country's geographic proximity to the North and suspicions that the North had kidnapped Japanese citizens from Japanese soil. The midget and mini-submarines (as well as disguised fishing vessels, described below) provided a clandestine infiltration capability to smuggle people into and out of Japan. Japan, moreover, had similarly experienced mysterious naval intrusions. One such intrusion in the fall of 1990 was known as the "Mihama Incident." On October 28 that year, a passerby discovered a boat that had washed ashore in Mihama, Fukui Prefecture. The boat had no name on the hull and no inspection certificate as required under Japanese law. Inside the pilothouse, police later found number tables and writings in Korean about the "Great Leader Comrade Kim Il-sung." The number tables were most likely code books, and the boat was thought to have been launched from a larger mother ship but had broken up due to the strong winds and waves that had been reported in the area. Police launched a wider search for crewmembers. Over the next four days, investigators found a deflated rubber boat 500 meters from the small shipwreck, and later found a blue naval jacket which had in its left breast pocket a notebook containing photos of Kim Il-sung and Kim Chong-il. The following day, a drowned body was discovered washed ashore near the area, and two more were discovered ten days later, all without any identifying marks. Other items found in the area included two inflatable life jackets, a bag with "Pyongyang, DPRK" on it, chewing gum with the label of the "Pyongyang Korea, Taedonggang Food and Chemical Plant," North Korean cigarettes, among other items. The items were later displayed to the public and press at the Tsuruga Police Station. While there were other instances of unknown or suspicious wreckage discovered along the Sea of Japan coast, this was considered the first time that espionage equipment was found near the wreckage of a presumed North Korean spy vessel in Japan.[363] The incident was especially alarming because Fukui Prefecture hosts a number of nuclear power plants that provide power throughout the central Honshu area of Japan. Moreover, rumors of kidnappings by North Korean agents persisted in communities along Japan's west coast for decades, rumors which were soon to be proven well-founded.

Thus, Japanese officials were keenly interested in the recent submarine incursions, for they marked a more sophisticated method of infiltrating operations personnel into neighboring countries' territories. Shortly after the June 1998 incident Korean Vice Defense Minister Ahn Byoung-gil met with his Japanese counterpart, Masahiro Akiyama, to discuss the North Korean submarine incursion during Akiyama's three-day official visit to Seoul.[364] A detailed investigation of the *Yugo* submarine, moreover, revealed hundreds of Japanese-made components, including active sonar for underwater navigation, a radar set, GPS navigator, plotter, and depth measurer all manufactured by Furuno, an HF radio set for long-distance communication by ICOM, a periscope camera made by Canon, and other equipment. These components were commercially available items sold in any developed country, but in these cases they were used to support clandestine operations. Some of the equipment was manufactured in the United States as well, such as the three engines used on the semi-submersible boat. The lawmakers were shown Japanese-made equipment from other North Korean vessels attempting to infiltrate South Korean territory as well. Two Japanese lawmakers who personally toured the North Korean vessels, later writing in Japan's monthly journal *Bungei Shunju*, suggested four methods by which North Korea could have procured the Japanese-made items: direct import as general-purpose items, import through a third party in Hong Kong, Macao or elsewhere, direct purchase in Japan and "hand-carrying" the items to North Korea (ie, smuggling), and smuggling them in bulk via container or other ships.[365] But neither South Korean nor Japanese officials knew exactly how Pyongyang procured the equipment. Most alarming, however, was that Japan would later discover that just as North Korea had conducted clandestine operations against South Korea, it was also conducting clandestine operations against Japan as well, using equipment similarly "Made In Japan."

Summer of WMD: Nuclear and Missile Tests in 1998

Contrary to trends in other regions around the globe, Asia was quickly becoming a center of WMD proliferation. Even as countries had renounced their nuclear weapons capabilities in the 1990s—Africa became a nuclear-free zone after South Africa had renounced nuclear weapons in 1993, South America became a nuclear-free zone after Argentina and Brazil gave up their nuclear weapon pretensions, and Kazakhstan and Ukraine both voluntarily gave up their nuclear arsenals left over from the days of the Soviet Union—countries in Asia were actively developing weapons of mass destruction and the means to deliver them.

Nuclear and missile tests became common in Asia in the 1990s: China had just completed a series of nuclear and missile tests in 1995 and 1996; Pakistan in July 1997 tested the Hatf-3 with an 800-kilometer range, and in April 1998 it tested a new 1,500-kilometer-range Ghauri missile that resembled North Korea's Nodong missile. In May 1998, India tested five nuclear devices, and Pakistan within weeks conducted its own nuclear tests. And the missile tests continued. In July, Iran tested several variants of the Shahab-3, which was also based on Nodong technology. Iran was also developing a 2,000-km Shahab-4. And while North Korea's plutonium production capability was officially suspended, Pyongyang would later admit to a clandestine uranium enrichment capability even as it continued to develop increasingly long-range missiles throughout the 1990s.

Although Iran and Pakistan seemed a half a world away from Northeast Asia, their work on WMD and missiles directly concerned Japan as they were suspected of trading in missile technologies with the Kim regime and thereby supporting North Korea's missile research and development programs.[366] Indeed, as missile tests were increasingly shown on television in North Korea, Iran, and Pakistan, analysts could compare the size and physical characteristics of the various missiles. In one example, *Mainichi Shimbun* noted a "striking resemblance" between a North Korean video of the Nodong and Taepodong missiles and video of Pakistan's Ghauri and Iran's Shahab-3 missiles. Military analyst Kensuke Ebata declared to the paper: "from the size and shape [of the Nodong engine shown in the video], it can be said that there is high credibility in what the United States has been pointing out" regarding the commonality between "the Ghauri, Shahab-3, and the Taepodong-1."[367]

As if to underscore the missile trade between North Korea, Pakistan, and Iran, Indian authorities on June 25, 1999 seized missile components contained in the 25,000 DWT North Korean freighter *Ku-Wol San* as it unloaded 13,000 tons of sugar at the port of Kandla in India. India claimed that the shipment was bound for Pakistan to be used in the construction and testing of short-range missiles such as the Hatf-2 and Hatf-3. The ship contained high-altitude testing equipment, optical protractors and theodolites, rolled steel metal frustum used to reinforce nose cones, generator condensers, and construction material for launching pads. Yet the ship's manifest described the shipment as water-treatment equipment.[368] Indian investigators also found 10 boxes of manuals, some with 15'x4' blueprints, all in Korean, detailing the manufacturing process for the 300-kilometer range Hwasong 5 and the 500-kilometer range Hwasong 6 liquid-propelled Scud missiles. A North Korean special envoy Jong Tae Hwa tried to persuade New Dehli in late July to release the freighter, her captain, and chief officer, both of whom were placed in jail as they were suspected of knowing about the undeclared cargo, but he was rebuffed.[369]

Japan remained alert for launches in the mid- and late-1990s as launch warnings became increasingly common. Following the missile tests in May 1993, work was observed at missile launch sites in North Korea four times in 1994 and ten times in 1995, although no launch was reported.[370] On October 17, 1996, Japan's Joint Staff Council Chairman Shigeru Sugiyama announced at a press conference that Tokyo expected North Korea to launch a Nodong-1 missile in the "near future."[371] In reply, North Korean radio and its *Nodong Sinmun* said that Japan was "recklessly making senseless remarks" as it "impudently" made "a fuss about our missile launching test." They also decried Japan's "spreading rumors about our sale of missiles to Middle East nations."[372] By November 12, however, North Korean officials at working-level talks in New York quietly promised to suspend the test launch of the missile, and they also reportedly took responsibility for dispatching the *Sang-o* submarine into South Korean waters in September that year.[373]

The Launch Over Japan

Suspicions that North Korea was about to test-launch a missile resurfaced in the summer of 1998. On August 21, 1998, *Sankei Shimbun*, citing "western military sources," reported that North Korea was preparing to test a medium-range missile into the Sea of Japan. This test, *Sankei* reported, might involve the longer range Taepodong-1, with a suspected maximum range of 2,000 kilometers or almost twice the range of the Nodong-1 launched five years earlier in May 1993.[374] This placed the entire Japanese archipelago within range of a missile attack from North Korea, including US bases in Okinawa. According to later accounts, the United States had informed Prime Minister Obuchi's administration as early as August 8 that North Korea was preparing a missile launch, and by August 28 Washington had informed Tokyo that North Korea was prepared to launch the missile within two days.[375] Thus armed with ample warning, Japan's Maritime Self-Defense Force dispatched the Aegis destroyer *Myoko* to the Sea of Japan to watch for a launch.[376] Japanese diplomats in Beijing, meanwhile, attempted to convince North Korea through back channels not to launch a missile.[377] These requests were ignored.

North Korea launched the Taepodong-1 Intermediate-Range Ballistic Missile (IRBM)—ostensibly to launch a small satellite—from a launch pad at Musudan-ri, North Hamgyo'ng Province near the coast on the Sea of Japan at 12:12 pm on August 31. Initial reports said that the booster stage of the two-stage missile landed in the sea approximately 300 kilometers southeast of Vladivostok, Russia, and 450 kilometers from the Noto Peninsula near the same splash area as the Nodong-1 test in May 1993. The second stage traveled over the Tohoku region of the main island of Honshu before landing several hundred kilometers east of Japan's Sanriku coastline.[378] This was the first-ever launch of a missile from North Korea over Japan. Worse, North Korea did not formally declare its intention to launch the missile at all, much less over Japan, and it refused official entreaties on the part of Japan and others to refrain from taking the provocative action of launching the missile. Japan's reaction to North Korea's flagrant test of the Taepodong-1 marked a watershed moment in its national security development.

US and Japanese units monitoring the area immediately communicated the launch to policymakers. In Japan, the MSDF's Central Command Post (CCP) contacted the personal secretaries of the Prime Minister, the Chief Cabinet Secretary, and the Deputy

Chief Cabinet Secretaries via *Otsutae-Kun*, or "Mr. Communicator" used for dedicated communications with the Prime Minister's Official Residence. They also contacted the office of the Deputy Chief Cabinet Secretary for Crisis Management, a new position that had just been created in April 1998 (detailed later in this book). Initial reports had the missile landing in the Sea of Japan, similar to the 1993 launch, causing some to conclude that North Korea test-launched a Nodong-1. Intelligence collected by the *Myoko*, tracking the launch in its Combat Information Center, contradicted these initial assessments however. The crew monitored the first stage separate, and a second stage began to accelerate, climbing in altitude. They quickly realized that the missile was going to fly over Japan, and watched helplessly as the second stage separated and fell into the Pacific on the far side of Japan. The *Myoko* transmitted its initial report via satellite telephone, and a short while later it transmitted a summarized flight path of the missile to the Electronic Intelligence Support Unit in Yokosuka, Yokohama. The *Myoko* was incapable of transmitting the actual flight path data, however, which would be critical in any future regional missile defense system. The summarized flight information was nevertheless hurriedly reported to the Operations Bureau and to the DA Vice Minister.[379]

An EP-3, meanwhile, had collected telemetry signals from the missile, but it could not transmit the information while in flight. It could only transmit the information to the unit in Yokosuka after it landed at Iwakuni airbase. SIGINT related to the launch was being collected at the Defense Intelligence Headquarters, but it was severely stovepiped and dissemination was severely limited.[380] The DA did not have access to a Japanese version of a classified "NOIWON" or National Operational Intelligence Watch Officer's Network system that would allow an immediate discussion of intelligence among the various watch offices in the national security community, thus preventing the sharing of most up-to-date reporting on the launch. All of these shortcomings would be reviewed in the subsequent years.

Intelligence stovepiping and a major procurement scandal hindered initial review of the situation. DA Director-General Fukushiro Nukaga was first informed of the missile launch by cell phone, and he received various briefings by staff once he returned to DA Headquarters. Only the head of Defense Operations, however, informed Nukaga of the possibility that part of the missile might have fallen into the Pacific Ocean, thus indicating the missile overflew the Japanese archipelago. The disparate, uncoordinated briefings indicated raw intelligence reporting had not been funneled through and consolidated at the Defense Intelligence Headquarters, established a year earlier as a one-stop intelligence shop for precisely this type of situation. Nor did the Defense Agency convene a special session of its internal Intelligence Committee, composed of the Vice Minister, Defense Policy and Operations bureau chiefs, and the chiefs of staff of the Ground, Maritime, and Air Self-Defense Forces, to examine the situation due to a procurement scandal then unfolding at the Defense Agency. The administrative vice minister who was responsible to call such a meeting was instead preparing for an imminent search of the agency's premises by the Tokyo District Public Prosecutors Office. (The scandal, which involved Japanese defense contractors overcharging the DA with the complicity of some DA employees, caused Nukaga's eventual dismissal and the prosecution of other high-ranking bureaucrats and contractors.) Additionally, MOFA, the DA, the National Police Agency, and the Public Security Investigation Agency were also attempting to collect information without coordinating with each other. There was no inter-governmental meeting such as a meeting of the JIC to coordinate collection efforts, despite knowing about a possible launch for almost two weeks. Nor did Japanese policy makers convene a special session of its Security Council; indeed, the council had never held an unscheduled special session since it was established in 1986, indicating that its sole purpose was bureaucratic in nature, coordinating routine policy and budget matters.

Japanese policymakers and the press severely criticized the timeliness of intelligence reporting immediately after the launch, and calls for further reforms were almost immediate. Chief Cabinet Secretary Hiromu Nonaka expressed disappointment in Japan's national security system during a live interview on *Close-up Gendai* a week after the missile test: "Regarding our country's future crisis management, I feel that we need to build a system that will enable us to give the people information for which we can take responsibility."[381] In a year-end series of articles on Japan's national security structure, titled "Is Japan Safe?", Japan's largest daily *Yomiuri Shimbun* called the response "sorely inadequate."[382] Japan's largest business paper *Nihon Keizai Shimbun* blamed bureaucratic infighting for the lack of a timely public announcement. When further information revealed that the missile had overflown Japan and part of it landed in the Pacific Ocean, inter-agency disagreement between MOFA and the DA prevented the publication of that information until 11 hours later, even as media outlets outside of Japan had reported the information hours earlier.[383]

Despite the confusion, Japanese policy makers did not give themselves or their slowly improving intelligence structure at least some credit for progress made since the May 1993 test-launch. Despite the fluid situation, Japan's intelligence structure collected and verified technical information related to the missile launch through their own channels. Multiple Japanese platforms observed the launch, tracked it, and reported it through their chain of command, and the fact that North Korea had launched a missile over the Japanese homeland had been reported to the Prime Minister's Office and other officials by mid-afternoon, even if the details were still unknown. The process was still slow because of the new structures in place to collect and transmit intelligence of this nature: the Aegis destroyers were new, the Defense Intelligence Headquarters was new, the Deputy Chief Cabinet Secretary for Crisis Management was a new position, and the scenario was new. The self-introspection, while important, was a sign that Japanese policymakers were still not comfortable with the "fog" of intelligence that comes with multiple, near-real-time intelligence collection platforms, even as bottlenecks prevented the transmission of that intelligence to policymakers in a more timely fashion.

The launch came at a particularly inauspicious time for talks on the North Korea nuclear situation. Japan immediately refused to sign a cost-sharing agreement with the United States, South Korea, and the European Union scheduled to take effect that day. Japan had previously promised to provide $1 billion of the $4.6 billion to pay for the construction of two light-water nuclear reactors in North Korea and interim deliveries of heavy fuel oil, but following the launch it balked at providing such a large sum given the circumstances. The agreement was to be completed before further US-North Korea talks, scheduled to begin the day after the launch on September 1, during which the two parties were to discuss (ironically) North Korea's missile developments. Japan also announced that it would freeze a year-long effort to restart normalization talks with North Korea and not provide food aid to the country.[384] The announcement was however a moot point since North Korea had already called off normalization talks, and in the absence of any breakthrough Japan had not publicized any plan to provide food aid prior to the missile test.[385]

Pyongyang timed the launch to coincide with major events to legitimize the new Kim Chong-il regime. On September 5,

North Korea's Supreme People's Assembly was scheduled to meet to elect Kim Chong-il as the chairman of the National Defense Commission, ahead of the 50th Anniversary of the DPRK founding on September 9. Following the August 31 launch, North Korean radio announced on September 4 that "our scientists and technicians succeeded in launching its first satellite into orbit with multi-staged delivery rockets."[386] The satellite, officially called the "Kwangmyo'ngso'ng-1" (referring to the constellation of Kim Chong Il's star) was transmitting "immortal revolutionary hymns" such as "song of General Kim Il-sung" and "song of General Kim Chong-il," as well as "the Morse signals 'Juche Korea'."[387] The following day, at the opening of the Supreme People's Assembly, Deputy Kim Yong-nam declared the "great leader Comrade Kim Chong-il" an "outstanding thinker" and "peerless great commander," and boasted: "[O]ur scientists and technicians successfully launched the first satellite with multi-stage delivery rockets. This is another historic, felicitous, pan-national event that vigorously demonstrates the unlimited potential of our republic, which advanced along the single road toward prosperity and development under the leadership of the respected and beloved general, as well as our republic's surprising development."[388] (The missile cargo, if indeed it had been a satellite, failed to achieve orbit and burned up in the earth's atmosphere.) The missile launch, then, was intended to show North Korea's technological developments in line with a policy emphasizing research and development, an undertaking ordered by Kim Chong-il when he emerged as the leader of North Korea in the mid-1990s. The SPA later that week abolished the title of President and re-elected Kim as the chairman of the National Defense Commission, solidifying Kim's control over the country four years after the death of his father, and it commemorated on September 9 the 50th anniversary of its founding. (The Taepodong missile would later be officially named the

"Paektusan-1," named for the famous mountain on the North Korea-China border where Korean propaganda claimed Kim Chong-il was born.[389])

Japan's reaction to the Taepodong missile test reflected a fundamental change in how the country perceived its security situation in Asia. While the previous Korean nuclear crisis and missile tests, the Aum Shinrikyo attacks, tensions in the Taiwan Strait, and the Peruvian hostage crisis were in their own ways challenges to Japan's national security, the August 1998 missile test represented a direct strategic threat to the Japanese homeland. The possibility that Pyongyang could launch a missile with a nuclear warhead toward Tokyo or a US base in Japan was increasingly real. Japanese policy makers felt this danger instinctively. LDP secretary general Yoshiro Mori—who would later serve as Prime Minister—said immediately after the launch that "it's quite fair to say that a war could have broken out" due to misperceptions immediately after the missile launch.[390] Prime Minister Keizo Obuchi called North Korea's attempts to justify the missile launch "unpardonable."[391] When a Pyongyang spokesman denounced Japan for "making a fuss over the matter" of North Korea's "national sovereignty," Chief Cabinet Secretary Nonaka declared: "We cannot tolerate remarks of a country which has fired a missile into the sky above another country without prior notice, in total disregard of international rules."[392] In a sign of both unity and concern, the Diet convened a special one-day session on September 2 during which both houses unanimously passed resolutions condemning North Korea's missile test over Japan as "thoughtless and dangerous" and that posed a "serious situation for [Japan's] security."[393]

Japan pressed its case against North Korea at the UN Security Council, but with no effect. Japan's ambassador to the UN, Hisashi Owada, declared that the missile test was a threat to Japan's security and called on the UNSC to hold official talks on the matter.

While the United States and United Kingdom supported Japan's position, China delayed any further action, claiming that the issue was bilateral in nature.[394] The ruling LDP dispatched a special delegation to New York on September 11 to meet with each of the UNSC permanent members to discuss the situation, but Shen Guofeng, deputy chief of China's permanent mission to the United Nations, said China accepted Pyongyang's explanation that the launch was an attempt to put a satellite into orbit, and the issue was therefore bilateral in nature.[395] With China blocking any UNSC resolution denouncing North Korea's launch, Japan's initiatives at the UN Security Council failed. Recurring failures to gain adequate redress in the UNSC would continue to stymie Japan and ultimately heighten its interest in gaining a permanent seat there.

Japan had greater authority in the Missile Technology Control Regime as its chair in 1998. Following the test, Japan sent letters to all MTCR member countries calling for improved measures to prevent the export of missile technologies by North Korea through third countries, and announced that it planned to discuss the matter at the MTCR general assembly scheduled for October.[396] As chair of the MTCR, Japan issued a statement declaring the MTCR member countries "were especially concerned about the potential of the rocket launched on August 31 to deliver weapons of mass destruction to increased ranges." "MTCR Partners will maintain special scrutiny over their exports of missile related material and technology in order not to support North Korean missile development in any way," the Chairman's Statement concluded.[397] Moreover, regime members placed North Korea's missile test in broader context: "Events in the current year, inter alia, in South and North East Asia and in the Middle East have come to illustrate eloquently the sensitive nature of missile technology development."[398] Japan also called on the International Civil Aviation

Organization to urge North Korea to observe the Aviation Safety Treaty, which requires countries to notify aviation authorities in advance of actions that might affect aviation services.[399] Indeed, the Flight Crew Unions Federation of Japan also pressed the case at the ICAO due to the "danger a missile could collide with a civilian aircraft."[400] ICAO obliged, adopting a resolution on October 2 condemning the missile launch—although the resolution did not mention North Korea by name.[401] But Japan's successes in these fora were little more than symbolic.

Government and ruling Liberal Democratic Party officials in the months following the launch established committees to investigate measures to improve its national security structure and intelligence collection capabilities, beginning with the LDP's "intelligence satellite project team," announced on September 4.[402] (The LDP had long been exploring the development of an indigenous intelligence satellite program, but the missile test made selling the program to the public far easier.) Even the opposition party leader, Yukio Hatoyama, was quick to jump on the intelligence satellite bandwagon by declaring on a Fuji TV Sunday News program that Japan should "definitely" deploy reconnaissance satellites, but with a twist: Japan should develop the satellites in cooperation with South Korea and China.[403] The proposal was a non-starter, of course, as the major missile tests of the 1990s were conducted east toward Japan and without warning, not toward China or South Korea, and thus Japan felt the threat most keenly. Moreover, events around the Taiwan Strait in 1995 and 1996 demonstrated that China itself was prone to launch missiles with little warning, thus causing similar concern in Tokyo.

Separately, the DA released a report within a week of the launch supporting the technological feasibility of missile defense, setting the stage for joint technical research with the United States a year later.[404] By year-end, Japanese defense planners began to review the need for aerial refueling aircraft, first broached in the 1980s but then considered unconstitutional as they would extend the range of Japan's fighters and could potentially be deemed as a power-projection capability in the region.[405] With proposals to build intelligence satellites and aerial refuelers, former defense "taboos" were quickly falling to the wayside in the wake of the unannounced Taepodong launch.

Perhaps the greatest defeat following the missile launch was felt by Hiromu Nonaka, the Chief Cabinet Secretary at the time. Nonaka had worked tirelessly to deepen relations with North Korea at the end of the Cold War through a strategy of active engagement. He first visited North Korea with former Deputy Prime Minister Shin Kanemaru in September 1990, until that point the highest-level Japanese delegation to have visited Pyongyang in the post-war era. The visit led to the first round of bilateral normalization talks in January 1991. Nonaka helped to establish the first commercial charter flight service between Japan and North Korea, which began in May 1991, and in October that year he traveled to the country again with construction company executives to explore joint development projects in the impoverished nation. The following year, he traveled to Pyongyang to observe Kim Il-sung's 80th birthday celebrations.[406] In all, Nonaka had traveled to the country six times since 1990, the most by an active LDP politician. Nonaka felt that small but symbolically important projects would increase everyday contacts with North Korea and lead to deeper understanding between the two countries, but the missile test shattered that work, with Japan cancelling on September 2 all charter flights between the two countries.[407] Diplomatic normalization talks were out of the question, as was the provision of food aid. Nonaka touched on his personal disappointment in his interview with NHK's *Close-up Gendai* a week after the launch: "[T]he country's latest action was very sad and disappointing and made me feel that it might take Japan-DPRK relations all the way back to the starting point…It was also sad enough to make me feel that at worst, it may take 50 years for the two nations" to improve ties, he concluded.[408]

Any goodwill that had been accumulated in the early 1990s was lost. Nonaka's North Korea engagement strategy would be replaced with the more hard-edge and no-nonsense engagement of younger LDP politicians such as Shinzo Abe. In the meantime, however, North Korea would continue its bellicose actions toward its neighbors.

March 1999: Suspected Special Ops Ships in Japanese Waters

Mere months after the second midget submarine was captured in South Korean waters, Japan discovered a similar clandestine operation in its waters. On March 19, 1999, Japanese officials in the Public Security Investigation Agency (PSIA) received information from counterparts in South Korea's National Intelligence Service indicating that North Korea had launched two ships from Ch'ongjin, North Korea, and that the ships were suspected to be heading toward Japan. The ships reportedly belonged to "Maritime Liaison Office" of the Operations Department under North Korea's Ministry of the People's Armed Forces.[409]

Officials at the PSIA contacted their colleagues at the National Police Agency's Security Bureau, who in turn activated a special SIGINT collection cell called the "Foreign Technology Investigation Office" (*gaiji gijutsu chōsakan shitsu*), sometimes called "Yama," which began to monitor for signals coming from the Sea of Japan. The DA, informed of the launch by their counterparts in the US DoD, PSIA, and NPA, on March 20 ordered

P-3C patrol planes to watch for the ships in the Sea of Japan. On Sunday, March 21, SIGINT sites run by the DA's Defense Intelligence Headquarters in Miho and elsewhere detected so-called A2 radio messages, numerical codes sent via short-wave radio that were consistent with North Korean signals, coming from the Sea of Japan. The multiple sites were able to triangulate the position of the ships in the Sea of Japan. The NPA's "Yama" office similarly detected the signals, and DA and Yama officials quietly contacted officials in the NPA's Security Bureau and the Maritime Safety Agency—later renamed the Japan Coast Guard—to inform them of the vessels' probable location. The Security Bureau in turn sent out an emergency notice to the Niigata Prefecture Police Headquarters to alert them of possible attempts to infiltrate Japan.[410]

On March 22, despite the holiday—most Japanese had the day off to celebrate *Shunbun no Hi* or Vernal Equinox—Maritime Self-Defense Force (MSDF) crews were recalled and supplies were hurriedly loaded onto three MSDF warships. The three ships were some of the best in the Japanese navy: the Aegis destroyer *Myoko,* which tracked the Taepodong launch the previous year and was awarded the "MSDF Chief of Staff's Citation" for its outstanding service, and the helicopter-destroyer *Haruna,* the flagship for the Third Escort Flotilla. They were joined by the *Abukuma,* a destroyer armed with a state-of-the-art 62-caliber, 76mm rapid-fire cannon from Italy's OTO Melara that had the longest range of its type in the MSDF.[411] The weather was bad and with temperatures hovering just above freezing, snow fell intermittently as the ships departed their home port of Maizuru. The Defense Agency explained the crews' unexpected holiday departure by announcing that a firing and helicopter control exercise had been moved forward by a day, citing "improving" weather conditions. The announcement was a cover to keep locals and the media from becoming suspicious.[412]

On the morning of March 22, two P-3C patrol planes—one each from the 2nd Fleet Air Wing out of Hachinohe and the 4th Fleet Air Wing out of Atsugi—were on station searching for the source of the signals. By nightfall, an EP-3 electronic intelligence plane had taken off from Kashima Base in Ibaraki Prefecture to join the group in the search. At 6:42 am on March 23, an MSDF P-3C discovered a suspicious vessel off the coast of Sado Island in the Sea of Japan. Two more were spotted at 9:25 am, 45 kilometers from Ishikawa Prefecture's Noto Peninsula. The MSDF ordered the helicopter destroyer *Haruna* to intercept the vessel near Sado Island and the Aegis destroyer *Myoko* to intercept the vessels near the Noto Peninsula to confirm the targets' identities. By mid-day, the Japanese destroyers had located each of the three fishing vessels in the area, including the *Daiichi Taisei-maru* and the *Daini Yamato-maru.* Their size, approximately 100 tons and 30 meters long, was consistent with fishing vessels in the area, but the P-3C pilots did not see any fishing gear on deck. Neither was flying a national flag. Moreover, they noticed several antennae on the decks of the two vessels, arousing the crews' suspicions. The *Haruna* and the *Myoko* contacted Maizuru District Headquarters with the information and requested verification of the boats' identities. One of the three boats identified in the area was quickly confirmed as a legitimate fishing boat. But an ominous report came from the MSA Guard and Rescue Department regarding the other two vessels: the *Yamato-maru* was actually fishing in waters off the coast of Hyogo Prefecture on the other side of Maizuru port, while the *Taisei-maru* had been scrapped in 1994 and its official registration voided. Both the ships discovered in the Sea of Japan were thus fakes.

The Maritime Safety Agency (MSA) had 15 ships and 12 airplanes in the area, and following verification of the boats as probable North Korean vessels, MSA airplanes attempted to order the two vessels to halt for inspection. At 1:18 pm, an MSA Falcon-900 in the area flew over the *Yamato-maru* and blinked its lights, signaling for the boat to stop, and the MSA helicopter-carrying patrol ship *Chikuzen* and the patrol boat *Hamayuki* headed toward the area to intercept the target that afternoon. Meanwhile, an MSA Sikorsky helicopter hovered over a slow-moving *Taisei-maru*, dropping smoke pots near the ship as a signal for it to stop. The MSA dispatched another patrol boat, ironically named the *Sado*, to intercept the *Taisei-maru*.[413]

In Tokyo, the DA's Bureau of Defense Operations contacted the Cabinet Security and Crisis Management Office—an expanded Cabinet Security Affairs Office that had been upgraded following the 1995 Hanshin Earthquake, the Aum Shinrikyo attacks, and the 1997 Lima hostage crisis—at 2:55 pm to inform the Prime Minister's Official Residence of the pursuits. Top NPA officials, meanwhile, were concerned that the boats had infiltrated armed agents into Japan. A number of nuclear reactors studded the Japanese coast along the Sea of Japan, including the Kashiwazaki plant in Niigata across from Sado island. The NPA's Security Bureau issued an order for local departments in Niigata and neighboring Ishikawa Prefecture to mobilize to conduct roadside checks and guard railways and coastal areas, and to inspect the grounds of nuclear plants for saboteurs. The Security Bureau also ordered a Special Assault Team (SAT) to deploy to Niigata.[414] If an armed force had indeed landed, the NPA wanted extra firepower prepared to respond in the area.

Early that evening, DA Director-General Hosei Norota, Foreign Minister Masahiko Komura, and Transport Minister Jiro Kawasaki—who had jurisdiction over the MSA—met at the PMOR's crisis management center, just as the MSA's *Chikuzen* and *Hamayuki* began to pursue the fake *Yamato-maru*. At 6:10, the "PMOR Office Concerning Suspicious Ships" was officially established. Prime Minister Keizo Obuchi joined the group shortly after to oversee operations, while Norota returned to his DA office to monitor the situation there. By this point, the *Chikuzen* had ordered the *Yamato-maru* to halt, but instead of halting the *Yamato-maru* speeded up to 24 knots and began to outdistance the *Chikuzen*, which had a top speed of 22 knots. Transportation Minister Kawasaki issued permission to the *Chikuzen* to fire warning shots toward the target. At approximately 8:00 that evening, the *Chikuzen* fired 50 rounds from its 20mm gun aft of the *Yamato-maru* as warning shots. The target did not halt. At 8:24, the *Hamayuki* fired 195 rounds from its 12.7mm machine gun across the bow of the *Yamato-maru*.[415] These were the first warning shots fired by MSA patrol vessels at another ship since 1953, when a patrol boat attempted to stop a suspected Soviet vessel in waters near Hokkaido's Cape Soya. The captain of the *Chikuzen*, Hiroshi Shimokawa, later explained that he did not use his larger guns so as to avoid possible escalation of the situation and armed retaliation from the *Yamato-maru*.[416] Yet, the MSA and MSDF ships at this time were limited by law to firing warning shots only. They could not shoot directly at the ships unless they were under direct attack and were ordered to respond in kind. The *Yamato-maru* increased its speed to 35 knots and was soon out of range of the *Chikuzen*'s guns. Just after 9 pm that evening, the MSA ships lost sight of the suspect vessels.

Separately, the medium-size MSA patrol ship *Sado* was joined by the patrol boat *Naozuki* at 5:20 in pursuit of the *Taisei-maru*, which had also refused orders to halt. The *Naozuki* later fired warning shots from a small rifle twenty minutes later. But the *Taisei-maru* began to outdistance the MSA patrol vessels. Running low on fuel, they gave up the chase by 9:30 pm.[417]

Free from MSA pursuit, the two vessels quickly approached the edge of Japan's Air Defense Identification Zone (ADIZ), the boundary within which Japanese air assets could respond to potentially hostile aircraft, or cover naval assets responding to potentially hostile ships or submarines. Only the large MSDF destroyers were in a position to intercept and halt the vessels at this point. But an intercept operation by a Japanese naval vessel, as opposed to a coast guard vessel, would require an order from Prime Minister Keizo Obuchi himself. The MSDF destroyers had been ordered to remain 2 kilometers away from the fleeing boats during the MSA pursuit. But at 11:46 that evening, the unexpected happened when the *Taisei-maru* suddenly stopped, apparently suffering engine troubles. The MSA patrol boats were over 100 kilometers away by this point, and it would take them three hours to reach the *Taisei-maru* at their current speeds. The MSDF's *Haruna* and *Abukuma,* however, were gaining on the *Taisei-maru,* and the *Myoko* continued to follow the *Yamato-maru.* At 12:30 am, after consulting with his cabinet that evening, Obuchi invoked the SDF Law's Article 82 to allow the SDF to take any necessary maritime patrol measures during this maritime incident. Minister of Transportation Kawasaki, based on Prime Minister Obuchi's decision, called Director-General Norota at the DA headquarters to formally request the MSDF assets to halt and board the vessels. It was the first time since the founding of the Self-Defense Forces in 1954 that Japan had invoked the Maritime Patrol provision.[418] Chief Cabinet Secretary Hiromu Nonaka declared at a news conference late that night: "The situation has come to a point where the capability of the Maritime Safety Agency is no longer enough."[419]

Based on Prime Minister Obuchi's decision and at Kawasaki's request, at 12:40 am, DA Director-General Norota ordered a *kaijō keibi kōdō*—a "maritime security action"—to stop and inspect the ships. Officials in the DA secretariat began calling cabinet ministers who were members of Japan's Security Council to keep them informed of the situation. Meanwhile, the destroyer *Asazari* based at the southwestern port of Sasebo was ordered to the area of engagement to reinforce the three destroyers, while the destroyers *Shirane*, *Amagiri*, and *Umigiri* based in Yokosuka were ordered to re-deploy to Sasebo.[420] Yokosuka was on the Pacific side of Japan and thus too far from the area of operation, so these MSDF ships would never see action during this operation; the redeployment order was rather a calculated over-reaction on the part of Obuchi to demonstrate Japan's commitment to protecting its territorial waters from incursions.

As their MSDF colleagues were preparing to set to sea, the Self-Defense Fleet commander, having received an order from Norota based on the Cabinet's decision, ordered the *Myoko* and *Haruna* to fire warning shots at the two vessels, which he detailed at a late-morning news conference the following day. At 1:19 am, the *Myoko* engaged the *Yamato-maru* first, firing a total of 13 rounds from its 5-inch gun forward of the *Yamato-maru*'s bow, and P-3Cs dropped four 150kg anti-submarine bombs forward of the vessel as well. The *Haruna* at 1:32 am fired six warning shots forward of the *Taisei-maru*'s bow from its 5-inch gun, which had already fixed its engine troubles and had resumed its escape. At 3:20 am, Norota ordered the *Myoko* to cease its pursuit of the *Yamato-maru* after it exited Japan's ADIZ. Norota then ordered the *Myoko* to engage the *Taisei-maru*, as it was lagging behind the *Yamato-maru* due to its previous engine troubles. The three destroyers fired another 22 rounds at the *Taisei-maru* in an attempt to force it to stop, and P-3C planes dropped a total of eight 150kg anti-submarine bombs forward of the vessel as well. The *Taisei-maru* crossed the ADIZ at 6:06 am, however, and Norota ordered all ships to disengage the target.[421]

Japanese government sources later that day reported the ships had entered North Korean territorial waters. As the SDF and MSA were standing down from their operations the previous evening, Foreign Minister Komura told a news conference that Japan, through its embassies in Beijing and at the UN in New York, "will request North Korea to hand over the ships if they are intercepted."[422] The public statement left the impression that the ships were operating separately from any North Korean military or government direction, but privately no one believed that. On March 25, Norota told a news conference that the two ships had entered a military port on the northeastern coast of North Korea, although he refused to name the port. Japanese missions in Beijing and New York meanwhile were having difficulty contacting their North Korean counterparts, but they sent faxes noting their concern. Chief Cabinet Secretary Hiromu Nonaka noted that the incident would not cause the Japanese government to freeze funding for the KEDO project, as the two issues were not linked. "Funding for the KEDO project...is a measure taken to tackle North Korea's suspected nuclear programs, so I think we must separate it from the incident," he said.[423] While the government had decided to freeze funding for KEDO following the August 31 Taepodong missile launch, it announced the resumption of funding in November.

Other vessels were suspected to have operated in concert with the *Yamato-maru* and the *Taisei-maru*. DA officials told *Tokyo Shimbun* that in addition to the two vessels discovered off the Japanese coast, signals from as many as five other suspicious vessels were detected in that area days earlier on March 21. The five other vessels made strange movements, according to the officials, such as circumnavigating Sado Island without entering a port. The vessels then headed in the direction of the Korean Peninsula while two vessels—the *Yamato-maru* and the *Taisei-maru*—remained behind.[424]

These were not the first suspected North Korean vessels to be spotted in waters near Japan. In addition to the October 1990

"Mihama Incident," in April 1985, a Miyazaki Prefecture fisheries department boat on patrol for illegal fishing discovered a small fishing boat called the *Koeimaru-31*. A subsequent check revealed, however, that a boat with the same name was operating in a different location. The fisheries department alerted the MSA, which pursued the vessel, but the boat escaped. After spotting it again the next day, the MSA resumed pursuit but lost sight of the vessel in the East China Sea after pursuing it almost 1,000 kilometers. On August 5, 1981, a Korean resident of Japan was arrested while attempting to land on the Wakimoto beach in Akita Prefecture, and authorities chased after a suspected North Korean agent who fled on a rubber boat from the area. (The arrested individual had returned from North Korea, where he was suspected of having received unspecified training.) The following morning, an MSA patrol boat caught a radar image of a vessel at the mid-way point between Japan and the Korean Peninsula traveling north at high speed. An MSA patrol came within seven kilometers of the unidentified vessel, but the 100-ton ship increased its speed to over 30 knots and escaped the area.[425] Japan, thus, was not immune to North Korean naval incursions despite the wide body of water that separated the two countries.

North Korea and the Illicit Drug Trade

The maritime intrusion incidents targeting South Korea and Japan represented threats on multiple levels. Aside from potentially infiltrating and exfiltrating North Korean agents into and out of neighboring countries or potentially smuggling kidnapped citizens to North Korea, they could also serve as a means to transport illicit items to and from North Korea. These would include items such as export-controlled technologies, counterfeit currencies, or narcotics and stimulants.

Indeed, the North Korean government was long suspected of engaging in the drug trade in Asia. A variety of reporting in media, in South Korean and Japanese government sources, and from testimony of North Korean defectors, indicate that North Korea began intensive, state-sponsored efforts to cultivate and process opiate- and amphetamine-type substances (ATS) in the late 1980s or early 1990s. Between 1976 and 1999, according to the *Bangkok Post*, police in 22 countries had arrested 70 North Korean officials on drug-related charges.[426] According to South Korea's National Intelligence Service (NIS) debriefs of former WPK Secretary Hwang Chang-yop, the North Korean government sanctioned a "Paektoraji" or "White Bellflower" campaign to cultivate opium poppies that were then refined at the Nanam Pharmaceutical Plant in Ch'ongjin, North Hamgyong Province in the early 1990s for export abroad. According to Hwang, a directive was issued by the State Council's Director of Narcotics calling for the "introduction of good seeds and proper cultivation methods from Southeast Asia, as well as establishing trade routes."[427] ("White Bellflower" is a pseudonym for opium in North Korea.[428])

The North Korean government also began to produce methamphetamine in the early 1990s for export, variously called "philopon," "shabu" (in Japanese), and "o'ru'm" and "pindu" (in Korean). According to another defector, An Myong-chin, who claimed he had worked for the Operations Department of the Workers Party of Korea, North Korea began in 1991 to experiment with the manufacture of ATS to supplement the export of opiate-based drugs. As with early attempts to produce opiates, the quality of its methamphetamine was bad, however, so the North Korean government invited members of crime syndicates and South Korean ATS "technicians" to the "15 September Hospital" on the Kim Chong-il Political and Military Academy complex in Pyongyang. There, North Korean technicians learned to produce more potent stimulant drugs. They then established mass-production facilities at Nanam Pharmaceutical Plant in Ch'ongjin and Sunch'o'n Pharmaceutical Plant in Sunch'o'n, South Pyongan Province, according to An.[429]

Many aspects of Hwang's and An's accounts have been corroborated elsewhere, although the timing of events as well as production capacity differ. According to an April 2004 National Intelligence Service report, "[e]specially since the collapse of the Soviet Union and Eastern Europe, North Korea has expanded poppy cultivation dramatically," and "since the 1990s, poppy cultivation has been carried out openly everywhere in North Korea." Moreover, "in August 1993, a special processing factory equipped with refining equipment with an annual refining capacity of 100 tons of opium was established inside Nanam Pharmaceutical Factory under the instructions from Kim Il-sung to expand drug production." NIS added that drug production in North Korea expanded to ATS in the 1990s, with manufacturing taking place at "small-scale secret manufacturing facilities scattered throughout the country."[430] South Korea's main daily *Choson Ilbo*, citing Chinese sources, reported in October 2004 that North Korean drugs manufactured at the Nanam Pharmaceutical Plant were flooding into China as well, creating drug problems in regions bordering North Korea.[431] In a September 2002 account, a Chinese drug dealer along the North Korean-Chinese border told a South Korean journalist posing as a drug dealer that the Nanam plant produces 1 metric ton of both heroin and "philopon" a month with the help of Thai technicians. A North Korean escapee in China told the journalist: "The largest amount of drugs has flowed into Japan," suggesting that Japan had become a significant customer in North Korea's drug trade.[432] Not to be outdone, a TV crew from Japan's TBS TV station also followed a drug deal in the border region in 2005 as a Chinese woman bought a substance labeled "White Bellflower" in a North Korean drug house along the China-North Korea border. "Nanam Pharmaceutical Factory" was printed on the label. The crew then filmed the woman light and smoke the substance immediately after she purchased it. TBS later interviewed two North Korean defectors in South Korea, who said the Nanam factory is the second-largest producer of drugs after another, unnamed factory in Pyongyang.[433]

To produce ATS, North Korea requires the key precursor material ephedrine, commonly found in cough medicine and diet pills. According to the NIS, North Korea attempted to import 8 tons of hydrochloric acid ephedrine from India in May 1995, but the International Drug Administration Committee allowed the sale of only 2.5 tons, as even 1.5 tons of ephedrine per year would be enough to make cough suppressants and medicine for treating bronchial asthma throughout the country. North Korea was then caught attempting to import 15-20 tons of the same substance from Germany in June 1995, in defiance of the IDAC.[434] Another 2.5 tons of ephedrine originating in India was seized in January 1998 in Thailand. North Korean diplomats in Thailand strongly protested the seizure, however, claiming the shipment was needed to manufacture cough syrup in North Korea. Thai authorities questioned the diplomats' explanation, as the amount was much more than the country's demonstrated need. Thailand released the shipment in August, however, after repeated complaints from the North Korean diplomats. Although Thai authorities could not prove any direct link between the shipment and the drug seizures in Asia later that year and the next, the *Bangkok Post* in May 1999 quoted a drug enforcement official saying cynically: "We haven't noticed any North Korean cough syrup exports."[435]

Japanese and South Korean law-enforcement officials began seizing larger quantities of ATS via maritime routes in the late 1990s. In April 1997, Japanese customs officials seized 70 kg of methamphetamine in 12 cans of honey on the North Korean freighter *Ji Song 2*, the first major seizure of ATS thought to have originated in North Korea. The stimulants had a street value of ¥10.9 billion, or around $100 million.[436] On August 12, 1998, six Japanese including members of the *Toyoda-gumi* organized crime group rendezvoused with a North Korean fishing boat flying a Japanese flag and with the Japanese name *Shojin Maru No. 12* in the East China Sea. They transferred an estimated 300 kilograms of stimulants to their boat and returned to Japanese waters, but when the Japan Coast Guard discovered them the group dumped the stimulants in waters off Kochi Prefecture in western Japan. Japanese officials later recovered over 200 kg of stimulants in plastic bags that had washed ashore in Kochi and Mie Prefectures.[437] A joint South Korean-Japanese team seized an amphetamine shipment in May 1999 at a South Korean port, where members of South Korea's *Sinsangsa Faction* and the *Sumiyoshi Kai*—one of Japan's three largest *Yakuza* groups—were caught with the shipment that was believed to have originated out of the North Korean port of Hun'gnam. The shipment was bound for the Japanese port of Sakai.[438]

Smugglers increasingly resorted to *sedori* or "transfers at sea" in the late 1990s as well. To avoid suspicion that a group of two or more vessels might arouse, the crew of one boat wrapped the drugs in plastic bags, attached floats to the packages, and placed the bags in the sea usually with a locational device for their accomplices to retrieve later.[439] But this method created another problem for traffickers, as the large bags were difficult to locate in the open sea and would sometimes wash ashore onto Japanese beaches.

Seizures spiked in 1999 when Japanese authorities discovered close to 1,975 kilograms of ATS, more than the five previous years combined. Of the 33 major seizures that year, 13 originated in

China for a total of 943 kilograms, but the two single largest seizures of ATS that year reportedly originated in North Korea and totaled 665 kilograms. These seizures included 100 kilograms discovered in April in Tottori Prefecture, and a huge seizure of 565 kg of amphetamines in Kagoshima Prefecture in southwestern Japan in October. While no North Koreans were arrested then—eleven Taiwanese, Chinese, and Japanese nationals were apprehended—chemical composition analysis suggested the substance's origin was North Korea. Approximately 1/3 of all ATS seizures that year were traced to North Korea.[440] And while authorities successfully interdicted many shipments, other shipments surely avoided detection. Indeed, the two North Korean vessels from Ch'ongjin disguised as fishing boats and chased out of Japanese waters in March 1999 could well have been involved in smuggling drugs into Japan.

Drug seizures by Japanese officials decreased in 2001-2003 according to National Police Agency statistics, possibly indicating more effective counter-drug policies. Authorities in other Asian countries continued to seize large quantities of drugs originating from North Korea. South Korean authorities seized a 50 kilogram shipment of methamphetamine in June 2003 from a ship that traveled from China through North Korea and docked in the southern port of Pusan. This seizure followed the confiscation of the 3,500-ton North Korean ship *Pong Su* after Australian police discovered 150 kilograms of heroin onboard in April 2003. (The Australian defense forces used the ship for target practice three years later.)[441] And in May 2006, Japanese police arrested a Japanese member of an organized crime group and a South Korean on suspicion of using the floating-drugs method of delivery at sea three times to transfer nearly a ton of stimulants, although police did not find the drugs.[442] In a sign that the ATS continued to hit the streets in the early 2000s, Toshikazu

Shigemura, a professor at Takushoku University, told the monthly *Gendai* that "street prices for stimulants have fallen to 1/3 of previous prices in the past four or five years, which implies the supply has expanded three-fold." He further suggested that "much of the supply originates from North Korea."[443]

Supporting this thesis, the US State Department highlighted the following in its mid-2000s *International Narcotics Control Strategy Report*:

> "[D]uring the 1970s and 1980s and into the 1990s, citizens of the Democratic People's Republic of (North) Korea (DPRK), many of them diplomatic employees of the government, were apprehended abroad while trafficking in narcotics and breaking other laws. More recently, police investigation of suspects apprehended while making large illicit shipments of heroin and methamphetamine to Taiwan and Japan have revealed a North Korean connection to the drugs. Police interrogation of suspects apprehended while trafficking in illicit drugs developed credible reports of North Korean boats engaged in transporting heroin and uniformed North Korean personnel transferring drugs from North Korean vessels to traffickers' boats. These reports raise the question whether the North Korean government cultivates opium illicitly, refines opium into heroin, and manufactures methamphetamine drugs in North Korea as a state-organized and directed activity, with the objective of trafficking in these drugs to earn foreign exchange."[444]

Following the March 1999 incursion by North Korean vessels, the JCG and MSDF were increasingly alert for unidentified or camouflaged vessels near Japanese waters. Less than two years after North Korea's first major naval incursion in the post-Cold

War era, the JCG pursued another unidentified ship in Japanese waters suspected to have originated in North Korea. This time, however, the JCG—on the orders of Japanese political leaders in Tokyo and supported by revisions in Japanese law—was prepared to engage the ship with deadly force.

2001: Aftermath of the Sinking of a Special Ops Ship

The JCG in late December 2001 fired upon a maritime vessel in international waters for the first time in Japan's post-war era, as detailed in the introduction of this book. The incident led to the sinking of the disguised North Korean vessel in waters inside China's Exclusive Economic Zone (EEZ). Coming so soon after the discovery (and escape) of two other disguised ships two years prior, and with North Korean special operations forces having been discovered in neighboring South Korea on multiple occasions in the late 1990s, the incident sparked intense concern in Tokyo that North Korea continued to actively target Japan as well. Tokyo was determined, therefore, to raise the vessel for definitive proof of the vessel's ultimate origin and mission. It would take almost a year to do so, however.

Within five days of the incident, the JCG announced that it was installing the advanced 20-mm, highly accurate gun system similar to that used on the *Inasa* on more JCG ships, as only eight of the 19 ships dispatched during the incident had the gun. It also announced plans to bullet-proof its ships, as the *Amami* did not have bulletproof glass installed in the pilothouse.[445] The Defense Agency was increasingly public in its case that the sunken ship was most likely North Korean, announcing that the signals it was emitting closely resembled those used by North Korea. The agency also cited other information suggesting the ship had originated from North Korea, although it did not elaborate on that information. The ship was also probably accompanied by two other ships, according to the DA.[446] The JCG, for its part, noted the ship's peculiar design also pointed to its North Korean origins. Officials found after studying infrared images of the ship that the engine room was located in the bow and not in the stern as in typical ships. North Korean ships used for clandestine operations were known to be built with the engine room in the bow, as the stern section was dedicated to launching and recovering small, fast boats. The JCG also said no smoke or heat was coming out of the main funnel, indicating it was a fake structure and further suggesting the engine room was forward. Indeed, during the chase, the *Mizuki* fired unsuccessfully at the stern believing that was the location of the engine room to force the boat to halt.[447] This information too would cause the JCG to change its interdiction tactics.

The JCG did not find the sunken ship for another two months. In the days after the sinking, 12 patrol boats and 11 planes searched the accident site when the weather allowed, but the JCG did not find much except scattered debris. On February 23, it dispatched the 550-ton coast guard survey ship *Kaiyo* and the 3,500-ton patrol ship *Izu* to the area. Two days after beginning its search, the *Kaiyo* recorded an echo response about 95 meters below the sea surface. The crew sent a remote-controlled underwater TV camera to the wreckage, and there they found two Chinese characters on the side of the ship—*Changyu*—along with the numbers "3705" and bullet holes on the sunken ship's port side.[448] Further probes discovered two badly decomposed bodies and weapons—two rocket launchers, an automatic rifle, a machine gun, several cartridge belts, and ammunition.

A potential salvage faced one major problem, however: the ship sank in China's exclusive economic zone in the East China Sea southeast of Shanghai. In Beijing, Chinese Foreign Ministry spokesman Kong Quan noted this fact bluntly shortly after the ship was found, and said Japan should adopt "a careful attitude" regarding possible salvage operations.[449] During Japan's search for the wreckage, Chinese ships monitored activities as Japan Coast Guard vessels probed the site, including the Chinese research vessel *Haijian 52*. The ship was rumored to actually be the *Shijian*, well-known for conducting multiple underwater surveys near the Senkakus and Amami. The ship and her crew thus knew the area well. China was concerned whether Japan was surveying the site itself, or using the incident as an excuse to conduct a more general survey for underwater natural resources since the area was reputed to have rich gas and oil deposits. While Beijing surely wanted to avoid undue publicity connecting the sunken vessel to Pyongyang—Beijing's primary emphasis was to keep Tokyo from doing what Chinese ships had been doing in the region for years, namely, meticulously surveying the sea bed topography for mineral and gas deposits. Mere months prior to the sinking, in February 2001 China and Japan had agreed on a "prior notification system" in which the two countries undertook to inform the other of the survey area and time-period two months before the survey, reflecting Tokyo's concern about Chinese survey vessels in Japan's EEZ. But Japan had already accused China of reneging on the system five times in 2001, thus raising questions about the efficacy of the system—and Beijing's commitment to prior notification—even before this incident.[450]

Complicating matters, allegations surfaced that the boat might have refueled in waters near Shanghai. The ship most certainly came from North Korea's western coast: defense commentator Shigeru Handa noted that for the *Changyu* to travel from Ch'ongjin (the suspected port of origin of the ships involved in the 1999 incident) on North Korea's eastern coast would have required the suspect vessel to travel through the narrow Tsushima Strait between the southern tip of South Korea and Japan, where both the JCG and MSDF patrol heavily, on its way to Kyushu and the Amami Islands where it was discovered. The *Changyu* therefore most likely departed from North Korea's west coast's port of Nampo, further supporting reporting by the US military.[451] (According to captured North Korean Yi Kwang-su's 1996 testimony noted above, Nampo was one of four bases under the direct control of the MPAF Reconnaissance Bureau used to support maritime operations against South Korea and elsewhere.)

Originating from a west coast port, the *Changyu* would have traveled close to the Chinese coast. The *Asahi Shimbun* reported on March 1 that reconnaissance satellite photos showed a ship similar to the *Changyu* near a port in the Zhoushan Islands 100 kilometers south of Shanghai and about 240 kilometers from where the *Changyu* sank.[452] Neither the US nor Japan could confirm that the ship resembling the *Changyu* in the image was the same ship, however.[453] (Later, following China's granting of permission to salvage the ship, the *Tokyo Shimbun* reported on July 3 that the *Changyu* most likely was refueled in the area by another North Korean vessel disguised as a freighter, although the DA was unable to verify that account.[454])

A week after the location of the sunken *Changyu* was confirmed, an *Asahi Shimbun* reporter in Beijing asked Foreign Minister Tang Jiaxuan at a March 6 news conference about China's position on raising the boat. Tang's reply was terse: China "expressed our strong dissatisfaction over Japan's indiscreet use of force in China's exclusive economic zone." He also extended a rather blunt warning to Tokyo: "I would like to emphasize once again that the Chinese side will safeguard, in accordance with law, the sovereign rights related to its exclusive economic zone and also jurisdiction over it."[455] Tang's comments were widely reported in

Japan. In public at least, Beijing certainly was not taking a cooperative stance on a Japanese-sponsored salvage operation.

While China certainly was concerned that raising the ship in its EEZ would provide conclusive evidence tying the operation back to North Korea, at issue was not the salvage site itself, but the natural resources located beneath it. The *Changyu* sank in waters 40-50 kilometers east of the Pinghu offshore gas field and 50-60 kilometers east-northeast of the Chunxiao offshore gas field group, which is comprised of four gas fields. China had built a drilling rig over the Pinghu offshore gas field in April 1998, and in December 2001—around the time the JCG sank the *Changyu*—China announced that it would begin exploitation of the Chunxiao gas field group as well.[456] These offshore gas fields were located immediately west-northwest of what Japan considered the "midline" in waters between the two countries, and as such part of the gas fields were potentially located on the Japan-claimed side as well. By unilaterally developing the gas fields, China was consuming natural resources that Japan claimed as well. China was therefore concerned that Japan would use the salvage of the *Changyu* as a pretext to conduct maritime surveys of the region to bolster Tokyo's claims that the natural resources in the East China Sea are located on both sides of the midline between the two countries and should therefore be developed jointly. A Japan-sponsored maritime survey could also be used to support Japan's proposed location of the midline itself, which China had yet to recognize.

Given Tokyo's overwhelming desire for proof that North Korea was behind the incident, however, Japanese officials were undeterred. Vice Foreign Minister Yukio Takeuchi was quoted as having told China's Ambassador to Japan Wu Dawei the next day that the JCG "did not [indiscreetly] use force. It was an action based on our right as a sovereign and constitutional state."[457] Japan's business daily *Nihon Keizai Shimbun* pointed out in its editorial supporting salvage operations that "the mystery boat…is not within Chinese territorial waters" and therefore "salvage operations do not legally require Beijing's permission, though diplomatically Tokyo would be well advised to obtain its approval."[458] *Yomiuri Shimbun* also countered by noting that the ship had first intruded into Japan's EEZ and refused orders to halt, and "the Chinese government should pay great attention" to the issue because "the security of waters surrounding Chinese territory was compromised" as well.[459] The incident concerned the security of both countries, in *Yomiuri*'s view.

A month later, perhaps in an attempt to calm Japanese reaction to Tang's remarks (or perhaps to play the "good cop" in Tokyo to Tang's "bad cop" in Beijing), Li Peng, chairman of the National People's Congress Standing Committee, during a visit to Tokyo reportedly told Japan's Foreign Minister Kawaguchi: "I can understand that the people of Japan have such high concerns over the suspicious ship issue."[460] Li met the next day with Prime Minister Koizumi, where the two agreed to "solve the matter in a manner satisfactory to both countries."[461] Li's friendly disposition regarding Tokyo's position on the sunken vessel during his visit—an unusually long eight-day tour to commemorate the 30th anniversary of normalization of bilateral relations—suggested Beijing was slowly moving toward allowing Japan to salvage the ship. Tokyo in turn showed patience on the matter as Kawaguchi stated the day after her meeting with Li that Tokyo was unsure whether it would raise the ship, citing a need to verify the ship's structural integrity later that month. With Li's face-saving comments to Japanese officials, Kawaguchi was thus able to buy some time for both parties to back away from harsh rhetoric while Japan prepared to investigate the site and the status of the sunken *Changyu* further.

The Japan Coast Guard hired a private salvage firm at the end of April to investigate the site of the ship, and two vessels arrived over the wreckage site on May 1. By May 4, the salvage team consisting of deep-sea divers and a submersible operated from two salvage ships had recovered two weapons and a bullet from the seabed and the remains of a human body near the wreckage. Two JCG patrol ships watched over the team's work. On a later dive that day, however, divers reported seeing several bodies lashed to the deck of the sunken vessel, and they discovered another mutilated body beneath the bridge. The divers also found a gaping hole just forward of the bridge, which the divers believed was the result of the crew scuttling the ship by blowing a massive hole in the ship's hull. The explosion also explained the mutilated body found below the bridge near the hole. To prevent any of the estimated 15 crew members from being captured alive—or else to prevent their bodies from floating to the surface for easy identification after the ship sank—someone tied at least a few of the crew to the railing on the deck before scuttling the boat.[462] The salvage team recovered another body and other technical information confirming the boat's structural integrity was intact, and the salvage ships and JCG patrol ships once again departed the area on May 8.[463]

Japan and China had been set to discuss salvage procedures shortly after the early May probe of the ship, but an incident at a Japanese consulate in China delayed discussions for a month. The same day as the salvage team departed the area, five North Koreans—a husband and wife, their three-year-old daughter, the husband's mother and his brother—rushed into the Japanese Consulate in Shenyang, northern China, seeking political asylum. Pictures of the scene showed Chinese guards at the gate forcibly wrestling the two women to the ground as the young daughter watched inside the gate. The two North Korean men, meanwhile, rushed into the visa application office on the grounds of the Consulate. Armed Chinese guards then entered the Visa application office and escorted the asylum seekers away. Some were relatives of Chang Kil-su, a high-profile North Korean who in June the previous year sought refuge at the United Nations High Commissioner for Refugees's Beijing compound and later resettled in South Korea. The situation contrasted with that at the US Consulate in Shenyang where two more asylum seekers successfully entered the Consulate, as Chinese guards refrained from entering the compound.[464] Following a two-week diplomatic dispute over whether Chinese officials intruded into the Japanese compound, China sent the five asylum seekers to South Korea via the Philippines.

Beijing, for its part, was still upset over Koizumi's April 22 visit to Yasukuni Shrine, his second as prime minister. The visit came one week after FM Tang specifically requested Koizumi to refrain from visiting, in line with long-held Chinese policy. (Yasukuni is a national shrine where, according to Shinto belief, the souls of almost 2.5 million Japanese war dead are interred, including 14 convicted of Class-A war crimes and over 1,000 convicted of Class-B and Class-C war crimes following World War II. The museum on the grounds of Yasukuni, the Yushukan, moreover blatantly whitewashes Japan's role in the East Asian conflicts, and prime ministerial visits lend tacit support to these erroneous historical views.[465])

After a month-long impasse, final discussions regarding the *Changyu* salvage commenced in mid-June, this time over the more prosaic matter of compensation should the *Changyu* leak fuel or cause other environmental damage to the sea as it is being raised. The two sides came to a basic agreement allowing Japan to commence raising the *Changyu*. When asked about China's response when a private Japanese salvaging company began preparations to raise the ship later that month, FM Tang said simply that "an agreement was reached between the two sides" and the "Japanese side will honor its commitments during and after the salvage operation as promised."[466] The concise statement was a marked contrast to Tang's posturing in early March.

The salvage operation finally commenced following the late June-September typhoon season. On September 11, 2002, Japan raised the 100-ton *Changyu* and transported the hull to shore. A senior JCG official called the boat "unusual…in all aspects."[467] Investigators found fake registration numbers on the bridge indicating the vessel was registered as a fishing boat in Miyagi Prefecture. These and other markings illustrated the degree to which the boat had been disguised as a fake fishing vessel, unseen until now. The ship was built for speed: the propeller blades were twice the size of normal propellers used on fishing boats, and the ship's keel was V-shaped, characteristic of high-speed boats. The Japan Coast Guard believed it had seen this type of ship before. The ship's design resembled another vessel monitored to have transported a large amphetamine shipment to a group of six Japanese men on a fishing boat in the East China Sea who were later caught with nearly 300 kg of amphetamine drugs in August 1998.[468]

Inside the ship, investigators found seven types of weapons and high-tech equipment in addition to the arsenal of weapons. They discovered several advanced Global Positioning Systems (GPS) units and a radar on the ship. The devices, manufactured by Furuno in Hyogo Prefecture, were the same ones discovered by South Korean investigators on the North Korean mini-subs that infiltrated South Korean waters in the summer of 1998 and again in December that year.[469] A computer found onboard contained a CD-ROM that displayed a marine chart made by the Japan Coast Guard. The charts first went on sale at Japanese marine shops in 2000 for ¥70,000, indicating that they were newly acquired perhaps from a location in Japan. The GPS plotter found onboard was used to integrate the GPS units and the radar, and all the devices together enabled the crew to verify their exact position, heading, surface conditions, and the existence of shallow reefs and other possible maritime hazards.[470]

The discovery of the ship and its many clandestine functions brought renewed focus to the issue of Japanese abductees. For decades rumors swirled that young Japanese who had suddenly vanished in the 1970s and 1980s had actually been kidnapped by North Korean operatives using vessels similar to the ones discovered in and near Japanese and South Korean waters in recent years. Tokyo would use the sinking of the *Changyu* as leverage to restart talks with Pyongyang on possible restoration of diplomatic relations, starting with the abduction issue.

The Return of the Abductees

The timing of the salvage operation in mid-September 2002 coincided with another momentous (and tragic) occasion in relations between Japan and North Korea. As the JCG was preparing to raise the North Korean spy ship in mid-September, government officials announced on August 30 that Prime Minister Koizumi planned to hold a bilateral summit with Kim Chong-il in Pyongyang. This would be the first ever visit by a Japanese prime minister to Pyongyang in the post-war era.

There had long been suspicions in Japan that North Korean agents were involved in the abduction of Japanese citizens in the late 1970s and early 1980s. Domestic political pressure had been building as North Korean defectors continued to allege in court and in South Korean and Japanese media that they had seen Japanese abductees in North Korea. In but one example, in early 1997 An Myong-chin, a WPK Operations Department agent who had defected to South Korea in September 1993, claimed that he had seen a young Japanese national at a ceremony commemorating the founding of the WPK in September 1988 and again on two separate occasions the following year. An said that an instructor named "Chong" pointed to the woman at the ceremony and said: "I brought her here from Niigata," a Japanese prefecture located on the Sea of Japan. Chong, according to An, explained that he and two other North Korean agents were near the Niigata beach when she came upon them. Not wanting their activities revealed, Chong claimed that they took her with them to their boat and then returned to North Korea.[471] The young girl, Megumi Yokota, was 13 at the time of her abduction, and she was returning home after playing badminton at her middle school in Niigata on November 15, 1977. Her friend said she last saw Yokota by the seashore 250 meters from her home.[472]

With defectors' testimony mounting, the Japanese Diet began to debate the abduction issue in February 1997 ahead of a possible resumption of bilateral normalization talks. Based on An's claim, Shigeru Yokota, Megumi's father and head of the Association of Families of Victims Kidnapped by North Korea, pressed Niigata Governor Ikuo Hirayama to lobby the Ministry of Foreign Affairs to investigate his daughter's whereabouts, and Yokota personally lobbied the National Police Agency and MOFA to revive efforts to investigate the whereabouts of other families' children who had similarly been abducted as well.[473] The Ministry of Foreign Affairs in April approached their North Korean counterparts in Beijing during unpublicized director-level talks to request an investigation of the latest allegation, but the North Korean side refused.[474] On May 1, 1997, Okiharu Date, head of the National Police Agency's Security Bureau, said at a House of Councillors session that his office now believed North Korea was involved in the disappearance of the 13-year-old Yokota in 1977.

The National Police Agency increased the number of Japanese nationals officially suspected of having been kidnapped by North Korean agents to ten.[475] By November 1997, at the request of a Japanese delegation led by future Prime Minister Yoshiro Mori, North Korea replied that it would review the abductee issue "as a simple case of missing persons." But in mid-June 1998, a spokesman for the North Korean Red Cross said that after an investigation, none of the 10 missing Japanese nationals were found to be residing in North Korea.[476] Announcing the "results" of the investigation, North Korea's Korean Central Broadcast Network declared: "[T]here is not and has never been even a single missing Japanese in our country," and any assertion to the contrary "is a defilement of our Republic, as well as an outspoken expression of a hostile policy against the DPRK."[477] North Korea's official KCNA continued the propaganda onslaught, this time attributed to "a spokesman for the Central Committee of the Red Cross Society of the DPRK," saying that use of the words "suspected abduction" is "an expression of a hostile policy toward the DPRK," an attempt "to hurl mud at the DPRK," and "is motivated by [Japan's] hostile policy toward the DPRK."[478] And this from North Korea's Red Cross! Later admissions from Kim Chong-il himself would reveal that these statements were all utter lies.

Following the sinking of the *Changyu* in December 2001, yet another former North Korean operative testified seeing abducted Japanese there. Megumi Yao, the former wife of a Japanese Red Army Faction terrorist who hijacked a Japan Airlines jet in 1970, told a court on March 16, 2002 that she helped lure a Japanese student in Copenhagen, Keiko Arimoto, to North Korea in July 1983. Yao said she handed over Arimoto to a North Korean diplomat and an associate of her husband's, one of nine Red Army Faction members involved in the 1970 hijacking. According to Yao, once in North Korea, Arimoto wed another Japanese kidnap victim.[479] Following Yao's testimony, Japan's NPA added Arimoto's name to its list of officially recognized abductees, bringing the total number of abducted Japanese to eleven.

In addition to Yokota, Arimoto, and Li Un Hye (the Korean name for Yaeko Taguchi discussed earlier in this book) there were eight other Japanese recognized by the Japanese government as having been abducted by North Korean agents. Kaoru Hasuike was a 20-year-old college student and Yukiko Okudo was a 22-year-old cosmetician when they vanished on July 31, 1978 from the town of Kashiwazaki in Niigata Prefecture (the same town that hosts a large nuclear power plant located on the Sea of Japan). They told friends and family they were going on a date that day, but they never returned. Hasuike's bicycle was discovered near a library by the seaside where they were supposed to meet. Yasushi Chimura was 23 and his fiancée, Fukie Hamamoto, was also 23 when they disappeared after exchanging engagement gifts at a local restaurant in Obama, Fukui Prefecture. Their car was similarly discovered abandoned near the sea. Tadaaki Hara, a cook in Osaka, disappeared from his village in Miyazaki in June 1980 when he was 43. A South Korean court ruled in 1985 that a known North Korean agent, Sin Guang Su, abducted Hara in Miyazaki and sent him to North Korea. (The NPA later suspected Sin had impersonated Hara to acquire a Japanese passport, and in August 2002 they placed his name on an international wanted list.) Shuichi Ichikawa and Rumiko Masumoto, 23 and 24 respectively, disappeared on August 12, 1978 from Fukiage, Kagoshima Prefecture. They told relatives they were going to watch the sunset but never returned. 52-year-old Tokyo security guard Yutaka Kume went missing in September 1977 in Noto, Ishikawa Prefecture, but his whereabouts were unknown. North Korean authorities later would say they had no record of entry to the country.[480] Yet beyond the list of officially recognized Japanese abductees, some families suspected the number was much higher, with up to 80 thought to have been abducted due to the mysterious circumstances surrounding their disappearance.

Following Yao's testimony and with preliminary discussions progressing secretly with North Korean representatives—and as Japan prepared to survey the sunken *Changyu*—on March 19, 2002 Prime Minister Koizumi established a special task force consisting of senior vice ministers and headed by Deputy Chief Cabinet Secretary Shinzo Abe to reexamine the abductions. Prime Minister Koizumi met with relatives following the announcement of the task force formation, where Shigeru Yokota told Koizumi, "We want the government to press North Korea hard, including applying sanctions." The father of another abduction victim summed up the frustration in the group with North Korea when he asked the Prime Minister, "Why is the Japanese government so weak?" Prime Minister Koizumi declared that the abduction issue "is not just a problem for these families," but "a problem that should be taken up by all of Japan."[481] The group also gave Koizumi a petition that they said contained 250,000 signatures supporting their cause. It was the group's third time meeting a sitting prime minister, and this prime minister, it seemed, finally had the evidence to act.[482]

Closely linked to the issue of Japanese abductions was the fate of nine Japanese hijackers who in March 1970 hijacked a Japan Airlines jet and flew it to Pyongyang. Called the "Yodo-go" incident in Japan, four of the nine hijackers involved were still residing in North Korea with their immediate family in what was reportedly called the "Japan Revolutionary Village."[483] While Japan had not demanded their return as part of the normalization talks, the group was suspected to have played a role in kidnapping some Japanese nationals, including Keiko Arimoto. But their numbers were slowly dwindling. Takamaro Tamiya, the group's leader, died in North Korea in November 1995, as did two others. Yoshimi Tanaka was arrested in Cambodia in 1996 for carrying counterfeit US dollars and was deported to Japan in June 2000, and was later sentenced to 12 years in jail.[484] Her mother, the wife of another hijacker, Shiro Akagi, returned to Japan in the previous September. In the summer of 2002, the remaining hijackers filed applications with the Ministry of Foreign Affairs for travel documents to return to Japan.[485] A North Korean Ministry of Foreign Affairs spokesman discounted any linkage to normalization in a July 27 statement, however, saying members of the group were making preparations "on their own initiative" and the government "has nothing to do with it."[486]

Talks to resume normalization discussions had begun shortly after Koizumi became Prime Minister in late April 2001 and after a bizarre incident when Japanese border control officials caught Kim Chong-il's oldest son, Kim Chong-nam, entering the country with a fake passport. The younger Kim, accompanied by two women and a young child, was reportedly going to Tokyo Disney World. Following a year of back-channel, secret negotiations, Tokyo received the necessary assurances that the abduction issue would be addressed at a summit between Kim and Koizumi, an obvious prerequisite for Japan. With this promise to address the abduction issue, the Japanese government announced on August 30 that the two heads of state planned to meet for a one-day summit in Pyongyang on September 17.

Prime Minister Koizumi departed Tokyo's Haneda airport aboard his official plane early in the morning on September 17. He was accompanied by a small entourage, including Deputy Chief Cabinet Secretary Shinzo Abe, Deputy Foreign Minister Toshiyuki Takano and Hitoshi Tanaka, director-general of the Foreign Ministry's Asian and Oceanian Affairs Bureau.[487] The three men shared both political and personal bonds of loyalty.

Takano served with a young Shinzo Abe as secretary to Abe's father and long-time politician Shintaro Abe when he was Foreign Minister. The younger Abe and Koizumi belonged to the Abe faction within the LDP, began by the late Prime Minister Nobusuke Kishi, Shinzo Abe's grandfather, and continued by the late Shintaro Abe. Also accompanying the group to Pyongyang was Kyoko Nakayama, the Cabinet Secretariat adviser on the North Korean abduction issue. The group would stay in Pyongyang only a few hours. The main goal was relatively modest. Japan wanted the return of all Japanese nationals kidnapped in the late 1970s and early 1980s. Only then would Japan restart normalization talks with the North. In the past, North Korea had immediately halted talks with Japan any time the subject of the kidnapped was raised, but this time would be different, Pyongyang promised. Tanaka had gained assurances that North Korea would provide information on the abduction victims.

The Prime Minister's Boeing 747 arrived at Pyongyang's Sunan airport at around 9:15 that morning. Koizumi's disembarkation was carried live in Japan. A blue and white stairway leading to the plane was placed at the plane's door, the words "Koryo Air" in Korean and Latin script clearly visible on the side, and Kim Yong-nam, president of the Presidium of the DPRK Supreme People's Assembly and North Korea's number two leader, walked to within a dozen paces of the plane. Other North Korean dignitaries milled about on either side of the wide red carpet leading to the plane, and a few other large passenger jets were visible in the distance. Japanese security officials in dark suits and black wires leading to small ear pieces watched vigilantly. After Kim took his place at the base of the stairway, Koizumi strolled out of the plane onto the top platform and surveyed the scene below as his deputies joined him. Koizumi seemed unhurried. An ASDF officer stood at attention on the platform immediately next to the door facing out, saluting as the group gathered in front of him. Once gathered on the platform, Koizumi started down the stairway, followed by Abe and then the others. Koizumi walked directly to Kim Yong-nam and shook his hand. Koizumi then shook hands with Kim Il-ch'ol, vice chairman of the DPRK National Defense Commission.[488]

Shortly after 10 am Ma Chol Su, Tanaka's interlocutor during the secret talks to set up this day's visit, revealed to Tanaka that an "investigation" into the situation of the missing Japanese nationals "confirmed five of them are alive." Eight other abductees, including Megumi Yokota and Keiko Arimoto, were dead. Two of the eight, Toru Ishioka and Kaoru Matsuki, were suspected of being abducted by North Korea after they went missing while in Spain in 1980, according to Ma. The Government of Japan had not included them on the initial list of eleven suspected abductees, however, thus raising the number of abductees the government would recognize as having been abducted. The North claimed that the others on Japan's list had never entered North Korea. The North Korean Red Cross Society would convey the information to the Japanese Red Cross Society, Ma said. The preparatory talks ended, and Tanaka and Abe informed the Prime Minister of the news.[489]

The Japanese delegation was stunned, not only about Ma's admission but also about the abduction victims' fate, since the abducted Japanese were simply too young for all eight to have died natural deaths. North Korea claimed, for example, that Megumi Yokota committed suicide while being treated for depression—Japan later called this story unconvincing. North Korea would later provide a vase in November 2004 that Pyongyang claimed held the cremated remains of Yokota. Following DNA analysis, however, Japan found that the remains were from two different people, neither of whom were Yokota.[490]

The group proceeded to Paekhawawon Guesthouse. Prime Minister Koizumi stood with his entourage at the entrance, surrounded by reporters, photographers, and cameramen, all shown live on television in Japan. It was now time to meet face-to-face with North Korea's "Dear Leader." Kim Chong-il entered opposite the group through large, heavy doors. He strode up to Koizumi and smiled slightly as the two shook hands: "I am pleased to meet you in Pyongyang." Kim then shook hands with Abe, whose position as Koizumi's right-hand man and potential successor was solidified that day. Koizumi and Kim then walked side by side to their meeting room along a long, large hallway covered with a lime green carpet, to a high-ceilinged meeting room. Koizumi, Abe, and Tanaka, and two others sat across from Kim Chong-il, Kang Sok-chu, first vice minister of foreign affairs, and their interpreter, Hwang Ho Nam. The table was long, made of a dark, well-polished wood. The three men on either side seemed dwarfed by the massiveness of the room. There were places for more than ten to sit on either side in high-backed leather armchairs. The two sides engaged in idle small talk as the cameras rolled.[491] The reporters were then dismissed and the cameras were turned off, and the summit talks began at 11:31.

During the initial meeting, Prime Minister Koizumi addressed the abductions. Asserting that as the Prime Minister of Japan, he was responsible for the safety of the Japanese people, and he expressed shock and reportedly remonstrated the North's actions. Kim did not address the abductions then, however, saying he would respond at the afternoon meeting. The encounter was brief, ending just over 30 minutes later as the delegations broke for separate lunches shortly after noon. Huddled together following the dramatic revelation that morning, the Japanese group debated whether to sign a joint declaration calling for the resumption of normalization. The group decided that if the North did not apologize, the Prime Minister would depart Pyongyang without signing the joint declaration.[492]

As the Japanese delegation discussed next steps, another Japanese MOFA official met with the four surviving abductees: Shiho Chimura, Fukie Hamamoto, Kaoru Hasuike and Yukiko Okudo. Koizumi wanted to meet the Japanese abductees in person, but the four said they were not psychologically prepared for such a meeting yet. He also met Megumi Yokota's 15-year-old daughter, Kim He-gyong.[493] Kim told Umemoto that she did not know how her mother died, though she thought she died of an illness when she was in kindergarten, and she did not know where the grave was located.[494]

The talks restarted after 2 pm. At the afternoon talks, Kim Chong-il surprised the Japanese delegation by admitting that North Korean agents had indeed abducted Japanese citizens. North Korea had until this day used the term "missing" to describe the Japanese nationals in question, but now, the North was officially admitting its agents' role in kidnapping Japanese citizens. According to a recounting of the day's events in the *Yomiuri Shimbun,* Kim told the group: "In the 1970s and 80s, there were some special agents who were driven by irrational impulses and a desire to be 'heroes' and ended up abducting the Japanese people. It's truly regrettable, and I offer my candid apology."[495] While Kim talked around possible government involvement in the kidnappings, he did nevertheless offer an apology as the Japanese delegation had required. The talks ended just after 3 pm as the two leaders prepared to sign the Pyongyang Declaration.

At 3:30 that afternoon, Koizumi again sat opposite Kim to sign the Pyongyang Declaration. The reporters and cameramen again gathered at one side of the room. The two sat alone this time, one aide standing behind each of the men on either side of the table. Koizumi and the two aides were dressed in well-tailored suits, while Kim Chong-il alone wore his signature brown Mao suit. Koizumi silently and expressionlessly opened a large black binder containing the declaration and signed his name on two copies, with camera flashes lighting his actions. He then slid the open binder to his aide. Koizumi's aide stamped the signatures to dry the ink, placed a thin paper in the binder to separate the two copies, and then closed it. He walked the binder to the end of the long table opposite the cameras, handed it to Kim's aide, who then placed it, open, in front of Kim. Kim, with a pen ready in his right hand, signed the first copy seemingly diagonally in wide strokes along the bottom half of the document, and sat back slightly to wait as his aide rearranged the thin paper dividing the two copies. He then signed the second copy, this time with less majesty. His aide then stamped the ink on the copies and closed the binder as Kim replaced the cap on his pen and handed it to his aide. The aide stuck the pen in his left inside coat pocket, his pressed and cufflinked sleeve clearly visible.[496]

The Pyongyang Declaration was thus signed. The Declaration focused on issues that in the past had prevented progress in the normalization talks, including Japan's colonial rule over the Korean peninsula, the abduction issue, and bilateral security: "Both sides determined that…they would make every possible effort for an early normalization of the relations," the document stated. Japan offered its apology for its colonial past: "The Japanese side regards, in a spirit of humility, the facts of history that Japan caused tremendous damage and suffering to the people of Korea through its colonial rule in the past, and expressed deep remorse and heartfelt apology." The Declaration touched upon the abduction issue without mentioning it by name: "With respect to the outstanding issues of concern related to the lives and security of Japanese nationals, the DPRK side confirmed that it would take appropriate measures so that these regrettable incidents, that took place under the abnormal bilateral relationship, would never happen in the future." Regarding security, "[b]oth sides confirmed that they would comply with international law and would not commit conducts threatening the security of the other side." In addition, "both sides" confirmed that they would "comply with all related international agreements," and importantly for Japan, "the DPRK side expressed its intention that, pursuant to the spirit on this declaration, it would further maintain the moratorium on missile launching in and after 2003."[497] (North Korea would break this pledge in July 2006, when it brazenly tested a half-dozen of short- and medium-range missiles.)

Kim's revelations regarding the abduction of Japanese nationals aroused deep distrust among the Japanese public toward North Korea. According to a *Yomiuri Shimbun* poll, while 44% gave the summit talks high marks and another 38% rated them positively, almost 68% thought that North Korea "will not...implement the agreements reached at the summit talks," and 91% believed that Kim's abduction admission required a thorough investigation ahead of normalizing diplomatic relations.[498] In an *Asahi Shimbun* poll, 81% rated Koizumi highly for the talks but 76% "expressed dissatisfaction" with Pyongyang over the abduction issue.[499] *Asahi Shimbun* lamented of the abductees, "more died than survived," and called North Korea's explanations that abductees died due to illness or natural disaster "hardly credible."[500] And as Japan prepared for possible talks in October, *Nihon Keizai Shimbun* noted: "It is typical for a country whose sovereignty has been violated by a third country in the form of abductions of its nationals to demand an apology, damages, [and] pledges that such an act will never be repeated."[501] But first, Japan had to secure the return of the Japanese nationals still held in North Korea.

The Tokyo-based National Association for the Rescue of Japanese Kidnapped by North Korea called on the government to investigate a further 60 abduction cases the group had investigated on its own. According to the group, apart from snatching Japanese nationals from shores along the Sea of Japan, North Korean agents lured Japanese into North Korea from other areas and then prevented them from leaving.[502] The National Police Agency for the time being added four names to its official list in early October, brining the number of Japanese officially recognized as abducted to fifteen. Toru Ishioka and Kaoru Matsuki were lured to North Korea while they were in Spain in June 1980. Two others, Hitomi Soga and her mother, Miyoshi, were kidnapped while on their way home from the grocery store on Sado Island in the Sea of Japan in 1978. The younger Soga, who was 19 at the time of her abduction, told investigators that three men assaulted her and her mother, dragged them to an area obscured by a tree, gagged them and stuffed them into large sacks. They were taken by small boat to a larger boat at sea. While Miyoshi had not survived, Hitomi was among the five survivors in North Korea presented to the Japanese delegation on September 17.[503]

Hitomi Soga's case would become more complicated because she was married to the US Army deserter Sgt. Robert Jenkins, who crossed the Demilitarized Zone in 1965 and was suspected of having assisted in the interrogation of crewmembers of the captured USS Pueblo.[504] Jenkins had met Soga when he was teaching English, and Soga was his student. The two married in 1980, and they eventually had two daughters together. Now, the abduction issue suddenly became a bilateral US-Japan issue, as the United States wanted to extradite Jenkins to face a Court Martial on desertion and possible espionage charges.

Japan requested the return of the surviving abductees and their children born there by mid-October. North Korea had initially wanted relatives of the survivors to visit them in North Korea, but the proposal was a non-starter for Japan. Tokyo sent a government team to Pyongyang in late September to interview the abductees more thoroughly and to get DNA samples. The team brought back a 10-minute video and pictures of the abduction survivors to show to their relatives, who naturally demanded their speedy return.[505] The relatives were understandably impatient. Preparations continued as Tokyo gained Pyongyang's consent for a temporary two-week return of the survivors to Japan on October 9. Tokyo had negotiated an unchaparoned visit—the returnees would not be accompanied by any North Korean minders. With no minders to exert any sort of influence, the returnees could make their own decision whether to stay in Japan. The Japanese Government chartered an All Nippon Airways 216-seat Boeing 767 for their return and issued special passports. The five returnees were the two couples, Yasushi Chimura, and Fukie Hamamoto, and Kaoru Hasuike and Yukiko Okudo, and a lone Hitomi Soga. When they arrived in Tokyo, all five deplaned wearing pins depicting the late Kim Il-sung. The reunion was emotional, and relatives who were in Tokyo to greet the returnees were surprised at how animated they were after so many years in captivity. The group had left behind close relatives, however, which would become a further sore point between Tokyo and Pyongyang. Soga returned without her husband, Robert Jenkins. Soga's two teenage daughters, Mika and Brinda, were studying at Pyongyang University of Foreign Studies and they too were not allowed to leave. In total, seven children and Soga's husband remained in North Korea. Pyongyang continued to maintain that the other eight Japanese citizens it had recognized as abductees were dead.

Following their arrival to their respective home towns, the five returnees worked quickly to reestablish their Japanese identities. One couple, Yasushi Chimura and Fukie Hamamoto, registered their marriage in their hometown of Obama, Fukui Prefecture.

They also registered the births of their daughter, 21, and two teenage sons, all born in North Korea. The other couple, Kaoru Hasuike and Yukiko Okudo soon followed suit in their hometown of Kashiwazaki, Niigata Prefecture.[506] Hitomi Soga, meanwhile, asked a local court to restore her name to her family registry: Soga's family had her listed as "missing" eight years after her abduction.[507] And the Government of Japan provided official recognition of their national identities when each of the returnees received a Japanese passport during their first week home.[508] They received the passports, moreover, based on their personal requests, indicating that they recognized themselves as Japanese citizens even after being held captive in a totalitarian state for over twenty years. In a sign Tokyo was attempting to secure the return of the survivors' next of kin, less than a week after the abductees' return it requested that Washington grant special amnesty to Robert Jenkins if he were to travel to Japan.[509] Tokyo feared that should Jenkins visit Soga in Japan, Washington would demand his extradition to the US to face desertion charges, and they were unsure of Jenkins's status under the US-Japan Status of Forces Agreement.

On October 24, ten days after the abductees arrived home, Chief Cabinet Secretary Yasuo Fukuda announced what many suspected all along. The Japanese abductees would not return to North Korea. Fukuda declared that the repatriated Japanese citizens would live in Japan "permanently." He also stated that Tokyo would request during the bilateral talks in Kuala Lumpur at the end of the month that they be reunited with their relatives still in North Korea.[510]

More details emerged about the abductions as government officials interviewed the victims. Hitomi Soga had gone shopping with her mother on August 12, 1979, the day they were abducted. After they left the shop at 7:00 or 7:30 that evening, they heard footsteps approach from behind, and when they turned they saw three men following them. The men followed for the two for several minutes. As the ladies passed a large tree along the road to their house, the men attacked the Sogas from behind and dragged them to beneath the tree. They covered Hitomi's mouth and forced her into a sack, and she lost sight of her mother. They put her on a small boat and then a short time later they transferred her to a larger boat, which then took her to Ch'ongjin. She was met there by a woman who could speak Japanese, and she was then taken by car and then by train to a spy facility, she told investigators. There, she stayed with Megumi Yokota during the first five to seven months as they learned Korean—she was given the Korean name Ming Hye-gyon. The two young girls played badminton and table tennis together. Japanese authorities believed she was kidnapped so that a North Korean agent could assume her identity and so that she could teach Japanese to North Korean agents.[511]

Speaking on the eve of the 25th anniversary of their 1978 abduction, Kaoru Hasuike explained how the couple was kidnapped. As he and Yukiko sat on the coast of Kashiwazaki, a man approached him to ask for a light. Three other men then approached, and the four beat him and stuffed him and Yukiko into sacks. They then transported the couple by rubber dinghy to a larger ship offshore, and they were taken to Ch'ongjin. Yukiko recalled that the abductors stuck adhesive tape over their mouths and eyes, but she was able to see through a small slit at the bottom of the tape as they took her away from her home. In the year following their return the couple had yet to visit the abduction site, as "[i]t is a bad memory and I will only feel depressed," Kaoru told reporters.[512]

Ch'ongjin was the common destination in these stories. Japanese and South Korean authorities believe Ch'ongjin is a major base of operations for the North's Operations Department espionage activities against the neighboring countries, and that it was the port of origin for the ships discovered off Noto Peninsula in March 1999. Two classified offices attached to North Korea's communist party, the Workers Party of Korea, were allegedly involved in the abduction: "Office No. 35" and the "Operations Division." The organizations were charged with committing abductions, terrorism and information and intelligence gathering. Operatives of "Office No. 35" were believed to have conducted the terrorist bombing of a Korean Air jetliner in 1987, for example.[513]

The Japan-North Korea bilateral normalization talks scheduled for late October were over almost before they began. Kim's abduction admission in September 2002 was quickly followed by another, more troubling one in early October when Assistant Secretary of State James Kelly visited Pyongyang on October 3-5 to discuss the North's violation of the 1994 Agreed Framework. The trip was the Bush administration's first senior-level contact with North Korea since early 2001. The United States had evidence that the North had procured hundreds of centrifuges since as early as 1997 for the enrichment of uranium. This effort represented a separate, parallel effort to its plutonium reprocessing capability. Diplomatic sources said the US suspected North Korea had procured up to 1,000 centrifuges, although they did not believe the centrifuges had been used by the time of Kelly's visit.[514] Following Secretary Kelly's presentation of evidence on October 3 that the North had a uranium enrichment program, North Korean officials initially denied that such a program existed. The following day, however, First Vice Foreign Minister Kang Sok-ju confirmed Secretary Kelly's assertions, telling Kelly that the North continued the program because of delays in the construction of the light-water reactors as agreed in 1994. Kang then blamed the US for the delays, asserting that they led Pyongyang to undertake the parallel program.[515] Kang then placed the program on the bargaining table, brazenly calling on Washington to meet three conditions. First, the United States had to guarantee that it would not launch a preemptive attack; second, the US had to negotiate a bilateral peace treaty; and third, the US had to accept North Korea's economic system.[516] The United States could not accept these "conditions," however, as Washington's position was that the program was counter to the 1994 Agreed Framework and illegal under the Nuclear Non-Proliferation Treaty. The program was therefore not open to negotiation. Prior to these talks, Washington officials had informed Tokyo of its suspicions even before Prime Minister Koizumi's Pyongyang Summit in September, and Kelly briefed Chief Cabinet Secretary Yasuo Fukuda on his meetings upon returning from Pyongyang in early October.[517] The news of Kang's admission did not hit papers in Japan until former Prime Minister Hashimoto told reporters following an October 16 meeting with Deputy Secretary of State Richard Armitage of the outcome of the US visit to Pyongyang as the US was preparing for emergency talks with Japan, China, and South Korea to discuss Pyongyang's admission.[518]

Despite the revelations on the nuclear front, bilateral normalization talks took place October 29 in Kuala Lumpur even as Pyongyang sank further under a cloud of suspicion on multiple fronts. With the return of Japanese abductees, momentum in Japan had built to the point that Tokyo wanted all the abductees' relatives returned as well and a full accounting of the deceased abductees, regardless of the nuclear revelations. The Japanese delegates also requested the return of Red Army Faction members who had a part in the 1970 Yodo-go hijacking incident. North Korea countered by demanding the return of the five Japanese abductees who were visiting Japan since October. The talks did not produce any major outcome, and Japan further asserted at informal meetings in November that it could not negotiate without the return of the abductees' families.[519] In late November, news arrived from Pyongyang that Robert Jenkins, Soga's husband, had been hospitalized for "extreme fatigue." Seizing on the opportunity—even if engineered behind the scenes—Tokyo quickly offered to bring Jenkins to Japan for treatment, which would set a precedent for bringing the other relatives home as well. Tokyo faced a different problem with the Jenkins case, however: Jenkins himself realized he could be extradited to the United States if he traveled to a US-allied country. He thought the statute of limitations for desertion was forty years, which he believed would come three years later, in 2005. The US Ambassador to Tokyo, Howard Baker, contradicted this, saying that the statute of limitations would not begin until he was in the United States or in US custody.[520] Defense Secretary Donald Rumsfeld also said that Jenkins would face legal proceedings if he went to Japan. Jenkins therefore equivocated, but his declining health would give Pyongyang a face-saving reason for sending him out of the country. The fate of Jenkins and the other relatives would not be decided for another year, however.

The North Korean nuclear issue was quickly turning into a major international crisis. In response to Pyongyang's October admission that it had a uranium enrichment program, Washington, which was providing the bulk of fuel oil to North Korea through KEDO, announced in November that it was halting all shipments of fuel oil due to Pyongyang's violation of the 1994 Agreed Framework. This did not please its partners in Tokyo and Seoul, however, as both understood that a halt to fuel oil deliveries would probably mean the end of both the Agreed Framework and KEDO. The announcement would allow Pyongyang to claim KEDO was not holding up its end of the bargain, use this as a reason to withdraw from the Agreed Framework, and restart its nuclear programs. Even though the opposite was in fact the case—Pyongyang was not adhering to the spirit of the agreement—Tokyo and Seoul nevertheless preferred more attempts at diplomacy within a nominally functioning KEDO framework. Seoul was especially adamant that the fuel shipments should continue parallel with diplomatic efforts to get North Korea to comply once again with the Agreed Framework.[521] Washington was firm, however, and the last shipment of fuel oil left Singapore in November 2002.

On December 24, Pyongyang announced that it would reopen nuclear facilities at Yongbyon, where workers began to remove IAEA surveillance equipment and seals from the 5-MW reactor, the radiochemical laboratory, a spent fuel storage pond and a fuel rod fabrication plant there. On December 27, Pyongyang ordered IAEA inspectors to leave the country by the end of the year. The two inspectors at Yongbyon, a Chinese and a Lebanese, departed Pyongyang for Beijing on December 31.[522] On January 6, 2003, the IAEA Board urged North Korea to return to compliance. The following day, the United States, Japan, and South Korea led to a US statement saying it was ready for dialogue (but not negotiations, since those had been completed with the Agreed Framework) with North Korea if it was ready to fulfill its international commitments. North Korea's ambassador to the United Nations, Pak Kil-yon, would later say of this proposal: "I view that it is not a sincere negotiator's attitude to have dialogue but not negotiations."[523] The North Korea nuclear problem was now center stage in Asia, even as the United States prepared for possible military engagements in Iraq.

On January 10, North Korea declared its intention to withdraw from the NPT. In a statement carried on North Korea's official news agency KCNA, Pyongyang declared "an automatic and immediate effectuation of its withdrawal from the NPT." It further stated that North Korea was now "totally free from the binding force of the safeguards accord with the IAEA." It also declared: "The withdrawal from the NPT is a legitimate self-defensive measure taken against the US moves to stifle the DPRK and the unreasonable behavior of the IAEA following the US." However, "[t]hough we pull out of the NPT, we have no intention to produce nuclear weapons and our nuclear activities at this stage will be confined only to peaceful purposes such as the production of electricity."[524] Of course, the international community could not be sure of this final statement without the ability to inspect the country's nuclear facilities. Given the Kim regime's repeated lies and obfuscations regarding its nuclear programs (not to mention the abduction issue), there was no reason to believe the North's "nuclear activities" would be "confined" to the "production of electricity." Choe Chin-su, the North's ambassador to China, continued the diatribe two days later, stating that the decision "is due to the US maneuver to crush the DPRK and the unfairness of the International Atomic Energy Agency, which is the US henchman." He then blamed the US for "pushing us to withdraw from the treaty."[525] With the North's latest announcement and with international attention focused on military preparations targeting the Hussein regime in Iraq, bilateral Japan-North Korea normalization talks were dead. Japan still sought the return of the abduction victims' families, but normalization of diplomatic relations would be impossible.

North Korea continued its provocative actions. In February 2003, it restarted the 5 MW reactor at Yongbyon. Later that month, it launched two short-range surface-to-ship missiles. While the missiles were 1960s-era silkworms with limited range and limited capabilities, the fact that North Korea tested them at the time without announcing the tests in advance or declaring its intentions was further evidence to the Japanese that the North

Korean regime was needlessly provocative. Tokyo, not wanting to precipitate another crisis, declared that the tests were not a violation of the Pyongyang Declaration halting missile tests since they were short-range cruise-type missiles. Japan and the United States were also concerned, however, that Pyongyang might launch unannounced a Nodong or other missile. In addition, one of the North's fighters intercepted a US reconnaissance aircraft in international airspace over the Sea of Japan, further heightening tensions. And North Korea not only restarted the Yongbyon reactor, by late spring it had begun to reprocess the fuel rods to extract plutonium.

North Korea's KCNA declared on April 18 in an English-language report that the country was in the "final phase" of "successfully reprocessing more than 8,000 spent fuel rods." Following a comparison of the English translation with the original Korean, however, US officials questioned whether this statement meant to indicate North Korea had begun actual reprocessing of the rods, or that it had almost completed *preparations* to reprocess the fuel rods. If actual reprocessing of the rods was almost complete, the North was that much closer to having the material to build a nuclear weapon. The extended quote from the original Korean carried by the Korean Central Broadcasting Station read: "As we have already declared that we have resumed our nuclear activities since December last year, and as we have given the United States and other related countries an interim notification in early March, even the reprocessing work of some 8,000 spent fuel rods is now successfully being carried out in the final phase."[526] Regardless of the semantics in the statement, clearly North Korea was moving forward with its nuclear program. At US-China-North Korea three-way talks less than a week after the statement, North Korean representative Ri Gun was quoted in *Asahi Shimbun* as telling Assistant Secretary of State Kelly: "We have a number of nuclear weapons," and "whether we test them or export them will depend on the stance the US takes."[527] If either Tokyo or Washington had any doubts about the reprocessing, they were dispelled when on July 11 US government sources announced the detection of Krypton 85, a gaseous byproduct emitted during the reprocessing of spent plutonium fuel, near the Yongbyon area.[528] This indicated North Korea had at least begun some reprocessing of plutonium fuel. How much remained a question, but if all 8,000 rods used in the Yongbyon reactor were reprocessed, North Korea would have enough weapons-grade plutonium to build a half-dozen nuclear devices.

Japan was of course highly concerned by these events, particularly due to the country's proximity to the Korean peninsula. In an article reviewing North Korea's nuclear and missile capabilities, the weekly magazine *Aera* noted that even the "rather primitive" Nodong had a 50-50 chance of hitting somewhere in Tokyo. Thus, "if two missiles were fired targeting the center of Tokyo City, one of them would fall somewhere in the city. Suppose the warhead of this one missile carried a nuclear weapon. That would devastate the city." *Aera* quoted defense analyst Keiichi Nogi: "I think North Korea has reached the stage of almost completing nuclear warheads, including the triggering devices. It could even have started to produce warheads."[529] *Asahi Shimbun* noted in April that North Korea's "[a]ssertions which include the 'possession of nuclear weapons'" could "be read as a diplomatic device in which, depending on what the US does, compromise is possible," which by the paper's own admission "is an excessively dangerous gamble."[530] In July, *Asahi* further declared following the announcement that the US detected Krypton 85: "If the reports are correct, North Korea has committed an outrage that erases its framework agreement with the United States." *Asahi* continued to advocate a peaceful, diplomatic solution, however, while declaring: "Japan can never tolerate North Korea's possession of nuclear weapons. But a military solution to the problem would demand far too high a price."[531] *Yomiuri Shimbun* declared in July: "The international community should take all possible measures to prevent Pyongyang from developing, possessing or proliferating nuclear weapons." The daily noted: "It is also necessary for Japan to establish a system whereby it can stop—at its discretion—North Koreans from trading with or receiving remittances from Japan immediately after it is confirmed that Pyongyang is reprocessing spent nuclear fuels."[532] Tokyo still had not addressed the issue of remittances, a topic of serious discussion during the first nuclear crisis in the spring of 1994. But even though Japan was highly concerned about North Korea's actions, all sober observers continued to advocate a peaceful response.

The Children Come Home

As the world community continued to grapple diplomatically with North Korea over its nuclear programs, Hitomi Soga and the other former abductees waited for the return of their kin. Soga, herself experiencing significant health problems, underwent lung cancer surgery in mid-March. She attempted to contact her husband Jenkins and their two daughters to tell them of the surgery via post, but the North Korean Embassy in Beijing, to which the letters were sent, would not accept them claiming that delivering mail was not a duty for their diplomats. The Japanese Cabinet Office sent the letters through other channels. Somehow they arrived, because Soga received a reply through the mail in mid-May. Yasushi Chimura and his wife Fukie also wrote to their children in North Korea telling them they were born to Japanese parents. The children had thought the parents were ethnic Koreans who had returned from Japan before they were born.[533]

Kaoru and Yukiko Hasuike wrote letters to their children asking them to be patient in waiting to be reunited. The North Korean Embassy in Beijing again refused to deliver them.[534]

Even as they waited for the return of their children, the former abductees began to make public appearances. They traveled to Geneva in April to address the UN Commission on Human Rights. They attended rallies, the largest one taking place in May 2003 in Tokyo where 5,000 supporters cheered their return. They also resumed their rights as citizens of democratic Japan by voting. Hitomi Soga and Yasushi and Fukie Chimura voted in the Niigata Prefectural elections, and it was indeed Soga's first vote cast in her adult life in Japan.[535] They met royalty. Emperor Akihito and Empress Michiko stopped for lunch at Kashiwazaki city hall where Kaoru and Yukiko Hasuike had begun working. The royal couple spoke with the Hasuikes briefly and encouraged them to remain supportive of each other.[536] The carefully staged encounter highlighted the royal couple's concern for the personal well-being of the former abductees while sidestepping the political dimensions of the abductee issue.

Rumors began to circulate in mid-summer that the North Korean regime was considering the return of the Hasuikes' and Chimuras' children. *The Korea Daily News* reported on July 31 that its Japanese and South Korean sources confirmed North Korea would soon hand over the children. A senior Japanese official later confirmed that North Korea floated the return through "informal channels."[537] Publicly, Tokyo continued to assert that it would not hold bilateral talks until the former abductees' family members were returned. Chief Cabinet Secretary Yasuo Fukuda told a press conference: "It will be difficult to continue talks unless" the issue of returning the relatives to Japan "is resolved before the normalization negotiations." Deputy Chief Cabinet Secretary Shinzo Abe made a similar announcement in early August.[538]

Tokyo Shimbun on August 19 reported that Japan and North Korea were conducting behind-the-scenes talks concerning the return of the children, but the North set two conditions for the children's return, namely, reaffirmation of the Pyongyang Declaration and food aid.[539] The provision of food aid would be especially difficult given the public mood in Japan toward North Korea. Many also believed that Kim had not been completely truthful about the abducted Japanese, with recent North Korean defectors making further sensational statements that Japanese abductees were still in North Korea. One former North Korean Korean People's Army official who defected to South Korea in 2001, An Yong-chol, claimed in the Japanese magazine *Gendai* that 108 Japanese were still alive in North Korea. The abductions were carried out on orders "and with the approval of Kim Chong-il himself," An declared.[540] Given the negative Japanese public sentiment and suspicion toward North Korea, the widely rumored "surprise September return" of the children to Japan to mark the year anniversary of Koizumi's Pyongyang summit would not be realized. Informal talks continued.

By this time also, preparations were underway for the first six-party talks concerning North Korea's nuclear weapons development. The United States refused to negotiate directly with North Korea while North Korea refused to allow inspectors to return to Yongbyon. The six-party talks provided an opportunity for a regional dialogue with Pyongyang by giving other countries in the region—China, Japan, South Korea, and Russia—greater responsibility working the issue. North Korea considered China and Russia friendly enough to its position to accept them at talks, while the US, Japan, and South Korea were united in their goal of ensuring that North Korea remained a non-nuclear state.

North Korea, for its part, established a new "Korea-Japan Exchange Association" in the fall of 2003 to take charge of bilateral talks with Japan. The association was established under Vice Foreign Minister Kim Yong-il, who was also serving at the time as Pyongyang's chief representative at the recently established six-party talks. The establishment of the association came around the time of WPK Party Secretary Kim Yong-sun's death. Kim Yong-sun had been in charge of talks with Japan until that time (tellingly, he oversaw other offices that conducted clandestine operations targeting Japan and South Korea), and the establishment of the association under the Ministry of Foreign Affairs signaled to some that talks would gain new momentum.[541] The nuclear and the abduction issues began to cross, if tangentially. The impasse on both the nuclear and the abduction issues continued through the end of the year, however, and the former abductees would celebrate their one-year anniversary marking their return home without their children.

Secret informal talks took place on December 20-21 at the Jinglun Hotel in Beijing, where five North Koreans including DPRK Ambassador for DPRK-Japan Negotiations Chong Tae-hwa and Deputy Director of the Foreign Ministry Song Il-ho met with a group of Japanese parliamentarians including Katsuei Hirasawa, secretary-general of a Diet members' league dealing with the abduction issue. The meetings were arranged by Kiyoshi Wakamiya, a freelance journalist with extensive contacts in Asia who was serving as a temporary advisor to Hirasawa.[542] Hirasawa was known as a hard-liner on the North Korean abduction issue, which made his involvement in the secret talks more surprising. Japan wanted the children still in North Korea reunited with their Japanese parents in Japan, with no strings attached. This was a prerequisite for bilateral normalization talks. The North Koreans offered to allow the children to return to Japan, but only if the former abductees returned to Pyongyang to retrieve them. The Japanese side did not know what to think of the offer. Could Japan trust a regime that just 16 months ago had confessed to kidnapping over a dozen Japanese citizens—eight of whom died in captivity—and that stood accused of kidnapping perhaps hundreds more Japanese, South Koreans, and others? Or was the offer an attempt to save face by drawing another Japanese delegation and the former abductees back to Pyongyang for a media relations campaign? Would Kim even allow the families to return to Japan, or hold them hostage in North Korea? Given the years of propaganda, spin, and lies out of Pyongyang on abductions and other issues, Tokyo simply could not trust the Kim regime.

With North Korea once again engaging the international community on the nuclear issue—the second round of six-party talks was scheduled to begin on February 25, 2004—and with North Korea sending signs that it wanted to resolve the immediate problem of the abductees' families still in North Korea, Japan continued to push for the unconditional return of the children. A four-day round of talks in Pyongyang in mid-February produced nothing. Bilateral talks also took place on the sidelines of the six-party talks at the end of February, but little progress was evident. Both sides stuck to their positions. Tokyo requested the return of the families unconditionally, while Pyongyang requested the former abductees' return to Pyongyang to personally ask their families if they wanted to move to Japan. Also in February, Japan finally finished revising its foreign exchange law to allow the imposition of sanctions against North Korea. Following the revision, Japan could legally halt financial transfers from individuals in Japan to their relatives in North Korea. Tokyo had a new legal stick to go along with the carrots of financial and material aid that it could offer.

The breakthrough came a month later, when Hirasawa and Taku Yamasaki, the former deputy president of the Liberal Democratic Party, traveled to Dalian, China for "secret" talks with the

North Koreans. The news of their mission and their arrival leaked almost immediately, however, placing the mission in jeopardy even before the two sides met.[543] (No longer a sitting member of parliament, Yamasaki was able to travel freely even during a Diet session. Representative Hirasawa, however, was reprimanded for traveling during the spring Diet session, as he was legally required to attend to Diet deliberations during that time.) Yamasaki, moreover, had visited the United States immediately prior to the Dalian trip to discuss the Jenkins case, indicating that Japan wanted to tie up this loose end before the families returned to Japan. Progress was in the air. While neither of the participants elaborated on their various discussions—silence itself in this case was a sign of progress—Hirasawa was later quoted saying: "The situation has moved forward considerably." Yamasaki, for his part, noted that working-level talks would take place again within the month.[544] A resolution seemed finally at hand.

Ultimately, the families did not travel to Pyongyang to meet their children. That task would be left to Koizumi himself, who announced on May 14 that he would return to Pyongyang personally to retrieve the returnees' kin and reaffirm the Pyongyang Declaration. Upper House elections were scheduled for July, and the brash prime minister wanted to deliver a major achievement for his party ahead of the elections.

Koizumi departed for Pyongyang on May 22, 2004. The second "summit" began at 11 in the morning and lasted a mere 90 minutes. An expected afternoon session was not held, although Kim reportedly told Koizumi at the end of the talks that they should "meet again."[545] Kyodo called the whole scene a mere "ceremony to pick up" the abductees' relatives.[546] Koizumi returned with five of the sons and daughters of the Japanese abductees and an agreement to establish a joint Japan-North Korea committee to reexamine the fates of the deceased abductees. Not everyone was happy, however. The Japanese relatives of those deceased abductees roundly criticized Koizumi for not gaining more information on their demise, the whereabouts of their remains, or information regarding their children or spouses possibly still alive in North Korea. "We must say it was the worst outcome," Shigeru Yokota told reporters, whose daughter Megumi had at least one child in North Korea. Shigeru's wife Sakie said Koizumi "left behind our children again."[547] The abduction issue would not disappear so easily, it seemed.

Koizumi returned with the Hasuike and the Chimura children, while Jenkins stayed in North Korea with his daughters. In return, Koizumi offered 250,000 tons of food aid and $10 million in medical aid to North Korea, which smacked of extortion. The families of the abduction victims and the Japanese press were getting impatient with Koizumi's high-level diplomacy with Pyongyang: "We find it difficult to say that Koizumi's meeting with Kim made any progress" on abduction, nuclear, or missile issues, Japan's largest newspaper *Yomiuri Shimbun* declared. "The abductions of Japanese must be seen as crimes committed by North Korea, which infringed upon this country's sovereignty and the fundamental human rights of the Japanese victims."[548] The Japanese public seemed to disagree with abductees' families and with the popular media, however: Koizumi's popularity soared almost 10 points in public opinion polls. A full two-thirds of respondents—66%—to a TBS Television "News 23" poll said they approved of Koizumi's second visit, and over 60% supported Koizumi's Cabinet. This latter figure was extremely high for a sitting Japanese prime minister in office for two years, and was especially high compared to his predecessor, Yoshiro Mori, whose polls dropped to single digits during his premiership. Seventy-one percent of respondents, however, said they did not trust the North's offer to cooperate in a joint reinvestigation of the ten deceased abductees.[549] The Japanese public still did not trust Kim, and for well-founded reasons.

While no one expected Koizumi to bring Jenkins to Japan with the other family members, Koizumi told a press conference that he was allowed to talk directly with Jenkins and their two daughters for an hour during his Pyongyang visit. Koizumi asked Jenkins if he wanted to return to Japan, but Jenkins replied that he would not go to Japan because he was concerned he would be handed over to US authorities. One of the daughters also told Koizumi that the two girls had been studying in Pyongyang "for many years" and that they wanted their mother to return to North Korea first before the family decided to travel anywhere. Koizumi said that the group talked about reuniting the family in a neutral site such as Beijing, which the three accepted.[550] Koizumi said in a statement after his return that Kim Chong-il had proposed the Beijing reunion.[551]

The children were reunited with their families in Japan, but the problem of the US Army deserter Jenkins festered. Japan could easily repatriate the children of the abductees as they were born to Japanese citizens who were held against their will in another country, but Jenkins was wanted by the US Government for treason, among other charges. As the spouse of a Japanese citizen, and given the high-profile nature of the issue, the Japanese Government could easily extend Japanese citizenship to Jenkins. But Japan also had an extradition treaty with the United States under the Status of Forces Agreement, requiring Japan to hand over US military personnel suspected of a crime. Given Jenkins's status as a US Army deserter, Jenkins was technically under that SOFA agreement. The US Government's position regarding Jenkins hit a snag in April 2003 when it was reported that the US Army Military Police Operations could not locate letters sent by Jenkins in which he allegedly suggested his intention to defect to North Korea. Some in Jenkins's family, moreover, began to raise doubts as to whether Jenkins had indeed defected or been abducted as had been his wife.[552] Soga, for her part, rejected a Beijing reunion within a week after Koizumi's return from his second trip to Pyongyang in May 2004. "I want us to be reunited in a place other than Beijing," Soga said in a statement. This surprised government officials, who thought after meeting Soga that she was willing to travel to Beijing for the reunion. Soga preferred to meet in a neutral, preferably English-speaking country farther from North Korea, however.[553]

Jakarta was floated as a neutral venue by early summer. While Japan's Ministry of Foreign Affairs initially planned to hold the reunion the week of July 12 due to Indonesian presidential elections scheduled for the prior week, Koizumi on the night of July 1 ordered Mitoji Yabunaka, director general of the Foreign Ministry's Asian and Oceanian Affairs Bureau who was in Jakarta negotiating a final date with North Korean officials, to set a reunion date before the upper house elections in Japan on July 11. The Ministry thus had to scramble to finalize the venue, transportation, and security arrangements. July 8 marked the 10th anniversary of Kim Il-sung's death and thus was ruled out.[554] The reunion was set for the following day, July 9. Taku Yamasaki, meanwhile, confirmed with US Deputy Secretary of State Richard Armitage and Assistant Secretary Kelly in Washington that the United States was not opposed to the reunion.[555] Soga departed Japan on a commercial flight for Jakarta on July 8, and the Japanese Government sent a chartered plane to Pyongyang to transport Jenkins and their two daughters to Jakarta the following day. The VIP security unit of the Greater Jakarta Metropolitan Police would provide security during their stay in Indonesia to include the use of armored cars to transport them throughout the city.[556]

The day of the reunion, Pyongyang's Korean Central Television provided extensive footage for Japanese audiences of Jenkins preparing to leave the country, a clever public relations campaign devised by the normally secretive Stalinist regime. The images were not broadcast in North Korea, however, a further sign that Pyongyang was attempting to influence the Japanese public specifically. At the airport in Pyongyang, KCTV showed a sprightly 64-year-old passing lithely through a metal detector and retrieving his baggage after it too was scanned. He showed no hindrance of movement. He then sat to wait for his flight, smoking a Marlboro, which he offered to his interlocutor standing just out of camera range. He seemed excited, almost quietly giddy, if pensive.[557] As he disembarked the plane in Jakarta, however, he looked frail and haggard. He had trouble walking down the stairs from the plane, holding tightly to the railing as he took each step carefully, one by one. His excited expressions seen in Pyongyang had been replaced by painful grimaces. The starkly differing images could perhaps be explained by his excitement and anticipation in Pyongyang ahead of his reunion with his wife in Jakarta, while his frail demeanor upon arrival to Jakarta could have been caused by the sudden onset of culture shock, or perhaps by a long and painful trip from North Korea. Or it could be that he was playing the part of a frail man to gain leniency before any possible legal action against him. Certainly, following forty years of self-imposed exile in North Korea, his life was sure to change. Soga embraced her husband and children on the tarmac of Jakarta's airport for the first time in 21 long months of separation.

The family stayed in a luxury suite at a hotel in Jakarta as a Japanese doctor examined Jenkins on Saturday and Sunday to check his health reportedly following abdominal surgery in April. The recent surgery did not prevent Jenkins from carrying out his normal daily functions but his abdomen needed to be monitored, the doctor declared. For their first outing on Sunday evening, two days after they arrived, the family dined on Japanese beef and pasta at Japanese Ambassador Yutaka Iimura's residence in southern Jakarta. The daughters, Mika and Brinda, watched four Japanese animated movies and the latest Harry Potter movie. The girls attended the dinner with North Korean badges pinned to their shirts, but Jenkins did not wear any badge on his new white polo shirt, which Soga gave him when they were reunited.[558] The three North Korean officials who accompanied Jenkins on the Japanese-chartered flight from Pyongyang remained a nuisance in Jakarta, however, as they continued to insist on a meeting with Jenkins during the weekend while he was ensconced in the hotel suite with his family. The Japanese minders turned them back repeatedly.[559] That part of Jenkins' and Soga's life was now officially over.

Another part was just beginning, however. On Friday, the day of their reunion, the US State Department spokesman repeated the US position: "As a humanitarian matter we thought [the family reunion] was appropriate. But it remains that Sgt. Jenkins potentially faces serious charges should he be in a place where he's subject to US jurisdiction."[560] A week following the reunion, US Ambassador to Japan Howard Baker on July 16 put forward the first compromise of sorts. Baker told Shinzo Abe and Tetsuzo Fuyushiba, secretaries-general of the Liberal Democratic Party and New Komeito respectively, that Jenkins will be spared the death penalty if he admits his guilt, gives himself up, and confesses everything. The statement came two days before Jenkins and his family were scheduled to leave for Tokyo for additional medical procedures.[561]

The family returned to Japan on July 18, and Jenkins and Soga went immediately to the Tokyo Women's Medical University Hospital for thorough checks of their post-surgery health. He had surgery in North Korea in April, and his health condition was publicly at least one of the reasons for being allowed to leave North Korea, while Soga had cancer surgery the previous year. By July 23, after a battery of medical tests had been conducted on Jenkins, the chief physician of a 15-doctor panel declared at a press conference that the abdominal wound from his surgery had "almost healed" and that "there is only a slight possibility that he has a serious disease." The chief physician noted, however, that "we believe he is suffering from severe stress due to various issues, and is no condition to return to normal life immediately."[562] In other words, Jenkins was stressed but physically ok, and doctors declared two weeks later that neither Jenkins nor Soga had cancer.[563]

Following further "treatment" and initial meetings with US military authorities at his hospital in Tokyo, Jenkins turned himself in to the US authorities on September 11. As part of the bargain struck between the Japanese and US governments and accepted by Jenkins, he was reactivated as an active-duty sergeant and performed day-to-day military duties while awaiting court martial proceedings at Camp Zama near Tokyo. He was charged with desertion, aiding the enemy, encouraging disloyalty, and soliciting other personnel to desert.[564] Despite the charges, Jenkins and his family were treated quite hospitably. He and his family were allowed to use the gym, indoor pool, and golf course on Camp Zama, and his wife and two daughters were given ID cards and were informed that they could move freely on base. The Jenkinses were assigned a married military couple who spoke English, Japanese and Korean to assist them while they stayed at Zama. Jenkins received an advance of one-month's salary—about ¥360,000, over $3,000—was given a haircut, and received new uniforms during his in-processing. By September 17, Jenkins was assigned light duties such as assisting in the coordination of unit training and maintaining files for an administrative support unit.[565] His in-processing and day-to-day status was broadcast on Japanese TV, and US military officials set up a special press room with a large liquid crystal display for briefings, a special webpage with pictures and video of Jenkins, and they allowed television crews to drive through Camp Zama for live broadcasts from inside the camp itself, rare permission during the early days of the "global war on terrorism."[566] The US government through public relations *Jujitsu* thus successfully turned a potential diplomatic spat between the US and Japan into a showcase highlighting US military civility.

At his general court-martial on November 3, Jenkins was found guilty of desertion and aiding the enemy by teaching English to North Koreans. The other charges of encouraging disloyalty and soliciting other personnel to desert were dismissed.[567] Jenkins pleaded guilty to the two charges, and prosecutors asked for a nine-month jail term and a dishonorable discharge. His defense counsel argued that no imprisonment was necessary (implying his almost 40-year stay in North Korea was enough prison time!) and indeed Jenkins received a reduced sentence because he had reached a plea bargain before the hearing began.[568] He was sentenced to a month's confinement at a facility in Yokosuka just outside of Tokyo, and a dishonorable discharge.[569] Jenkins served just over three weeks as he was released on November 27 and was officially dishonorably discharged.[570] Jenkins then traveled with his family to Sado Island in Niigata Prefecture—his wife's childhood home—where he began a new life as a free man in Japan. Jenkins book of his experiences in North Korea, published in Japanese as *Kokuhaku* ("Revelation of the Truth"), sold over 300,000 copies in just over a year.[571]

Thus, the immediate families were reunited, and for a time Tokyo was optimistic that a true breakthrough with North Korea had occurred. But Tokyo wanted more details about the circumstances surrounding the deaths of the other abductees and their remains. The remains that Pyongyang claimed were those of Megumi Yokota were identified following a DNA analysis to be the remains of two other unknown people, thus creating more distrust. Tokyo continued to call for Yokota's true remains to be returned, while Pyongyang continued to claim the remains were Yokota's. And while Japan listed eleven unsolved abduction cases, Pyongyang only recognized eight. Further creating difficulties between Tokyo and Pyongyang, residents of other countries began to lobby Japanese officials to inquire about members of their families who were suspected of being kidnapped by North Korean agents. Relatives of a Thai, a Lebanese, and two South Koreans alleged to have been kidnapped by North Korea traveled to Tokyo in late 2005 to discuss the cases ahead of bilateral Japan-North Korea talks scheduled several weeks later.[572] And Shinzo Abe, by this time Japan's Chief Cabinet Secretary, told Thailand's Deputy Prime Minister that Tokyo's delegates would try to resolve the case of Anocha Panchoi. Panchoi was believed to have been kidnapped from Macao in 1978, and her case resurfaced after Jenkins claimed in *Kokuhaku* that he and Soga lived in the same apartment complex with her in 1984. Jenkins further claimed that North Korean authorities offered her to Jenkins as a potential partner after Soga left for Japan in 2002.[573]

Thus, contrary to Kim's expectations, recognition of the North's role in the abduction issue remained a serious constraint to Japan-North Korea relations. The true fate of other suspected abductees of all nationalities remained a mystery. While normalization talks started again in February 2006, they again ended without any agreement. Similarly, the Six-Party talks would continue off and on from the fall of 2003, but with no tangible results. North Korea remained cut off from the world under a

Stalinist dictatorship as the country raced to develop—and eventually test—its nascent nuclear and missile capabilities.

Yet, just as some of the lingering questions related to the abductee issue had been answered, another incident served to highlight Japan's national security dilemma on a separate front. A Chinese submarine passed provocatively submerged within a few miles of Japanese islands without warning and against international laws prohibiting such actions. The incident was but one in a series of worrying incidents in the region, as China continued to modernize and build its military capabilities at a rapid pace and with little transparency.

China and the 'First Island Chain'

On November 10, 2004, a Chinese submarine cruised submerged through Japanese territorial waters near the Sakishima islets in Okinawa Prefecture. The submerged passage through Japanese territorial waters was in contravention of the Law of the Sea Convention, which requires a submarine to surface and show its flag.

Tokyo first learned of the submarine's general location and heading on the night of November 8, based on information passed by the US Navy. The MSDF dispatched P-3C patrol aircraft to the area to follow the submarine's activities by dropping passive—and later active—sonobuoys. At 0400 on November 10, a P-3C discovered the submarine 33 kilometers south-southeast of Ishigaki Island heading east-northeast. The P-3C and other aircraft monitored the *Han*-class submarine as it entered Japanese territorial waters at 0548. It passed along a route that snaked between Ishigaki and tiny Tarama islands through the Ishigaki channel, and it exited Japanese waters almost two hours later at 0740. It re-entered international waters in the East China Sea north of the islands. At 0845, Tokyo issued a *kaijō keibi kōdō*—maritime security action—but by this time the submarine had already departed Japanese territorial waters.[574]

The timing and location of the submarine's passage through Japanese territorial waters was particularly sensitive. Nine US and twenty-five Japanese ships were just commencing week-long joint naval exercises that day. The Japanese destroyers *Kurama* and the *Yudachi*, about to take part in the exercises, instead followed the Chinese sub. Four SH-60J helicopters from the two destroyers located the sub at approximately 0900 on the northern side of the Ishigaki channel. As the MSDF units continued to follow the sub, it changed direction several times and stopped to circle, seemingly in an attempt to avoid being tracked. The MSDF units maintained contact, however. It continued north seemingly on an intercept course with Taisho Island—part of the Japan-controlled and China-claimed Senkaku Islands—but before reaching the area it turned east running parallel with the Nansei island chain and then turned north again. (The ASDF launched an AWACS Airborne Warning and Control System over the sea near Okinawa to watch for the approach of Chinese aircraft as the MSDF followed the Chinese submarine.[575]) Nansei literally means "southwest," and it includes the islands stretching from the main island of Kyushu southwest to the Senkaku islands and Yonaguni near Taiwan.

The *Han* submarine exited Japan's Air Defense Identification Zone at 0710 on November 12. Tracking was halted at 1300 that afternoon, as the submarine continued to head north-northwest, back to China. Japan had known from initial contact that the target was most likely a *Han*-class submarine based on acoustic signatures of its turbines and the propeller. As defense journalist Shunji Taoka observed in his recounting of events, *Han*-class submarines are "extremely noisy." Sometime before dawn on November 16, the submarine entered port at Qingdao, headquarters for the North China Sea Fleet.[576]

The submarine's transit was a violation of Article 20 of the UN Convention of the Law of the Sea, which states: "In the territorial sea, submarines and other underwater vehicles are required to navigate on the surface and to show their flag." The *Han* submarine did not surface, nor did it show its flag. On November 16, China's vice foreign minister and former ambassador to Japan Wu Dawei blamed the pass-through on "technical" troubles experienced while the submarine was conducting regular drills in the area. He further stated that China would take measures to prevent similar incidents from occurring in the future.[577] Perhaps lending support to Wu's explanation, the MSDF had since November 5 followed a Chinese submarine rescue ship and a Chinese tugboat in the East China Sea north of the Nansei island chain. On November 8, they were again spotted in waters near the coast of Kagoshima Prefecture, although it was impossible to know if the ships traveled to the area due to the submarine's "technical" issues cited by Wu, if they were involved in exercises with the submarine, or whether their presence was coincidental.[578] Moreover, they were located northeast of the submarine, relatively removed from the submarine's area of operation. One DA official complained that "citing a technical error is the same method used by the former Soviet Union when its aircraft infiltrated our airspace." Any "technical" issues that were purely mechanical in nature would have shown up in the submarine's navigational track, but the MSDF detected no deviation as it passed straight through Japanese waters.[579]

The defense journalist Taoka suggested the "technical" issue cited by Beijing was actually a mistaken navigational track. Ishigaki is the central island in a cluster of islands between Okinawa and Taiwan. Yonaguni is the western-most island in this cluster, while Miyako is the eastern-most. Tarama is located between Ishigaki and Miyako. According to Taoka's theory, the sub mistook Ishigaki Island for Miyako Island and attempted to pass northeast along the outer edge of Japan's territorial waters to approach the U.S.-Japan joint naval exercises undetected from the south. However, by grazing Japan's territorial waters extending east of Ishigaki Island—which it thought was Miyako—the submarine passed through waters extending west from Tarama Island. Between Ishigaki and Tarama Islands, Japan's territorial waters intersected along the narrow Ishigaki channel, through which the sub passed. Had it passed east of Miyako Island instead—located on the opposite side of Tarama Island—the sub would not have passed through Japan's territorial waters extending from any other island as there is a large expanse of water extending northeast from Miyako Island to Kome Island near the main island of Okinawa. The sub would have thus passed through the Nansei Island chain in international waters.[580]

Beijing called the incident "regrettable" in a meeting with Japan's Ambassador to China Koreshige Anami, and China's Foreign Ministry Spokesman Zhang Qiyue told a regularly scheduled press conference that "the problem has now been settled in a proper manner." He quickly changed the subject, saying "the present difficulties in bilateral political relations is the issue of Japanese leaders paying respects at the Yasukuni Shrine."[581] This was China's only public statement on the submarine issue as Japanese and Chinese relations were increasingly strained. "We'll urge China to make sure that similar incidents do not happen so that it will not mar the development of Japan-China friendship," Prime Minister Koizumi said following Beijing's explanation of the event.[582] From China's point of view, the submarine issue was but a blip on the radar screen in Sino-Japanese relations: Prime Minister Koizumi's yearly visit to Yasukuni Shrine, where the souls of 14 WWII Class-A war criminals and some 1,000 Class-B and Class-C war criminals are interred, was the true constraint to deeper relations between the two regional powers.

While the November 2004 Chinese submarine mission was unsuccessful because it was discovered well in advance of passing through Japanese waters, China had been preparing intensely for these types of operations since 1996. Former National Institute for Defense Studies professor Shigeo Hiramatsu, who has written and lectured extensively on China's maritime operations around Japan, noted that China began methodically conducting maritime surveys in Japan's exclusive economic zone that year, when it conducted 15 such missions. It conducted four more in 1997, 14 in 1998, 30 in 1999, and 24 in 2000. Indeed, some of these operations were conducted along the strip of water between the main island of Okinawa and Miyako Island, and these operations included seabed topographical surveys using sonar, water temperature and salinity measurements, and the collection of other information vital to submarine operations. China started naval exercises in the late 1990s in waters near Japan as well. In July 1999, a Chinese fleet comprised of *Luhu* and *Luda* missile destroyers, a naval supply ship, and a submarine support ship conducted naval operations close to Japanese waters. The exercises followed a smaller naval exercise in May comprised of several outdated warships: although the ships were technologically inferior to those in Japan's MSDF, the proximity of the exercises to Japan marked a new precedent.[583]

In May 2000, China conducted its most provocative maritime survey to date: A *Yanbing*-class intelligence collection ship, the *Haibing 723*, circled Japan's Honshu, Shikoku, and Kyushu islands, and it even passed through the narrow Tsugaru Strait separating the main island of Honshu from Hokkaido. (The newly launched *Haibing 723* was first been spotted surveying waters in the Tsushima Strait in April 1999 and in the Osumi Strait in May 1999.[584]) In July and November 2001 the *Haibing 723* cruised waters near Tanegashima—the location of Japan's space launch facilities—to the Ogasawara Islands, a Japanese island chain that leads to the Mariana Islands and to the US territory of Guam. In February 2001, China and Japan agreed to give a two-month prior notification of surveys via "verbal notes," but Japan complained that China failed to give notification on five separate occasions later that year.[585] The Chinese maritime surveys continued unabated: Takushoku University Professor Ikuo Kayahara counted 13 in 2001, 12 in 2002, 11 in 2003, and 31 by July 2004, shortly before the *Han*-class submarine was discovered in Japanese territorial waters in November 2004.[586]

Following the *Haibing* and other maritime surveys in the late 1990s and into the early 2000s, China began a series of submarine navigation exercises in waters near Japan from the Nansei Islands to the Ogasawara Islands between 2001 and 2003. These exercises culminated in November 2003 with the passage of a *Ming* submarine in international waters through the narrow Osumi Strait between the southern tip of Kyushu and Tanegashima in Kagoshima Prefecture. Unlike the November 2004 incident the following year, the *Ming* submarine surfaced, exposing its rusted, aged hull, and it raised the PRC national flag. But the *Ming*'s passage through the Osumi Strait—widely regarded in Japan as a "showing the flag" exercise—could only be taken as a signal from China that its submarines could now navigate Japan's narrowest water passages.

The PRC submarines had a very specific mission among many, according to defense analysts. China's purpose in surveying maritime passageways around Japan, conducting underwater navigation exercises, and deploying its submarines on the Pacific Ocean side of Japan was to prepare to engage US aircraft carriers that might sail from Yokosuka to Taiwan, similar to the mission the US Navy conducted in 1996 when it dispatched the *USS Independence* carrier battle group from Yokosuka Naval Base immediately prior to Taiwan's first direct presidential elections. While the noisy *Ming* submarine itself posed no threat to the Japanese or US Navies, it was merely confirming navigable routes in the area. More advanced submarines soon to be commissioned—the eight Russian *Kilo*-class submarines China purchased in 2002, for example, and the Type-093 and Type-094 submarines China was building—certainly would not be so visible during future operations. Additional extensive maritime surveys were begun in 2004 in the sea areas south of Okinotori, another possible deployment route for US naval assets from Guam.[587]

Moreover, as Japan's *Defense Whitepaper 2004* observed, submarines are not the only concern: "China intends to transform its navy from a brown-water navy to a blue-water navy," extending its reach to the Pacific Ocean. Chinese naval vessels conducted their first crossing of the Pacific Ocean in 1997, and in 2002, two Chinese naval vessels completed a four-month, round-the-world voyage, the first ever for the Chinese Navy.[588]

Indeed, China has in recent years placed significant emphasis on a stated policy of extending its naval superiority 500 miles from its coasts. This strategy, once implemented, would give China control over what Chinese defense strategists call the "first island chain"—the Nansei island chain extending from Kyushu to Taiwan and down to southeast Asia—and China would extend its influence to the "second island chain"—the Ogasawara islands extending south from Tokyo to the Marianas, Saipan, and Guam. Reunification with Taiwan is the unifying lynchpin to this strategy, according to some Chinese strategists. Guo Longlong, director of the Shanghai Institute of International Studies, wrote in the PRC-owned Hong Kong paper *Ta Kung Pao* in October 2001: "[R]eunification [with Taiwan] is where China's fundamental interests lie…Taiwan is an important pivot point of the first island chain close to the Mainland. It is also the only link that China can control." Guo emphasized China's need to reunify Taiwan as a means to break out of a Western-backed "encirclement": "For a considerably long period of time, China was within a crescent-shape encirclement formed by the West with this island chain as the pivot point. Whether or not China can break this line, correlated to its future interests from this island chain and change its secluded image of several thousand years in the world and its international status, depends to a large extent on whether Taiwan's future can become part of China's master plan for revitalization, for becoming an ocean power, and for heading toward the world." Guo declared: "China will be forever incarcerated on the Mainland if it ever loses Taiwan."[589]

China's People's Liberation Army echoed Guo's commentary. The PLA paper, *Jiefangjun Bao*, in its June 23, 2003 edition, for example, called Okinawa "an enormous lock clamped tightly in the center of" the first island chain. The first and second island chains form a "pincer" on Chinese forces in the Pacific: "[T]he role in the western Pacific of the US military's 'second island chain,' which centers around Guam, is becoming increasingly prominent, while the base of Okinawa, with its northwesterly orientation [eg, towards the Chinese mainland]...serving as a supporting 'bridgehead' for the 'second island chain' and the most forward position of the US military in the Asia-Pacific region."[590] The PLA Navy by 2004 was actively reorganizing itself to meet this perceived blockade. According to another Hong Kong daily *Sing Tao Jih Pao* in July 2004: "The PLA has made long-term strategic plans for breaking the island chain blockade. Military experts pointed out that the strategic task of the PLA over the next 10 years is to achieve 'absolute supremacy within 500 nautical miles of the coastline to protect the coastal economic circles.' This is an important strategic objective for China's economic development." Further, "in order to achieve this goal, the Chinese

Navy is continuously expanding the combat effectiveness of its three fleets," and China by 2010 will have in operation the eight *Kilo*-class submarines procured from Russia, an additional eight submarines built in China, and "eight advanced domestic or Russian-made destroyers joining the service." Indeed, the article marked the entry into service of four Chinese ships, including two "Chinese Sovremenny" vessels, a "Chinese Aegis" ship, and a stealth frigate.[591]

The PLA Navy built these and other naval units to form three layers of "defense" through the "first island chain" along two main lines—one to the north in to the Pacific Ocean up to the "second island chain" and beyond and one to the south of Taiwan to the South China Sea and Indian Ocean. The July 14, 2004 edition of *Jiefangjun Bao* described the PLA Navy's ongoing modernization with this strategy in mind: "In accordance with the strategic aim of coastal waters defense and the aim of Taiwan Strait combat missions, the navy will organize its combat ships into three layers for dealing with different combat missions and functions." The first layer will consist of "frontline ship units... and naval air force long-range combat planes." "In particular, the destroyer detachments and nuclear and conventional submarines can also undertake blue-water combat missions; at present they can fight up to the first island chain, and the submarines can fight up to the second island chain," the paper asserted. The second layer "consists of the units undertaking coastal waters combat missions...[such as] the sea area within the first island chain," while the third layer "consists of support vessels." These three layers, in turn, will follow "two lines" to the Pacific Ocean, one in the north through the Nansei Islands, and one to the south: "In controlling these two lines, defense dispositions for the northern line (Pacific exit) have been nearly completed, and the southern line (South China Sea and Indian Ocean exits) is still being built." But according to the PLA daily, Taiwan is the key "obstacle" preventing the PLA Navy's fleets from uniting in the Pacific: "Of the two sea lanes vital to the national destiny, going through the northern line is mainly for entering the Pacific, and the obstacle at present is Taiwan controlled by Taiwan independence; so long as Taiwan is overthrown, the problem will be readily solved. The North Sea Fleet and East Sea Fleet can naturally join forces in a Pacific fleet."[592]

Since Japan consists of a major chain of islands separating the northern half of mainland China from the Pacific Ocean, Japan will invariably experience an increase in Chinese naval traffic traversing its waters to and from the Pacific Ocean particularly as China expands its naval capabilities and ambitions. Thus the maritime and intelligence surveys all around Japan, submarine navigation exercises through Japan's narrow straits and even through its territorial waters, and the growing frequency of naval exercises near Japan provoked increasing concern among Japanese analysts and the public by the early 2000s: "[T]he appearance of Chinese submarines is a matter of concern for the future of Japan," Hiramatsu declared in late 2004, for example.[593] A glossy magazine published in September 2005, *Jieitai vs Chugoku Gun* ("The SDF vs the Chinese Military"), summed up Tokyo's view of China's naval developments: "The possibility of a direct confrontation between Japan's MSDF and the Chinese Navy, which is strengthening its capability to advance into the open sea to secure natural resources and expand China's exclusive economic zone [EEZ], is becoming more and more realistic every year." To "counter a fleet of US aircraft carriers, the Chinese Navy has been" improving "the fighting capabilities of its submarines." But for Japan, "a conceivable scenario is a direct confrontation between surface warships of Japan and China because of the territorial rights issue concerning the Senkaku Islands and the desire to secure sea areas," according to the magazine in an allusion to China's "first island chain" strategy.[594]

By 2005, moreover, the skies over the East China Sea suddenly became more crowded as well. Japan's ASDF scrambled more flights in 2004 and 2005 to intercept Chinese planes near Japan's Air Defense Identification Zone (ADIZ) than at any time since 1998. In 2002, ASDF planes did not scramble once, a significant drop from the 30 scrambles in 1998. ASDF planes scrambled twice in 2003, and thirteen times in 2004. By the first half of 2005, they scrambled 30 times. In early 2006, General Hajime Massaki, chief of Japan's joint staff office, announced that for all of 2005 the ASDF scrambled 107 times against Chinese planes (and another 116 times against Russian planes in the north).[595] Additionally, the DA asserted that the PRC was now flying electronic intelligence planes along Japan's ADIZ in the East China Sea—near areas where China had built a number of rigs to exploit gas fields there—allegedly probing for information on radar signal frequencies emitted by SDF aircraft and radars. With this information, the DA feared, China would be in a better position to neutralize Japan's air defense systems should hostilities erupt in the region.[596] Chinese air activity in the region had increased notably and rapidly.

Given its increasingly expansive maritime activities in the region since the late 1990s, China's opaque defense budgets and training have sparked further unease in Tokyo. China's defense budgets, for example, have increased at double-digit rates since 1990, faster even than the PRC's Gross Domestic Product (GDP). This compares with Japan's stagnant defense budgets during the same post-Cold War period. China's budgets, moreover, do not include major weapons purchases from Russia such as the eight *Kilo* submarines in 2002 and Su-27 fighters, or research and development costs of programs under development, for example. China's total defense budget surpassed Japan's by 2003, according to the

CIA's *World Factbook*, with an estimated defense budget of $55.91 billion that included purchases abroad and defense R&D, compared to Japan's $40 billion defense budget. By 2006, according to that year's *World Factbook*, China's defense budget reached $81.48 billion, almost double Japan's defense budget for that year. China thus has the second largest defense budget in the world after the United States, and its defense budget was moreover concentrated in one geographic area. China was quickly emerging as a regional power, and Japan, on the front lines in northeast Asia, increasingly experienced China's emergence first-hand.

Further hindering confidence building in the region, China in 2002 stopped granting observer status to US or Japanese military attachés during major military training exercises. In 2005, for example, China and Russia conducted major joint exercises near Vladivostok and the Shandong Peninsula in August. Dubbed "Peace Mission 2005," close to 2,000 Russian troops and almost 8,000 Chinese troops took part in the exercises, which included major weapons platforms such as Tu-22M, Tu-160, and Tu-95MC mid- and long-range bombers, Il-76 and Il-78 aerial transports and refueling tanker aircraft, Su-27 interceptors, submarines, and destroyers and showcased a major amphibious assault. The two countries invited military observers from members of the Shanghai Cooperation Organization (Kazakhstan, Kyrgyzstan, Uzbekistan, and Tajikistan), as well as SCO observer states Iran, Pakistan, Mongolia, and India. The US and Japan were not invited. Sergey N. Goncharov, Charge D'affaires of the Russian Embassy in Beijing, was quoted as saying of the exercise: "The wargame showcasing the two countries' military might is aimed to help them get ready for a joint fight against international terrorists, national separatists and religious extremists." But if the exercises targeted "international terrorists," as one Indian observer wondered skeptically, "why the strategic bombers and submarines?"[597] Immediately after the exercises were completed, one senior Russian general suggested expanding the exercises to include SCO members and observers as well.[598]

The 2006 DoD report to Congress, *Military Power of the People's Republic of China,* echoed Japan's *Defense Whitepaper* regarding China's rapidly expanding defense budgets: "China's leaders have yet to adequately explain the purposes or desired end-states of their military expansion. Estimates place Chinese defense expenditures at two to three times officially disclosed figures. The outside world has little knowledge of Chinese motivations and decision-making or of key capabilities supporting PLA modernization." Thus, "[t] his lack of transparency prompts others to ask…Why this growing investment? Why these continuing large and expanding arms purchases? Why these continuing robust deployments? Absent greater transparency, international reactions to China's military growth will understandably hedge against these unknowns."[599]

Indeed, the year 2006 served to cement Tokyo's sense of strategic unease. In addition to China's increasingly active military deployments in the region, North Korea tested a series of missiles in the summer, and in October of that year, it tested its first nuclear device and thus became a defacto nuclear power. By this time however, many of the initial reforms and reorganizations had taken shape, and Japan was well on its way to modernizing its national security and defense capabilities to meet the newly emergent threats of the 21st century.

Summer-Fall 2006: A Nuclear North Korea, pt. 2

In contrast to its experiences in the early 1990s, Tokyo was prepared for North Korea's provocative missile and nuclear tests in 2006.

North Korea publicly restarted its nuclear program in 2002, after a US delegation presented evidence that the country had maintained a clandestine uranium enrichment program even as it froze work at Yongbyon from the mid-1990s. US officials publicly announced in mid-October that regime officials initially admitted to maintaining the program in private, only to later deny it publicly. Nevertheless—and confident in the evidence—the US administration called the clandestine program a "material breach" by North Korea of its obligations, and subsequently the U.S., South Korea, the European Union and Japan agreed to halt the shipment of heavy fuel oil that they had jointly provided in exchange for North Korea freezing its nuclear program in 1994. The IAEA in the meantime adopted a resolution calling on North Korea to "clarify" its "reported uranium-enrichment program." Pyongyang not only rejected the resolution, it informed the IAEA weeks later that it was restarting its functional reactor and reopening the other nuclear facilities frozen under the Agreed Framework.[600] One month later, in early 2003, North Korea announced its immediate withdrawal from the NPT citing pressure by the US and IAEA, among other parties: "Under the grave situation where our state's supreme interests are most seriously threatened, the DPRK Government declares an automatic and immediate effectuation of its withdrawal from the NPT... now that the US has unilaterally abandoned its commitments to stop nuclear threat[s] and renounce hostility towards the DPRK."[601]

Diplomatic pressure on Pyongyang increased significantly through the end of 2005 on a variety of fronts. The UN General Assembly took a greater interest in North Korea's dismal human rights record at this time, for example. Following mass famine in the 1990s and early 2000s, the regime's admission in 2002 of the state's role in abductions, various allegations of involvement in the drug trade, and claims by various political refugees and non-governmental organizations focusing on North Korea, the UN Commission on Human Rights appointed, based on a UNGA resolution, a "Special Rapporteur" in 2004 to investigate the human rights situation in North Korea more systematically. While a full investigation into the Stalinist regime's human rights record was impossible, the resulting report on the "situation of human rights in the DPRK" documented, among many issues, "distortions" in feeding the population "caused by the high military budget," "detention without access to credible courts," "punishment based upon 'guilt by association'," and "increased penalties for anti-State crimes."[602] Even though the report was written in bureaucratese in an attempt to avoid being overtly confrontational, it led the UN General Assembly in December 2005 to pass a resolution denouncing "continuing reports of systemic, widespread and grave violations of human rights in" North Korea, including "torture," "severe restrictions on the freedoms of thought," and "violation of…fundamental freedoms of women."[603]

What hurt Pyongyang the most, however, was Washington's public focus on an obscure Macao-based bank, Banco Delta Asia, beginning in 2005. On September 15, the US Treasury called the bank a "primary money laundering concern" and "a willing pawn for the North Korean government to engage in corrupt financial activities." It handled North Korea's precious metal sales, helped North Korean agents conduct multi-million dollar cash deposits and withdrawals, and in a "special relationship with" North Korea, it "specifically facilitated the criminal activities of North Korean government agencies and front companies," according to the Treasury Department.[604] Indeed, Washington merely warned that it might block Banco Delta Asia from accessing the US financial system because of possible ties to North Korean money laundering activities, and this in turn led to a run on the bank. Customers withdrew over a third of their deposits held at the bank within a week. Treasury's move was followed by official requests to other banks throughout the region to cut banking ties with North Korea.[605]

The moves obviously hurt Pyongyang. Almost daily in the ensuing months, North Korea publicly derided the "financial sanctions" in increasingly blustery language. By May 2006, US and Japanese authorities began to monitor preparations for major missile tests. The size of components observed suggested a new, longer-range Taepodong-2 missile might be tested. Any major missile test would be a violation of the September 2002 Pyongyang declaration between Japan and North Korea. Kim Chong-il, moreover, had told European Union representatives in May 2005 that North Korea would continue to observe a freeze of missile testing. Reports through June suggested a large missile was in position at a test site in North Hamg'yong Province, the same site from which the Taepodong-1 was launched in 1998.

As reports increasingly indicated that a major missile test was likely, Tokyo and Washington began to prepare. The MSDF dispatched the Aegis destroyer *Chokai* to the Sea of Japan to monitor any future missile tests. Taking lessons from the 1998 launch, it also dispatched the Aegis destroyer *Kirishima* to waters near the Sanriku coast in the Pacific Ocean—the same waters where the first Taepodong landed. Should North Korea launch a missile over Japan, this destroyer would be in a position to monitor its flight into the Pacific Ocean. The United States, too, dispatched two additional Aegis destroyers to monitor any missile tests, and additionally flew aircraft from Kadena Air Base in Okinawa to monitor for any indications of imminent missile launches.

Tokyo had taken additional legal precautions since the early 2000s to prepare for a possible missile strike in Japan or on Tokyo itself. Prime Minister Koizumi, at the start of his administration in Spring 2001, had designated a list of five successors if he were to become incapacitated for any reason. His first designated successor was Chief Cabinet Secretary Shinzo Abe, followed by the finance minister and then the foreign minister. Also, the Prime Minister had a range of legal options under recently enacted "Citizen Protection" legislation authorizing him to dispatch the SDF domestically and use public facilities as civilian shelters in responding to armed aggression aimed at Japan, which would necessarily include a missile strike on the country. This was particularly relevant in case the missile or missiles were tipped with weapons of mass destruction or otherwise hit a sensitive facility such as one of Japan's 48 nuclear power plants.[606]

It was therefore no surprise when North Korea launched a series of missiles early in the morning of July 5. While most of the missiles were variants of the short-range Scud missile, at least one was a Nodong missile and another was a new Taepodong-2 missile. None of the missiles were reported to have landed near Japanese territory, and the Taepodong-2 was later deemed a failure. North Korea issued a statement the following day linking the tests to military exercises, but it also hinted at taking "stronger physical actions of other forms" if further "pressure" were put on it.[607] North Korea watchers quickly understood that, given the high level of the official government statement, Pyongyang was hinting at conducting a test of a nuclear device.

While the missile tests took place on July 5 in Asia, they coincided with Independence Day festivities the evening of July 4 in the United States. Moreover, the launches took place hours after the US Space Shuttle *Discovery* launched from the Kennedy Space Center in Florida. While the shuttle itself was certainly not in any danger, the symbolic meaning of launches' timing was noted in Japan as well as in the United States. Symbology aside, the primary concern was focused on North Korea's advancing technical capabilities in launching increasingly longer-range missiles, and its increasing willingness to use them in defiance of bilateral and multilateral agreements that Pyongyang itself signed.

At his initial news conference immediately after the missile tests, DA Director-General Fukushiro Nukaga—who ironically headed the DA during the August 1998 missile launch—called the series of launches "a grave issue" and "a serious concern" for Japan. He said he was informed at 3:50 that morning of the launches, almost immediately after the tests had taken place. When asked how these tests differed from eight years prior, he said that in 1998 "it was difficult for us to decide how to judge the information," whereas in the run-up to these tests Tokyo had developed "various analytical capabilities" and "vigorous measures on ballistic missile defense." As a result, "we were able to analyze it properly and calmly respond to this incident." Chief Cabinet Secretary Abe, during his press conference that day, outlined initial discussions at the Security Council that morning, which was chaired by Prime Minister Koizumi, and the sharing of information with the US ambassador.

Missile defense naturally became a focus of attention in the immediate aftermath of the tests. The prolific defense analyst Atsuyuki Sassa called the Japanese government's management of the situation "unprecedentedly expeditious," although he noted that Japan's meager PAC-1s were no match for North Korea's 200-plus Nodong missiles. "There is no way to defend our citizens in the current situation," he declared in calling for immediate deployment of a national missile defense system.[608] Japan was well on its way to deploying its first missile defense capabilities, but the individual systems were months away from being fielded and operational. The country's first PAC-3s were scheduled to be operational by the beginning of the following year, and the new SM-3s would be deployed on Japanese destroyers next spring. Moreover, the ASDF was just completing its upgraded FPS X-band radar site in Aomori Prefecture. Once operational, the upgraded radar would play a central role in Japan's missile defense system, together with the MSDF's Aegis destroyers. But Japan's missile defense network had yet to come on line by the time North Korea conducted its missile tests.

Another lingering legal issue was the prospect of shooting down a missile that flew over Japan but targeted Guam, Hawaii, Alaska, or the US west coast. The recently passed legal framework that enabled the SDF to shoot down a missile in the very short timeframe necessary was limited to missile strikes specifically targeting the Japanese archipelago. Shooting down a missile that overflew Japan—presumably targeting North America or US territories in the Pacific—was not interpreted as legal because to do so would be considered an act of "collective self-defense." That is, Japan would be using its own military forces to assist an ally outside the territorial boundaries of the Japanese archipelago. Intervening with armed force during an attack on an ally was still considered to "exceed the limit of use of armed strength as permitted under Article 9 of the Constitution," in the words of the Ministry of Defense.[609] The issue would be left unresolved.

In the immediate aftermath of the July 5 launches, Japan again lobbied the UN Security Council to pass a resolution censuring the missile launches as it unsuccessfully did in 1998. This time however, in a fateful coincident, Japan had become a non-permanent member of the UN Security Council in 2005. While any of the five permanent members could certainly veto any UNSC resolution, Japan now had additional clout and access to other member states—not to mention the ability to address the council during debates—that UNSC membership imparts. Moreover, Japan's international lobbying efforts received a major boost when Prime Minister Koizumi attended the G-8 summit in St. Petersburg, Russia, mere days after the missile tests. Since four of the five UNSC permanent members were also members of the G-8, Koizumi and his diplomatic team had direct access to the heads of governments in the immediate aftermath of the missile tests—and immediately after North Korea hinted at testing a nuclear device. Only China, a permanent member of the UNSC with veto rights, was a nonmember of the G-8, but Tokyo had significant back-channel access to Beijing on the North Korea nuclear issue due to the six-party talks.

Moreover, while China effectively blocked any attempts at passing a UNSC resolution following the 1998 launch, by 2006 its patience with Pyongyang was wearing thin after years of ultimately fruitless six-party talks. Thus all the permanent members of the UNSC—China included—supported some sort of council resolution addressing North Korea's missile tests. While Japan and the United States were forced to delete references to Chapter VII in the draft resolution invoking enforcement mechanisms, the UNSC unanimously passed Resolution 1695 ten days after North Korea's launches. The resolution "condemned" the missile tests and "demanded that the North-East Asian country suspend all ballistic missile related activity." The resolution also asserted "that such launches jeopardize peace, stability and security in the region…particularly in light of the country's claim that it has developed nuclear weapons."[610] The resolution called for North Korea's immediate return to the six-party talks.

The resolution was a major diplomatic victory for Japan. While Tokyo had lobbied the UNSC for weeks to take action after the first Taepodong launch in 1998, the UNSC this time took swift action in passing the strongly worded resolution. Shintaro Ito, Japan's Vice Minister for Foreign Affairs who attended UNSC deliberations, praised the council as acting "swiftly and robustly in response to the condemnable act," particularly since "the nature of the threat had become more serious in light of the country's claim that it had developed nuclear weapons."[611]

Yet little came from the resolution. Not only did North Korea ignore calls to re-join the six-party talks, it proceeded with plans to test a nuclear device mere months later.

On October 3, North Korea's Foreign Ministry issued a definitive statement in which it declared in unequivocal language that "the DPRK will in the future conduct a nuclear test under the condition[s] where safety is firmly guaranteed." It claimed that the upcoming nuclear test was due to the United States specifically: "The US extreme threat of a nuclear war and sanctions and pressure compel the DPRK to conduct a nuclear test, an essential process for bolstering nuclear deterrent." Moreover, addressing significant concerns about the country's nuclear doctrine, the Foreign Ministry claimed that "the DPRK will never use nuclear weapons first but strictly prohibit any threat of nuclear weapons and nuclear transfer."[612]

The no-first-use statement served to emphasize how serious the regime was in conducting a nuclear test. If the statement were pure bluster, it would have been issued by a lower-level official focusing almost exclusively on the destructive capabilities of its "nuclear deterrent," in line with previous hyperbolic threats to turn regional cities into a "sea of fire," for example. In contrast to previous propaganda, this high-level official statement was straightforward and specific about North Korea's plans to test a nuclear device. The fact that the Foreign Ministry itself issued the statement—not a proxy such as a newscaster on North Korean television or through an unnamed "spokesman"—meant the statement was official policy. Finally, the statement was found to emphasize the same points as China's statement prior to its first nuclear test in 1964, another confirmation of Pyongyang's intent to test a device of some sort imminently.[613] North Korea was going to test a nuclear device, it was just a matter of time.

In yet another twist of fate, not only was Japan a member of the UNSC at the time, it had taken over as President of the council for the month of October. It naturally used its additional clout by issuing a Presidential statement immediately after North Korea announced its intent to test a nuclear device. The UNSC Presidential Statement declared that if North Korea carried "out its threat of [testing] a nuclear weapon," the test "would jeopardize peace, stability and security in the region and beyond."[614] The statement served to put North Korea on notice that the UNSC would take further action in the wake of any test. Additionally, newly elected Prime Minister Abe used the occasion to improve ties with South Korea and China by issuing joint statements calling on North Korea to avoid testing a nuclear device. Abe visited Beijing on the eve of the test, calling any future test by North Korea "unacceptable." Tokyo's lobbying on the issue in advance of the test, coupled with holding the presidency of the UN Security Council that month, smoothed condemnation of the test in the immediate aftermath.

Japan prepared measures to verify any future nuclear test. In addition to having full access to the ten monitoring stations in Japan in support of the Comprehensive Test Ban Treaty Organization (CTBTO), Tokyo also closely monitored the 1,500 or so seismic monitoring stations throughout the archipelago for indications of a test.[615] It also began flying EP-3s out of Iwakuni Airbase to monitor communications for any indications of a test, and it separately flew T-4s specially configured with devices to collect atmospheric samples potentially containing signs of radioactive noble gases. Because they seep through layers of rock into the atmosphere shortly after an underground nuclear test, they are the only atmospheric evidence of a well-contained underground nuclear explosion. Tokyo coordinated its monitoring with US forces in Japan, which similarly monitored for a possible test.[616]

Despite international pressure, North Korea tested a nuclear device on October 9. The test occurred one day before North Korea would mark the 61st anniversary of the Workers' Party of Korea.

Over twenty of the CTBTO's seismic stations in the International Monitoring System (IMS) detected signals originating from the test site in northeastern North Korea. Unlike a natural seismic event such as an earthquake, an explosion features a very impulsive, large onset of compressional waves and smaller surface waves compared with an earthquake of similar size. This was indeed what the CTBTO monitoring stations observed during the seismic event—the nuclear test—originating in North Korea. The organization was able to source the event to an area to within several hundred square kilometers in North Korea. Moreover, its radionuclide noble gas monitoring station at Yellowknife, Canada—one of only ten in the world then in operations—registered a higher concentration of Xenon 133 within weeks of the test. The CTBTO backtracked the dispersion of the gas and found it to be consistent with a hypothesized release from the test in North Korea.[617] Subsequent analysis confirmed that the underground explosion was nuclear, but that the test produced a yield of less than one kiloton.[618]

With Japan serving as president of the UNSC, the UNSC subsequently condemned the nuclear test in yet another unanimous resolution passed on October 14.[619] The UNSC reiterated demands that North Korea refrain from both missile and nuclear tests, rejoin the six-party talks and bilateral talks with Japan, and return to the NPT. The resolution this time invoked Chapter VII on enforcement—although it barred "automatic military enforcement," as the accompanying press release made clear.

Members of the Six-Party talks would meet again in December where the US would present a multistage denuclearization plan.

The talks made no progress towards implementing a previous September 19, 2005 joint statement, however, and North Korea would continue to call for an end to "financial sanctions" and restoration of frozen Banco Delta Asia funds. The Six-Party talks would continue periodically until North Korea announced its complete withdrawal from the body in April 2009 following further UNSC condemnation after launching a three-stage rocket earlier that month. Pyongyang subsequently announced its intention to "boost its nuclear deterrent for self-defense in every way," "restore…nuclear facilities" to "their original state," and "fully reprocess" the 8,000 spent fuel rods from its Yongbyon reactor in order to extract plutonium for nuclear weapons.[620] It would conduct its second nuclear test one month later.

North Korea was well on its way to becoming a nuclear power.

• • •

Following successive national security crises after the Cold War ended in 1991, Japan's national security strategies slowly evolved to focus on developing capabilities to defend the Japanese archipelago and Japanese interests abroad against a new era of threats. Japanese national security specialists beginning in the early- and mid-1990s called for reforms to enable intelligence and warning and, if necessary, robust defenses against three broad types of threats: the use or threat of use of nuclear, chemical, and/or biological weapons; state-sponsored insurgent/terrorist networks and organized smuggling networks that could support WMD R&D programs; and threats to remote islands such as encirclement, seizure or a mass influx of refugees. Response to natural disasters dovetailed with these strategic concerns, and indeed all of these threats were intricately linked as potential adversaries could employ multiple threat scenarios to support a particular strategic objective.

The first major post-Cold War national security evolution involved a restructuring of Japan's national command and control structure. In the mid- and late-1990s, sub-cabinet-level positions were created to handle national security affairs, and the Prime Minister's Official Residence underwent major refurbishment that included the establishment of a 24-hour operations center. Moreover, command of the Self-Defense Forces was unified under one uniformed officer under the direct command of the Prime Minister through the Minister of State for Defense.

As maritime incursions increased in the late 1990s, Japan began to emphasize defense of its outer islands, the second major national security evolution. This evolution marked both a shift in geographic conceptualization of threats to the Japanese archipelago and a resultant shift in force structure. The process was slow to evolve at first, since heavy mechanized units stationed on or near Hokkaido formed the basis of much of Japan's conventional ground forces to defend Japan's northern frontier from a Soviet conventional invasion. In contrast, providing for adequate defense of the hundreds of medium- and small-size islands in the Nansei Island chain and in other areas near Kyushu and southern Honshu would require a lighter, quick-reaction force structure that would be capable of responding to contingencies on multiple islands far from major Japanese bases if necessary. This shift in emphasis in turn required greater service interoperability, as the MSDF would be called upon to transport battalion- or brigade-sized ground units to these areas of possible conflict, with ASDF units providing air cover and possibly air-to-ground support of landing GSDF forces. This new force structure gradually developed into mini-amphibious battle groups as part of Japan's "Defense of Remote Islands" strategy.

The consolidation of Japan's intelligence structure—the third major evolution—actually began in the late 1980s. Japan unified its intelligence structure in a newly constructed Defense Intelligence Headquarters in January 1997, and it launched reconnaissance satellites in the early 2000s. In addition, a scandal involving the misuse of off-budget funds highlighted Tokyo's use of shadow budgets in the Ministry of Foreign Affairs and in the Cabinet Office revealed intelligence collection was taking place through the use of HUMINT-type techniques as well. Yet, as rivalries in Asia continued to build, by the early-2000s calls increased for more expansive intelligence capabilities including the overt establishment of a special HUMINT collection agency to better understand the evolving threat environment around Japan.

Finally, the issue of preemptive strikes resurfaced in the early 2000s. The debate was not new: the Japanese cabinet under Prime Minister Hatoyama in 1956 declared preemptive strikes theoretically constitutional during Diet debates. However, technologically Japan could not conduct a preemptive strike during the Cold War years because of its greatly limited defense capabilities and because, at the time, a preemptive strike necessarily meant a nuclear strike or carpet bombing of the area in question, or otherwise an invasion of enemy territory by ground troops. Japan was certainly in no position to conduct such operations even through the 1990s. New military technologies developed during the so-called "Revolution in Military Affairs" such as precision-guided weapons and the advent of Network Centric Warfare made preemptive strikes technologically an increasingly realistic option. As a new generation of post-war politicians came into power that had no memory of Japan's defeat in World War II or of Japan's reconstruction period in the 1940s or 1950s, the topic of developing advanced preemptive strike capabilities was increasingly broached even as Japan's defense forces acquired basic precision strike capabilities. As the basic foundation of Japan's 21st Century defense structure was being completed by the early 2010s, discussions of preemptive strikes were becoming more than theoretical.

The first steps on the road to reform were taken in the mid-1990s, when the LDP reconsolidated its power in the Diet and Prime Minister Hashimoto retook the *Kantei*.

SECTION 2:
New National Security Structures

3) Japan's National Security: Reforming the Structure

Momentum to reorganize and strengthen Japan's national security structure intensified in the mid-1990s with each successive national security crisis. While Japanese leaders became intimately aware of shortcomings in the country's *kiki kanri shisutemu* or national security structure following the first North Korean nuclear crisis, the Great Hanshin Earthquake in January and the Aum Shinrikyo attacks in 1994 and 1995, each successive national security crisis created increasing impetus to reform and reorganize Japan's national security and defense capabilities.

Early government-sponsored reform studies examined possible reorganization of various government functions to include national security, but the studies had little if any lasting impact. Following similar studies in 1964 and 1982, the third Ad Hoc Council for the Promotion of Administrative Reform in October 1993 proposed reorganizing the 22 ministries and agencies into six ministries, while tinkering with the national security structure.[621] When nothing happened as a result of those proposals, Prime Minister Hosokawa established the Administrative Reform Promotion Headquarters in late 1993 that met through 1995 under Prime Minister Murayama. It too produced almost no tangible results.

Indeed, the political revolving door of successive prime ministers and poor leadership through the mid-1990s hindered any nascent efforts to reorganize the government. Prime Minister Murayama and the Japan Socialist Party were novices at governing Japan, having taken the helm for the first time in 1994 after spending almost forty years as a perpetual opposition party. Party leadership therefore had almost no governing experience and was completely unprepared to handle the security crises at hand. Taking power during the dénouement of the North Korean nuclear crisis, the septuagenarian Murayama was visibly tired by the end of his term after 18 months in office. Not only did Murayama have to deal with the immediate aftermath of the nuclear crisis and the death of Kim Il-song, in order to maintain power he prodded his party to recognize the constitutionality of the Self-Defense Forces, which in turn created a rift in the party on the eve of the Great Hanshin earthquake. Criticism of his administration continued unabated following what was seen as a slow government response to the natural disaster and, mere months later, to the Aum Shinrikyo attacks and the prolonged investigation into the various cult dealings afterward. On January 5, 1996, the 71-year-old Murayama announced his resignation of the premiership at an impromptu news conference. "I was hounded by one incident and accident after another," Murayama said of events during his 18-month tenure.[622]

In parallel with proposals to re-organize government functions, defense analysts and recently retired senior officials and officers increasingly focused on emerging national security needs by the mid-1990s. In one prime example, 17 retired staff officers of the Morino Military Research Institute in 1996 published the book *Jiseidai no Rikujo Jieitai* [*Next Generation GSDF: Fighting Future Wars*], in which they assessed that "[f]uture threats to our nation's security will not be clear, as in the Cold War era." They declared that Japan should prepare defenses against "low-intensity threats such as terrorism, guerrillas/commandos, and armed refugees to island attacks, strategic attacks on significant areas [of the Japanese homeland], and even nuclear missile attacks."[623] Similarly, retired GSDF two-star general and former professor at the National Defense Academy Etsu Kuwada highlighted the three main emerging threats of nuclear-tipped missiles, local and regional low-intensity conflicts, and guerrilla warfare/terrorism. Countries around Japan could be prone to instability and conflict under competing regimes, Kuwada assessed, so that "we should be especially concerned with…remote islands such as Okinotorishima, Tsushima, Ikinoshima, the Goto Islands off Kyushu and the Ryukyu chain, which could be inundated by waves of refugees arriving by sea," Kuwada wrote in mid-1995. And if China were to take military action against Taiwan or enact a blockade, "there is a real danger that armed conflict could spread to the vicinity of the Ryukyu chain (in particular the Senkaku Islands) and other areas," and "in an almost total absence of an SDF presence, it would invite the belligerents to use the area to their advantage, making it difficult for us to maintain strict neutrality."[624] Kuwada urged improved command, control, communications, and intelligence (C3I) capabilities and the establishment of robust capabilities to mobilize and transport troops to "remote islands" for their defense.

And while the U.S.-Japan security relationship remained strong during these initial post-Cold War years, Japanese defense commentators nevertheless supported the development of national security and defense capabilities completely independent of the United States in case Washington was unable or unwilling to provide substantial assistance in a national security matter. Retired General Kotaro Kamei, a former director of the GSDF Staff College Research Department, emphasized this point in the July 1996 military journal *Gunji Kenkyu*: "[T]he basis for US involvement in Asia is less 'existence' than the pursuit of 'prosperity'," while "our nation's involvement with Asia is an issue of 'existence.'" US and Japanese interests could potentially diverge, in Kamei's perspective. Therefore Japan should be prepared to act alone if necessary under three "limited warfare" scenarios, according to Kamei: China's seizure of the Senkaku islands or South Korea's "occupation and rule" of Takeshima; limited warfare in which a foreign power seeks to temporarily occupy a part of Japanese territory in the pursuit of other objectives (i.e., China's use of remote Japanese islands to support operations against Taiwan); and "large inflows" of "armed refugees" to seize territory or destroy facilities in Japan to advance political demands, as if to predict North Korean operations against South Korea and Japan in 1996, 1998-9, and 2001. According to Kamei, "we should assume that US aid and intervention" in these three situations "would be at the diplomatic level and not extend to the military level."[625]

Just as Murayama was preparing to leave the premiership, the new leader of the LDP, Ryutaro Hashimoto, had just been voted president of his party in late 1995. In the days after Murayama's resignation, Hashimoto garnered a majority of votes in both houses of the Diet after the three coalition parties—the LDP, the JSP and the New Party Sakigake—agreed to support him for the premiership (a number of JSP members cast blank ballots because of the perception that Hashimoto was conservative and hawkish, however).[626] With Hashimoto in the *Kantei*, however, the LDP was better positioned to take a leadership role in reforming the government and Japan's national security structure, with a stated goal of improving "crisis management."

In his first major policy speech at the Diet on January 22, 1996, almost a year to the day after the Kobe earthquake, Prime Minister Hashimoto opened his speech by expressing his "deepest condolences to the victims and the bereaved families of those who perished." He then outlined his broad policy goals, including his intention to reform the bureaucracy and "strengthen" Japan's crisis management system:

> "With the major earthquake last year, the Aum-related incidents, and other violent crime, a cloud has come over the civil safety in which Japan took such pride, and it is thus

> important to strengthen crisis management so as to keep our society safe. It being difficult to anticipate what crises will occur when and where, people and systems are the important thing in crisis management, and we will make every effort to buttress safety measures and crisis management arrangements."[627]

He outlined an ambitious plan. Citing Japan's growing debt burden, a moribund economy, the graying of Japanese society, and the need to streamline the central bureaucracy, Prime Minister Hashimoto announced his intention to reorganize not just Japan's basic national security structure, but the entire Japanese government along with its financial and retirement systems and schools.

Pre-Reform: Offices at the Cabinet Level

Until the mid-1990s, the prime minister and chief cabinet secretary headed a cabinet secretariat composed of five cabinet offices, three of which had a specified "crisis management" role: the Cabinet Security Affairs Office (CSAO), the Cabinet Information Research Office (CIRO), and the Cabinet Office on Internal Affairs (COIA). The Cabinet Office on Foreign Affairs (COFA) and the Public Relations Office rounded out the five offices. While CIRO had been created in 1952, the four remaining offices were organized in their then-current form in 1986 under Prime Minister Nakasone. Career officials on two-year assignments from other ministries served as directors of the cabinet offices. Under normal circumstances, a career Defense Agency official headed CSAO, while career officials from the Ministry of Foreign Affairs and the Finance Ministry directed

COFA and COIA respectively. A National Police Agency official headed CIRO, and this individual usually had a slightly longer tenure than the directors of the other offices. The office director positions were equivalent to ministerial bureau directors, which complicated policy coordination among the various ministries and agencies since the office directors had little actual authority over their counterparts in any given ministry. Those officials in other agencies reported directly to their respective administrative vice minister and not to the cabinet offices in the *Kantei*. The office directors certainly had no authority over the administrative vice ministers, who were several ranks higher than the office directors. Given the rapid turnover among cabinet ministers and parliamentary vice ministers—the politicians who were elected and appointed to oversee the ministries—the administrative vice ministers who were career bureaucrats thus wielded an inordinate amount of power in developing and driving day-to-day policy.[628]

While the Chief Cabinet Secretary was the visible face of the cabinet secretariat under the Prime Minister, his deputy, the administrative deputy chief cabinet secretary, runs the day-to-day activities in the secretariat and oversees each of the cabinet offices. This individual is the highest-ranking career government official, and as such he is said to "manage Kasumigaseki," the area of Tokyo just outside of the grounds of the Imperial Palace that is famous for its concentration of government office complexes. While Prime Ministers and Chief Cabinet Secretaries come and go, the administrative deputy chief cabinet secretary remained in place to span multiple administrations.

Two administrative deputy chiefs held especially long tenures in the late 1980s and 1990s: Nobuo Ishihara and Teijiro Furukawa were the longest-serving administrative deputy chief cabinet secretaries in Japan's post-war history. They thus played significant roles in shaping Japan's post-Cold War national security structure.

Ishihara, a former vice minister of the Ministry of Home Affairs, served in the position from November 1987 until March 1995 and helped to coordinate Japanese government policy during the North Korean nuclear crisis (Ishihara personally leaked news of the May 1993 missile tests to the press), the Great Hanshin Earthquake, and the initial response to the Aum Shinrikyo terrorist attacks. Given his long tenure, he was sometimes called "the behind-the-scenes prime minister."[629] Ishihara ran for governor of Tokyo in April 1995, but he lost despite active LDP support. Furukawa, another career Ministry of Home Affairs bureaucrat, became the longest-serving administrative deputy chief in post war history, serving from early 1995 until late 2003. Furukawa oversaw subsequent crises, such as the hostage crisis at the Japanese embassy in Lima, Peru, North Korea's Taepodong missile test in 1998, and the spy ship incidents in 1999 and 2001. Furukawa also oversaw the structural changes in the cabinet and government between 1998 and 2001.

The Cabinet Information Research Office (CIRO) provided intelligence to the Prime Minister through the Chief Cabinet Secretary. CIRO was established under the Shigeru Yoshida cabinet in 1952 when Deputy Prime Minister Taketora Ogata, himself an intelligence officer during the war, proposed the creation of a cabinet intelligence bureau. While Ogata envisioned the creation of a true intelligence organization directly under the Prime Minister's Office, efforts to enlarge the office lost momentum upon Ogata's untimely death in 1956. CIRO remained small, and the number of full-time personnel remained between 70-80 officials throughout the Cold War with a similar number of personnel seconded to CIRO for two-year tours. The head of CIRO briefed the chief cabinet secretary once a week, but during the Nakasone administration in the 1980s, Chief Cabinet Secretary Gotoda suggested that the head of CIRO brief the Prime Minister as well.

This set a precedent, but unlike the President's Daily Briefs in the United States, the CIRO briefing took place only once a week for thirty minutes. The briefings, sometimes referred to as *Go-Shinkō*—a special term for "educating" an extremely high-ranking individual such as the Emperor or the Prime Minister—continued into the 1990s to take place once a week on Thursday afternoons.[630] While the prime ministerial briefings indicated a greater interest in international security affairs, the perfunctory nature of the briefings and the fact that briefings took place but once a week showed that senior Japanese policymakers still concentrated overwhelmingly on internal or trade matters. Intelligence remained fragmented, with individual ministries normally providing intelligence through their own cabinet ministers and vice ministers, and prime ministers at any rate had few policy tools to act on intelligence once received.

While one would expect the head of CIRO in his capacity as briefer to the Prime Minister and the Chief Cabinet Secretary to be plugged into the intelligence establishment, this had not been the case historically. Yoshio Omori, the head of CIRO during the turbulent period between 1993-1997, complained in his book *Japan's Intelligence Structure* that he did not see one cable from the Ministry of Foreign Affairs during his tenure at CIRO, nor, he claimed, did he receive any information of importance from the National Police Agency—this despite serving an entire career in the NPA, including a stint as the Commandant of the National Police Academy. Rather, according to Omori, each of these organizations would relay information to the Prime Minister's office through their respective ministers, who would often bring the division heads of the office overseeing that particular issue to separate meetings with the prime minister and without Omori present. While this was perhaps understandable depending on the issue—Prime Minister Hashimoto received much of his early information regarding the Peru hostage crisis through MOFA during that time, as MOFA had senior representatives present in Lima—Omori felt the stove-piping of information hindered his role in the immediate aftermath of the Aum Shinrikyo attacks in Tokyo, for example. In that case, the NPA did not want to share information with Omori on the grounds that the attack took place on domestic soil, but Omori argued that he needed the information to pursue Aum Shinrikyo's international connections, especially those in Russia. Ultimately, Omori simply did not have the authority to demand information from other government entities since CIRO as a *shitsu* or "office" did not rank as high as a *chō* or *shō*, "agency" or "ministry" respectively. Attempts were made throughout Omori's tenure to establish CIRO as the main intelligence pipeline into the Prime Minister's Office, but these all failed according to Omori.[631]

In contrast to CIRO's intelligence functions, the Cabinet Security Affairs Office helped to shape policy on national security issues and was also tasked to deal with serious security incidents such as hijackings, terrorist incidents, or other situations involving national defense. CSAO was established in 1986 under Prime Minister Nakasone ostensibly to assist with security treaty negotiations then taking place with the United States to further strengthen U.S.-Japan security relations. By law, its work was limited to "important matters relating to national defense" and "important matters concerning the handling of critical situations." CSAO handled crises such as the Soviet downing of a Korean Airlines passenger jet in 1988 and the Gulf crisis in 1990-1991 (although Japan did not provide any tangible assistance to the war effort). CSAO also helped to manage the Peru hostage crisis at the cabinet secretariat as that crisis dragged on, although the Ministry of Foreign Affairs was clearly in command of the situation on the ground. CSAO had approximately 20 staff and was headed by a career Defense Agency official on a two-year assignment. His four deputies or councilor-level officials consisted of officials from the Defense Agency, National Police Agency, Ministry of Finance, and the Ministry of Foreign Affairs, also on two-year rotations.[632]

On the other end of the crisis management spectrum, the Cabinet Councillors' Office on Internal Affairs (COIA) handled emergency response to natural disasters in addition to helping to shape domestic policy. COIA shared responsibility with the Fire Disaster Management Agency and the National Land Agency, and in the aftermath of the Great Hanshin Earthquake, the reputations of all three offices were severely tarnished. Since all three offices shared responsibility, there was no clear line of authority to actually coordinate efforts from the Prime Minister's Official Residence, thus delaying the response. COIA also provided guidance on some policy issues related to the Aum Shinrikyo cult immediately after the sarin gas attacks in early 1995 such as providing for the care of 60 children found at Aum facilities, but the COIA was criticized even in this effort when it could not handle media requests seeking more disclosure about the children's whereabouts.[633] COIA, managed by a career Ministry of Finance official, was also involved in a range of domestic policy issues such as the economic revitalization of Okinawa Prefecture, the development of telecommunications policies in the mid-1990s, the formulation of policies related to climate change, and government reform itself. As the incongruity of disaster response and domestic policy formation within the same office became noticeable following the 1995 crises, calls for the transfer of disaster response to the Cabinet Security Affairs Office intensified considerably.

High-ranking Japanese officials in the Cabinet Secretariat increasingly complained of information overload during times of crisis in the 1990s. The journalist Iku Aso quoted Kazo Watanabe, a member of the JSP who was appointed parliamentary deputy chief cabinet secretary during the Hashimoto administration, as complaining: "I get so many phone calls at night. I am really tired from lack of sleep. Fax messages pour in. The sound of fax machines gets on my nerves and keeps me awake" at night. With the establishment of a 24-hour watch office in the PMOR in 1996, Watanabe described an incident when he was awoken by a watch officer at the Prime Minister's Official Residence with information about a suspected Chechen hijacking of a Turkish tourist passenger boat. Watanabe asked whether any Japanese were on board, and the watch officer replied in the negative. He said of the incident, "Why am I woken up when something happens about which the Japanese government does not need to do anything?" Aso also noted that Watanabe's colleague, Administrative Deputy Chief Cabinet Secretary Furukawa, would wake up early in the morning each day to sort through fax messages—with the help of his wife—that arrived over night and skim through them before his day began. One official was quoted as saying of Furukawa: "[T]he volume of messages was so large that he and his wife simply could not deal with them all."[634]

Lastly, a Joint Intelligence Council (JIC) was formed in 1986 along with the five cabinet offices described above in an attempt to coordinate policy across ministries and agencies. Chaired by the Deputy Chief Cabinet Secretary and composed of bureau-level chiefs from national security-related offices in the various ministries, the JIC met once a month and discussed issues related to policy. It was colloquially—and derisively, according to Aso—termed the "Deputy Chief Cabinet Secretary's Study Group," implying that nothing actionable came out of the council. Further hampering the JIC's impact, council members were barred from taking notes during meetings as the discussions were considered classified. Beginning with the Korean nuclear and missile crises in 1993, however, Deputy Chief Cabinet Secretary Nobuo Ishihara used the council to a much greater extent to coordinate policy responses to possible scenarios on the Peninsula. The JIC began to meet twice monthly that autumn with the expectation that each member would bring more finished intelligence to meetings. Also, non-permanent members were invited, such as representatives from the Maritime Safety Agency (later renamed the Japan Coast Guard) who were brought in to discuss responses to a possible refugee crisis, for example. Based on this experience, Ishihara proposed institutionalizing a series of changes to the JIC at its meeting on November 11, 1994, to include the continuation of twice-monthly meetings and the permanent inclusion of the bureau-level heads of CIRO and CSAO, the National Police Agency's Security Bureau, the Defense Agency's Defense Policy Bureau, the Public Security Investigation Agency deputy director, and the Ministry of Foreign Affairs International Intelligence Bureau. In addition, representatives from other offices would be invited to discuss intelligence or policies related to their area of expertise. CIRO would provide secretariat support to the JIC. The JIC would be granted greater authority to provide opinions to the Prime Minister.[635]

The JIC remained a target of criticism both before and after a late-1990s government-wide reorganization. One unnamed government official complained to the *Yomiuri Shimbun* in April 1998 that "participating ministries and agencies...do not present any important information, and the officials just exchange views."[636] Six years later, little changed as an unnamed member claimed that "we never provide really important information to the panel," but rather just use the meetings as "introductions to each other." Instead, several members admitted to passing truly critical intelligence through their ministries to the Prime Minister's Office, bypassing the JIC.[637]

The JIC has sometimes been referred to in English as the "Cabinet Joint Information Exchange Panel," highlighting the different translations of *jōhō* in its Japanese name, *gōdō jōhō kaigi. Jōhō* can be translated as either "information"—its more common English term—or "intelligence." Thus the many Japanese offices involved in the collection, analysis, and dissemination of intelligence in the traditional sense often used the English term "information" instead of "intelligence" until the early 2000s. The Cabinet Information Research Office similarly used the word "information" in its English title, until it officially (if quietly) changed its official English translation to "intelligence" in 2003 to emphasize the greater role it was attempting to take on in the realm of intelligence.

Reform Movement Takes Hold

One of the first actions taken under the new Hashimoto administration in February 1996 was the establishment of guidelines on government succession and response to a major natural disaster in central Japan. Called the "Initial Actions To Be Taken by the Cabinet in the Event of a Major Tokyo Earthquake," this basic "crisis manual" as it was often called delineated a line of authority should the prime minister become incapacitated during an earthquake. The prime minister would be replaced by the deputy prime minister, followed by the chief cabinet secretary and the director general of the National Land Agency. The manual also delineated priority assembly locations for cabinet meetings in times of emergency: the Prime Minister's Official Residence came first on the list, followed by the National Land Agency, Defense Agency Central Command Center, and lastly the Tachikawa Wide-Area Disaster Base, all of which were in the greater Tokyo region. The procedures were approved at a cabinet meeting on February 23, 1996, a month after Hashimoto assumed power.[638]

Because this "crisis manual" was based on a specific event—an earthquake in the Kanto region—it was not applicable to Prime Minister Obuchi's sudden stroke and death on May 14, 2000. Rather, his successor was chosen by an opaque intra-party decision-making process among senior LDP leaders, much to the consternation of the Japanese public. To increase transparency, subsequent administrations voluntarily established their succession plan shortly after any new cabinet was formed. In September 2003 when Prime Minister Koizumi's second cabinet was inaugurated, for example, the new cabinet agreed to make Chief Cabinet Secretary Yasuo Fukuda Koizumi's immediate successor, followed by Finance Minister Sadakazu Tanigaki, Agriculture Minister Yoshiyuki Kamei, Public Management Minister Aso, and lastly Minister of Economy Shoichi Nakagawa.[639]

While the impetus for discussions of government reorganization was created by Japan's continuing economic malaise in the mid-1990s following the collapse of the real estate and stock market bubbles in the late 1980s and increasing US pressure to open its markets, by late 1997 discussions focused actively on reform of Japan's national security structure as well. Reform of Japan's national security system took place in two stages in the late 1990s. The hostage crisis in Peru during Hashimoto's first year in office, following so quickly after the Great Hanshin Earthquake and the Aum Shinrikyo attacks in 1995, spurred the Hashimoto administration to create a new Deputy Chief Cabinet Secretary for National Security and Crisis Management position in late 1997. The first designee, Tadao Ando, took office at the beginning of Japan's next fiscal year in April 1998. Meanwhile, legislation to reorganize the entire Japanese government reached the Diet in early 1999, and following successful passage, the reorganization took effect in early 2001.

The Increasing Importance of National Security and Crisis Management

The LDP took the first concrete step toward government reorganization with the formation of its own Administrative Reform Promotion Headquarters (ARPH) in mid-December 1995 shortly after Hashimoto became president of the LDP. This was not the first such "Headquarters" established to review possible government reorganization, as a similarly named group met multiple times during Hosokawa's and Murayama's tenures, but that Headquarters accomplished little. The LDP this time appointed 15 industry and business leaders to its own party-sponsored ARPH with committees on deregulation and fiscal reform among others, suggesting that it too was initially focused overwhelmingly on economic reforms.[640] By May 1996, the ARPH issued its recommendations centered on reducing the size of the government and, though it was only hinted at in the "Vision," transferring the Diet and government functions outside of Tokyo altogether—a widely floated proposal at the time. Indeed, the Hashimoto Cabinet on May 28 endorsed a separate study by the National Land Agency that recommended moving Japan's capital out of Tokyo to reduce overcrowding.[641] The transfer of the capital functions could not be accomplished until after 2010 according to the NLA outline, however, and at any rate the cost of moving the capital would have been astronomical. The proposal later died.

Hashimoto increasingly engaged CSAO directly on matters of national security as well. Following a Summit meeting with President Clinton in April 1996—one month after the Taiwan Strait crisis—when the two leaders agreed to expand bilateral defense cooperation and signed the "Japan-US Joint Declaration on Security," in May Hashimoto directed CSAO to begin a study in four specific national security issues together with MOFA, the DA, and other ministries and agencies. They included: the rescue of Japanese nationals from areas outside Japan, measures to handle a large number of refugees in Japan, countermeasures against terrorist activities (in Japan), and support for the US military in areas surrounding Japan. Tokyo assessed these to be realistic scenarios during the 1993-1994 Korean peninsula crisis and again during the 1995-1996 Taiwan Strait crisis. In August, Hashimoto additionally directed CSAO to submit a monthly report on the international security situation. Until that point, only the MOFA vice minister and the head of CIRO submitted monthly reports.[642]

The internal studies in conjunction with working-level talks with the United States over the next year led to the revision of the Japan-US Guidelines for Defense Cooperation, signed on September 23, 1997. The revised guidelines were the first attempt to define Japan's support of US military operations during "situations in areas surrounding Japan." The Guidelines specifically noted that the concept was "not geographic but situational" in an effort to allay concerns by Japan's neighbors so soon after the Taiwan Strait crisis. To implement the strengthened cooperation guidelines, in early 1998 Tokyo drafted legislation to support the various measures stipulated in the revised guidelines, such as a bill to support Japan's logistical support for US forces during "situations" around Japan, revision of the Acquisition and Cross Servicing Agreement (ACSA) to apply it to emergency as well as peacetime situations, revision of the SDF Act to enable the dispatch of SDF ships to rescue Japanese nationals abroad, and a law to allow for the inspection of suspicious vessels.[643] It would take a number of years to pass these bills into law—indeed, not until several years after the 9.11 attacks in the United States would the Diet pass all the legislation. But the new guidelines were a seminal shift for Japan: no longer was Japan's defense posture focused exclusively on defending its own territorial possessions as Japan slowly began to take a more outward, cooperative, and active defense posture.

Hashimoto maintained his electoral mandate following successful elections in November 1996. After the subsequent inauguration of his second Cabinet, Hashimoto established an Administrative Reform Council (ARC) under his direct control to finalize government reorganization. The ARC had 13 members and included the heads of former government reform study groups, such as the Administrative Reform Committee—chaired by Yotaro Iida, who also headed *Keidanren*'s Defense Production Committee—and the Committee for the Promotion of Decentralization, headed by Chichibu Cement Chairman Ken Moroi, a close friend of Hashimoto.[644] Kiyoshi Mizuno, formerly the chairman of the LDP's Administrative Reform Promotion Headquarters, was also appointed to the ARC and was made a "prime ministerial aide in charge of administrative reform." Evoking a sense of crisis, Hashimoto declared at the inaugural meeting on November 28: "Our country is at a turning point… the economic and social systems that have supported the development of our country for 50 years after the war have exposed their limits amid changes in the domestic and external environment. We should reconstruct them into ones to suit the 21st century." Hashimoto also declared that this Council would make its recommendations within one year, with submission of legislation to the Diet planned for early 1998 and with the ultimate goal of completing government reorganization by New Year's Day 2001. The council was scheduled to meet twice a month for the next year to hammer out a final reform plan.[645]

While much of the discussion centered on reorganization of the entire government, the hostage crisis in Peru the following month turned the spotlight of reform onto the national security structure as well. On December 21, days after the hostage crisis began, the LDP established a special "Subcommittee on Measures Against International Terrorism" in its Foreign Affairs Research Commission to examine security at Japanese embassies and legal issues relating to the dispatch of counter-terrorism "task forces" abroad.[646] The subcommittee—a separate group from the ARC—also examined reform of Japan's cabinet-level security bureaus. Tomoharu Yoda, the subcommittee chairman and a former director of CSAO under the Kaifu Administration, told the *Sankei Shimbun* soon after the subcommittee's establishment that "crisis management is the best form of welfare we can provide to the Japanese people."[647] The subcommittee on May 9, 1997 released an advisory report calling for a reorganization of Japan's cabinet-level security bureaus. Among the LDP commission's recommendations: establish an upgraded crisis management bureau in the cabinet secretariat by merging the crisis response functions of COIA with those of CSAO. The recommendations called for the strengthened office to be placed under a new deputy chief cabinet secretary for crisis management. The report also called for a revision of the Police Law to enable SAT counter-terrorism teams to train and operate overseas and to allow smoother cooperation between police and the SDF.[648]

The ARC continued to meet as well, and in May 1997 it too published an interim "Synopsis of Opinions on Improving the Cabinet's Crisis Management Capability." The "Opinions" proposal also suggested designating a deputy chief cabinet secretary position that specialized in crisis management, which it foreshadowed in press leaks during the Peru hostage crisis.[649] In August, the ARC published its full plan to trim Japan's 22 ministries and agencies into one cabinet office and 12 ministries, which if approved would take place in January 2001. The council also proposed a staff and a "network" to enable "the crisis management specialist and his staff to communicate on a regular basis with other crisis management specialists both in Japan and abroad."[650] This would entail consolidating functions in three offices in a reorganization of the Cabinet Secretariat: one dealing with national security and crisis management, one dealing with information/intelligence, and one dealing with social and economic issues.[651] This cabinet-level reorganization, however, would take place together with the government-wide reforms in early 2001. Before the full reorganization occurred in 2001, and given the increasingly frequent occurrence of crises, the Hashimoto Administration decided to create the "Deputy Chief Cabinet Secretary for National Security and Crisis Management" three years ahead of the government-wide reforms.

Deputy Chief Cabinet Secretary for National Security and Crisis Management

Based on the LDP subcommittee's recommendations in May 1997 and the ARC's recommendations in August, CSAO was expanded into the "Cabinet Office for National Security Affairs and Crisis Management" (CONSACM) in 1998. CSAO's crisis management section—which dealt with defense and terrorism-related issues—merged with the COIA natural disaster section. A new post, the Deputy Chief Cabinet Secretary for Crisis Management (DCCS/CM), was created to oversee the new cabinet office and to manage response to national crises. The post was officially inaugurated in April 1998, with Tadao Ando appointed as Japan's first DCCS/CM. Ando had formerly served in the Tokyo Metropolitan Police Department from 1959 until his retirement in 1993 as chief of police, and he headed the Japan Road Traffic Information Center when his appointment was announced.[652]

Ando came to the post aiming to break down organizational barriers preventing information-sharing between agencies: "We hope officials on the front line convey information, not through their ministries' administrative vice ministers, but directly to us, whenever necessary."[653] Prime Minister Hashimoto fully supported Ando's plans and ordered his cabinet ministers to provide their complete support: "I want government ministries and agencies to provide him with information, not only in the event of an actual crisis either at home or abroad, but also when there exists the possibility that a crisis may occur."[654] Yet, as with any new organizational structure, there were bound to be difficulties in establishing authority and even simple lines of communication with the myriad offices having any disaster response function, and the process would require both tenacity and patience on Ando's part.

At the Crisis Management Council's first meeting a month later (just as riots in Indonesia threatened to become Ando's first crisis), he began to assert his new role in the bureaucracy. "I would like to play a role in boosting coordination among concerned ministries and agencies," since in his previous career at the Tokyo Metropolitan Police Department, "I experienced some cases in which 'reluctance' to provide information resulted in irreparable misjudgment," he said.[655] He planned to improve cooperation between the SDF, police, firefighters, and other local first-responders and to create "crisis manuals" so that the government was better prepared for future emergencies. Ando visited former Deputy Chief Cabinet Secretary Nobuo Ishihara shortly after taking office for input on government-wide crisis response measures. Ishihara reportedly told Ando that the 1993-4 Korean Peninsula crisis was the most difficult one he faced, during which time his only source of information was US intelligence services.[656] In contrast, by the time Ando took office five years later, the *Kantei* had a nascent 24-hour watch office, the Defense Agency had created a centralized Defense Intelligence Headquarters, and the LDP was examining the possibility of building and launching reconnaissance satellites. Japan was gradually modernizing its own intelligence gathering capabilities, which would later provide Ando's successors with a wider range of sources.

Ando planned to hold CONSACM's first crisis management drill in May 1998, a month after he took office. Real world events, however, forced Ando to postpone the drill. Mass rallies and demonstrations in Indonesia against rising public utilities charges devolved into anti-government riots protesting the country's long-time ruler, President Suharto. Indonesia was strategically significant for Japan given its location along shipping lanes to and from South Asia and the Middle East and as a growing market for Japanese goods. On May 11 Ando held the first meeting of the Liaison Council for Crisis Management with 14 directors-general in charge of disaster response from ten agencies and ministries including the NPA, the DA, the National Land Agency, the Maritime Safety Agency, and others. Kazuhiro Sugita, director of CIRO, also attended. At their first meeting the group discussed the situation in Indonesia, a series of earthquakes on the Izu Peninsula in Shizuoka Prefecture, and agreed to work on producing crisis manuals on dealing with emergencies.[657] As the rioting in Indonesia escalated, Ando held another meeting on the evening of May 14, and by this time, as Hashimoto was preparing to depart for the G-8 Summit in the UK, Chief Cabinet Secretary Kanezo Muraoka ordered extra personnel to monitor the situation at the Cabinet Information Collection Center, the new 24-hour monitoring center at the *Kantei*. MOFA Administrative Vice Minister Shunji Yanai also established a 24-hour watch center at the Ministry of Foreign Affairs.[658] On May 16, ahead of a major rally in Indonesia to mark a symbolically important 1908 independence rally, Prime

Minister Hashimoto raised from level three to level four the danger warning for Japanese nationals living in and traveling to the country—level three indicated that Japanese should not travel to the country, and level four indicated that Japanese nationals should evacuate their families from the region. With the expected mass exodus from Indonesia, the Japanese government asked Japan's major airlines to provide extra flights for the next three days so that Japanese nationals could return home safely. Japan Asia Airways, All Nippon Airways and Japan Airlines scheduled 14 non-stop flights to Japan in the following three days, and the Japanese Embassy set up a special consulate general booth at the Jakarta airport to issue necessary documents for Japanese who lost their passports.[659]

A day later, as an estimated 500 Indonesians had been killed in riots during that week, Hashimoto ordered the dispatch of six ASDF C-130 transport planes to Singapore to stand by in case the political situation deteriorated further, and he ordered the dispatch of two Maritime Safety Agency vessels, the *Mizuho* and the *Echigo*, to the region as well. (While a dispatch to actually evacuate Japanese citizens was considered illegal at the time without Diet approval, the planes and ships could legally wait for such approval at points outside the country, thus cutting down on travel time if an evacuation order came; this real-life scenario starkly illustrated the need for legislation that would allow Japanese defense units to evacuate non-combatants—whether Japanese or other nationals—from areas of strife outside of Japan.) Tokyo also chartered flights from non-Japanese airlines—Garuda Indonesia, Cathay Pacific Airways and Malaysia Airlines—to evacuate Japanese nationals, and asked shipping companies for their help if airports became unusable.[660] By May 20, over 13,000 Japanese had left the country, but with often-violent protests continuing, Tokyo remained concerned that the Indonesian government might escalate their crackdown of protests in the country. Tokyo estimated that despite the mass exodus of Japanese, some 4,745 Japanese still remained in Indonesia, including 2,565 in the Indonesian capital, Jakarta. Thus Hashimoto met with Ando, Foreign Minister Keizo Obuchi, and DA Director General Fumio Kyuma that day as Tokyo secured 15 charter flights with a 4,900-seat capacity to evacuate the remaining Japanese.[661] Two days later, however, Suharto stepped down and was replaced by new president Bacharuddin Jusuf Habibie. As some stability returned to the country, the six ASDF transport planes and two MSA ships departed Singapore to return to Japan on May 27.[662]

Following these events in May, the two-hour drill, taking place at the end of June, seemed rather tame in comparison. The drill was held at the PMOR's Crisis Management Center and involved the disappearance of a commercial flight with 192 people on board over the Izu Peninsula soon after it departed from Narita airport. With Ando's official announcement that a special *Kantei taisakushitsu* or PMOR countermeasures office was being established, over 70 government officials gathered in the CMC and officials from five ministries including the Ministry of Transportation and the Defense Agency posted maps of Izu on the wall and attempted to collect the latest information from DA units conducting virtual searches in the area. The Minister of Transportation took over as head of the *hijō saigai taisaku honbu* or Natural Disaster Task Force, in line with established procedure at the time.[663] Although the entire exercise was scripted, it served the important function of getting everyone on the same operational page as attention was increasingly focused on the *Kantei*'s leading role in crisis management. With this and future drills, agencies and ministries would increasingly look to the *Kantei* for guidance during future crises.

Ando was closely involved with other mini-crises and exercises during his three-year tenure. Ando attended meetings on government response measures following a series of food poisoning incidents in Japan during the late summer and fall 1998.[664] As the United States initiated "Operation Desert Fox" against Iraq in December 1998 and with Prime Minister Obuchi on an official visit to Vietnam, Ando established a *Kantei taisakushitsu* to follow the situation in the background as government spokesman Hiromu Nonaka told an emergency press conference that morning that Japan supported US and UK actions.[665] And while Ando and his office were bypassed in the immediate aftermath of the Taepodong missile launch in August 1998,[666] he took part in the inaugural meeting of the Cabinet Intelligence Committee meeting that met in January 1999.[667] In September 1999, following a nuclear criticality accident at a nuclear fuel facility in Tokaimura north of Tokyo, Ando briefed Chief Cabinet Secretary Nonaka on the situation that afternoon, and later that evening Ando personally visited the site with a GSDF chemical unit dispatched to the area.[668] Ando became involved in the aftermath of a commuter train collision in Tokyo when initial reports suggested an explosion had occurred on one of the trains, perhaps pointing to foul play. It was later determined that the collision was an accident (Prime Minister Obuchi himself suffered some political damage when the press learned that he went to get his hair cut five minutes after ordering the establishment of the task force).[669] And for the first time since the Great Hanshin Earthquake, Prime Minister Obuchi ordered the establishment of a Natural Disaster Task Force on March 31, 2000, following major eruptions of Mt. Usu in Hokkaido. Although the task force was led by National Land Agency Head Masaaki Nakayama as the SDF provided relief operations in the area, Ando was also involved with the task force in Tokyo, helping to brief reporters.[670] And Ando met with the Liaison Council for Crisis Management and established a task force, for example, after 33 Japanese tourists were taken hostage on a bus in Greece in November 2000 when a local man, after having a fight with his wife, stormed out of the house with a rifle and hijacked the bus that happened to be passing by at the time.[671] (Following talks with the police and a popular Greek TV talkshow host, the gunman that evening surrendered himself after handing his rifle to the driver and bowing to the hostages in apology. As the emotionally distraught man was being fingerprinted at the police building, he suddenly ran out a window and plunged to his death in an apparent suicide.[672])

In the first years after the creation of the DCCS/CM position in 1998 and as security issues came to the fore more often, the CONSACM attempted to improve preparation for any potential crisis by writing crisis manuals. By 2003, however, senior policymakers were faced with a proliferation of crisis manuals: some 15 disaster-response manuals in the previous five years on how to respond to crises such as major earthquakes, volcanic eruptions, and accidents at nuclear power plants at the central government level, often following real-life crises. Many prefectural authorities, moreover, were compiling their own disaster response manuals. After the 9.11 attacks in the United States and the SARS epidemic in Asia, however, the central government at the end of 2003 moved to incorporate information contained in the 15 separate manuals into one overarching crisis response manual that detailed procedures to be followed at the initial stage of each crisis.[673] Yet despite the growing pains, the long-serving Deputy Chief Cabinet Secretary—Ando's boss—Teijiro Furukawa would later recall that the creation of the DCCS/CM decreased his workload tremendously.[674]

Ando retired from the post after three turbulent years. Kazuhiro Sugita, the director of CIRO and formerly a career National Police Agency bureaucrat, was appointed Ando's successor just as newly elected Prime Minister Koizumi took office in the spring of 2001 and shortly after a government-wide reorganization that included the reorganization of cabinet offices at the *Kantei.*[675]

Post-Reform Cabinet Structure

The government-wide reform package was adopted by Prime Minister Keizo Obuchi's Cabinet on April 27, 1999. The Diet then passed the 17 reform-related bills as part of the Administrative Reform Law on July 8, 1999. The government would be officially reorganized on January 1, 2001. On that day, the existing cabinet secretariat and 22 ministries and agencies were reorganized into 13 entities—a strengthened Cabinet Office and 12 ministries and agencies. The reform stripped the authority to formulate fiscal policy from the powerful Finance Ministry and transferred that authority to the new Council on Economic and Fiscal Policy in the expanded Cabinet Office. The reform created an expanded Ministry of Economy, Trade, and Industry in the place of the Ministry of International Trade and Industry, and it elevated the Environment Agency to Ministry status.[676] The Defense Agency, however, remained an Agency under the oversight of the new Cabinet Office. The LDP dropped the idea in October 1997 after its coalition partner the Social Democratic Party—the renamed JSP—strongly objected to upgrading the DA to ministry status. The LDP made the move to keep overall talks on government reform on track.[677] The Defense Agency would not be upgraded to Ministry status until late 2006 (see below).

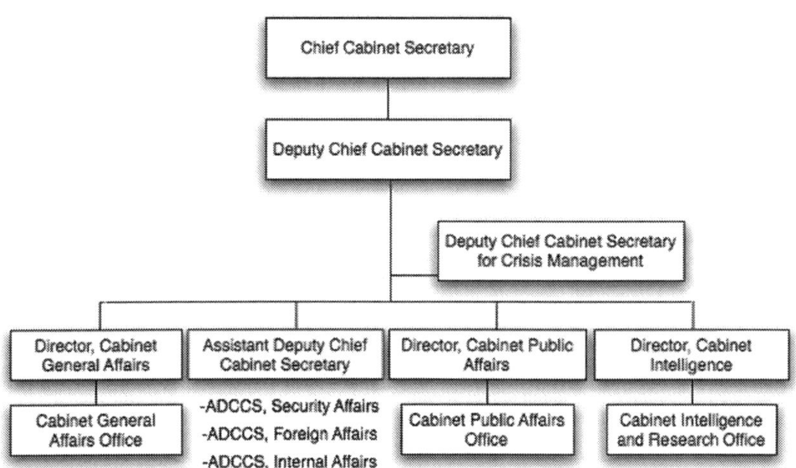

Source: Cabinet Office, "Outline of the Country's Government Organization"

Once the full government reorganization took effect in January 2001, cabinet office director positions were elevated to Assistant Deputy Chief Cabinet Secretary (ADCCS) positions, one each for Foreign Policy, Security, and Social and Economic Affairs. The director of CIRO was elevated to Cabinet Intelligence Officer (*Naikaku Jōhōkan*—sometimes also called the Director of Cabinet Intelligence). The post of Deputy Chief Cabinet Secretary for Crisis Management (DCCS/CM) remained separate from and one level above the ADCCS positions, and this position's role continued to focus on coordinating immediate government response to crises. He (the first three DCCS/CMs were male) also manages the Crisis Management Center at the Prime Minister's Official Residence.

Their elevated ranks, coupled with the more centralized role of the *Kantei*, theoretically gave the ADCCSs greater clout to form policy and guide interagency coordination among Japanese ministries and agencies. Each ADCCS now had a support staff usually referred to as the "Office of the Assistant Deputy Chief Cabinet Secretary Omori" (for example, referring to the first ADCCS for Security) to assist with issues related to their portfolios. As under the prior system, officials from the Defense Agency, Foreign Ministry, and Finance Ministry normally fill the ADCCS positions. Since their positions are the equivalent of the vice minister rank, the individuals filling these positions had more or less equal bureaucratic status with career ministerial leadership at the various ministries and agencies outside the new Cabinet Office structure, although the ADCCSs lacked direct authority over personnel in each ministry or agency. Symbolizing their central roles in the Japanese government under the auspices of the Prime Minister and his Cabinet, the ADCCSs have offices on the fourth floor of the newly renovated *Kantei*, one story below the offices of the prime minister and the chief cabinet secretary.[678]

Keiji Omori, former head of the DA's Defense Facilities Administration Agency, became the first ADCCS in charge of national security issues. Omori served as ADCCS from January 2001 until March 2004, during which time he helped to shape policy related to SDF dispatches to the Indian Ocean and to Iraq, and he helped to write legislation that legalized Japan's basic crisis response capabilities (such as enabling the Japan Coast Guard and the MSDF to fire directly at suspected ships in waters near Japan). Omori also had a deep interest in intelligence matters, as his brother Yoshio Omori directed CIRO in the mid-1990s. After a brief stint back at the DA he was named Japan's Ambassador to Oman, a critical posting for Japan given its geographic location near the Strait of Hormuz and Musqat's quiet diplomacy with both Tehran and Washington.

Career diplomat Kazuyoshi Urabe was appointed ADCCS in charge of foreign policy in January 2001. Urabe came to the post with extensive diplomatic and administrative experience, having served as ambassador to Bangladesh, headed MOFA's Ministerial Secretariat, and served on rotation as head of the Toyama Prefectural Police Department.[679] The ADCCS for foreign policy played central roles in some of Japan's highest-level diplomatic efforts in the years after the position was created: Shotaro Yachi, Urabe's replacement in September 2002, headed Japan's delegation on Free Trade Agreement (FTA) talks with Mexico, and Yachi's replacement, Shin Ebihara, spearheaded Japan's diplomatic efforts to gain a permanent seat on the U.N. Security Council, although those efforts ultimately failed.

The ADCCS for national security and for foreign affairs sometimes share watch duties during crises. During the Japanese hostage crisis in Iraq in 2004, for example, ADCCS Omori's successor, Kyoji Yanagisawa took turns with DCCS for Crisis Management Takeshi Noda, staying overnight at the PMOR to follow the situation until it was resolved.[680]

Cabinet Intelligence and Research Office

Shortly after the government-wide reorganization, the Cabinet Information Research Office quietly changed its official English translation to the Cabinet Intelligence and Research Office, pointing to a conscious change in identity. The Japanese name, *Naikaku Jōhō Chōsashitsu* or *Naicho*, stayed the same, as *jōhō* can be translated as either "information" or "intelligence." And while discussion of an expanded intelligence capability would gain momentum in the late 1990s and early 2000s, the post-reform CIRO employed the same number of personnel as before the 2001 government reorganization—just fewer than 200 personnel with only half of those full-time careerists at CIRO. The rest served on multi-year rotations to CIRO from their home agencies, with approximately 40 from the National Police Agency, 20 personnel from the Public Security Intelligence Agency, 10 from the Defense Agency, and a few from remaining ministries and agencies such as the Ministry of Foreign Affairs.[681] Iku Aso, writing immediately after the government-wide reorganization, noted that in total 188 personnel worked at CIRO as of June 2001.[682]

CIRO's main office is located on the sixth floor of the Cabinet Office Building across from the *Kantei*. Following government reform, CIRO had five departments and one center: a General Affairs Department (*sōmubu*), Domestic Affairs Department (*kokunaibu*) which handles domestic information/intelligence, an International Affairs Department (*kokusaibu*), and an Economics Department (*keizaibu*) which is in charge of economic analysis based on intelligence from abroad.[683] The Cabinet Information Collection Center, the *Kantei*'s 24/7 watch office (detailed below), was originally the International Affairs Second Department, but following the demonstrated need in the mid-1990s for a dedicated watch office, the department was reorganized to perform watch duties.[684] The Cabinet Satellite Intelligence Center (CSIC—pronounced "C-Sice" in its first years of existence) falls administratively under CIRO as well, but because of the Defense Agency's deep involvement in tasking Japan's reconnaissance satellites (CSIC is indeed located behind the Defense Agency Headquarters in Ichigaya, Tokyo) and because the center's 300-plus personnel outnumber the number of personnel at CIRO, CSIC therefore reports directly to the Cabinet Intelligence Officer.

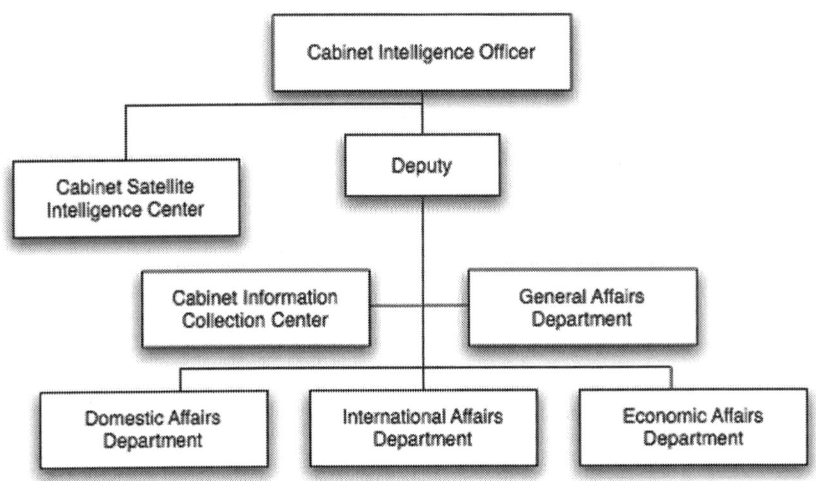

Source: Buntaro Kuroi's "Naikaku Jōhō Chōsashitsu to Nihon no Jōhō Komyuniti," in September 2006 Gunji Kenkyu, p 25.

The International Affairs Department, headed by an official from the National Police Agency, handles foreign intelligence. Following the 2001 reforms it was divided into thirteen teams or *han*, the first of which is the Trading Company Team. This team handles research contracts with Japanese commercial trading companies that have an international presence and therefore, in the words of Iku Aso, offer an "intelligence network that spans the entire world." A separate team liaises with foreign government intelligence services. A majority of the remaining teams are based on geography, including the Korean Peninsula Team, the China Team, the Americas Team, the Africa and Middle East Team, the Europe Team, the Southeast Asia Team, and the Russia Team. The latter team also covers Ukraine, the three Baltic countries, according to Aso. Rounding out the teams are the Military Affairs Team, the Counter-Terrorism Planning Team, and a so-called *Tokumei-han* or "Special Missions Team" that conducts classified missions, according to Aso.[685]

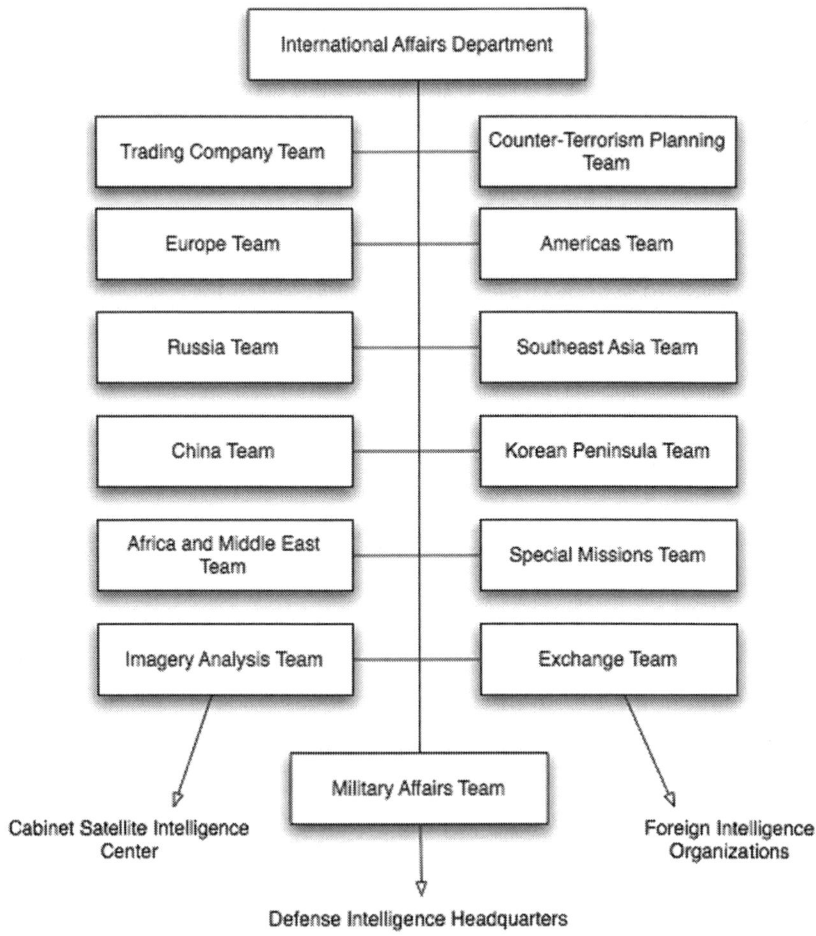

Sources: Iku Aso's Jōhō Kantei ni Tassezu and Buntaro Kuroi's "Naikaku Jōhō Chōsashitsu to Nihon no Jōhō Komyuniti," in September 2006 Gunji Kenkyu, p 29.

Besides supplying a majority of rotating personnel to CIRO, the National Police Agency also normally provides the Director of Cabinet Intelligence. Yoshio Omori and Kazuhiro Sugita, two prominent figures from the NPA, played central roles in Japan's post-Cold War crisis management operations in CIRO. A third figure, Takeshi Noda, took the mantle just after the government reorganization.

Yoshio Omori, who took over CIRO in April 1993, was typical of an NPA-appointed director. Omori entered the National Police Agency after graduating from Tokyo University in 1963 (a not insignificant number of those serving in the PMOR—and in senior positions throughout government—graduated from *Todai* or Tokyo University), and served stints in several leadership positions such as the chief of the regional Police Headquarters in Tottori Prefecture and head of the Tokyo Metropolitan Police Department's public safety section. Omori's appointment to CIRO was announced following a short six-month tour as head of the National Police Academy—then a typical stop for future CIRO directors. Perhaps unlike other directors, however, Omori was met with a baptism by fire when he took office, following so soon after North Korea announced on March 12 that it intended to leave the Nuclear Nonproliferation Treaty and become a nuclear power. During his tenure, Omori not only directed CIRO during the North Korea crisis in 1993-1994, he also headed CIRO during the Great Hanshin Earthquake and Aum Shinrikyo attacks in 1995, and during China's missile and nuclear tests in 1996. And just as Omori was preparing to leave CIRO in late 1996, the Shinning Path Guerrilla group seized the Japanese Ambassador's residence in Lima, Peru, taking scores hostage. Omori would spend the next four months dealing with the situation before his successor, Kazuhiro Sugita, officially took over as the head of CIRO. (Omori described his experiences as head of CIRO in a 2005 book, discussed in a later chapter.) Omori joined the major defense contractor NEC after his retirement from government service and remained active in intelligence matters, serving on a number of commissions examining the possible restructuring of Japan's intelligence organizations.

Cabinet Intelligence Council

While the JIC remained an active council after the government-wide reorganization, the Administrative Reform Council proposed the establishment of the Cabinet Intelligence Council (CIC) in June 1997 to coordinate intelligence and information sharing at the subcabinet level.[686] The CIC actually began to meet in January 1999, two years before the government-wide reorganization took effect in 2001, as a direct result of the August 1998 Taepodong missile test. Meetings are held twice a year with a stated purpose of discussing ways to increase intelligence sharing among ministries and agencies—and improve Japanese intelligence capabilities in general—and after each meeting the council provides the prime minister with a classified report of their discussions.[687] Chaired by the Chief Cabinet Secretary, the CIC is composed of deputy chief cabinet secretaries (for political and administrative affairs); the Cabinet Intelligence Officer and the ADCCS for Security and Foreign Affairs, the commissioner-general for the National Policy Agency; director-general of the Public Security Intelligence Agency; and vice ministers of foreign affairs and the Defense Agency. Later reform efforts would focus on enhancing the functions and oversight of this council to further improve Japanese intelligence and national security capabilities.

Security Council of Japan

Established in 1986, the Security Council of Japan was the country's highest deliberative forum on issues related to national security both before and after the government reforms. Council members included the Prime Minister, the Defense Agency Director General, the Foreign and Finance Ministers, the Minister of Public Management, Home Affairs, Posts and Telecommunications, the Minister of Economy, Trade and Industry (METI), and the Minister of Land, Infrastructure, and Transport—which oversees the Japan Coast Guard. The body historically did not have a core decision making function for day-to-day formation of foreign and national security policy in Japan, but rather was used to debate budgets and strategic policy. The council met in 1995 to discuss the National Defense Program Outline then under review, for example, but it left the wording of contentious passages to be debated and finalized among the defense affairs councils in the three ruling parties at the time.[688] The Security Council never met to deal with an actual emergency situation prior to the government reorganization, a significant criticism after the North Korean launch of the Taepodong missile in August 1998, for example.[689]

In an effort to increase the relevancy of the Security Council, however, in August 2003 the Japanese Government established a permanent panel within the special committee to deal with emergency situations (*jitai taisho senmon iinkai*) in an attempt to unify the *Kantei*'s control over security issues. The new panel theoretically would provide an additional forum by which information could be shared among the DA, the Ministry of Foreign Affairs, the police, and other government offices (thus indicating, however, that information-sharing was still severely stovepiped even up to the prime ministerial level), and some officials hoped that the permanent committee with its associated secretariat would one day morph into a Japanese version of the National Security Council.[690] As one unnamed government official was quoted as saying: "We are now standing at the starting line to make strategic decisions on complicated security issues."[691]

Reform continued slowly, however, prompting the Araki Report, completed in the summer of 2004 ahead of the country's third review of the National Defense Program Outline (detailed below), to again highlight the need for a Japanese National

Security Council: "The government should use the Security Council as a forum for in-depth discussion of security strategy by Cabinet ministers and, for that purpose, seek to build up the current Cabinet Secretariat staff and sponsor policy studies by internal and external experts." The Araki Report pointed to the US as a model: "The National Security Council within the Office of the President of the United States can serve as a useful model."[692]

The Security Council would indeed form the nucleus of a Japanese National Security Council ten years after the Araki Report was published, although that formation is outside the scope of this writing.

Prime Minister's Official Residence and the Cabinet Information Collection Center

With an assertive Prime Minister Koizumi in office immediately after the government reforms were enacted in 2001 and the higher profiles of the assistant deputy chief cabinet secretaries, a newly renovated Prime Minister's Official Residence or *Kantei* became a new focal point of power in Tokyo. The financial daily *Nihon Keizai Shimbun* in April 2004 highlighted the *Kantei*'s expanding functions by asserting that "security and crisis management, which bears on the very survival of the nation, is the *Kantei*'s job."[693]

As the *Kantei* asserted greater power in policy formation and took greater responsibility in crisis management, it needed to have the facilities necessary to properly perform its duties. Although it was coincidental, major renovations on the old two-story brick PMOR began in 1998 just as discussions of government reform proceeded in earnest between 1998-2001. While the original decision to renovate the residence came under the Nakasone administration in the 1980s, the actual renovation symbolized the transition from a post-WWII era to a post-Cold War one.

The completely renovated Prime Minister's Official Residence opened for business on April 30, 2002 marking the one-year anniversary in office of Prime Minister Junichiro Koizumi—one of Japan's most assertive and longest-serving prime ministers in the post-war era. The renovations included a hi-tech Cabinet Information Collection Center (CICC) or *naikaku jōhō shūshū senta,* and a dedicated Crisis Management Center adjacent to the CICC. (Since the CICC functions as a watch office and not as a collector of finished intelligence as such, it is probably most appropriate to translate *jōhō* in its title *naikaku jōhō shūshū senta* as "information.") The new PMOR is 2.5 times as big as its older version and has five stories above ground and a basement. The building sits on a sloping hill so that the main entrance in the front is actually on the third floor. While it is in the heart of Tokyo, the building is surrounded by bamboo, lush green trees and a high bamboo fence so that pedestrians can see only the top floors.[694]

The prime minister and senior cabinet officials sit on the fifth floor, but contrary to past practices when reporters could walk up to the prime minister's office door, the entire fifth floor is off-limits to the media. As a compromise, the government installed a camera system next to the PM receptionist's desk so that reporters can observe who enters and exits the prime minister's office, but that system has its limitations. Reporters soon complained that the pictures were too small and unclear. Moreover, there is an inner corridor that connects all the offices of the fifth floor but is not visible to the camera. It is therefore possible for senior officials to visit the chief cabinet secretary, for example, and then meet with the prime minister whose office is connected to the chief cabinet secretary's office via a private door.[695] An elevator sits directly outside the Prime Minister's office, and this allows immediate access to all floors and to the CICC and CMC, which occupy the entire basement. Moreover, an underground tunnel approximately 200 meters long connects the Cabinet Office building across the street to the *Kantei*'s second floor, providing direct and protected access between the two buildings. Until the tunnel was built, officials had to walk across the street outside, sometimes carrying classified documents from the Cabinet Office building (where CIRO is located, for example) to the PMOR. The documents would be exposed to the elements and or could be stolen, which of course posed a security hazard.[696]

Theoretically, if the *Kantei* were intent on keeping the identity of a visitor secret, that person could enter the Cabinet Office building and walk through the underground tunnel to the second floor of the *Kantei* and then take the private elevator to the fifth floor (to visit the prime minister or chief cabinet secretary) or to the basement (to attend meetings in the CICC/CMC). The press and other observers would be unaware of the visitor's presence. Occupants of the *Kantei*'s fifth floor could do the same in reverse.

Other floors contain committee rooms for cabinet meetings and cabinet secretariat offices (fourth floor), a media room for government briefings (first floor), and a reception hall for formal occasions (second floor). VIPs can be transported via helicopter to and from the *Kantei*'s rooftop heliport. A small pond in the garden adjacent to the building is designated an emergency landing point that can be drained should the heliport be damaged. The building itself was designed to withstand an earthquake with the same magnitude as the Great Hanshin Earthquake and with a solar power generation system and heavy oil reserves to provide power during a major natural disaster as long as the building remains intact.[697] The Prime Minister's actual living quarters, the *Kōtei*, is located adjacent to the PMOR and renovations on it were completed in 2004.

The renovations were intended to both update the *Kantei*'s working space and to improve security of the building. Political leaders were afforded little protection since the original residence was first constructed in 1929. On May 15, 1932, Prime Minister Tsuyoshi Inukai was assassinated in the building during a coup attempt, and several others were killed in another coup attempt on February 16, 1936, although Prime Minister Keisuke Okada survived. Following the war, in 1978 a man armed with a knife snuck into the PMOR and tried to assassinate Prime Minister Masayoshi Ohira in the entrance hall, though the assassination attempt failed.[698] The old PMOR building was also said to have little protection from bugging, and the Prime Minister's phone was rumored to be unsecured from eavesdropping. Iku Aso related in a 1996 *Bungei Shunju* article that in February 1994, when Prime Minister Morihiro Hosokawa was meeting with senior officials in preparation for a Summit on contentious trade issues with President Clinton in the United States, Hosokawa would make phone calls to Japanese correspondents stationed overseas using an open phone line from his office in the *Kantei*—not one phone in the PMOR was protected by security devices, Aso chided. Aso quoted one high-ranking National Police Agency official as saying: "Everybody knows the phone calls are being monitored by SIGINT…Japan's national secrets are completely exposed."[699] A prime goal of the PMOR renovation, therefore, was to improve both physical and technical security at the residence.

Following complaints that the government was slow in responding to the Hanshin Earthquake and the Aum gas attacks, a 24-hour Cabinet Information Collection Center (CICC) was inaugurated in an annex building of the old Prime Minister's Official Residence on April 11, 1996. It was established organizationally under CIRO and was first headed by Nobuo Narijima, former director of CIRO's First International Department. The CICC at that time offered only basic watch office capabilities, however, since the original center was located in a make-shift camera room in the annex building.[700] As discussed previously, this caused great difficulty coordinating operations from the *Kantei* during the initial months of the hostage crisis in Lima, Peru. By March 1997, however, equipment was installed in a larger dedicated control room in the annex before the permanent center was completed in the new PMOR.

There are actually two areas available to manage crises in the new *Kantei.* The CICC acts as the 24-hour operations center that watches for breaking events and monitors reporting from Japanese government entities all over the globe, while the Crisis Management Center (CMC) serves as a dedicated situation room and can host meetings with other officials and offices to deal with particular events as they occur. The CICC monitors television and news agencies, radio, and the internet, and has contact with Japanese utilities and telephone companies. Five shifts of four people manned the CICC around the clock in its first years of operation.[701] The CICC has six large screens to watch footage of disaster sites sent from SDF units or from the Japan Coast Guard on the scene in real time. The CICC is linked via fiber optic cable to various ministries and agencies and has teleconference capability. The center also features a separate sleeping area and extra supplies of food and water.[702] While CIRO manages the CICC, the CMC falls under the supervision of the Deputy Chief Cabinet Secretary for Crisis Management. During extended crises, various representatives of government offices involved in the crisis du jour form a specially convened PMOR Liaison Office, which would usually work out of the CMC and would be in charge of providing situational reports to political leaders.[703]

Established as a result of the Kobe earthquake, the CICC is tasked to report immediately on natural disasters. Should an earthquake strike anywhere in Japan measuring a weak six or higher on Japan's *shindo* scale of 0-7, or if an earthquake measuring a strong five occurs in the Tokyo region, the CICC is tasked to inform the Deputy Chief Cabinet Secretaries, the Chief Cabinet Secretary, and the Prime Minister immediately. The CICC is also tasked to report hijackings, accidents and incidents at nuclear facilities, oil spills, and other major incidents that might impact Japan's national security.[704] These events, incidentally, mirror the crises that occurred in Japan as the new *Kantei* was being planned and constructed, such as the summer 1995 plane hijacking; the grounding of the Russian oil tanker *Nakhodka* near the Noto Peninsula, causing a massive oil spill in late 1996; and the careless mixing of low-enriched uranium that caused a criticality accident at the JCO uranium enrichment facility in the fall of 1999.

As construction on the PMOR was about to begin in the mid-1990s, the Ministry of Posts and Telecommunications planned to connect the CICC/PMOR to the Kasumigaseki WAN, a communications network connecting ministries and agencies in the Tokyo region then under development. The new PMOR would also be able to communicate via any of several communications satellites, according to the Telecommunications Ministry plan.[705] This and other networks developed over the next decade were direct results of an acknowledged lack of real-time information sharing capabilities during times of crises and a push in the mid- and late-1990s to transfer many government services to an internet-based system.

Kasumigaseki WAN

Local Area Networks (LANs) at Japanese government offices—including the Cabinet-level offices discussed above—were first connected via the Kasumigaseki Wide Area Network (WAN) in the late 1990s. The Kasumigaseki WAN became operational on

January 6, 1997 among ten ministries and agencies including the Cabinet Secretariat, Ministry of Foreign Affairs, and the Science and Technology Agency. The Defense Agency and four other agencies joined the Kasumigaski WAN in February, and by March 1998 thirty ministries and agencies were connected to the network.[706]

The WAN is managed by the "Kasumigaseki WAN Operations Center," sometimes called the "NOC" or Network Operations Center. The network is connected via fiber optic cable using a loop link method that would allow alternate communications channels should one be disconnected. Moreover, adding redundancy to the system, PDAs and laptop computers for government use had access by the late 1990s to two N-STAR communications satellites, owned by Japan's largest telecommunications company NTT, which facilitated wireless communications as well.[707]

Upgrades to government communications networks continued as the networks were expanded to include local government offices as well. The Kasumigaseki WAN by 2003 was connected to the "Local Government Wide Area Network," the central network that links governments of cities, towns, and villages in Japan. The "LG WAN" was established as part of the "e-government" program aimed at offering government services via the internet such as tax filing and passport applications, and was completed in 2005.[708] After experiencing great difficulty in communicating with local communities in the immediate aftermath of the Kobe earthquake, however, the initiative will most likely serve the role of providing expanded communications capacity with local communities as well: the crisis management offices in the Cabinet therefore most likely connect to local governments via this network.

The Defense Ministry and Japan's National Defense Posture

As plans for the extensive renovation of the *Kantei* were finalized, a completely new and expansive Headquarters of the Defense Agency—upgraded in 2007 to a Defense Ministry—was constructed in the late 1990s. The DA moved into its new five-building complex in Ichigaya, Tokyo, in May 2000, having been located in Tokyo's Roppongi district (among other locations) in the post-WWII period. Construction on the new DA Headquarters in Ichigaya was originally scheduled to begin in 1988, but artifacts from the ancient Owari clan were discovered on 14 of the 23 hectares during site surveys.[709] The construction was thus delayed until May 1994 while the artifacts were safely excavated. The total construction cost ¥250 billion—some $2.5 billion—which was offset when the DA sold some of its land holdings elsewhere in Japan.

The DA Headquarters' five main buildings are designated by letters of the alphabet, with Building A, the central building, sitting in the middle. The 19-story Building A houses the Defense Minister's office and the secretariat, the internal bureaus, the Joint Staff Council, and staff offices for the Maritime, Ground, and Air Self Defense Forces. The Defense Minister sits on the 11th floor, while high-level meetings are conducted in one of several executive conference rooms located on the 13th floor of Building A.[710] A central command center is located in the third-level basement of Building A as well. Other buildings house communications units (Building B), the Defense Intelligence Headquarters (Building C), Defense Facilities Administration Agency, the Technical Research and Development Institute, and procurement offices (Building D and Building E). Akio Fujii of the DA's Construction Planning Division told the weekly defense newspaper *Asagumo* that the DA buildings and compound as a whole were inspired by Buddhist temple architecture.[711]

The Ichigaya area in Tokyo has a deep link historically with Japan's military modernization efforts since the Meiji era. Japan opened its first modern Military Academy in Ichigaya in 1874. Following the start of World War II, Japanese leaders concentrated the Ministry of War, the General Staff Headquarters, the Department of Military Education, and the Imperial Army's Central Government Agency in Ichigaya. Following the war, the Tokyo Trials were held in Ichigaya, and 30 years later the prolific Japanese author Yukio Mishima and several followers held the SDF's Eastern Regional Army commander hostage at the regional headquarters with swords until the commander allowed Mishima to read his manifesto, "Rise, Members of the Self Defense Forces," from the rooftop. He then committed *seppuku* by slitting his belly as first one then another of his followers attempted to lop off his head during the dramatic ritual.[712]

There were 65 DA directors general between the DA's founding in 1954 and its 50th anniversary in 2004, and the very short average tenures pointed to the relatively low status accorded to the position among power-seeking politicians in the post-war years. One Japanese commentator cynically opined that politicians viewed the post as a way to win SDF and family votes during elections or to gain repeat posts in cabinets.[713] This changed in 2001 when Gen Nakatani became the first DA Director General to have graduated from Japan's National Defense Academy and to have served as an officer in the Ground Self Defense Force. Nakatani (whose given name is actually "Gen," pronounced with a hard "G") ultimately served as an instructor for an elite ranger unit before he left uniformed service in December 1984. He then worked as a political secretary to three Diet members before winning a seat in the House of Representatives in his native Kochi Prefecture in 1990.[714] Nakatani's successor, Shigeru Ishiba, was known to quiz his subordinates on nomenclatures of various weapons systems and built models of jet fighters and ships, which he displayed in his office. *Asahi* called him "one of the best-known experts on defense policy in defense circles" when he took over the DA.[715] Both would remain active in defense policy discussions following their respective tenures.

National Defense Program Outline: Defining Japan's Defense Posture

The National Defense Program Outline (NDPO) describes Japan's general threat perception and details the country's overarching defense policy, force levels and types of units. Based on the NDPO, five-year mid-term defense plans are developed that set budgets for major defense systems to be procured and fielded over that time period.

The first National Defense Program Outline was published in 1976 during a period of détente between the United States and the Soviet Union. The document reflected the entrenched Cold War struggle between the United States and the Soviet Union in assuming that "the international political structure in this region...will not undergo any major changes for some time to come," and further declaring that "equilibrium between the super-powers and the existence of the Japan-US security arrangement...play a major role in maintaining international stability." At the same time, the document hinted at security threats besides the Soviet Union in the Asian-Pacific region: "Tension still persists on the Korean Peninsula...and military buildups continue in several countries near Japan."

The 1976 NDPO outlined ambitious numerical targets for pacifist post-war Japan's defense forces. The total number of uniformed personnel in the three services would total approximately 270,000 personnel, while the GSDF would consist of 12 divisions and 2 combined brigades, the MSDF would consist of 4 flotillas, and the ASDF would maintain 28 Aircraft Control and Warning Units and 10 interceptor squadrons. The NDPO also provided numerical targets for the number of major weapons systems such as ships, tanks, artillery pieces, and jet fighters: the MSDF would have 60 surface ships, 16 submarines, and 220 aircraft, while the GSDF would field over 1,000 tanks and artillery pieces, and the ASDF would operate 430 total aircraft.[716]

Predicated on the possibility of a major invasion from the north, Japan's Self-Defense Forces fielded heavy equipment such as tanks and self-propelled howitzers to defend against a ground invasion from the Soviet Union, while the MSDF emphasized antisubmarine, sea-lane defense, transport, and counter-mining operations as part of its maritime strategy. A full four GSDF divisions were deployed in Hokkaido, and the MSDF would transport additional divisions northward to meet an invading force as necessary.

Symbolizing the very real threat from the north at the time, the ASDF scrambled fighter jets and other aircraft over 400 instances each year from 1976 into the 1980s to intercept Soviet reconnaissance planes, bombers, and jet fighters as they flew along—and sometimes intruded into—Japan's airspace. In addition to reconnaissance and intelligence collection missions, some were assessed to be training missions to simulate strikes against radar sites in Wakkanai, Abashiri, and Nemuro on the Pacific side of Hokkaido, and against Tobetsu and Okushiri on the Sea of Japan side. By the late 1980s, ASDF jets scrambled over 800 times each year to intercept Soviet military planes: 825 times in 1986, 848 times in 1987, and 879 times in 1988, for example.[717]

In late 1987, ASDF F-4s even resorted to firing warning shots at Soviet Tu-16 "Badger" bombers, the first warning shots fired since the ASDF took over air patrols from the United States in 1964. Two ASDF F-4s scrambled to intercept four Badger bombers flying as far south as Okinawa. One of the four left the formation and intruded into Japanese territorial airspace during two separate occasions that afternoon. As the errant plane entered Japan's airspace, one of the F-4s first warned the Badger to leave Japan's airspace over the radio, and then waved its wings visually to warn off the Badger crew. There was no response, so after receiving orders from ASDF command the F-4 fired tracer shells as warning shots from its 20mm gun towards the Badger.[718]

With the sudden collapse of the Soviet Union, however, the number of ASDF scrambles dropped precipitously. In 1992, they dropped to 331, the first time that number fell below 400 in a year since 1976.[719] That number fell to 263 in 1994.[720] It was still clear, however, that while the number of required scrambles fell the Russian Federation nevertheless continued to train its military forces to an extent around northern Japan. Moreover, a significant amount of former Soviet military hardware remained in the Russian Far East. Thus in the early 1990s at least, Tokyo was unsure to what extent the threat from the north had really dissipated.

1991-1995 Review

In the fall of 1990, with the ASDF still scrambling hundreds of time a year, Japanese policymakers were unsure which direction a future defense review should take. The international security situation was clearly changing in Europe and to some extent in the Soviet Far East, but with US and allied troops in the Middle East for Operation Desert Shield and Soviet bombers and fighters flying near Japanese airspace an average of once or more a day, threats clearly persisted. Thus the 1991-1995 Mid-Term Defense

Buildup Plan, passed in December 1990, contained nuanced language calling for a study of Japan's defense power in the future: "The government will study Japan's defenses and will provide a conclusion in the last year of the study," that is, in 1995.[721] The Defense Agency established an internal study group in 1991 to examine the future of warfare. The study was not an official review of the NDPO, but it would ultimately inform the future NDPO.

The first hints that Tokyo was preparing to review its overarching defense policy came in December 1991, following the overwhelming US and allied victory in Desert Storm and the demise of the Soviet Union that very month. The newly elected Prime Minister Miyazawa solicited input at a Security Council of Japan meeting as to whether a reduction of the GSDF by one division was possible. Miyazawa, a former (and future) Minister of Finance, saw the reduction of the SDF as a means to stem Japan's rising debt levels in the 1980s and early 1990s, and the question paralleled those being posed in other capitals including Washington. With the collapse of the Soviet Union, Miyazawa wanted *heiwa no haitō* or "peace dividends" for Japan.[722]

But as a new Prime Minister—Miyazawa had been in power only a month—and as head of the conservative LDP, he had to balance fiscal policies with long-term defense priorities in an increasingly uncertain era. While the Finance Ministry wanted to cut defense spending, the Defense Agency, for its part, wanted to keep its strength at current levels even as it prepared to modernize its command, control, communications, and intelligence (C3I) systems. Sohei Miyashita, the DA Director General, told *Sankei Shimbun* in November 1991: "Just because of changes in the world, we should not decide that the [mid-term defense] program…should be reduced." Moreover, Miyashita implied that the Soviet Union remained the main security challenge despite its imminent demise at the end of 1991: "Despite a quantitative reduction, there has been no qualitative degradation" of the former Soviet forces in the Far East.[723] The DA even took the step of creating a separate Operations Bureau in charge of operational matters and training from its former parent, the Defense Policy Bureau, to better prepare itself for the dispatch of Japan's first uniformed personnel abroad the following year for so-called "Peace-Keeping Operations" or PKO under United Nations auspices. The reorganization, announced on December 2, 1991, would enable an unencumbered Defense Policy Bureau to concentrate on strategic studies and policy matters as it was freed from day-to-day operational issues.[724] However, with the demise of the Soviet Union, a full review of the NDPO was inevitable.

Tokyo moved closer to an official NDPO review in early 1992 when, at a plenary Diet session on January 28, 1992, Miyazawa said in response to an opposition JSP member's call for a reduction in defense spending that the Defense Agency was currently studying Japan's future defense capacity. The study "may lead to changes in the...NDPO," he said.[725] Two days later, DA Administrative Vice DG Akira Hiyoshi tempered that statement somewhat, saying that an actual revision of the NDPO was not likely until the end of the current five-year plan in FY1995 due to the complexities involved in such a revision.[726] On February 4, Hiyoshi's boss, Sohei Miyashita, told a Diet session that the Defense Agency would indeed review the NDPO, although the review would take time and it would include consultations with friendly countries.[727] Moreover, the Defense Agency's *Defense of Japan 1992*, published in August that year, hinted at a study of defense policy, which in turn created further calls for a formal review. Declared pacifist *Mainichi Shimbun* shortly after the publication of the *Defense of Japan*: "There are growing voices that say Japan should review its defense capability in line with changes in the international situation...Post-Cold War changes are bound to transform the security framework of Asia and the Pacific. Such being the case, now is the time for Japan to cut and rationalize its military strength."[728]

At the same time, Japan in 1992 was finally reaching the upper limits of its authorized defense strength in the 1976 NDPO. The MSDF, for example, on March 25 commissioned its 16th submarine, the Hayashio, for the first time reaching the NDPO's authorized limit of 16 submarines that year. Director General Sohei Miyashita noted this situation in an August 1992 interview with *Yomiuri Shimbun*: "Quantitatively speaking, the [1976] Program has nearly been completed. Therefore, based on such factors as restrictions on personnel resources, the change in the international situation, and also changes in military technologies, we should review our overall defense capability."[729] With 1976 NDPO priorities nearly fulfilled and following the dramatic changes in the international security environment, a review of Japan's defense policies was certainly in order, but Tokyo had yet to set a clear timetable for its first official review of defense policy in the post-Cold War era.

This changed in early 1993 when the Defense Agency finally revealed plans to undertake an internal review of the NDPO ahead of a possible revision. The new Defense Agency Director General, Toshio Nakayama, who had replaced Miyashita in a cabinet reshuffle two months earlier, told reporters on January 21 that Japan planned to review and revise the 1976 NDPO by 1995.[730] The review would begin with the establishment of a council comprised of prominent Japanese leaders in business, academia, and retired officials that would be chaired by the DA Director General himself.[731] But having the head of the Defense Agency chair a nominally private advisory council on defense policy could invite charges of excess influence or bias, and at the same time would make it difficult for defense officials to distance themselves if a preliminary report was not well received by the public. Moreover,

Japan's domestic political situation devolved into turmoil when the LDP lost the premiership in the summer of 1993. These domestic polical issues, coupled with the suddenly unstable regional security environment beginning in the spring of 1993, led to delays in establishing the council. With Tokyo intensely preoccupied with these domestic and regional matters, there was little momentum forward even on selecting candidates. Only in September 1993 did the DA and the Cabinet Office began to review lists of possible nominees for the nine-member council.

In February 1994, Prime Minister Hosokawa officially appointed members to the "Advisory Council on Defense Issues" (*bōei mondai kondankai*). Instead of appointing the DA Director General, Hosokawa appointed Hirotaro Higuchi, honorary chairman of Asahi Breweries, to head the council. The Defense Agency had representation on the council, however: Seiki Nishihiro, former Administrative Vice Minister of DA who was reverently called "Mr. Defense Agency" because of his extensive institutional knowledge of the organization (he was the first career Defense Agency staffer to be promoted to vice minister), sat on the council as did Admiral Makoto Sakuma, retired Chairman of the Joint Defense Council. This was indeed the first time a retired uniformed member of Japan's armed services sat on a defense-related council. Former Ambassador to the US Yoshio Okawara, several notable professors, and a number of chairmen at well-known Japanese companies were also named to the council. And in a further sign that the council had official backing of the government, it was also announced that the council would receive administrative support from the Cabinet Security Affairs Office.[732]

The council held its inaugural meeting on February 28, 1994 and met throughout the spring and summer as tensions on the Korean peninsula intensified significantly. In August 1994, the council submitted to the Hosokawa Cabinet perhaps the most forward-leaning policy documents for Japan's national security structure since the end of World War II, titled "The Modality of the Security and Defense Capability of Japan: Outlook for the 21st Century." It was informally called the "Higuchi Report" after the chairman, Hirotaro Higuchi. The Higuchi Report advocated for a comprehensive security strategy based on three areas of emphasis: multilateral cooperation, the US-Japan alliance, and a modern and efficient military. The Report defined the threats that Japan would increasingly face in the 1990s and beyond. Japan might experience "violation of its territorial airspace, limited missile attack, illegal occupation of a part of the country, terrorist acts, and influence of armed refugees." And it presciently emphasized the need for the Government of Japan to respond more effectively to crises, as Japan would face significant difficulties responding to crises in the coming years.[733] The Higuchi Report was ahead of its time, however.

Highlighting the continuing tensions in northeast Asia at the time, the United States had completed its own review of its military posture in Asia that emphasized its bilateral security ties in the region. Assistant Secretary of Defense for International Affairs Joseph Nye directed the drafting of the "East Asia Strategy Report," what became called the "Nye Report." As Assistant Secretary Nye himself explained at a news conference on February 27, 1995, the East Asia Strategy Report was written with input from the US military commands in Asia, the State Department, the National Security Council, and was edited by staff in the Department of Defense's International Security Affairs office. The report superseded recommendations to cut US troop strength in the region in prior East Asia reports of 1990 and 1992, and thus reaffirmed the US "commitment to maintain a stable forward presence in the region at the existing level of about 100,000 troops for the foreseeable future." In a subtle reference to an increasingly fashionable view of multilateral cooperation as discussed in the previous year's Higuchi Report, the Report emphasized: "The strategy is not based on multilateralism, the strategy is based on reaffirmation of the bilateral alliances we have: Japan, Australia, South Korea." In contrast with Europe, where NATO formed the core multilateral security organization, Asia ended the Cold War without any similar security apparatus. The United States supported the creation of multilateral institutions, but it wanted multilateralism to form "around this core of the bilateral relationships." "[T]he core of the strategy is first and foremost to maintain the bilateral security alliances, then to add on—where possible—multilateral fora to increase confidence and transparency in the region," the Report declared.[734] Thus while the Higuchi report placed multilateral cooperation ahead of its bilateral alliance with the United States, the United States emphasized its bilateral relationships with its partners in Asia, including Japan, almost to the exclusion of multilateral cooperation as popularly conceived at the time. The two governments then entered intense consultations that resulted in the Hashimoto-Clinton Summit and the April 17, 1996 "Japan-US Joint Declaration on Security."

The Nye report was completed as Japan entered the final deliberative stage on the revision of its NDPO. Members of Japan's highest-level defense policy board, the Security Council of Japan, held a series of 10 meetings from June 1995 to discuss the revision. The Murayama Cabinet approved the revised National Defense Program Outline on November 28, 1995, and two weeks later it passed the Mid-Term Defense Buildup Plan. Because the NDPO provided an outline of SDF troop strength and capabilities planned for the next 10 years, there was a tacit understanding that the NDPO would be reviewed again by 2005.

Given events in and around Japan as the NDPO was finalized in the summer and fall of 1995, the new NDPO took into account the changed international security environment with the demise of the Soviet Union as well as nascent issues of large-scale disasters and domestic terrorism as a result of the Kobe earthquake and Aum Shinrikyo attacks early that year. The 1995 NDPO noted decreased international tensions, declaring: "With the end of the Cold War, which led to the demise...of military confrontation between East and West backed by overwhelming military capabilities, the possibility of a global armed conflict has become remote in today's international community." Moreover, the NDPO de-emphasized what had been a major threat to Japan until the early 1990s: "[T]he collapse of the Soviet Union has brought about a reduction of the military force levels and changes in the military posture in Far East Russia." With the Soviet threat greatly diminished, the NDPO hinted at the possible future challenges of China without naming it: "[M]any countries in the region are expanding or modernizing their military capabilities mainly against the background of their economic development." Moreover, "uncertainty and unpredictability" continued in northeast Asia "such as in the continued tensions on the Korean Peninsula," and "the possibility of a situation in this region, which could seriously affect the security of Japan, cannot be excluded."[735] The NDPO therefore suggested that a major national security threat to Japan—the Soviet Union—had diminished, while other possible national security challenges emerged on the horizon. It could only hint at subsequent threats, since the Peru hostage crisis, North Korean intrusion and kidnapping issues, regional missile tests, intensifying territorial and maritime disputes, and nuclear tests were yet to occur.

The 1995 NDPO emphasized defense capabilities in three major areas: "national defense," e.g., the prevention of indirect or direct aggression against Japan; "response to large-scale disasters and various other situations" including acts of terrorism "when needed"; and "contribution to the creation of a more stable security environment," such as participation in international peace cooperation activities and security dialogues, although this NDPO did not expressly note the dispatch of Japanese troops abroad. "The security arrangements with the United States," moreover, "are indispensable to Japan's security and will also continue to play a key role in achieving peace and stability in the surrounding region of Japan and establishing a more stable security environment," according to the NDPO. Yet despite the post-Cold War uncertainty and Japan's emerging support to operations in "the surrounding region," the NDPO pointed to some force reductions: "This review needs to reflect such factors as...a decreasing proportion of young people and increasingly severe economic and fiscal conditions." The NDPO called for restructuring "Japan's defense capability...both in scale and functions by streamlining, making it more efficient and compact," and at the same time "enhancing necessary functions and making qualitative improvements to be able to respond effectively to a variety of situations and simultaneously ensure the appropriate flexibility to deal smoothly with the development of the changing situations."

The 1995 NDPO cut some military forces while maintaining essentially the same structure as during the Cold War. The GSDF was forced to reduce the number of tanks and artillery pieces by a few hundred each to 900 pieces, while the ASDF maintained 400 combat aircraft including 300 jet fighters. Many of the MSDF units were similarly unchanged. There was a slight reduction of SDF personnel as well, but this was partially off-set by an increase in reserve personnel strength, a recognition of the increasing number of retirements from active duty in the 1990s and a dearth of young people willing to serve in the military.

In an official statement issued the same day the NDPO was released, the Chief Cabinet Secretary highlighted both the dramatic changes in the international security environment as well as

Japan's essentially unchanged defense structure. "Almost 20 years after the formulation of the National Defense Program Outline, the international situation has greatly changed" with the "end of the Cold War," and "[e]xpectations for the role of the Self-Defense Forces have also expanded from the principal mission of defending Japan to coping with large-scale disasters and other situations, and contributing to building a more stable security environment." Yet, despite these expanded roles, "Japan will essentially continue to adhere to the existing concept of a basic and standard defense capability."[736] Peppered with words like "rationalization," "compactness" and "qualitative improvements," the NDPO in reality suggested a slight decrease in capabilities during an era of "decreasing proportion of young people" and "increasingly severe economic and fiscal situations." Thus, with the North Korean nuclear issue seemingly solved and other national security threats and regional tensions yet to emerge, by the end of 1995 Tokyo planned a gradual decrease in its Cold War military force structure while modernizing communications networks and deployability in and around Japan.

The revised National Defense Program Outline was essentially a transitional defense policy document bridging Japan's Cold War defense posture with post-Cold War national defense capabilities. While defense policymakers understood that Japan had entered a new era of devolved security threats, these threats were still minor in number and scale. They were not of sufficient magnitude that created wide public support for whole-sale change of Japan's defense capabilities. The latent threat from North Korea was a possible exception, but the creation of KEDO and a new safeguards regime seemed to have averted a nuclear North Korea. The Aum Shinrikyo attacks were domestic in nature and thus a police matter, affecting the Self-Defense Forces only tangentially. The attacks and subsequent hijacking did demonstrate, however, that catastrophic terrorism was a real security challenge even for pacifist Japan. And in a land of earchquakes, tsunamis, and volcanos, the SDF showed that it could play a major role in disaster response after the January 1995 Kobe earthquake, and this disaster-response role was highlighted in both the 1976 and 1995 NDPOs.

However, even as the Defense Agency and Self Defense Forces began to adjust their force structures in accordance with the 1995 NDPO, analysts increasingly pointed to a gradually expanding array of asymmetric threats to Japan in the post-Cold War environment. Former chairman of the Joint Staff Council Akihiko Ushiba criticized the newly revised NDPO, saying: "I think that threats from missile attacks and the seizure of sea lanes are significant possibilities." He did not offer any creative solutions, however, and instead called for a return to the Japanese Navy's heyday of operating aircraft carriers: "[I]t is imperative for us to have small carriers in view of our sea-lane defense."[737] After North Korean submarines were caught in South Korean waters attempting to infiltrate special operations forces and after its 1998 missile launch over Japan, retired GSDF General Toshiyuki Shikata suggested that "Japan should gradually shift its defense system so that the present capability is developed into one that can respond to new kinds of threats."[738] He highlighted North Korea's employment of "ballistic missiles so as to impose a psychological threat" and the resorting "to terrorism through the use of special forces." Even as piecemeal changes were made to Japan's operational capabilities and legal structure, Japan prepared for yet another review of the NDPO following a series of security challenges in the late 1990s and early 2000s.

2001-2004 Review

When Prime Minister Junichiro Koizumi took office by mid-2001, Japan's post-Cold War security environment had changed significantly. Since the 1995 NDPO review, Japan had experienced missile tests near its islands bordering Taiwan in 1996, a prolonged hostage crisis at the Japanese Ambassador's Lima residence in 1997, further missile and nuclear tests in 1998, and a suspicious ship incident near its shores in 1999 that had followed several North Korean attempts to infiltrate special operations forces into South Korea in 1996 and 1998. The 1995 NDPO revision was, moreover, widely perceived as an interim measure and was therefore open to further review. Immediately after the Defense Agency and the LDP announced preparations for a future review in the fall of 2001, however, they experienced added urgency following the 9.11 terrorist and subsequent anthrax attacks in the US followed shortly by yet another suspicious boat incident. The violent end to this incident and the evidence collected later proving North Korea's involvement starkly demonstrated the continuing activities of North Korea around Japan's shores.

Following Koizumi's assumption of the premiership in April 2001, the LDP established a "Subcommittee to Examine Self Defense Policy" at the end of May. The new subcommittee, under the direction of the former Defense Agency Parliamentary Vice-Minister Yasukazu Hamada, was initially established to review the Constitutional interpretation that Japan was not allowed to engage in collective security and to examine the possible upgrade of the Defense Agency to Ministry status, both of which would be contentious issues in the coming years.[739] Then in early August, the *Nihon Keizai Shimbun* reported that the Defense Agency was preparing "a substantial revision of the current NDPO by 2003, with a view to shifting the Self-Defense Forces' main presence to the southern regions of Japan." The paper said the DA would review policy ahead of a possible decision to join a US missile defense program, streamline the command system, and "sharply" enhance the SDF's transport capabilities "to speedily dispatch forces to the southern areas" if necessary.[740] In line with this, the Defense Agency announced plans to establish a council in early September 2001 under newly appointed Director General Gen Nakatani to reformulate the NDPO, although according to *Asahi Shimbun* the new NDPO would not be completed until 2005. Echoing the *Nihon Keizai Shimbun* report, *Asahi* also noted that the DA planned to "shift priority...from large scale military invasions to [defending against] guerrilla incursions, sea intrusions, nuclear accidents and natural disasters" as well as to "reassign SDF units and reinforce the SDF's presence in Okinawa and the southern areas where Chinese navy vessels...have appeared."[741]

As reports of a possible NDPO review circulated, *Asagumo*, a weekly paper devoted to defense issues, outlined what many in Japanese defense circles were thinking: "Since the [1995] revision...there have been incidents such as North Korea launching a missile over Japan and spy ships found invading the territorial waters of Japan...In the meantime, China has continued to raise its military spending by more than 10 percent a year for the past 13 years in a row, and the Chinese military's brisk activities have become visible not only in the Taiwan Strait but also in the waters surrounding Japan."[742] The dramatic change in emphasis in the lead-up to the new review from the northern areas surrounding Japan to the southwestern areas, missile defense, and terrorism and guerrilla warfare was a direct result of the security incidents taking place since the 1995 NDPO.

Additionally, the September 11, 2001 terrorist attacks on the World Trade Center and the Pentagon, followed by the anthrax attacks in the fall of 2001, further highlighted the potential lethality of asymmetric threats such as terrorism in the world at large. That very day, on September 11, Nakatani told reporters during an official visit to Indonesia (before the attacks had taken place) that the Defense Agency panel might hold its first meeting on

NDPO review as early as September 18. Indicating that this review would be more comprehensive than the previous one in 1995, he told reporters: "We need to go back to the drawing board and hold discussions from scratch...Following the end of the Cold War, we need to think about the structure for the next 50 years."[743] The first meeting was delayed only a few days following the 9.11 attacks and was held at the Defense Agency headquarters on September 21. Nakatani re-emphasized the new threat paradigm: "Given the current situation caused by new types of threats, we must review our defense capability that will provide us with [adequate] readiness."[744]

Ineed, in the immediate wake of the 9.11 attacks, Japanese policymakers began to review a greater range of defense capabilities. Taku Yamasaki, Secretary General of the Liberal Democratic Party, asserted in early October that because of 9.11 Japan "should consider establishing special forces" terrorism response capabilities.[745] Diet members in November established two supra-partisan "policy study groups" to examine Japan's national security. "The catalyst" of these various study groups at the DA, the Diet, and later in the LDP, according to *Asahi Shimbun*'s sober commentator Yoichi Funabashi, was "the September 11 terror shock." Japan had to take greater responsibility to promote stability in the world, according to Funabashi: "Japan should work together with the international community to promote social stabilization, economic development, and nation building in disputed regions that bring about such threats as ethnic cleansing, terrorism, drugs, refugee exoduses, and AIDS...[C]ollective defense and preventive diplomacy need to be the two pillars of national security and human security," he concluded.[746]

The discovery and subsequent sinking of the *Changyu* on December 21-22, 2001, highlighted Japan's vulnerability to state-sponsored terrorism just three months after the 9.11 and anthrax attacks. It was the second time in a little over two years that Japan had discovered suspicious vessels in waters near the archipelago. Thus the DA group conducting a preliminarily review of defense recommendations added terrorism to the top of a list of six priority areas for a new NDPO at its January 2002 meeting. The new NDPO would promote: 1) measures to deal with large-scale terrorism, guerrilla attacks and cyberterrorism; 2) measures to strengthen intelligence gathering and analysis; 3) international cooperation in peacekeeping operations; 4) measures related to the "Revolution in Military Affairs"; 5) integrated operations of the Ground, Maritime, and Air Self-Defense Forces; and 6) further strengthening of the Japan-US alliance.[747] Nakatani, chairing the group, declared when the meeting convened on January 18: "This is an opportune time for us to discuss the role of defense capabilities from a clean slate."[748] With national security-related incidents occurring one after another in and around Japan, it was thought that the Japanese public would be more supportive of a new and more robust NDPO.

Paralleling the DA effort, the LDP officially conducted its own internal review of the NDPO in early 2002. The ruling party's special subcommittee in its Defense Division policy research group held more than 20 sessions to discuss possible new defense postures. The group then conducted on-site visits at GSDF, MSDF, and ASDF installations, followed by five sessions with former Defense Agency directors general. This process took two years and culminated in the Defense Division's March 29, 2004 document outlining LDP proposals for the future National Defense Program Outline. Following the review, Hiroshi Imazu, head of the LDP's Defense Division, spoke of new security challenges in an interview with *Kankai*, a Japanese political affairs journal: "When the constitution was compiled and when the SDF was established, we did not foresee that individuals would hijack airplanes and fly them into buildings, resulting in the death of more than 4,000 people [sic]. The times have definitely changed, and the nature of defense has evolved from dedicated defense [of Japan] to international contributions, measures to deal with terrorism...and guerillas, and to new activities in response to changing times."[749]

In spring 2002, the Defense Agency released advanced drafts to media outlets of its *Defense of Japan 2002* (probably to gauge public reaction to potentially controversial sections) scheduled for official publication in June 2002. The draft *Defense of Japan* had a number of new DA-sponsored policy initiatives in addition to reporting on the activities of Nakatani's internal Council to Examine the Proper Approach to Defense Capability, the precursor of the official government review of the National Defense Program Outline. The draft *Defense of Japan* also called for the creation of a Defense Ministry: "It is important to establish a ministry as an administrative organization in charge of national defense, as the importance of defense is increasing in national politics... As the Defense Agency, we hope for the enactment of a law on establishing a defense ministry at an early date."[750] Moreover, the Defense Agency in April 2002 began discussions of drastically reforming the geographic commands of the three forces. As initially envisioned, the five or six regional groups under separate Ground, Maritime, and Air SDF commands would be abolished and replaced by regional commands that control all the forces in that region. Regional defense bureaus would also be created to strengthen coordination with local governments, a key lesson of the 1995 Great Hanshin Earthquake.[751] This far-reaching plan was not enacted, although a plan to improve joint operations by giving greater Joint Staff Council authority over the staff offices of the individual services, which was discussed at the same time from April 2002, was ultimately enacted in early 2006.

Yet, despite the internal DA and LDP reviews that began in early 2002, an official government review of the NDPO had yet to be announced. The dates reported in the press for possible completion of a final review ranged from the end of 2003 to as late as the end of 2005. Given events of 2001 both in the United States and in Japan, the process was entirely too slow for *Nihon Keizai Shimbun* by summer 2002: "Considering that the simultaneous terrorist attacks on the United States occurred in September 2001, if the next NDPO were to be completed in December 2003, it would have taken less time than the current NDPO [completed in November 1995]. However, that still means that it would take two more years to complete the new NDPO. Why does it take so much time?" The daily also called into question Japan's expensive and unwieldy weapons systems, which was an increasing topic of discussion: "[T]he GSDF possesses the Type-90 Tank, which is said to be the most expensive tank in the world, and the ASDF possesses the F-2 support fighter, which is plagued by malfunctions despite its being the world's most expensive fighter aircraft. These weapons were acquired in preparation for possible invasion of Hokkaido by Soviet troops." Yet, new threats require different weapons systems, and "calls favoring missile defense systems will likely gain strength," the paper declared.[752] The business daily called into question whether the coming revision would be soon enough or radical enough to truly provide for Japan's national security needs.

Missile defense did indeed become a topic of active debate in late 2002, as the *Nihon Keizai Shimbun* and other papers had predicted. The United States by this time had withdrawn from the bilateral Anti-Ballistic Missile (ABM) Treaty with Russia and upgraded the Ballistic Missile Defense Organization to the Missile Defense Agency. The US was also preparing to deploy its first anti-missile missiles at a base in Alaska by January 2004. Japan, for its part, had watched helplessly as North Korea fired missiles towards its shores and over the country on multiple occasions in the 1990s, and as China conducted multiple tests as a political statement aimed at Taiwan. Japan's possible participation with the United States in building missile defense systems became a matter of open discussion in early December, when DA Director General Shigeru Ishiba declared following a meeting with Secretary of Defense Rumsfeld that he would "consider the missile defense issue with a view of future development and deployment," while noting that such a decision "needs approval of the Japanese government."[753] Following some criticism that Ishiba had overstepped his political authority, Ishiba later backtracked, telling reporters: "I only said that we have reached a phase where we need to debate and judge issues such as whether it is an appropriate system for Japan, taking into consideration the costs and legal issues involved." An "official close to Prime Minister Koizumi" also backtracked, declaring that "there has been no such debate as described by Ishiba."[754]

Such political obfuscations would not continue for long, however. The DA announced plans weeks later—during the year-end holidays—to "accelerate" study of missile defense "for practical use." One unnamed official was quoted as saying: "It has finally become possible to promote detailed studies on the legal aspects of and the costs for the missile defense system."[755] The US missile defense systems then under development consisted of a ground-based midcourse missile defense program, the Sea-based midcourse Missile Defense (SMD) system based on Aegis destroyers and the Patriot Advanced Capability PAC-3 system for point defense. Tokyo at this time was discussing the deployment of the SMD system and PAC-3s in addition to enhancing its ground-based and Aegis radars to better track missile launches: the SMD system would intercept short- and medium-range ballistic missiles at sea, while the PAC-3s would intercept any remaining missiles targeting major metropolitan areas or important bases in Japan.[756] The SMD system based on Japan's Aegis destroyers would be the "pillar of Japan's missile defense," according to Kyodo.[757]

On April 5, 2003, the DA began an official review of its missile defense policy and budgets ahead of possible incorporation of missile defense, and by the end of May unnamed government sources began to assert that Tokyo had indeed decided to proceed with the introduction of missile defense systems. The accelerated review had added urgency because Pyongyang reportedly claimed in talks with US diplomats in April that it possessed a "nuclear arsenal," in the words of one unnamed senior Japanese diplomat.[758] While the threat was unsubstantiated because North Korea had yet to test a nuclear device—Pyongyang's claim was more than likely a ploy to prevent Washington from undertaking military action against North Korea as it was then undertaking against Iraq—Tokyo could not take a chance that Pyongyang was bluffing (North Korea tested a nuclear device three years later). The government added as much as ¥100 billion in the JFY2004 budget to begin the introduction of missile defense. The multiyear effort would cost at a minimum ¥500 billion, with ¥200 billion allocated for the PAC-3s and ¥180 billion for Aegis and other radar upgrades. The cost was expected to reach ¥1 trillion—around $10 billion—as it was further expanded.[759] It would cost a total of ¥500 billion just to upgrade all four Aegis destroyers over a four-year timeframe, with the first Aegis destroyer ready by JFY2006 at the earliest.[760] Funding was added to the budget by the end of the summer, but a formal government decision on introducing missile defense would be required along with the approval of the budget at the end of the year to proceed.[761]

That approval came on December 19, 2003, when the Koizumi Cabinet approved a "Cabinet Decision" titled "On the Introduction of Ballistic Missile System and Other Measures."

The Cabinet also passed the FY2004 budget, which included funding for the program. The defense budget in fact listed multiple budgetary areas to meet new challenges facing Japan, including missile defense, defense against "guerrilla" incursions, the implementation of a joint operations capability (for greater mobility in defending remote islands), a renewed emphasis on defense R&D, and the improvement of its IT infrastructure.[762] Given the continuing belligerent claims from North Korea, opposition Democratic Party of Japan members supported missile defense as well. The *Nihon Keizai Shimbun* in fact highlighted "nearly unanimous" support: "The government is…changing past defense policies because of new threats related to the terrorist attacks on the United States and the lack of transparency in North Korea. During the Cold War, public opinion in Japan was split on whether or not the Soviet Union posed a threat, but opinion is nearly unanimous regarding these new threats."[763] And in an understated tone, Japan's largest daily *Yomiuri* noted: "As there are no effective countermeasures, it is reasonable for Japan to introduce a defense system to intercept such missiles."[764] There were, of course, some dissenting voices, reflected for example in the pacifist *Mainichi Shimbun*, which called on Japan to solve specific "issues" such as the technical feasibility of MD, operational issues, and impact on neighboring countries ahead of deployment.[765] But these were operational and procedural issues, indicating that dissenting voices did not outright oppose missile defense, just the rush to deploy an untested and expensive technology.

Moreover, the cabinet approved a review of the National Defense Program Outline—by this time, the internal DA and LDP reviews were nearing completion. Detailed in the Cabinet Decision on missile defense, the decision announced a "Direction for Reviewing Defense Capabilities," with an outline of the NDPO to be completed by the end of 2004, just one year later. Because of the significant preparation within the DA and LDP since 2001 and 2002 respectively—largely out of the public eye—the official review of Japan's national defense capabilities progressed relatively quickly. On March 29, 2004, the LDP Defense Policy Studies subcommittee briefed their recommendations to Prime Minister Koizumi (who was no doubt already aware of the subcommittee's discussions) and the following day posted the recommendations on the LDP website. According to the subcommittee:

> "In the new security environment, two distinct types of threats coexist. On the one hand, there are conventional, traditional threats and on the other, there are what can be called the 21st century-type threats. Cases in point for the former are the Iraq and North Korea issues, where the state plays a prominent role. In these cases, dictator states strive to possess such weapons as missiles and biological and chemical weapons and also present the world with the danger of proliferation. The 21st century-type threats, on the other hand, are those posed by elusive, non-state actors such as terrorist groups: these threats can transcend national borders with ease and may inflict catastrophic damage upon the states by the use of biological, chemical or, in the future, even nuclear weapons."

The group listed 15 recommendations, with amending Article 9 of the Constitution at the top of the list. Next came legalizing the ability to exercise the right of collective self-defense—aiding an ally, for example, if it were attacked. According full ministry status to the Defense Agency was third, followed by improving Japan's national crisis management regime. Other recommendations included the reorganization of the Defense Agency command structure for better decision-making and enhancing intelligence collection.[766] These types of expansive recommendations were beyond the scope of previous NDPOs, which focused more specifically on outlining specific force structures and troop numbers based on Japan's security environment, and they would require separate legislation to be realized.

After the LDP's Defense Division policy subcommittee outlined their recommendations, Koizumi established an advisory organ, the "Council on Security and Defense Capabilities," in April 2004. The council was made up of civilian leaders drawn from corporate and public sectors to include retired civil servants, all of whom specialized in national security affairs. Hiroshi Araki, a senior advisor at Tokyo Electric Power Co., chaired the council, and Fujio Cho, President of Toyota Motor Corporation, served as the deputy chairman. Other members included Teijiro Furukawa, the former deputy chief cabinet secretary, former SDF Joint Staff Council Chairman Tetsuya Nishimoto, former DA Administrative Vice Director General Ken Sato, and Shunji Yanai, former Japanese Ambassador to the United States. The four remaining members were drawn from academia. The group met for a total of 13 sessions, including an introductory session with remarks from Prime Minister Koizumi and three wrap-up sessions before the group presented its final report—nicknamed the Araki Report—to Koizumi on October 4 during its final session.

Titled "Vision for Future National Defense and Security Capabilities," the report, at 32 pages, was similar in length and scope to the 1994 Higuchi Report. The Araki Report highlighted the wide range of threats to Japan's national security: "Japan faces security problems unique to its location in East Asia." While "[t]he end of the Cold War has certainly reduced substantially the risk of a full-scale invasion...two nuclear powers [Russia and China]" continue to exist "in this region," as well as "one country that has not abandoned its ambition of developing nuclear weapons"—North Korea. "The problem of WMD development including North Korean nuclear weapons, and the development and deployment of ballistic missiles could represent a direct threat to Japan, and instability on the Korean Peninsula may yet become a major destabilizing factor affecting international relations in East Asia." Also, "the possibility of armed clashes across the Strait of Taiwan can not be ruled out." And citing the Aum Shinrikyo attacks and suspicious boat intrusions into Japanese waters, "it is obvious that the country faces threats from endogenous terrorist forces and criminal organizations" in addition to the "illicit entry into territorial waters of armed special-operations vessels." Finally, "protecting the life and wealth of Japanese nationals from major natural disasters" and from "disturbances abroad also comes under the rubric of security," according to the report.[767] Each of these points drew from specific national security crises Japan experienced over the previous decade.

The Araki Report also recognized, however, that due to Japan's extremely low birthrate and rapidly aging society—Japan's population officially began to shrink the following year—Tokyo was severely limited in shaping and modernizing its defense capabilities. To respond to these various scenarios, the Araki Report advocated a "Multi-Functional Flexible Defense Force" that can "perform many functions without enlarging the size of the force by learning lessons from the streamlining efforts of business enterprises, utilizing state-of-the-art information technology, overhauling the chain of command, and implementing educational, training, and other improvement programs."[768] "The pivotal requirement" of this force "is the ability to collect and analyze information," according to the report. "The level of the nation's intelligence capability is critical to meeting new threats, such as the threat of terrorism." Thus, the report advocated an improved intelligence capability to support a modernized and mobile—but necessarily limited—force structure: "a Multi-Functional Flexible Defense Force, equipped with sophisticated intelligence capabilities and highly networked weapons systems…should be put in place to deal with complex and diverse future threats."[769] Japan's revised defense strategy would echo many of the recommendations in the Araki Report.

Moreover, as the council met ahead of the NDPO revision, commentators increasingly highlighted the now-obvious changes in Japan's security environment and outlined possible force structures in response. Discussing this new era, the Japanese political journal *Foresight* noted that "[t]he nature of the security threat has changed, and focus has shifted from symmetrical nation-versus-nation situations to asymmetrical terrorism and guerrilla situations."[770] Kazuhiko Nakagawa, editorial board member of the economics magazine *Toyo Keizai* and supporter of stronger defense capabilities, called the 1995 NDPO incomplete: "In retrospect, the current outline, which was drawn up in response to the end of the Cold War, was unfinished. It discusses the issue of international contributions and terrorism, but its main policy focus centered on how to make the SDF more compact." Nakagawa pointed to basic defense capabilities he felt Japan should maintain, including mini-fleets with sea-based missile defense systems and mini-carriers to protect Japan's sea lanes and distant islands. He also advocated aerial refueling capabilities to respond flexibly to provocations: "[T]anker planes will be introduced gradually starting in fiscal 2006," and "if they are combined with fighter planes, attack planes, and aerial control planes, there will be enough elements for counterattack capabilities."[771]

Japan officially revised its defense posture a mere two months after the early October submission of the Araki Report. The new National Defense Program Guideline—the official English rendering for the NDPO was changed to NDPG, although the Japanese title remained the same—was approved by the Security Council and the Cabinet on December 10, 2004. This revised NDPG bluntly outlined potential threats to Japan, bluntly naming both North Korea and China. "North Korea is engaged in the development, deployment and proliferation of weapons of mass destruction and ballistic missiles, and it maintains a large number of special operations forces. Such military activities by North Korea constitute a major destabilizing factor to regional and international security," it declared. Further, "China, which has a major impact on regional security, continues to modernize its nuclear forces and missile capabilities as well as its naval and air forces. China is also expanding its area of operation at sea. We will have to remain attentive to its future actions."[772]

The NDPG also detailed Japan's strategic "vulnerabilities": "limited strategic depth; long coast lines and numerous small islands; a high population density; the concentration of population and industry in urban areas; and a large number of important facilities in coastal areas, in addition to frequent natural disasters due to Japan's geological and climactic conditions, and the security of sea lines of communication which are indispensable to the country's prosperity and growth." With these vulnerabilities in mind, the NDPG listed five priority defense capabilities necessary for the SDF: 1) defense against ballistic missiles; 2) defense against guerrillas and special operations forces; 3) defense against invasion of Japan's offshore islands; 4) patrol and surveillance in the sea and airspace surrounding Japan; and 5) response to large-scale and/or special-type (nuclear, biological, chemical, and radiological) disasters. (The Araki report also listed these issues as its top five priorities.) According to the NDPG, a "full-scale invasion" of the Japanese archipelago "is expected to remain modest in the foreseeable future."

The 2004 NDPG stressed an overt shift away from Japan's Cold War defense structure: "[W]e will modify our current defense force building concept that emphasized Cold War-type anti-tank warfare, anti-submarine warfare and anti-air warfare, and will significantly reduce the personnel and equipment earmarked for" defending against "a full-scale invasion." Echoing the Araki Report's Multi-Functional Flexible Defense Force concept, "Japan will develop multi-functional, flexible, and effective defense forces that are highly ready, mobile, adaptable and multi-purpose, and are equipped with state-of-the-art technologies and intelligence capabilities measuring up to the military-technological level of other major countries," the NDPG declared. But this transformation "cannot be accomplished in a short period of time" and "Japan will continue to maintain the most basic capabilities of its defense forces, while also taking into account developments in neighboring countries and making use of technological progress." Additionally, and in line with the Araki Report, the NDPG emphasized greater intelligence capabilities across the government: "[T]he Government will improve its ability to collect and analyze intelligence which serves as the basis of the Government's decision-making. The Self-Defense Forces, police, Japan Coast Guard and other relevant organizations will improve their close cooperation through increased intelligence sharing, joint exercises, and other activities, while appropriately sharing their roles, and improve their overall performances."[773]

The NDPG expressed Tokyo's desire to maintain an autonomous defense capability even as it continues its alliance with the United States: "Japan's defense forces are the ultimate guarantee of its national security, representing Japan's will and ability to repel any threat that might reach its shores...[G]iven the new security environment...future defense forces should be capable of effectively responding to new threats and diverse situations."

Not only would Japan's SDF prepare for possible security contingencies in and around Japan, they would also be deployed abroad with greater frequency: "Japan will, on its own initiative, actively participate in international peace cooperation activities as an integral part of its diplomatic efforts." But the NDPG certainly did not downplay the Japan-US alliance: "The Japan-US Security Arrangements are indispensable in ensuring Japan's security... the US military presence is critically important to peace and stability in the Asia-Pacific region, where unpredictability and uncertainty continue to persist."[774] Yet it was clear that Japan planned to take an increasingly active role in both providing for the defense of its homeland as well as assisting other countries during times of crises.

The 2004 NDPG made it readily apparent that Japan was beginning a major, long-term transformation of its military forces that Japanese policymakers could use increasingly as a policy tool. Defense Agency Director-General Yoshiro Ono underlined Tokyo's intention of becoming more proactive on national security issues: "From now on, we shall place more importance on our ability to effectively deal with threats instead of maintaining a policy of deterrence, as in the past."[775] Reflecting the rapidly changing security environment in the 21st century, the NDPG explicitly stated that it could be reviewed within as few as five years, by 2010: "In order to better adjust our defense policy to the changing security environment, we will review and, if necessary, revise the NDPG five years from now, in accordance with the security environment at the particular point of time."[776] The new NDPG recognized Japan needed to be prepared to adapt readily to further changes in its national security environment in the coming years.

Japan's budgeters also foresaw a change in major defense procurements. As the Cabinet approved the revised NDPG, Satsuki Katayama, the official in charge of the country's defense budget at the Ministry of Finance, described Japan's defense restructuring plans in the widely read journal *Chuo Koron*: "[W]e now have to respond to new threats, including the proliferation of weapons of mass destruction and ballistic missiles and international terrorism," and "therefore, our plan is to have precision-guided munitions and radars, including the BMD program, and improve our intelligence and communications capabilities." Moreover, "rapid-response units" will be established with increased "mobility so as to enable them to cover a wider area" than "conventional troops… attached to specific regions." These efforts were "in line with the Revolution in Military Affairs." In a sign of entrenched opposition in some parts of the uniformed forces, Katayama bemoaned that "the GSDF was extremely unwilling to undertake RMA-style innovation and reform" as the NDPG and the mid-term defense plan were being finalized, suggesting the service was deeply wedded to its traditional weapons systems. Nevertheless, "frontline equipment designed for the Cold War" such as tanks, artillery pieces, and anti-tank helicopters were "subject to restructuring."[777]

Despite some lingering parochialism in some parts of the GSDF, however, it was clear that Tokyo's defense policies and budgets were now aligning to provide for major response capabilities to asymmetric threats in the beginning of the 21st century. Tokyo had made the decision to proceed with the construction of missile defense systems and the development of more robust counter-terrorism and counter-guerrilla capabilities. GSDF light infantry units were preparing to deploy to Iraq—the service's first "boots on the ground" in a war zone since 1945—and within several years Japan would establish several rapid reaction units based partly on its experience deploying to Iraq. As Japan began to embrace the force structure necessary to actively engage perceived threats in the region and beyond, it required a more capable defense bureaucracy. Japan required a Defense Ministry.

Creating The Defense Ministry

The first attempt to raise the DA's status to a ministry came in 1964, when the Ikeda Cabinet approved the "Defense Ministry Establishment Bill." The Ikeda Cabinet opted not to submit the bill to the Diet, however, in recognition of the staunch opposition from the Japan Socialist Party.[778] The prospect of elevating the DA to a ministry was broached again when the Hashimoto Administration began to discuss a government-wide reorganization from 1996. A panel of LDP lawmakers publicly proposed elevation of the DA's status at a meeting in November 27, 1996. The panel happened to be chaired by Gen Nakatani, one of the few LDP lawmakers who graduated from Japan's National Defense Academy and would later serve as DA Director General. The Social Democratic Party opposed the idea, arguing that it would create distrust among Asian countries. The proposal was dropped due to a lack of SDP support, but the elevation of the Environment Agency to ministry status in 2001 established a precedent for the DA's possible elevation at a later date.

Shortly after the government reorganization, the ministry issue came up again when the LDP's small coalition partner New Conservative Party submitted the "Bill to Establish a Defense Ministry" to the Diet in June. The September 11 attacks in the United States caused debate in the Diet to shift to possible Japanese support of Operation Enduring Freedom in the fall of 2001. Debate on the Defense Ministry bill was thus postponed. Debate of the bill was again postponed in 2002 as lawmakers took up debate on three emergency legislation bills. Moreover, the LDP's other new coalition member, the New Komeito, was not at all eager to debate the bill, since the party had significant connections to and the backing of the pacifist Buddhist organization Soka Gakkai.

Following 18 months of inaction on the Defense Ministry bill, the ruling parties discussed the bill at a leadership conference in December 2002. Despite New Komeito's reluctance to support the bill, the policy chiefs declared the bill "a top priority after the emergency bills are enacted"—a reference to another series of bills to address legal deficiencies in providing for Japan's national security to be submitted in early 2003.[779] But with the US military actions in Iraq from March 2003, debate on the Defense Ministry bill was again postponed due to extended debate on legislation to support Iraqi reconstruction in the summer of 2003. This debate, moreover, came amid rumors that Prime Minister Koizumi would dissolve the lower house of the Diet and call a snap election, in which case the bill would become null and void. Months of political turmoil continued until the Diet was indeed dissolved and lower house elections took place in November 2003.

Yet, given the unique threat environment in northeast Asia, the DA's upgrade to Ministry status had been gaining grass-roots political support. The "Society to Support National Defense"—chaired by the LDP parliamentarian Taku Yamasaki—had reportedly collected 500,000 signatures in 1999 supporting the DA's elevation following the Taepodong missile launch. The signatures were presented to upper house parliamentarians, but to little effect. Undeterred, the Society pressed again following the submission of the Defense Ministry bill in June 2001.[780] In 2003, Fumio Yunoki, a representative of another support group, the "Association To Urge the Promotion of the Defense Agency to Ministry," presented a petition containing over 17,000 names urging the support of granting the DA ministry status to the upper house's 50 members of the "House of Councilors League To Promote the Establishment of the Defense Ministry." Moreover, more than 20 local assemblies by the summer of 2003 passed a resolution calling for a defense ministry, and the Kagoshima

Prefectural Assembly (with its string of islands stretching from the main island of Kyushu to Okinawa bordering the East China Sea) and Sasebo City Assembly (a major MSDF port near Nagasaki) passed similar resolutions by the end of the year.[781] While the resolutions were non-binding, they cited recent national security events such as the Taepodong launch in 1998 and the North Korean incursion incidents in 1999 and 2001. With this swelling grass roots support, the Defense Agency itself openly declared support for elevation to ministry status in the *2002 Defense of Japan*: "It is important to indicate, domestically and internationally, Japan's attitude to tackle the issues of national security and crisis management...As the DA, we hope for the enactment of a law on establishing a Defense Ministry at an early stage."[782]

Moreover, the Japan's largest defense industry association comprising 128 Japanese defense-related firms took the unusual step of advertising its support for granting ministry status in full-page ads in its monthly publication, an unprecedented show of political support as such ads normally did not appear in the journal. The ads declared members' "unanimous" support of "the Defense Agency's promotion to 'Ministry'," highlighting various threats to Japan such as proliferation and "suspicious vessels" around Japan.[783] This active lobbying was important as the defense arms of some of Japan's largest firms were members including Mitsubishi Heavy Industries, NEC, and Kawasaki Heavy Industries. The visible show of support for a Defense Ministry by major Japanese companies complemented the grass-roots initiatives and provided sustained momentum for the final passage of the bill three years later.

A new Defense Ministry bill was submitted following the late 2003 elections only to be shelved weeks later. Support remained strong among LDP parliamentarians, however, with Shinzo Abe, the LDP's Secretary General, declaring in the spring of 2004 that "our party pledged to upgrade the Defense Agency to a ministry, so we would like to start discussions at the Diet in one way or another."[784] Yet the bill continued to languish as other more politically pressing legislation was discussed, including the possible privatization of Japan's postal service, Prime Minister Koizumi's major policy goal during his administration. Many in his own party did not support the privatization of the Postal Service—it was a major supporter of and fundraiser for the LDP, and postal savings accounts served as an enormous source of over $3 trillion from which politicians borrowed to pay for large state-directed construction projects. Following failure to pass legislation to privatize the postal service—even some LDP parliamentarians voted against it—Koizumi again dissolved the lower house and held snap-elections on September 11, 2005. Voters were impressed with Koizumi's resolve and gave him a resounding victory: the LDP and the New Komeito took a combined 327 seats in the election. With his mandate secured, the postal privatization bills sailed through the Diet a month later. But following passage of this major piece of legislation, Koizumi seemingly became disinterested in major legislation through the end of his tenure in the summer of 2006, and the Defense Ministry bill again languished during the last Diet session that spring.

North Korean provocations again becamse a catalyst for change in Japan's national security policy when it test-launched seven short- and medium-range missiles in early July, and in October, it tested a low-yield nuclear device. The bill was again submitted to the Diet in the fall of 2006, and with the LDP firmly in control of the Diet, it passed the lower house in late November and the upper house on December 15, the final day of the regular Diet session. The Defense Agency would become a Defense Ministry on January 9, 2007.[785] Perhaps because the bill had been submitted so often to the Diet over the previous five years—and perhaps because North Korea's actions provided clear justification—the final passage into law garnered relatively little reaction. The significance of the bill had already been debated in public since the late 1990s, and as supporters of the bill noted, Japan was the only major country in the developed world *without* a ministry-level defense organization. In the eyes of supporters, Japan was merely becoming a "normal" country.

The new status as a ministry would serve a number of purposes. First, ministry status legitimates national security as a prime policy and budgetary issue for Tokyo. The new Defense Ministry has equal bureaucratic rank with the Ministry of Foreign Affairs, MITI, the Ministry of Finance, and other ministries. The Defense Ministry also gained control over its own budgets. As an agency, it had to go through the Finance Ministry to request a budget before being approved by the cabinet. As a ministry, it can submit its budget directly to the cabinet. Defense Ministry budgets could also increase, if it follows the example of the Environment Ministry. In its budget request for JFY2000, the final year as an Agency, the Environment Agency requested just under ¥100 billion, plus approximately ¥28 billion as part of that year's special supplemental budget.[786] Seven years later, in its budget request for JFY2007, the Environment Ministry requested more than twice that amount—¥264.4 billion.[787] Whether the Japanese government and politicians can fund increases in defense budgets with a shrinking population—and thus a shrinking tax base—is a separate issue dealt with in a later chapter. But a Defense Ministry has the same bureaucratic clout as other ministries in lobbying for budgets.

Perhaps the most important aspect of the upgrade is in the Defense Ministry's ability to assist in operationalizing aspects of Japan's foreign policy, as dispatches abroad became a primary role of the Self-Defense Forces according to the legislation. The

Defense Ministry can serve a pseudo-diplomatic role as it oversees the dispatch of Japanese troops abroad for UN humanitarian missions, even as SDF units gain important experience in deploying beyond Japanese shores. Defense Ministry assets will be called upon, for example, to evacuate Japanese citizens from areas of strife, as happened in Indonesia in May 1998. And as the Korean peninsula remains divided, the Defense Ministry will take an increasingly visible role in contingency planning to evacuate Japanese citizens from the area and to manage the influx of refugees if necessary, a stark contrast to Defense Agency quiet behind-the-scenes contingency planning in 1993-1994. Also enshrined in the legislation was SDF assistance to US forces in times of emergency. As the Self-Defense Forces increasingly train alongside its American counterparts, an increasingly confident Defense Ministry will seek to play a greater role in the bilateral defense relationship, in which the Defense Agency had traditionally played a junior role due in no small part to its lesser organizational status in the Japanese government. Moreover, the Ministry of Foreign Affairs will begin to cede some its diplomatic functions abroad, as the Defense Ministry participates in UN functions and as attachés in Japanese Embassies abroad become increasingly independent, a situation discussed more fully in a later chapter.

• • •

The national security events of the 1990s and especially early 2000s provided the impetus for Japan's gradual improvements in its national security policymaking and crisis response structures. Policymakers drew lessons from each national security event that in turn informed subsequent reforms. The 1993-1994 Korean nuclear crisis revealed a government structure incapable of truly planning for a national security event off Japan's own shores, while the 1995 earthquake and subsequent terrorist attacks demonstrated to the public that the government was seemingly unprepared to respond to the needs of its citizens in a time of crisis. The 1996-1997 hostage crisis caused the government to speed some of those reforms, and the reforms were tested early during an evacuation of Japanese citizens from Indonesia in 1998. The multiple suspicious vessel incidents on the heels of special operations forces intrusions into South Korea and the 9.11 attacks in the United States further demonstrated the danger of guerrilla warfare and state-sponsored terrorism. Other events such as North Korea's unannounced missile tests, its declaration in 2003 that it was a nuclear power, and China's yearly double-digit growth in military spending further confirmed that the Asia-Pacific region remained remarkably insecure. It would indeed have been irresponsible for Tokyo to ignore these obvious threats to its own citizens and to its sovereignty as a nation. Given all that occurred in the 1990s and 2000s, then, the Japanese government had no choice but to modernize its national security and crisis response structure.

Similarly, with the national security events of the 1990s and 2000s in mind, Japan's uniformed services have gradually modernized their force structure as well to better respond to these multifaceted challenges. These modernization efforts are detailed in the next chapter.

4) Towards Jointness: Building a More Mobile Defense Force

In early February 1997, over two-dozen illegal immigrants were discovered and arrested in a three-day period on several islands in Kagoshima Prefecture in south-western Japan. The largest number of immigrants—twenty—was discovered on Shimokoshiki-jima, one of Kyushu's thousands of islands along the East China Sea.[788] Local authorities were concerned that more illegal immigrants had entered undetected, and police, fire fighters, and the Japan Coast Guard began a search for others in the region.

Shimokoshiki was no ordinary island, as it happened to host a major ASDF radar installation that monitored for possible air incursions into Japan's southwestern air space. Given the growing concern that foreign agents could infiltrate Japan—the South Korean military had just caught over two dozen North Korean special operators near Korean bases months earlier—Shimokoshiki island, with its major radar installation, would certainly be a target.

Given the sensitive military installation on the island, local officials conducted a thorough search. Hundreds of fire fighters divided into ten groups to search the beaches and roads for any signs of additional immigrants, and in the afternoon an additional 30 ASDF personnel joined the search. The technical legality of the search was immediately questioned, however, as SDF personnel could only be "mobilized" upon the order of the prime minister or following a request from the prefectural governor, neither of which had occurred. A local ASDF official defended the action, linking it with other training in the area: "We conducted military drills outside the area while keeping the search in mind and operating apart from police."[789] Defense Agency Director General Kyuma defended the action more directly, asserting he did not think it was "inappropriate."[790] Japan was already on edge. The discovery of the illegal immigrants occurred less than five months after a North Korean *Sang-o* "Shark" submarine was discovered grounded near Kangnung city in South Korea in late September 1996, and 25 commandos were captured or killed during an intensive two-month search in the region. The Defense Agency thus took a stronger stance than it might have in previous years, as it was indeed becoming more vocal regarding the proliferating national security threats facing the country in general.

The major daily *Yomiuri Shimbun* would later highlight the Shimokoshiki island incident as illustrating how exposed the country was to possible infiltration: With some 2,522 remote islands in the Kyushu area—only 191 of which are inhabited—the geography of southwestern Japan is markedly different from that in Hokkaido, requiring a mix of light forces capable of traveling long distances by sea or by air, the paper noted. "Japan should always be prepared for the possibility of spies or terrorists approaching by sea and landing on remote islands with the aim of launching guerrilla warfare in the nation's main islands," it opined.[791]

By the late 1990s, Japan's security environment had clearly changed. The threat of an invasion force landing in northern and central Japan receded, while terrorism and guerrilla warfare threats intensified. The DA began to highlight the threat of terrorism in its annual publication *Defense of Japan* in 1998, and it further emphasized the threat from foreign "guerrillas" and "special operations forces" in addition to terrorism from 2000. The potential use of isolated islands as staging grounds for operations in Japan—as well as outright seizure—similarly concerned the DA.

The DA institutionalized its strategic shift away from the threat of a conventional invasion in the 2003 *Defense of Japan*, when it asserted for the first time that "in the near future, the possibility of a landing invasion of Japan is thought to be low."[792] This strategic assessment was further codified in the 2004 NDPG. By this time, the DA had begun a major effort to improve its defenses against more probable threats such as guerrilla incursions and outright seizure of remote islands in its southwestern territories by creating highly mobile forces operating jointly in the region. The official recognition from 2003 of the improbability of a full military invasion of Japan's main islands represented an important shift in Tokyo's publicly declared threat perception that allowed it to shift scarce resources from maintaining heavy mechanized and tank units in central and northern Japan to developing and maintaining lighter and more mobile units capable of responding quickly to any of a variety of threats along the archipelago.

Based on this new threat perception and its island geography, Japan at the dawn of the 21st century began to develop modern rapid-reaction forces capable of providing what Tokyo has dubbed "defense of remote islands" or *ritō bōei*, and "emphasis on the southwestern region" or *nansei hōmen jūshi*. The Ground Self-Defense Force has established light and mobile forces capable of operating in forested and mountainous island geographies, while the Maritime Self-Defense Force has upgraded its so-called "8-8" fleets into mini-task forces capable of transporting and landing ground units to defend or retake distant islands in response to hostile incursions. The MSDF and the Japan Coast Guard, moreover, have built compact pursuit boats capable of intercepting high-speed vessels that might attempt to insert clandestine agents or other special operations forces onto Japanese islands. And Japan's Air Self-Defense Force capabilities have been enhanced to provide long-range patrol and transport capabilities with the introduction of aerial refuelers and basic precision strike capabilities. Each of the forces is increasingly capable of participating in joint operations, with the introduction of a more robust joint staff structure in 2005. While many challenges remain—Japan's services remain wedded to large and expensive domestic development of weapons programs that hinder funding of further modernization efforts, for example—Japan has introduced a force structure more capable of responding flexibly to asymmetric threats in the region and beyond.

The GSDF's Increasingly Mobile Forces

In the early 1990s, the GSDF had approximately 180,000 uniformed personnel divided among 12 divisions and 2 brigades, and its main responsibility under the slogan *hoppō jūshi* or "emphasizing the north" was to defend Hokkaido and northern Japan from a Soviet invasion. While GSDF units were stationed throughout Japan under five GSDF Armies—the Northern Army in Hokkaido, the Northeastern Army on northern Honshu island, the Eastern Army that included Tokyo, the Middle Army that covers the southern half of Honshu and Shikoku islands, and the Western Army on Kyushu and the Okinawan island chain—summer training exercises included a major deployment exercise from southern Japan to Hokkaido to practice reinforcement of the northern region ahead of any invasion attempt. The *hoppō jūshi* concept was tank-heavy, and the GSDF was authorized to procure a staggering 1,200 tanks, including the 38-ton T-74 tank and the more powerful 50-ton T-90 tank, and close to 1,000 artillery pieces such as the T-99 28-ton self-propelled howitzer and the 25-ton Multiple-Launch Rocket System.[793] Such equipment could only be fully employed on the relatively flat plains of Hokkaido, as the rest of Japan consisted of mountainous terrain, steep ravines, and thousands of islands.

Following the demise of the Soviet Union in the early 1990s, however, Japan no longer faced the threat of a full-scale conventional invasion and thus had little need for over 1,000 tanks and artillery pieces. In stark contrast to Japan, the United Kingdom, similarly an island nation with a comparable defense budget, maintained approximately 260 tanks. Indeed, Japan's T-90 tank and T-99 howitzer were too big and too heavy to operate anywhere beyond Hokkaido, and they were certainly useless against emerging threats such as ballistic missiles, terrorists' use of weapons of mass destruction, the clandestine insertion of special operations units on high-speed boats, or the defense of Japan's thousands of islands from seizure. While defense planners and analysts in Tokyo increasingly understood the new threat paradigm, high-ranking GSDF officers in the mid-1990s lobbied to keep the heavy equipment given the uncertainty of the immediate post-Cold War era and because of the significant budgets they controlled in purchasing and maintaining this major military equipment.

The 1995 NDPO revision pared these numbers slightly, but the GSDF successfully lobbied to maintain its basic force structure overall. Moreover, new threats to the archipelago were just beginning to emerge when the NDPO was revised, so Tokyo had less incentive to force change. Units were slowly reorganized as a result of the NDPO review, with the GSDF's 13 divisions cut to 9—eight infantry divisions and one tank division—and the number of lighter (and cheaper) mixed brigades were increased to six. The GSDF force structure continued to reflect Cold War perceptions, however, as it remained heavily reliant on tanks and self-propelled howitzers at over 900 pieces each. The GSDF continued to be organized into five Armies, though the number of armor divisions in Hokkaido was pared to one—the 7th Division. The GSDF suffered a 20% cut in personnel strength, dropping from 180,000 to 145,000 full-time uniformed personnel, plus a further 15,000 ready reservists. While this reduction partly reflected the demise of the Soviet Union and the increasingly difficult fiscal situation in Japan, it was also a de facto bureaucratic recognition of the difficult recruiting environment for the GSDF, which historically was able to fill only 80-90% of its authorized manpower. (In 1993, for example, the GSDF could only fill 81% of its slots, but after the revised NDPO by 2003 the GSDF was able to fill over 93% of its available positions.[794])

The term "defense of remote islands" or *ritō bōei* began to appear in the popular press a year after the NDPO was revised in 1995. On September 21, 1996, three days after the North Korean agents were discovered in South Korea, *Asahi Shimbun* reported that the GSDF would create light ranger-type units based in the Western Army's 8th Division to defend "remote islands" in Japan's southern and western region.[795] The announcement of the unit's creation indicated that despite having one of the largest defense budgets in the world at the time, Japan did not have a robust capability to defend remote islands. As former GSDF trainer Saburo Takai wrote in the November 1997 military studies journal *Gunji Kenkyu*, "even reconnaissance activity to warn of threats" near remote islands "is prohibitive," and therefore, "a large-scale operation to recapture Uotsuri Island"—one of the larger islands in the remote Senkaku island chain— "remains confined to the realm of military fiction."[796] Takai's comments foreshadowed events in 1999 and 2001, when the simple process of sending photos taken by P-3Cs of suspicious vessels in waters near remote Japanese islands took almost half a day to reach Tokyo, and these events in turn drove the decision to speed up the eventual establishment of the Western Army Infantry Regiment. The DA-affiliated Defense Institute, meanwhile, in early 1997 listed "remote island defense" as one of many capabilities that Japan should consider developing, in addition to improved intelligence, more robust sea-lane defenses (to include the possible introduction of nuclear-powered submarines), theater missile defense systems, and long-range transportation capabilities.[797]

Counter-guerrilla warfare and defense of remote islands became official policy with the publication of the Midterm Defense Buildup Plan (MDBP) at the end of 2000, spurred by North Korea's multiple incurssions into South Korea and Japan to that point. The plan included a section outlining the development of "capabilities to deal with special forms of attack" such as by "guerrillas" and other non-conventional troops: "The SDF shall activate, train, and equip special-purpose units in order to effectively deal with attacks by guerrillas and special operations units," the MDBP declared. Moreover, given the unconventional nature of this emerging threat, these units would rely on greater use of tactical military intelligence: "The SDF shall also activate units with high-level capabilities for initial actions and intelligence collection so that it can appropriately deal with invasions of remote islands."[798] Tokyo also budgeted ¥3.5 billion for counter-guerrilla training in the first year and planned to budget more funds throughout the five-year period. Counter-guerrilla warfare and defense of remote islands were thus closely linked in the eyes of Tokyo.

The popular press cited the multiple incursions as a primary reason for the emphasis on *ritō bōei*. *Yomiuri Shimbun*'s national security correspondent Hidemichi Katsumata pointed to the March 1999 North Korean ship incident as a primary reason for the creation of the new rapid reaction units, so that Japan "was now emphasizing [more] frequent operations in waters surrounding Japan" rather than preparing for an invasion from the north. Because "remote islands" represented 90% of the western and southern parts of Japan, these new forces required "new, lighter weapons and armored vehicles capable of being loaded onto helicopters to improve maneuverability," according to Katsumata.[799] Atsushi Nakamura, staff writer for the left-leaning *Mainichi Shimbun*, commented in late 2000 that "the need for counter-guerrilla and counter-terrorism policies in Japan were highlighted by events such as the DPRK's spy ship incursion in March 1999," but Nakamura also noted that "debate of the SDF's role" in providing for counter-guerrilla defense "has been poor," a recognition that the SDF was just at the beginning stages of its new emphasis on *ritō bōei* both operationally and legally.[800]

With new funds allocated for counter-guerrilla training and "defense of remote islands," 2001 became a watershed year as the GSDF began to actively examine the establishment of new light infantry organizational structures, tactics, and equipment. On March 28, 2001, the GSDF established the Ground Self Defense Force Research and Development (R&D) Institute at Camp Asaka near Tokyo. The R&D Institute consolidated the disparate GSDF research organizations in one organization, and it included a 350-person Development Test Group headquartered at the GSDF base in Fuji, one of the main GSDF training facilities in Japan.[801] The consolidated R&D Institute indicated that the GSDF was serious not only in considering new force structures and equipment, but also in testing them on a simulated battlefield.

At the same time, the GSDF began to slowly reorganize its core regimental structure into one of five types, depending on what role they played in the defense of Japan. The "Type A" regiment consisted of an anti-tank company, four infantry companies and a mortar company, with a core coastal defense mission. These regiments would be located mainly in the northern parts of Japan, as the 2nd Division in northern Hokkaido and the 10th Division in Ishikawa have three of these infantry regiments, while the 6th and 8th Divisions on northern Honshu and Kyushu respectively have a reserve regiment in addition to the three infantry regiments. The "Type B" infantry regiment is slightly lighter without the anti-tank company (one anti-tank company, however, remains at the Division level). Regiments in the 4th and the 9th Divisions in northern Kyushu and northern Honshu consist of these types of regiments. And indicative of the switch from tank and heavy-mechanized units, only the 7th Division's 11th Infantry Regiment in Hokkaido retained a mechanized designation as a "Type C" regiment with five mechanized infantry companies and one mechanized heavy mortar company—the 7th Division, based in Hokkaido, remained Japan's lone armored division.[802]

Of special note are the "Type D" and "Type E" infantry regiments: the Type D regiment is a special configuration of five infantry companies, and it is designed to defend the major metropolitan regions of Kanto (Tokyo) and Kansai (Osaka), while the Type E regiment is a specially designated light infantry regiment with three companies of 600 personnel for high mobility. Type D regiments assigned to the 1st Division (assigned to defend Tokyo) and the 3rd Division (assigned to defend the Kansai region) receive special urban warfare training to defend against guerrilla/special operations forces or terrorists discovered in densely populated areas. The 12th and 13th Brigades in southwestern Honshu contain Type-E infantry regiments, and the 5th and 11th Divisions in Hokkaido were restructured into Brigades containing Type E regiments as well.[803]

Indeed, the 1st Division is a prime example of the modernized force structure in the GSDF. Headquartered in Nerima Ward, Tokyo, the 1st Division is in charge of defending the Kanto region—the political and economic heart of Japan—and thus incorporated "Type D" regiments emphasizing counter-SOF/counter-terrorism in an urban environment. The division was rapidly reorganized into a light infantry division, reducing its tank complement from 44 to 30 and the number of howitzers from

60 to 20. The division in turn increased the number of lightly armored wheeled vehicles—the Japanese version of HMMWVs—to 300 and increased the size of its chemical corps unit attached to the division enabling response to three chemical or biological incidents at once. Shortly after the reorganization, elements of the 1st Division's 34th Infantry Regiment spent a month in the fall of 2002 training with the US Army's 25th Infantry Division in urban warfare tactics at Schofield Barracks in Hawaii.[804] The 1st Division (and its twin 3rd Division) is thus emphasizing a new role in counter-guerrilla operations in urban environments in addition to significantly improving CBRN response capabilities.

Urban Warfare and Counter-Guerrilla Training

While the GSDF had first built a facility to simulate urban combat and hostage rescue training in 1975 at its Fuji School in the Higashi Fuji training area, it merely consisted of a two-story building with few support facilities. By 1994, the GSDF had begun using the building as temporary barracks for troops during exercises at the school, symbolizing the reduced importance of urban warfare training at the time. In October 1999, however, shortly after the North Korea spy boat incident in March that year—and prior to the official changes in the 2000 MDBP—the GSDF announced plans to improve its urban combat training capabilities by budgeting ¥200 million to build an urban combat facility consisting of three buildings at its Sone training grounds near Kita Kyushu City in the northern part of Kyushu. This was part of ¥2.7 billion put aside for counter-guerrilla training that year.[805] The GSDF then proceeded to build urban warfare training centers in each of its regional armies.

The new urban combat facility at Sone was completed in February 2002. While not expansive, the complex features move able interiors for a variety of training scenarios. The smaller Building One has two stories and 242 square meters of space, while the larger Building Two has two stories and a total space of 744 square meters. Building Three is the smallest, at 100 square meters. Each of the buildings is essentially hollow inside, and plywood panels can be positioned and repositioned to change the layout. The buildings can also be equipped with moveable mannequin targets on rails and controlled remotely. Cameras are also positioned throughout the facility, recording trainees' every move.[806] Sone was chosen to host Japan's first modern urban combat training facility precisely because of its strategic location: northern Kyushu is geographically closest to the Korean Peninsula, and the Western Army Infantry Regiment, the GSDF's first rapid reaction force inaugurated a month after the completion of the Sone facility, would also be stationed in this area.

Other urban combat training facilities soon followed. The GSDF budgeted funds for a large urban combat training facility at its main Fuji School to completely replace its pre-existing two-building complex and announced plans to send units—beginning with those from the 1st Division—for urban combat training with US 25th Infantry Division in Hawaii in 2002.[807] A third urban combat training facility was built on the Aibano training grounds in Shiga Prefecture, and the facility hosted the first joint U.S.-Japan urban combat training in March 2006.[808] Other facilities were built at Yausubetsu in Hokkaido for use by the Northern Army, Ojojihara in the Northeastern Army area, and Kirishima for the Western Army.[809] The urban warfare training facility at Higashi Fuji is by far the largest. Measuring over 30,000-square meters, the facility has eleven urban mock-up buildings including a three-story apartment building, a supermarket, and a restaurant. Cameras are installed throughout the area for use in after-action reviews in an adjacent administrative building. The facility began to host platoon-size units in the summer of 2005 and company-size unit training began as of spring 2006, when it became fully operational.[810]

Rapid Reaction Forces: the WAIR and Central Readiness Force

The GSDF by this time also began to organize rapid-reaction units with defense of remote islands as a primary role, starting with the Western Army area of operations. As the defense journalist Naoya Tamura wrote in the December 2003 *Gunji Kenkyu*: "In response to the threat from North Korea, more attention is being directed to the Western Army, which is responsible for Kyushu/Okinawa...[and] toward dealing with lightly equipped guerrilla and/or commando units such as armed agents from North Korea." Because of the thousands of islands in the region, "priority is being placed on improved mobility."[811] The first rapid response unit created in the region was called the Western Army Infantry Regiment (WAIR), placed under the direct control of the commander of the Western Army. Officially established in March 2002 at Camp Ainoura near Sasebo, Nagasaki Prefecture, the WAIR's primary responsibility is the defense and security of remote islands in southwestern Japan, and over half of the 660-man unit is Ranger-qualified. The WAIR was established based on the GSDF's Type E infantry regiment, as noted above, and according to the *2002 Defense of Japan*, the unit is designed to be able to rapidly deploy to remote islands in response to an enemy commando or guerrilla insertion.[812]

The WAIR's area of responsibility covers 2,600 islands along a 1,200 kilometer stretch of maritime territory from the large Tsushima island near the Korean peninsula to Yonaguni Island in the south near Taiwan. Mobility is thus critical to the successful defense of remote islands in this region. While this is not the only unit that defends southwestern Japan—the 4th Division, the 8th Division, and the 1st Combined Brigade are also stationed in the region—the WAIR is the most mobile.

With the increasing reliance on joint operations and interoperability with other forces, members train with MSDF units—taking the scuba course at the First Technical School at the MSDF's nearby Etajima facility, for example—and shortly after inauguration they trained with the modernized MSDF transport *Shimokita.*[813] The WAIR's main mode of transportation is the CH-47 and UH-60J (although analysts added the V-22 Osprey to their wish lists when US forces began to employ them), and the WAIR has rappelling towers at Camp Ainoura to practice rappelling from helicopters as a main insertion method. To extend the range of its helicopters, the GSDF also began to experiment with the use of C-130Hs as aerial refuelers for its helicopters in its five-year plan from 2006, with the GSDF budgeting funds to modify some UH-60Js to receive fuel from a C-130H in-flight.[814] In line with the 2000 MDBP's emphasis on greater intelligence capabilities, the Western Army also established new tactical intelligence units—the Western Army Communications Intelligence Unit and the Western Army Intelligence Processing Unit—in 2004 to further support operations in this maritime territory and especially to guard against the possible clandestine insertions of special operations or other forces. The units collect and process tactical SIGINT and had a total strength of approximately 100 personnel at their inauguration.[815]

To improve its limited amphibious landing capabilities, the WAIR began to train with the US Marine Corps in early 2006 as well: 125 personnel from the WAIR trained with the 1st Marine Expeditionary Group at the Amphibious Base Coronado near San Diego, California from 9-27 January. This training was also directly linked to *ritō bōei* in the eyes of Japan, as *Nikkei Shimbun* reported shortly before training was to begin that this was "the first joint remote island defense exercise with US Marines."[816] The Marines put the unit through "an extremely drummed down version of a Marine Expeditionary Unit training package," according to a public affairs officer at Camp Pendleton. Dubbed "Iron Fist" and led by Col. Yoji Yamanaka, the exercise culminated in a nighttime landing from the USS Comstock, a 609-foot amphibious transport similar to the *Shimokita* noted above.[817] Following the nighttime amphibious landing, the unit was to undertake a map exercise that included exchanging gunfire with enemy units.[818] Col. Yamanaka later told the *Mainichi Shimbun* that the unit would train other units in Japan as well: "We are going to apply the skills we learned from the US Marines to drills in Japan."[819]

The WAIR was but the first of Japan's several rapid reaction units. The 2004 National Defense Program Guideline announced plans to create a new type of unit from early 2007 capable of deploying anywhere in Japan or abroad to "respond to new threats and diverse situations." Called the *Chūō Sokuō Shudan* or "Central Readiness Force" (CRF), a major focus of the force is counter-guerrilla operations, and reflecting Japan's frustration with its inability to deploy any counter-guerrilla forces during the 1997-1998 Lima hostage crisis, the unit can also be deployed abroad. The new organization fell under a newly created "Central Rapid Response Command," (CRRC) also established in early 2007 under the Minister of Defense and headquartered in Utsunomiya, Tochigi Prefecture. The CRRC took over command of the 1st Airborne Brigade and a newly formed Special Operations Group—both in Narashino near Tokyo—and the 1st Helicopter Brigade in Kisarazu, Chiba Prefecture.[820] The Command also oversees the 101st Special Weapons Group in Omiya, an International Operations Training Unit in Komakado, and Headquarters in Asaka. The headquarters would eventually move to Camp Zama to be collocated with the US Army's headquarters in Japan, indicating deepening defense relations with the United States. In addition, the CRF will be able to rely on the GSDF's consolidated 600-person intelligence unit, called the "Central Intelligence Unit" (*Chūō Jōhōtai*), which can form 10-person teams to be dispatched prior to a CRF deployment.[821]

Research on new GSDF equipment since 2001 has also reflected a growing emphasis on small-unit networks and mobility. In 2003, Japan's Technical Research and Development Institute (TRDI) began development of a "High-Tech Outfit System" for use by individual infantrymen. The outfit consists of a bulletproof jacket that contains a small computer, GPS, and communications equipment connected to a helmet and night-vision camera and head-mount display. The outfit allows individual personnel to be connected in real-time at the squad, platoon, and company level.[822] This would most likely be networked to the "3CT IT Network" system, which links the company commander with individual units in the field and is discussed further below. TRDI also began development of a Future Wheeled Combat Vehicle, a multi-purpose vehicle capable of supporting various weapons systems—Japan's version of the Swiss Piranha and the Canadian LAV. The vehicle would be able to employ a variety of turrets interchangeably depending on mission needs, including a TRDI-developed 40-mm telescopic projectile machine gun to serve as the vehicle's main weapon, and other turrets for anti-tank, anti-air, and howitzer-type missions as well. The GSDF planed to field the Wheeled Combat Vehicle by the end of the decade.[823] These vehicles would be capable of being transported by Japan's new C-X airplane, a military cargo plane with greater capacity than its C-130s or its indigenously produced C-1s. The C-X and its sister P-X patrol plane are also discussed further below.

Even as the GSDF embraced greater mobility, however, it continued to procure expensive legacy weapons systems such as the T-90 tank, thus prohibiting greater investment in more urgent programs such as counter-guerrilla training or newer and lighter weapons systems. The T-90 tank remained one of the GSDF's major platforms, but it was also one of the most expensive tanks in the world at a cost of approximately ¥805 million per unit—over $8 million.[824] This was almost twice as expensive as the US-made M-1 Abrams battletank, which cost $4.3 million per unit.[825] From 1996 to 2004, the total number of tanks in Japan dropped from 1,110 to 976, but the number of T-90 tanks in Japan's arsenal increased from 136 to 277 as Japan replaced older T-74 tanks, reducing their number from 873 to 699.[826] As the discussions over the 2004 NDPO progressed, elements in the GSDF lobbied heavily for only a small reduction in the number of authorized tanks in the draft 2004 NDPO—civilian defense officials (and presumably MSDF and ASDF personnel) pushed for a 50% reduction in the authorized number of tanks, while the GSDF opposed any reduction greater than 10%.[827] While the number of authorized tanks was indeed cut substantially to just over 600, Japan continued to build the newer T-90 tanks even when it has little use for them. TRDI in 2003 established a new tank research division in its Ground Systems Development Department to develop a lighter tank that can be transported without removing its 120-mm smoothbore gun[828]–which eventually became the Type-10 tank—but one wonders how effective even this somewhat lighter tank will be in the mountainous terrain of islands in Kyushu and Okinawa prefectures.

The SDF relationship with local communities in Kyushu and Okinawa, moreover, remained complicated. Perhaps due to lingering post-war pacifist sentiment, or perhaps due to local political dynamics, some local elected leaders continued to refuse to allow the SDF anything more than token access to facilities such as airports and maritime ports. Debate in southwestern Okinawa's Miyako island was a case in point. Host of the region's largest airport on neighboring Shimoji island that features a 3,000-meter-long runway, local leaders for years prevaricated over whether to allow the SDF use of the airport. As Japan Airlines began to plan upgrades for the facility beginning in the late 1960s in hopes of developing a "Hawaii of the orient," Chobyo Yara, then-chief executive for Okinawa, negotiated the so-called "Yara Memorandum" with Japan's Transportation Ministry in 1971, the year before reversion of the islands to Japanese control, limiting the use of the airport to "civilian purposes."[829] With its large airport facility and important radar facilities in the Sakishima chain of islands, Miyako is central to the MOD's plans to defend the region, however, according to plans revealed as Tokyo was reviewing its National Defense Program Guideline in mid-2004. According to leaked military documents, should an armed dispute erupt between regional powers "X" and "D," the GSDF had developed plans to dispatch 7,200 ground troops to Miyako, Ishigaki, and Yonaguni islands, augmented by 2,000 airborne troops, to prevent the islands' seizure by power "X".[830]

The US military had used the airport on a limited basis for refueling helicopters during flights between Okinawa and the Philippines during the Cold War, but US use of the facilities ceased following closure of the US Navy's Subic Bay base in 1992. The mayor of Irabu town, where the airport is located, had briefly supported the SDF's use of the airport in the early 2001 to promote economic development, and then-DA Director General Gen Nakatani said that the mayor recognized the Shimoji island airport "is in a location necessary for our national security"—a bare popular majority supported the mayor's proposal at the time, according to a poll taken by the left-leaning *Mainichi Shimbun*. But the mayor was in the political minority even then, as the Okinawa Prefectural Assembly passed a resolution declaring "we will never allow the SDF to use [the airport]."[831] Following the crash of a US helicopter on Okinawa's main island in August 2004, he joined with five other mayors in opposing the military's use of the airport.[832]

Contingency legislation passed in 2003 and 2004 provides the legal foundation for the SDF's emergency use of the airport and other transportation facilities. The Diet passed a total of 10 laws by June 2004 that clarified the legal basis for defense mobilizations, among other things. Perhaps the most important law empowers the prime minister to authorize the Self-Defense Forces' use of port facilities. Indeed, the law gives the prime minister authority to replace port masters should they refuse SDF use of the facility. Another law implemented the Japan-US "Acquisition and Cross-Servicing Agreement," giving the SDF the legal authorization to provide supplies to US forces in the region. Thus the SDF might transit Japanese ports not only to defend Japanese territory, but also to transport supplies for US forces—a somewhat more contentious issue due to lingering negative sentiment following US military actions in Iraq. Because of local political opposition to military use of the airport, however, and because of lingering anti-military sentiment in general, the SDF had little opportunity to train along the Sakishima island chain even as it inaugurated the WAIR and similar units, however.

The MSDF's Evolving Role and Mini-Taskforces

While the GSDF's rapid reaction WAIR relies primarily on helicopters for quick deployments, the MSDF provides transportation of heavier reinforcements and supplies in addition to being able to provide island and sea-lane defense. With a force of 120 ships and over 200 aircraft, the MSDF by the early 2000s was divided into five regional districts—Yokosuka Regional District, Kure Regional District, Sasebo Regional District, Maizuru Regional District, and Ominato Regional District—that were responsible for patrolling and providing security in waters surrounding Japan. MSDF vessels based in each of these districts also formed one of four Fleet Escort Forces for special deployments in Japanese waters and beyond. Called the "8-8" fleet structure, each fleet was comprised of 8 destroyers and 8 helicopters. The eight destroyers consisted of two helicopter-carrying destroyers capable of carrying three helicopters each, two destroyers with one helicopter each, and three guided-missile destroyers, at least one of which is a *Kongo*-class Aegis destroyer. The Fleets could also include one or more of Japan's 16 submarines—based out of Kure and Yokosuka—as well as one or more transport ships that operate Landing Craft Air Cushion (LCAC) platforms for ship-to-shore landing operations.

The MSDF in the early 2000s began to expand its "8-8" basic fleet structure to provide greater support to the emerging "Island Operations" and the "Defense of Remote Islands" (*ritō bōei*) concepts. The MSDF's contribution to joint operations grew to consist of four main elements: a new "16DDH" command-and-control ship capable of providing flight operations; a transport force capable of conducting amphibious landing to reinforce Japanese units or reclaim territory from enemy combatants; surface-attack capabilities from the sea and from air to provide cover for landing forces; and submarine and destroyer forces capable of providing task force and sea lane protection. This mini-task force would be able to both transport and command in-theater mobile GSDF "Type E" regiments (such as the WAIR) and other units to reinforce or retake island territory and ASDF units in support of island operations. Retired Vice Admiral Makoto Yamazaki, a former Maritime Self-Defense Force (MSDF) fleet commander writing in the monthly journal *Sekai no Kansen,* wrote that Japan's emerging "Island Operations" consisted of securing "air and sea superiority and then combin[ing] various land, sea, and air forces for…amphibious operations and ground combat" which would include "ground strikes from the sea and air."[833] To support island operations, 8-8 fleet functions are being significantly upgraded with the addition of the 16DDH-type helicopter carrier into a mini-task force capable of commanding joint operations.

Japan's Mini-Taskforce and the Hyuga-Class Command Ship

Retired admiral and former Maritime Self-Defense Force Chief of Staff Hiroshi Nagata was an early vocal proponent of a robust and multifunctional naval capability in the post-Cold War era. Nagata has written a series of articles since the mid-1990s describing his vision of Japan's future naval capabilities. In the December 1995 edition of *Sekai no Kansen,* a monthly journal that covers Japanese and other navies around the world, Nagata lobbied for the MSDF to expand beyond "conventional concepts" such as "defense of Sea Lines of Communication": "There is a need to broadly consider response to threats and scenarios ranging from low-intensity conflicts (LICs) to saturated missile attacks, Theater Missile Defense (TMD), and countering invasions, including island defense." Moreover, in the 21st century, "the standards in the Cold War era based on Japan-US joint operations should be modified to also consider independent operations," according to Nagata.[834] Nagata consistently opined that the US might not be in a position to defend Japan in an era of asymmetric threats, an underlying fear common among many Japanese defense experts since the 1990s.

Following the Taepodong launch and multiple incursions by special operations units in the late 1990s, Nagata opined that "as an island country," Japan is "very vulnerable militarily." Nagata again highlighted the importance of remote island defense: "Japan must build up defense capabilities to deal with situations like local and small-scale invasions," and he stressed that Japan "cannot expect joint actions" with the United States. "The fact is that the Japan-US joint defense system can never be built up in a short period of time to deal with all situations even including invasions of limited areas like islands," Nagata asserted.[835] With island defense in mind, Nagata lobbied for the construction of a light helicopter-carrier, "a vessel to replace the DDH [helicopter-destroyer]...that would be able to carry three modified SH-60Js and about eight V-22s." This new vessel would be built specifically "for the purpose of defending islands." Nagata featured a conceptual diagram showing spots for simultaneous flight operations along a long flight line, with eight V-22s and three SH-60Js hovering above it. With a long flat deck in both the front and back, separated only by a narrow island in the middle, the ship bore a striking similarity to a light helicopter-carrier, and it further served as the command ship of a small Japanese fleet.[836] The new class of "DDH," as envisioned by Nagata, more closely resembled a smaller version of the US Marine's Wasp-class Landing Helicopter Dock (LHD) than Japan's 1960s-era helicopter-destroyers.

Nagata's proposal came during a critical time, as the Maritime Staff Office was preparing conceptual plans for a new type of helicopter-destroyer to replace the 5,000-ton *Haruna* DDH and a second to replace its sister ship the *Hiei*, both commissioned in the early 1970s. Given the air complement of Nagata's proposed vessel, it would not only be much larger than the *Haruna* or any other MSDF ship then in service, it would in fact be one of the largest ships in Asia then in service.

While Nagata was by this point retired, his writings nevertheless mirrored the thinking of the MSO, as this was exactly the kind of ship Japan would later build.

In September 2000—a year after Nagata's article appeared in *Sekai no Kansen*—the MSDF publicly proposed three alternative versions of a larger helicopter-carrying destroyer to replace the *Haruna.* One of the three versions would be built as part of the next five-year defense plan. The first two conceptual schematics merely resembled extremely large destroyers, as each had helipads forward and aft of a large superstructure. The third, however, featured a superstructure on the port side and a long, flat deck spanning the entire length of the ship. It was undeniably a continuous flight line. Each of the proposed designs would allow four helicopters to take off and land simultaneously according to the official description of the vessels' capabilities, although speculation among defense analysts immediately turned to possible Harrier V/STOL and other flight operations particularly related to the third proposed design. The five-year defense plan approved funds for the development of what would be called the "16DDH"—the ship's initial designation based on the Japanese year (*Heisei 16*, corresponding to the year 2004) when construction on the ship was due to commence—but the five-year plan did not specify which version would be built. All that was known at the time was that the new 16DDH would be able to carry over a dozen helicopters—in contrast to helicopter-carrying destroyer *Haruna,* which operated three helicopters—and the 16DDH would be able to launch and recover multiple helicopters simultaneously.

Nagata's colleague, former MSDF fleet commander retired Vice Admiral Makoto Yamazaki, writing in *Sekai no Kansen* before the official version was chosen, compared this new class of ship to the USS *Coronado,* an Auxiliary Command Ship (AGF) and at one time the flagship for the US Navy's Third Fleet. The comparison was a subtle attempt to deflect comparisons from larger and more capable amphibious assault ships such as the *Wasp*, since the *Coronado* did not have a long flight deck and its design outwardly resembled a larger version of the old *Haruna* DDH.[837] Regardless of the difference in size, the new 16DDH would serve a core command-and-control function in Japan's new mini-task forces.

By the end of 2003, Nagata's envisioned fleet structure was coming to fruition. The MSDF announced that it had decided to construct the third version of the 16DDH with a deck running the length of the ship. The JFY2004 budget for the Defense Agency included ¥105.7 billion to start construction on the 16DDH that was scheduled to be launched in 2008.[838] Moreover, the MSDF would procure a second ship of the same class, designated the 18DDH. The 16DDH—which would become the *Hyuga* when commissioned in 2009—would measure 195 meters long and 40 meters wide and had a fully loaded displacement of over 18,000 tons.

The 16DDH would serve as a "'command and control ship' where the commanders of the various ground, sea, and air units—including the joint commander of theater operations…manage theater intelligence," according to Yamazaki, and serve as the command ship during operations to "defend islands or retake them." Yamazaki depicted the 16DDH as the command ship of a Japanese fleet consisting of large *Osumi*-class transport ships operating landing-craft air-cushion (LCAC) boats to transport ground troops ashore, Aegis destroyers providing air defense for the fleet, a new advanced destroyer—the 18DD—to provide covering fire for landing ground troops, submarines for counter-submarine warfare, and ASDF units such as F-15s and AWACs planes to gain and maintain air superiority.[839] By 2003, it was clear that Japan was building its own mini-task force for the defense of remote islands and other operations, and with the start of construction of the sister ship 18DDH in 2006, Japan would eventually have two such mini-task forces.

The *Osumi*-class transport is another key element to the mini-task force capable of conducting joint operations. The three in service by the time of the *Hyuga*'s launch have a standard displacement of approximately 8,900, with a rear dock well featuring two Landing Craft Air Cushion (LCAC) hovercraft for ship-to-shore transport of troops and equipment such as one T-90 tank or four type-73 armored vehicles. While the MSDF officially designates the Osumi-class vessels an LST—or "landing ship, tank"—in line with its older and smaller transports such as the *Atsumi*- and *Miura*-class transports, *Jane's Fighting Ships* asserts that this class of ship should be designated an LPD or LPH—which stand for "amphibious transport, dock" and "amphibious assault ship, general purpose" respectively. *Jane's* even noted that the "through deck, flight deck and stern docking well make this more like a mini-LHA than an LST," or mini-landing helicopter assault ship.[840]

Whatever its designation, the *Osumi*-class ship is almost five times larger than the MSDF's Cold War-era *Miura*-class transport, with living quarters for over 1,000 troops and a crew of 130. Large vehicles can be raised to the deck from the through-deck below via two elevators, and equipment can also be secured to the main deck during long voyages. Its deck can support and refuel rotary aircraft such as the CH-47 transport helicopters.[841] The deck could presumably also support other assault helicopter operations as well, such as the GSDF's AH-1 Cobra and AH-64 Apache helicopters. (*Jane's Fighting Ships* noted that the *Osumi*-class transport can carry 330 troops in addition to its 135-man complement, 10 T-90 tanks, and 1,400 tons of cargo.[842]) Nagata compared the importance of the *Osumi*-class transport ship to the British landing forces during the 1982 Falkland Islands War who "succeeded in recapturing the Falkland Islands because they succeeded in a counter-landing maneuver at San Carlos Bay." And "if, as in the Falkland Islands War, there were to be a sudden attack on territory that Japan governs in practice, then it would be the responsibility of those in charge of defense to...be able to properly carry out the measures needed for territorial integrity," according to Nagata. The *Osumi*-class ship would help to enable a landing function similar to that conducted by British forces at San Carlos Bay, according to Nagata.[843]

The MSDF's smaller *Miura*-class transports thus took on secondary transport roles, with a standard displacement of 2,000 tons and transport capacity of 200 troops. The six *Miura*-class transports together are capable of transporting no more than 30 percent of a GSDF regimental combat team consisting of approximately 2,000 troops, tanks, and howitzers.[844]

For missions involving the transport of supplies over longer distances, the MSDF also has three *Towada*-class AOE fast combat support ships with a displacement of 8,100 tons empty and over 15,000 tons fully loaded that entered service in the early 1990s. More recently, Japan has launched a new *Mashu*-class 13,500-ton (empty) multi-purpose transport ship. The *Mashu* also doubles as a small hospital ship, with a two-bed surgical unit, an eight-bed hospital unit, and a secondary infirmary with 30 beds.[845] These ships would provide vital resupply and in-theater medical support for a Japanese mini-task force engaged in operations at sea. Separately, both the *Mashu*- and *Osumi*-class ships can also provide significant relief to areas affected by natural disasters.

Surface-Strikes and Missile Defense

As Japanese defense commentators have noted, the mini-task force commanded by the 16DDH will have to be able to provide for its own air defense even as it provides covering fire for an amphibious landing. Nagata highlighted the need for three layers of defense: point defense—the defense of "High Value Units" in the MSDF fleet such as the 16DDH—makes up the inner layer of defense; area defense is defense of the fleet from 10 to 100 nautical miles away, and outer defense is defense from targets 100-300 nautical miles from the fleet. The fleet will rely on medium-range missiles fired from destroyers and other platforms in the fleet for area defense, while according to Nagata, the fleet will rely on ASDF units such as interceptors in conjunction with airborne early warning aircraft under the command of the fleet to provide the outer layer of defense.[846] Although the 16DDH as originally conceived will not have the ability to launch interceptors or other fixed-wing aircraft (the MSDF has all along denied the capability to launch Harrier jets, for example), the range of Japan's interceptors and AWACS aircraft will be increased in and around Japan with the introduction of aerial refuelers so that any mission to provide for the defense of outer islands will be within range of ASDF assets.

The *Kongo*- and new *Atago*-class Aegis destroyers and the 19DD stealth destroyer will provide area and point defense respectively for the fleet. Indeed, Japan's Aegis destroyers are perhaps the MSDF's most valuable assets in an era of asymmetric threats, as they not only provide for fleet defense but are also integral components in Japan's missile defense system. The four *Kongo*-class DDGs, launched in the early 1990s, were refitted from 2005 to launch the new SM-3 anti-ballistic missile. Funding for the construction of the two *Atago*-class DDGs, delivered to the MSDF in March 2007 and 2008, was approved before the Cabinet approved the implementation of a missile defense system from 2004, but like the *Kongo*-class destroyers they too would undergo refitting to provide ballistic missile defense functions as well. As *Sekai no Kansen* pointed out in 2004, with only four Aegis ships available to participate in the missile defense system, "there is a considerable likelihood that gaps would develop in the rotation." Therefore, "giving the [*Atago*-class] 14DDG and [the follow-on] 15DDG BMD capabilities will be an important issue in the future."[847] Unlike the *Kongo*, however, the *Atago* features an aft hangar and helicopter pad, allowing basic air operations from this Aegis destroyer platform. The helipad would also allow for basic resupply during long deployments in waters around Japan.

Each of these ships features a Mk41 vertical launch system (VLS) with a total of 96 cells, two type-90 surface-to-ship missile launchers, torpedo launchers, two triple-mount torpedo launchers, and two 20-mm CIWS for point defense and a 127-mm single-mount gun for surface fire. The Mk41 VLS is the key weapons system for these vessels, as it can fire a variety of missiles for air defense and surface strikes such as the Seasparrow, the Standard Missile 2 (SM-2) and Standard Missile 3 (SM-3), and potentially missile systems similar to the Tomahawk land-attack cruise missile. While Japan had not publicly introduced any long-range surface strike capabilities similar to the Tomahawk missile system for use on its Aegis destroyers, political debates regarding the possible incorporation of such capabilities increased markedly in the early 2000s, as discussed in chapter 6. Thus, these or similar ships in the future could become key platforms for the launch of longer-range surface strike missiles as well.

The SM-3 plays a key role in Japan's nascent national missile defense system. While Japan already operated the surface-to-air Standard Missile 2 from its *Kongo*-class destroyers and had 27 PAC-2 missile systems, these weapons systems were dated and their effectiveness against longer-range missile systems such as the Nodong and Taepodong was questionable. The United States and Japan commenced joint research of the SM-3 in 1999, even though at the time Tokyo had not decided to introduce any missile defense system. Japan decided to proceed with joint development of the Standard Missile 3 in late 2003 following the Cabinet decision to build a missile defense system.[848]

To protect the archipelago from a missile attack or threats of attack, the SM-3 deployed on Aegis destroyers in the Sea of Japan would be the first of a two-stage missile defense system. The Aegis destroyers would attempt to destroy a ballistic missile during its midcourse flight with SM-3s, and the Patriot Advanced Capability 3 (PAC-3) system deployed near major urban centers and other strategic areas throughout Japan would engage any remaining warheads during their terminal stages. Japan began deploying the newly developed SM-3s on the *Kongo* at the end of 2007, while Tokyo began to deploy PAC-3 missile systems at Iruma Base outside of Tokyo and nine other bases throughout the country that same year.

One sticking point for missile defense, however, was the fact that the Prime Minister had to meet with the Cabinet before ordering the Minister of Defense to deploy any military units or launch any military action, including any launch of anti-missile missiles as part of missile defense. However, a full meeting of the cabinet was not feasible as a missile launched from the Korean peninsula could hit a target in Japan in as few as 10 minutes, so the decision to engage a ballistic missile had to be automatic. Thus in 2005, the Diet added provisions on missile defense to the Self-Defense Forces Law that allowed the defense minister to mobilize missile defense units to stand by for any sudden attack and order an intercept under emergency guidelines approved in advance by the prime minister.[849]

Apart from the *Kongo*- and *Atago*-class destroyers, the "19DD" destroyer is Japan's next-generation general-purpose destroyer that would replace *Takanami*- and *Murasame*-class destroyers from 2011. The 19DD—the *Akizuki*-class destroyer—provides point defense of the 16DDH command ship and Aegis destroyers and other high-value targets in the Japanese fleet, and it will also have advanced surface-strike capabilities and "will probably be called on to have greater capabilities than those of traditional individual-ship defense," according to *Gunji Kenkyu*.[850] As with the 16DDH, the Defense Agency issued two proposals for the 19DD in 2003: "Plan A" for the 19DD program incorporated a 127-mm Mk-45, and the more stealthy "Plan B" that featured an Italian OTO-Melara made by Japan Steel Works under license. Both versions were "operationally" expected to "support landing units in coastal waters," according to *Sekai no Kansen*.[851] Thus the 19DD *Akizuki* will be multi-functional, providing point-defense of Japanese fleet units as well as surface fire support during landing operations.

Moreover, Tokyo was at this time developing its own extended-range guided weapons for possible use from MSDF ships and other platforms. After the construction of the 19DD was first announced in late 2003, *Sekai no Kansen* assessed that "one can anticipate the introduction of extended range guided munitions" fired from these ship-based weapons systems.[852] According to the gun's US manufacturer—United Defense—the Mk-45 can "provide Naval Surface Fire Support (NSFS) range in excess of 21 nautical miles (37 km)," and can "also provide over-the-horizon NSFS range of more than 60 nautical miles (120 km) with the near-term integration of the 5-inch Extended Range Guided Munition."[853] As will be discussed in greater detail in a later chapter, defense researchers in the early 2000s began to develop an extended-range guided munition capable of being fired from howitzers. A Japan Association of Defense Industry committee proposed the development of a 105-mm rocket-assisted projectile with GPS capability for use in future Japanese artillery systems in 2003.[854] This same technology could conceivably be used with rounds fired from naval platforms as well. Pointing to a continued debate in defense circles on the issue, however, defense journalist Isamu Okabe denied that the MSDF was examining any such extended range system, writing in 2004 that "there are no signs to indicate the MSDF will take the step of adopting a 155mm gun" or "extended-range guided munitions" (ERGMs). Okabe nevertheless conceded that if ever "the MSDF is considering land bombardment to prevent landings or repulse units which have infiltrated, there would probably be the possibility that the adoption of guided munitions to improve strike accuracy, not to mention extended-range munitions or bomblet-scattering munitions, would become a topic for study."[855] These functions fall squarely within Japan's expanding *ritō bōei* concept as it was being developed through 2006, and moreover Tokyo would not wait until after an outside force has infiltrated Japanese territory before introducing advanced munitions such as ERGMs. As Japan's precision strike technological capabilities progress, such technologies will surely be developed proactively for naval use as well.

AIP Submarines

The MSDF as of the early 2000s operated 16 conventional submarines out of the MSDF ports of Kure and Yokosuka. Japan launched a submarine on average once a year, built by the major contractors Mitsubishi Heavy Industries and Kawasaki Heavy Industries at Kobe City—and submarine construction did not experience delays even following the earthquake in the region in 1995. Japanese submarines, moreover, have grown steadily larger. The *Yushio*-class submarines, built 1976-1988, displaced 2,200 tons—2,450 tons dived—and measured 76 meters long. The *Harushio*-class submarine, built between 1987 and 1995, displaced 2,450-2,750 tons and measured 78 meters in length. The newest conventional submarine, the *Oyashio*-class submarine, displaces

2,700 tons and 3,000 tons dived and measures 81.7 meters in length. Each of these classes has six torpedo tubes amidships and fires the McDonnell Douglas Sub-Harpoon with a range of 130 kilometers.[856]

Signaling the incorporation of a generational leap in submarine technology, TRDI began to experiment with Air-Independent Propulsion (AIP) systems in 1995 when it procured two Stirling AIP systems from Kockums Company, a Swedish defense firm widely known for its AIP technology. Major submarine manufacturer Kawasaki Heavy Industries also experimented with the Stirling engine on the *Oyashio*-class submarine in the late 1990s.[857] In 2000, the DA modified the training submarine *Asashio*—the last *Harushio*-class submarine built in Kobe—to accommodate four Stirling engines, increasing the sub's displacement by 400 tons and increasing its length by 9 meters in doing so. The sub tested well, and the Defense Agency requested ¥60.4 billion for a new AIP-based submarine—called the "16SS"—in the JFY2004 budget.[858] The Diet approved ¥59.8 billion for the project on March 26, 2004.

The 16SS "*Sōryū*-class" submarines were designed to run on two diesel engines, four Stirling engines, and one main motor. The Kockums V4-275R Mk II Stirling engines have a continuous rated output of 65 kilowatts that produce 88 horsepower. They will mainly be used when cruising at slow speeds (up to five knots) and when halted underwater.[859] The AIP engines allow the 16SS to remain submerged for weeks at a time, instead of having to snorkel every few days to discharge the fumes from the diesel engines and to recharge the batteries. Stirling engines also run quiet since there are fewer moving parts, and they have a smaller heat signature. Japan's submarines will provide a key role in defense of the new fleet structure as well as in playing its traditional role in defense of sea-lanes.

High-Speed and Missile Boats: Responding to Suspicious Maritime Vessels

The MSDF historically maintained missile boat units at three bases along the Sea of Japan: Sasebo MSDF Base near Nagasaki, Maizuru MSDF Base near the Noto Peninsula—the approximate area where the suspicious vessels were discovered in 1999—and Yoichi MSDF Base in Hokkaido. While the primary role for MSDF missile boats during the Cold War period had been to defend against invading warships, the additional task of responding to suspect vessels was added to the missile boat units following the March 1999 suspicious vessels incident.

The 1st Missile Boat Squadron is based at Yoichi MSDF Base. The unit was originally created in 1971 as a torpedo boat unit, but it was reorganized into the 1st Missile Boat Squadron in 1993, and the unit was supplied with three hydrofoil vessels 1993-1995, each with a 50-ton displacement and equipped with SSM-1B anti-ship missiles and a 20-mm six-barrel machine gun. The MSDF originally planned to build up to 18 of these missile boats to form six missile boat units, but it dropped the plan due to stagnating budgets in the 1996-2000 mid-term defense plan. Moreover, *Gunji Kenkyu* suggested the 50-ton vessels were too small and incapable of operating at full capacity in the rough Sea of Japan.[860]

Following several years of study, the Defense Agency requested funding for two larger 200-ton missile boats in the fiscal 1999 budget, which was compiled in the summer of 1998 and passed the Diet just prior to the suspicious vessels incident in March 1999.[861] Once it received budgetary support, the MSDF had to make modifications to its proposed design through the summer of 1999 taking into account the new threat before it could order the first two boats' construction at Mitsubishi Heavy Industry.[862]

The first two of six boats to be delivered, the *Hayabusa* and the *Wakataka*, were launched on March 25, 2002 and were transferred to the 2nd Missile Boat Division in the MSDF's Maizuru Regional District. Ironically, their construction was completed shortly after the second suspicious vessel incident that occurred in December 2001, further emphasizing the need for high-speed patrol boats. Sturdier than the hydrofoil boats based at Yoichi, the 200-ton *Hayabusa*-class missile boats can reach a speed of 44 knots (81.4 km) per hour and carry four SSM-1B anti-ship missiles with a range of over 150 kilometers and armed with a 76-mm gun and two 12.7-mm guns. The vessels are also equipped with a smaller craft capable of carrying up to ten for boarding suspect vessels.[863] The ships were built by Mitsubishi Heavy Industries at its Shimonoseki shipyard in Yamaguchi Prefecture at a cost of ¥10.8 billion.[864] With the completion of the *Umitaka* and *Shirataka* in March 2004, the fifth and sixth *Hayabusa*-class missile boats, the MSDF's three missile boat divisions were complete. The missile boat divisions of the Maizuru Regional District and Sasebo Regional District operate the new *Hayabusa*-class missile boats. At least one of the three boats in each missile boat squadron was kept on alert 24 hours a day after they entered active service.[865]

The Japan Coast Guard has also deployed special high-speed patrol boats to JCG bases at Niigata, Kanazawa, and Maizuru. Two high-speed 1,000-ton *Aso*-class and two 2,000-ton *Hida*-class ships were completed in 2006. The JCG in 2006 planned five more high-speed vessels at just under 1,000 tons, and all were scheduled to be completed by 2009. This new class of vessel would feature remote-operated 30-mm gun and a high-pressure water hose, as well as four small- and large-composite boats for use against small protest boats. This class would also incorporate an extended aft heliport and storage area for helicopter fuel, allowing relief for the crew during long deployments near remote islands.[866] Using lessons learned following the attempted deployment of JCG SSTs during the December 2001 spy boat incident—discussed further below—the heliports could also serve as a potential staging platform for SSTs.

The ASDF's New Air Platforms: Fighters, Refuelers, and Transports

Japan has a robust but aging air force, with F-15s, F-4s, and a joint U.S.-Japan developed fighter aircraft, which Japan designates the F-2. By the early 2000s, the Air Self Defense Force operated 202 F-15s, 91 F-4s, 23 indigenously produced F-1s, and 47 of the newest F-2s. In addition, the ASDF operated 16 C-130H and 26 C-1 transports, 13 E-2C early warning aircraft, and 4 E-767 AWACS aircraft. The Maritime Self Defense Force separately flies the P-3C, 99 of which were in operation in the early 2000s.[867] The ASDF also began to incorporate aerial refuelers into its force structure, significantly increasing the range of its fighters and other aircraft. With the increased emphasis on mobility and defense of remote operations, Japan has begun to introduce replacement aircraft with greater range and carrying capacity compared to the aging C-130s and P-3Cs.

Japan's Aging Tactical Fighters

Following a series of Chinese naval movements through the Nansei island chain culminating with the *Han*-class submarine incursion in late 2004, and with the dramatic increase in ASDF scrambles to intercept Chinese military flights—a total of 146 between June 2004 and June 2005, as noted previously—the ASDF accounced plans to redeploy up to 40 F-15s to Okinawa's Naha Airbase to replace 24 F-4s stationed there. The redeployment was scheduled to take place over several years and would be complete by 2009.

One unnamed Defense Agency official told the conservative *Sankei Shimbun* that "there is a capability gap" between the aging F-4s and China's Su-30s and newly developed J-10s, which the F-15s would help to fill. As *Sankei* noted, the F-15 has a 50% greater range than the F-4, allowing for longer patrols over the Senkaku and Sakishima island chains, for example. Moreover, the redeployment represented another "shift" from "emphasis on the north" (*hoppō jūshi*) to "emphasis on the southwestern region" (*nansei hōmen jūshi*) for "remote island defense," according to *Sankei*, and the redeployment would be further augmented with the incorporation of aerial refuelers later in the decade.[868]

Yet, with Japan's F-15s themselves aging—the bulk of the fleet was acquired in the 1980s—the ASDF began an F-15 modernization program from 2004 to extend their service lives by 20 years. As part of this modernization program, the F-15s were to receive a Tactical Data Exchange System (MIDS-FDL) Terminal which allows data links between the ASDF BADGE air defense system, E-767 AWACS aircraft, Patriot units, and other F-15s. The modernized F-15s would thus be part of an improved networked environment. The system would also potentially improve interoperability with US Air Force assets, as the Air Force is scheduled to outfit all of its fighters and bombers with Link 16 using MIDS-FDL (Multifunctional Information Distribution Systems-Fighter Data Link) terminals.[869] The modernization program also included the installation of a domestically developed IRST (Infrared Search and Track) system emplaced over the nose section in front of the cockpit that would improve detection of stealthy targets and targets at night and in bad weather. The system was to be integrated with air-to-air missiles such as the recently developed AAM-5.[870] The modernization program fell behind schedule as the ASDF used the funds to complete its bulk acquisition of 20 F-2s by 2007, however. This brought the total number of F-2s to 96, but it meant that only eight F-15s had completed their upgrades, compared with 26 as originally stipulated in the 2005-2009 Mid-Term Defense Plan. The F-15 modernization program continued into the 2010s.

The F-2 *shien sentoki* or "support fighter" is Japan's most recently acquired tactical aircraft. Based on the US F-16 tactical fighter-bomber, the F-2 was developed in the 1990s to replace Japan's aging F-1 support fighters. As a tactical fighter-bomber, the F-2 can carry air-to-surface bombs including the Joint Direct Attack Munitions (JDAMs) and short-range anti-ship cruise missiles to target both ground-based and maritime units. The F-2 thus serves a key support role in remote island defense by preventing enemy naval units from approaching an island or by attacking enemy ground units after they have seized territory. However, the F-2 is one of the most expensive fighter aircraft in the world, with a unit cost of ¥12 billion—over $100 million per aircraft—compared with $15-$20 million for the F-16.[871] The Defense Agency originally planned to procure 130 F-2s, but given the soaring production costs, Tokyo halted procurement after purchasing its 98th plane as the ASDF looked ahead to other aircraft to replace Japan's F-4s.

Moreover, the F-2 has faced significant structural issues during flight tests in the late 1990s. The F-2s incorporated a new single-piece composite material wing that theoretically was both lighter and stronger. The F-2's wingspan was increased compared to the F-16 so that the F-2 could carry up to four air-to-ship missiles (ASM-2s). But during an initial test flight in 1998 with four ASM-2s carried under the wings, cracks suddenly developed on the right wing during flight causing the Defense Agency to extend the development phase another nine months.[872] The following year, engineers discovered small cracks in the middle rib of the right wing after a test flight in May 1999, and further cracks and peeling on both wings. These developments further delayed deployment of the F-2.[873] And again a year later, in May 2000, engineers discovered cracks in the horizontal tail wing. Ultimately, the Defense Agency resorted to securing the wings in place with hundreds of rivets. The additional weight detracted from the light-weight composite material, however, and the aircraft was less maneuverable when fully loaded.[874] The Defense Agency added flight control program software to correct the defects in 2002 and with the work-arounds deployment proceeded later that year, though slower than anticipated.[875] The aircraft experienced further problems following deployment, as the F-2's new radar system also experienced "a number of technical glitches": the phased-array radar, which is supposed to be able to identify targets over 100 kilometers away, had a less-than-expected range, and targets would sometimes just disappear.[876] Despite these setbacks, Japan proceeded—slowly—with the deployment of F-2s. The first set of F-2s arrived at Misawa in October 2000, but they were not activated until February 2004 due to the series of structural and other technical issues.

The ASDF during this time also took a keen interest in Russian jet fighters, most likely due to China's acquisition of the Su-27 in the mid-1990s. The Defense Agency in 1997 sent two pilots to Russia to train with the Russian Air Force on the Su-27, and it reviewed the possible purchase of a Su-27 for research purposes. *Sankei Shimbun* cited China's introduction of licensed production of Su-27s since late 1995 and subsequent deployment of Su-27s near the Senkaku Islands as the main reason for the training.[877] The Japanese trading company that brokered the deal, Mitsui Bussan, was also rumored at the time to be involved in negotiating a deal to sell one of the jets to Japan as the pilots were training in Russia.[878] However, following the ASDF pilots' approximately six-week training, Director General Kyuma was quoted as saying the Agency had "no plans to buy" a Su-27.[879] The ASDF sent two more trained pilots and a technical officer to Russia the following year to attend a two-month pilot course that would include include weapons and radar systems training and the firing of short- and medium-range air-to-air missiles.[880] The training certainly provided insights into Su-27 operations just as China was incorporating them into its air force.

In addition to researching neighboring countries' fighter capabilities, and as the F-2 moved from the research to the development phase in the mid-1990s, the Defense Agency began to look ahead to its next-generation fighter project. TRDI and Mitsubishi Heavy Industries at this time began basic research on yet another advanced fighter, called the "Advance Technology Demonstration Aircraft" or *senshin gijutsu jisshoki*. TRDI began its preliminary research 1992, and in 1995 TRDI and MHI requested significant funding to develop key technologies such as conformal radar, stealth, fly-by-light fiber-optic controls, and new engines. Reporting on the program stopped in the mid-1990s, but the program came to light again in 2001 when a desktop computer was reported stolen from an office of Mitsubishi Heavy Industry's Nagoya Aerospace Systems Works. The computer reportedly contained information on the Defense Agency's "study on a future fighter jet" and data on a simulator used to design the future fighter. The future fighter—if developed—would replace the F-15 and incorporate stealth technology, new radar systems, and fiber-optic controls, according to reports about the incident.[881] Within months, yet another computer related to the program was lost. Following a visit to TRDI's 3rd Research Center in Tachikawa, an MHI employee left a computer containing data related to research on a new engine for a "future fighter" on a train in Tokyo in April 2002—the incident was not made public until December 2002, however.[882] Also by this time, MHI by 2003 had begun advertising its ability to build a future jet in the defense industry journal *Gekkan JADI* with the opening of a "new IT laboratory" a few blocks away from the Defense Agency HQ in Ichigaya, declaring: "Now we can use modeling and simulation methods to make attractive proposals concerning equipment such as the future fighter program."[883] The DA displayed various mock-ups and models of an indigenous future fighter as late as 2006, in fact.[884]

As F-2 development and procurement costs continued to skyrocket in the early 2000s, it was clear that any indigenously developed fighter program would be enormously expensive. Speculation increasingly turned to Japan's procurement of a future fighter from the U.S., Europe, or elsewhere: Isamu Miyamoto, an aerospace journalist writing in the September 2001 *Gunji Kenkyu*, highlighted TRDI research on future fighter technologies but noted that the Defense Agency would be unable to design, research, develop, and introduce a successor to the F-4 or F-15 in the 2008-2013 timeframe, when the F-4s would begin to reach the end of their natural lifecycles. Miyamoto instead suggested that the Defense Agency would most likely purchase the F-22, the F-35 Joint Strike Fighter, or possibly the F/A-18.[885] By 2006—even as some in the DA continued to advocate a domestically designed and produced advanced fighter—the Air Staff Office did indeed begin a formal review of six future fighter candidates: the F-15X, F/A-18E/F, F-22, F-35, the Eurofighter, and the Dassault Rafale, with procurement set to begin by the end of the decade.[886] (The F-35 was ultimately selected, although funding concerns continued to plague procurement into the mid-2010s.)

Current and future ASDF fighters have dramatically increased range with Japan's introduction of its first aerial refuelers from 2007. The Security Council of Japan authorized the acquisition of four refueler airplanes in December 1999, citing four points (three of which were completely benign): refuelers will increase flight training time and reduce noise around SDF bases; refuelers make Combat Air Patrols (CAPs) more efficient by extending patrol times; they allow for extended flight time during unexpectedly bad weather; and personnel and equipment can be more readily transported during "international cooperation assignments" by reducing the number of transit landings.[887] Tokyo decided to procure a refueler based on Boeing's 767-200, called the KC-767J, that features a remote aerial refueling operator II (RARO II) system. With the RARO II, the operator is located at the rear of the cockpit enhancing coordination with the cockpit crew during refueling operations. The aerial refuelers also serve dual functions, as fuel is stored in the bottom half of the 767 and the top deck of the 767 features a 30-ton cargo carrying capacity.[888] In anticipation of the aerial tankers, ASDF pilots began aerial refueling training with US counterparts 2003, discussed in a later chapter.

Modernizing Airlift Capabilities

With no significant international missions until the 1990s, the ASDF had little reason to maintain long-range transports. Three ASDF units provided the force's airlift capability: the 401st Airlift Division at Komaki Airbase, the 402nd Airlift Division at Iruma Airbase, and the 403rd Airlift Division at Miho Airbase, which flew C-130Hs, C-1s, and YS-11s. The US C-130Hs were Japan's only platforms capable of providing an international airlift capability, as the indigenous C-1s and YS-11s did not have the range or the capacity for international flights. However, as the SDF increasingly emphasized mobility and international deployments—and as Tokyo operationalized the remote islands defense concept—Japan's airlift capabilities have taken on an important role in transporting units and supplies to remote locations both within

Japan and to locations around the world. Japan, therefore, requires increasingly long-range transportation aircraft.

The YS-11, a turboprop plane that can seat up to 60 people, was Japan's first indigenously produced passenger plane after World War II. Developed in the 1960s, serial production began in 1964 and ran until 1973. Separately, Japan's indigenously developed C-1 cargo plane was purposely designed in the late 1960s with a limited range and cargo capacity to avoid any misperception that Japan was developing a capability to transport military equipment beyond the Japanese archipelago. The C-1 was originally designed to transport up to 8 tons of cargo approximately 1,300 kilometers. However, the distance between Tokyo and Okinawa is over 1,500 kilometers, so the C-1 would have to land and refuel to complete even this flight, and it could not carry even one T-73 armored vehicle. With the reversion of Okinawa to Japanese rule in the early 1970s—and as Tokyo began to station SDF troops in the southwestern islands—the range of the C-1 was extended through make-shift additions of fuel tanks to empty spaces in the aircraft, allowing it fly between Tokyo and Okinawa without refueling. The cargo capacity was reduced even further with the alterations and the C-1, therefore, could provide only limited transport capabilities. Japan would eventually manufacture 26 C-1 transport aircraft.

By the late 1970s, Tokyo debated whether to develop a replacement for the C-1 indigenously or to purchase the US C-130 transport aircraft. The ASDF had followed development of the C-130 since the program began in the 1950s, dispatching pilots and navigators to the US to investigate its progress. In 1981, Japan made the decision to procure the first of 16 C-130Hs, but at a rate of approximately one per year, procurement was not complete until 1998.[889]

The Technical Research and Development Institute, in cooperation with Japanese industry, began research on the new replacement aircraft, dubbed the P-X and C-X programs, in the spring of 2001. The C-X cargo plane was designed to carry up to 26 tons of cargo at a range of 6,500 kilometers. Unlike the C-130H, the C-X featured jet engines and will be able to fly 890 kilometers per hour. As development was completed, Tokyo planned build over a dozen C-X aircraft by 2013 and complete fielding of the aircraft by 2018.

Intelligence Collection Platforms

Japan has collected intelligence from airborne platforms such as the ASDF's YS-11E and YS-11EL propeller planes based out of Iruma Air Base, and EP-3s based out of Iwakuni Air Base. The EP-3s were the primary collection platform against North Korea when North Korea's Kim Il-song died in 1994 to collect intelligence on North Korea's intentions and track aircraft that might be launched. As no one knew at the time whether Kim Il-song had died of natural causes, was assassinated, or whether there was a coup, Japan and other countries closely observed the situation on the Korean peninsula immediately after Kim's death.[890] In another incident in March 1997, the newly opened DIH received two reports that a coup had taken place in North Korea and that the country was under martial law. The DIH dispatched an ASDF YS-11EL aircraft to the Sea of Japan to monitor North Korean military radio communications.[891] While the YS-11 reached retirement age—besides the YS-11s deployed in the SDF, the few remaining YS-11s in commercial service were scheduled for retirement by 2006[892]—the EP-3s are relatively new with just over a decade of experience in the ASDF.

Two YS-11s were initially modified as ECM trainers in 1976 and 1979. In 1982, according to Enji Rai, the former director for TRDI's Plans and Programs department, the YS-11 became Japan's first plane to conduct electronic intelligence when it was fitted out with the J/ALR-1 ELINT suite in 1982. Three YS-11Es were later upgraded with the improved J/ALR-2 units, manufactured by Toshiba.[893]

Japan operates five EP-3 ELINT aircraft belonging to the 31st Air Unit based at Iwakuni.[894] The first two EP-3 aircraft were ordered from Lockheed in the late 1980s and delivered in 1991; the next three were ordered in 1992, 1993, and 1995 and delivered in September the year following their order. After delivery, the EP-3s underwent further modifications with Kawasaki the main contractor and NEC and Mitsubishi Electric providing the low- and high-frequency detector systems.[895]

In addition to the earlier deployments noted above, a separate incident illustrates the danger these planes sometimes face in the current security environment. Just after 1000 the morning of March 2, 2003, two North Korean MiG-29 fighters locked on to an MSDF EP-3 during its routine mission monitoring North Korea in international airspace. The ASDF scrambled two F-15s from Komatsu airbase in response to the situation, but the MiG-29s quickly switched their attention to the US RC-135S reconnaissance plane instead for about twenty minutes until the RC-135 returned to Kadena Airbase in Okinawa. The planes were not equipped with chaff or flare dispensers, making them easy targets for the North Korean fighters.[896]

Hostage Rescue Teams and Special Operations Forces

Japan created its first tactical teams in the late 1970s following a series of attacks and hijackings in the Middle East and Asia by the Japanese Red Army. These initial tactical teams fell under the jurisdiction of the National Police Agency (NPA) and, given their domestic focus in major metropolitan areas, they functioned more like SWAT teams rather than counter-guerrilla or counter-terrorist response units. The Transportation Ministry and its Maritime Safety Agency—later renamed the Japan Coast Guard (JCG)—established two security teams in the mid- and late-1980s that would form the nucleus of Japan's first special operations-type unit in 1996. Indeed, 1996 was a watershed year for Japan's counter-terrorism units, as both the JCG and NPA units were consolidated and upgraded after the Aum attacks and a series of copy-cat attacks in 1995, including the hijacking of an ANA flight in Japan that summer. The Ground and Maritime Self Defense Forces began to contemplate the formation of their own special operations units in the late-1990s following the discovery and capture of North Korean agents in South Korea in 1996 and 1998, and planning accelerated following the North Korean ships discovered in waters near Japan in 1999 and 2001. By 2003, both the GSDF and the MSDF had nascent special operations units, and pointing to highest-level interest in counter-terrorism, the units fell under the direct command of the Minister of Defense.

NPA Special Assault Teams

Japan's first tactical units were created within the National Police Agency in 1977 following a series of hijackings and attacks by the Japanese leftist organizations Red Army Faction of the Communist League (*Kyosando Sekigunha*) and its more radical offshoot the Japanese Red Army (*Nihon Sekigun*), which was allied with the Middle East terrorist group the Popular Front for the Liberation of Palestine (PFLP). In the Red Army Faction's first infamous attack on March 31, 1970, nine members wielding swords, pipes, and a bomb hijacked Japan Air Lines flight 351 from Tokyo to Fukuoka. With 122 passengers on board, the hijackers ordered the pilot to fly to North Korea. Stopping at South Korea's Kimpo

Airport, where the hijackers released the passengers, the plane then flew to Mirim Airport in North Korea, where they released the crew of the plane. The hijacking is commonly referred to in Japan as the "Yodo-go" incident.[897]

Members of the Japanese Red Army, founded by Fusako Shigenobu in Lebanon in 1971, carried out attacks almost yearly in the 1970s. After attacks in Israel, Europe and Southeast Asia, the 1977 "Dhaka Incident" led to the creation of a domestic hostage rescue team. On September 28, 1977, five JRA members hijacked a JAL plane, Flight 472 from Paris to Tokyo, as it flew over India and ordered it to land in Dhaka, Bangladesh. The Japanese government ultimately acquiesced to the hijackers' demands, releasing six Red Army members and paying a $6 million ransom for the release of the hostages.[898]

Initially called the "Special Armed Police" (SAP), this hostage rescue unit was first used during a hostage incident in Osaka in January 1979, when a man held up a Mitsubishi bank with a hunting rifle and then took the customers hostage when he could not escape. Following a two-day standoff, the SAP stormed the bank and freed the hostages but fatally wounded the hostage taker, who died on the way to the hospital.[899] An SAP unit was also dispatched to Hakodate Airport in June 1995 in response to a hijacked ANA plane, although once it was determined that there was only one hijacker, the unit allowed local Hokkaido police to storm the plane as the SAP unit watched.[900]

The Japanese government publicly revealed the existence of the special NPA units when it announced their expansion in May 1996 to five more prefectures, and it officially renamed them the "Special Assault Team" or SAT. While SAP units had been located in Osaka and in Tokyo—although the units could respond to incidents in other areas of the country—the government had decided to expand the new SATs to regional police headquarters in five other prefectures: Hokkaido, Chiba, Kanagawa, Aichi, and Fukuoka. Of the 200 SAT personnel, 60 would be based out of NPA's Tokyo headquarters, 40 out of Osaka, and twenty personnel based in each of the five prefectures named in 1996. Additionally, there are special training facilities in Tokyo's Tachikawa city. The SAT had also reportedly built a mock-up of the Ambassador's Residence in Japan during the 1996-1997 hostage crisis in Peru to practice storming and firing exercises, but actual dispatch of SAT units to Peru was hotly contested in Japan at the time (and Peru's Fujimori wanted his forces to do the job alone, as subsequent events demonstrated).[901] The SAT also trained with Germany's GSG9 during this time.[902] Additionally, "Special Investigations Teams" (SIT) were established in 1992 to conduct investigations related to hijackings, hostage situations, and kidnappings. They are also adept at conducting surveillance operations and providing other support to SAT operations.[903]

The SAT's first hostage rescue following its 1996 establishment occurred in early May 2000, when the SAT based in Fukuoka and Osaka deployed in response to a bus hijacking situation in western Japan. On May 3, a 40-year-old woman calling from the restroom of a moving bus first alerted the Japan Highway Public Corporation's operations center about the bus's hijacking. The hijacker, a 17-year-old boy wielding a knife, allowed her to use the restroom, and she reported that the boy had already stabbed another female passenger. Unsure of its location, Yamaguchi and Fukuoka police searched the major thoroughfares for the bus for several hours, when it was finally spotted cruising along the Chugoku Expressway. Two passengers jumped from the moving bus, and perhaps realizing that he could not control all the passengers, the hijacker subsequently released four others but kept the bus moving. The police forced the bus to stop at a rest area adjacent to the expressway, where three women were pulled from an open bus window. The hijacker injured two in the escape (one of whom later died from a stab wound). The hijacker then held a knife to the throat of a six-year-old girl in the halted bus preventing police from trying anything further. He demanded that the bus be allowed to go to Tokyo, which police initially allowed while following the bus. Less than thirty minutes later, however, the bus pulled into Kodani rest area in Hiroshima Prefecture to refuel. Negotiations began for fuel and a new driver, but with the arrival of the boy's parents, the police dragged out the negotiations to try to convince him to give up peacefully.[904]

Meanwhile, Hiroshima police had borrowed a similar bus from the bus operator to review ways of breaking into it to free the passengers. The easiest way to gain entry was through the front windshield, but attempts to break it ended in failure as the glass merely cracked into spider web-like pattern. Police determined that they did not have the expertise or the tools to carry out a hostage rescue of this nature, and thus requested the dispatch of SAT units from Osaka and Fukuoka. The SAT also deployed a sniper team, but because the hijacker kept the window curtains closed inside the bus, they could not see where he was at any given time.

As the late afternoon turned to night, the police decided to deliver pillows to the passengers, hoping that the hijacker would also fall asleep. The passengers could also use the pillows to shield themselves in case the police tried to break the side or rear windows the get inside the bus, it was thought. At around 3 am, as the bus was being refueled, the hijacker placed his 6-year-old hostage behind the driver's seat as he sat down in the front-row seat immediately behind her. The negotiator, standing at the front of the bus, watched for an opportunity to signal a rescue operation, as it had already been decided to rescue the remaining hostages if the boy did not signal his intention to give up soon. At 5:30 that morning, the negotiator dropped his left-hand white glove, a signal to start the operation. A fifteen-man hostage rescue team quickly moved into place from the rear of the bus, moving low and quietly along both sides. The boy noticed some activity, but he reacted too slowly: the team broke the windows and tossed a stun grenade at the hijacker, which exploded at his feet. One of the team members then pulled the little girl away from the hijacker and handed her to a waiting officer outside the window as others moved in, white smoke billowing from inside the bus. They quickly swarmed the boy, taking the knife from him and subduing him. The operation lasted less than two minutes, and the remaining nine passengers and driver were freed unharmed following the almost 16-hour ordeal.[905] The boy, it turned out, had just been released from a state-run psychiatric hospital, and had earlier that year written incoherent letters to NPA headquarters, the Prime Minister's Official Residence, and other offices claiming that he would "start a revolution" in Japan.[906]

In addition to managing the SAT, the National Police Agency also takes the lead in providing armed police officers to act as sky marshals on select international flights, in coordination with Japan's Transportation Ministry and US sky marshal officials when applicable. Japan initially placed sky marshals on select flights during the 2002 World Cup soccer games, which it cohosted with South Korea.[907]

JCG Special Security Teams

The Japan Coast Guard created its first counter-terrorism unit in 1985 (when the JCG was still called the Maritime Security Agency or MSA) when planning for the construction of the Kansai International Airport was underway. To prevent sound pollution in the densely populated Kansai region, the airport was to be built on a small artificial island five kilometers from land outside of

Osaka. Because there would be only one major thoroughfare to and from the island, officials soon realized that they would have to provide security around the perimeter of the island at sea, not on land as at other major airports in Japan. Thus the MSA established an eight-man security team, called the *Kansai Kokusai Kūkō Kaijō Keibitai* ("Kansai International Airport Maritime Security Unit" or *kaikeitai* for short, at MSA's closest base in Kishiwada, Osaka Prefecture, to provide for perimeter security once the airport opened. The team was increased to 24 members in 1987 when construction began that year. Members were selected from *tokkeitai* or Maritime Security and Rescue Units in each of the MSA's 11 regions. These units were in charge of responding to the scene when the MSA discovered illegal fishing boats or other suspicious vessels that refused orders to halt. The new *kaikeitai* unit was so secret that, once selected to serve in the unit, the 24 members were stricken from the MSA roster of personnel as if they had resigned.[908]

One incident occurred on August 14, 1989, when the MSA received an SOS from the *EB Carrier*, a Panamanian-registered freighter transporting iron ore in the East China Sea some 500 kilometers from Okinawa. The 34 Philippine crewmembers had locked four British crew in a cabin, threatening them at knife point. The MSA dispatched seven patrol boats and five aircraft to the scene.[909] Coincidentally, the MSA and the Japanese Shipowners' Association both had warned Japanese shipping companies and freighters the previous day that pirate attacks had increased in the South China Sea, after a Liberian-registered gas tanker owned by a Japanese company had been attacked and robbed by pirates off the Anambas Islands near Indonesia on August 6, and days later a Panamanian-registered Japanese freighter was robbed in the same area by four pirates. Greek and Norwegian ships were robbed in the area the same week, according to the warnings.[910]

Thus the MSA was already on alert for security incidents. While the Maritime Security and Rescue Unit from Fukuoka accompanied the patrol ships dispatched to the scene, MSA officials debated whether to dispatch the *kaikeitai* as well, as it was still a secret unit. While the MSA did not want to expose the unit given its classified counter-terrorism function at Kansai International Airport, the MSA at the same time wanted to test response capabilities as it was in the process of establishing another special security unit to guard shipments of plutonium for reprocessing in Europe. Therefore, the MSA ordered the unit to mobilize. An eight-man team immediately headed to Osaka's Itami Airport and boarded a YS-11 plane bound for Okinawa. Once on board, they were greeted by senior MSA officers who were observing the unit's response capability. When the plane landed at Okinawa's Naha Airport, the crew checked the location of the *tokkeitai* en route to the scene, which was also dispatched with the seven patrol boats. The team had not yet reached the *EB Carrier*, however.

The team chief on the YS-11 decided to proceed to Ishigaki Island, where the eight-man team would divide into two four-member squads and transfer to two Bell 212 helicopters waiting there. The two squads did not have the firepower necessary for a full operation, however, as they were armed only with Smith & Wesson M19 revolvers and new MP5s just delivered the previous year. Indeed, these were the only eight MP5s available for the entire 24-man *kaikeitai* at the time. And each team member on this operation had just one spare clip, making a flawless operation critical. Moreover, once the two helicopters reached the freighter—by that time surrounded by MSA patrol vessels—they could not rappel directly onto the deck, as the only boarding method available to the teams short of landing on the deck was the rescue basket used to hoist people from the sea below to the helicopter. They would have to use this system in reverse to lower themselves onto the deck below. The helicopters hovering over the *EB Carrier* were running low on fuel, so the team leader ordered his squad leader and one more experienced member to be lowered down first. The descent was excruciatingly slow as it was not designed for a quick delivery of special operations personnel to a target below—had the mutinous crew possessed weapons, the *kaikeitai* team would surely have taken significant casualties. But as they gathered on deck the *kaikeitai* could see that the crew only carried axes and rods as weapons sixty meters away from where they were landing.

On deck, the two held their MP5s at the ready as the rescue cages were slowly raised back to the helicopters. While this was an unprecedented operation in post-war Japan—this was the first active boarding operation on a non-Japanese vessel—their MP5s were empty: The JCG personnel were not allowed to use force unless directly fired upon, and they were ordered to keep their clips disengaged from their weapons. Obviously the crew did not know this, or they surely would not have remained so docile.

The team leader and another member landed behind the first two *kaikeitai*, and four other MSA personnel approached the freighter via patrol boat. Now, however, the team leader ordered his three men to load their MP5s as the gathering crew hooted and hollered at them. They then began to walk forward toward the crowd, shouting "Maritime Safety Agency!" and asking "where is the captain?" in Japanese and English. Seeing the four men in helmets and bulletproof vests pointing weapons in their direction, the mutinous crew surrendered. The eight MSA personnel—four others had just boarded from a patrol boat—freed the four British crew and locked the mutineers in empty rooms on the ship. The unit and the freed crew guided the 86,000-ton freighter *EB Carrier* on a two-day journey to Okinawa.[911]

At the time of the *EB Carrier* incident late in the summer of 1989, Tokyo was preparing to assume responsibility for the transshipment of plutonium from their civilian reactors in Japan to Europe for reprocessing. Such transshipments had taken place since 1969, with the most recent shipment being delivered by the 16,910-ton *Seishin-maru* in late 1984. The *Seishin-maru* carried six containers with 251 kilograms of plutonium onboard and was under heavy French Navy escort when it departed Cherbourg, France. While the shipments were historically controversial, a larger number of environmental groups protested this shipment because the *Montlouis*, carrying uranium hexafluoride, sank the previous year after colliding with a ferry off the coast of Belgium. After departing France, the *Seishin-maru* then headed for the Panama Canal, where US Navy ships assumed escort duties. Following a forty-day journey across the Pacific, the *Seishin-maru* arrived to Tokyo's Odaiba Pier 13 in the early morning hours of November 15, escorted during the final leg of its journey by an MSA patrol ship.[912] The six containers were then offloaded and taken by trailer to Tokaimura in Ibaraki Prefecture to be loaded into the experimental Joyo fast-breeder reactor.[913] Tokyo grew increasingly concerned of protest activity related to the shipments, however, and it also wanted to take more responsibility for security of its own nuclear material.

Tokyo considered multiple options for the transshipment of spent fuel to Europe for reprocessing in the late 1980s. It floated a proposal to fly the material to Europe, but dropped it given the stringent specifications for the airplane and the possible official protests of countries over which the nuclear material would fly. Maritime transshipment remained the only other viable option. While the ruling Liberal Democratic Party wanted to have the MSDF transport the material, the Japan Socialist Party and the Japan Communist Party—still major opposition parties in the

Diet—wanted the MSA to transport the material instead. With the pirate threat increasing particularly around the Malacca Strait—a major transportation route for the shipments—and because the shipments would be a potential high-profile target for terrorists, security took highest priority. After Parliamentarians observed MSA exercises to judge the Agency's capacity to secure future shipments, it became obvious that the long-range transportation operations would require a separate, dedicated unit to guard the material. The MSA thus established the Plutonium Transport Countermeasures Office to oversee a special team of 13 security personnel based at the *Kaikeitai*'s Kishiwada base near the Kansai Airport, beginning in April 1990. The selection process for this elite force took place over the next six months, and by October all 13 were in place at Kishiwada.[914]

The 13-member team—called the *Keijōtai* or boarding guard team—was divided into three squads of four men each and one team commander. In 1991, the team received training in Japan by US Navy SEALs, preparing them for the MSA's first cross-ocean active operation to Europe. On August 24, 1992, the team assembled on the pier next to the *Akatsuki-maru*—the new Japanese name for the previously British freighter *Pacific Crane*, which was scheduled to transship reprocessed plutonium to Japan—their home for the next six months. Taking the 1989 *EB Carrier* operation as a lesson, the *Keijōtai* was more heavily armed. The team now carried SIG P228s automatic pistols instead of the Smith & Wesson M19s, and each team member was issued a type-89 rifle and three MP5A5 sub-machineguns with one MP5SD6 sound suppressor. They were also allowed a minimum of six clips for the sub-machineguns and two for their pistols.[915] A newly constructed MSA ship *Shikishima* escorted the plutonium shipment, which proceeded without incident. The existence of the *Keijōtai* security team was kept secret at the time.

Thus by the mid-1990s, the MSA had developed a basic capability to deploy and operate maritime security teams in and around Japan, and these teams would serve as the nucleus for expanded capabilities in the coming years. When the National Police Agency announced the consolidation and expansion of the Special Assault Teams in the spring of 1996, on May 11 that year the Maritime Safety Agency too announced the establishment of the Special Security Team (SST) by combining the *Kaikeitai* based at Kansai International Airport and the Plutonium Transport Countermeasures Office. The SST would comprise of five 8-man teams for a total of 40 personnel, plus support staff. Team members were picked from throughout the country and were trained in a variety of counter-terrorism techniques, explosive ordinance disposal, and while the SST fell under the 5th Region Coast Guard in Osaka, teams could be deployed anywhere in Japan. They would be armed with counter-terror equipment such as Heckler & Koch MP5 submachine guns, sniper rifles, SIG-Sauer P226 9mm semi-automatic pistols, domestically manufactured type-89 rifles, silencers, flash grenades, and night-vision devices.[916]

SST personnel train at the Special Security Station, located across from Kansai International Airport in Rinku Town, Izumisano city, outside the major metropolitan city of Osaka. The facility, completed as the SST was inaugurated in 1996, has a pool, two boats to practice shore landings, indoor training facilities, a martial arts *dojo*, and other facilities.[917] They can be flown to any major airbase in Japan on one of the Japan Coast Guard's fixed-wing aircraft, and with the JCG's purchase of the EC225 helicopter, fully equipped teams can be transported intact to one of several new JCG high-speed patrol ships that can handle helicopter operations, a significant improvement following the unsuccessful dispatch to units attempting to halt and board the *Changyu* in

December 2001. This is also a primary reason why even the JCG's smaller high-speed patrol vessels are equipped with helipads.

SDF Special Operations Group

The Self Defense Forces began to take steps in the late 1990s to establish special operations units. The GSDF established a preparatory cell within the 1st Airborne Brigade in 1998 and dispatched personnel to train with British SAS and US special operations units. The GSDF's first special operations unit—the "Special Operations Group"—was created at the end of 2003 and was formally inaugurated on March 29, 2004. It has a force strength of 200 personnel and 100 support personnel, and falls directly under the command of the Minister of Defense.[918] Perhaps due to its recent formation and lack of operational experience, little was reported about the GSDF's SOG in its first years of existence.

Similarly, the Maritime Self Defense Force on March 27, 2001 inaugurated a Special Guard Team (*tokubetsu keibitai*—sometimes referred to in English as "Special Boat Unit"). The ceremony was held at the unit's training base on the island of Etajima, Hiroshima Prefecture—the former home of the Imperial Naval Academy. The unit was initially fairly small, consisting of 10 officers and 60 NCOs divided among three platoons.[919] Based on the history of the SAT and SST, however, the unit is sure to grow in numbers. Personnel began to train with the British Special Boat Squadron in early 2000, and although the unit was placed on alert during the 2001 spy boat incident, it was unable to deploy to the immediate area of operations in time.[920] Little has been written about this unit, however.

• • •

Defense Agency Director General Ono, marking the new National Defense Program Guideline in 2004, declared a significant shift in the Japanese mindset on defense: "From now on, we shall place more importance on our ability to effectively deal with threats instead of maintaining a policy of deterrence, as in the past"[921]

As Japan moved from passive deterrence to actively engaging threats, Tokyo needed the ability to command its forces in a centralized, joint fashion. Japan could no longer afford to maintain three separate uniformed services on the ground, in the air, and in the oceans, all with different commanders and non-integrated roles. This was particularly true given the shift of Japan's defense strategy from its northern territories to southwestern areas focusing on "remote island defense" and the establishment of corresponding units in each of the forces. These forces needed to work together under one commander who had the responsibility as well as authority to accomplish a given mission. Japan's three Self-Defense Forces needed to operate jointly.

Joint Operations and the New Joint Staff Structure

Japan's ability to conduct joint operations is a critical element of the "defense of remote islands" concept, as each of the uniformed services increasingly relies on interoperability to accomplish the central mission of defending or, if necessary, retaking a remote island. Missile defense also requires clear command authority over missile defense units from multiple forces. Until recently, however, and despite the overlapping regions for the three forces, no one commander had authority over forces belonging to another force. The head of the Ground Self-Defense Force's Northern Army in Hokkaido, for example, did not have any operational control over (and often could not communicate with) ASDF or MSDF units in the area, and vice versa. There was little need for unified commands during the Cold War, as each of the services' functions during an attempted invasion of Japan's northern regions were well-defined. The GSDF would attempt to repel a land invasion, while the ASDF would defend against heavy bombers and fighters and the MSDF would protect sea-lines of communication and conduct anti-submarine and mine-clearing operations as necessary.

The idea of creating a joint operations structure was first advocated in the late 1980s by Administrative Vice Minister Seiki Nishihiro (the aforementioned "Mr. Defense Agency") and Masao Ishii, the Chairman of the Joint Staff Council, shortly after the US Congress imposed a joint structure on the US armed services with the passage of the Goldwater-Nichols Act. However, Nishihiro and Ishii spent significant political capital in the late 1980s to win funding for a new Defense Agency Headquarters to be built in Ichigaya, Tokyo, and once construction began there was little momentum and little perceived need to establish a more joint structure within the SDF. The SDF thus retained its original command structure into the 1990s: Chiefs of Staff for the Ground, Maritime, and Air Self Defense Forces commanded respective units in each of the forces, and they in turn reported to the Defense Agency director general. Joint units could be formed temporarily based on a defense mobilization order, but the process under the Joint Staff Council (made up of each of the chiefs of staff) was time-consuming and would necessarily become parochial, although it had never been tested.[922]

Only after the 1995 Great Hanshin Earthquake and a subsequent spill from the Russian tanker *Nakhodka* near the Noto Peninsula in late 1996 did the Defense Agency take the first concrete step toward jointness when, in July 1997, the agency formally gave the Joint Staff Council authority to coordinate each of the forces during peacetime following major disasters and during UN peacekeeping missions. JSC support staff was also expanded to enable greater liaison and coordination with US forces in preparation for a contingency situation around Japan, in line with the new Japan-US Defense Cooperation Guidelines that were finalized that year.[923] Passed in April 1998, the revised Self-Defense Forces Law permitted the Joint Staff Council chairman to execute orders of the Defense Agency director-general to deploy joint units for maritime patrol actions, disaster relief, and other actions. Concurrently, the Defense Agency Establishment Law was revised and the Joint Staff Council was empowered to prepare joint patrol plans.

Further revisions to the SDF law, passed in 1999, allowed all Self-Defense Forces units including maritime and helicopter units to evacuate Japanese citizens (and citizens of other countries based on requests from their respective governments) from areas of strife outside of Japan—the SDF would no longer have to wait for permission from the Diet to evacuate Japanese citizens, as was the case during riots in Indonesia the previous year. This too required the coordination of units from multiple forces, as both the ASDF and the MSDF could potentially be involved in the evacuation of civilians from a particular area of the globe. However, each of the SDF forces remained constrained to single-force commands during hostilities. A Ground Self-Defense Force commander had no authority over a Maritime Self-Defense Force unit, for example, rendering operational coordination of units from more than one force practically impossible under the defense of remote islands concept. Transportation by sea or by air could potentially devolve into squabbles between commanders of different forces, each with a different operational goal in mind. Missile defense posed a similar problem since both the MSDF and the ASDF had disparate missile defense units with no peacetime unified command to oversee their operations if missiles were fired suddenly toward Japan.

With the increasing emphasis on defense of remote islands and response to asymmetric and other non-conventional threats, the Defense Agency recognized the need to enable unified operational control over units from multiple forces. In April 2002, the Joint Staff established a thirteen-member "joint project team" that published its *Results of the "Study of Joint Operations"* in December, and the Joint Staff also established a Joint Operations Planning Office in the J-5 to manage a potential transition. Citing C4ISR and increasingly accurate and long-range strike technologies, the study observed that the modern battlefield was changing rapidly. The report laid out legal steps to realize this new joint system, including the revision of the Defense Agency foundation law, the Self-Defense Forces law, and laws governing SDF mobilization.[924]

In early 2004, the Defense Agency took the first steps to establish a new structure charged with overseeing joint operations. On February 7, 2004, the Defense Agency drafted legislation that would abolish the Joint Staff Council and the position of "Chairman of the JSC" and create a new head of the Joint Staff. The operations divisions of the Air, Ground, and Maritime Staff Offices would be consolidated under the new head of the Joint Staff, and a "Defense Intelligence Bureau" would be established in the Intelligence Headquarters. The Chief of Staff of each SDF service would continue to control administrative affairs in day-to-day operations of their respective forces.[925] In March 2004, the Defense Agency's Joint Operations Planning Office—which was now in charge of planning the new structure—began to brief field units and to host commanders and others at their Tokyo office to "painstakingly explain" the envisioned joint operations structure, as some still "misconstrued the new approach by saying, 'Joint operations will be handled by the chief of the joint staff, while operations will be handled by the respective chief of staff in each Self-Defense Force branch,'" in the words of Commander

Toru Nishio, a member of the Joint Operations Planning Office. Instead, it was explained that one commander from one of the forces would be given over-all tactical command of a joint task force drawing units from two or more forces of the SDF.[926]

The Diet on July 22, 2005 approved revisions to the Self-Defense Forces Law to give the joint chief of staff command authority over the GSDF, MSDF, and ASDF. Whereas the DA director general previously had to convey orders through the chiefs of staff of the GSDF, MSDF, and ASDF separately, under the revisions the director general issued orders directly to the head the joint chief of staff. The chiefs of staff of the individual forces would oversee equipment and personnel matters, but they were excluded from the chain of command. The Diet also approved revisions to the Office, headed by a "Chief of the Joint Staff" and a deputy joint chief of staff, detailed below.[927]

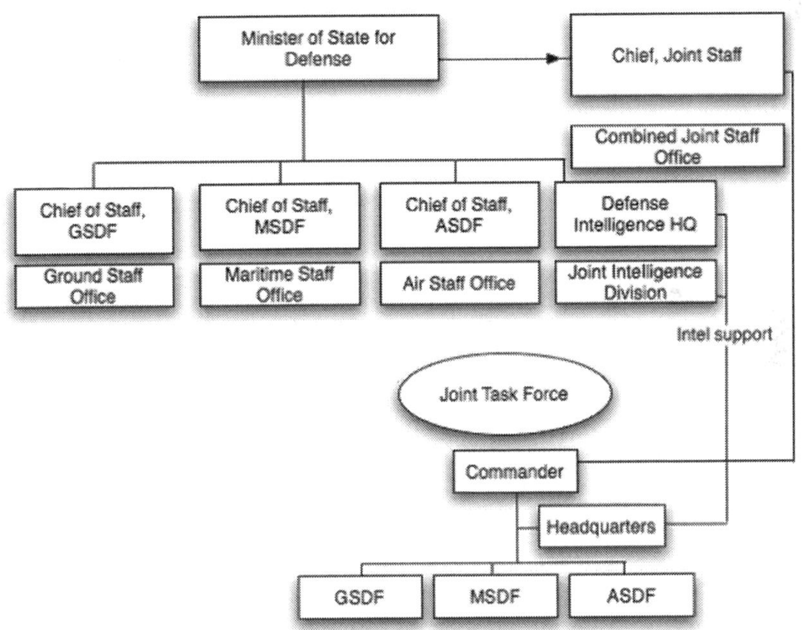

Source: Defense White Paper 2004, Japan Defense Agency

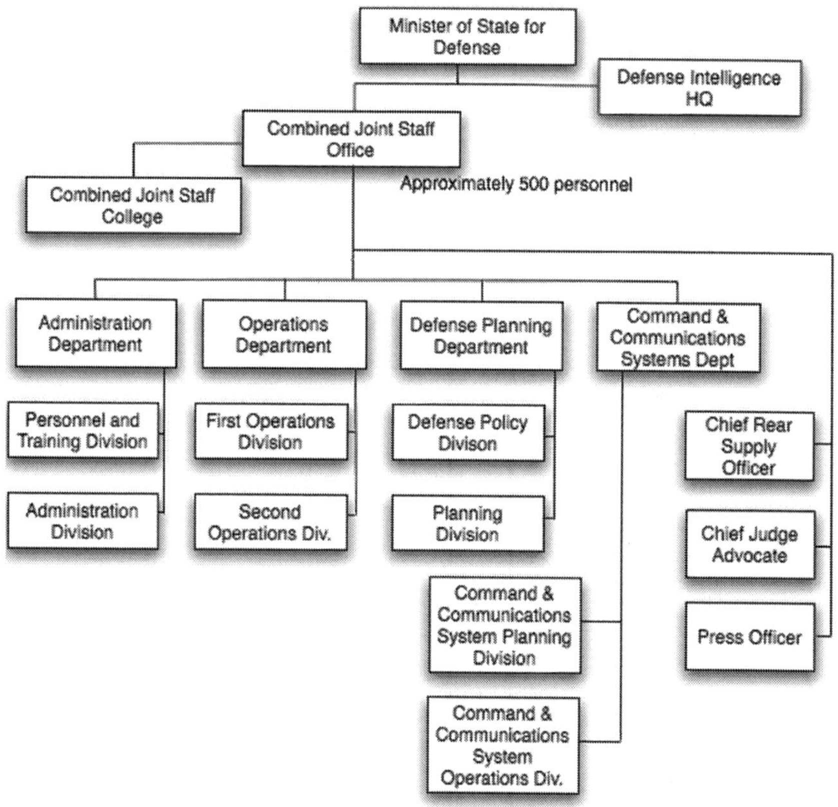

Source: Asagumo, July 21, 2005

Missile defense was a primary driving force behind the change. Since a missile launched from North Korea could reach the Japanese archipelago in 10 minutes or less, the Prime Minister simply could not consult with the Diet or even with his cabinet prior to ordering Japan's missile defense assets to engage an incoming missile or warhead. Thus, the revision of the Self-Defense Forces law included a provision added to Article 82 to allow the interception of "ballistic missiles" and similar types of systems such as cruise missiles and rockets. The provision stipulated that the Defense Agency director general, with the approval of the prime minister, can order a unit to intercept a missile over territorial airspace or in international airspace. If there is no time, however, the director general can issue an interception order immediately without obtaining the prime minister's approval. The director general would have to report to the Diet after an interception order.[928] Under the new joint operations concept, one commander has authority over missile defense units in both the MSDF and the ASDF. He would first order Japanese Aegis destroyers at sea to fire at any ballistic missiles aimed at Japan, and if those attempts failed, the commander can then order ASDF PAC-3 units to fire at missiles targeting their respective air defense zones.[929]

The Chief of the Joint Staff and the DA director general are empowered to designate a joint task force commander from one of the forces with tactical command authority over all units in the joint task force. As part of the reorganizations, the Defense Intelligence Headquarters also established a standing joint intelligence bureau to support any future joint task forces. As an indication of the new joint structure's growing functions, the joint staff was more than doubled from approximately 300 to over 650 billets. Of the 650, approximately 130 serve in the Operations Bureau, 100 serve in the Intelligence Bureau, 60 serve in the Defense Plans Bureau, 230 serve in the Communications Bureau, 60 serving in the Rear Logistics Bureau, and 70 serve in the General Affairs Bureau.[930]

The system will certainly evolve over time as the SDF continues to experiment with and test integrated operations capability. A year following the Diet's revision of the Self-Defense Forces Law to create the new structure, "work still needs to be done to establish a system providing for the ability to actually perform [joint] activities at the on-site level," in the words of Joint Operations Planning Office staffer GSDF Lt. Col. Kazunori Manabe in the defense monthly *Securitarian*. His colleague, ASDF Lt. Col. Hiroshi Kimura, added that Japan's joint operations structure will "improve gradually in the future to a system applicable to our country," and MSDF Commander Toru Nishio further noted that over "the next 10 to 20 years, we can improve the system further."[931] Thus, Japan's joint operations capabilities will surely evolve over time.

C4 Support for Joint Operations

Until the early 1990s, Japan had a fairly static command, control, and communications system. The Self-Defense Forces began construction on the country's first modern national defense communications network in 1977, which was called the *bōei mikurokaisen* or Defense Microwave Communications System (DEMICS). When it was initially completed in 1982, the main trunk and communications branches covered over 4,000 kilometers of territory along the length of Japan's main islands. Most major SDF bases were connected to the system, including Obihiro GSDF Base in Hokkaido, Misawa ASDF Base in Aomori, Kanoya MSDF Base in Kagoshima, and the Ichigaya GSDF Base in Tokyo. Defense authorities however feared that, should an attack take out one portion of the network, the entire analog communications system could collapse. There was also concern that the system was easy to tap. Defense Agency officials therefore began in the mid-1980s to consider the construction of a new digital network soon after DEMICS construction was completed.[932] Despite concerns for the viability of the system following a catastrophic event, DEMICS proved effective in the aftermath of the January 1995 Kobe earthquake as it was the only major communications system that remained undamaged, and because it was an analog SHF microwave communications system—a standard that had been adopted by other government entities—local authorities were able to tap into the DEMICS network as well.[933]

By the late 1980s, Japanese officials had decided to proceed with the construction of the modernized digital communications network, and in 1987 it budgeted ¥80 billion for the digital network. The new network, called the Integrated Defense Digital Network (IDDN), was to consist of 100 relay stations situated across Japan and was scheduled to be completed within ten years. Because the Defense Agency had to build 70 new stations that stood between 30-40 meters high, however, a number of local civic groups disapproved of the construction due to concerns the towers would negatively impact the local landscape.[934] The Defense Agency ultimately dropped the number of new stations to around 40, but the completion of the network was still delayed until shortly after the year 2000.

In addition to the terrestrial DEMICS and IDDN communications networks, the Self-Defense Forces increasingly relied on communications via the "Superbird" communications satellites. Although not characterized as such at the time, the SDF's early use of satellites for communications purposes represented Japan's first attempts to improve defense of remote islands, as they enabled communications with units on Iwo Jima and in other remote locations. Japan's first government use of satellite communications for defense purposes came in 1983. That year—just as DEMICS was completed—the Defense Agency was allowed access to NTT's "test" communications satellite CS-2/Sakura-2 for communications between the Defense Agency headquarters and units in Iwo Jima. This created a public stir since it was the first time the Defense Agency had used a space-based system for defense purposes. In 1985, the Maritime Self Defense Force used the 1983 precedent as grounds for a request to use the US Navy's communications satellite Fleetsat.[935]

The main reason for the public unease in 1983 was due to a 1969 cabinet decision that, with the establishment of the National

Space Development Agency (NASDA), Tokyo would limit its use of space for "peaceful" purposes.[936] When the Defense Agency requested permission to use a communications satellite in 1983, the Cabinet at the time ruled that the use was "generalized" and therefore did not violate the "peaceful objectives" of the resolution.[937] The SDF could use satellites as long as the satellites also served a general, commercial purpose as well. Because the NTT satellite and later communications satellites were multi-purpose—they primarily provided commercial communications services—the Defense Agency deemed them "generalized" and therefore in compliance with the original "peaceful uses" provision.

Following early successes using the NTT and Fleetsat satellites for communications purposes, the Defense Agency decided to contract with a new Japanese commercial group, called the Space Communication Corporation, to use their "Superbird" satellites for communications purposes as well. The Space Communication Corporation (SCC) is a joint venture among the 28 companies in the Mitsubishi Group, with Mitsubishi Corporation and Mitsubishi Electric Co. (MELCO)—both of which are also major Japanese defense contractors—taking the leading roles in the business and developing the critical shipboard systems as well.[938]

Despite the involvement of Japan's most experienced high-tech companies, SCC experienced a series of failures early in the organization's existence. While Superbird-A was successfully launched on June 6, 1989, the second Superbird, launched months later in February 1990, failed to achieve orbit due to a launch failure. Moreover, Superbird-A was lost in December 1990. The company's third attempt was successful: Superbird-B was successfully launched on February 27, 1992, and it commenced operations in April that year.[939] The satellite was dual-purpose, thus allowing Tokyo to assert that the satellite was "generalized" and could be used by the Defense Agency as well. It was developed from the beginning with defense purposes in mind, since in addition to its commercial communications equipment the satellite had on board two transponders dedicated for SDF use—one for the MSDF, one for the GSDF. The SDF began to use Superbird-B for defense communications in July 1992. The MSDF equipped 52 ships with special receivers for the X-band satellite transponder at a cost of ¥18 billion, and ships could communicate via the Superbird satellite with the MSDF's anti-submarine center in Yokosuka.[940]

SCC successfully launched several more satellites in the 1990s, including another Superbird-A in December 1992. Superbird-C was launched from Cape Canaveral, Florida, in July 1997 by Lockheed Martin Commercial Launch Service.[941] Superbird-C was also mainly used for commercial services—the satellite broadcast digital television for DirecTV in Japan—but it covered a much wider area over the Pacific including Japan, Northeast Asia, Southeast Asia, Hawaii, and a steerable beam that covered Australia and New Zealand. The ASDF joined the GSDF and MSDF in acquiring a satellite communications capability, and all three services were able to use the Superbird-C by October 1998.[942]

Two more satellites were launched in 2000: Superbird-B2 was launched on February 18, and Superbird-D was launched on October 7, 2000.[943] The Superbird-D by that point was the most advanced of the Superbird satellite family, with a high-output 120W Ku-band transponders that covered the entire Japanese archipelago, and the MSDF upgraded its communications equipment to allow communications links via Superbird D by 2003.[944] The Superbird-A2, launched in April 2004, took over for the decommissioned Superbird-A in July, although it was more advanced and was reportedly capable of providing high-speed communications with regions as far as India and the Middle East from its orbit 36,000 kilometers above the earth's surface.[945] The

Ku-band satellite enabled communications with MSDF units in the Indian Ocean supporting Operation Enduring Freedom and, separately, GSDF units stationed in Samawah, Iraq from 2004 via satellite videophone and satellite cellular phone.[946] Thus, Japan's real-time defense communications network reached as far as the Middle East.

As the new Defense Agency Headquarters was under construction in Ichigaya, Tokyo, the DA in 1996 began construction on the so-called "New Central Command System" (NCCS) to replace the system in use at the Agency's former facility in Roppongi. The NCCS officially became operational in March 2001.[947] The NCCS main command/control facility is located on the third basement floor of the Ministry of Defense headquarters Building A in Ichigaya, Tokyo. The NCCS is linked to the command/communications systems of each of the SDF services via a fiber optic cable network.[948] The NCCS is also linked to the Prime Minister's Official Residence and other relevant government entities.[949]

Japan's 21st Century 'Info-RMA'

While the Defense Agency's use of the earliest Superbird communications satellites represented an attempt to establish basic communications with units in remote areas of the Japanese archipelago, the latest and significantly more robust "Superbird" satellites can be seen as an extension of Japan's nascent embrace of the "Revolution in Military Affairs." The "Revolution in Military Affairs" in the United States began in the 1970s and 1980s when the US military began to leverage information technology and real-time communication networks such as the Global Positioning System and communications satellites to enable greater awareness on the battlefield and, ultimately, highly accurate strikes on military-related targets, for example. RMA became a vogue term in the 1990s following coalition forces' lopsided victory over Iraqi forces in Operation Desert Storm, and Japanese strategists began discussing concepts related to RMA in the mid- and late-1990s. While it fell out of use in the US military in the early 2000s,[950] Japanese media continued to highlight US military dominance in Afghanistan and Iraq as examples of "RMA." *Yomiuri* for example proclaimed: "The power of RMA was proved in the recent Iraq war. Information on enemy forces obtained by spy satellites and unmanned reconnaissance planes was transmitted through digital communications systems, followed by attacks with precision guided munitions."[951]

As Japan began to emphasize defense of remote islands and greater mobility, the Defense Agency in 2000 conducted an initial study of RMA concepts as a guide to modernizing its command, control, and communications capability. The Defense Agency in September 2000 published its first official policy paper concerning the indigenous development of an advanced defense information-sharing network. Titled "On Info-RMA," the paper provided a sweeping discussion of the need to improve information networks in the Self Defense Forces to facilitate rapid response capabilities. "[W]e cannot deny the possibility of attack by weapons of mass destruction by [traditional] militaries and attacks utilizing unconventional means such as terrorism and guerrilla warfare," and "therefore, an ability to respond to unconventional warfare is necessary." Information and intelligence are the keys to responding to unconventional warfare in the 21st century: "In order to improve battlefield identification and response capabilities, it is necessary that troops of the Ground, Maritime, and Air Self Defense Forces share sophisticated and large volumes of information through an information network and possess so-called C4ISR."[952] The main focus of early Defense Agency efforts in the field of RMA would center on the sharing of information among the different forces, a major prerequisite for joint operations.

"On Info-RMA" identified the need to develop RMA concepts in Japan. In December 2000, the Defense Agency outlined its plan to operationalize info-RMA and upgrade the country's defense C4ISR capabilities. Titled "Outline of the Defense Agency's Comprehensive Program for Gaining Information Superiority," the plan focused on three main elements: the development of a nationwide defense computer network called the "Defense Information Infrastructure," accompanied by a common software system called "Common Operating Environment"; improvements to command, communication and intelligence capabilities; and improvements to information security.

Even as the Defense Agency undertook its first efforts to introduce info-RMA concepts and modernize its C4ISR capabilities, the December 2001 spy ship incident once again highlighted the overriding need for a near-real-time tactical defense information network in Japan. The P-3C that discovered the suspicious vessels was unable to transmit images of the ships directly to shore, as the P-3Cs in that region had yet to be outfitted with the communications equipment necessary for the transmission of digital imagery. It had to return to base to have the images delivered to Tokyo—the return trip took one and a half hours, and the delivery of the 10 images to Tokyo took another three hours. It would take 9 hours altogether for the images to reach policymakers in Tokyo and to be delivered to the Japan Coast Guard for further action.[953] The basic inability to send pictures in near-realtime from Japanese P-3Cs further highlighted the need for improvement of Japan's C4ISR networks.

Based on this incident, the Koizumi administration in 2002 moved to implement comprehensive measures to improve its capabilities to identify and respond to threats from suspicious vessels, which included improving communications capabilities. In April 2002, a special commission led by Chief Cabinet Secretary

Fukuda released the "Investigation Results of Measures to Deal with Spy Ships in Southwest Seas Near Kyushu." Its first policy recommendation was to supply units at sea—including P-3Cs—with equipment capable of sending photos electronically and instantaneously not only to the respective unit's headquarters, but also to policymakers in Tokyo. The special sets to be installed in the P-3Cs would send information to higher echelons and to Tokyo via Japan's "Superbird C" communications satellite.

Improvement of C4ISR was considered central to enabling a robust joint operations structure. DA Director-General Ishiba said in an interview in 2003 that "the foundation of joint operations is a common and integrated communication and information system."[954] A National Defense Academy instructor asserted that improvements in technology are indispensable in joint operations: "If we further install data links necessary for operations among the three Self-Defense Forces and share central command centers, we will be able to provide for efficient joint operations." Further, "Japan is scheduled to launch an independent intelligence satellite next fiscal year, enabling the Self-Defense Forces to aim for a full-fledged C4ISR system."[955] A description of RMA in the monthly *Sentaku* in October 2002 further illustrated the importance defense commentators placed on new information technologies: "Battlefield Intelligence collected in realtime using satellites and special forces would enable precision guided weapons to expose the enemy to pinpoint aerial attacks."[956] Thus, policymakers and defense commentators alike pointed to a modernized C4ISR system as providing the foundation for joint operations and precision-strike capability.

As part of Japan's emphasis on RMA-based concepts to enable joint operations, each of the forces began to upgrade their tactical C4I capabilities in the early 2000s. Following the submission of legislation to create the new joint operations structure in

2004, the Defense Agency budgeted funds from 2005 to improve the Agency's "information and communications posture to support the smooth execution of joint operations and international operations" in each of the forces.[957] These upgraded systems include: the "Maritime Operations Force System"—commonly referred to as the "MOF System"—in the MSDF; the Base Air Defense Ground Environment (BADGE) system in the ASDF; and the Regimental Command and Control System in the GSDF. Moreover, the Technical Research and Development Institute in 2004 inaugurated a new "Department of Integrated Advanced Technology Development," a 21-person office that develops advanced IT and networking technologies for joint use among the SDF branches.[958]

MSDF: 'MOF System'

Given their extended areas of operations, both the MSDF and the ASDF rely heavily on C4I capabilities.

The Maritime Self Defense Force maintains command and control functions via the Maritime Operations Force (MOF) System out of the MSDF Headquarters in Yokosuka City south of Tokyo. Regional MSDF bases in Yokosuka, Maizuru, Ominato, Sasebo, and Kure, as well as the Maritime Air Center of the Air Command HQ at Atsugi, were also connected to the system as of the early 2000s.[959] (The MSDF's Fleet Intelligence Command, which began operations in January 1997, is also located at the MSDF HQ in Yokosuka City.[960])

In late 2002, the MSDF budgeted funds to enhance "IT functionality…to respond to the IT revolution and RMA" and to improve "the sophisticated network environment connecting the Defense Agency and the SDF." This "enhanced" effort included renovating the MOF System and improving C2T "Command

and Control Support Terminals"—the sea-based terminal of the MOF System. Each flag ship of the MSDF's four flotillas would be equipped with an upgraded C2T.[961] Most new ships now coming on line are also equipped with the C2T, giving the MSDF more flexibility in commanding individual ships. New ships equipped with the C2T include the new *Takanami*-class destroyers, the 14DDG guided destroyers, and the new 16DDH helicopter destroyer.[962] (The new 16SS class submarines, the *Soryu*, would have a "submarine version" of the C2T terminal, and a newly developed "Multi-Function Intelligence Control Console.[963])

Further, the MSDF funded upgrades to satellite communications equipment to link with satellites capable of transmitting in Ku-band wide-area, high-capacity spectrum such as the Superbird-D communications satellite launched in 2000. The MSDF also began to upgrade its HF multicast communications system and began modernizing the submarine broadcast system. And following the December 2001 inability to transmit photos of a suspicious vessel, the MSDF budgeted funds to improve photo transmission capabilities for its P-3C platforms and a modification of the OP-3 imaging equipment.[964] The MSDF also upgraded its communications capability with the Japan Coast Guard in 2006, upgrading teletype communications link between the MSDF Central Communications System command and JCG headquarters with an encrypted communications system.[965]

The heart of the MSDF flotilla, however, is the *Hyuga*-class 16DDH. The 16DDH will serve the role as an at-sea tactical command and control headquarters for an MSDF Flotilla. As early as 2001, planning was underway to equip the ship "with C2T terminals that are more advanced than those at the fleet flagship level" given its central role in providing fleet "command and control." It also features an Advanced Combat Information Processing System, the MSDF's new combat direction system for integrated control over different types of sensors, a new anti-submarine information processing system, and a new electronic warfare control system.[966]

ASDF: 'BADGE' and Missile Defense

The ASDF's main national level command and control network centers on the Base Air Defense Ground Environment or "BADGE" System, which the SDF define in its 2002 *Defense of Japan* as "a nationwide computer system whose capabilities are divided into an air warning and control capability, a command and communication capability and a communication line control capability." The four command centers and 28 radar sites across Japan form the ASDF's "eyes," "central nervous system," and "brains."[967] The BADGE System is "designed to convey and process command orders and information on aircraft tracks to identify and allocate targets to fighter intercepts or surface-to-air missile units."[968] As such, BADGE plays an integral part in air defense from foreign hostile aircraft and also serves as the basic backbone of Japan's nascent missile defense system.

The initial network of radars in Japan that formed its first modern, post-war early warning system was built by the United States. The network of 23 sites was handed over to Japanese control in the 1960s, and that number grew to 28 sites by 1973 with the return of Okinawa—where three additional sites were located—and the hand-over of additional sites in Amami Oshima Island that year. The whole network was modernized in the mid-1980s under Prime Minister Nakasone, and the new BADGE system was operational by 1989.

One of the primary missions for Japan's Air Self Defense Force during the Cold War was to provide early warning of an attack from the Soviet Union. Throughout the Cold War, the ASDF was on constant guard for intrusions into Japanese air space of Soviet fighters and bombers. The intrusions numbered in the hundreds each year, peaking at nearly 900 incidents a year in the mid- and late-1980s. The number of intrusions began to fall with the demise of the Soviet Union to 488 in 1991 and ultimately to 151 incidents in 2001.[969] Thus, during the Cold War, intrusions by foreign aircraft into Japanese airspace were the main focus for Japan's air defense system. Missiles, however, presented a more complex problem because they were much smaller and traveled much faster and at a different trajectory than conventional aircraft. The BADGE system was unable to track missile launches or trajectories around Japan, such as North Korea's Taepodong missile launch in 1998. Only Japan's Aegis destroyers had a radar powerful enough to track missile launches.

Prior to the August 1998 Taepodong missile launch, 18 radar sites had J/FPS-1 and J/FPS-2 fixed three-dimensional radar systems developed by Mitsubishi Electric and NEC respectively, but those radars could not track missiles. Radars at ten other sites were being upgraded to J/FPS-3 systems developed by Mitsubishi Electric that could discern distance, azimuth and altitude of targets. The system had antennas for two types of active phased-array radars to detect targets at short and long distances, and were capable of communicating via the US military's Link 16 Joint Tactical Information Distribution System (JTIDS) and link with MILSTAR satellite via secure UHF.[970] Seven J/FPS-1 radar sites were scheduled to receive a newly developed J/FPS-4 radar, which would enable the tracking of a missile launch.[971] The radars were not installed in time for the August 1998 Taepodong missile launch, however, leaving MSDF Aegis destroyers to track the missile as it flew over Japanese territory.[972]

Following the 1998 Taepodong launch, the Defense Agency immediately pushed for funding to modernize the entire BADGE system. In its 1999 budget, the DA hastily requested funding to upgrade six radar sites along the Sea of Japan, and the Agency later won funding to upgrade the entire network. In early 2002, the Air Self Defense Force awarded a contract to NEC worth ¥70 billion to upgrade the BADGE network as part of a defense modernization effort. The upgrades began that year and were scheduled to be complete by 2007, with the new BADGE system set to be operational by 2008. Six other companies were reportedly interested in the project, including Fujitsu and Hitachi, but NEC was the only company that submitted a formal bid for the work.[973]

Separately, the Technical Research and Development Institute began to research a new FPS-XX radar at its research center in Iioka City, Chiba Prefecture, specifically to track ballistic missiles. The system entered a two-year testing phase by April 2004, and deployment of the radars (designated the J/FPS-5) began by 2007.[974]

Should one or more of the fixed radar sites be damaged, the ASDF can rely on wheeled vehicles outfitted with the J/TPS-100, 101, or 102 three-dimensional mobile radar systems that are deployed to each of the Aircraft Control and Early Warning Wings. The six-by-six platform carries cylindrical active phased array radars that can link directly to the BADGE system. Like the fixed sites, the mobile systems are also capable of communicating via VHF and UHF radio frequencies, Link 16, and secure UHF via MILSTAR.[975]

The BADGE system displays the range, speed, bearing, and altitude of aircraft in its area. Friendly and "known" aircraft are identified with an "F," while unknown aircraft are identified with a "U." While the ASDF tries to keep the exact range of the J/FPS-4 classified, the popular magazine *Yomiuri Weekly* reported that it can identify objects, "several hundred kilometers away," and the first J/FPS-4 installed in the BADGE network with the 7th Early

Warning Squadron in Mihonoseki, Shimane Prefecture, could reportedly identify objects over the Korean peninsula.[976]

Radar blind spots are covered by E-767 Airborne Warning and Control (AWACS) Aircraft and E-2Cs. The ASDF bases 4 E-767s at its Air Base in Hamamatsu, Shizuoka Prefecture, and 12 E-2Cs at the Air Base in Misawa, Aomori Prefecture. The E-767 AWACS planes were acquired in the 1993 and 1994 defense budgets, costing approximately ¥57 billion each, or four times as much as an F-15 jet fighter.[977] Two were initially deployed to Hamamatsu Air Base in March 1998, and two more in March 1999.[978] The planes provide air defense during major events in Japan, such as the World Cup soccer games hosted jointly by South Korea and Japan in the summer of 2002 (the AWACS planes even had soccer ball stickers on the planes that designated which city they covered during the World Cup.)

The information is coordinated at ASDF command posts called "Direction Centers" (sometimes termed "DCs"). There were four in Japan as of the early 2000s, located at Misawa in the north, at Iruma air base outside of Tokyo in central Japan, at Kasuga in Kyushu, and at Naha in Okinawa in the southwest. The DC receives flight information from BADGE radar sites and, in the event of an airspace violation, they give intercept orders to fighter and surface-to-air missile units.[979] The system operates 24 hours a day, seven days a week.[980] There are also ten communications centers in the BADGE network—the locations also happen to correspond with Japan's SIGINT centers, discussed later in this book.

The DCs are connected to Patriot missile batteries. Four squadrons of the 1st Air Defense Missile Group cover the Kanto region, where Tokyo is located. The 4th Air Defense Missile Squadron, for example, is located in a restricted area in the Iruma ASDF air base. While the PAC-2s were reportedly effective against bombers and most modern aircraft, the commander of the 1st Air Defense

Missile Group was skeptical in an interview with *Yomiuri Weekly* that the system would be effective against a ballistic missile attack from North Korea or elsewhere: "I think that it is possible to a certain degree. However, I believe that the response is quite limited."[981] Because of concern that the PAC-2s initially deployed in Japan were ineffective against ballistic missiles, Japan began deploying the PAC-2GEM—used effectively against scud missiles during the second Gulf War—in the summer of 2003. The PAC-2GEM has an improved radar and missile body, though as one popular magazine noted, "there is virtually no hope of shooting down a No Dong missile" with even the improved PAC-2s.[982] Because of doubt that these systems could engage longer-range missiles such as the No Dong, Tokyo decided in 2004 to deploy PAC-3s at ten sites in Japan.

However, the PAC missile system is a point defense system that engages ballistic missiles in the terminal phase. Thus Japan must maintain a series of PAC-3 missile defense units across Japan, a difficult prospect given the country's geographic expanse. The range of the No Dong missile is around 1,300 kilometers and enters its terminal phase from an altitude of 300 kilometers or more at Mach 7. Moreover, the reentry vehicle itself would have separated from the two or three stage missile body, and in its terminal mode the reentry vehicle—which contains the warhead and other technical gear—represents a considerably smaller target moving at very high speeds.[983] Tokyo is therefore certainly interested in a regional defense system that could defend larger areas from missile attacks than the Patriot system.

GSDF: "G-Net" and the Regiment C2 System

The Ground Self Defense Force operated a basic command and control system until the early 1990s called the *yagai tsūshin shisutemu* or "Field Communications System." By 1995 the GSDF completed the first portions of a more complex network that would eventually link each of the GSDF divisions with the Ground Staff Office in a Central Command System. The GSDF inaugurated the first portion of the system, called the "Ground Self Defense Force Command System," at the Northern Army Headquarters in Sapporo in March 1995.[984] The Northern Army receiving the first operational portion of the system demonstrated the lingering strategic emphasis on defense of Japan's northern regions. As the new command system was completed over the next two years, the DA contracted with Japanese communications companies to build a "Division Communications System" for use among GSDF divisions from 1997. By utilizing a new fiber optics network, this system would allow a greater amount of information to be passed from front-line units to higher headquarters units and vice versa.[985]

The GSDF placed greater emphasis on C4I improvements in the early 2000s based on the concept of a "Ground Self Defense Force Network"—popularly called "G-Net." G-Net, according to the military analyst Naoya Tamura, "is an integrated computer network which links the Ground Staff Office to first line units" that features "sophisticated C4I functions." G-Net would streamline communications from headquarters units to units on the front line. The "Regiment Command and Control System" operates as a subset of the G-Net that connects individual units at the regiment level. This includes the "Inter-Vehicle Information System" (IVIS) linking tanks and other weapons systems in a local network.[986] (The RCCS was finally fielded in 2007.[987]) Also in the early 2000s, the GSDF began to field a tactical satellite communications system called "TASCOM-X" (*eisei tanitsu tsūshin shisutemu*), which was developed by NEC and can link with Superbird communications satellite.

The GSDF's Colonel Koichiro Bansho was a leading implementer of C4I systems in the early 2000s. Col Bansho in 2003 commanded the 3rd Infantry Regiment of the GSDF's 2nd Division, which twice tested a tactical "3CT IT Network System" at the unit level. The system incorporated computer links between combat teams and command posts that allowed the commander to monitor events via cameras at observation points.[988] (Little else has been reported on the "3CT IT Network," however.) A year later, as commander of the first unit that deployed to Iraq in early 2004, he established and communicated with Defense Agency headquarters via real-time satellite communications link, the first for a GSDF unit deployed outside Japan.[989] Bansho, a rising star in the GSDF, would eventually be promoted to lieutenant general and take over the high-profile command of GSDF's Western Army.

Computers: The Defense Information Infrastructure

The backbone of the Ministry of Defense's computer network is the "Defense Information Infrastructure" (*bōei jōhō tsūshin kiban*–DII), which connects the ministry with each of the Self Defense Forces. Before the DII became operational in 2003, each of the forces and the DA maintained separate systems, requiring separate operations and maintenance budgets. The DII has both an "open" and "closed" networks, with the "open" network able to connect to the internet. The open network operates on what is called the JIPNET-N system, which stands for "Joint IP Network-N" (*tōgō IP netowaku-n*), while the classified network operates on the JIPNET-S or "Joint IP Network-Secure" (*tōgō IP netowaku-s*).[990]

The system runs on a "Common Operating Environment" (COE) software system, through which software and upgrades are provided to workstations and mobile units throughout the system. Construction of the non-classified network began the following year in 2002, with users gaining access to the system later that year; development was scheduled to continue through 2006. Construction on the secure JIPNET-S system began two years later, in 2004, and users were able to access the system by 2005.

Fujitsu won the contract to develop the DII and COE in late 2000, but the new network experienced growing pains. Just as users were beginning to log onto the system in August 2002, information on the unclassified but sensitive network leaked. The information concerned the Local Area Network (LAN) that linked computers at approximately 160 stations between the ASDF, the GSDF, and the DA Headquarters in Ichigaya, sparking fears that "military experts could determine chains of command within the SDF" according to one SDF official.[991] The DA banned Fujitsu from competing for defense contracts for a time following the incident.

The open system was used to support GSDF units deployed to Samawah, Iraq, as well as MSDF units in the Indian Ocean supporting Operation Enduring Freedom. The secure network, in contrast, uses separate terminals to link MoD headquarters with unit commanders, thus limiting the number of accounts. From the time of its deployment in 2004, the system was designed to require digital ID cards or fingerprints to access the system in addition to passwords. The secure network also enabled secure voice and teleconferencing capabilities. The DII is administered by the Joint Staff's "DII Management and Operations Office."[992]

Cyber attacks remain a major concern for the DII. Even when it was established in the 2002-2005 timeframe, the DA reported dozens to hundreds of attacks a day in 2004, and up to 10,000 virus penetration attempts a month.[993] Each of the forces established units to defend against cyber attacks, with the GSDF establishing a 60-person unit that year for example at the DA's headquarters.[994] The problem continued to grow, however, with the DII as a whole requiring "drastic improvements" by 2011, according to the Ministry of Defense.[995] Cyberdefense will remain an increasingly pressing issue for Ministry of Defense and the Government of Japan.

• • •

In the two decades after the end of the Cold War, Japan's defense forces have transitioned from *hoppō jūshi* or "emphasis on the north" to *ritō bōei* and *nansei hōmen jūshi* or "defense of remote islands" and "emphasis on the southwestern region" respectively. The transition was slow to emerge at first, but the new strategic emphasis quickly grew in importance following maritime and special operations incursions and missile threats in the late 1990s and early 2000s. While *hoppō jūshi* centered on a heavy mechanized ground force, the new "defense of remote islands" strategy required a lighter mix of forces able to deploy rapidly and operate jointly.

Yet, even after this change in strategic emphasis, Japan's military remains small relative to its Asian neighbors. Japan has around 250,000 active-duty uniformed personnel and reservists, compared with over 2 million uniformed members of China's People's Liberation Army, South Korea's over-600,000-strong active uniformed military, and a North Korean military and paramilitary numbering in the millions. Moreover, as an island nation consisting of thousands of small- and medium-sized and sparsely populated islands, Japan's large geographic expanse requires significant resources to defend that, if not deployed appropriately, could be easily overwhelmed.

In this new era of asymmetric threats, timely intelligence is a critical component of Japan's national security. As Takemasa Moriya, former deputy director of Japan's Defense Intelligence HQ, asserted in late 1997: "Japan truly realized the importance of intelligence only after the end of the Cold War."[996] Intelligence reforms thus paralleled defense reforms in the late 1990s and 2000s.

The next chapter details Japan's intelligence reforms in the post-Cold War period through 2006.

5) Japan's Intelligence Community

In the Japanese language, *jōhō* can mean either "information" or "intelligence." The Japanese translations for US intelligence agencies all use *jōhō* in their titles. The Central Intelligence Agency rendered in Japanese is *Chūō Jōhōkyoku,* and the Defense Intelligence Agency is rendered *Kokubō Jōhōkyoku,* for example

In contrast, the titles of Japanese intelligence organs are more difficult to render into English. Japan's CIRO—*Naikaku Jōhō Chōsashitsu*—until recently was rendered with the rather innocuous official title "Cabinet Information Research Office" in English. In a sign of Japan's increasing acknowledgement of its intelligence capabilities, Tokyo quietly changed the official English title to "Cabinet Intelligence and Research Office" in 2003 without changing the Japanese designation. Similarly, Japan's reconnaissance satellites are called in Japanese *jōhō shūshū eisei,* which can be rendered as either "information-gathering satellites" or "intelligence-gathering satellites." (While Japan's space agency JAXA prefers the English translation "Information Gathering Satellites," the satellites are used almost exclusively by Japan's intelligence offices, so this author chooses to render the translation as "*Intelligence* Gathering Satellites" or intelligence collection satellites in line with changes in the CIRO English title.)

Chōsa, meaning "investigation," "survey," or "research" used in some intelligence-collection activities, can similarly be rendered as "intelligence": *Koan Chōsa-chō,* until recently the "Public Security Information Agency," was renamed in English the "Public Security Intelligence Agency" without any change to its Japanese title.

The defense analyst Kensuke Ebata noted this linguistic challenge in differentiating "information" from "intelligence" in the opening pages of his book *Jōhō to Kokka: Shūshū, Bunseki, to Hyoka no Otoshiana* ("Intelligence and the State: Pitfalls of Collection, Analysis, and Evaluation"), published in 2004. Ebata complained that the lack of a precise term to differentiate the concept of intelligence from information is "evidence" that "the importance of *jōhō* is not truly understood in Japanese culture." The difference, according to Ebata, is in how the information is sifted and used: information must be collected (*shūshū*), analyzed (*bunseki*), and then evaluated (*hyoka*) before it can be considered "intelligence." Information as such does no good without specificity, timeliness, and contextual reference. Nor is "intelligence" necessarily a matter of stealing secrets, according to Ebata. Such a concept would be designated *chōhō* or "espionage" in Japanese, but this is different from *jōhō*/intelligence as even stolen bits of information must be analyzed and evaluated to be properly understood. Ebata repeated the popular refrain that 80%-95% of "intelligence" is derived from publicly available sources, especially as the "information revolution" progresses. However, even correct bits of information can lead to incorrect conclusions—and thus, incorrect "intelligence"—when incompletely collected, improperly analyzed, or insufficiently evaluated. These are what Ebata calls *otoshiana* or "pitfalls" of the intelligence process.[997]

Ebata was attempting to imply that Tokyo spent the post-war years focused on collecting "information" but ignored the more crucial aspects of "intelligence." Tokyo had the basic structures to access and collect information in both the public and non-public domains, but until recently at least, the structures were not robust enough (such as having the personnel to craft the intelligence on a timely basis), nor did they have the advanced collection technologies and techniques that would allow a more complete collection capability in the modern information age. That situation began to change in the 1990s.

The first political efforts to reestablish an indigenous intelligence capability following World War II came in 1952, when then-Deputy Prime Minister Taketora Ogata proposed the creation of a Cabinet Information Bureau under the Cabinet Office. Ogata was an experienced intelligence officer, having been the director-general of the prewar Cabinet Intelligence Bureau. Ogata appointed Jun Murai, head of the National Police HQ's Security Bureau, to recruit specialists for the new organization. (The National Police HQ later became the National Police Agency, and its Security Bureau oversees the NPA's robust intelligence capability.) In April 1952, the Cabinet Research Office (using the term *chōsa* instead of *jōhō* in its title)—predecessor to CIRO—was created with Murai as its head and a staff of seven. Murai attempted to recruit former Japanese intelligence specialists who served in consulate police forces in foreign countries under the former Home Affairs Ministry to beef up his office. Ogata, however, passed away during this time, and opposition to a strong intelligence organ in post-war Japan in both the ruling and opposition parties caused Murai to scale back the plans and let go of some of those he had already hired, although he ultimately built a staff of 70.[998]

The Self-Defense Forces began to develop its own intelligence capability shortly after its founding in 1954. According to once-classified documents cited by the *Asahi Shimbun*, six years after the establishment of the CRO, the *Nibetsu* or "Second Annex" was established in 1958 in the Second Division of the Ground Staff Office (GSO). This office was in charge of intercepting and decoding signals intelligence (SIGINT) from other countries in the region, specifically the Soviet Union and the Peoples Republic of China (PRC). And although the *Nibetsu* belonged organizationally to the Ground Self-Defense Force and consisted primarily of uniformed staff, it was managed by and supplied much of its information to the Cabinet Research Office. Moreover, the newly formed National Police Agency maintained close links with *Nibetsu* as NPA officials were forward deployed to leadership positions in the *Nibetsu.* With an NPA official assuming the top post at *Nibetsu,* organizational ties between the NPA's security bureau, the Ground Staff Office's *Nibetsu,* and Murai's CRO were further deepened. The *Nibetsu* was later expanded and renamed the *Chōbetsu* (short for "*Chōsabu Dai-Nika Besshitsu*" or 2nd Intelligence Division [G-2] Annex) following a reorganization of the Ground Staff Office's Intelligence Divisions in 1977, by which time the *Chōbetsu* had a staff of some 1,000 personnel and nine SIGINT collection facilities in Japan.[999]

Also during this time, the Public Security Information Agency—later to become the Public Security Intelligence Agency—was established as far left-wing and far right-wing groups became increasingly active after the war. Mitsuhiro Suganuma, former director general of PSIA's Second Investigation Department, wrote following his retirement in 1995 that the Japanese Government in the 1950s recruited former members of the Imperial Army signal corps who had served in mainland China to monitor wireless communications of these groups with outside advisors in the Soviet Union and elsewhere. Many of those recruited, according to Suganuma, had served as military advisors to the Chinese Nationalist Army after World War II and had followed Chiang Kai-shek to Taiwan to become part of the "Pai Division." In 1952, the newly established PSIA set up a wireless monitoring section in Nerima Ward, Tokyo, under the cover of a private research institute called the "Terada Technology Institute," to monitor clandestine communications between Communist countries and groups within Japan. Within two years the staff had increased from two to 120 and was under the direct control of the PSIA director general. "Terada" was fully operational by the late 1950s, according to Suganuma, and it monitored wireless messages of domestic organizations suspected of being engaged in subversive activities as well as communications by "pledgers"—former Japanese prisoners who had pledged to spy for the Soviet Union in return for their release to Japan—with locations in Khabarovsk, Vladivostok, the Kurile Islands, and other locations along the Kamchatka Peninsula. PSIA also interviewed many former Imperial Army soldiers returning from captivity in the Soviet Far East who had been involved in the construction of many remote and little-known military sites in the Soviet Union. Suganuma noted that the "Terada Technology Institute" was dissolved in August 1976.[1000] PSIA remained active, however, as detailed below.

By the early 2000s, most of Japan's intelligence services had been upgraded and expanded to meet policymaker needs in the post-Cold War period. In addition to the gradual expansion of CIRO and PSIA outlined above, MOFA's Intelligence and Analysis Bureau was upgraded to the Intelligence and Analysis Service, and the National Police Agency's intelligence offices were similarly reorganized and upgraded to form the Foreign Affairs and Intelligence Department. In perhaps the most significant reorganizations since the Cold War, the Defense Agency's intelligence organizations were consolidated in 1997 to form the Defense Intelligence Headquarters. With the Defense Agency's upgrade to Ministry status in early 2007 and further consolidation within the MOD's intelligence organization, and with the co-location of the Cabinet Satellite Intelligence Center at the MOD Headquarters in Ichigaya, the DIH plays an increasingly central role in Japan's intelligence establishment. The histories and organizational make-up of Japan's intelligence community through 2006 are detailed further below, beginning with the Defense Intelligence Headquarters.

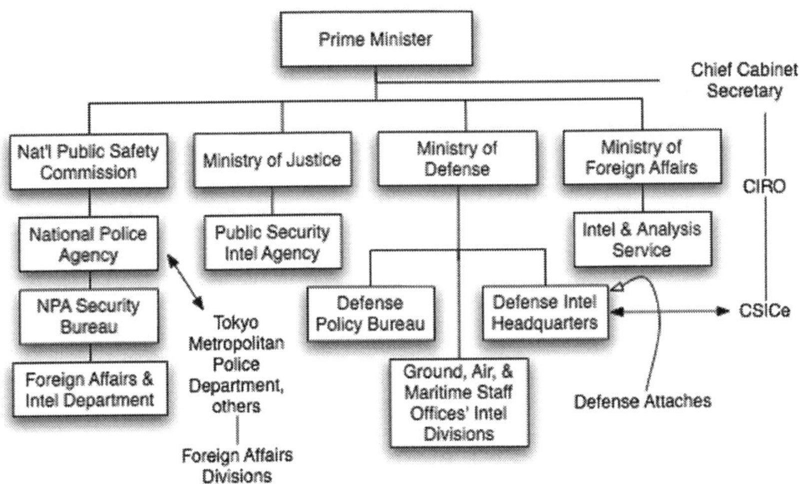

Japan's main intelligence services, based on "World Intelligence, Vol. 2," Gunji Kenkyu, September 2006, p 195, and other sources.

The Defense Intelligence Headquarters

By the early 1970s, a number of offices within the Defense Agency conducted intelligence functions of some kind, but sectionalism and internal rivalries prevented the sharing of collection capabilities. The resultant duplication of effort increasingly wasted resources. Besides the Ground Staff Office's 1st and 2nd Intelligence Division Annexes (responsible for domestic and foreign intelligence collection respectively), the Maritime and Air Staff Offices maintained their own intelligence offices, as did the Joint Staff Council with its J-2 and the Defense Policy Bureau.

The first serious attempt to unify intelligence within the DA took place under the leadership of Director General Yasuhiro Nakasone, who headed the DA from January 1970 until July 1971 and later served as Prime Minister in the mid-1980s. The DA under Nakasone established a provisional "Joint Intelligence Headquarters Study Preparatory Office" in the Joint Staff Council (JSC) to examine the establishment of a consolidated intelligence headquarters. Colonel Chikara Sakamoto, the deputy director of the GSO's *Chōbetsu* G-2 annex, was appointed director of the office. Sakamoto had studied at the prestigious Tokyo Imperial University before the war and served as an infantry lieutenant during WWII. Following the war, he covered the Tokyo Metropolitan Police Department as a reporter for NHK, but upon the founding of the National Police Reserve—the predecessor to the Self-Defense Forces—he re-enlisted and served in the NPR's Intelligence Department and studied psychological operations in the United States in the early 1950s. He later became Japan's first defense attaché in Thailand, and served as commandant of the GSDF Staff College. The plan to consolidate intelligence functions within the DA was shelved, however, following Nakasone's departure from the DA to become Secretary-General of the Liberal Democratic Party in July 1971, as the offices in question wanted to retain their intelligence functions. The idea reemerged briefly after a Soviet fighter pilot flew his MiG-25 Foxbat through Japan's early warning system almost unopposed and landed at Hakodate Airport in 1976.[1001] While the strengthened *chōbetsu* was created in the late 1970s, the proposal for a consolidated intelligence headquarters sat dormant for another decade.

Moves to consolidate intelligence functions were renewed in 1988 when "Mr. Defense Agency" Administrative Vice Minister Seiki Nishihiro led an internal DA study on the issue while the agency prepared the 1991-1995 mid-term defense plan. Masao Ishii, chairman of the Joint Staff Council and Japan's highest-ranking uniformed officer, actively supported the idea. A variety of intelligence structures were studied, including the US National Security Agency, the Central Intelligence Agency, the Defense Intelligence Agency, and the UK's MI6.[1002] The study group outlined for Prime Minister Takeshita a unified intelligence organization within the Defense Agency that would be created with the construction of a new Defense Agency Headquarters in Ichigaya by 1994.[1003] Due to inter-agency squabbles, however, the Agency announced on December 19, 1990 that the plan would be "postponed" until the next mid-term defense plan after 1995.[1004]

The August 1991 coup in Moscow presented the Defense Agency with a unique opportunity to revive the DIH proposal. *Yomiuri Shimbun* reported that the Defense Agency had decided on August 25, days after the coup failed, to proceed with the creation of the centralized Defense Intelligence Headquarters by the end of 1995, merely one year later than Nishihiro had originally proposed in 1989.[1005] Consolidation received further support from the "Advisory Council on Defense Issues," which highlighted the need to consolidate intelligence in its Higuchi Report in September 1994. The report suggested "strengthening" "joint operations" to support "strategic intelligence functions" and "command and communication functions." As the basic planning had already taken place under Nishihiro's guidance and with the construction of the DA Headquarters just beginning in the late 1980s, the Higuchi Report lent additional support to the consolidation effort. The Defense Agency formalized the DIH proposal on June 10, 1995, and inserted a request for funding in the JFY1996 budget in August that year.[1006]

Following its establishment in January 1996, the Hashimoto Cabinet quickly proceeded to introduce legislation in the Diet on February 9 to amend the Defense Agency Establishment Law to consolidate intelligence activities within the DA. On May 22, 1996, the Diet passed the bill, creating the Defense Intelligence Headquarters in the Joint Staff Council. The new law read: "A new intelligence headquarters shall be established within the Joint Staff Council as an organization for the collection and analysis of defense-related intelligence, while the DA's intelligence organizations shall be revamped and reorganized to make the intelligence functions of the Defense Agency as a whole more complete and efficient." Under the new law, the DIH initially took control 520 GSDF personnel, 333 MSDF personnel, 349 ASDF personnel, and 18 Joint Staff Council personnel, for a total of 1,220 uniformed personnel, all under the command of a general officer. With this legislation and with funding approved in the JFY1996 budget, the Hashimoto Cabinet on December 27 issued orders officially establishing the Defense Intelligence Headquarters on January 20, 1997. Once inaugurated, the DIH would become "Japan's largest intelligence gathering and analysis organ," in the words of the defense newspaper *Asagumo.*[1007] The DIH would be home to a total of 1,582 personnel including civilian workers in its first year, and this number would grow over the years.

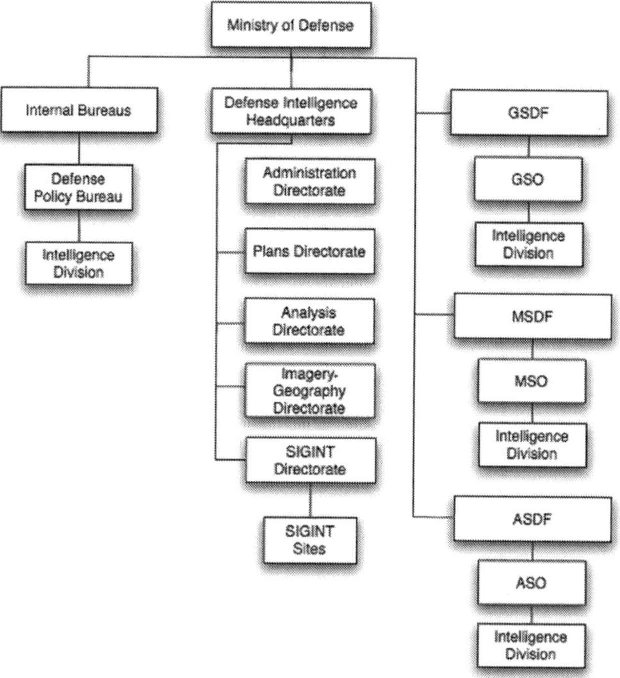

Ministry of Defense intelligence-related offices, based on "World Intelligence, Vol. 2," Gunji Kenkyu, September 2006, and other sources.

Interestingly, even though the DIH was organized within the Defense Agency's Joint Staff Council, according to the amended Defense Agency Establishment Law the Prime Minister's Office (PMO) retains key authority over the organizational structure and senior personnel appointments in the DIH. While the amended law states that the DIH falls under a "serving uniformed SDF officer" and organizationally under the Joint Staff Council, the DIH's "internal structure shall be decided by the Prime Minister's Office," according to article 18-2 "Formation of the Intelligence Headquarters." The PMO also has a say in lower-level personnel as well, as it is allowed by law to designate the civilian officials, including the DIH's civilian deputy director.[1008] Thus the PMO can shape the DIH to fit its intelligence needs as well as those of the uniformed services. The DA Director-General at the time of its formation, Fumio Kyuma, highlighted this dual role when he declared at the DIH's inauguration: "The first objective of the DIH is to contribute to policy-making not only by the agency but also by the government through analysis of high-quality strategic information."[1009]

The *Jōhō Honbu* or "Defense Intelligence Headquarters" was officially inaugurated on January 20, 1997. Lt. General Masahiro Kunimi was appointed the DIH's first director and Takemasa Moriya served as its first deputy director. (DIH had to wait until 1999 to move into its new building at the DA HQ complex in Ichigaya, since construction was still underway. Until then, it remained in Roppongi, Tokyo.) General Kunimi had significant intelligence experience, having served as the resident defense attaché at the Japanese Embassy in Beijing for three years in the early 1980s and later commanding the GSDF's 10th Division and the GSO's *Chōbetsu* intelligence division annex. Indicative of his successful tenure as the first commander of the DIH, following his retirement from the GSDF in the late 1990s, Kunimi was later asked to serve as the inaugural director of another new intelligence collection organization, the Cabinet Satellite Intelligence Center (CSICe). Moriya, a career civilian official, was well-placed to manage more prosaic organizational and personnel issues at the newly created DIH, having worked on personnel and finance issues in the 1970s and in the Defense Operations Division in the 1980s. Moriya, a rising star at the Defense Agency, worked his way through the ranks after joining the agency in 1971 and would later serve several terms as the Administrative Vice Minister of the agency. He also supported active use of the SDF as necessary, as his profile in *Gunji Kenkyu* quoted him as saying in 2006: "[T]he Self-Defense Forces are here to be used."[1010]

Under the director and deputy director of DIH, the Chief Technical Officer (CTO) is the third-highest post and has overall responsibility for technical operations related to intelligence. The CTO in turn manages three Defense Intelligence Officers—two SDF uniformed officers and one civilian official. The two uniformed DIOs are responsible for collecting and processing defense intelligence on regions around Japan and the civilian DIO is responsible for intelligence regarding security and defense policies of foreign governments. In turn there are five directorates: Administration (with two divisions and a staff of about 60 at its founding in 1997), Planning (three divisions and a staff of 60), Analysis (eight divisions with a staff of about 120), Imagery (two divisions and a staff of about 30), and SIGINT (ten divisions with a staff of about 350).[1011] There are also nine SIGINT sites, as noted above, with a total of 970 personnel. Intelligence cooperation between the former *Chōbetsu* and the NPA continued, as the DIH's new SIGINT directorate was still headed by a senior official assigned from the NPA.[1012]

Although the Defense Agency consolidated most of its major intelligence functions within the DIH, each of the Ground,

Maritime, and Air Staff Offices and the Defense Policy Bureau retained some of their intelligence functions to provide tactical intelligence. The Defense Policy Bureau in 1997 consolidated the 1st and 2nd Intelligence Divisions into one division, called the *Chōsa-ka* or "Intelligence Division," and it established a new "International Planning Division" as well, pointing to increased Self-Defense Force deployments abroad.[1013] The MSDF created the Fleet Intelligence Command directly under the MSDF Chief of Staff that consolidated tactical intelligence units, while the ASDF abolished the air intelligence units under its chief of staff and created new Intelligence Service Units under the Air Defense Command.[1014] Perhaps the largest intelligence division among the three services with 150 personnel, the GSDF's Central Data Unit (*Chūō Shiryotai*) was in charge of collecting open source intelligence (OSINT) from foreign media outlets and the Internet. The Defense Agency announced in 2005 its intention to combine this unit with remnants of the Central Geography Unit in Tachikawa to form a 600-person "Central Intelligence Unit" (*Chūō Jōhōtai*) in the GSDF to provide tactical intelligence support to GSDF units dispatched abroad. The new unit would have 10-person teams who could be sent abroad to assist in collection efforts as the GSDF units prepared to depart. (*Asahi* quoted one unnamed GSDF commander expressing frustration with the difficulty in determining the source of mortar rounds fired at GSDF units in Iraq as one reason for the decision.) The new intelligence unit would be created as the GSDF planned for multiple 1,300-person international rapid-deployment units beginning in 2007.[1015] In 2007, when the GSDF formed the fledgling intelligence unit, it created an "intelligence specialist" occupational designation, and planned to train 1,300 officers and 1,900 non-commissioned officers as "intelligence specialists" by 2014.[1016]

Kunimi explained the importance of retaining intelligence capabilities in each of the uniformed forces in an interview with *Gunji Kenkyu* shortly after its founding: "The DIH is responsible for strategic intelligence while each staff office intelligence department handles tactical intelligence." And although the DIH falls organizationally under the JSC, "the annual intelligence programs…are conducted in line with basic instructions appropriate to the operational guidelines from the Defense Agency Intelligence Committee chaired by the administrative vice minister," thus in theory keeping all of the intelligence offices aware of counterpart collection efforts.[1017] Moreover, the Defense Policy Bureau retains key control over the dissemination of intelligence through its "Intelligence Division" to other government offices outside of the Defense Agency, and the director of the Defense Policy Bureau often accompanies the DIH director when they brief the Prime Minister's Official Residence and when they attend the biweekly Cabinet Joint Intelligence Committee meetings.[1018]

The Analysis, Imagery, and SIGINT directorates are located in Building C in the DA Headquarters complex—the building between the main A Building and the communications building on the far right as one faces the complex. Building C is in turn divided into three main sections designated C1, C2, and C3 with eight stories above ground and four stories below. Building C also houses the ASDF's Intelligence Service Unit, while the MSDF's Fleet Intelligence Command (FIC) established operations at its new headquarters in Yokosuka's Funakoshi district on January 20, 1997.[1019] Two other DIH directorates—Administration and Planning—are housed in the main Tower A of DA's Headquarters complex, where DIH senior management also sit.[1020]

The DIH also controls a number of SIGINT collection sites throughout Japan. The facilities are located at Higashi-Chitose and Higashi-Nemuro in Hokkaido, with detachments at the remote Wakkanai and Nemuro radar sites also in Hokkaido; Kobunato, Niigata Prefecture, Takaoyama Radar Site at Miho in Tottori Prefecture, and Oi in Saitama Prefecture on the main island of Honshu; and Tachiarai in Fukuoka Prefecture and Kikaishima in Kagoshima Prefecture in Kyushu. Two of these sites, Higashi-Chitose and Miho, host large circularly disposed antenna array (CDAA) "elephant cages" used for the collection of COMINT.[1021] Japan's SIGINT facilities are "on the front line of intelligence gathering for the newly formed Defense Intelligence Headquarters," in the words of Ishikawa Iwao, an expert on Japanese and US basing issues.[1022] Japan's SIGINT facilities can not only receive foreign communications, they can also use its various SIGINT stations located around Japan to triangulate the location of transmission sources, as when the DA triangulated the location of the source of transmissions in the Sea of Japan during the first spy ship incident in 1999.[1023]

The facilities have claimed some notable successes. The detachment at Wakkanai in Hokkaido Prefecture intercepted the communications on September 1, 1983 between the Soviet fighter pilot and the air control center in Sakhalin when the Korean Airlines passenger airliner was shot down over Sakhalin island.[1024] Chinese specialists at the detachment in Tachiarai, Fukuoka Prefecture intercepted information that former Chinese Communist Party Vice Chairman Lin Biao was attempting to leave the country aboard a Trident airplane, which later crashed as it was flying to the Soviet Union.[1025] And in a third incident made public a decade later, Japanese SIGINTers picked up communications from a helicopter transporting doctors from Pyongyang to Mt. Myohyang on the death of Kim Il-so'ng in July 1994.[1026]

The DIH has been adding personnel since its inauguration. Despite zero growth in procurement in its 1998 budget, the DIH added 41 personnel in 1998 mainly to the SIGINT directorate.[1027]

The following year, the DA requested ¥1 billion in additional funding to ramp up intelligence collection efforts primarily on Asian countries such as Cambodia and Indonesia. The money was earmarked for up to 100 personnel at DIH. The DA cited as an example the Japanese government's surprise at the resignation of Indonesian President Suharto in May 1998 and the resulting need to plan for a possible evacuation of Japanese citizens in Indonesia at the time.[1028] Additionally, the imagery center at the DIH had approximately 30 personnel devoted to imagery analysis in 1997, but once Tokyo approved the development and launch of intelligence satellites, that number was more than doubled to 70 in 2000. By 2003, the DIH reorganized the Imagery Directorate into an Imagery and Geography Directorate with added responsibilities, further increasing the number of personnel there to approximately 160. Thus, the DIH had grown by a third in the decade after its inauguration in January 1997, with over 2,000 personnel dedicated to military intelligence operations in Japan and abroad.

Intelligence Training at Kodaira

Most intelligence personnel in the SDF attend the Kodaira Intelligence School. Located organizationally within the GSDF, the school trains some 2,500 students a year. Kodaira is commanded by a two-star general who oversees 300 personnel at the school as well as the SDF student population. The Kodaira School was founded in September 1954 as a *Chōsa Gakko*—literally "Investigation" or "Research School," but as noted above the term *chōsa* in post-war Japan commonly refers to intelligence-related activities. Thus, it could be called an "Intelligence School." The school taught students counter-psychological warfare techniques to prevent a foreign force from using psychological operations during an invasion or occupation. The school also taught GSDF personnel to infiltrate leftist organizations in Japan until the early 1980s, but the *Yomiuri Shimbun* later reported that the school stopped such training and destroyed the textbooks to avoid an opposition-led Diet inquiry into the school's activities.[1029]

The Kodaira school was reorganized and consolidated in March 2001 to include the operations school, intelligence school, and an accounting unit, and the school offers 93 courses in 59 subjects in intelligence, foreign languages, personnel, security, and accounting, among others.[1030] The Kodaira School offers intensive year-long language courses in Russian, Chinese, and Korean, and the school also offers courses in English as a second language, a standard course of study for a majority of Self-Defense Force personnel. Foreign language course graduates are sometimes sent abroad for further study. Graduates of the Korean language course, for example, are sometimes sent for further study to South Korea's National Defense College or South Korea's National Defense Research Institute.[1031] The school also teaches cartography and the analysis of aerial photography, increasingly important subjects after Japan launched its own reconnaissance satellites.[1032] With these and future additions to the curriculum, the Kodaira School will surely play a central role in training Japan's future intelligence professionals as defense intelligence becomes an increasingly important job category within the Ministry of Defense.

Reconnaissance Satellites[1033]

It is commonly asserted that North Korea's August 1998 test launch of its Taepodong missile over the Japanese archipelago spurred Tokyo to undertake a crash program to build and launch its own reconnaissance satellites. In reality, however, the Liberal

Democratic Party, CIRO, and the Defense Agency had been actively studying the possibility of establishing such a program for a number of years prior to the launch, and these prior studies coupled with Japanese technology firms' decade-long research in satellite and remote sensing technologies provided the basis for the immediate construction and deployment of reconnaissance satellites.

Japan's possession of reconnaissance satellites was gaining greater political support in the early 1990s, given the fall of the Soviet Union and the impact of Iraq's invasion of Kuwait on oil prices. On March 6, 1991—shortly after the successful conclusion of Operation Desert Storm—during interpolations at the House of Representatives' Foreign Affairs Committee, Foreign Minister Taro Nakayama, speaking of the sometimes-difficult process of gaining information from counterparts abroad, rhetorically supported the idea of introducing of reconnaissance satellites. "If we don't receive intelligence from America we won't know anything," he said, and therefore "of course it would not be strange for Japan to have its own so-called diplomatic satellite [*gaikō eisei*]." He continued: "For example, one thing to think about is watching the military situation and military maneuvers in the entire Asian region using reconnaissance satellites [*teisatsu eisei*]."[1034] In fact, CIRO began a "top secret" study of reconnaissance satellites in 1991, according to the security affairs journalist Tsuyoshi Sunohara.[1035]

In October 1993, the DA's Defense Policy Bureau studied the possibility of introducing reconnaissance satellites following North Korea's test launch of its Nodong missile in May that year. The Bureau subsequently finalized a classified report, called the "Outline for Photo-Reconnaissance Satellites," at the end of January 1994. The study examined the possibility of building indigenous satellites with help from four major Japanese defense contractors—Mitsubishi Heavy Industries (MHI), Mitsubishi Electric (MELCO), NEC, and Toshiba—with MHI providing the H2 rocket technology to launch the indigenous satellites and the latter three companies developing and building the satellites and components. Remote sensing technology developed by Japan's Science and Technology Agency could also be used on the satellites, according to the outline. It noted, however, that a constellation of five to seven satellites would cost up to ¥1 trillion, not a small sum for a country mired in recession. The fact that this study took place was leaked to the *Mainichi Shimbun* in August 1994, as Tokyo neared completion of its revised National Defense Program Outline.[1036]

Japanese government-sponsored basic satellite and remote-sensing technologies were coming to fruition by the early 1990s as well. The Science and Technology Agency (STA) had been deeply involved in research and development of remote sensing technologies for Japan's earlier research observation satellites, as one of STA's primary responsibilities since the mid-1980s was to support research and development of "earth observation" and "satellite remote sensing" technologies. In partnership with Japan's National Space Development Agency (NASDA), STA supported development of the Marine Observation Satellites (MOS-1 and MOS-1b) launched in February 1987 and February 1990; the Japan Earth Resources Satellite (JERS-1) launched in February 1992; and the Advanced Earth Observation Satellite (ADEOS).[1037] STA was also in the preliminary stages of developing the Advanced Land Observation Satellite (ALOS), which would have a resolution of several meters and at that time was scheduled to be launched in 2002. The Agency would draw heavily from technology developed for ALOS in building its reconnaissance satellites in the early 2000s.

Indeed, Tokyo had already employed its indigenously developed observation satellites at times for reconnaissance purposes in the late 1980s and early 1990s. In August 1993, an unnamed "military official in Tokyo" provided the *Yomiuri Shimbun* with three overhead imagery photos of Chinese airfield and port construction on Woody Island in the disputed Paracel chain of islands taken from the MOS-1. The overhead imagery, taken on November 14, 1987, June 14, 1989, and April 17, 1991, showed the progression of construction activities on the island during that time period. The first photo showed no activity, while the second photo from 1989 showed evidence that China had commenced construction of an airstrip and a port facility sometime in 1988. The final photo showed dredging operations had been completed, and the port facility was large enough to support a 4,000-ton frigate or submarine, according to the unnamed "military official" quoted by *Yomiuri*.[1038]

While the resolution of the imagery was poor, the implication was clear: a Japanese-built satellite was being used to produce overhead imagery of possible foreign military sites in Asia. And while the *Yomiuri Shimbun* did not report the specific offices using the imagery, the Defense Agency had surely seen the photos and was most likely obtaining other overhead imagery from Japan's indigenous satellites, just as the Agency purchased imagery from commercial vendors, such as from Landsat (with a resolution of 30 meters) since at least 1985 and from France's Spot satellite (with a resolution of 10 meters) since 1987.[1039] The GSDF had also ordered reconnaissance photography from Landsat in the early 1990s of regions around Japan including the Russian-held Northern Territories.[1040] By the time Tokyo launched its own reconnaissance satellites in 2003, it had close to two decades of experience in using overhead imagery.

Leak of the DA's 1993-1994 reconnaissance satellite study came a week after the release of the rather forward-leaning "Higuchi Report" on August 12, 1994. The report, as discussed previously, suggested that Japan should develop reconnaissance satellites, strengthen its C4I capabilities, build a missile defense system, and incorporate midair refueling capabilities. In the summer of 1994, however, the newly inaugurated Murayama Administration, the first JSP to lead Japan in over a generation, was not in a position to support such wide-ranging proposals as the development of high-resolution reconnaissance satellites. Murayama, who had just personally recognized the constitutionality of the Self-Defense Forces, could barely convince his own party to accept the constitutionality of the SDF. Murayama was in no position politically or ideologically to support new intelligence programs or the development of reconnaissance satellites. A possible reconnaissance satellite program would not be discussed openly for another 18 months, following the inauguration of an LDP-led government.

Shortly after the LDP regained power in January 1996, its Research Commission on Foreign Affairs and the Research Commission on Security began to hold joint meetings on the possibility of acquiring indigenously built reconnaissance satellites. Their first joint meeting on the subject, on May 15, 1996, was attended by officials from the Foreign Ministry, the Defense Agency, and Japan's electronics giant NEC. The NEC representatives stated that a reconnaissance satellite, a second satellite to serve as a spare, a data transmission satellite, and the ground station would cost roughly ¥210 billion and could be operational by 2003 if Tokyo were to support the program. The planned reconnaissance satellites would have 30-centimeter resolution—very near US capabilities—according to the NEC representatives.[1041]

NEC's participation at the meeting indicated discussion within the LDP had moved beyond *whether* to build reconnaissance satellites to *how* they could be built. Following these initial discussions, the Ministry of Foreign Affairs requested money to study the reconnaissance satellite issue in the JFY1997 and JFY1998 budgets, although the requested amounts—a mere ¥5.24 million in the JFY1998, for example—were miniscule.[1042] Moreover, MOFA stressed that the money was to review the idea only and would not be used for research or development purposes. Part of the reason MOFA could not budget more money for the program was political. The LDP was still in a coalition government with the JSP at this time, and without a Diet- or cabinet-approved policy document such as the NDPO calling for the incorporation of reconnaissance satellites or a significant exogenous event to draw public support for the plan, the LDP was limited to providing seed funding only for small government studies of a reconnaissance satellite program. The LDP remained hopeful, however, and continued to review plans in 1997 and 1998.

Indeed, as the Defense Intelligence HQ was established in early 1997, it was increasingly clear that Tokyo envisioned some sort of reconnaissance satellite program in the medium-term. As the well-connected *Sankei Shimbun* noted ahead of the DIH inauguration on January 4, 1997, "The DIH's imagery division will start as a section to buy commercial imagery and conduct imagery data processing. The DA, with a plan to possess its own satellites in the future, will accumulate analytical know-how" in this division.[1043] With Japan's technological base and the analytical structure in place, all that was needed was a political decision to fund and launch reconnaissance satellites and build the ground stations to support the satellites, but this in turn required solid public backing.

The commissions met jointly again in the summer of 1998. On August 15—a mere two weeks before North Korea tested its Taepodong missile—NEC representatives again submitted a study on a reconnaissance satellite program asserting that the company could build two reconnaissance satellites and one data relay satellite with "initial funding of approximately ¥210 billion."[1044] But by this point, two years after the LDP began actively entertaining proposals for a reconnaissance satellite program, NEC's rival, MELCO, had also prepared a proposal of its own. A week after NEC gave its presentation, MELCO's President Ichiro Taniguchi on August 25 presented his company's ideas on building reconnaissance satellites at the LDP's "Science, Technology, and Information Roundtable Discussion."[1045] He told the 18 representatives that not only would his company's satellites provide for greater national security, they could also be used to ascertain damage after large-scale natural disasters and keep watch over Japan's long coast lines.[1046] Following the 1995 Great Hanshin Earthquake and the recent DPRK infiltrations into South Korea in 1996, these were tantalizing merits and sellable to the public. The price, however, remained about the same at just over ¥210 billion.

Less than a week after Taniguchi's presentation, North Korea on August 31 launched a Taepodong missile over Japan. The launch provided all the justification the LDP needed to proceed with the reconnaissance satellite program. At a specially convened LDP meeting of local representatives in Tokyo to discuss the missile launch, Prime Minister Keizo Obuchi, who had recently taken over the premiership from Hashimoto, declared it "outrageous" that North Korea had "launched [a missile] over Japan without prior notification." Obuchi informed the representatives that day that his administration had ordered a review of reconnaissance satellites: "[W]e have instructed ministries and agencies concerned to study what [kind of satellite] we would be able to launch and what functions it would be able to carry."[1047] A reconnaissance satellite, it was widely argued at the time, would provide Tokyo with advanced notification of preparations for future launches. The LDP established a "project team to study the feasibility of introducing an intelligence satellite," which held its first meeting on September 10, the very day of the Obuchi gathering.

By this point, however, despite NEC's head-start in the reconnaissance satellite program bid, executives at NEC had been implicated in a scandal of overcharging the Defense Agency and NASDA for contracts. On September 10, four senior executives at companies including NEC were arrested and charged with bilking the Defense Agency out of millions of yen in defense contracts over the past several years. Although NEC was not out of the running for the satellite contract—it had significant technical experience due to its work on the ALOS—MELCO was becoming the early, untainted favorite among LDP officials eager to establish the reconnaissance satellite program quickly. By November, when the LDP officially announced that it would proceed with the satellite program, 11 NEC executives had been arrested in connection with the scandal, ruining its chances for winning the satellite contract.[1048]

Review of the proposed reconnaissance satellite programs moved quickly in the fall of 1998. Officials from MELCO submitted their detailed reconnaissance satellite proposal, titled "Study Concerning Multipurpose Information-Gathering Satellite System," to the LDP on October 14, 1998.[1049] NEC and MELCO were the only Japanese companies with experience building observation satellites. With NEC caught in a scandal and therefore out of the running for the satellite contract, MELCO was the only choice left to LDP officials eager to launch reconnaissance satellites. The LDP approved MELCO's plan in November, and the Cabinet approved the construction of four "intelligence-gathering satellites" (*jōhō shūshū eisei*)—two optical and two synthetic-aperture radar satellites—on December 22, 1998.[1050] By spring of 1999, the Space Activities Commission, in charge of setting Japan's space policy—and more importantly, budgets—formally approved the reconnaissance satellite program and programmed money into the JFY2000 budget to start their construction.[1051]

Japan was officially on the road to building its own reconnaissance satellites, at an initially projected cost of over $1.5 billion.

During the final stage of the approval process, Japan experienced another security challenge that served to underscore the need for better intelligence: US reconnaissance satellites and Japanese SIGINT facilities had discovered suspicious vessels off the coast of Noto Peninsula in March 1999. The vessels were ultimately believed to have originated from North Korea. The incident served as an exclamation point to the Japanese perception of a growing threat from North Korea, and Japanese media began to cite yet another reason to launch reconnaissance satellites. As the conservative newspaper *Sankei Shimbun* observed in an article on the intelligence satellites: "Japan has so far had no choice but to rely on US military reconnaissance satellites to make its initial move to deal with a crisis involving national security...Japan's plan to launch its own reconnaissance satellites was prompted by North Korea's launching of the Taepodong missile in August 1998," and with the spy ship incident off the Noto Peninsula, "there emerged a heightened need for using the reconnaissance satellites" to watch for "spy ships" originating out of North Korean ports.[1052]

ALOS, "Parent" to Reconnaissance Satellites

Japan immediately turned to another domestic satellite project then under development for technology and expertise: ALOS. First conceived in the early 1990s, ALOS was to be Japan's most advanced observation satellite yet. It would have three main sensors onboard allowing three-meter resolution using its optical sensor and ten-meter resolution using its synthetic aperture radar (SAR). Moreover, the optical sensor would allow three-dimensional mapping. MELCO happened to be a major contractor on the project. Thus, once the project was given the green light, MELCO proceeded to build the reconnaissance satellites using technologies developed initially for ALOS.

The LDP publicly announced Japan's intention to use ALOS technologies for the reconnaissance satellite project in its "Proposals on the Introduction of Intelligence Satellites" published in early November 1998, which noted that it is possible to develop the satellites based on "the technology developed for the Advanced Land Observation Satellite."[1053] One month later, after the LDP formally decided to proceed with an intelligence satellite program in December, the first director and acting program manager of the "Preparatory Office for Intelligence-Gathering Satellites" at NASDA happened to be the former chief of development for the ALOS project.[1054] On April 1, 1999, the first day of the new fiscal year, Chief Cabinet Secretary Hiromu Nonaka announced the decision to proceed with development of the satellites using indigenous technologies. That same day, NASDA upgraded the "Preparatory Office" to a "Research Office," and transferred 13 personnel from the ALOS project to the "intelligence-gathering satellite" (IGS) project as NASDA "will apply ALOS technology" to the IGS project, according to the industry newspaper *Nikkan Kogyo Shimbun*.[1055] Non-government defense analysts also noted heavy reliance on ALOS technologies. Keiichi Nogi, a well-versed military affairs commentator, in the December 1998 edition of the defense journal *Gunji Kenkyu* called ALOS the "parent satellite" of the information-gathering satellites and noted that "if the performance of the charge-coupled devices and optics is improved, achieving one-meter ground resolution at the original altitude [of 700 km] would not be impossible."[1056]

Thus many of the technologies used in the first-generation reconnaissance satellites were essentially dual-use technologies originally developed for other government-supported research satellites.

Launch

Tokyo originally scheduled the launch of all four satellites in mid-2002, but citing a delay in parts procurement, it postponed the launch until early 2003 for the first pair and late summer 2003 for the second pair.[1057] On March 28, 2003, Japan successfully launched two indigenously produced IGSs on its indigenously built H-2A rocket from the Tanegashima Space Center. The March launch placed two IGSs into orbit: one with an optical system with a one-meter resolution and the other with a synthetic aperture radar (SAR) with a resolution of 1-3 meters. While the SAR satellite produces only monochrome images, unlike the optical system it can be used at night and during inclement weather. The first SAR satellite operated in the L-band with a frequency between 0.4 gigahertz and 1.5 gigahertz, which accounts for the three-meter resolution.[1058] However, Sunohara quoted a Japanese imagery specialist as saying that achieving a one-meter resolution would be quite difficult with the L-band radar, and a three-meter resolution was more likely. For better resolution, the satellite would have to use a higher frequency C-band or X-band radar at 8-9 gigahertz, which Sunohara suggested might be included in third-generation satellites after 2011.[1059] The satellites orbit the earth in a solar synchronous quasi-revolution orbit at 400-600 kilometers in altitude 15-20 times a day. (Sunohara, citing "multiple" sources, placed the orbit at 470 kilometers.[1060]) Thus, the two satellites can take an image of any place on earth at least once a day. Following the March 2003 launch, another optical satellite and a SAR satellite were scheduled to be launched in August 2003, while the Japanese government planned to launch two more "reserve satellites" in JFY2006 and two second-generation satellites in JFY2008. The second-generation satellites will reportedly have a 0.5 meter resolution.[1061]

The satellites began transmitting imagery in late May, and the preponderance of early imagery was reportedly taken of targets in North Korea, including nuclear facilities at Yongbyon and missile launch facilities at Musudan-ri. The satellites also photographed facilities in Russia, China, and the Middle East, according to initial press reports.[1062] In one reportedly successful use of the satellites, Tokyo captured imagery of a rail line 150 km north of Pyongyang where a massive explosion took place on April 22, 2004, shortly after a train carrying Kim Chong-il home from China had passed by. Pyongyang initially explained that the accident was caused by contact of electrical wires with ammonium nitrate fertiziler loaded on a train at the station, but Japan's monthly *Gendai* interviewed an unnamed North Korean official who claimed that theblast had been an attempt to assassinate Kim: "The blast at Ryongchon was simply not an accident—it was a terrorist assassination attempt on the Dear Leader," the unnamed official declared.[1063] Whatever the case, the state-run television station in North Korea reported that the explosion damaged buildings as far as two kilometers away from the epicenter, with extensive damage especially in a 1.5-kilometer radius of the blast. The damage was not as great as the north led on, Japanese authorities determined after viewing the photos, and they judged the damage area to have a maximum radius of one kilometer. Once Japanese policy makers—including Prime Minister Koizumi—viewed the photos and independent damage assessments, Tokyo concluded the north exaggerated the damage to gain more international aid.[1064]

The second launch to place two more intelligence-gathering satellites into orbit was postponed until November 29, 2003. The postponed launch was ill-fated, however. The satellites failed to reach orbit when a procedure to jettison a side tank failed to operate properly. Instead of detaching from the body of the rocket, the tank remained partially attached and the resultant extra weight caused the rocket to fail to reach orbit. NASDA was forced to destroy the rocket at an altitude of 422 kilometers to keep the rocket and its cargo from crashing down to the earth's surface.[1065] The launch failure in November 2003—the first failure of the H-2A rocket after five successful launches—also caused a setback to Japan's growing space-launch program. Before the launch failure the Japan Aerospace Exploration Agency—JAXA for short, the result of a merger of the NASDA, the Institute of Space and Astronautical Science, and the National Aerospace Laboratory April 2004—was scheduled to launch up to 17 satellites by 2007 on the H-2A and M-5 space launch vehicles. All planned launches would be significantly delayed, however. The launch failure greatly disappointed DA and other government officials, who had hoped to use four reconnaissance satellites for robust coverage of potential trouble spots in Asia. But Japan still had two satellites in orbit, and it planned to build and launch additional satellites.

While initial satellites had to transmit their imagery while in visual range of Japan, future reconnaissance satellites probably have data-relay capabilities, giving Japan real-time coverage over a wide area of the globe. Because reconnaissance satellites orbit the earth at low altitudes, their window of opportunity to transmit images to ground stations is limited to times when they are above stations that can receive the transmissions. A data-relay satellite maintains geo-stationary orbit at a high altitude, sometimes as high as 22,000 miles or more. If they are out of range of the ground stations, reconnaissance satellites could send imagery data to a data-relay satellite, which would then send the information to a ground station below, reaching analysts in near real-time over much greater ranges.

Immediately prior to the launch of the reconnaissance satellites, Japan successfully tested on February 20, 2003 the "Kodama" Data Relay Test Satellite (DRTS) to relay images of the

Indian subcontinent and Ceylon taken by the Advanced Earth Observation Satellite (ADEOS-II) to the Tsukuba Space Center and the Earth Observation Center in Japan. The Kodama DRTS, moreover, was built so that it could relay images captured by ALOS.[1066] As noted above, much of the technology used in the ALOS served as the basis for the reconnaissance satellites, and NEC's original proposal included a data-relay satellite in its ¥210 billion proposal—as NEC's main competitor, MELCO most likely included a similar provision in its proposal. This all suggests that data relay capabilities were built into the reconnaissance satellites using technology similar to the Kodama DRTS (if not Kodama itself) to transmit images to ground stations in Japan. Thus if Japanese reconnaissance satellites do have a relay capability, they could conceivably provide Japanese analysts and policy makers with near real-time imagery of areas as far as Central Asia, the Indian Subcontinent, and perhaps the Middle East without passing over a ground station in Japan.

Ground Facilities

Japan has data reception centers in the north at Tomakomai, Hokkaido and in the south at Akune, Kagoshima Prefecture. Each data reception site has one receiving antenna—covered by a giant greenish-bluish dome—and a two-story building adjacent to it, as reported by local papers that provided pictures of the facilities.[1067] The subcenter, which has two receiving antennas and a two-story building, is located north of Tokyo in Kitaura, Ibaraki Prefecture, and serves as a back-up to the main control and analysis center in Ichigaya, Tokyo.[1068] The construction of the facilities was completed in December 2001, more than a year ahead of the launch of the first pair of satellites in March 2003.[1069]

Another satellite reception station is located on the western side of Australia near Perth.

Imagery analysis is conducted in the Cabinet Satellite Intelligence Center (CSIC: pronounced "C-Sice," which rhymes with "slice"), under the Cabinet Intelligence and Research Office. Retired General Masahiro Kunimi was appointed the inaugural director of the center, and his position is approximately equal to the CIRO deputy director given the special "center" designation of CSIC. Kunimi, the first head of the Defense Agency's DIH, was called out of retirement to head CSIC because of his experience in intelligence matters. When it became operational in the summer of 2001, CSIC had approximately 20 SDF personnel and 180 personnel from other ministries and agencies, and Kunimi told *Sankei Shimbun* that summer that CSIC full strength would be approximately 300 personnel.[1070] An additional 80 personnel would be needed to operate the four reception centers, bringing the total number to 380 personnel, but *Nihon Keizai Shimbun* questioned whether this would be enough for 24-hour operations.[1071] A career Ministry of Foreign Affairs official was promoted to deputy director from his position as the first chief of the imagery analysis department on August 5, 2003 as the satellites were becoming operational.[1072] CSIC's five-story "core center" that operates the satellites was constructed on the north side of the Defense Agency Headquarters in Ichigaya, Tokyo. Indeed, a sign adjacent to the back gate of the Defense Agency Headquarters identifies the incongruously deep silver building rising above the walls as the Cabinet Satellite Intelligence Center. The facility was specially built to protect it from eavesdropping on electromagnetic signals emanating from the building.[1073] The CSIC building is connected to the Defense Intelligence Headquarters' Imagery Directorate via high-capacity data cable, and thus can share imagery with the DIH's Imagery Directorate.

As noted above, the DIH Imagery Directorate was created in 1997 by merging the "Central Geography Unit" of the GSDF, based in Tokyo's Higashi-Tachikawa, with the Satellite Imagery Analysis Divisions of the other SDF branches. When the directorate was first established, analysts worked mainly with imagery purchased from US companies, although even in 1997 it was "rumored" that Japan "will eventually receive its own reconnaissance satellites," according to *Sentaku*.[1074] The Imagery Directorate was expanded to an "Imagery and Geography Directorate" with 40 additional imagery analysts in April 2003, bringing the total number of imagery analysts there to 160. The number of personnel devoted to imagery analysis—civilian and uniformed—rose to 321 by mid-2004.[1075] The expanded Imagery and Geography Department would perform "three-dimensional map intelligence" in addition to imagery analysis, in the words of defense analyst Buntaro Kuroi.[1076]

To support IMINT operations, the DA in March 2001 inaugurated the Imagery Intelligence Support System (called the *gazō jōhō shien shisutemu*).[1077] According to the DRC's Isao Ishizuka, this system provides reconnaissance photographs from IKONOS satellites (owned by Space Image) as sharp as 82 centimeters in resolution to imagery analysts.[1078] Construction began on the system in 1997 with a projected cost of ¥16.1 billion. The IISS went operational in March 2001, working with such satellite imagery acquired by Quickbird IKONOS commercial satellites, and it connects CSIC and the Imagery and Analysis Directorate at DIH via high-capacity data cable.[1079] Japan also orders imagery from the commercial imaging satellites Radarsat (Radarsat International), Landsat (Space Imaging), and Spot (Spot Imaging).[1080] Obviously, if the system can be used with commercial satellite imagery, it can be used with imagery obtained from Japan's reconnaissance satellites as well.

Future Intelligence Satellites

While still considered first-generation satellites, Japan successfully launched a third satellite on September 10, 2006, and a forth launch followed in February 2007. The industry newspaper *Nikkan Kogyo Shimbun* reported in late July 2000 that the additional satellites were planned as a "contingency" for a launch failure during either of the first launches in 2003.[1081] While still considered first-generation satellites, the back-up satellites launched in 2006 and 2007 included improvements not found on the two already in orbit. The Charged-Coupled Devices or CCDs employed on the back-up optical satellite were scheduled to be upgraded by 2005 from 8-bit to 11-bit radiometric resolution, thus increasing the grey values (and therefore the image quality) in the black-and-white images from 256 to 2048. The optical satellite would be capable of taking one-meter black-and-white images and five-meter color images, and have a more powerful "pointing" or slewing capabilities. The SAR satellite was also to have a 1-3 meter resolution, although it would continue to employ L-band radar and thus its resolution was probably limited to around 3 meters as discussed above.[1082]

The next generation of satellites was officially approved on June 13, 2001, when the "Intelligence-Gathering Satellite Promotion Committee" headed by Chief Cabinet Secretary Yasuo Fukuda approved the indigenous development of second-generation satellites capable of acquiring imagery with 50-centimeter resolution.[1083] Second- and later-generation satellites to be launched after 2009 were to have improved, shorter solar panels that will allow for greater maneuverability. The satellites will also be equipped with improved reaction wheel capabilities to allow slewing along all three axises. The reaction wheels, essentially weighted spheres that cause the satellite to turn when they spin in a particular direction, are part of the attitude control system that adjusts the satellite's position for precision targeting. While the first-generation satellites were equipped with reaction wheels limited to slewing on one axis, the next-generation satellites will be capable of slewing along all three axises, thereby expanding the number of potential surface targets within range at any given moment in orbit. The satellites will also be lighter than the two-ton first-generation satellites, with an expected weight of around 1.2 tons.[1084]

One interesting question for speculation would be whether Japan ultimately builds non-IMINT satellites, such as SIGINT, MASINT, or launch-detection satellites. Whether Japan will develop these other types of satellites in addition to reconnaissance satellites will depend for policy direction on the Expert Panel on Space Development and Utilization (*Uchū Kaihatsu Riyō Senmon Chōsakai*) under the Council for Science and Technology, an advisory panel to the Prime Minister.[1085] The Expert Panel was established in October 2001, and although it has the benign-sounding objective to "find ways to strengthen the international competitiveness of Japan's space industry" and examine "matters such as the fundamentals in tackling space development and utilization," the panel's guest speakers suggest that defense uses of space is not a taboo subject: the panel spoke for two hours with Toshiyuki Shikata, a retired GSDF Lt. General and former commander of Japan's Northern Army, during its third meeting in January 2002, for example.[1086]

Indeed, Shikata has consistently called for the development of a constellation of satellites, telling the *Yomiuri Shimbun*: "[T]his country should have at least eight satellites to be able to take photos" of missile and other sites "twice a day."[1087] He has made similar calls in his monthly column in *Securitarian*,[1088] and he has proposed the construction of a SIGINT satellite to intercept communications and of a launch detection satellite.[1089] Masahiro Matsumura, a professor at Momoyama Gakuin University who writes extensively on Japanese national security issues, suggested Japan "develop national infrared early warning satellite technologies" and launch at least two EW satellites over Asia as a next step in its missile defense system. Kensuke Ebata, a well-known expert on defense issues in Japan, pointed to increased SDF use of satellites in *Securitarian,* writing in April 2002: "Even though there is the problem of interpretation of 'Peaceful Utilization of Space,' in the future it will probably be necessary to continue to actively pursue the utilization of space, whether it involves the civilian sector or the SDF."[1090]

The "Peaceful Utilization of Space" policy, promulgated in 1969, will not be a factor slowing Japan's future satellite capabilities. In a further sign of Japan's intentions to build additional satellites, the Liberal Democratic Party in June 2006 began to plan the submission of a bill enabling Japan to use space for military purposes within the range of self-defense rights. As Kyodo reported, the bill would enable the development of high-definition reconnaissance satellites and of a satellite capable of detecting the firing of ballistic missiles, and it would establish a headquarters in the Cabinet headed by the prime minister to coordinate space development strategies in the various government agencies.[1091]

The bill had broad bipartisan support, as all three major parties—the governing LDP, its coalition partner the New Komeito Party, and opposition Democratic Party of Japan—supported the legislation in the Diet in early 2008. The bill became law—the *uchū kihonhō* or "Space Basic Law"—in mid-2008, after it was passed by both houses of Japan's Diet. Of particular interest is Article 3, which states that Japan's continued development of space is necessary for its own "national security" as well as the preservation of international community's "peace and security." The new law thus sanctioned the use of space-based systems specifically for national security purposes, opening the door for the legal development of a wider range of intelligence-related satellites.

Yasuaki Hashimoto, writing for the Defense Ministry-affiliated National Institute of Defense Studies, noted that the enactment of the law indicated that Tokyo was moving away from the use of space strictly for "peaceful purposes equal to nonmilitary purposes" to a "nonaggression" policy of the use of space. In other words, Tokyo can now legally develop the full range of space-based platforms for national security purposes such as "early warning satellites, communications satellites, data relay satellites," and SIGINT satellites in addition to reconnaissance satellites, according to Hashimoto. While the enactment of this law makes the use of space-based platforms for national security purposes legal, there are multiple hurdles to their indigenous development and operation, not least of which is cost. But with this law, Tokyo "will be able to examine the merits and demerits of various national security systems" that operate in space, according to Hashimoto.[1092]

Following a public debate on the "merits" and "demerits" of future satellite systems in the spring of 2009, the Japanese government in June approved a panel recommendation that included the launch of an additional reconnaissance satellite and the development of sensors to be employed on a future early warning satellite.[1093] Japan continues to launch reconnaissance satellites periodically in an attempt to maintain a constellation of four or more active reconnaissance satellites.

Intelligence and Counter-Terrorism at the National Police Agency

The National Police Agency has historically maintained a strong intelligence capability in post-WWII Japan. These efforts were focused overwhelmingly on intelligence targets from the Soviet Union, and to some extent from North Korea and China as well. The NPA's Security Bureau oversees the Agency's intelligence collection efforts.

The NPA's post-war involvement in SIGINT collection is demonstrated by the fact that a career NPA senior official has historically headed the Defense Agency's SIGINT operations. The NPA's own SIGINT efforts are run by the Foreign Affairs Division's *Gaiji Gijutsu Chōsakanshitsu*—the "Foreign Technology Intelligence Office" (FTIO)—a little-known entity in the Security Bureau that was established to monitor Morse code and other clandestine communications from Communist countries in Asia. Demonstrating the Defense Agency's and NPA's overlapping SIGINT collection capabilities, Iku Aso reported in the Japanese journal *Bungei Shunju* that the FTIO—known colloquially as *Yama*—received transmissions from the North Korean spy ships in 1999 at the same time as the DA.[1094] Buntaro Kuroi, who writes on intelligence matters in *Gunji Kenkyu*, further noted that the NPA manages at least two main monitoring facilities, both in Tokyo: one in a building next to the NPA's Police Academy in Nakano Ward (where the NPA Technology Center and the Tokyo Metropolitan Police Department's Police Academy are also located), and another in Hino Town, a suburb of Tokyo.[1095]

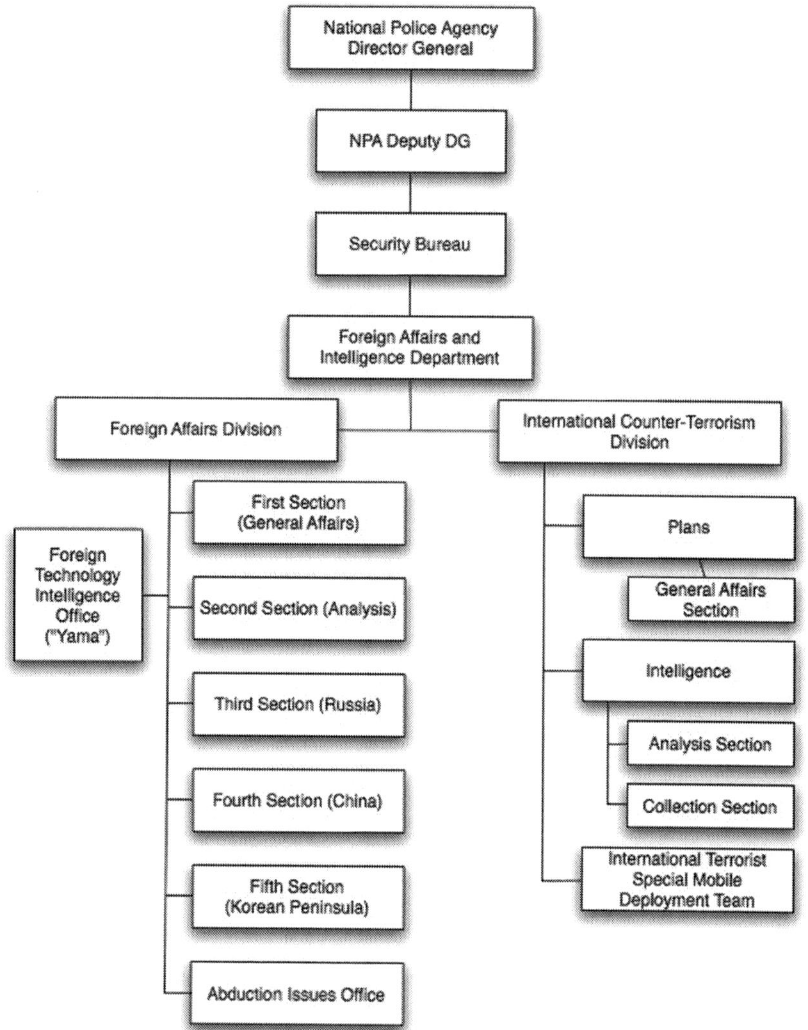

"World Intelligence, Vol. 2," Gunji Kenkyu, September 2006, p 60; Police Law revision bill.

Following the Aum Shinrikyo attacks and Lima hostage situation in the mid-1990s, the 9.11 attacks in the United States, and the Kim regime's admission that North Korean agents had kidnapped

Japanese citizens, the Diet in 2004 passed revisions to the Police Law to reorganize the NPA's intelligence and counterterrorism offices and to further empower the agency to respond to terrorist acts in Japan and abroad. Other attacks, such as the Bali bombing in Indonesia on October 12, 2002 and the commuter train bombings in Madrid on March 11, 2004 (as the Police Law revision bill was being debated in the Diet), further reinforced Tokyo's alarm that similar terrorist attacks might target Japan directly or else involve Japanese citizens who traveled and lived abroad. The Diet unanimously passed revisions to the Police Law on March 31, 2004, with even Communist Party representatives supporting the bill so closely after the Madrid bombings. The revisions took effect the following day.

The 2004 restructure was particularly noteworthy as it demonstrated anew the importance of intelligence in Japan's counterterrorism efforts. In the most significant change, a new Foreign Affairs and Intelligence Department (*Gaiji Jōhōbu* or FAID) was created under the Security Bureau to oversee the Foreign Affairs Division and an upgraded International Counter-Terrorism Division (ICTD). Initially established as the "International Terrorism Countermeasures Office" in 1977 following the hijacking of a Japan Airlines flight over India—now popularly referred to as the Dhaka Incident—the office had only two or three personnel in its first years. The office's importance increased somewhat in the 1990s, but it wasn't until the 2004 reorganization that it was upgraded to a division, giving new organizational clout to the NPA's counterterrorism efforts. The 2004 law also strengthened legal support for dispatching police units abroad to coordinate counter-terrorism response with police authorities in other countries and established the International Terrorist Special Mobile Deployment Unit. The International Terrorist Special Mobile Deployment Unit, falling under the International

Counter-Terrorism Division, would be a collection of experts on a variety of terrorism-related subjects, and would therefore help lead Japan's tactical intelligence collection and coordinate response efforts on-site during a crisis.[1096]

Indeed, the Diet's unanimous passage of revisions to the Police Law came just in time for Japan's next crisis. On April 8, three Japanese citizens—Soichiro Koriyama, a freelance photographer, freelance writer Noriaki Imai; and social activist Nahoko Takato—were kidnapped and held for ransom as they traveled through Iraq. The 18-year-old Noriaki Imai traveled to Iraq to oppose the alleged use of depleted uranium in munitions during the 2003 Iraq war, while Koriyama had been photographing events in Iraq for a year and sometimes supplied photos to the *Weekly Asahi* and other news outlets. Takato had been helping Iraqi children in Baghdad prior to her abduction.[1097] The group who seized the three Japanese called itself the Saraya al-Mujahideen, and they demanded that Tokyo withdraw its Self-Defense Force contingent from Iraq within three days or they would burn the hostages alive. In response—and supported by the new Police Law revisions—the NPA dispatched a nine-member terrorism response team and police investigators from the Tokyo Metropolitan Police Department and the Hokkaido Prefectural Police to investigate the kidnappings and liaise with coalition partners in the region to secure the release of the three.[1098] Mikio Shiokawa, head of the ICTD, led the police team with Senior Vice Foreign Minister Ichiro Aisawa as head of the delegation.[1099] The three were released a week later, although the Japanese tabloid *Shukan Posuto* insinuated days later that the government paid up to $3 million ransom for their release.[1100] (The payment of ransom was not unprecedented, as Japan paid a $6 million ransom during the 1977 Dhaka incident.) Aisawa and others in the government immediately denied the accusation, although he did not provide further details as to how his team, working from Amman, Jordan, secured the hostages' release through a clerics' association in Iraq.[1101]

Following interviews with the three former hostages and local eyewitnesses, their kidnapping was pieced together. The three departed Amman, Jordan late on April 6 to travel overland to Fallujah. When they stopped at a gas station to refuel some 15 kilometers from Fallujah, a group of 7 or 8 men with automatic rifles, antitank rockets, and grenades seized the three. The kidnappers drove them to a location ten minutes away, but they did not blindfold or handcuff the Japanese hostages. The kidnappers then moved the hostages eight times during that week before releasing them unharmed in Baghdad.[1102] Kyodo quoted one NPA official declaring after the three were released: "Thank heaven for the enactment" of the law.[1103] With the changes to the law, Japan could now send counter-terrorism units to the site of a terrorist incident outside of Japan.

Since the kidnapping occurred so soon after the revision of the Police Law, the team sent to the Middle East in April 2004 was somewhat haphazardly assembled as the NPA had not yet actually organized international terrorism response units. On July 1, the NPA announced the establishment of a permanent unit—the "Terrorism Response Team Tactical Wing for Overseas"—the following month. The initial terrorism response wing consisted of approximately 110 personnel with expertise in forensics, explosive devices, terrorism and hostage negotiations. Moreover, the NPA expanded its Special Assault Team to 250 personnel from 200, and the NPA also established a special CBRN response team.[1104]

Despite the "national" in its title, the National Police Agency held only tangential investigative and supervisory authority over prefectural police agencies limited to cases concerning hijackings and hostage situations. With the revision of the Police Law on April 1, 2004, NPA's authority was explicitly expanded to terrorist attacks involving bombings and chemical/biological/radiological/nuclear devices. Under the revised Police Law, the NPA has the authority to assemble and dispatch investigative and counter-terror teams from large prefectural police departments such as the Tokyo Metropolitan Police Department and Osaka Prefectural Police Department to other areas of Japan or abroad, as during the Iraqi hostage situation in April. The NPA's Security Bureau can also alert local police forces to specific security threats, as it did in Ishikawa and Niigata Prefectures during the 1999 spy ship incident. The bureau also provides guidance as to what local police units will monitor—in September 2002, for example, the Security Bureau instructed local authorities to "significantly reduce" the number of officers monitoring Chinese operatives and put renewed priority on investigating the activities of possible North Korean agents in Japan.[1105]

The Human Factor

While Japan is not known for its capabilities to collect human intelligence (HUMINT), an embezzlement scandal in early 2001 at the Ministry of Foreign Affairs revealed a number of off-budget accounts both at MOFA and within the Cabinet Office that pointed to the use of paid informants. While some of the funds were used for domestic political purposes, the use of these off-budget accounts for intelligence-collection purposes was later even acknowledged by Shinzo Abe, deputy chief cabinet secretary at the time who eventually succeeded Koizumi as Prime Minister in the fall of 2006 and again in 2012. Beyond the off-budget accounts and apart from the Ministry of Foreign Affairs and the Cabinet Office, the Defense Ministry's defense attachés based at several dozen Japanese embassies give the Defense Agency a basic HUMINT capability abroad as well, a fact that is openly acknowledged by several former attachés themselves. While the off-budget accounts and the number of defense attachés stationed abroad are limited, Japan nevertheless has its own HUMINT collection methods that should not be underestimated. Moreover, these basic capabilities will most likely serve as a baseline as Japan works to expand and improve its intelligence collection efforts in coming years.

'Compensation Funds' at the Cabinet Office and Ministry of Foreign Affairs

The existence of off-budget "compensation funds" first became a topic at the Diet in 1990, when a member of the Japan Communist Party questioned the existence of secret funds controlled by the Chief Cabinet Secretary. On June 14 that year, Japan Communist Party Representative Iwao Teramae asked Chief Cabinet Secretary Misoji Sakamoto during an audit committee hearing about the existence of secret slush funds, declaring that according to documents he had obtained, Sakamoto was using funds from MOFA's budget as well as from Cabinet discretionary funds to give Diet members gifts as they departed for trips abroad. Sakamoto refused to discuss the issue.[1106]

The issue reemerged in January 2001 when Katsutoshi Matsuo, head of MOFA's Overseas Visit Support Division, was dismissed on charges of embezzling over ¥500 million from 1993 to 1999. His scam worked like this: ahead of a prime ministerial trip abroad, in addition to regular budget accounts at MOFA, a MOFA official working on rotation at the Cabinet Secretariat would allocate funding to Matsuo's support division to cover accommodations and other expenses for the premier's entourage during the trip. At least some of the money from the Cabinet Secretariat, however, was allocated from confidential accounts. Matsuo would travel to the Cabinet Secretariat and physically take possession of cash to pay for Cabinet Secretariat officials' travel and lodging. With no oversight, he then deposited the money into one of nine personal bank accounts he had established since 1993. He then paid for many of the expenses using his personal credit cards, often providing the government with receipts he himself had prepared. Chief Cabinet Secretary Fukuda later told the House of Representatives that the Cabinet Secretariat had provided Matsuo in total with ¥965 million for 46 prime ministerial visits from 1993-1999. In its initial investigation, MOFA discovered ¥560 million in two of Matsuo's accounts, and later investigations would discover more. Matsuo embezzled on average tens of millions of yen from each PM trip abroad. With the embezzled money, Matsuo reportedly bought 14 racehorses and paid ¥80 million in cash for a condo in Tokyo.[1107] Matsuo was later sentenced to seven years and six months in prison for embezzlement.[1108]

Others were implicated in kick-back scams at MOFA as well. Akio Asakawa, assistant director at the First West Europe Division of the ministry's European Affairs Bureau, was convicted and sentenced to two years in prison for defrauding MOFA of ¥422 million as he helped organize such events as the Okinawa G-8 Summit in the summer of 2000. Hiromu Kobayashi, 46, former assistant director in the office of the deputy director general for general affairs at the ministry's Economic Affairs Bureau and his subordinate Tsutomu Okuma were also convicted of embezzling ¥21 million during the 2000 G-8 Summit in Okinawa. They had at one time worked for Matsuo, and because the embezzlement scam had been in place before they arrived, Kobayashi and Okuma received suspended sentences.[1109]

As the Matsuo incident unfolded, much was revealed about how the classified funds were transferred around official Tokyo.

MOFA received classified funding that was overseen by the director of the MOFA secretariat, and most funds went directly to Japanese embassies abroad.[1110] Part of these funds was also returned to the Cabinet Secretariat each year as a kick-back from MOFA. During the MOFA's budget compilation in the fall of each year, the ministry designated a specific amount for the Prime Minister's Official Residence. Following Diet approval of the entire budget, MOFA's Financial Affairs Division compiled a document for the ministry's expenditures for that year and transfered the classified funds to a special account, from which the PMOR withdrew the transferred funds.[1111]

As further evidence of the classified funds, on February 9, 2001, shortly after the scandal broke, Communist Party Chairman Kazuo Shii presented a document titled "About Compensation Funds" to the Lower House Budget Committee, which he asserted proved the existence of off-budget accounts transferred from the Ministry of Foreign Affairs to the Cabinet Secretariat. The document was allegedly written in May 1989 by Teijiro Furukawa, chief cabinet councilor at the time and later the administrative deputy chief cabinet secretary, to assist in a high-level personnel transition following a political scandal. In his position as Chief Cabinet Councilor, Furukawa was the official charged with spending the compensation funds at the direction of the chief cabinet secretary. The document explained that the funds "take the form of delivering money, which was appropriated for the Foreign Ministry, to the Cabinet Secretariat." After Shii presented the document in the Diet, however, both Furukawa—who was by this point the senior bureaucratic official in Tokyo—and Chief Cabinet Secretary Fukuda denied the veracity of the document.[1112]

Other former officials were more forthright about the existence of the off-budget funds, however. Former Japanese Ambassador to Lebanon Naoto Amaki confirmed in his 2003 book *Saraba Gaimushō* ("Farewell, Foreign Ministry") that MOFA diverted approximately ¥2 billion to the Cabinet Secretariat each year. Amaki said the transfer of funds from MOFA to the Cabinet Secretariat began during normalization talks with South Korea in the mid-1960s, when Prime Minister Eisaku Sato requested the transfer of funds from Foreign Minister Etsusaburo Shiina after the Prime Minister's Office ran out of its budgetary share of funds. (Amaki also claimed that he was fired for not supporting the allied effort to overthrow the Hussein regime in Iraq, and his dismissal was probably a motivating factor in confirming the existence of the off-budget funds.)[1113]

Indeed, following the Matsuo revelations, "compensation funds" became a hot topic as Japanese papers gradually revealed many aspects of the off-budget accounts. According to an investigative report by the left-leaning *Mainichi Shimbun*, in FY2000, the chief cabinet secretary was allocated ¥1.624 billion for undisclosed purposes (tens of millions of which the chief cabinet secretary allegedly kept in cash in his office safe). In addition, the Ministry of Foreign Affairs was allocated ¥5.57 billion in FY2000 in secret funds, of which ¥1.92 billion was reportedly allocated to the MOFA headquarters in Tokyo and ¥3.65 billion was distributed to Japanese Embassies.[1114] The off-budget funds had continued for much of Japan's post-war era: MOFA in 1975 received ¥3.76 billion in secret funds and that sum gradually increased through the late 1980s, but the amount allocated to MOFA stagnated at around ¥5.57 billion between FY1992 until at least FY2001, perhaps reflecting the Japanese government's fiscal difficulties during that decade. And the funds were primarily intended for intelligence purposes: as Kyodo observed in explaining the off-budget funds, the "compensation" funds "are intended to cover costs for classified government activities such as intelligence gathering and are allocated to a number of ministries and agencies." Kyodo reported that even the Defense Agency receives some off-budget funds, but far less than MOFA and the Cabinet Secretariat.[1115] Moreover, following a review of government documents from November 1997 to March 2001, *Yomiuri* reported that 80% of Cabinet Secretariat compensation funds were used by the chief cabinet secretary, and the remaining amount went to CIRO. In FY1998, for example, the chief cabinet secretary used ¥1.21 billion and distributed ¥310 million to the director of CIRO. The highest amount paid out in one month during that time period was ¥200 million in November 1997, and the same amount was paid out again in May and October 1998.[1116] Yet despite the embezzlement scandal and subsequent revelations, officials insisted on maintaining the system for "compensation funds": "I want [the government] to approve a certain amount of compensation money," Foreign Minister Kono declared shortly after the scandal.[1117] Kono of course did not clarify what was being "compensated."

Yoshio Omori, the former head of CIRO, acknowledged CIRO's use of compensation funds in his book *Nihon no Interijensu Kikan* ("Japan's Intelligence Structure"). Omori preferred the term "compensation fund" (*shohohi*) to "secret fund" (*kimitsuhi*) commonly used by the Japanese media because the funds are used to "compensate" (*sharei*) sources for sharing information and their opinions in areas related to their field of study. Thus Omori implied that the funds are not used to acquire information clandestinely, but they are merely used to pay informed individuals for their insights into an intelligence-related matter. Omori told of an occasion during which he was involved in providing "compensation" to an individual he identified as "Cheng," who resided in Taiwan. Omori first met Cheng—the Chinese version of "Mr. Smith" as the name is widely used in Taiwan—when Omori was serving as a young National Police Agency official in Okinawa in 1967. Cheng often traveled between Okinawa's

Yonaguni Island and Taiwan on business. In 1993, when Omori was named head of CIRO, he registered Cheng as an "intelligence cooperator" (*jōhō kyōryokusha*) and paid him "several tens of thousands of yen"—several hundred dollars—a month, as Omori had come to trust Cheng's "intelligence sense." MOFA and the PMOR were not interested in Taiwan's military situation during Omori's first three years, according to Omori, and information provided by Cheng was "ignored." But Omori was barred from having an overt relationship with Taiwan, so during the 1996 Taiwan Strait crisis Cheng was one of Omori's primary covert sources of intelligence. Omori claimed he had no knowledge of Cheng's sources in Taiwan, however, which if true would raise questions about Japanese source vetting and validation procedures.[1118] The secretive nature by which Cheng was paid does not seem to support Omori's claim that the fund was used merely to "compensate" Cheng in return for his expertise on Taiwanese matters, however. And Omori himself admitted that Cheng was probably using him as a channel to voice Taiwan's concern over the missile tests to official Tokyo. Omori's experience, however, highlighted Tokyo's limited paid use of human assets during times of crisis.

According to *Foresight*, the compensation funds have been used to support unspecified actions during the hostage crisis at the Japanese Ambassador's Residence in Peru, prepare the groundwork for officials investigating the kidnapping of Japanese in Kyrgyzstan (in 2000), and the funds were allegedly used to provide weapons for anti-Soviet guerrillas in Afghanistan following the 1979 Soviet invasion. Compensation funds presumably were also used to pay the $6 million ransom to hijackers in the 1977 Dhaka incident and to support secret negotiations with North Korea, *Foresight* judged. Yet in many other instances the funds have been used to support non-intelligence related policy initiatives such as the introduction of the consumption tax in 1989. Funds were also used to buy souvenirs during the Naples Summit in 1994 and the Halifax Summit in 1995 to give to PMOR staff, for example.[1119] *Asahi* reported that a Japanese ambassador to an unnamed Southeast Asian country used money from his embassy's compensation fund to install cable television at his residence to watch Japanese dramas and music shows, while another ambassador used the off-budget funds to host an overseas wedding reception at a favorite restaurant.[1120] Given the lack of oversight, then, portions of off-budget compensation funds were diverted to non-official uses, which led to the embezzlement scandals in the early 2000s.

Shinzo Abe addressed the "misappropriation issue" in a 2004 discussion of intelligence issues with former head of the Cabinet Security Affairs Office Atsuyuki Sassa, which was reprinted in the monthly journal *Voice*. Abe explained that the vague definition of the "compensation fund" designation when it was conceived after the war led to problems associated with the Matsuo case:

> "After Japan's defeat in war, GHQ [the US General Headquarters in Tokyo] …dismantled the army and navy and simultaneously stripped the country of its intelligence-gathering capabilities. In that connection, confidential funds used as resources were discontinued, but an individual in the then-Ministry of Finance realized the importance of intelligence strategies and somehow retained such funding by labeling it as compensation funds. However, changing the designation made the nature of the funding very vague, and led to the so-called confidential funds misappropriation issue. It was said, 'If these are supposed to be funds to reward those who dedicate themselves to the country, it should be acceptable to use them to purchase wine for ourselves.'"[1121]

Despite the "misappropriation" incident, Abe in the interview expressed continued support the use of undocumented payments for intelligence purposes: "The purchase of intelligence will at times require the use of money without the need for a receipt. Intelligence cannot be obtained without a cost." Abe's comments demonstrated his staunch support for autonomous intelligence capabilities and foreshadowed Japan's future build-up of HUMINT collection capacity.

As an aside, one should note the particularities of HUMINT intelligence collection techniques employed by countries in Asia can often differ from the traditional image of running paid agents and informants, most of whom are to some degree knowingly engaged in espionage activity (i.e., knowingly passing information to a foreign party in return for payment of some kind). Many intelligence collectors in Asia are true masters in the art of subtly coaxing bits and pieces of information from often unsuspecting targets. Indeed, the title "intelligence officer" is itself not appropriate in many cases because the HUMINT collectors themselves are usually well-regarded practitioners in the targeted areas of expertise, and their reputations help to establish rapport and respect between collector and unsuspecting targets. For example, if Tokyo were targeting a particular unmanned vehicle technology, it dispatches its own engineers and scientists in the field of unmanned vehicle technologies from a variety of offices to visit UV offices in target countries and to attend international conferences on the technology in question. The collectors establish as targets highly knowledgeable officials, political figures, scientists, or businessmen to collect piecemeal information that, when put together, form a remarkably precise picture to fulfill a given intelligence need. Naoki Ehara, head of TRDI's maritime guided missile system development, for example highlighted the ability to glean information at scientific conferences in the July 2006

Securitarian: "The high classification of missile system specifications in each country means there are few opportunities to compare with other countries, but technical information pointing to the most recent trends can be collected at scientific meetings."[1122] As will be noted in the next chapter, retired defense personnel belonging to a variety of Japanese think tanks such as the Defense Research Center and defense contractors from Mitsubishi, Sumitomo, Toshiba, and a variety of other companies often travel on coordinated trips abroad to investigate technologies under development in other countries.

In the final analysis, however, while classified budgets clearly exist, MOFA's and the Cabinet's HUMINT capabilities were minimal in the early 2000s, and some have expressed increasing dissatisfaction with the seeming inadequacy of HUMINT collection capabilities in general. As the new Deputy Chief Cabinet Secretary for Crisis Management, Tadao Ando, took his post in April 1998, an unnamed LDP politician complained: "The intelligence-gathering abilities of the Foreign Ministry's embassies and other overseas offices are inadequate."[1123] Iku Aso, moreover, pointed to a lack of training in how to use the funds for intelligence collection: "Japanese foreign legations possess confidential operating funds for collaborators," but "most Japanese diplomats are not trained in intelligence matters."[1124] In the future, as Japan improves and expands its HUMINT intelligence collection capabilities, it will no doubt expand training at facilities such as the Kodaira School as well.

Defense Attachés

Even in the 1990s, the Defense Agency made no attempt to hide the fact that it uses its attachés stationed at embassies abroad to "collect information" (*jōhō shūshū*) on foreign militaries. Their numbers have steadily grown since the mid-1990s: according to the *1996 Defense of Japan*, the DA had 42 officers seconded to the Ministry of Foreign Affairs at 33 overseas diplomatic missions "collecting military information." The DA began to increase the number of defense attachés stationed abroad in 1997 after the hostage crisis at the Japanese ambassador's residence in Lima, Peru, because the DA had been criticized for not having a presence in the country and therefore being caught unaware of the local security environment. Besides the hostage crisis, the Defense Agency also used the Hong Kong reversion—another major event in 1997—as a reason for announcing a review of its military attaché requirements. By August 1997, the DA announced that it would increase the number of military attachés at its embassy in Beijing "due to China's increased military significance following the July 1 reversion of Hong Kong to China."[1125] The DA also announced plans to increase its attaché presence in Southeast Asia, and had just opened a military attaché office in Vietnam in 1996. By 2000, according to Toshiyuki Shikata—himself a former defense attaché to the United States—Japan had 54 defense attachés stationed abroad, including three each in South Korea, Russia, Indonesia, and China, and nine in the United States. Shikata himself noted in his book on the Self-Defense Forces that the main purpose for the attachés was "to collect military intelligence in each country."[1126]

In January 2003, Japan established a de facto attaché office in Taiwan by dispatching a retired GSDF officer to the island. *Mainichi Shimbun* called the retired officer an "OB" or "Old Boy," a common term for officially retired personnel who retain connections with their former organization. One unnamed DA official was quoted as saying about the posting: "We have to provide against China as a potential threat." Another unnamed official from Taiwan's Presidential Office highlighted the tension between diplomacy vis-à-vis the PRC, and geopolitical tensions between the three governments: "[Japan's] Defense Agency understands strategic relations between Japan and Taiwan, but I think people in the Foreign Ministry are 'yes men' to Beijing out of concern of its reaction."[1127] The posting to Taiwan would give the DA an additional channel of communication to the Taiwanese government.

Until recently, the Foreign Ministry had complete organizational control over Defense Agency personnel stationed at embassies, and by custom, the Defense Agency was obliged to loan up to three of its information analysts to the Foreign Ministry in exchange for ministry approval for each additional defense attaché.[1128] In return, SDF officers were forced to leave their positions with the Defense Agency and join the Ministry of Foreign Affairs to be stationed abroad. The attaché offices, therefore, did not have an official presence as such in the embassies. One major way to control the attachés was to control their communications systems with the DA in Tokyo. Throughout the Cold War era, defense attachés did not have their own communications system and had to rely on MOFA to transmit classified reporting back to Tokyo. Information had to go through—and hence be vetted by—diplomats in the Ministry of Foreign Affairs.

Despite being embedded in MOFA until the early 2000s, the system had not kept Japanese defense attachés from being accused of spying on military targets—mainly in China. A number of defense attachés were recalled in the 1990s and 2000s after being accused of collecting militarily sensitive information in foreign countries. In 1996, for example, Col. Kenji Maetani, a defense attaché with the Japanese Embassy in Beijing, was recalled to Japan in January that year after China claimed that he "snuck into Hainan Island and the Fuzhou area several times…where the Chinese military conducted missile test-firing exercises in the Taiwan Strait," in the words of one Hong Kong paper.[1129] He allegedly trespassed into restricted military zones in the southern provinces of Hainan and Guangdong and took photographs. (A

US Defense attaché had also been recalled that year.)[1130] The Maetani incident took place immediately prior to the Taiwan Strait crisis in March 1996. In another case in November 2002, Hiromasa Amano, a defense attaché also stationed in Beijing, was sent home after being accused of entering an "off-limits area" near a Chinese naval base.[1131]

The Japanese attaché posting system began to change in the early 2000s, however. In 2002 the Defense Policy Research Subcommittee of the LDP's National Defense Division submitted a five-point proposal for revamping the military attaché system, including: 1) military attachés should retain their status as SDF officers under the command and control of the DA; 2) adequate communication systems should be installed and secured so that defense intelligence can be quickly transmitted to the DA; and 3) the status of Japan's military attachés at diplomatic stations should be equal to attachés of foreign countries.[1132] The subcommittee was headed by Yasukazu Hamada. (Hamada, active in defense policy circles, had the year before been dubbed part of the "Gang of Four" in Japan's defense policy circles, together with Gen Nakatani, Shigeru Ishiba, and Kenzo Yoneda. Hamada was often quoted as saying of Japanese defense policy: "Japan should be an 'ordinary' state like all other countries."[1133]) The recommendations would be enacted in piecemeal fashion, beginning with the attaché communications system. In 2004, it was announced that the DA would receive special funds in the 2005 budget to introduce a new communications system that would allow defense attachés to send information directly to the Defense Agency Headquarters without going through MOFA channels.[1134]

Upon their return to Japan after serving in a defense attaché post abroad, Japanese SDF officers often take on significant intelligence-related posts. A prime example is Colonel Chikara Sakamoto, one of Japan's first post-war intelligence officers noted above who ultimately was instrumental in shaping Japan's future intelligence capabilities as head of the "Joint Intelligence Headquarters Study Preparatory Office" in the Joint Staff Council.[1135] Other examples include retired Lieutenant General Masahiro Kunimi, who headed both the Defense Intelligence Headquarters when it opened in 1997 and later the Cabinet Satellite Intelligence Center in 2001. Prior to those posts, Kunimi served as an attaché to China in 1983, and upon returning he became a section chief in the Ground Staff Office's Intelligence Department—at that time the home of Japan's SIGINT capabilities. He later headed the GSO's Intelligence Department in 1993.[1136] Retired Lieutenant General Toshiyuki Shikata (whose writings have been cited a number of times in this book) served as a defense attaché in the United States. A prominent commentator on military and intelligence matters, Shikata writes regular columns for such journals as *Gunji Kenkyu* ("Military Studies") and the DA journal *Securitarian*, and he often gives speeches and talks with journalists on military matters. He has also been a member of a number of government-sponsored panels on defense and intelligence issues, such as the high-profile government panel to review the possible introduction of intelligence satellites.

As an aside, the Defense Agency is not the only organization to station its personnel at Japanese embassies: NPA officials also often serve at Japanese embassies and consulates abroad. The aforementioned Atsuyuki Sassa, former head of CSAO, gave the following account of his experience in Hong Kong in the May 2004 *Voice*:

> "I was placed on loan from the National Police Agency to MOFA to serve as a consul in Hong Kong...Intelligence was completely controlled on a centralized basis by the in-country consul general and ambassador. If I were to bypass

> those officials and submit a report directly to my own parent agency, the action would be followed by immediate repatriation orders…I submitted reports on any intelligence I had obtained directly to the consul general, but the problem encountered was that the consul general was delegated authority to assess the value of the intelligence. Since this was the heyday of the Ministry of International Trade and Industry (MITI), the most significant issue was the handling of Japan-China trade. Thus, intelligence concerning that issue would be expeditiously transmitted to Japan via top-secret telegrams. However, not once did intelligence concerning the Red Guard, obtained by myself, undergo such handling. In the case of consul generals who exercise an interest in only economic affairs, if one were not careful, intelligence concerning diplomacy and security would be discarded in the wastebasket."[1137]

Sassa apparently experienced similar difficulties as defense attachés with passing intelligence to Tokyo, although he admitted that at times NPA officials would circumvent official communications procedures: "There were times when an individual on loan from the National Police Agency would directly submit a telegram to the agency without going through the consul general and create a major issue." And Sassa's comments clearly illustrate that perceived national priorities on the part of the chief of mission—in this case, trade with China—dictated what intelligence was passed expeditiously. Priorities change, however, as will be noted below.

Japanese Diplomats and Defense Attachés as Targets

The first major spy incident involving Self-Defense Forces personnel in Japan occurred in 1980, when General Yukihisa

Miyanaga and two SDF staff members were charged with violating the Self-Defense Forces Act by passing sensitive information to a Soviet military attaché. The incident came at an especially sensitive time as his arrest followed immediately after the Soviet invasion of Afghanistan. The invasion reignited concern in Japan that the Soviets might be planning to invade Hokkaido as well, possibly using information provided by Miyanaga. Miyanaga, moreover, was considered one of the SDF's premier Soviet expert having served on the front with the Soviet Union during World War II and had been held prisoner in Siberia; he later re-entered Japan's security forces in 1952 following his return. In addition to Miyanaga, there were many other returnees still serving in the SDF, thus raising the question of their loyalties to Japan. Miyanaga was found guilty and sentenced to a year in prison.[1138]

In an incident more political in nature, a MOFA Intelligence and Analysis Bureau analyst on Russia, Masaru Sato, was charged in 2002 for passing classified information to a powerful LDP politician, Muneo Suzuki, without obtaining proper approval and without declassifying the reports. Sato was reported to have contacts in both the Israeli Mossad and in Russia's SVR intelligence agency, and had traveled to Israel, Russia, and elsewhere to meet with his counterparts abroad, a sign of growing intelligence ties between MOFA and other intelligence organizations. Suzuki, a representative from Hokkaido who had taken a special interest in Japan-Russian relations due to Hokkaido's proximity to Russia, had access to MOFA's classified information as a deputy chief cabinet secretary, with Sato delivering classified reporting as part of his normal duties. But Suzuki's access was automatically revoked when he lost his deputy chief cabinet secretary position following a Cabinet reshuffle in September 1999. Despite Suzuki's new status, Sato continued to provide classified reports to Suzuki. Ultimately, despite the questions regarding intelligence security (aside from Suzuki's lack of need-to-know, the classified information would have been most likely provided to Suzuki in an unsecured facility), Sato was arrested for using ¥33 million budgeted for an international aid panel to pay for a trip to Israel.[1139] After serving a brief prison sentence, Sato was released and now writes prolifically on intelligence matters.

The most dramatic attempt to turn a Japanese consulate worker against his country took place in Shanghai in 2003-2004. Shortly after he arrived to his post in Shanghai, a 46-year-old communications officer working at Japan's Consulate General there developed a relationship with a hostess at a local karaoke bar called *Kaguyahime*[2] in the Hongqiao district of western Shanghai. The officer was in charge of the transmission of top-secret cables between the consulate and MOFA headquarters in Tokyo, and as such he had access to highly classified information originating out of the consulate. The karaoke bar was a known Japanese expat hangout as many Japanese living in Shanghai frequented the bar, and thus it was a logical target for China's security services.

As the relationship evolved, a Chinese man calling himself "Tang" and identifying himself as working for a "public security" office struck up a casual acquaintance with the communications officer. At first his interactions were innocent, though he soon began to ask subtle questions about the consulate official's work environment such as how Consul General Nobuyuki Sugimoto was rated among consulate general staff members. Feeling increasingly uncomfortable in the situation, the communications officer

---

[2] *Kaguyahime* or "Radiant Evening Princess" is the main character in one of Japan's oldest folk tales, *Taketori Monogatari*, about a bamboo farmer who discovered a young princess in a bamboo stalk. Not knowing who her parents were, the farmer adopted the young princess. As she grew many princes tried to woo her, but knowing that she would one day return to her home *Tsuki no Miyako* or "Capital of the Moon," she gave the princes impossible tasks to fulfill. She rejected even the Emperor's marriage proposals. Kaguyahima is finally taken back to her home *Tsuki no Miyako*, an event her parents and the Emperor lamented deeply.

soon requested and obtained a transfer to another consulate in Russia, where he had served previously, and by late April 2004 he was preparing to leave for Yuzhno-Sakhalinsk. When Tang learned about the coming transfer, he attempted to coerce the consulate officer into revealing more specific information, claiming his relationship with the hostess was considered a crime in China. Tang said he would reveal the relationship to his superiors at MOFA and to authorities in Beijing. The woman would certainly be punished, Tang threatened. Tang pressed for information such as the names of consular staff at the consulate and their original agencies and ministries, and the flights Japanese couriers use to hand-carry classified documents to and from Shanghai. Tang also demanded specific information on the Japanese government's policies on territorial issues involving Uotsurijima, one of the Senkaku islets claimed by China. Then, in an effort to elicit a continuing relationship with the PRC, Tang resorted to a common tactic, telling the officer that his colleagues would be in contact with him once he arrived in Russia: "We are lifelong friends, right?" Tang reportedly added. The Japanese officer could take no more: on May 6, 2004, mere days before he was scheduled to depart for his next assignment, the communications officer committed suicide. He left several notes for Consul General Sugimoto, fellow consulate workers, and to his family saying "I cannot sell out my country." In his notes, however, he admitted to passing the names of other consular personnel to the PRC intelligence officer. No other information was passed, he claimed in his notes. The extent of information passed to the Chinese side could never be precisely determined, but one fact was obvious: the communications officer had allowed himself to be compromised.[1140]

Japan's Shanghai Consulate played a key role in Japan's diplomatic efforts in China at the time. According to an investigative report by *Shukan Bunshun* shortly after the suicide was publicly revealed, Consul General Sugimoto had built a network of connections among individuals who belonged to Jiang Zemin's major support organization called the "Shanghai Faction." While Jiang Zemin had retired as Secretary General of the Communist Party of China (CPC), he still retained influence at the time as Chairman of the Central Military Commission, and many wondered whether Jiang would attempt to maintain his influence on Chinese domestic affairs through this faction. Sugimoto had reportedly obtained information from high-level sources in the Shanghai Faction, and the Chinese security officials reportedly wanted to know what that information was. Moreover, China was concerned that the consulate was collecting information on military bases in the region, including information on two submarine bases in Zhejiang and Jiangsu provinces near Shanghai. But most of all, China wanted Japan's cryptologic codes. Tokyo started a quiet investigation into the suicide, dispatching teams from MOFA and CIRO to interview consulate staff. Junichi Ihara, MOFA's councilor in charge of inspections, conducted interviews for a week while personnel from MOFA's Information and Communications Division checked the Consulate General's classified communications system and the coded cables themselves for signs of a leak, and then they checked for bugs. When all systems were verified as untampered, they changed the codes. MOFA then expanded its investigations to all six Japanese diplomatic missions in China. They found a few similar cases, but none as extreme as the one in Shanghai.[1141] News of the suicide did not become public until over a year later, when *Yomiuri Shimbun* first reported details in late December 2005.[1142]

Similar incidents followed. In August 2006, it was reported that an MSDF petty officer first class had traveled to Shanghai eight times in a 15-month period without taking leave and without informing his superiors at his base in Nagasaki Prefecture.

He traveled to Shanghai to meet a Chinese hostess working at the same Karaoke bar—the *Kaguyahime*—as the Chinese woman involved with the communications officer. He sent letters and as much as ¥3.5 million to the woman. Moreover, MSDF investigators found official-use-only documents and CDs at his home containing identification reference data used to monitor military vessels of other countries. While the materials were not classified—he merely took them home to study, he said—if his Chinese interlocutors convinced the 45-year-old sailor to deliver the documents to Shanghai or otherwise discuss their contents, skilled intelligence officers could use that as psychological leverage against him to gain access or insight into other more sensitive Japanese operations or technologies. The petty officer denied taking any documents to China, and investigators found no evidence that he had transferred the material to the Chinese.[1143] However, given the ties of the Karaoke bar in Shanghai to suspected Chinese intelligence, there could be no doubt that he was being cultivated as a possible intelligence source. As *Shukan Bunshun* noted regarding the 2004 communications officer incident: "It was their old trick to first ask for harmless information and then gradually draw out confidential information."[1144] The intelligence wars were heating up in Asia.

MOFA's Intelligence and Analysis Service

MOFA's intelligence and analysis capabilities were expanded significantly in stages following the end of the Cold War. Citing the rapidly changing international security environment, MOFA established the Intelligence and Analysis Bureau during a major reorganization in the summer of 1993. Indeed, symbolizing the need for increased intelligence collection in the new era, one commentator noted that the IAB was to be established on the three-year anniversary of Iraq's invasion of Kuwait in early August 1990, and at a time when the nuclear crisis on the Korean peninsula was just heating up.[1145] MOFA's intelligence shop was renamed from its original "Intelligence and Research Bureau" (*Jōhō Chōsakyoku*) to the more outward-focused "International Intelligence Bureau" (*Kokusai Jōhōkyoku*), often called the Intelligence and Analysis Bureau by counterparts in English. The Bureau was divided into three divisions including an international intelligence division and two analysis divisions further subdivided along geographic areas of expertise.[1146]

Eleven years later, the bureau was upgraded in a Ministry-wide reform from August 2004 and renamed the "Intelligence and Analysis Service," with a fourth division added to the service. A specially appointed Intelligence Officer—a deputy foreign minister-level official—was appointed to head the Service, and four director-level officers were in turn appointed to head each of the Service's four divisions. Reforms of MOFA's intelligence capabilities continued in a piecemeal fashion the following year, as Foreign Minister Machimura announced the establishment of a private round-table conference on intelligence issues consisting of five members to advise him on intelligence matters. Following their recommendations, in November MOFA announced plans to establish some 30 resident "Intelligence Managers" (*Jōhō Tantokan*) at its embassies in Europe and the Americas, the Middle East, and China. The managers would be drawn from the Intelligence and Analysis Service and would "cultivate intelligence sources," in the words of *Tokyo Shimbun*.[1147] By this time also, the Ministry was discussing the option of implementing a more robust human intelligence collection capability.

Indicative of the key role the Intelligence and Analysis Service plays in Japan's foreign policy, many of the IAB/IAS senior leadership are later appointed to significant posts abroad immediately after serving in the IAB/IAS. Tadashi Imai, who headed the IAB starting in early 2001, was named Japan's ambassador to Israel in April 2002 and later ambassador to Malaysia in April 2004.[1148] Imai's successor at IAB was Takaaki Kojima, a rising star at MOFA before taking the IAB helm in 2002: Kojima had served in senior-level positions at the Japanese embassies in China and the United Kingdom before becoming minister at the Japanese embassy in the United States.[1149] Kojima was named ambassador to Singapore in July 2004 following two years leading the IAB, while Norihiro Okuda, IAB deputy director under Kojima, was named as ambassador to Afghanistan in July 2004 as well.[1150] In turn, Japan's ambassador in charge of Iraqi reconstruction, Shigeru Nakamura, replaced Kojima, becoming the first head of the upgraded IAS. Following his two-year stint as head of the IAS, Nakamura was appointed Japan's ambassador to Saudi Arabia in April 2006.[1151]

Public Security Intelligence Agency

A relatively small organization under the Ministry of Justice, the PSIA followed ultra-right and ultra-left-wing groups in Japan, communists, cultists, and other individuals perceived to be politically radical in Japanese society. Since its inception in the 1950s, the PSIA's primary targets in Japan had been communists, intelligence agents in Japan from other countries, and Japanese returnees from the Soviet Union, North Korea, and China. Following the demise of the Soviet Union, the PSIA focused on North Korean elements in Japan, and after the 1995 Aum Shinrikyo attack it also focused on that cult as well.[1152]

By the time government-wide reforms were seriously being discussed in 1997 it employed as many as 1,754 personnel, and some reform plans since then have called for cutting PSIA positions to as few as 200 and adding staff to an expanded CIRO.[1153] It remained relatively intact into the 2000s, however, and it changed its English title from the Public Security Investigation Agency to the Public Security Intelligence Agency in the early 2000s.

In addition to the Defense Agency and the NPA, PSIA also has a basic SIGINT capability. According to Mitsuhiro Suganuma, former director general of PSIA's second intelligence department in charge of collecting foreign intelligence, "[t]he PSIA is generally known as a government agency intended to keep public peace by controlling organizations that carried out terrorist subversive activities. However, from the very beginning, the PSIA has performed functions of an external 'intelligence agency.'...The PSIA in the past carried out information-gathering activities both within and outside of Japan in various forms, but few of the facts are publicized: 'Wireless monitoring' activities were especially concealed." According to Suganuma, PSIA established a SIGINT facility called the "Terada Technology Institute" in Nerima Ward, Tokyo, in 1952, noted at the beginning of this chapter. By the mid-1960s it was monitoring communications from Khabarovsk, Vladivostok, the Kurile Islands, Sakhalin, and the Kamchatka Peninsula. The Terada Technology Institute could also monitor communications as far as Tibet, according to Suganuma, and PSIA monitored the "repeated clashes with the troops of the People's Liberation Army dispatched from China" to Tibet during the 1960s. The Institute was dissolved in August 1976 after monitoring 3.81 million pieces of traffic, filling 41,000 reports, and deciphering 31 codes.[1154]

Suganuma also claimed that the PSIA had obtained "highly reliable information beforehand that an invasion by Soviet troops" of Afghanistan in late 1979 "was imminent." PSIA obtained this information through *Kudankai,* a "detached corps of the PSIA" that was headed by former WWII intelligence operative

Saburo Nomura. Nomura had developed an intelligence network in the Soviet Union during the war, and later as head of PSIA's *Kudankai* in the 1970s, Nomura discovered the plans to invade and informed Tokyo. Tokyo, however, was not in a position to do anything with the intelligence, according to Suganuma, because Japan was powerless to stop it.[1155] How much Tokyo knew beforehand of the invasion is difficult to confirm, but Suganuma's boastful claims at least point to organizational efforts to obtain foreign intelligence via human sources.

PSIA was also involved in efforts in the 1950s to interview Japanese repatriates from the Soviet Union. Many of these returnees had been sentenced to 25 years' hard labor and worked in construction projects at important facilities in the Soviet Union. Following Khrushchev's rise to power in the mid-1950s and diplomatic efforts during the resulting thaw in relations, Tokyo secured their return. With these interviews, the PSIA "amassed detailed top secret data, ranging from the private lives of important figures of the Communist Party to major military installations," Suganuma wrote. The project "laid a foundation for later HUMINT activities by the PSIA" targeting the Soviet Union. By the mid-1990s, however, attention had turned primarily to North Korea, and "at present, the PSIA places its utmost emphasis on the effort to collect North Korean intelligence."[1156]

With the decline of ideologically motivated groups in Japan and as the strength of Aum Shinrikyo (which renamed itself Aleph) wanes, PSIA as an intelligence organization is gradually losing bureaucratic standing in Tokyo. Among national security-related offices in Japan, PSIA will be most vulnerable to personnel cuts should efforts to bolster intelligence capabilities at other intelligence organizations such as MOFA, the Defense Ministry, CIRO and others be realized, as billets are shifted among agencies.

Seeking Greater Intelligence Autonomy

Less than a year after the establishment of the DIH in 1997, the deputy director at the time, Takemasa Moriya, gave an extensive interview with the defense journal *Gunji Kenkyu*, during which he highlighted the increasing importance of intelligence in a newly multipolar world. According to Moriya, "During the Cold War Japan's defense policy was stable; it would not be able to make a big mistake as long as it acted as a member of the Western side." However, "When the structure of two rival poles crumbles and becomes multi-polar, a point of view begins to become necessary which ponders what each country, in planning for its survival and prosperity, will consider to be its national interest, and what kind of measures it had best take for that purpose." In essence, a number of powers have emerged in the post-Cold War environment, with some harboring national goals that are at odds with Japan's national values and perceived interests. Intelligence in this environment thus is critical in warning of and possibly preventing national security challenges to Japanese interests before they appear. While calls in Japan for improved intelligence capabilities are not new—conservative forces have supported strengthening intelligence functions since the early 1950s—support for improved intelligence deepened in the mid-1990s in response to crises during that decade and also due to fears that Japan's only major military ally, the United States itself, might withhold, manipulate, or be unable to provide intelligence.

Calls for better intelligence have sometimes invoked famous intelligence figures in Japan's history, particularly that of pre-World War I figure Colonel Motojiro Akashi. Jitsuro Terashima, the head of Mitsui's Global Strategic Studies Institute and the non-profit Japan Research Institute, pointed to the "Akashi Operation" of 1904-1905 in calling for improved intelligence capabilities. The

Akashi Operation refers to Colonel Akashi's efforts to undermine Czarist Russia militarily and politically while Akashi served as defense attaché with the Japanese Imperial Army's General Staff Office in a number of European countries while Japan was at war with Russia. Operating out of Berlin, Geneva, London, Paris, and other cities, Akashi collected information on Russia and is reputed to have provided substantial funds to Russian opposition groups including underground Leninist revolutionaries around the time of Russia's first revolution in 1905. Most of the funding, however, came toward the end of hostilities in 1905, and Akashi eventually returned 30 percent of the funds provided by the Meiji government, according to popular retelling of the story.[1157]

For Terashima, the contrasts with post-war Japan were stark. Japan had a "clear concept of national interest" at the time, but "in post-World War II Japan, diplomacy and intelligence activities have evolved without a clear concept of national interest." Japan became "excessively dependent on the United States, and thus there has not been any need to take the initiative in thinking about our own concept of national interest." He called for a robust and independent intelligence capability to be built in post-Cold War Japan.[1158]

Following the 9.11 attacks in the United States, former PM Nakasone, a vocal supporter of improved intelligence capabilities, suggested that Japan should create a "Ministry of National Intelligence to collect, analyze, and take action on intelligence," because "aggressive intelligence activities of the sort conducted by Colonel Motojiro Akashi during the Japanese-Russian War" have been "non-existent in postwar Japan."[1159] The Akashi image was again cited following the death of two diplomats who were ambushed in Iraq in late 2003, with conservative daily *Sankei Shimbun* calling Akashi "a role model for Japanese professional intelligence officers." "The lesson Colonel Akashi handed down to future generations has to do with the vital importance of human intelligence obtained by interacting with the locals in an area in turmoil, and that the work of one brilliant intelligence officer alone can be sufficient to move history," *Sankei* declared. *Sankei* called on Tokyo to devote "ample funds" for HUMINT operations "even at the expense of cutting back on the exorbitant cost of housing and entertainment at diplomatic missions overseas," an allusion both to MOFA's slush-funds scandal and to perceived posh living standards for Japanese diplomats in general.[1160] Shinzo Abe, during a discussion on Japanese intelligence capabilities, declared: "Before World War II, Japan too was aware of the importance of intelligence strategy and...representative of such activities was that of Colonel Motojiro Akashi."[1161] Yet, as Abe's interviewer noted, "Japan is in the process of gradually improving its capabilities in the areas of COMINT and ELINT [but] Japan is highly deficient in the area of HUMINT."[1162] These periodic references to Akashi highlight Tokyo's increasing interest in creating an organization dedicated to the active collection of intelligence from human sources.

Diversification of and independent control over intelligence sources is a particular goal for Japan in the 21st Century. Indeed, many officials and commentators hold Terashima's opinion that Japan is "excessively dependent on the United States" for its intelligence needs. Some officials in Japan fear the United States would withhold vital intelligence if US and Japanese national interests were perceived to diverge. One unnamed Japanese official justifying the launch of its reconnaissance satellites stated simply: "The US would not give information when Japanese national interests conflict with US national interest."[1163] The academic Masahiro Matsumura similarly feared that as Japan became ever more integrated with US missile defense systems, reliance on US-controlled launch warning systems "would further skew the already asymmetrical bilateral power relationship in favor of the United States, to such a decisive and irreversible extent that Japanese security and foreign policy would be geared to appease the United States so as to secure continuation of satellite information flows." According to Matsumura, Japan could find itself in a situation where it disagrees with the US on a particular security matter, but in order to secure continued access to the system, Tokyo might feel compelled to follow the US lead on the matter. Matsumura thus advocated "a separate and parallel structure" including "a reliable level of early warning information" in order "to secure sovereign control" over its own missile defense systems.[1164]

Tokyo is similarly wary that resource constraints will limit how US intelligence assets are allocated. As the United States is deeply involved in security matters across the globe, in Tokyo's view a compelling tactical need elsewhere might require the redeployment of particular platforms or capabilities directly supporting both US and Japanese intelligence needs to other areas of the globe, such as the Middle East. And even US intelligence is not omni-present. The retired General Shikata pointed to this reality in a 2003 article in the conservative monthly *Shokun!*, in which he called on Japan to become an "information superpower" and develop "an intelligence-gathering capability that would enable [Japan] to collect information even the United States is not able to collect."[1165] While only implied, under both Matsumura's and Shikata's proposals Japan could become a true ally sharing a greater burden in the region, allowing the US to redeploy assets to other areas of the globe as necessary.

These sentiments were increasingly gaining support among the policy community in Tokyo, leading to a number of studies on intelligence reform in the early 2000s. The Liberal Democratic Party on March 30, 2004—following shortly after the Madrid bombings—issued a policy paper entitled "Recommendations on Japan's New Defense Policy: Toward a Safer and More Secure Japan and the World," compiled by the LDP's Defense Policy Studies Subcommittee. The report called for the improvement of Japan's main intelligence organizations, the CIRO and the Defense Intelligence Headquarters: "The Defense Intelligence Headquarters, the sole organization in charge of collecting and analyzing intelligence from a military perspective, should continue to be strengthened." It also called for an expansion of intelligence ties with multiple countries, not just the United States: "While intelligence cooperation with the United States should be furthered, expanded contacts with other countries should be sought."[1166] As the political party in power at the time, the LDP certainly did not want to be perceived as overtly advocating "independence" from intelligence-sharing with the United States, so they instead focused on diversifying intelligence "contacts."

Months later, the Araki Report—published in preparation for review of the National Defense Program Outline in 2004—echoed LDP's recommendations particularly in the field of human intelligence: "There is also a growing need to counter the new, externally unrecognizable threats posed by non-state actors through first-hand human intelligence. Consequently, the government should promptly take steps to fully exploit human intelligence resources, including area study specialists and overseas intelligence experts."[1167]

Not to be outdone, the Ministry of Foreign Affairs, no doubt hoping to position itself to expand its own intelligence capabilities, in the spring of 2005 hosted a high-level advisory panel on intelligence reform. Advisory panel members included intelligence expert Kensuke Ebata, former Japanese Ambassador to Thailand and Saudi Arabia Satoshi Morimoto, and former CIRO head Yoshio Omori. The advisory panel's "Toward the Strengthening of Japan's Foreign Intelligence-Gathering Capabilities" explicitly highlighted the importance of intelligence in a new era of asymmetric threats: "[I]n light of the increasing number of new threats, such as international terrorism and the proliferation of weapons of mass destruction, in which the strength of intelligence-gathering capabilities can play a decisive role in solving problems, the strengthening of Japan's foreign intelligence-gathering capabilities is an urgent issue that must be tackled without further delay." And while national technical collection means such as reconnaissance satellites "play an important role in pursuing objectivity through the process of cross-checking information with human-based intelligence-collection activities," it is necessary "to expand human" intelligence collection as well. The panel advocated the creation of an intelligence organization like Britain's Secret Intelligence Service, "placed under the foreign minister to perform its own specialized activities." The panel suggested this organizational approach—a HUMINT service outside of MOFA—because "[f]oreign intelligence-gathering activities sometimes involve activities that are incompatible with usual diplomatic activities." The panel recognized the obvious duality of this proposition, since MOFA would necessarily host at least some personnel from a HUMINT service in undercover capacities. Without explicitly saying as much, the panel noted that "MOFA already has the basis for foreign intelligence-gathering activities, such as embassies and legations abroad" and "[t]he time has come for the MOFA to strengthen its foreign intelligence-gathering capabilities thoroughly and qualitatively."[1168]

Thus, these official statements and studies demonstrated deep support for the formal creation of some type of HUMINT collection service, most likely within the Cabinet Office. The Liberal Democratic Party declared its staunch support in its 2004 report, although further intelligence reform stalled in the waning years of the Koizumi administration due to his focus on the unrelated postal privatization issue. Prime Minister Abe has made a number of statements strongly supporting improved HUMINT intelligence capabilities prior to taking over as prime minister in September 2006, although he used his first years to consolidate his political base before attempting piecemeal reforms in a variety of areas. Both the Defense Agency and the Ministry of Foreign Affairs support such a capability, as demonstrated by their respective advisory panel reports. Indeed, the creation of a formal HUMINT organization could be said to complete Japan's basic intelligence collection capabilities.

6) Preemptive Strikes and Precision-Guided Weapons

Japan has long debated the issue of limited preemption. The administration of Prime Minister Ichiro Hatoyama first made a statement in 1956 supporting the theoretical constitutionality of a preemptive strike on a foreign missile base if an attack on Japan were imminent. However, subsequent statements questioned the constitutionality of actually maintaining the force structure necessary to carry out a preemptive strike. Of course, there was only minimal debate at the time since post-war Japan was in no position to develop the overwhelming military force—long-range bombers or conventional forces to invade and seize an objective—required at the time for preemptive strikes. Following the 1954 Yoshida Doctrine, moreover, Tokyo had emphasized Japan's economic development. Thus, throughout the Cold War Japan maintained a policy of "defensive defense": Japan kept the minimum conventional strength necessary to defend its homeland and avoided expensive, offensively oriented defense systems such as attack aircraft carriers, heavy bombers, and long-range missiles.

By the 1990s, however, information and defense technologies had progressed to the point that overwhelming force was no longer required to carry out a limited preemptive strike. The United States had in the 1970s-1990s developed a range of precision strike technologies that could accurately hit and destroy targets with conventional explosives and other non-nuclear munitions. Prior to this time, a preemptive strike required the carpet-bombing of a target, the use of a nuclear weapon, or the seizure of a target by a massive number of troops. By the late 1980s, a greater ability to distinguish militarily relevant targets through improved intelligence coupled with the ability to actively guide a weapon to those targets with improved information technologies made a preemptive strike using conventional weapons an increasingly viable option. This capability was based on what was popularly called at the time the "Revolution in Military Affairs." New defense technologies and networks now allowed greater and extremely accurate strike capabilities without resorting to a nuclear strike or carpet-bombing and with little collateral damage. This in turn reduced the risk of escalation—in theory at least.

Yet the United States itself was still at the early stages of developing the full potential of "RMA" at the end of the Cold War. Japan's Self Defense Forces at this time had not yet begun to incorporate the platforms, networks, or precision-guidance technologies necessary to carry out precision strikes, and thus as a practical matter Japan could not conduct a preemptive strike outside of the Japanese archipelago. While the Air Self Defense Force flew F-4s, F-15s, and F-2s—a variant of the U.S. F-16—possible targets for preemption were located outside the range of these aircraft. As long as Japan did not have an aerial refueling capability, its fighter-bombers could not fly sorties to distant targets in East Asia with a full compliment of weapons and return following a mission. And neither the ASDF nor the Maritime Self Defense Force operated long-range cruise missiles. Although the MSDF was armed with short-range anti-ship cruise missiles such as the Harpoon and a domestically produced anti-ship short-range cruise missile SSM-1b, the declared range of both weapons systems was less than 200 kilometers—enough perhaps to strike targets along the coast from a naval asset (as the US Navy Web site notes, the Harpoon's GPS-assisted inertial navigation "enables the system to have both an anti-ship and a land attack capability"[1169]), but not a long-range precision-strike capability. Japan also did not have the intelligence structure or the surveillance and reconnaissance capabilities that could provide near-real-time target information required prior to and during a preemptive strike.

As Japan's "Info-RMA" progressed—with its emphasis on timeliness, intelligence and, increasingly, precision—the contradiction in Japan's policies became increasingly obvious in the early 2000s as the perceived threat especially from North Korea grew ever more real: Tokyo continued to assert the constitutional legality of a theoretical strike against a target that showed imminent signs of preparing for an attack even as it declared the forces necessary to carry out such a strike unconstitutional. Moreover, without the capability to carry out a limited preemptive attack, declarations that Japan could constitutionally conduct a preemptive strike on a missile base if Japan felt threatened were meaningless.

Yet in the background of public debates on the pros and cons of preemptive strikes in the early 2000s, Japan's Self-Defense Forces began the piecemeal introduction of a basic capability to carry out such strikes. Japan began to adopt precision technologies and the infrastructure necessary to operate them. As previously noted, Japan had in the 1990s already begun to centralize its defense intelligence functions within the SDF, but this was only a start. Japan sought an ability to operationalize the collected intelligence if it so chose. As retired LTG Seiyu Mori wrote on the eve of the formation of the DIH in the October 1996 *Rikusen Kenkyu,* "The problem…is in 'using' in a timely and appropriate manner the intelligence obtained." Mori called the use of RMA—the foundation of a precision strike capability— "victory through intelligence."[1170] With its improved and near real-time ISR capabilities represented by its reconnaissance satellites and improving UAV capabilities, Japan was ready to proceed to the next step in the "Revolution in Military Affairs": Japan in the early 2000s began to acquire a limited precision strike capability, which in turn could serve as the basis for an offensively oriented preemptive strike capability.

Japan Debates Preemptive Strikes

The Japanese Government adopted the stance in 1956 that an attack on an enemy base can be considered self-defense when there is no other way to defend Japan from an imminent missile or other attack. In a statement by Prime Minister Ichiro Hatoyama, read by then-Defense Agency Director General Naka Funada in the Diet on February 29, 1956, Hatoyama asserted: "It cannot be thought that it is the aim of the Constitution that we should sit and wait for self-destruction in the case of an attack by guided missiles or other means. In such a case, in order to prevent such an attack... attacking a guided missile or other base is legally within the scope of self-defense and should be considered possible."[1171] Of course, precision weapons did not exist in 1956, so a "preemptive strike"—*sensei kōgeki*—was limited to either a nuclear attack (or similar mass destruction of the target such as with carpet-bombing) or, practically speaking, seizure of the enemy area in question by ground troops. The first option was categorically out of the question for Japan, as only four countries had nuclear weapons at the end of the 1950s and nuclear weapons and missile technologies were quite unavailable to Japan. Japan could not exercise the second option—dispatching troops to the area—even if Tokyo determined an "enemy base" or *teki kichi* was preparing an imminent attack on Japan, as the recently established Self-Defense Forces were extremely limited at the time. Recognizing this, Funada further clarified Hatoyama's statement during Diet discussion that day in 1956: "I am not saying that conducting a so-called preemptive attack, such as sending many troops to an enemy base and attacking it, is included [in this statement]."

The difference between the theoretical constitutionality of conducting a preemptive attack and the possession of the forces necessary for such an attack was further highlighted during a Diet debate on March 19, 1959. Then-Defense Agency chief Shigejiro Ino repeated the Japanese government's position that "legally… it is within the scope of the right of self-defense to attack an enemy base to defend from an attack by guided missiles when there is no other means to do so." But Ino also declared that "it is not the aim of the Constitution to possess offensive weapons that pose a threat [to other countries]." These were, according to Ino, "two separate issues" and "not at all contradictory."[1172] Thus while Japan considered a preemptive attack on an enemy base to be constitutional in theory if the enemy base showed signs of preparing an imminent attack on Japan, it considered the development or possession of a capability to conduct a preemptive attack to be offensive in nature and thus unconstitutional. Tokyo continued to support this policy line for the next fifty years.

Precision and Preemption

In the 1980s, countries were increasingly conducting preemptive strikes against specific targets strongly suspected of developing weapons of mass destruction or supporting international terrorism. In one of the most notable early preemptive strikes, the Israeli Air Force destroyed Iraq's Osirak nuclear reactor at the al-Tuwaitha Nuclear Center near Baghdad in a June 1981 air raid using conventional bombs delivered by F-16 fighter/bombers and escorted by F-15s. Israel feared—quite rightly it turned out—that Iraq would divert the fuel to a nuclear weapons program.

Five years later, the United States bombed Moammar Ghadafi's bunker in April 1986 in retaliation for Libya's role in bombing TWA flight 840 and the La Belle discotheque in Berlin in April 1986.[3] The military use of precision weapons came into stark relief at the end of the 1980s, when the United States demonstrated its "Revolution of Military Affairs" in Panama in December 1989 and during Desert Shield/Desert Storm in 1990-1991. The U.S. military during these conflicts showed an astonishing capability to hit targets extremely accurately with precision-guided conventional munitions, even if the percentage of such weapons used during the conflicts was small.

This precision-strike capability in turn was based on several supporting capabilities. Platforms capable of providing tactical intelligence, reconnaissance, and surveillance (ISR) such as reconnaissance satellites and J-STARS (Joint Surveillance and Target Attack Radar System) were able to locate the precise location of enemy units and other targets and communicate that information in near-real time to targeters, who in turn were able to input the coordinates into guidance systems. The guidance systems themselves relied on coordinates provided by the GPS satellite constellation built in the 1980s and, in some cases, terrain contour mapping of the area. While these internetworked technologies were new—only 10% or so of the conventional munitions used during Desert Shield/Desert Storm was precision-guided—they demonstrated an astonishing ability to determine where a bomb landed.

Suddenly, with the advent of precision guidance technologies coupled with tactical ISR platforms and the communications

---

[3] In explaining the airstrike, W. Hays Parks, a legal adviser in the Reagan Administration during the time, wrote in the *New England Law Review*: the airstrike "was neither a peacetime reprisal nor an act of retaliation. It was a limited act of self-defense against a continuing threat for the purpose of deterring Libya's continued reliance upon illegal acts of terrorism as a foreign policy tool."

networks to provide that information quickly to combat units, a limited preemptive strike did not require nuclear weapons or an invasion by ground troops, as demonstrated by NATO's air campaign over Kosovo in the spring of 1999. A military employing precision weapons and the networks to support them could now target specific military targets and destroy them with conventional weapons (assuming they were not in hardened bunkers). Civilian casualties could be dramatically reduced by employing precision-guided weapons, as long as targeters could discern a military target from a civilian one and communicate any changes in the target environment to combat units as they engaged the targets.

Japanese defense commentators writing in the mid-1990s were just beginning to realize the full implications of the "Revolution in Military Affairs." While they did not overtly assert so at the time, they hinted at the fact that increasingly long-range precision weapons systems and what would later become known as "network-centric warfare" could ultimately alter Japan's core policy of "defensive defense." Writing in *Rikusen Kenkyu* in January 1996, four officers from the ASDF and GSDF declared that RMA "will likely render meaningless distinctions between front line and rear area; tactics, operations, and strategy; and soldier and civilian. Beyond a doubt, there is a great possibility of a major revolution in military thought taking place around the year 2020."[1173] The disappearance of "distinctions between front line and rear area" was even more important for Japanese defense policies because in traditional warfare Japan could isolate its forces in rear areas performing support roles for U.S. offensive operations on the front lines and thereby avoid combat. Once the distinction between the rear area and the front line disappeared, the concept of "defensive defense" was no longer applicable, as rear echelon units would be just as vulnerable to direct attacks—and increasingly capable of engaging directly in combat—as those on the front line. The easily delineated front line thus disappears, and with it, Japan's ability to neatly separate constitutionally acceptable defense from unacceptable participation in "collective self-defense."

Nevertheless, "defensive defense" remained a catch-phrase in most writings on Japanese security policy with the writers themselves using the term even as they called on Japan to study RMA: "Our nation, too, from a viewpoint of exclusively defensive defense, should begin without delay to study in earnest, government officials and private citizens together, the possibility and essence of RMA as well as its effects on our nation's defense," according to the *Rikusen Kenkyu* article. Only later, in the early 2000s, did the first articles to discuss broader implications for the concept of "defensive defense" appear.

Indicative of their deepening interest in the concept, Japanese defense journals in the late 1990s were increasingly detailing RMA developments then underway in the U.S. military. *Gunji Kenkyu* in 1998 published a series of articles detailing the U.S. "Force 21" concept promulgated by the U.S. Army's Training and Doctrine Command in August 1994, with articles on intelligence, networks, and sensor technologies. "Without a doubt, the armies of the United States and the other great powers are promoting… reforms in organization and equipment" that will be complete by "the early part of the twenty-first century," the introductory article declared. These reforms would include the ability to share "[r] eal-time, high-volume, and accurate information," the possession of "precise, long-range, and powerful firepower" based on "guided weapons technology [and] high-output energy technologies," and battlefield units that will incorporate "small-scale armor, light air transport, and stealth," and will be "highly versatile" and "functional" with "efficient logistics support."[1174] Major General Masahiro Shigemura, commander of the GSDF's Signal Brigade, in a July 1996 *Rikusen Kenkyu* article called on the GSDF "to tackle in a positive manner the changes" represented by RMA to make units hi-tech and "highly mobile." Shigemura also noted that for the GSDF, "in times of both peace and emergency, information warfare potential will grow increasingly important."[1175]

Mainstream Japanese journalists began to notice aspects of the Revolution in Military Affairs in the late 1990s as well. The widely read columnist Yoichi Funabashi pointed out following the "Operation Desert Fox" airstrikes against Iraqi targets in December 1998 that a "new war mode is emerging which integrates the most state-of-the-art technology in the aspects of hi-tech, space, information, and others." Funabashi highlighted that this new "high-tech" warfare capability in turn leads potential adversaries to rely increasingly on "dirty" or asymmetric warfare capabilities: "The more the United States sets out on a 'clean' RMA system, the more the nations opposing the United States will specialize in 'dirty' warfare methods."[1176] Japan offers a case-study of how the opposite would happen, however: because other countries such as North Korea were increasingly relying on asymmetric capabilities and 'dirty' warfare methods, Japanese policy makers began in 1999 to contemplate in public the development of technologies that would make possible the use of precision-guided weapons by the SDF.

With precision-strike technologies rendering a conventional attack on an enemy base increasingly feasible, by the late 1990s Japanese defense policy makers again began to broach publicly the topic of preemption. Following the 1998 Taepodong launch, the National Defense Division of the LDP's Policy Research Council in early 1999 established a "crisis management project team" to review contingency plans in case North Korea prepared a second launch of a missile toward Japan. The team was headed by Fukushiro Nukaga, who had been the head of the

Defense Agency at the time of the Taepodong launch but who had resigned in November to take responsibility for an unrelated procurement scandal at the Agency. Other members included a who's-who of Japan's young political Turks—many in their young 40s the sons and grandsons of Japanese politicians—on Japanese security issues such as future Prime Minister Shinzo Abe, Kenzo Yoneda (who later quoted Hugo Grotius in advocating a Japanese preemptive strike capability: "To kill those who are preparing to kill is lawful"[1177]), Norihiko Akagi, and former Defense Agency Director-General Kazuo Aichi, who later became head of the National Council for Making a New Constitution. The team met twice weekly from late January to June 1999 and examined a range of possible policy actions, from prohibiting money transfers to North Korea and further restricting trade to allowing Japan Coast Guard and MSDF ships to fire directly on suspected North Korean ships to halt and inspect them. At its February 24 meeting, the group discussed the theoretical possibility of conducting preemptive strikes. (Ironically, the discussion included a review of possible preemptive response scenarios conducted by Hajime Funada, the grandson of Naka Funada, who made Japan's original statement on the constitutionality of preemptive strikes in 1956.) While the project team did not come to any conclusion regarding the development or procurement of precision-guidance technologies for use in preemptive strikes—leaks to the media of the discussion were probably trial balloons to test the public's appetite for such an option—the group that day called for further examination of a preemptive strike option.[1178] Shinzo Abe was quoted to have said at the meeting that Japan "uses only carrots and no stick" in dealing with North Korea. "Without the stick, the choices of diplomacy are narrow," he declared.[1179]

The project team's interim report, released on June 3, stated: "[W]e should establish on an expedited basis a new crisis management system including radical changes in laws, with the broad approval of the public." In addition to highlighting the Cabinet's recent decision to build reconnaissance satellites, the project team called for "early warning satellites to track ballistic missiles." The team praised the Defense Agency and SDF "intelligence-gathering services" for "their earnest efforts," but recognizing Japan's still-limited capabilities, the team called on the government to "establish a system for accurately collating, analyzing, and evaluating intelligence." The team called for a robust ballistic missile defense system and further studies of a more offensive capability: "[W]e must study whether it will be permissible to conduct an attack on the enemy missile base and define what we will do in such a situation under the Japan-U.S. security system."[1180]

Perhaps in support of these objectives, in July 1999, the Defense Agency established an "RMA study group" in the Defense Policy Bureau's Defense Policy Division, which in September 2000 published its first official policy paper concerning the indigenous development of an advanced defense network. Titled "On Info-RMA," the paper provided a sweeping discussion of the need to introduce a networked environment in the Self Defense Forces to enable C4ISR capabilities on par with the United States. The paper stated: "In order to improve battle field identification capability and response capability, it is necessary that troops of the Ground, Maritime, and Air Self Defense Forces share sophisticated and large volumes of information through an information network and possess so-called C4ISR."[1181]

While it did not discuss precision-guidance technologies or preemptive strikes directly, the policy paper highlighted RMA as providing a capability to reduce non-combatant casualties in hostile engagements while at the same time reducing the need for defense personnel. "In Japan, the consciousness of honoring life above all things is high, and given the trend of households having a smaller number of children, we need to pay attention to the fact that the social demand for minimizing the number of victims in disputes and so on is great," it asserted. And pointing to a shift in Japanese thinking on the use of force, the document declared: "This is even more so when a dispute does not involve Japan's vital existence." The statement indicated that the Defense Agency began to view the use of force as a legitimate policy tool in response to a variety of threats in its geographic vicinity even as it continued to employ the "defensive defense" catchphrase in other parts of the document. A precision-strike capability was a primary way to minimize collateral damage and to achieve a precision strike capability one needed a robust C4ISR capability.

2003: The Preemption Debate Begins Anew

The issue of preemptive strikes became a topic of debate again shortly after North Korea announced its withdrawal from the NPT on January 10, 2003. The next day, opposition Democratic Party of Japan lawmaker Yoshinori Suematsu declared during debate in a House of Representatives Budget Committee meeting that North Korea was suspected of developing or possessing a range of asymmetric weapons such as chemical and biological weapons, nuclear weapons, and dozens or perhaps hundreds of missiles capable of reaching Japan's main islands. This was causing "tremendous concern" in Suematsu's home district in Tokyo, he declared. Foreign Minister Yoriko Kawaguchi responded diplomatically, saying that the international community was also concerned about North Korea. Shigeru Ishiba, director general of the Defense Agency, added that the "threat" of North Korea consisted of both capability and intent. "It is reasonable to say [North Korea] has the capability," but "we don't know" the North's intent, Ishiba stated. "In the case of a normal democratic country," Ishiba explained, "intention" is reflected in "public opinion," "mass media," "parliament," and similar civil institutions. North Korea does not have these institutions and is moreover run based on a "military first" ideology, making its intentions difficult to discern. Suematsu asked them more emphatically: "If one warhead were to fall on Tokyo…we would all die. Are you going to think about this after it happens? Are you saying you are going to think about it after Japanese citizens die?" Suematsu also asked Kawaguchi and Ishiba whether Japan could conduct a preemptive attack or if Japan could request the United States to conduct one. At this point, Kawaguchi repeated almost verbatim Ino's 1959 statement. Ishiba, for his part, delineated a number of hypothetical steps that might indicate North Korea's intention to fire missiles at Japan, such as declaring its intention to "turn Tokyo into a sea of fire" and fueling its missiles.[1182]

While Diet debate moved to other issues that day, the public debate regarding preemption was only beginning, with papers the following day suggesting Ishiba implied an attack on North Korea would be justified if certain conditions were observed—a mischaracterization of the day's debate and Ishiba's comments. Yet Suematsu's comments once again touched on Japan's policy dilemma: while official policy still recognized the constitutionality of a military strike on a foreign base that shows signs of preparing an attack, it did not regard the possession of a capability to carry out that strike to be unconstitutional. Tokyo was increasingly placing itself in a rhetorical bind. As it increasingly asserted its constitutional right to carry out a military strike if signs of an attack were imminent, it would eventually have to develop the capability to carry out such a strike if it indeed considered an attack from North Korea or elsewhere remotely realistic. Otherwise, a potential enemy would view such rhetoric as an idle threat and could potentially proceed with an attack regardless of Japan's domestic arguments on the constitution.

The following month, in the run-up to U.S. military actions targeting the Hussein regime, Ishiba's reported comments on the North Korea situation with several non-Japanese media outlets caused further speculation. On February 13, Reuters quoted him saying: "It is too late if" a missile "flies towards Japan." "Our nation will use military force as a self-defense measure if [North Korea] starts to resort to arms against Japan." However, "[w]e differentiate this from the concept of a preemptive strike," he noted in the Reuters report. Again attempting to walk the fine line between hypothetical capabilities and Japan's defense policies, at a news conference the day after the Reuters interview was published, Ishiba clarified that "it is not true that…we are making special preparations" for a "preemptive strike." His statements paralleled those he and FM Kawaguchi made in the Diet several weeks earlier: "Nothing is different from what I have been saying at Diet meetings," Ishiba said of the Reuters report.[1183]

Two weeks later, in an interview with London's *The Times* published on February 26, Ishiba seemingly hinted that the Defense Agency might examine the acquisition of longer-range precision-strike weapons: "It has been agreed that Japan is the shield and the U.S. is the arrow, but we have to discuss whether this is adequate or not," he told the paper. "[T]his will be discussed in parliament." Ishiba highlighted the democratic aspect of any future changes in defense policy: "This is not just what I think. It should be decided according to popular opinion and from listening to the Japanese people." After all, "Japan's constitution doesn't intend that we just wait and be attacked," he asserted, repeating a refrain from almost 50 years ago.[1184] When asked about Ishiba's comments, Japan's Ministry of Foreign Affairs spokesman explained that "Minister of Defense Shigeru Ishiba was answering to questions of a very hypothetical nature, and he tried to explain the Japanese stand on the right to self-defense. Since Japan, as a sovereign nation, has a right to defend itself, if another nation clearly shows signs of attack, we would not stand idly and accept any sort of attack. We can take the necessary measures, which are within the framework of our Constitution. It is a matter of what the clear sign would be that attack is being prepared and is imminent."[1185] Indeed, as *The Times* noted, the Ishiba interview took place less than 24 hours after North Korea launched the first of several 1960s-era shore-to-ship Silkworm missiles into the Sea of Japan and as the U.S. prepared a ground offensive into Iraq the following month. "I wasn't surprised by it," Ishiba coyly informed his interviewers of North Korea's tests.

As the Diet discussions and Ishiba's comments foreshadowed, Tokyo began an active and open debate of the possible possession of preemptive strike capabilities a month later. On March 27, Ishiba instructed the DA to begin an investigation into the possible introduction of weapons "capable of attacking missile launch bases, such as the U.S. cruise missile 'Tomahawk.'"[1186] In a rather friendly debate with opposition DPJ's hawkish Seiji Maehara that day in the House of Representatives Committee on Security about the possibility of possessing capabilities of attacking "enemy bases," Ishiba replied: "It is worth considering." Indeed, it wasn't much of a debate at all, as Maehara, noted for his deep interest in national security issues, asserted matter-of-factly at the same meeting that "if it appears that we're about to be attacked, then the Constitution allows for us to attack their base."[1187] Maehara agreed with Ishiba, indicating that at least some opposition party members supported a preemptive strike capability as well.

The next day, the Koizumi administration clarified the study's intent. Chief Cabinet Secretary Yasuo Fukuda, Koizumi's chief spokesman, noted that "we cannot use any [missiles such as the

Tomahawk] in light of the defense-oriented policy based on the Constitution." He did not deny the DA was studying the issue of cruise missiles, but rather contended the DA "is not doing so to realize it." Prime Minister Koizumi himself said simply that his "government does not have the intention" to possess such arms.[1188] Yet this scenario paralleled what took place in Tokyo prior to officially proceeding with the construction of reconnaissance satellites and, later, missile defense: the government denied an intention to build such systems, asserting that the studies were just studies. But when the political decision was finally made, the studies and related R&D efforts provided the foundation for the new programs, which were quickly funded and built within a few years. Ishiba himself pointed to this possibility by asserting: "It would be irresponsible if we do not know anything about how much it may cost and how long it may take to possess offensive capabilities."[1189] Thus, Tokyo was laying the groundwork for some sort of offensively oriented but limited precision-strike capability in the future.

Ishiba and Maehara were certainly not alone among Japanese politicians in advocating the development of both passive and active defense capabilities in response to North Korea's actions. On June 23, all 103 members of the bipartisan "Group of Junior Lawmakers To Establish a Security System for the New Century" adopted a statement calling North Korea "an extremely serious threat." The statement declared: "Not only has North Korea not adhered to agreed matters in the 'Pyongyang Declaration by Japan and North Korea'…it has also repeated provocative actions over and over since then: the unilateral refusal of nuclear inspections by international organizations, withdrawal from the NPT, conducting missile launch tests, and making statements that it would develop nuclear weapons. As a result, North Korea has come to pose an extremely serious threat to peace and stability, not only to Japan but to all of Northeast Asia." The group called on the Japanese government to "hasten" a "missile defense concept" (which was still under "joint study with the United States"), and a "restructure" of Japan's "defense only" concept "in a way appropriate for the times." "[W]e should make it possible to have the necessary, albeit minimum, 'offensive capability against an opponent's base' in the event of an impending attack on Japan," the group declared in the statement.[1190] Ishiba and Maehara were among the 15 organizers of the group.

Also in the summer of 2003, Ishiba explained the particularities of possessing a capability to strike "enemy bases" in a wide-ranging interview with the weekly magazine *Sekai Shuho*—the same publication that carried the Junior Lawmakers' statement in full. Ishiba continued to assert that Japan's Constitution would allow a limited preemptive strike capability:

> "The philosophy of our nation's constitution gives three necessary conditions for exercising the right to self-defense: there shall be an imminent unlawful armed invasion; there should be no other measures that can be taken to prevent the attack; and the force exercised should be kept to a minimum. We are not talking about, for example, a missile striking us, and then reducing the country that fired it to ashes....In cases where no other measures are available, it is unthinkable the constitution planned for us to sit on our butts and wait to die. I combined those two and made my statement [in the Diet on March 27], so there is nothing about it that deviated from former government remarks in the Diet."

When asked whether Japan presently has the capability to strike a base before a missile is launched, Ishiba replied simply: "We have nothing of the kind." He further stated that the Koizumi administration did not have a policy supporting a preemptive strike capability. "However, if that debate were taken up by the Diet...and the cabinet were to make that choice, then it would not necessarily be precluded by the constitution. The present cabinet has not chosen to possess that kind of strike capability."[1191] Ishiba's last comment pointed to one possible solution to Tokyo's seemingly contradictory stance on the constitutionality of a preemptive strike versus maintaining the forces to conduct a strike: instead of revising the constitution, Tokyo could simply restate how it interprets the constitution. And similarly with the reconnaissance program in the mid-1990s—when Tokyo brushed aside concerns that the satellites contradicted Japan's 1969 "Peaceful Utilization of Space" policy—Tokyo could simply reinterpret the constitution once all the pieces were in place by simply stating that just as a limited preemptive strike itself was constitutional, maintaining the means to carry out that strike was also constitutional, and then it could set the budget for mass-production of longer-range precision weapons and support programs.

Ishiba certainly recognized the difficulty in implementing a preemptive strike capability. During the *Sekai Shuho* interview, he explained the steps necessary to put in place a robust preemptive strike capability:

> "[S]upposing that the members of the Diet thought we should have that capability: in order for F-15s to be able to fly, for example, first we need to have air tankers or there is no way the planes could fly [to the target]. It would still be totally impossible only with air tankers. If we were to fly somewhere, first we would have to take out their radar network and then make our move, just like the United States

> did when it attacked Iraq. Then, we must have accurate information about where the radar and missile bases are. Then, it is necessary to have pilots with enough skill to reach those enemy missile bases. Then—we do not presently have any—air-to-surface missiles would be needed. Just thinking about it, in order to do all of that, a huge amount of money and time would be required."[1192]

At the time of Ishiba's interview in 2003, Japan did not have any of these capabilities aside from the F-15s. The defense commentator Isaku Okabe phrased the situation another way in the April 2004 *Sekai no Kansen*: "Just because you have some guns or can put a missile in a VLS [vertical launch system] or on the main wing of an airplane does not mean that you have land-attack capabilities."[1193] A land-attack capability requires a variety of supporting systems and training before it can be considered operational which both Ishiba and Okabe recognized, and even with the required infrastructure and highly trained pilots, success is by no means assured. Precision strike capabilities remained theoretical during the Koizumi administration.

The issue of capability aside, the Japanese government in 2003 continued to reserve the right to conduct a preemptive strike if it considers an attack on the Japanese homeland to be imminent. The official policy on preemptive strikes, as read by Minister of State for Defense Ishiba at the 156th ordinary session of the Diet in 2003 and quoted in the *2003 Defense of Japan*, is the following:

> "In the event that our country faces a danger of imminent and unfair invasion of its territory by missiles, etc., the Constitution should not be interpreted that Japan shall do nothing until it is destroyed. In the case of an attack by missiles, it should be interpreted that Japan can take the

> minimum necessary measures to prevent such an attack, and if it is deemed to be the only method to prevent the attack, the country should be able to attack the missile base, etc., as a legal invocation of its self-defense rights."[1194]

The Best Defensive-Defense is a Good Offensive-Defense

North Korea's provocative actions in 2003 and Ishiba's subsequent remarks regarding the constitutionality of limited preemptive strikes against missile bases sparked significant public debate on the issue over the next several years. Aside from the desire to develop a credible response to North Korea's provocative actions during that time—it declared on January 10 that it was no longer bound by the NPT and it conducted three unannounced shore-to-ship missile tests toward Japan between February and April that year—arguments centered on two main issues: the need for an active complement to passive missile defense capability, and a wish to have an independent option should the United States be perceived to demure from being willing to conduct a preemptive strike in defense of the Japanese homeland.

One major proponent of a new security doctrine was retired Vice Admiral Hideaki Kaneda, a former commander of Japan's Self-Defense Force Fleet. Although Kaneda was forced to retire following an accidental weapons discharge by sailors under his command in 1999, Kaneda quickly became influential in the defense policy community by becoming the deputy director of the Okazaki Institute, a visiting scholar at Harvard University, and visiting professor at Keio University, where he helped to establish periodic exchanges between Keio and National Defense Academy students. Kaneda began to write publicly of the need for an "offensive defense" strategy in early 2003, when he advocated Japan's adoption of the "5 Ds" in the world affairs weekly *Sekai Shuho*—the same publication that published Ishiba's extensive interview on preemptive strikes and that reprinted the Junior Lawmakers call for a preemptive capability. He also published a book advocating the "5 Ds" published that same year. The five Ds were: dissuasion, deterrence, denial or "offensive defense," defense or "active defense," and damage confinement or "passive defense." Dissuasion employs diplomacy and defense policies to prevent other countries from proliferating or otherwise expanding their military capabilities, "preventing threats from becoming actual realities." Deterrence is the ability to project the image that Japan is capable of responding to an act of military aggression in kind (Kaneda, however, noted that with regard to nuclear deterrence specifically, Japan should remain under the US "nuclear umbrella").

Denial and defense—or "offensive defense" and "active defense"—are interrelated capabilities for Kaneda. "Offensive defense" is "a measure to neutralize the enemy's ballistic missile capability by destroying its ballistic missile launchers and silos," Kaneda wrote. As "Japan examines the security conditions in its surrounding areas...where ballistic missile threats may emerge unexpectedly and by surprise...Japan will come to realize the need to possess the denial capability in its own conventional forces to some extent." "Offensive defense" therefore is Kaneda's term for a limited preemptive strike capability. "Active defense," on the other hand, is the ability to "intercept ballistic missiles in flight...before they reach their points of impact in Japan proper." Kaneda, an expert on and supporter of a national missile defense system, asserted that "Japan needs to build and become ready to operate a system that enables it to take responsive action within around 10 minutes of the detection of the pertinent missiles" (it should be noted that within two years of writing this article, Tokyo had embarked on the path of "active defense" by budgeting for several missile defense systems). The "passive defense" concept refers to civil defense measures to be taken following an attack "to limit the damage as much as possible in case ballistic missiles reach their points of impact"—"an area where Japan is in an extremely delayed preparatory condition," according to Kaneda.[1195] Thus, at the time of Kaneda's early 2003 article, Japan maintained limited capabilities in just two of the "5 Ds": dissuasion and damage confinement. By early 2005, Japan began to develop a third "D": defense or "active defense" by beginning construction of missile defense systems. A fourth "D," deterrence, was not possible without the fifth "D"—denial or "offensive defense." Indicative of his influence, Kaneda was invited to speak during Diet deliberations on the issue in April 2005 and again in April 2006, and he continued to speak in public on his five "Ds".

Moreover, Kaneda increasingly focused on the "offensive defense" aspect of his "5 Ds," noting in the naval journal *Sekai no Kansen* that because the United States "is engaged in military operations in the Middle East" and elsewhere, it might be "difficult" for the U.S. to compose a sufficient attack force to exercise 'offensive defense' measures in the area around Japan," and therefore "it is perfectly conceivable to expect Japan to have a partial role." Moreover, it might become "necessary" to eliminate "a direct threat before it materialized…by Japan on its own." Kaneda thus advocated for Japan to acquire "stand-off precision strike capabilities" such as "land-attack cruise missiles" and "ground-penetrating warheads," and "new technologies such as lasers or high-powered microwave devices which employ electromagnetic pulses."[1196]

Masato Ushio was another vocal advocate of a preemptive strike capability. Ushio, a lecturer at Seigakuin University with prior service in the Air Self Defense Force, published articles in April and May supporting such a capability as his book titled *People Who Refuse To See the North Korean Threat* (*Kitachosen no Kyoi wo Minai*

Hitotachi) was about to be published in that summer. Citing U.S. and Japanese inability to shoot down a missile during its boost phase—the most opportune time to do so, Ushio asserted—he declared in the May 2003 *Sekai Shuho* that "the best deterrence available today against ballistic missiles is nothing other than to upgrade the capability to strike missile launch facilities in North Korea." Ushio declared: "What the government is obligated to defend is the peace and independence of Japan, not official remarks made by the governments of the past. Now is the time for our country to set about having 'offensive capabilities.'"[1197] And in the April 2003 *Voice*—in which he gave Japan's Self Defense Forces barely passing grades in providing for the defense of Japan—Ushio declared: "It is precisely because the situation on the Korean peninsula is becoming more tense that I would like to call for decisive action by the Koizumi cabinet, embarking on the introduction of precision-guided munitions."[1198]

Other retired high-ranking officers also called for a preemptive-strike capability. Former Chairman of the Joint Staff Council Hajime Sakuma, commenting on what he saw as a need to develop a basic, independent strike capability, in June 2003 told the *Yomiuri Weekly*: "[E]ven if it is not 100%, we should have the ability to attack on our own and not rely on the U.S. military... Today's support fighters can only support ground attacks, but they should be outfitted to be able to attack underground missile installations. Furthermore, we should introduce Tomahawk cruise missiles, because that would serve as a deterrent force."[1199] The well-connected retired Lt. General Toshiyuki Shikata echoed Sakuma in his regular *Gunji Kenkyu* column: "It is understood that Japan will rely on the United States" for a "strategic attack capability," but "if neighboring countries take a militarily arrogant attitude towards our country, the SDF must also consider possessing medium-range cruise missiles, escort carriers, and a precision air-to-ground bombing capability."[1200] Thus, former officers were advocating a conventional deterrent capability in line with Kaneda's "offensive defense" argument.

Moreover, contradicting Ishiba's comments in *Sekai Shuho* that same summer, the *Yomiuri Weekly* itself asserted that Japan was indeed developing a basic infrastructure to support such a capability: "As a practical issue, even if intelligence gathering satellites launched by the [Japanese] government cannot detect the launch of a ballistic missile, it will be able to determine the location of the missile base accurately. The aerial tanker that the ASDF will introduce in JFY2006 will certainly be helpful in improving the efficiency of fighter aircraft training and will also be able to ensure that they have the cruising range to get to an enemy country and back. No one is saying outwardly that 'this will make it possible to attack enemy missile bases,' but in terms of the result, it is certain that the ability to attack enemy missile bases is gradually being acquired."[1201] This insight highlighted the increasing dissonance between politicians' statements on preemptive strike capabilities—namely, that Tokyo was merely "studying" the issue—and what Japan's defense establishment was actually developing, similar to the situation in 1996 and 1997 when politicians studied the possible introduction of reconnaissance satellites even as they downplayed the possibility in public. By the summer of 1998, all the satellite studies had been conducted and all Tokyo had to do was approve funding for their construction. And *Yomiuri Weekly*'s sister publication, the *Yomiuri Shimbun*, called on Tokyo in its March 6, 2004 edition to consider increasing its defense budgets and further develop a preemptive strike capability: "To be fully prepared for possible launch of ballistic missiles, the country needs to consider, without taboo, its relationships with neighboring countries, a drastic reform of its defense budget, means of attacking enemy bases, and so forth."[1202]

Perhaps the lengthiest discussion of the issue appeared in the semi-official *East Asian Strategic Review 2004*, published in February 2004 by the National Institute for Defense Studies, the Defense Agency's think tank. It succinctly detailed Japan's security dilemma regarding the ballistic missile and nuclear threat: "Given the unprecedented lethality and destructive power of nuclear weapons, Japan understandably cannot afford to wait until a WMD-armed ballistic missile actually hits the country to determine that such an attack has occurred." The problem lies in recognizing "an imminent and illegitimate act of aggression against Japan." Such a recognition would necessarily be made "on a case-by-case basis," according to the *Review*, and Tokyo would obviously not publicize the exact indicators it would use to assess whether an attack were "imminent" because "if published, such criteria would reveal Japan's hand to its adversaries."

Echoing Kaneda's differentiation between "active defense" measures such as missile defense and "offensive defense," the *East Asian Strategic Review* continued: "The use of force…fulfills a role complementing missile defense. As with other threats, it is desirable to take multiple countermeasures against ballistic missile attacks." And as Japan improves its missile defense network, "[a]n adversary contemplating a ballistic missile attack on Japan is likely to mount an attack that overwhelms Japan's missile defense capability." Thus the *Review* places deterrence—the threat of armed retaliation—on an equal level with passive forms of defense. As for Japan's alliance with the United States, "[a]s long as U.S. forces constantly maintain their capability to attack the missile sites of a country contemplating a missile strike, then this will play a role of complementing the missile defense of Japan." The unstated implication of this last statement, however, hinges on the word "constantly": if U.S. forces were perceived to cease to "constantly" maintain their capability—if U.S. forces were perceived to be bogged down in the Middle East, or were perceived to lack the political will to engage militarily—Japan would want alternative capabilities as a hedge. The question of how much to hedge increasingly weighs heavily on the minds of Japanese strategists.

Ultimately, "the defense posture from which one can launch simultaneously offensive operations against an adversary's missile sites and defense operations of intercepting incoming ballistic missiles will go a long way toward shoring up the defense of Japan against missile attacks," the *East Asian Strategic Review* concluded.[1203] This final statement was perhaps the clearest sign yet that Japan was preparing to shift from a strategy of defensive-defense to a more active security posture that included developing its own basic precision strike capability that could be projected beyond its own shores.

There were of course dissenting voices, especially by the summer of 2006 as North Korea prepared yet another series of short- and medium-range missile tests. Shunji Taoka, a journalist who covers Japanese national security, noted that "even if Japan were to possess strike capabilities, it is basically impossible to destroy ballistic missiles before they are launched."[1204] The head of the opposition Democratic Party of Japan, Ichiro Ozawa, was quite blunt in his opposition, telling Fuji Television's "News 2001" that Japan's possession of a preemptive strike capability "is a completely absurd argument."[1205] And a poll taken after North Korea's missile launches indicated at best mixed support for a preemptive capability among the public: 22% indicated Japan "must possess" such a capability, while almost 30% said that Japan "should consider possessing" such a capability, according to Jiji. However, 53% did not support the actual use of a preemptive strike, and only 26% of those polled supported such use.[1206] While a bare majority supported at least considering a preemptive *capability*, a larger majority opposed its actual *use*. Japan's development of longer-range precision-strike weapons at any rate was moot politically, as the LDP had been unable to secure its partner Komeito's support for such development in the 2005-2009 five-year defense plan. Thus, Nukaga's "National Security Project Team," which was in charge of establishing the Japan's next five-year defense plan, announced that any development of precision weapons would be limited to "ranges under 300 kilometers" with no consideration for "attacking other countries," only as a means to "defend remote islands."[1207]

Yet, by this time, Japan had already begun to move away from mere debates of the constitutionality of a limited preemptive strike to acquiring basic precision strike capabilities and the infrastructure to support such capabilities. This interest in developing basic precision strike capabilities dovetailed with Japan's new emphasis of outer island defense. The precision capabilities would be used to fend off a limited attack or invasion of Japan's remote islands while avoiding as much as possible extensive destruction of the surrounding environment and civilian infrastructure. To paraphrase Ishiba and the *Yomiuri Weekly* above, in order to carry out a land-attack mission on a military base in foreign territory, Japan would need aerial refuelers, several flights of F-15s, F-4s or F-16s and accompanying command and control aircraft to conduct counter-radar operations, and precision bombs or air-launched cruise missiles to engage ground targets effectively. Separately, Japan could introduce land-attack cruise missiles launched from platforms at sea. Japan also would need sensors to monitor for real-time threat indicators and target locations and a means to communicate assessments of potential threats to policymakers in a timely fashion. And as the *Yomiuri Weekly* noted in mid-2003, Japan was indeed developing a capability in each of these vital areas: Japan's ASDF was preparing to introduce aerial refuelers beginning in early 2007; Japan already had a number of reconnaissance satellites and it began building the analytical base to identify missile bases and nuclear facilities—potential targets—in neighboring territories. Japan's ASDF already flies F-15s, F-4s and F-2s (Japan's F-16), although their counter-radar capability is unknown. Japan also flies AWACS E-767s and E-2Cs, which can provide command and control functions during an offensive counter-air/-land strike. As *Yomiuri Weekly* assessed, "it is certain that the ability to attack enemy missile bases is gradually being acquired."[1208] The final pieces to a basic land-attack capability, essentially, are the precision weapons themselves and the training to carry out the mission. Japan started incorporating these on a limited basis in 2004, as the next section will show.

First Introductions: Japan Acquires JDAMs

Japan's first well-publicized acquisition of precision weapons technology came in 2004, when Tokyo budgeted funds to acquire the U.S.-developed Joint Direct Attack Munition (JDAM). JDAM, according to Boeing—the company that manufactures them—is "a low-cost guidance kit that converts existing unguided free-fall bombs into accurately guided 'smart' weapons" and "consists of a new tail section that contains an Inertial Navigation System/ Global Positioning System."[1209] This low-cost kit gives an otherwise "dumb" gravity bomb the maneuverability necessary to guide it to a target of choice. The DA inserted ¥1.2 billion into its JFY2004 budget request for the JDAM guidance kits that would fit the ASDF's Mk-82 225-kg bombs, and it requested additional funding to upgrade five F-2s so they could carry the JDAM-fitted Mk-82 bombs. Eventually, all F-2s would be equipped to carry JDAM-fitted Mk-82s. The intended target of a possible precision bombing run was an invading or guerrilla force in Japan, as

Yomiuri Shimbun reported: "The SDF apparently plans to carry out counterattacks using JDAMs in contingency situations, such as if foreign guerrillas or special task forces invade Japanese territory and secure positions outside the range of arms such as artillery used by Ground Self-Defense Force troops."[1210] And with the introduction of aerial refuelers, the Air Self Defense Force could conduct precision strikes of ground targets at much longer ranges.

As Japan prepared to introduce the first of four aerial refuelers starting in early 2007, Japanese F-15 and F-4 pilots in 2003 began to train with U.S. Air Force counterparts in aerial refueling techniques in preparation for the major bilateral air exercise "Cope Thunder" scheduled to take place in early June that year. The first aerial refueling training session took place on April 21 and again on May 14.[1211] Following the initial training in Japan, six Japanese F-15DJs flew the 5,400-kilometer distance non-stop between Chitose Airbase in Hokkaido to Elmendorf Airbase in Alaska, refueling in the air from a U.S. KC-135. This was the first ever non-stop flight by Japanese fighters to a foreign land. A Japanese AWACS and three C-130s also flew to Elmendorf to participate in "Cope Thunder," where Japan's F-15s flew eight sorties a day as the AWACS conducted electronic warfare missions and ASDF airmen practiced surface-to-air missile firings on six SAM kits. Following the training, a KC-135 refueled the Japanese jet fighters on the return flight at the end of June as well.[1212] Later that year, in November 2003, 10 ASDF F-4EJs from Naha, Okinawa participated in "Cope Thunder Guam" at Andersen AFB in Guam where the F-4s practiced flying under electronic warfare conditions, which was impossible to practice in Japan given the restrictive environment there.[1213] The following year, "Cope Thunder" joint training took place from June 6-18 in skies near Okinawa and again included aerial refueling exercises, this time with six Japanese F-15s, ten F-4s, and an AWACS. Indeed, joint U.S.-Japan aerial refueling training continued on multiple occasions in each year thereafter, with four such training sessions taking place in the first half of 2006 as Japan's first aerial refueler neared completion.[1214]

Yet Japanese ASDF bombing practice around this time was very limited in both Japan and in joint exercises abroad. Japan's population density and local aversion to live-fire exercises in general hindered ASDF live-fire exercises at multiple locations in Japan. Illustrating the dangers of live-fire training near expanding urban areas, a June 2001 training flight misfire over a major firing range in Hokkaido caused the ASDF to halt training at one of its main air-to-ground firing ranges for over two years. On June 25 that year, four Phantom F-4EJ-Kai fighter jets from the 83rd Air Wing had just fired four rocket rounds and four practice rounds over the Shimamatsu Air-to-Ground Firing Range, located south of Hokkaido's capital, Sapporo. They began to ascend to an altitude of 2,250 meters to prepare for cannon live-fire target practice over the range, but as one of the F-4s repositioned for a firing run, it suddenly fired 188 rounds from its 20-mm cannon even as the crew reported that the trigger's safety was still engaged. At least 13 rounds hit vehicles parked outside the Kitahiroshima Rehabilitation Center on the outskirts of the training range, and one more round hit a golf course a kilometer away. Luckily no one was injured. An Air Staff Office investigation committee said later that they thought the misfire was due to a buildup of electricity in the F-4's firearms control system, perhaps sending an electrical signal that caused the cannon to fire.[1215] *Yomiuri Shimbun* noted that the population in areas immediately adjacent to the range had increased since the firing range became operational in 1959. In fact, low-flying approaches to the firing range were halted in the 1970s as the population had begun to build up noticeably around the training area.[1216] After the June 2001 misfire, ASDF target practice at Shimamatsu was halted while the facility relocated targets further away from urban areas, and training flights were then resumed in September 2003 using a new flight path.[1217]

The ASDF at this time operated one other live-fire facility near Misawa in Aomori Prefecture, where it conducted live-fire training about 100 days a year. The ASDF in the early 1980s returned a third live-fire training area in Fukuoka Prefecture to local authorities. It has requested the use of other unpopulated islands in Japan and over the GSDF's Yausubetsu Training Range—Japan's largest ground training facility, also located in Hokkaido—but the requests have been turned down following local protests.[1218] While there have not been any reports of ASDF training specifically involving JDAM-fitted bombs at Japanese ranges, such training would presumably take place at the facilities listed above, at the firing range on Sekibisho island in Okinawa Prefecture used by U.S. forces. Training could alternatively take place in Australia, which offered to host F-15 and F-2 air-to-ground training from 2001.[1219]

Additionally, ASDF pilots began to train at a U.S. target range in Guam in 2005. In June 2005 and again in June 2006, F-4EJs practiced dropping 500-pound bombs over the Farallon de Medinilla Target Range during "Cope Thunder Guam." In 2005, the F-4s practiced unfettered solo bombing runs, but in 2006 the bombing runs were conducted along side U.S. F-15s that were divided into coalition and enemy units. The ASDF F-4s conducted their bombing runs as their F-15 counterparts conducted aerial intercept and engagement operations.[1220]

Japanese training remained rather limited in the first few years after the introduction of JDAMs in 2004, but at the same time Tokyo continued to explore other precision-guided technologies quietly behind the scenes.

Beyond JDAMs: Indigenous Extended Range Missiles and Munitions

While Japan first acquired a precision-guided technology (the JDAM) in 2004, Japan had actually been researching precision technologies for use in weapons systems since at least the 1990s and therefore had already developed the technological base to develop its own precision weapons indigenously. Indeed, the Defense Agency developed a kit resembling the Joint Direct Attack Munition in the 1990s called the Type-91 "*yudo bakudan GCS-1,*" which stands for "guided bomb Guidance Control Set-1." GCS-1 fin stabilizers and an infrared guidance system can be attached to a Mk82 or a JM117 gravity bomb much like the JDAM, and the sets are sometimes on display at airshows and a set is on permanent display at the Technical Research and Development Institute's 3rd Research Institute museum in Tachikawa.[1221] While the stated targets of the GCS-1 are "enemy warships" approaching Japan by sea, it goes without saying that what can be used against ships at sea can be targeted against buildings and other objects on land. In addition, Japan in 2004 allocated some ¥179 million in funding for basic research on the follow-on XGCS-2, which resembles the AGM-154 Joint Stand-Off Weapon (JSOW), according to Defense Agency budget documents (at less than $2 million for the project that year, however, the funding represented a mere fraction of the development costs for U.S. development of the AGM-154A, which totaled some $417 million![1222]). The XGCS-2 like the U.S. AGM-154 Joint Stand-Off Weapon will be launched at much greater distances than the GCS-1 or JDAM—from 15 nautical miles from its target at a low altitude or from 40 nautical miles from the target at high altitudes—and pictures of an F-4 flying test XGCS-2s have also appeared on the internet and in Japanese special-interest magazines such as *Air Wings.*[1223]

In addition to the XGCS-2, Japan began development of a longer-range air-launched cruise missile in the early 2000s, the air-to-ship XASM-3. The XASM-3, under development by TRDI, uses an integral rocket ramjet for propulsion and will have a composite seeker (infrared imaging and radar) guidance system and was scheduled to be fielded in the early 2010s, according to the project outline. To illustrate the desired capabilities, the DA compared the XASM-3 to Russia's Kh-31A and Kh-41 missile systems and France's super-sonic ANF anti-ship missiles.[1224] (The Kh-31A is a short-range air-launched cruise missile and the Kh-41 "Moskit" is a supersonic anti-ship missile, designated the SS-N-22 "Sunburn" by NATO.) The XASM-3 will be able to engage a target along multiple tracks, according to the project outline, including a direct sea-skim track, a sea-skim pop-up track, and a high-altitude approach-and-dive track. The missile is thus highly maneuverable, and as noted above, such maneuverability is conceivably applicable to targets on land as well. ASDF aircraft were sometimes spotted conducting tests of the XASM-3 from a test range in Gifu from 2006, as on August 10, 2006 when an F-2A belonging to the Flight Development Test Group flew with new test ASM dummies under each wing that were equipped with supersonic ramjets. *Koku Fan*, an aircraft enthusiast magazine, noted that the two dummy missiles were "larger than the conventional ASM-1/-2," and given the checkered paint on the dummy missiles, they were test variants.[1225] According to Junichi Ishikawa, an expert on Japanese aerospace issues, one intended use for the missile is suppression of enemy air defense (SEAD), a key capability during any preemptive strike. If Japan were to embark on the development a land-attack capability, according to Ishikawa, "ASM-2 and 3 anti-surface attack models would be most expeditious."[1226] Although they are designated anti-ship missiles, nothing precludes them from being adapted for use against ground targets as well.

Tokyo remains interested in an over-the-horizon cruise missile capability as well. The Defense Agency's study of cruise missiles almost led to official incorporation of the technology into the 2004 National Defense Program Guideline. A draft summary was released on July 24, 2004, perhaps as a trial balloon to gauge public reaction. While the outline gave few specifics, the MSDF section of the outline referenced the possibility of developing a capability to strike surface targets using precision-guided weapons.[1227] Following the release of the summary, *Asahi Shimbun* reported in late July 2004 that a DA council headed by Ishiba said Japan should "consider" acquiring such weapons systems as the Harpoon 2, the Tomahawk cruise missile, and light aircraft carriers (something he had been advocating for over a year by that point).[1228] But Takemasa Moriya, the administrative deputy director general of the DA, talked down such reports at a press conference on July 27, saying: "I think there's no need for us to possess equipment intended to strike enemy bases" and "there is no truth to reports that we are studying such a matter." And an unnamed Japanese defense official also asserted that a large outlay of funds would be required to build an infrastructure that would allow a strike against a target in another country.[1229]

But by this point, Tokyo had undeniably begun to review the various preemptive strike options, and indeed Japan was already in the process of developing basic operational capabilities in each of the areas of infrastructure cited by the unnamed official as necessary for preemptive strikes: it had already launched its first reconnaissance satellites, it had already budgeted for JDAMs and aerial refuelers, it already operated AWACs and other support aircraft, and it was researching other precision technologies. While these technologies themselves were not sufficient to conduct a robust preemptive strike (for example, against hardened targets), they pointed to a new mentality among defense policymakers that supported the gradual build-out of more meaningful capabilities. Moreover, all signs also pointed to Japan eventually incorporating cruise missile systems into its defense capabilities precisely due to officials' concern about the "enemy's air defense capability": most importantly for Japan, long-range cruise missiles are unmanned, thus if they were shot down or otherwise failed in-flight, Japanese aircrews would not be in danger. Long-range cruise missiles do not require support aircraft to provide electronic counter-measures, aerial support, or refueling necessary for a long-range strike mission. And cruise missiles are relatively cheap compared to the price of a jet fighter or bomber and its aircrew. And although there was much discussion of purchasing Tomahawk cruise missile system, Japan was also researching indigenous cruise missile technologies as well.

XSSM-2: Japan's Over-the-Horizon Cruise Missile

Japan developed an indigenous surface-to-ship cruise missile system in the late 1980s, designated the SSM-88, and a ship-based cruise missile system designated the SSM-90. (They are also sometimes referred to as the SSM-1 and SSM-1b). These missiles, with a reported range of 150 kilometers, are deployed with GSDF artillery units as defense against a maritime invading force, and on MSDF combatants such as on the *Hayabusa*-class missile boats as anti-ship missiles. And the systems were reportedly quite advanced even employing 1980s technology. Retired Lt. General Naruhiko Ueda, the former head of the Ground Staff Office's R&D division who worked on Japan's missile systems, wrote of the SSM-1 in 1996: "[E]ven when launched behind a mountain, it can follow a programmed course, skim the ocean's surface, approach a target at a low altitude, and strike" its target, indicating an in-flight guidance capability.[1230] Thus, by the mid-1990s Japan had a working guided cruise missile capability.

TRDI began development in the late 1990s of an upgraded version of the SSM-88, designated the SSM-88-Kai, and sometimes referred to as the XSSM-2 (as in the January 2001 edition of *Jane's Missiles and Rockets*).[1231] The new missile incorporates "terrain-contour tracking flight capabilities," according to defense journalist Naoya Tamura. Tamura also noted that it was "conceivable" researchers would extend the range of the missile system.[1232] As water does not have any set terrain, a guided missile with "terrain-contour tracking" technology would obviously be used against land-based targets. Moreover, contour-tracking technology coupled with detailed three-dimensional imaging from Japanese satellites and extremely precise positioning coordinates from GPS satellites and Japan's regional Quasi-Zenith Satellite System (QZSS)—discussed below—would theoretically give Japan an extremely capable, if regional, precision strike capability.

Extended Range and "Smart" Munitions

Japan's active interest in using GPS for domestic defense purposes dates to the mid-1990s. Lt. General Ueda, the retired GSDF lieutenant general and former assistant director general for ground equipment development at the Technical Research and Development Institute quoted above, wrote in the defense magazine *Securitarian* in October 1996: "The GSDF is adopting a variety of high-tech equipment, mainly produced domestically, that can support the performance of effective defensive combat and overcome the challenges posed by a Japanese topography more complicated than that in other countries." Moreover, "studies are being made to improve the accuracy of mortar shells, which are light and easily portable, by incorporating GPS in them to provide guidance." Inline with growing discussion of the "revolution in military affairs" at that time, Ueda called GPS the "key to information warfare."[1233]

One of the systems to which Ueda referred became public in 2001. According to Defense Agency project documents made public that year, the DA was funding research on a smart munitions project called the "*chinōka dan*" or "smart round." The DA compared the *chinōka dan* to the U.S. 155-mm H-SADARM "Sense and Destroy Armor" and Germany's SMArt 155 "Sensor-fuzed Munitions for Artillery 155mm."[1234] The SADARM is fired and, according to the U.S. Army description, "when a target is identified within the sensor scan area, an Explosively Formed Penetrator (EFP) is fired into the target."[1235] Unlike the U.S. and German versions, the Japanese project will incorporate rocket-assisted projectile technology to extend its range, according the DA's project outline.[1236] The munition was not scheduled to be completed until the 2010s, however.[1237]

The Japan Association of Defense Industry's "Gun and Ammunition Technology" subcommittee highlighted this and other possible future smart munitions technologies in a variety of proposals in the early 2000s. Extensive conceptual diagrams showed possible future munitions such as a reconnaissance round, an advanced armor-piercing round, and a cargo munition, while other schematics showed UAVs and individual soldiers on the ground "painting" targets with laser target designators to provide final guidance to the target. Other schematics showed the munitions receiving coordinates from GPS satellites in a networked environment.[1238] As official DA documents indicated, Japan was developing at least some of these technologies.

Moreover, while the *chinōka dan* is being developed to be fired from howitzers on land, the technology once perfected can be applied to munitions fired from sea-based platforms as well. New Japanese destroyers such as the 19DD are being equipped with Mk 45 Mod 4 5-inch guns, which are capable of firing extended-range guided munitions. The defense journalist Isaku Okabe, writing in the April 2004 *Sekai no Kansen*, noted that while the Aegis destroyer *Kongo*'s 127-mm 54-caliber gun can fire a projectile to a distance of 24 kilometers, a Mk 45 Mod 4 firing an ERGM would increase that range almost five-fold to 117 kilometers. While Okabe suggested that "it is probably safe to say that land attack capabilities have hardly been envisioned by the MSDF at all," other *Sekai no Kansen* contributors (including retired flag officers) suggested otherwise.[1239] It is of course safe to conclude that Japan's Association of Defense Industry *has* envisioned land attack capabilities, and such capabilities are hardly foreign to other retired MSDF officers. According to retired Vice Admiral Makoto Yamazaki writing in the same periodical, "island operations" will require some sort of land attack capability to support landing forces: "The insertion of various land, sea, and air forces for...amphibious operations and ground combat" will be supported by "mine countermeasures and ground strikes from the sea and air." As "ground units" are transported "by sea, either for reinforcement purposes or to retake [a position]," according to Yamazaki, it is therefore "necessary to conduct ground strikes by aircraft and ships to neutralize enemy ground forces on the island before amphibious forces land."[1240] By firing highly accurate "smart" munitions, the number of volleys fired could be greatly reduced while Japanese maritime units could remain at a safer distance from shore, and the Japanese fleet would not have to be resupplied as often. As the MSDF expands its capabilities to support "island operations"—a central mission of the SDF in the 21st Century—it is quite conceivable that the MSDF will explore extended range land-attack capabilities as well as cruise missile capabilities to support amphibious landing and other operations.

QZSS: Japan's 'Complement' to GPS

The U.S. Global Positioning System (GPS) plays a critical role in precision strike technologies. Early precision-guidance technologies developed from the late 1950s and 1960s required a local human presence to guide the ordnance in some way, such as visually by joystick or by "painting" or pointing a laser at a target. Visual guidance and laser target designators were limited to fair weather, however, and heavy fog, rain, or smoke hindered accuracy. The GPS, funded and developed by the U.S. Department of Defense starting in 1973 with the goal of enabling a user anywhere in the world know his or her location to within tens of meters, helped to solve the visibility issue when targeting fixed positions by providing location coordinates and guidance based on GPS signals. The first Block I GPS developmental satellite was launched in February 1978, while the operational Block II GPS satellites were launched beginning in February 1989. Over a dozen satellites were in orbit for use during Operation Desert Storm two years later. The GPS constalation of 24 satellites was complete and operational in 1993, and the US Air Force declared the system fully operational on July 17, 1995.[1241]

The GPS satellites orbit 20,200 kilometers above the earth and broadcast a constant radio signal. Four GPS satellites are located in each of six orbital tracks and are equally spaced approximately 60 degrees apart in 12-hour intervals. A user must be able to receive signals from four GPS satellites for greatest accuracy, with the signals indicating the user's locations on the X, Y, and Z axes, and accurate time. With this information, a user can know position, velocity, and time. This information is crucial for precision guidance: location of a target could be programmed before ordnance is released or missile fired, which would then receive the GPS signals during flight and, coupled with an Inertial Navigation

System, it could travel to the target without human intervention. GPS can also be used in conjunction with other guidance systems, such as a laser target designator: the guided weapon could be launched from at a distance from the target, guide itself to the area of the target, and then locate the laser target designator pointed at a target to home in on its exact location. While this method still requires some human interaction, the aircrew's time over target is greatly reduced or eliminated.

To avoid possible enemy use of GPS signals in an attack against the United States, the original GPS constellation had "Selective Availability," (SA) a deliberate degradation of signal that reduced the accuracy of the reading available to non-U.S. military users. Commercial users around the globe could access the Standard Positioning Service (SPS) free of charge or regulation, although the accuracy was intentionally degraded from a normal 30-meter accuracy to a 100-meter accuracy. The U.S. military and other U.S. Federal Government and allied users could access the Precise Positioning System (PPS) with access to cryptographic equipment and keys. The PPS was accurate to within tens of meters.[1242] On March 28, 1996, as the United States was preparing to upgrade the GPS satellite constellation, President Clinton issued Presidential Decision Directive NSTC-6 announcing the U.S. government's intention to discontinue use of Selective Availability within the next ten years.[1243] In 2000, following a yearly review of possible security issues related to the discontinuance of SA, the United States government stopped employing Selective Availability to reduce accuracy and gave unhindered access to the more accurate signal.

Japanese companies began introducing commercial applications using GPS such as car navigation systems in 1991, and by 2000, 1.5 million car navigation sets were sold in Japan alone, representing two-thirds of global sales of 2.35 million sets.[1244] Thus by the mid-1990s, Japan had a vested interest in maintaining access to free, unhindered, and accurate GPS signals. In line with President Clinton's 1996 PDD, the U.S. Department of State initiated bilateral talks with Japan, a major user of GPS signals, in August 1996 as part of an international effort to discuss harmonization of GPS standards and prevention of misuse. Talks led to a September 1998 joint statement between Prime Minister Keizo Obuchi and President Clinton pledging to work together on GPS standards, technology, and infrastructure. (The summit took place less than one month after North Korea launched the Taepodong missile.) In the joint statement, the United States declared that it "intends to continue to provide the GPS standard positioning service for peaceful civil, commercial, and scientific use on a continuous, worldwide basis, free of direct user fees." Japan, in turn, "intends to work closely with the United States to promote broad and effective use of the GPS standard positioning service," while both parties "are convinced of the need to prevent the misuse of GPS and its augmentation systems without unduly disrupting or degrading civilian uses."[1245]

At the same time, Japan was beginning its own research into positioning technologies in a variety of fields. Following the first U.S.-Japan bilateral discussions on GPS in August 1996 and as the Europeans began to conceptualize its own GPS-type constellation called Galileo, the Japanese government began a significant review of GPS technologies and uses. In support of this review, the Defense Research Center, a private think-tank partially funded by the Defense Agency, dispatched a six-person "military technology inspection team" (as described by the Japanese industry newspaper *Nikkan Kogyo Shimbun*) to the United States in late 1996 to examine GPS technologies and policy. The research mission was led by the aforementioned retired Lt. General Ueda, lead technologist for TRDI who called GPS "key to information warfare."

Ueda had become head of the Defense Research Center (DRC) following his retirement and led research missions several times a year to the United States and elsewhere to examine how defense technologies were being incorporated in foreign militaries, including this mission to examine defense uses of GPS. He was accompanied by a number of retired general officers who were then advising major Japanese defense corporations. The group met with civilian and uniformed officials at North American Space and Air Defense Command and other bases in Colorado, the Departments of Defense, Commerce, Transportation, the National Mapping Office, and the Defense Information Systems Agency in Washington and the GPS main control station.[1246] Ueda's colleague Akiji Yoshida, a retired major general in the Ground Self Defense Force and director of the Radar Systems Technology Department for Toshiba Corporation, wrote following the research mission: "[W]e had the distinct impression that there will be spectacular improvements in GPS in the near future" and "GPS will play an indispensable role during the age of information warfare."[1247] The GPS represented a perfect dual-use technology: commercialized GPS technologies could thrive even as defense technologists researched military applications for the system. Japan quickly embraced the system and all its possibilities.

The DRC research group's report to the Japanese government and other government-sponsored investigations had notable impact. In March 1997, three months after the group returned to Japan, the Space Activities Commission's Satellite Positioning Technology Working Group recommended to Prime Minister Hashimoto the construction of an indigenously developed satellite-based navigation system, called the Quasi-Zenith Satellite System (QZSS).[1248] While initially not funding the program in full, in August 1999—one year after North Korea's Taepodong missile launch and Obuchi's agreement with Clinton on the unhindered provision of GPS signals—the Japanese government budgeted funds for research on three essential technologies for a highly accurate regional positioning system: atomic clocks installed on satellites, satellite group time control, and technologies for determining satellite orbits. The Communications Research Laboratory (CRL) in the Ministry of Posts and Telecommunications conducted the initial research beginning in 2000.[1249]

As the CRL research proved successful enough to proceed to the next stage, members of the Liberal Democratic Party (LDP) in the summer of 2002 formed a "League of Diet Members Promoting a Next Generation Satellite System" to promote a Japanese version of a regional GPS. The League was headed by LDP parliamentarian Fukushiro Nukaga, who as former director general of the Defense Agency maintained a keen interest in national defense issues. (Nukaga also happened to be the lower house representative of Ibaraki Prefecture's Kashima city, the host city of the Communications Research Laboratory, where scientists were actively developing the "Quazi-Zenith Satellite System.") In contrast to Europe's fully independent Galileo satellite constellation, the QZSS as envisioned would supplement the U.S. GPS with only three satellites orbiting over Asia. Yet, the League's letter of invitation to its inaugural meeting on July 4 specifically highlighted the country's lack of an independent positioning system: "Japan's positioning data is wholly reliant on the U.S. GPS...In order to enhance information safety and security, it is necessary to create a next-generation satellite system that can function as a backup to the U.S. system." While "backup" can mean "alternate" in case of degradation or failure, it also can mean "substitute." There was no reason why, once the technologies were verified, the QZSS could not become the basis for a fully independent regional positioning system if Tokyo made the decision to build additional satellites. Thirty-two members of the Diet attended the July 4 meeting, where the group requested ¥8 billion for the JFY2003 budget to launch the system.[1250] The final amount approved for the QZSS dropped to ¥5.8 billion in March 2003, immediately before the start of Japan's 2003 fiscal year on April 1.[1251] But development of the system was going forward.

Under the plan, three QZSS satellites would be launched and operational by the early 2010s and would orbit in a figure-eight pattern at an altitude of 36,000 km from northern Japan to Southern Australia. The figure-eight orbit would intersect in space over southern of Japan. Each satellite would be in orbit above Japan during any given eight-hour period: as the satellite over Japan proceeds south toward the equator and then to a position above Australia, another moves into position above Japan to continue the provision of accurate signals over Japan, while the third satellite over Australia begins its rotation back to the equator. With one satellite almost directly over Japan during any given time, consumers in mountainous regions or near tall buildings in Japanese cities would have direct access to the signals. The entire system as planned would be accurate to 15 centimeters. It would also provide high-speed communications and broadcast services to complement its extremely accurate positioning capabilities. The Ministry of Science and Technology estimated that a total of seven satellites would be necessary to completely replace Japanese dependence on the U.S. system.[1252] Japan planned to build only three satellites due as much to the price of the system as to deference to its U.S. ally. The system was costly, according to 2003 estimates: one satellite would cost an estimated ¥50 billion, while the basic constellation of three satellites and ground-based equipment was estimated to total ¥210 billion.[1253]

As development plans were finalized, the Japanese Government announced that it would share the costs of the QZSS program with a consortium of Japanese companies that planned to develop an array of commercial uses for the QZSS. In July 2002, obviously in coordination with Nukaga's League of Diet Members Promoting a Next-Generation Satellite System (the league had met days earlier), the Japan Federation of Economic Organizations established a study group for the commercial potential of a QZSS. In August 2002, the Ministry of Economy, Trade, and Industry (METI) Industrial Science and Technology Policy Division announced a project called "Focus 21," a three-year effort that would provide a total of ¥37 billion for projects in the fields of biotechnology, information technology, nanotechnology, and the environment. Funding for a quasi-zenith satellite system was specifically mentioned in the plan.[1254] In November 2002, a consortium of 42 companies headed by Mitsubishi Electric—developer of Japan's intelligence-gathering satellites—Hitachi Ltd, and Toyota Motor Corporation established the Advanced Space Business Corporation to run a positioning and broadcast business based on services provided by the QZSS.[1255] The public-private partnership was expected to cost a total of ¥210 billion—¥160 billion for satellite development and launch and another ¥50 billion for systems operations—with METI and the Ministry of Public Management, Posts and Telecommunications providing ¥100 billion for the project and private industry providing the remaining ¥110 billion.[1256]

The commercial applications of the QZSS are numerous: fishermen and boating enthusiasts can use the QZSS for both precise navigation and communications; emergency workers can use the system to pinpoint the exact location of a cell-phone user who is calling for help, and navigate to and from the scene of an accident based on concise traffic information; and gas and electric utilities can know the exact location of their meters and make remote readings using the systems communications capabilities.[1257] Once successfully miniaturized, a QZSS receiver could be embedded in golf balls and golf clubs so that golf enthusiasts could map out their game or those of their favorite pros; the same could be done for any sport, for example. The commercial applications of this multifunctional satellite system are seemingly endless, and precision location services coupled with broadcast capabilities would create a vast market according to some estimates: the Japanese Federation of Economic Organizations at the start of the program in 2002 anticipated that the QZSS would become a ¥1.1 trillion market in communication and broadcast devices.[1258]

Quite obviously, an extremely accurate positioning system has military uses as well. Just as the U.S. military relies on the GPS for guidance information, Japan's SDF could also use the QZSS for its precision-guided weapons, as Akira Sasao, a retired ASDF colonel and consultant to Furuno Electric Company, emphasized in the February 2004 *Gekkan JADI.* The QZSS, according to Sasao, will "increase the ability to inflict casualties against hard targets" through "improved accuracy." "[W]eapons that are guided by GPS and a quasi-zenith satellite will have better survival characteristics because they have the capability to be fired at a distance without being aimed at any particular target," Sasao explained. New weapons could use several guidance systems in what Sasao called "coordinated attack weapons": "[C]oordinated attack weapons (weapons that use GPS and quasi-zenith satellites) that are laser- or TV-guided can be used in poor, very cloudy weather conditions" with the addition of QZSS-guidance capabilities. The combination of the QZSS's high-capacity communications service, its high-quality broadcast service, and its high-precision positioning capability give the system a "synergistic" effect, Sasao wrote, and he noted that the QZSS can be used in a number of areas "near Japan" such as the Koreas, Philippines, Indonesia, Papua New Guinea, and Australia.[1259]

Indeed, the QZSS's figure-eight pattern places a satellite almost directly above the Korean Peninsula and runs parallel to the coast of China during any given eight-hour period, giving unparalleled accuracy over all of the eastern Pacific rim. In fact, monitoring stations are located as far west as Hawaii, as far south as Guam (in the northern hemisphere) and Canberra, and as far west as Bangkok and Bangalore, India.[1260]

Although the deployment schedule has slipped, the first QZSS satellite (the "Michibiki") was launched in 2010, and the QZSS will be fully operational sometime in the late 2010s.

Capability vs Capacity: Can Japan Make Enough Missiles and Munitions?

As former Defense Agency Director-General Ishiba noted in 2003, attacking a missile base on foreign territory is not merely a matter of flying an aircraft to the area and dropping a few precision-guided bombs onto a target. Rather, the attacking force must destroy or render harmless multiple targets such as radar and air-defense sites and opposing air assets before reaching the main target, and in turn be prepared for any counter-attacks. Moreover, as history has demonstrated, modern conflicts often continue much longer than originally envisioned. Thus the importance of the military-industrial complex and its ability to provide sufficient supplies to ongoing operations. While Japan can surely develop increasingly sophisticated weaponry, another question must be addressed: can Japan manufacture or acquire enough precision weapons and missiles if aggressions do break out? While Japan has not been in a major conflict since WWII, there is always the chance, if slim, that Japan could be involved in an altercation requiring significant stores and manufacturing capacity of ammunition and guided weapons.

However, several of Japan's weapons manufacturers have experienced major accidents since the mid-1990s that have slowed or halted production, bringing into question even Japan's limited peacetime manufacturing capacity.

In 1996, Chugoku Chemical Co. suffered two major explosives accidents at its Etajima facility. The first explosion took place in the morning of April 16, killing three people and injuring several others. Following the explosion, which affected the HMX production line[4], the Chugoku Bureau of the Ministry of International Trade and Industry reviewed safety procedures with the plant's safety officers and management to avoid further accidents.

The safety reviews apparently had little impact at the plant, since another major accident occurred in November the same year. The November accident occurred in a trinitrotoluene (TNT) processing room where sulfuric acid was added to mononitrotoluene to produce liquid trinitrotoluene. The TNT was piped to a holding tank where it would cool and crystallize. The tank at the time held over 1,300 liters of TNT. On the day of the accident, according to a year-long investigation, as the processing work was taking place repair work to a pipe that happened to be filled with carbonic acid was also taking place. The carbonic acid leaked and mixed with the TNT in the room creating a chemical reaction that ultimately caused a fire to break out in the room and led to large explosions at the facility. Luckily, before the explosions, one of the workers spotted black smoke rising from near the crystallizing tank and instructed workers in the area to get out, saving many lives. He did not, however, warn plant operators in time to halt operations.[1261] Although the facility's managers had instigated a series of safety measures

[4] HMX or "High Melting Explosive" is a high-energy solid explosive and is used as a component of plastic-bonded explosives, as an ingredient for rocket propellant, as a high-explosive burster charge, and, in the United States, to implode fissionable material in nuclear devices.

following the April accident in which three people died, an additional seven workers were seriously injured as a result of the Novmber explosion. The resulting damage forced the facility to halt operations for several years until a new one could be built. But Chugoku Chemical was Japan's only indigenous producer of TNT, and the plant's shutdown halted all domestic production of the product. Despite declaring shortly after the accident that it had several years' supply, the Defense Agency began to import TNT from South Korea in February 1997 to continue manufacturing various munitions, and it continued to import the product for several years until a newly renovated facility was opened several years after the accident.[1262]

Chugoku Chemical has been a major manufacturer of explosives since shortly after WWII. It began operations in 1947 to reprocess former Imperial Army and Navy munitions, and it opened the Etajima facility in 1950 at a former Imperial Navy facility in Hiroshima Prefecture. In 1953, the Etajima facility began to supply the U.S. military with munitions, greatly expanding the company's operations. By the 1990s, the Etajima facility was Japan's only manufacturer of TNT, making on average 690 tons of the substance each year, eighty percent of which went to defense purposes.[1263] The facility supplied TNT as booster and burster charge material for bombs, torpedoes, mines, and other explosives such as HMX for major Japanese munitions and rocket manufacturers such as Daikin, Komatsu, and Japan Steel Works—JSW, incidentally, is Japan's only manufacturer of major gun and howitzer turrets. Chugoku Chemical processes the TNT and fills the various cartridges at its Etajima facility, and then sends them on for final processing at the main contracting companies before they are delivered to the SDF. The plant also helped to manufacture anti-personnel land mines until Japan signed the international treaty banning anti-personnel land mines in 1997.[1264]

Highlighting the importance of the Etajima facility, Japan Steel Works' Hiroshima Machinery plant, Japan's only domestic manufacturer of munitions larger than 40mm, is located just up the road from the Etajima facility, and the Etajima facility itself maintains a tunnel-like firing range to test some of the munitions on-site before they are transferred to JSW and elsewhere.[1265] In the words of a special commission established by the Japan Association of Defense Industry to look into the explosion, the facility's shutdown had a "substantial impact on the Defense Agency's procurement of ammunition and guided missiles."[1266] (Kidney stone patients were also affected. The plant supplied tiny amounts of gunpowder for pellets used in small plastic devices called "AG Cartridges" to break up kidney and ureter stones. It supplied enough for 48,000 pellets, but the Etajima accident cut off those supplies for a time thus affecting kidney stone procedures in several hospitals in Tokyo and Miyazaki Prefectures following the plant's shutdown.[1267])

Immediately following the accident, the Japan Association of Defense Industry on November 29, 1996 established the Chugoku Etajima Accident Liaison Council in its Munitions and Explosives Branch, which established contingency plans, surveyed other ammunition plants for safety, and inquired into accident insurance.[1268] Japan's METI also held hearings and sponsored a panel of experts to review the accidents. While the Etajima facility was partially opened by July 1997, the company was finally granted permission to build a new facility in May 2001, based on a Swedish design. The new plant would operate 24 hours a day for 100 days a year, but would manufacture smaller quantities of TNT to avoid too much explosive material on-site at any given time.[1269] The new facility was completed in June 2002, and during its 100 days of operation the facility could produce 600 tons of TNT supplying all of Japan's needs, 80% of which would be used to supply the

Ministry of Defense needs. Almost six years had elapsed since production of TNT was halted at the facility, and in that time Japan had imported over 3,200 tons of TNT from South Korea.[1270]

Despite both government and industry scrutiny of plant safety, another major accident occurred four years later at the Taketoyo Plant in Aichi Prefecture, run by Nippon Oil and Fats. On August 1, 2000, an explosion occurred at a temporary storage facility containing 7.7 tons of smokeless gunpowder. While the explosion occurred at night when the plant was closed, 161 houses and other buildings were damaged and 63 people were injured. It was the eighth accident at the factory, according to NHK TV's account the following day.[1271] The explosion was strong enough to damage on-site processing facilities that disrupted M-5 solid rocket fuel production, another major product of the plant. Immediately following the accident JADI again established an "accident working subcommittee" to review safety procedures at the Taketoyo plan. In addition to separate investigations by the Defense Agency and Ministry of Economy, Trade, and Industry, members of JADI's Guided Weapons Branch also looked into ways to get operations at the plant up and running again.[1272]

The Taketoyo plant, like the Etajima facility, had a long history of manufacturing explosive materials. It was originally founded in 1919 and manufactured explosives for the Imperial Navy. Following the war, the plant produced dynamite and other explosives for industrial and defense uses as well as rocket propellant. Of Nippon Fats' eight manufacturing plants, Taketoyo is the only to produce explosives-related materials, and it is the only plant in Japan that manufactures solid rocket propellant, which includes propellant used in guided missiles and the M-5 rocket.[1273] With the damage to the M-5 solid rocket fuel production, the accident thus disrupted Japan's guided missile production capacity for a time as well.

Issues of safety procedures aside, these accidents highlight Japan's limited domestic ordnance and missile manufacturing capacity. Japan's already limited capacity to manufacture key explosive and solid rocket materials are concentrated in just a few facilities in the heart of Japan. The manufacture of these key ingredients was disrupted for months—and in one case years—following accidents at the sites, which forced the government to turn to sources outside of Japan for their supply. Given these incidents, and should Japan develop indigenous and robust precision-strike capabilities, Japan's military industrial complex in its present state is not in a position to support a sustained supply of the munitions and missiles necessary should Japan become involved in a prolonged military engagement. Given this state, a military commander will always have in the back of his or her mind: if our forces run out of ammunition and missiles, what could we do next?

Japan's Final Option?

A number of politicians and commentators have from time to time highlighted Japan's latent nuclear capability. In post-Cold War Japan, the first such instance came in the summer of 1994, when debate raged in the Diet concerning a proposal in the International Court of Justice to outlaw nuclear weapons and the nuclear crisis on the Korean peninsula. Prime Minister Tsutomu Hata told reporters on June 17, 1994: "[I]t is certainly the case that Japan has the capability to possess nuclear weapons but has not made them." Hata was attempting to point out that many nations including Japan choose not to develop nuclear weapons. Because Prime Minister Hata himself made the statement, however—prime ministers had until then avoided public discussion of Japan's latent nuclear weapons potential—*Asahi* quoted an unnamed

Defense Agency official calling the prime ministerial statement "unprecedented."[1274] Chief Cabinet Secretary Kumagai, however, immediately clarified to reporters the same day that Japan "limits its use of nuclear energy to peaceful purposes, abstains from military utilization and does not endeavor to possess nuclear weapons technology or know-how."[1275]

The comments lingered in the media for days, however. Two days later, following complaints from Beijing, Hata called his remarks "trivial" and then made a veiled reference to China's nuclear arsenal: "We have never even imagined going to war with nuclear arms." He clarified that "as a politician, I have never once thought about possessing" nuclear arms.[1276] Moreover, an unnamed "Japanese government source" further asserted that based on "Japan's scientific know-how and economic power," Japan's latent nuclear capability "is obvious," but "intention and capability are different"—Japan according to this view had the technological *capability* to build nuclear weapons, but in lacking the *intent*, Tokyo had no desire to move forward with a nuclear weapons program.[1277] A Ministry of Foreign Affairs statement four days after Hata's initial comments put the issue to rest: "It is true that Japan has highly advanced technology for the peaceful use of nuclear energy. However, mere possession of high-level nuclear technology does not signify the capability of producing nuclear weapons. Japan does not have any expertise or experience in producing nuclear weapons. This means that Japan does not have the capability to produce them." Yet it would not be long until nationalist politicians would again point to Japan's latent capability to produce nuclear weapons if it so desired, and one even argued that Japan *should* go nuclear.

In a more notorious incident five years later, Shingo Nishimura, who had just been appointed parliamentary vice minister of the Defense Agency, was asked during a highly provocative interview with Japan's *Weekly Playboy* magazine in October 1999 about the tit-for-tat nuclear tests in India and Pakistan a year earlier: "No nuclear war will occur now that both countries have become nuclear powers." Rather, "the danger lies with non-nuclear powers. In this sense Japan is in the most dangerous situation. The Diet should consider the fact that if Japan armed itself with nuclear weapons it may be better off." Adding fuel to his already fiery rhetoric during the interview, he compared deterrence theory vividly with rape: "Nuclear weapons are a 'deterrent.' If there were no punishment for rape, we would all be rapists. However, that is not the case because punishment acts as a deterrent." And personalizing his rape comments further while at the same time subtly hinting at Japan's precarious situation in northeast Asia, he continued: "That is precisely why I told a female SDF member (who opposes the right of collective self-defense), 'If you were being raped, I would never try to save you.'" At another point in the interview, Nishimura even stated regarding the possible "global" deployment of defense forces: "I would say, 'We can expand the Greater East Asia Coprosperity Sphere'"—Japan's name for its sphere of influence before and during World War II—"'or the idea of the whole world under one roof to other countries of the world.' I am a nationalist, otherwise I would not be qualified as a politician."[1278]

Nishimura obviously did not remain long at the Defense Agency. Prime Minister Obuchi "immediately dismissed him because of his inappropriate remarks," Obuchi declared in a policy speech to the Diet. Obuchi reaffirmed that he had no intention to change Japan's nuclear policies: "As a nation that has taken the initiative in the international community in promoting nuclear disarmament and nonproliferation, Japan has not changed its policy a bit on continuing to maintain its three non-nuclear principles." And Obuchi apologized to the Diet for Nishimura's rape remarks, which had created a further backlash: "As to his comments that were taken as contempt for women, they were extremely inappropriate since they trampled down women's feelings and human rights. As the person who appointed him to the post, I apologize to the people from the bottom of my heart."[1279]

Later comments by politicians did not result in dismissals, however. In 2002, several politicians addressed the nuclear issue.

During an April 2002 political speech in Fukuoka, the popular opposition politician Ichiro Ozawa told an audience that "Northeastern Asia, in which both China and North Korea are located, is the most unstable region in the world," and "China is applying itself to the expansion of military power in the hope of becoming a superpower." If China "gets too inflated, Japanese people will become hysterical." To deter an "inflated" China, "it would be so easy for us to produce nuclear warheads" since "we have plutonium at nuclear power plants in Japan, enough to make several thousand such warheads." But in an effort to soften his own comments, Ozawa noted that he made the assertions to "encourage a society where Japan and China can coexist," as a democratized China would create greater global security.[1280] Echoing this speech, Ozawa the following day said that he "told a deputy chief of staff of China's People's Liberation Army that Japan could become a nuclear power with its technology and economic might but that it would be tragic if such a thing occurs and we must not let it happen." With China's opaque military modernization, the nuclear argument "could apply to any nation" facing a similar situation "and prompt some Japanese to insist on a further buildup for self-defense and nuclear armament." But ultimately, "I'm against nuclear armament" as "[t]here's nothing beneficial to Japan politically," Ozawa asserted.[1281] Ozawa made his comments as Japan's relations with China were quite tense: Japan and China were in the spring of 2002 negotiating access to the modified North Korean fishing boat sunk in China's EEZ, and Junichiro Koizumi was promising to visit Yasukuni Shrine each year as Prime Minister.

Chinese officials, of course, did not appreciate Ozawa's comments. Foreign Ministry Spokesman Zhang Qiyue called the comments "entirely provocative" and "a typical manifestation of the Cold War mentality." Zhang noted that Ozawa's remarks were made on the 30th anniversary of the normalization of Sino-Japanese relations, and were "completely contrary to the wish of the broad mass of the Japanese people to take the path of peace and development."[1282] Ozawa's comments were barely noted in Japanese media at the time, however, and Chief Cabinet Secretary Fukuda's assertion that Japan's nuclear policies were unchanged was only carried by AFP: "There will be no changes to the fact that we faithfully abide by the policy and that we wish all nuclear weapons will disappear from the world."[1283] And as head of the Liberal Party, Ozawa was certainly free to make comments as he wished without fear of being dismissed from any position.

Another politician revisited the nuclear issue a month later, but this politician was a high-profile member of the ruling LDP. On May 13, 2002, then-Deputy Chief Cabinet Secretary Shinzo Abe—who would later become Prime Minister in September 2006—gave a lecture on "crisis management and decisionmaking" at the prestigious Waseda University, extensive parts of which were reprinted in the weekly *Sande Mainichi*. Answering a question on preemptive strikes, Abe noted: "We will not engage in preemptive strikes. However, although we do not deny preemptive strikes altogether, essentially, we view 'initiation of attacks as attacks imposed on us.'" Visiting professor and noted political commentator Soichiro Tahara then asked Abe a rather surprising question: "Does that mean it is acceptable for Japan to manufacture intercontinental ballistic missiles?"

The question was surprising because the thrust of the public debate just beginning at the time in Japan revolved around the possible possession of a conventional preemptive strike using aircraft or cruise missiles as delivery vehicles. Discussion of Japan's ICBM possession was almost never broached, as ICBMs tipped with conventional explosives held little tactical advantage and provided no strategic deterrence, but they risked major escalation of any conflict by the mere possibility of delivering a nuclear warhead. Abe's answer was even more surprising, as he did not skirt the issue: "Intercontinental ballistic missiles are no problem from the standpoint of the constitution." Moreover, according to Abe, "Constitutionally, there is no problem with even a nuclear bomb...as long as they are small." This had been official policy since 1960, according to Abe: "[T]he late Nobusuke Kishi during prime minister interpolations in 1960 stated the use of strategic nuclear weapons 'would not violate the constitution'"—and Abe knew Kishi's policies well, as Kishi happened to be Abe's grandfather. Indeed, as *Sande Mainichi* pointed out, Prime Minister Kishi first stated during a House of Councilors Cabinet Committee session on May 7, 1957 in response to a question: "Assuming we are speaking of nuclear weapons, it would probably be excessive to state that they are all in violation of the constitution." However, Abe also noted that "since Japan is restricted by the three principles concerning a ban on nuclear weapons, it will not resort to such actions."[1284] He did not mention that it would certainly be easier to revise or abolish the three non-nuclear principles (and associated domestic laws) than to revise Japan's Constitution.

Abe's remarks gained little attention at the time, and Chief Cabinet Secretary Fukuda discussed Abe's remarks at a *kondan* or off-record meeting with reporters after the *Sande Mainichi* was published. But where Abe's speech garnered little attention, Fukuda's off-record comments did. On May 31, a *seifu shuno* or "top government official"—the usual media reference to the Chief Cabinet Secretary—noted that "in the face of calls to amend the Constitution, the amendment of the principles is also likely." Fukuda also said during a regular Friday press conference that same day that Japan was not necessarily bared from possessing ICBMs but later backtracked: "Japan will not possess ICBMs as they exceed the defense-only policy."[1285] This time, the comments were taken more seriously, as the four opposition parties called for Fukuda's resignation and China and South Korea called on Japan to maintain the three non-nuclear principles.[1286] "[S]uch remarks made by high-ranking officials of the Japanese Government are shocking," China's Foreign Ministry Spokesman Liu Jianchao declared, and "China hopes Japan will solemnly and seriously abide by its solemn commitment."[1287] The following Monday, Fukuda admitted that the remarks were his and clarified: "I meant it could be possible that the Japanese people discuss the nation's security on any level in line with international situations and eras...but I did not indicate any direction that the government should take in the future."[1288] Prime Minister Koizumi, for his part, reiterated throughout the weekend that there was no change in Japan's nuclear policies, declaring on a visit to Seoul to watch the opening match of the World Cup: "My cabinet will keep the nonnuclear weapon principles...Japan will not possess a nuclear arsenal because we have these principles."[1289]

Abe later complained about the publication of his excerpts of his speech. Waseda University "agreed not to publicize" his remarks, Abe told the *Asahi Shimbun,* and he called *Sande Mainichi*'s actions "regrettable." "The university has also lodged a protest against the magazine," Abe declared. Abe explained: "I never said the possession of ICBMs does not violate the Constitution" and "my answer" quoted in the *Sande Manichi* "was cut off halfway." "Later, I clearly said that ICBMs that target cities are unacceptable," Abe said. Moreover, "I have never thought that Japan should possess nuclear weapons. With the NPT, Japan has permanently renounced the option of possessing nuclear weapons and shown its strong determination to the world." Abe was merely presenting "the government view and explanations given by Prime Minister Nobusuke Kishi in 1959 and 1960 to the effect that the Constitution does not necessarily ban the possession of nuclear weapons as long as they are kept to a minimum," he reiterated. In other words, at no point was he or Fukuda advocating Japan's arming with nuclear weapons. They were merely pointing out long-held Japanese policy that Japan's Constitution did not necessarily ban the country's possession of nuclear weapons, and that while Japan maintained policy of not possessing, building, or introducing nuclear weapons, this policy too could theoretically be revised based on international events.

As Japan debated preemptive strikes the following year in 2003, a related debate began as well: *Shokun!*, a nationalist monthly that often addressed controversial themes using sensationalist tones, invited a number of well-known national security specialists to describe their views in its special April 2003 edition on whether Japan should develop nuclear weapons. Kan Ito, a political analyst, wrote for example that a "minimum required level of nuclear armament for Japan…would be to possess 200 to 300 cruise missiles with nuclear warheads that could be launched from small destroyers and submarines." Japan did not need intercontinental or submarine-launched ballistic missiles, strategic bombers or large aircraft carriers, Kan asserted, "as Japan will never invade other countries." Kan suggested simply purchasing nuclear-tipped cruise missiles from the United States—which of course was an absurd suggestion—but "if the United States does not want to sell the technology, Japan will simply have to develop such technology. Considering Japan's outstanding technological capabilities, it would not be difficult to produce small nuclear warheads and cruise missiles." Ito noted that Japan was a signatory to the NPT, and it had a right to withdraw from the treaty based on article 10. Moreover, "as Chief Cabinet Secretary Fukuda said last year [2002], 'Japan's nuclear armament is not prohibited by the Constitution of Japan'," Ito added.[1290]

While the rhetoric in Japan indicated an increasing willingness to at least consider a nuclear Japan, there are many domestic, technical and other treaty-based hurdles preventing Japan from arming itself with nuclear weapons. Japan, of course, does have the right to withdraw from the NPT, as North Korea attempted in 1993 and again in 2003. The NPT's article X paragraph 1 cited by Ito declares that "each party" to the NPT "shall give notice of such withdrawal to all other Parties to the Treaty and to the United Nations Security Council three months in advance" of its withdrawal. Any hint at a withdrawal would be met with significant domestic and international pressure.

Moreover, in response to Ito's suggestion that Japan could somehow acquire from the United States a nuclear explosive device or the know-how to build one, it is important to note that the United States is bound by treaty *not* to provide Japan with any sensitive nuclear technology or material for a nuclear weapon. As written in the bilateral "Peaceful Uses of Nuclear Energy" Agreement signed between Japan and the United States in November 1987 (among other bilateral agreements), "restricted data and sensitive nuclear technology shall not be transferred."[1291] Restricted data refers to the "design, manufacture, or utilization of nuclear weapons" and "the production of special fissionable material," while sensitive nuclear technology includes "any data which are not available to the public and which are important to the design construction, fabrication, operation or maintenance of enrichment, reprocessing or heavy water production facilities."

Moreover, Article 8 states: "Cooperation under this Agreement shall be carried out only for peaceful purposes" and material transferred from the United States to Japan "shall not be used for any nuclear explosive device, for research specifically on or development of any nuclear explosive device, for research specifically on or development of any nuclear explosive device, or for any military purpose." In other words, the United States would in no way assist Japan in building a nuclear weapon, and Japan is bound by this treaty to refrain from using nuclear material supplied by the United States in any nuclear explosive device. The United States can, moreover, request additional safeguard arrangements under Article 9, and it has a right to "require the return of any material" if Japan is not complying with any of the provisions in the Agreement. Japan has similar bilateral agreements on the peaceful uses of nuclear energy with Canada and Australia as well, two major exporters of uranium and nuclear energy technologies. And since Japan has no significant uranium deposits, it has had to import virtually all of its uranium from abroad under these bilateral safeguards agreements. Thus, virtually all of Japan's fissionable material, whether it is enriched uranium or plutonium, remains subject to these bilateral treaties as well as to Japan's commitments to the Nuclear Non-Proliferation Treaty.

Japan is also subject to inspections of its nuclear-related facilities and material under the Nuclear Non-Proliferation Treaty. The NPT states: "Each non-nuclear-weapon State Party to the Treaty undertakes to accept safeguards, as set forth in an agreement to be negotiated and concluded with the International Atomic Energy Agency...for the exclusive purpose of verification of the fulfillment of its obligations assumed under this Treaty with a view to preventing diversion of nuclear energy from peaceful uses to nuclear weapons or other nuclear explosive devices." Japan thus has a safeguards agreement with the International Atomic Energy

Agency, and if Japan withdrew from the NPT, it would have to abrogate its agreements with the IAEA as well.

The IAEA, with major regional offices in Tokyo, indeed spends a significant amount of time and a significant portion of its budget inspecting and monitoring Japanese nuclear-related facilities and measuring nuclear material on an on-going basis. IAEA inspectors also audit facilities' accounting and operating records to verify the country's nuclear material inventory. Moreover, Japan was one of the first countries to ratify the IAEA's Additional Protocol in the early 1990s, which grants IAEA inspectors expanded inspection authority to the country's entire nuclear fuel cycle, from the mining and processing of uranium ore, fuel fabrication and enrichment plants, to its nuclear waste sites. Any area where nuclear material may be present is subject to short-notice inspections, and inspectors even have the right to take environmental samples from areas outside declared locations when deemed necessary.[1292] The Additional Protocol thus gives IAEA inspectors complete and unhindered access to Japan's nuclear-related facilities and to information on its nuclear material. And apart from Japan's international commitments under the NPT and its bilateral agreements with the United States and other nuclear exporters, Japan's domestic policy is based on the three non-nuclear principles promulgated by the Sato government in 1968. Beyond this Cabinet-approved policy, however, Japan's peaceful uses of nuclear energy is indeed the law of the land, as the Atomic Energy Basic Law, which established the Atomic Energy Commission and the Nuclear Safety Commission in January 1956, limits Japan's nuclear use to peaceful purposes. The law declares: "The research, development and utilization of atomic energy shall be limited to peaceful purposes." Domestic law would have to be revised to allow for the development of nuclear weapons.

Thus, prior to establishing a nuclear weapons program, Tokyo would have to take a series of well-publicized actions. Domestically, Japan's lower and upper houses of the Diet would have to revise or repeal the Atomic Energy Basic Law and restate (or abolish) the three non-nuclear principles in a clear manner that would allow the manufacture and possession of nuclear weapons. These changes would require Diet debate and would certainly cause a public uproar in Japan as opposition parties, no matter how small, would not only attempt to block debate of legal revisions but also try to pass votes of no-confidence in the government. A significant segment of the public would surely actively oppose any decision to acquire nuclear weapons, placing additional pressure on any sitting government. Once such a policy decision had been made, and if implementing legislation were passed in the Diet, Japan could withdraw from the NPT and abrogate its agreements with the IAEA. Separate from the NPT, Japan would have to give the United States government written notice six months in advance that it was abrogating the "Peaceful Uses of Nuclear Energy" Agreement, according to Article 16, during which time the U.S. government would most likely request the return of all nuclear material and equipment it transferred to Japan during the period of the nuclear safety agreements. During this time, domestic and international pressure would of course continue in order to convince the governing party in Japan to rethink its radical change in policy.

Should the Government of Japan weather all of this in its pursuit of a nuclear weapons capability, it would then have to research, develop, and build the nuclear weapons, the triggers and safety mechanisms, the delivery systems, command and control, and develop the tactics for their possible employment. Once built, Japan would want to make sure its nuclear weapons were reliable: while Japan would not necessarily have to test a nuclear weapon once a *basic* capability has been acquired—South Africa did not test its nuclear devices before it gave them up in the early 1990s, nor has Israel tested a nuclear device—if Japan were to minitu-rize any future nuclear devices to fit on a submarine-launched cruise missile, for example, it would most likely want to verify—and demonstrate to its nuclear-armed neighbors—that such a nuclear capability actually worked. This in turn would require Japan to withdraw from the Comprehensive Test Ban Treaty, which it ratified in July 1997, and to find a test site to conduct a nuclear weapons verification test. This is not so easy, for as an *Asahi* editorial made clear, "topographically, the Japanese archipelago is not suited to be defended with nuclear weapons,"[1293] and it is not suited to testing a nuclear device either. But for the nuclear option to serve as a true deterrent, it must be demonstrated to potential adversaries, since nuclear weapons serve as a deterrent only to the extent that adversaries believe that they can be reliably used. Only at this point would Japan have a basic, credible nuclear weapons capability.

• • •

It is true that Japan possesses a theoretical *capability* to build nuclear weapons, as conservative media and hawkish politicians point out from time to time. However, there are significant impediments to Japan's *actually building* them. As long as the U.S.-Japan alliance remains strong, Tokyo will most likely continue to calculate that nuclear weapons will simply not provide for Japan's security needs, and they could potentially *increase* the threat of a nuclear or other preemptive attack by regional powers. As an archipelago, Japan does not have the geography to withstand a nuclear attack. Two nuclear strikes, one centered on Tokyo and the other centered on the Kansai/Osaka region—the most densely populated regions of the world—would devastate the country.

While domestic rhetoric on the topic will no doubt increase, Japan appears to be fully entrenched in bilateral and multilateral nuclear non-proliferation regimes. As long as the current nuclear non-proliferation structures remain sound and U.S. nuclear assurances are perceived to be credible, Japan will have little geostrategic incentive to pursue nuclear arms.

On the other hand, given the geographic realities, Tokyo will continue to seek to improve the country's "active defense"—missile defense—as an alternative to a nuclear weapons capability. Tokyo also has every incentive to continue to develop and expand its "offensive defense" capabilities—precision strike technologies and the networks and platforms needed to employ them—to provide for a basic and visible deterrent to potential adversaries targeting the island nation. While the development of a conventional preemptive strike capability remains contentious in Japan, the option has a 60-year history of political support dating to 1956.

Yet, despite its technological expertise, Tokyo will face increasing difficulties in maintaining modernized conventional capabilities to defend the archipelago in the 21st century, as Japan is experiencing a shrinking population and with it a contracting tax base. Japan's severe demographic situation increasingly strains the fiscal foundation necessary to support increasingly complex and expensive conventional systems. A heavily indebted Japan will have to make painful choices such as easing immigration laws to expand its tax base or cutting social services to support defense modernization programs and expanded intelligence collection capabilities. Without drastic measures to stabilize its shrinking population, in the future there will be few Japanese to protect. These issues will be examined in the next chapter.

SECTION 3:

Demographics as Japan's Long-Term Threat

7) Sleep-Walking to Dusk? Japan's Rapidly Shrinking Population

Japan is experiencing a demographic crisis. Barring an outbreak of war in northeast Asia, Japan's dire demographic situation represents the true mortal threat to Japan's national security in the medium- to long-term. Due to decades of below-replacement birthrates since the late 1970s, in 2005 Japan's population shrank for first time since the 1960s. Japan reached a peak population in 2007-2008, but its population began to shrink on a consistent basis just as the deaths now outnumber births. As birthrates have continued to drop, coupled with the rapidly aging baby boomer generation and nonexistent in-migration into Japan, the decreasing population will only accelerate in the coming years. If the current population trends continue, according to official statistics, in 65 years there will only be half as many residents of Japan compared to peak population in 2008. Almost half of those will be over the age of 65, well beyond the age of military service.[1294]

Japan's demographic outlook increasingly poses fiscal as well as personnel constraints for national security policymakers in Tokyo, as there will be fewer and fewer able-bodied Japanese to support the increasing numbers of elderly while also participating in what was once a vibrant economy. As the current workforce ages and retires, an increasingly larger proportion of younger workers will be required to care for them in a very literal sense: hospitals, long-term care facilities, and nursing homes all will compete for dwindling numbers of workers to serve as doctors, nurses, and aides, even as companies and the public sector attempt to replace the wave of retirees in the 2010s and beyond.

The decreasing proportion of workers to retirees also portends steadily decreasing tax revenue for the central government—even as Japan is already one of the largest debtor nations in the developed world—and a larger proportion of taxes will go to supporting Japan's elderly, who rely overwhelmingly on the state to meet their retirement and elder care needs. This in turn will create greater budgetary constraints as growing entitlement expenditures compete with national security requirements, particularly as the complexity and expense of defense technologies grow in the 21st century.

Tokyo has few options to respond to this slowly evolving – yet completely predictable – demographic crisis. As birthrates continue to drop despite over a decade of policy initiatives to revive them, only one other option remains: allowing more migrants to work and settle in Japan. Yet for a variety of reasons, this remains anathema to the current generation of policymakers.

Japan's Long Demographic Decline

Like the United States, Japan experienced a baby boom in the post-war years. According to Japan's National Institute of Population and Social Security Research, in 1950, the typical Japanese woman gave birth on average to 3.65 children. This number represented Japan's Total Fertility Rate (TFR), or the average number of children born to a woman of child-bearing years.

For any given population to sustain itself – that is, for the population to remain static – the TFR needs to remain slightly above 2.1, meaning that the average woman would need to bear slightly more than 2 children each. Following a post-war baby boom in the late 1940s and 1950s, Japan's TFR hovered around the minimum needed to sustain the population in the 1960s. Birthrates slightly increased by 1970, to 2.13 children per woman, and peaked in the mid-1970s in an "echo baby boom" when baby boomers gave birth to their first children.[1295]

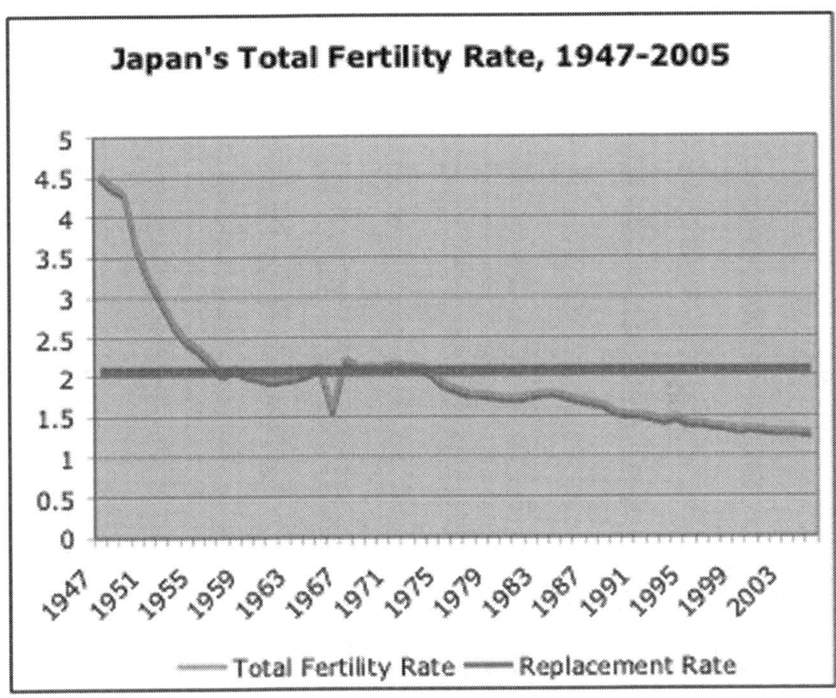

Source: National Institute of Population and Social Security Research

Japan experienced an anomalous dip in births during this initial post-war period in 1966, when births fell from 2.14 to 1.58 in one year, only to recover the following year to an average of over two births per woman again. Superstition most likely drove this sudden drop, as 1966 was the year of *hino'e-uma* – the Fire Horse – in the Chinese Zodiac. Each year of the Chinese Zodiac is divided into one of twelve animal signs with certain attributes, and these in turn are governed by one of five elements, such as wind, water, fire, etc. People born under the horse sign are considered to be energetic, independent, ambitious, and sometimes hot-tempered, and the fire element serves to accentuate these features. The traits were considered undesirable for girls and potential wives, since fire horse women were said to have troubled marriages and to mistreat men. A disproportionate number of women born under the fire horse sign in 1906 experienced delayed marriage compared to their peers born in other years, most likely due to their birth year.[1296] Thus at least some couples avoided giving birth in 1966 most likely to avoid stigmatizing their daughters and negatively impacting a daughter's future marriage possibilities.

Following its recovery into the 1970s, the birthrate in Japan began a precipitous decline from the mid-1970s. By 1980, the average number of births per woman had dropped to 1.75 children, and by 1990 to 1.54 children per woman. As birthrates in Japan consistently remained below replacement rate through the end of the Cold War, the impact on the number of youth as a percentage of the population became increasingly pronounced by the early 1990s. According to figures compiled by the Ministry of Internal Affairs and Communications, while Japan's 1940s-1950s baby boom produced nearly thirty million children—a full third of the population at its peak—by 1990 the youth demographic dropped to 22 million and represented less than 20% of the population. The downward trend continued into the early 2000s: by 2005, there were only 17.5 million children under the age of 15 in Japan, representing a staggeringly low 13% of the total population. Moreover, the percentage of population over 65 increased during the 1990s and into the 2000s as well, surpassing the percentage of children in 1997. In 2005, while children under 15 made up 13% of Japan's population, those over 65 made up almost 20% of the population, and this demographic continues to increase both in raw numbers and as a percentage of the population (see chart below).[1297]

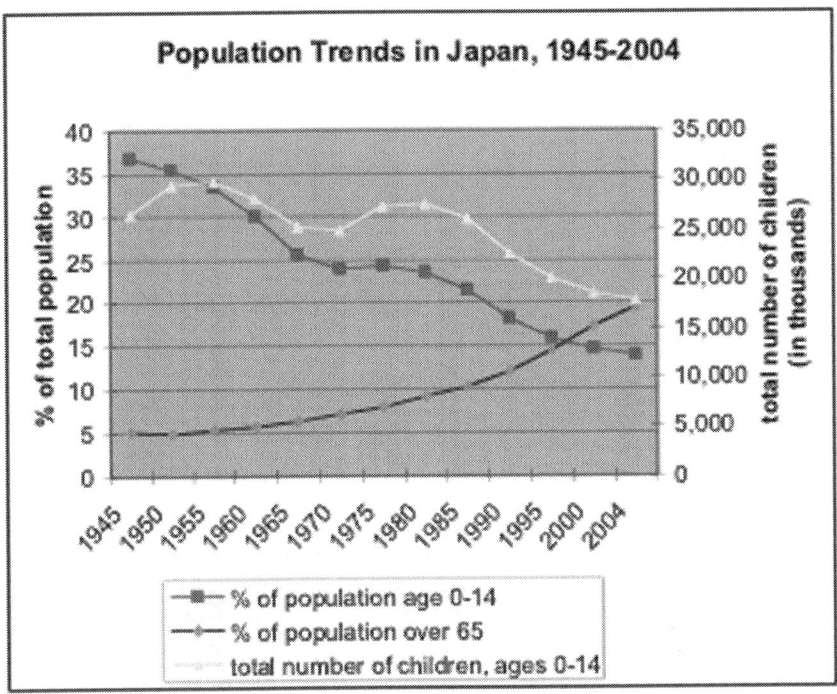

Source: Ministry of Internal Affairs and Communications, Population and Growth Trends, 2005, p 14.

By the late 1980s, as members of the baby boom generation moved into the highest echelons of power in Tokyo, policymakers and business leaders were growing increasingly concerned about the persistently low birthrates. Unlike 1966, when births suddenly dropped below replacement rates but then recovered the following year, by the late 1980s birthrates in Japan showed no signs of recovering. According to Teijiro Furukawa, the deputy chief cabinet secretary and senior government bureaucrat at the time, discussion of policies to promote higher birthrates in Japan had been taboo since the end of the Second World War because of that era's emphasis on coercive policies and slogans such as *umeyō fuyaseyō*: "have children, increase the population." But according to Furukawa, policymakers knew this taboo had to change and that policies needed to be enacted to improve "the environment in which children are born and raised."[1298] As an indication of the increasing attention the issue was being given, by this time the term *shōshika shakai*—low birthrate society—was coined. This term was soon modified to *shōshi koreika shakai*—low birthrate and rapidly ageing society—a further indication of demographic trends in Japan.

Prime Minister Toshiki Kaifu brought the issue to the national spotlight in his first speech to the Diet on October 2, 1989. While Kaifu devoted only a few lines to the issue, declaring "I will work to create a healthy environment in which children will be born and raised," Kaifu's speech represented the first time a politician pledged to emphasize policies designed to ameliorate the decrease in birthrates. The conservative *Sankei Shimbun* highlighted precisely this aspect of the prime minister's speech on its front page, calling the low birthrate phenomenon the "1.57 Shock"—a clear reference to Japan's below-replacement TFR. But despite the theme appearing again in the following year's prime ministerial address to the Diet—and despite a number of studies by committees in the related ministries and agencies shortly thereafter—Furukawa lamented that it was "difficult to say that policies to respond to low birthrates were widely promoted."[1299]

The first initiatives aimed at increasing Japan's birthrate were formed in early 1992. With a goal of increasing the TFR to 1.8, Tokyo initiated the "Welcome Baby Campaign"—complete with its own "Baby's Song" campaign tune—which encouraged symposia across the country such as the "21st Century Baby and Family Forum" and the "Committee To Create Great Environments for Children" to discuss measures to improve birthrates.[1300] While one proposal led to the construction of a few wilderness preserves where young children living in densely populated areas could enjoy a more natural setting, little else came of this initial campaign as evidenced by the continuing decline in birthrates.

The Japanese government at this time also undertook the first of many revisions to a system of providing monetary compensation for families with children to include first-born children, as support had previously begun with the third and later second child born in the family since the system was established in 1972. In 1991, families would receive a monthly allowance of ¥5,000 for the first child until he or she turned 1, and ¥10,000/month until second and subsequent children turned 5. In 1992, the monthly payments were extended until the first-born child turned 2, and by 2006 the payout continued until the child was 12.[1301] While it was perhaps the most concrete and direct policy initiative undertaken in the 1990s, the amount was the equivalent to around $100 and thus did little to offset the costs of rearing a child.

Following the failure of the "Welcome Baby Campaign," the government instituted the "Angel Plan" for 1995-1999, focusing on improvements to child care centers and maternity health. This, coupled with increased payments for rearing children, again failing to increase the TFR to 1.8, Indeed, the birthrate declined to such an extent that the government in 1997 revised downward its TFR goal to 1.61 and also attempted to reinforce a 40-hour (vice longer) workweek.

New policies were initated each year in the early 2000s. In December 1999, the Japanese government launched the "Basic Guidelines to Halt the Declining Birthrate" or simply the "New Angel Plan," with the slogan *wouldn't you like another little angel?* "Guidelines for Measures to Support Working Parents" were approved by the Cabinet and included improved access to childcare facilities especially for working parents. In September 2002 the Ministry of Health, Labor and Welfare initiated the "Plus One Measures to Halt the Declining Birthrate," with a new slogan *have a child plus one.* This policy sought, among other things, to ease financial burdens during parenting, set child-care leave targets for both men and women, and reduce overtime work during child-rearing years. In a sign of the increasingly dire situation, the government also lowered its target TFR yet again, this time to 1.39. In July 2003, the Diet enacted the "Basic Law on Measures for a Society with a Decreasing Birthrate," which declared: "We are being strongly called upon to halt the decrease in children by creating an environment where parents can feel secure in giving birth and raising children who will be the next generation of society." With this goal in mind, the "Law for Measures to Support the Development of the Next Generation" was passed requiring local government and business owners to create "action plans" to build an environment for the next generation of children to be born and raised in good health. If companies achieved whatever targets they set in their action plans, they would receive a certificate to use in advertisements indicating such.[1302] But by 2004, in a review of the "New Angel Plan," the *Kantei* noted that overall results "cannot be said to be satisfactory."[1303] Yet another Angel Plan, called the "New New Angel Plan" for 2005-2009, followed the *Kentei*'s finding, but given the abject failure of previous policy initiatives, this one too was doomed from the outset.

These initiatives have had absolutely no impact in actually fostering a desire among young couples to have more children. Toru Suzuki, writing in the *Japanese Journal of Population,* noted that these "prenatal measures are not as effective as expected" and have "not succeeded in preventing fertility decline." Moreover, "there is no reason to expect that policy intervention can induce sustainable recovery of fertility."[1304] By 2004, according to the Ministry of Health, Labor, and Welfare, the birthrate per woman in Japan as measured by the Total Fertility Rate (TFR) fell to 1.29 children – below even the lowered government target rates and still well below replacement rate of just over two per woman. Together with Italy, Japan continued to exhibit one of the lowest birthrates in the world.

Politicians' deeply paternalistic treatment of the issue, with references implying or even outright stating that a woman's sole function was to have more babies, certainly did not serve to increase young families' desires to have more children. Prime Minister Koizumi implicitly compared women to dogs in his 2006 New Year's address, relating the act of giving birth to the Year of the Dog in the Chinese Zodiac in a misguided attempt to entice women to get pregnant: "Dogs…are said to have an easy labor."[1305] According to this warped logic, women should have an easier time giving birth in the Year of the Dog. While Koizumi was introducing the topic to declare that he will do his best "to create the environment where people can think raising children is delightful and being parents enriches human lives"—a standard political mantra since the early 1990s—his implicit comparison of young women to dogs certainly did not produce the desired effect of increasing their desire to give birth. And in early 2007, the Minister of Health, Labor, and Welfare Hakuo Yanagisawa was quoted calling women "birth-giving machines": "The number of women aged 15 to 50 is fixed. As we have a fixed number of birth-giving machines and devices, all we can ask of them is that each do their best." Yanagisawa later apologized for the remark.[1306] The patronizing imagery and slogans used by (predominately male) politicians in Tokyo was not the best way to gain support among women and young families to have more children.

In a sign of continuing low birthrates, according to a Cabinet Office-sponsored survey of 1,000 men and women in five countries in late 2005, respondents in Japan wanted to have fewer children in general than those in other countries: only 42% of women wanted to have more children, the fewest among surveyed respondents in the United States, Sweden, South Korea and France. This contrasted with high positive response rates—81%—among women surveyed in Sweden and the United States as wanting to have more children, while a relatively high 69% of French women said they wanted more children. Only South Korean women—43% of respondents—tied Japanese women in replying positively that they wanted more children (South Korea too suffers from exceedingly low birthrates).[1307]

Additionally, young Japanese are increasingly delaying marriage. This magnifies the problem because those who choose to enter into marriage at a relatively young age shrinks even more as the sheer number of youth in Japan shrinks, causing the total number of young married couples in their childbearing years to decline even more rapidly. This phenomenon is often cited as a main cause of declining birthrates in Japan, since giving birth out of wedlock is frowned upon.[1308] As an increasing number of young people in Japan delay marriage, they thereby delay giving birth to their first children and reduce their chances of having subsequent children, causing Japan's birthrate to shrink more rapidly than officials have predicted.

Japan's population declined for the first time in its modern history in 2005, shrinking by 19,000 to 127,768,000. That year, the birthrate declined by 39,000 to a new low of 1,087,000 babies born in 2005. Instead of increasing as the government had hoped—and indeed planned—the average birthrate per woman in Japan fell again, to 1.29. Following a brief uptick in population through 2008, Japan is now experiencing sustained year-over-year declines in its population as deaths now outnumber births. In 2012, Japan's population dropped to 127,515,000, and deaths outnumbered births by over 200,000.[1309] Japan's population was projected to drop below 100 million in thirty years, a staggering drop of almost one-quarter of Japan's peak population.[1310]

On the other end of the age spectrum, Japanese experience the highest life expectancy rates in the developed world. According to the Ministry of Health, Labor, and Welfare, the average male in 2004 lived on average 78.6 years, and the average female lived to be 85.6 years of age. Sweden boasted the next-longest lived population, while in the United States average life expectancy rates were some four to five years less than in Japan.[1311] Coupled with decades of below-replacement birthrates, however, a large and growing proportion of the population is aged. The Cabinet Office defines a nation with more than 7% of the population over 65 "aging," and when the ratio reaches 14% the nation becomes "aged"—Japan crossed this threshold in 1995. In 2005, 20% of the Japanese population—25.6 million people—was over the age of 65. That ratio rose to over 24%—31 million people—in 2012. Japan has become what demographers term a "super-aged" nation.[1312]

Ominously, the aging trend has accelerated faster than demographers predicted since focusing on the issue in the early 1990s. In 1992, the National Institute of Population and Social Security Research, an institute affiliated with the Ministry of Health and Welfare, predicted that the population would begin to shrink in 2011. But by 1997—when the number of Japanese over 65 outnumbered those under 15 for the first time ever—that prediction was moved forward by four years to 2007. The institute further predicted in 1997 that by 2050, one in three Japanese would be over the age of 65, an upward revision from the 1992 forecast of just over 28%. By 2050 as well, the population would have shrunk by 20%, from 125 million to fewer than 100 million, according to the institute's 1997 projections.[1313] Already the *Japan Statistical Yearbook 2014* has moved those predictions forward by several years. One in three Japanese will be over 65 by 2035, and Japan's total population is predicted to fall below 100 million by 2048.[1314]

On a nation-wide scale, by the early 2000s hundreds of communities were disappearing throughout rural Japan. According to a joint survey by the Construction and Transport Ministry and the Internal Affairs and Communications Ministry, between 1999 and 2006, 191 communities vanished, while another 2,643 communities were considered likely to disappear in the near future. Over 400 were deemed likely to disappear within a decade of the 2006 study.[1315] The National Institute of Population and Social Security Research also predicted in 2007 that 19 of Japan's 47 prefectures will experience a 20% decline in population by 2035 (preceding the 20% national decline by 15 years), and 20% of the populations in 39 prefectures will consist of people aged 75 or older. The number of prefectures with fewer than 1 million people would rise from seven prefectures to 15 by that time as well.[1316] The continuing urbanization in Japan intensifies the declining birthrates in rural communities, as the younger populations leave their rural towns to find jobs and social opportunities in Japanese cities.

Amazingly, even as Japanese researchers were predicting the gradual demise of an entire nation, Tokyo has been unable to devise creative and workable policy initiatives to halt the decline in birthrates beyond raising subsidies to families with young children by a few thousand yen per month. The only measure that is likely to succeed is the one Tokyo avoids implementing: to maintain its population through the next century, Japan would need to allow greater numbers of migrants to work and settle in the archipelago.

Immigration as the Answer?

With a drastically declining birth rate and an aging population, the only other way for Japan to maintain its population is to import labor. Yet Japan has some of the most restrictive immigration policies in the developed world, as reflected in its immigration statistics. At the end of 2004, Japan hosted some 1.9 million non-Japanese residents, less than two percent of its total population. However, over 600,000 of these—30% of foreign residents of Japan—are registered as Korean, a large majority of whom are descendents of forced laborers imported from the Korean peninsula during Japan's decades-long occupation. Given the persistence of national versus civic tests for citizenship in practice if not in law, these descendents remain registered as "Korean" nationals even though many of them were born and raised in Japan.

Reflecting Tokyo's attitude towards immigration in general, Japan accepts only a miniscule number of asylum seekers. A report on Japan's asylum record commissioned by the United Nations High Commissioner for Refugees noted that Japan "was a closed country from 1639 to 1867 and subsequently has been a country of emigration rather than immigration." As Tokyo slowly began to review whether to accept asylum seekers based on the 1951 Convention Relating to the Status of Refugees—Japan acceded to the Convention in 1981— "government and public opinion adhered to the fact that Japan was mono-ethnic, homogeneous and unique and therefore to encourage immigration would disrupt social cohesion."[1317] But despite formalizing procedures to handle asylum seekers following a surge of refugees from Vietnam, Cambodia, and Laos since the 1970s, Japan accepts refugees and asylum seekers only on a very limited basis. According to UNHCR statistics, 426 cases for asylum were submitted in Japan in 2004, but the government accepted only nine. That compares with close to 28,000 submitted in the United States, over 25,000 submitted in Canada, and over 3,000 submitted in Australia—with the latter two countries having only a fraction of Japan's population. Japan's recognition rate was also by far the lowest in the developed world, accepting only 2.9% of the asylum requests that year. Even Germany accepted more both in total numbers of applications as well as by percentage, recognizing 1,760 requests for asylum out of a total of 35,607, a rate of 4.4%.

In the two decades after the end of the Cold War (1992-2012), Japan experienced a net out-migration of 220,000 people. Japan experienced net out-migration in thirteen of those years, net in-migration in seven of those years, and no change in one.[1318]

Under current trends, Japan would require a staggering number of immigrants to maintain population rates in Japan. The United Nations Population Division in 2000 released a study of the potential impact of in-migration on low-birthrate societies in the developed world, including Japan. Titled *Replacement Migration, Is It A Solution To Declining and Ageing Populations?*, the study projected four scenarios to 2050: status quo (no in-migration), steady-state population (ie, projecting how many migrants would be required to maintain 2005 population levels), steady-state working population, and a final scenario aimed at maintaining a worker-to-retiree ratio of 4.8 – a ratio last seen in Japan in 1995.

According to UN projections in the late 1990s, with no net immigration—essentially the status quo for Japan—Japan's population would peak in 2005 and then decline by 20% to 104 million residents by 2050. Japan's working age population (those between 15-64 years of age) would decline "continuously" from 87 million to 57 million people, while those over 65 years of age would almost double from 18 million to around 33 million and would make up almost 32% of the population.[1319] This is already an optimistic scenario even by Japanese government's own statistics.

To maintain a steady 2005 population of 127 million residents, Japan would need to accept 17 million net immigrants between 2005 and 2050, or 381,000 immigrants per year (see chart below). Under this scenario, by 2050 the immigrant population would total 22.5 million (a twelve-fold increase of the current immigrant population) and make up over 17% of the total population of Japan, compared with less than 2% today. Yet the working age population would continue to decline even under this scenario, from 86 million to just under 73 million residents. While the youth population (those under 15) would begin to recover, growing from 18.5 million to just over 19 million in that time period, Japan's elderly population would continue to grow, from 21 million to over 35 million residents.

Under yet another scenario, Japan would need to attract 33.5 million immigrants through 2050—over 600,000 per year—to maintain the size of its working-age population, and under this scenario the entire population of Japan would grow to over 150 million residents. Finally, in order to keep the ratio of working-age population to the retired-age population at its 1995 level of 4.8, the country would need to attract 553 million immigrants – a staggering 10 million people per year – through 2050. However, the support ratio has already dropped below 4 since the study was published, so the number of immigrants in the final scenario would need to grow even further to maintain 1995 support levels. These final two scenarios are extremely unlikely, as Japanese policymakers have yet to view immigration as a serious response to Japan's declining population.

Yet, birthrates in Japan have slowed more quickly than even the UN could have calculated. The UN study predicted in its median variant projection that Japan's population of 0-14 year olds would number just over 16 million in 2025, and 14.5 million in 2050. By 2012, however, according to Japan's official statistics the number of those under 15 had already dropped to 16.5 million, and with the current decline averaging just over 170,000 children a year, Japan's under-15 population could fall to 16 million by 2015, a full ten years before the UN predicted. This means that the future number of workers will also shrink more rapidly than predicted. And as the pool of workers shrinks, so too will the amount of taxes paid to the central government, assuming tax rates remain static. But in the face of the rapidly increasing elderly population, tax rates in fact have already begun to rise.

Fiscal Effects: Japan's Shrinking Tax Base

A lower birthrate, coupled with Japan's world-leading longevity rates, mean there are fewer young workers who can support the elderly population through payments into the national pension plan and other transfers.

Japan has two major pay-as-you-go pension programs dating to the 1950s: the *kokumin nenkin* or National Pension program mainly for the self-employed, and the *kosei nenkin* or Employees' Pension program for private sector employees. Until recently, the percentage of one's salary paid into the *kosei nenkin* was similar to those paid in the United States. Workers generally paid 6.79% of their salary and bonuses up to a maximum amount adjusted periodically for inflation, and the employer contributed a similar amount. Self-employed workers depending on their situation paid a flat ¥13,300/month into the national pension plan, although their benefits were smaller in retirement. To be eligible to receive any payments after the age of 65, a worker must have paid at least 25 years' worth of premiums into the system, and workers were generally expected to contribute 40 years into the system for full benefits.

The modern state-run pension system was formalized in the 1950s when the ratio of workers to pensioners was quite favorable for a pay-as-you-go system. Again according to the UN population study, in 1950, the ratio of workers to retirees stood at 12 to 1, and taxes paid by those 12 individuals more than covered the pension for that one retiree. By 1975, the support ratio fell by one-third, to eight workers for every retiree in Japan. The ratio dropped by half again by the year 2000, with just under four workers supporting each retiree. And by 2025 the ratio is projected to drop by half yet again to around 2 workers supporting each retiree.[1320]

As projections indicated that the shrinking support ratio would fail to provide adequately for the national pension system, the Diet in 2004 passed legislation that gradually increased mandatory payments into the social welfare system from 13.58% (6.79% each from the employee and employer) of income to 18.3% (or 9.15% each from the employee and the employer) by 2017. The new law was intended to maintain pension benefits for the current workforce equivalent to at least 50% of average take-home pay. But this legislation was based on a projection that the fall in total fertility rate would stop at just over 1.3 in 2007, and increase to 1.39 thereafter. Less than a week after the enactment of pension reform, however, the government released figures for 2003 indicating that the TFR had fallen to 1.29—already breaking the projections set forth in the legislation. This obviously portended still more increases in pension payments—essentially, further tax increases—or cuts to pension payouts. The largest circulation daily *Yomiuri Shimbun* called for further "drastic reform of the country's entire social security system" and the need for "the public to accept a certain increase in their premium burden and a decrease in benefits."[1321] Thus, not only will payments into the system most likely rise after 2017, benefits are likely to fall.

According to official statistics, pension payouts have doubled from around 7% of national income in the early 1990s to over 15% in 2010. Total social security benefits—pension payments, medical care, welfare, and other payments—more than doubled from around 14% of national income to 30% in 2010.[1322] These upward trends will only continue as Japan ages rapidly.

Complicating matters, the Social Insurance Agency has proven surprisingly inefficient in collecting national pension premium payments in recent years. The agency reported in 2003 that the amount of unpaid premiums in 2000 and 2001 totaled ¥1.88 trillion—about $18 billion. This was not an anomaly, as the amount of nonpayments had risen steadily since 1982, with over ¥1 trillion owed on average each year since 1994. Businesses also owed ¥430 billion in fiscal 2001. Indeed, 37.2% of workers failed to pay into the national pension system in 2002, a sharp increase from the 29.1% who had not paid into the system in 2001. Over half of those in their 20s reportedly did not pay into the pension system, most likely fearing that they were paying for an entitlement they would never be able to enjoy their old age. Following these revelations in 2003, Minister of Health, Labor, and Welfare Chikara Sakaguchi highlighted growing distrust of the system among the public and especially by younger generations: "I think young people have uneasy feelings about how much they will receive from the pension system in the future…We'll try to craft a new system that gives them a solid answer."[1323]

Less than a year later, as the Diet began to debate pension reform to provide some "answers" to younger generations of taxpayers (in the form of higher mandatory payments into the pension system), it was revealed that many Japanese politicians *themselves* were not paying into the system despite a requirement for all Diet members to do so since 1986. In April 2004, Prime Minister Koizumi, Chief Cabinet Secretary Fukuda, and six cabinet members (including Shigeru Ishiba, the director-general of the Defense Agency) were found to have missed payments into the national pension plan at various times during their political careers. Minister of Economy, Trade and Industry Shoichi Nakagawa said he had "forgotten" to pay his pension premiums for over twenty years—Nakagawa later repaid two years' worth of premiums, but the remaining period of non-payment was exempted due to the statute of limitation on past arrears. Many current and former political leaders of the Ministry of Health, Labor, and Welfare—which oversees the Social Insurance Agency, the administrator of the public pension system—were caught having missed significant payments into the system. These included former welfare ministers Yuya Niwa and Ryutaro Hashimoto, and the former parliamentary vice minister Jinen Nagase, all of whom were actively engaged in proposing reforms to the pension system. Fourteen members of the New Komeito—a staunch advocate of robust social welfare programs—were caught having missed payments into the system as well, including party head Takenori Kanzaki, Secretary-General Tetsuzo Fuyushiba and Kazuo Kitagawa, chairman of the party's Policy Research Council. The opposition Democratic Party of Japan was also affected, as opposition leader Naoto Kan was discovered to have missed payments. Part of the nonpayment problem was due to the fact that companies were required to withdraw pension premium payments automatically from paychecks, but the Diet did not have an automatic payment system in place. While "failure to pay the mandatory premiums no doubt was an oversight," in the words of *Asahi Shimbun*, it was "a disgraceful state of affairs" that no doubt created more ill-will toward the pension scheme especially among younger generations of Japanese.[1324] Chief Cabinet Secretary Yasuo Fukuda and opposition leader Naoto Kan eventually resigned to take responsibility for the fact that many in their parties had missed payments. His reputation seemingly untarnished, three years after the scandal Fukuda became prime minister of Japan.

Mismanagement and high-profile nonpayment into the system has caused significant lack of confidence among the Japanese public, particularly younger generations. In a survey conducted by the Japan Institute for Social and Economic Affairs (JISEA) in 2005, when various age groups were asked whether they planned to rely on government social welfare programs such as the national pension system in retirement or mainly on personal resources, over 90% of those in their 60s and 70s responded that they would rely or already were relying completely or to a major extent on government-sponsored social welfare programs, and 85% of respondents in their 50s said they planned to rely on government sponsored programs in retirement. In contrast, half of those under the age of 30 said they expected to rely entirely on personal resources to fund their retirement.[1325] A 2007 poll cited by JISEA authors indicated that 76% of the public distrusted the public pension system, while 87% of those in their 20s distrusted the system.[1326]

Complicating the fiscal situation, Japan also owes more relative to other industrialized nations following two decades of recessions and extremely low growth. Japan's debt more than quadrupled between 1990 and 2012, rising from ¥216 trillion to over ¥1 quadrillion in the early 2010s.[1327] Japan had a debt-to-GDP ratio of 143% in 2002, second only to Italy 106% debt-to-GDP level. A decade later, the International Monetary Fund projected Japan to reach a debt-to-GDP level of 242% in 2014.[1328] Taxes were set to increase in 2014 as well, with Tokyo raising the sales tax from 5% to 10% in two stages through 2015.

To meet the increasing demand for workers and taxes in the coming decades, the Japanese government would either have to increase birth rates or increase immigration. But young Japanese couples show few signs of wanting more babies, and the government continues to maintain a very low immigration rate due to restrictive immigration policies. Ultimately, fewer workers and more elderly mean the Japanese economy will continue to stagnate barring any dramatic increase in productivity. Lack of growth coupled with a smaller proportion of taxpayers to pensioners mean that the government will collect less revenue from taxes even as an increasing proportion of total tax revenue is earmarked for social welfare programs. Pressures on government revenue will thus increase inexorably, with a shrinking percentage of the budget going to "discretionary" expenses (ie, non-entitlements) such as defense spending in the long term.

In addition to the dire fiscal situation, labor is increasingly becoming a challenge for Japan's defense planners, especially given the increasing competition with the private sector for young Japanese workers. It goes without saying that Japanese companies need younger workers to replace retirees. As the old grow older, they will need to be cared for, and the increasing number of elder care facilities will also require more workers. The result: fewer workers to fill positions, but for less take-home pay due to increasing taxes being levied for social welfare programs. In 2002, the Ministry of Economy, Trade, and Industry predicted that the working-age population will drop 30.3% to 47 million workers between 2000 and 2050, which is 10 million fewer than the 15-64 working-age population predicted by the UN.[1329] (In comparison, the number of retirees was projected to grow by 25% to almost 38 million through 2050.) As an initial harbinger of Japan's future employment woes, Japanese schools are already experiencing lower enrollment. In the 2005 academic year, for example, 160 private universities—30% of the nationwide total—failed to meet their student recruiting targets.[1330] Public schools are experiencing a similar contraction in student populations, and those in rural regions are having to consolidate or close.

Indeed, signs have begun to emerge that suggest the Japanese government itself is directly affected by the demographic challenges, as only 26,268 young high school and college graduates applied to take the standardized test to qualify for work with the

Japanese government in 2006, a drop of 15.9% from the year before and its lowest point in Japan's modern history. The highest number of applications was recorded in 1996, when 45,254 people applied to take the examination in the midst of economic recession. The number of applicants in 2006 was lower even than in bubble-era 1989, when the number of applicants was 27,243, the second lowest number of applicants in modern history.[1331] But at the height of the bubble economy, many talented young Japanese then wanted to work for large Japanese corporations, not the government. The increasing number of jobs available in the private sector of a muddling Japanese economy cannot fully explain the drop in applications. With a smaller pool of labor available to both the government and the private sector, the number of young applicants to all job vacancies will surely continue to decline.

What is true for the civilian public sector is true for Japan's uniformed armed services. Simply stated, there will be fewer young Japanese willing and able to serve. While Japan's total uniformed forces number under 300,000 personnel, a relatively small number compared to the overall public sector, the Self-Defense Forces will compete for the dwindling number of civic-minded young Japanese with other public safety-oriented occupations such as local police forces, first responders, fire fighters, medical personnel, and the Japan Coast Guard. Mindful of the demographic crisis since the early 1990s, the Self-Defense Forces have taken steps to focus its efforts in attracting young talent as it increasingly targets college students and young women. It has also highlighted new missions for the 21st century, in particular domestic and international response to natural disasters and Peace Keeping Operations under UN auspices. And the SDF has also relied on cutesy mascots to broaden its appeal to young children in an attempt to influence their future career decisions. While potentially effective, these efforts might also have the adverse consequence of softening a warrior spirit, which is ultimately the prerequisite for any fighting force.

Recruiting: Finding the Men–and Women–to Serve

While rarely an easy task in any democratic country with a volunteer defense force, recruiting for the armed services has at times been especially tough in post-war Japan. Very few young graduates wanted to serve in the Self Defense Forces, which was apparent in the chronic shortage of personnel in each of the services during the Cold War. Toshiyuki Shikata, the former commander of the GSDF's Northern Army in Hokkaido, recalled that during his first tour in Hokkaido in the late 1960s—when Japan's economy really began to take off—he had to walk the streets "day and night" trying to recruit personnel for his units rather than train "because the SDF…faced difficulties in recruiting." Competition with the private sector for personnel intensified in the 1970s as the economy continued to expand, Shikata noted.[1332] Taosa Ochiai, a recruiter posted to Okinawa after it reverted to Japanese home rule in 1972, recalled being met by 200 protestors with signs reading "Destroy the recruiting office" and simply "no SDF," and the door to his office was sealed shut with concrete. Taosa, who retired from the MSDF after attaining flag rank, said: "It was just impossible to recruit in that environment."[1333] While this was due in part to Okinawa's wartime experiences, recruiters in other areas faced extremely difficult recruiting environments as well, especially because Japan's rapidly growing economy through the 1980s provided potential recruits with significant opportunities in the civilian world.

Service with Japan's Defense Agency, both uniformed and civilian, was never popular in post-WWII Japan in comparison to careers in other government ministries such as the Ministry of Finance or Ministry of Foreign Affairs, or to careers in large companies. Bureaucratically, the Defense Agency offered ambitious young Japanese few opportunities for political or bureaucratic clout later in their stovepiped careers. And with U.S. forces stationed in Japan and in the region, there was little perceived need for the Self-Defense Forces. Shikata early in his career felt he was looked upon as a "thief of taxpayers' money." More prosaically, life in the SDF was not easy: post-war recruiters often lamented younger generations' increasing aversion to anything involving the so-called "3 Ks" – *kiken*, *kitanai*, or *kitsui* – which translates into English as the 3 Ds, "dangerous," "dirty," or "difficult."

Thus, the Self Defense Forces consistently fell short in filling their ranks each year, with GSDF units often falling more than 10% below authorized strength on a consistent basis. As the GSDF Chief of Staff Yuji Fujinawa noted in a 1997 interview with *Gunji Kenkyu*, a "low personnel recruitment rate has been a long-standing issue for the GSDF." The ASDF and MSDF, with smaller authorized force levels, often fell between 5-10% below authorized strength each year. Recruitment in general was projected to get worse, according to Fujinawa, as "around 2011, the 18-year-old population will be about 60 percent of that population in 1992."[1334] The following year, Defense Agency Director-General Kyuma declared in 1998 that the "decline in the number of children is a serious problem for the SDF."[1335]

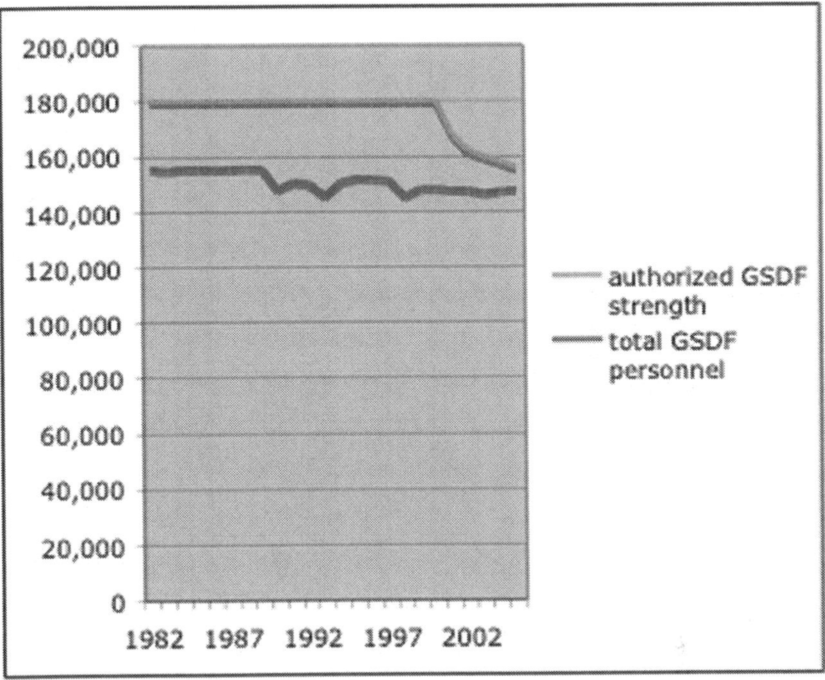

Personnel actually serving in the GSDF – Japan's largest defense force by personnel strength – has consistently remained below its authorized strength of 180,000 personnel. In response to this, and as each of the forces faces a decreasing population of youth in Japan, the GSDF increased the number of reserve personnel in the early 2000s and reduced its number of full-time service members to 155,000 (Source: Bōei Handobukku, 2007).

Indeed, the Defense Agency began to highlight the demographic crisis in its annual *Defense White Paper* (*Bōei Hakusho*) in the mid-1990s. The Defense Agency noted that 1994 marked the peak in the number of eligible male recruits who were 18 years old and high school graduates, with 900,000 eligible for service in the SDF that year. The *White Papers* projected the total number of 18-year-old males to decline to under 700,000 by 2008, while the total number males aged 18-26 was projected to decline by one-third from a peak of nine million in 1994 to six million in 2008. The number is projected to continue to fall well below 6 million thereafter, a dramatic fall from the early 1990s peak. Similarly, the total number of 18 year-olds was projected to fall below 600,000 by the early 2010s.

At the same time, the larger numbers of baby boomers serving in the SDF were approaching retirement. The number of retiring uniformed service personnel in 2001 reached its highest level in over ten years, according to the *2003 Defense White Paper*, and it was projected to increase further as the baby-boomer generation neared retirement age. "We are in the midst of a time when a majority of SDF personnel are reaching retirement age and are leaving," it declared bluntly.[1336] And according to the defense weekly *Asagumo*, by 2007 over 60% of GSDF company grade officers—lieutenants and captains—were approaching the mandatory retirement age of 52. Reporting this, *Asagumo* contrasted the situation in the GSDF with that in the U.S. and British militaries, in which a large majority of company grade officers in those countries were in their 20s. Moreover, a majority of officers over 45 in the SDF were in the lowest rated "C" category, meaning their physical activity was limited compared with those in the "A" and "B" categories.[1337] Thus, they were less ready to deploy than their physically healthy colleagues. And because Japan's private sector was also increasing efforts to replace the same rapidly aging workforce, the SDF projected increasing competition to recruit younger workers to take the place of the large number of retirees. *Asagumo* noted in the summer of 2007: "As the baby-boomer generation retires in large numbers and companies increase their [young] employee ranks…in the medium- and long-term the recruitment environment is expected to become even tougher."[1338]

According to recruiters, gone are the days of scouring downtown shopping districts, asking young kids whether they would like to join the SDF. "That's the old way," Major Kidoguchi was quoted as saying in the monthly *Securitarian*. "We don't use that method."[1339] The SDF in the late 1990s began to target more educated and career-minded young recruits through targeted ad campaigns and outreach programs. But this required improvements in the SDF image as well as the environment in which young SDF personnel live. Improving the "brand" of the SDF became a significant theme among recruiters and SDF image-makers. When asked about the declining birthrate in Japan, then-GSDF Chief of Staff Fujinawa, for example, highlighted the need to improve the GSDF's image in the 1997 interview: "[S]ecuring and developing good-quality personnel on a long-term and stable basis will require that we convert the GSDF into an attractive organization permeated by the sentiment best expressed in phrases such as, 'We think the GSDF is worthy of our presence! We would like to join!'" In addition to highlighting the need for innovative recruitment programs, Fujinawa also noted the need to improve management and pay systems, housing and working conditions to retain skilled SDF personnel.[1340] All three Self Defense Forces and the Defense Agency (later, the Ministry of Defense) focused more intently on improving their respective images in the 1990s and into the 2000s, and these efforts were tied directly to recruitment efforts.

In the late 1990s, SDF personnel began to experiment with new media to emphasize the positive aspects of service, portraying the SDF as a first responder during natural disasters and a major provider of humanitarian assistance abroad. The services also began to openly target school-age kids for recruitment through outreach programs and by inviting students on various "tours" of SDF bases. The SDF actively expanded opportunities for young women to serve and incorporated positive images of women serving in the SDF in various ad campaigns. Finally, the GSDF, which has historically suffered the most from yearly personnel shortages, implemented a new reserve system allowing civilians to serve in the GSDF part-time, thereby expanding the pool of interested but otherwise busy SDF candidates.

Getting in: the PLOs and PCOs

In the post-war era, the Defense Agency recruited new personnel for the Self Defense Forces using a network of uniformed recruiters at SDF Prefectural Liaison Offices (*jieitai chihō renrakubu*—often called "*chiren*"). With 50 main offices nationwide—four in Hokkaido Prefecture and one in each of the remaining 46 Prefectures—the offices are responsible for recruiting candidates for active and reserve duty in the Ground, Air, and Maritime Self Defense Forces. The PLOs also recruited students for the National Defense University (*bōei daigakko*), as well as professionals such as doctors and nurses.

Reflecting the need for improved and consistent liaison relationships with local governments following the 1995 Kobe earthquake, in the summer of 2006 the PLOs were reorganized into "SDF Prefectural Cooperation Offices" (*jieitai chihō kyoryoku honbu*—often termed "c*hihon*" or PCOs in English). Instead of focusing strictly on recruiting, the PCOs were charged with comprehensively engaging with local communities on issues ranging from recruiting and job placement services for discharged SDF personnel, to natural disaster response preparation and other efforts in coordination with local authorities to "protect Japanese nationals," and to manage local public relations more systematically.[1341] Before they were upgraded, the Defense Agency called the Prefectural Liaison Offices the "bridge between society and the Self Defense Forces," a statement that took on even greater meaning after the upgrade to PCO status.[1342] Building liaison relationships with local communities went hand-in-hand with recruitment efforts, as the PCOs developed a wider network of influencers who could suggest the SDF as a possible career choice to younger area residents. The PCOs also began to provide greater job-placement services, another role that was growing in importance as more SDF personnel were retiring or nearing retirement.

As in the U.S. armed services, Japanese can choose to serve on a two or three year contract and then be released to civilian life—with a further option to serve in a reserve component—or they can choose to make uniformed service a career, retiring by the early- or mid-50s depending on rank. New recruits with a middle school education join as a Private, and those with a high-school education join as Private Second Class. While many new recruits choose to serve as privates in a typical SDF occupation, others join as Sergeant Candidates or attend nursing school as members of the SDF, and upon graduation with some additional training become either a sergeant or staff sergeant. Still others, with a college education, can attend one of three Officer Candidate Schools.

The contract system, called *ninkisei* or "term system," is the most popular option among enlistees, while the career track is called *hininkisei* or "non-term system." This track is also sometimes referred to as the *jakunen teinensei* or "system of retirement at a young age," which reflects the idea that the retirement age in the uniformed services is lower than retirement ages in the civilian world due to the physically demanding nature of the job.[1343] As SDF retirees are not entitled to full government retirement benefits until the age of 60, however, they must usually work a few additional years until they are eligible to receive full retirement benefits, but according to the 2003 *Defense White Paper* recent SDF retirees faced a "difficult employment situation" and "it is necessary to strive for complete policies that support employment."[1344] Hence the increasing importance of the *chihon* PCO in assisting the large wave of baby-boomer retirees find jobs.

Enhancing the Image of the SDF

Self Defense Forces image-makers began to broaden efforts to advertise a more modern SDF image in the late 1990s and early 2000s via new media platforms. One early effort employed large video billboards in major cities to advertise SDF missions. Some local SDF PLOs increasingly sponsored video billboard ads in a number of city shopping districts in the late 1990s to complement traditional advertising efforts via posters, ads in newspapers and magazines, and on television and radio. One early basic theme was "local boy doing good," in which one or two recent recruits from the region were shown in crisp SDF uniforms with proud smiles on their faces. The videos focused on the lives of local recruits in the SDF.

These local initiatives quickly evolved into more organized efforts to highlight wider roles of the services. In 2002 the GSDF public relations department ran an ad on the 13-meter color screen in Tokyo's Shinjuku shopping area featuring "combat training," an airborne brigade parachuting from a transport, heliborne operations of a CH-47, and troops participating in PKO in Cambodia and East Timor. The billboard ad ran for a week in December and was billed by the defense weekly *Asagumo* as "the first trial of its kind to advertise the GSDF in ways other than classified ads."[1345] This was followed six months later by a broader ad campaign in five major cities: in May 2003, the SDF sponsored video PR campaigns featuring training and PKO in five major cities including Fukuoka and Sapporo, for example.[1346]

While recruiters had traditionally employed VHS videos to highlight life in the SDF—and videos of SDF training exercises were sold in bookstores—video tapes were an aging technology with limited interactivity. Recruiters who relied on VHS videos made specifically for recruitment purposes found them unwieldy during presentations to high school and other students, and they complained that it took too much time to fast-forward or rewind to specific video segments highlighting particular jobs in the SDF. Pausing on particular scenes caused the image to become fuzzy and distorted. Recruiters were complaining that the technology was increasingly *dasai*—uncool in Japanese slang—and kids quickly grew bored with the presentation. Thus in 2001 and in 2002 the SDF developed interactive DVDs featuring vignettes at different military occupation schools and interviews with young recruits. Instead of having to play the entire video or waste valuable time fast-forwarding to particular segments, recruiters could access any section quickly through a menu list of contents based on audience interest.

Together with this effort, the SDF turned to digital methods to project a more modern image. The SDF digitalized images of major military "new weapons" (*shinheiki*) such as the T-90 tank, the *Kongo* destroyer, and F-15s, making them appear almost "manga-like" in the words of *Asagumo*, referring to the popular comic books popular among young Japanese. Also digitized were images of SDF personnel in various uniforms such as combat uniforms and helmets, pilot's suits, and formal uniforms. "Mamoru-kun" and "Mirai-chan"—Mr. Defense and Miss Future as they were called—were animated and could perform a variety of actions such as saluting and giving a thumbs-up sign. The SDF even developed a catchphrase similar to the "Be all you can be" slogan of the US Army: the SDF's slogan at this time was "Realize your capabilities" (*jibunrashisa wo jitsugen suru*). Recruitment headquarters personnel in Tokyo distributed the digitized images to local PLOs for use on their individual web sites and on CD-ROMs, and they were used in SDF calendars, posters, and for animated commercial spots.[1347]

Although the digitized characters were described as "*manga*-like," they nevertheless represented a more realistic version of the SDF mission than in the past. Previously conceived *manga* characters were more child-like as the SDF had attempted to project a child-friendly image using actual cartoon characters. This was in part due to the overwhelming popularity of *manga* comic books and cartoons among very young readers but also an effort to influence potential recruits at ever-earlier ages. One character, "Prince Pickles," first appeared in the late 1980s and is still used into the early 2000s. The Defense Agency contracted with graphic artist Taro Tomonaga to develop the characters for public relations purposes in 1988 and began selling character products in 1992.[1348] A boy with big cheeks and large saucer eyes, Prince Pickles is from "Paprika Kingdom" and is now on an exchange program to learn about the SDF, according to his bio. He is often seen riding around GSDF equipment, such as a rather undersized cartoon tank or bulldozer. He has two friends similarly exploring the SDF: Mr. Paprika, a pilot in the ASDF, who is often shown flying around in a small jet plane, and "Parsley-chan" or Miss Parsley (from the neighboring "Broccoli Kingdom) is often depicted in a sailor's outfit representing the MSDF. She happened to be the girlfriend of Prince Pickles. The Defense Agency Web site even offered several comic books featuring Prince Pickles, including "Prince Pickles's SDF Diary." The Ministry of Defense features the characters during family day at its Tokyo headquarters and as trinkets such as charms for cell phone straps, and they feature in the MoD's "kids' site" as well.[1349] The services have adopted their own characters, with the GSDF's "Mr. Takuma" and "Miss Yu" having their own Twitter feeds.[1350]

While cutesy, the characters are effective tools to attract the attention of young children. The SDF headquarters in Ichigaya, Tokyo, for example sponsors "Prince Pickles Tours" every summer for children in grade and middle schools. While the Defense Ministry advertises this as a singular event, the 1999 tour was held alongside 19 other government offices during the "Kids' Kasumigaseki Tour Day."[1351] The SDF has sponsored Prince Pickles Tours fairly regularly ever since then.

Highlighting a growing emphasis on recruiting women, the Defense Ministry also sponsors overnight "Miss Parsley Tour" for women in their early 20s to tour several bases, ride a helicopter, and observe "Ranger" training in late July each year (discussed below). Not to be outdone, local *chihon* offices sometimes create their own mascots. In one example, the PCO in Hokkaido came up with its own mascots in 2003: "Bikki," a deer, representing the GSDF; "Hikki," an owl, represents the ASDF; and "Rokki," a squirrel, represents the MSDF. They were designed by one of the PCO's own officers.[1352]

According government-sponsored population surveys, posters remain one of the SDF's most visible means of advertising in the 1990s and early 2000s. Images used in posters and other ads in major urban centers generally feature close-ups of SDF members such as young pilots or smart-looking uniformed men and women with bright smiles on their faces. While posters sometimes included static images of military equipment in the background or the image of a stoic-faced young recruit, these are generally not the focus of ad campaigns. The ad campaign in the summer of 2000, for example, featured two pilots—a male and a female—clasping hands with T-90 tanks and F-15s in the background. Clearly focusing on the smiling pilots, the catchphrase "Big Stage: Your World is Here in the New Century" (*Big Stage: Shinseki, Kimi no Seikai wa Koko ni Aru*) was written in large letters beneath them. Posters for this campaign were hung in major cities including in train stations and subway cars and a 15-second billboard video featuring several prideful-looking SDF personnel was displayed in Shibuya, Tokyo for several weeks in July that year.[1353] The Ministry of Defense sometimes employs actors and pop stars to advertise the SDF, as well. One campaign that received significant attention featured 15 members of the female pop star group "Morning Musume" in August 2003 as part of a late-summer recruitment campaign. As part of this campaign, 130,000 recruiting posters featuring the uber-happy young girls proclaiming "Doing one's best feels good" in Japanese and "GO! GO! PEACE!" in English were hung up throughout Japan.[1354] Unlike other recruiting posters featuring *tarento* or entertainers, however, the group was not photographed in SDF uniforms.[1355]

Indeed, the 2003 and 2006 Cabinet Office "Opinion Survey Concerning Self Defense Force and Security Issues," which is conducted every three years, suggest video billboards attracted relatively little attention compared with traditional advertising media. The surveys, taken after the billboards' increasingly widespread use, found that only 1.4% of respondents had seen the SDF advertisements on electronic billboards in 2003 and 2.6% had noticed the electronic billboard ads by 2006. (The question did not appear in the 2000 survey because the SDF had not made a concerted effort to use that medium before then.) In contrast, much higher percentages of respondents had seen SDF advertisements via traditional static media with nearly 70% identifying SDF posters as a primary SDF advertising source, 32% noting signboards and 25% pointing to public notice boards as primary advertising sources. The 2006 survey saw big jumps in other traditional media as well, with 20% of respondents having read newspaper ads compared to 12% in 2003, and 13% having seen SDF ads on television, twice the number (6%) in 2003. The jump most likely pointed to an increased focus on advertising through those media as well.

Outreach Programs Targeting Students

While the SDF continue to employ passive advertisement campaigns, the Forces at the same time have increasingly and actively targeted college-aged young adults in their recruitment efforts since the late 1990s. Japan's uniformed services, like those in the United States and other advanced militaries, increasingly rely on highly technical systems to perform the job of defending the country. These systems, in turn, require a highly literate and intelligent workforce to operate them. The SDF has therefore tried to recruit educated youth who can more readily handle the demands of a technologically advanced military force. The increasing engagement has included sending uniformed officers to conduct outreach activities at universities, working with SDF-friendly university professors to set up tours of local bases, and the general promotion of short tours of SDF bases for college-age young adults.

As part of their combined public relations and recruitment efforts, the services in coordination with recruiters in the area established outreach programs with eight universities in the Tokyo region beginning in 2000, including with the prestigious Keio and Waseda Universities. This built on exchanges already established locally, with Keio's economics department sponsoring an exchange with Yokosuka since 1997, and Shizuoka Prefectural University's international relations department having established a yearly exchange with Fuji base personnel since 1993.[1356] These activities were also highlighted in SDF journals, with the Keio-MSDF exchange program profiled in the DA's *Securitarian* each year since 2001, for example. According to the 2005 profile, for example, over 50 students attending lectures at Atsugi Naval Base listened to lectures on Japan's security environment and participated in round-table discussions with young MSDF officers, toured aircraft, and finally were treated to a banquet before returning to school.[1357] The SDF during this time also grew increasingly active in sending uniformed personnel to give lectures at local colleges and universities. Outreach efforts took place outside of the Tokyo region as well: SDF officers participated in lectures on security issues at 22 universities in Aichi Prefecture in 2001, which *Asagumo* billed as the "first trial" lecture series "of its kind in Japan." Some of the lectures were also open to the public. The programs gradually expanded into other major metropolitan areas, with SDF officers participating in security seminars at universities in Kobe and Osaka in 2002. The seminars at Kobe University were the first in its 100-year history, according to *Kobe Shimbun.*[1358]

The SDF also invites college and graduate students to experience life in the Self Defense Forces, sponsoring "tours" coinciding with spring and summer holidays. The first five-day August "summer tour" was held in 1990 and includes rides in a CH-47, a P-3C, a C-1 transport, a destroyer, observation of "Ranger" training, bivouacking, and tours of several SDF bases. The students are treated as if they were in the SDF, wearing uniforms, walking in formation, and learning to salute and make their beds according to regulation. A separate two-day "Spring Tour" began in 2002 and is a truncated version of the summer tour. And the tours are not unpopular: over 600 students participated in the 2005 summer tour, for example.[1359]

Recruiters in the early 2000s increasingly and openly targeted students at Japanese high schools as well. SDF officials began visiting high schools to talk with new students in Aichi Prefecture in 2000, for example, in coordination with principals of each high school in the prefecture. In the summer of 2001, recruiters held a round-table discussion with high school principles in the prefecture to discuss strengthening efforts, emphasizing that the SDF mission included responding to natural disasters and the personal development of new recruits.[1360] This message was surely a winning formula for the recruiters in the region, as Aichi Prefecture is located immediately northeast of Kobe, which had experienced a major earthquake in 1995. Similarly, the PLO in Shizuoka Prefecture began to send uniformed speakers to talk with students at middle schools and high schools in January 2001 – a lecture by a uniformed SDF officer at a Shizuoka public middle school that year was reportedly the first of its kind in the country.[1361] Recruiters in Saga Prefecture in late 2001 moved their central office to a building 150 meters away from the main Saga train station, through which many high-school and middle-school kids commuted to and from school each day. "I'd like to create a fun environment to draw in students," one of the recruiters was quoted as saying after the opening.[1362] And in the Tokyo region, citing a "subpar" performance in recruiting Tokyo high-schoolers into the SDF, the Tokyo PLO in August 2003 expanded its collaboration with local government organizations and schools in the metropolitan area, with a stated purpose of establishing "a strong organizational recruitment system in response to the low-birth-rate times."[1363]

Due to these renewed efforts at the local level, the Defense Agency became embroiled in some controversy in April 2003 when close collaboration between PLO recruiters and many local government authorities reportedly involved the provision of personal information beyond what was permitted by law. Indeed, almost 900 cities, towns, and villages freely provided Defense Agency officials with information on young school-age residents, including name, address, date of birth, and gender for recruitment purposes, and over 300 municipalities supplied further information such as health, family situation, and special technical qualifications of young potential recruits. The information was used primarily to target households for direct mailing campaigns, the DA claimed, and was conducted based on the Basic Resident Register Law. While the practice dated in some cases to the 1960s, it came to light shortly after Ishikawa Prefecture and the local PLO standardized guidelines in November 2000 on the provision of further information such as the health condition and technical qualifications of potential recruits.[1364]

The Defense Agency defended its recruiting operations and indicated it would continue to collect the name, address, date of birth, and gender of potential recruits, which it asserted is allowed under the Basic Resident Register Law. Indeed, the head of the DA at the time, Shigeru Ishiba, strongly supported close relations with local governments, saying: "We must actively get the word out there by asking local public bodies to cooperate in our recruiting. Otherwise we won't be able to fill our positions."[1365] The controversy died shortly thereafter with the DA's promise to use only information that is available under the Basic Resident Register Law, specifically: name, address, date of birth, and gender.

Not only did the Defense Agency continue to elicit the assistance of local authorities for recruitment purposes, they continued to expand their efforts to recruit high school students. The Defense Agency in 2003 established a program allowing high schoolers to experience life in the SDF with rides on military equipment, unit training sessions, and invitations to view firearms exercises on short visits to SDF bases, much like the programs targeting their older college-age brothers and sisters.[1366] And with SDF units serving in Iraq and elsewhere in the world, the SDF began an entirely new video-phone interview program for select high school and middle school students. Starting in February 2006, the Ministry of Defense allowed younger students to attend satellite video conferences with SDF personnel in the field, during which the students can ask questions such as "how have the Iraqis reacted to the SDF's presence?" According to the

Defense Agency-affiliated *Securitarian*, the 30 students at this first session heard "raw information from Iraq" that even "news agencies did not know."[1367] Two months later, the Ministry of Defense sponsored a similar satellite video teleconference for Tottori prefectural junior high school students with SDF units in the Golan Heights, where the SDF had just marked its tenth year of participation in the multinational UN Disengagement Observation Force (UNDOF).[1368] Similar video teleconferences between students and various units continued regularly after these successful events. While not recruitment events per se, the video teleconferences certainly help to improve the SDF's image among that key youth demographic and ultimately might influence some to choose to serve in the SDF in later years.

The increased engagement efforts appeared to meet with some success. The percentage of university and junior college graduates who joined the Self Defense Forces rose from 1% in 1994 to 12% by 2004 among male recruits, and from 6% to 20% among female recruits.[1369] The SDF still continued to face difficulties in filling all of its billets, however.

The Ministry of Defense and the SDF will certainly increase its emphasis on targeting teenage and college-age students in its PR efforts given the increasingly dire implications of Japan's demographics. In the summer of 2007, the LDP National Defense Division advocated increased efforts to improve the SDF's "brand image" as the SDF "is competing with companies and other public organizations to recruit younger generations" due to the "decreasing birthrate and increasing educational experience" of young Japanese. The committee called on the SDF to "strengthen cooperation with universities" and other schools more uniformly as "cooperation with high schools and universities varies by location." Similarly, "depending on location, there is a significant difference in the amount of cooperation on the part of local organizations," and as the SDF "relies on" these local organizations for information on possible recruits, the SDF "should try to obtain the needed cooperation" of "all local organizations" to assist in recruitment efforts. Ultimately, the panel declared that recruitment efforts should be part of a wider campaign to engage the Japanese public as the job of the SDF "differs from that of other public officials...[P]olicies that deepen the people's understanding concerning the honorable duties of SDF personnel are important."[1370] Thus, Japanese recruiters will surely engage Japanese society more visibly in the years to come as competition with other Japanese companies and organizations intensifies.

Recruiting Young Women to Serve

Japanese women have slowly gained acceptance in performing an increasing variety of SDF roles since the late 1960s. The GSDF first allowed women to serve in non-health-related professions from 1967, when seven females entered the GSDF that year in non-health-related roles.[1371] The ASDF and MSDF followed seven years later, allowing women to serve in non-health-related professions beginning from 1974.[1372] Paralleling Japanese government efforts to stem the decline in birthrates in the early 1990s, the Defense Agency began in 1993 to make a concerted effort to attract women into both uniformed and civilian positions. The SDF that year opened all professions to women. The Defense Agency also began a program to allow young civilian women to experience life in the armed services. Called the "Parsley-chan Tour," the tour allows young women in college and recent graduates to spend a few days climbing ropes and riding in tanks and CH-47 transportation helicopters, all the while wearing Self Defense Forces battle-dress uniforms (*meisaifuku*) and helmets.

Japanese women broke multiple gender barriers in the Self-Defense Forces in the late 1990s and 2000s. The first female pilots earned their wings in both the MSDF and ASDF in 1997. The first female helicopter pilot began flying from MSDF ships that year, necessitating the installation of "special accommodations" on ships to prepare for additional "Waves," the MSDF's promotional term for its female pilot cadre.[1373] And First Lieutenant Kazue Kashiji became the ASDF's first female pilot of a fixed-wing aircraft, while thirteen other females were in training to become pilots in the ASDF.[1374] (Later, in 2003, Kashiji became the ASDF's first female pilot instructor.[1375]) The first female to attain flag rank, Hikaru Saeki, was promoted to rear admiral in 2001.[1376] In March 2002, Prime Minister Koizumi specifically mentioned the 32 female graduates of the National Defense Academy during his commencement speech, adding that the total number of female National Defense Academy graduates reached 200 that year.[1377] Moreover, seven women participated in the 680-personnel-strong Peacekeeping Operation mission sent to East Timor in 2002, the first time females were involved in a PKO mission.[1378] And in 2002 as well, the Defense Agency directed that female SDF personnel be referred to as "women Self Defense Force member," instead of the rather belittling label "lady Self-Defense Force member."[1379] The latter reference was similar to the "OL" or "Office Lady" title often heard in Japanese companies, a title that implicitly imparted a lower, menial status on female office workers compared to their male counterparts.

Indeed, recruitment campaigns have increasingly shown women in realistic SDF roles, often alongside or even in the lead of their male counterparts. The Big Stage campaign in the summer of 2000 featured a female pilot standing alongside her male counterpart, for example, and in the summer of 2001 the Aichi PLO sponsored a video billboard commercial spot showing three

SDF personnel standing in formation, with a uniformed female in the lead.[1380] In late 2001 a young actress served as a model for posters to recruit JROTC-type student-applicants for the SDF school system. The 15-year-old Suenaga was photographed for posters and a calendar in various uniforms including a battle-dress uniform and LBEs and a pilot suit, her hair up in a tight bun as if she were actually a student studying to become an SDF officer.[1381] Unlike typical pin-up girls in the tabloids, Suenaga was completely clothed and did not pose provocatively. Even the "Morning Musume" ad campaign two years later avoided any provocative poses, although the girls were not featured in specific SDF roles most likely because they were already well known as a pop-star group.

Of course, some local PCOs were not above using their young female SDF personnel to target young men in their recruitment efforts. In 2007, for example, the Tochigi PCO highlighted the fact that it sent its young female SDF personnel to distribute pamphlets outside train stations specifically targeting young males.[1382] But in general, the SDF has undertaken to project an integrated role of women serving in the defense forces.

In an additional sign that the Defense Agency and now the Defense Ministry takes SDF servicewomen seriously, formal societies have been established to support women in each branch. The "Japan Women's Air Society" (*nihon josei koku kyokai*) gives awards to women pilots in each branch of the SDF, as well as to women pilots in other government agencies. While the first recipients of the award—called the "Award to Promote Women Who Love the Sky"—in 1997 were female pilots in the Air Self Defense Force, the society awarded four female helicopter pilots in the GSDF for the first time in 2003.[1383] And in 2001, the Defense Agency established the Office to Promote Gender Equality and Participation to promote opportunities for women to serve in the SDF and in the Defense Agency. The office in 2002 announced plans to increase the number of female SDF service members 10 percent to over 10,000 by 2007 and create more daycare facilities on SDF bases for service members, for example.[1384]

The effort proved successful: within five years, the SDF surpassed its goal of 10,000 females serving in the SDF. In 2006, 11,161 women were serving in the SDF, of which 9,735 were outside the health professions.[1385] While this number continues to grow, total female participation rates represent less than 5% of the total SDF population, indicating further opportunities for greater participation by women in the SDF.

The New Reserve System

If the SDF cannot recruit enough personnel to serve in the forces—and historically this has been the case—another option is to reduce the total number of slots to fill. The GSDF did this in the late 1990s, although in a way that appeared that the force continued to maintain total strength levels the same since the 1970s, on paper at least.

The revised 1995 National Defense Program Outline posed as a solution to the yearly shortfall in personnel the idea of allowing civilians to join a reserve component directly without having to serve a full-time stint first. The plan would shift personnel from one regiment to other short-manned units within a given division to create full-strength units. The remaining regiment would be manned with trained reservists. While the total number of GSDF personnel would remain the same—around 180,000 authorized billets—the number of full-time personnel gradually shrank by 10% or so with the remainder fielded by reserve personnel. Ultimately the new system created 15,000 reserve slots as part of the 180,000 billets in the GSDF.

The GSDF reserves were initially limited to those who had already completed two years or more of active service. Following recommendations in the 1995 NDPO, the first changes to the law were passed that would allow civilians to join the reserves directly. The new changes expanded the types of reserve service after 2001 to three: *yōbi jieikan, sokuō yōbijieikan,* and *yōbi jieikanhō*. The *yōbi jieikan* position, Japan's traditional reserve system in the post-war period, is similar to the U.S. "individual ready reserve" system, in which former active duty personnel are still eligible to be called up for duty in the armed forces during a set period of time. Once released from active duty, a former member of the SDF can choose to join the individual ready reserve system, during which time he or she has agreed to be called up as necessary. Unlike the U.S. IRR system, where individual ready reservists have no obligation to train unless they are activated, Japanese individual ready reservists train for a few days each year—in 2002, the first full year of the system, training amounted to five days a year. This system allows for at least some continuation of training and takes into account private employers' traditional post-war reluctance to allow their employees additional time off for reserve training. For each day of training, the individual ready reservist received ¥8,100. Each month, the reservist receives another ¥4,000 just for agreeing to serve in IRR status.

The *sokuō yōbijieikan* system—equivalent to the U.S. selected reserve system—gives the SDF a reservoir of civilians in a time of need who maintain their basic military readiness by drilling 30 days out of the year. The reservists are volunteers who formerly served full-time in the GSDF and would be the first to be called to duty should the need arise. By March 2003, shortly after the system was established, there were approximately 5,300 Japanese serving actively in the reserves.[1386] An individual can join the reserves between the ages of 18-34, while people with specialized skills such as an ability in foreign languages or a needed medical profession can join between the ages of 18-53 years of age.[1387] The reservist earns a base ¥16,000 a month and between ¥10,400 and ¥14,200 per day of active training. The reservist also receives ¥120,000 bonus for successfully serving a three-year term.[1388] And because companies were often reluctant to allow their employees significant time off to train in the reserves, the Japanese government, as part of the *sokuō yōbijieikan* ready reserve system, established a compensation system for companies to allow their employees to train during the allotted times: ¥42,700 a month or ¥512,400 a year, which amounts to over $5,000 for each reservist employee.

Until 2001 the SDF only allowed former full-time service members to join the reserve system, but the Diet passed a law that allowed civilians to join the SDF reserve system directly as a "Ready Reserve Candidate" or *yobi jieikanho.*[1389] By definition, the Reserve Candidate is still in training, so the SDF cannot call the candidate reservist to active duty for immediate service. However, once the candidate has served sufficient amount of time as a candidate reservist, he or she is eligible to serve as a *sokuō yōbijieikan* selected reservist and will have a legal obligation to serve on active duty if ordered. To qualify for either *sokuō yōbijieikan* selected reserve or *yōbi jieikan* ready reserve status, the candidate reservist must complete 50 days of SDF training within three years. With the expanded reserve service, the SDF began recruiting reserve personnel in the Tokyo area with the catchphrase "A New Way of Contributing to Society" in January 2002.[1390]

Those interested in joining the reserves directly, without serving several years of full-time duty in the SDF, can take the basic qualification exam in each of the Prefectures, while tests are offered in five locations across Japan for those with specialized skills.

There are also five locations across Japan where candidate reservists train: Hokkaido, Miyazaki Prefecture, Kanagawa Prefecture, Shiga Prefecture, and Nagasaki Prefecture. The candidate would receive ¥7,900 for each day of training at the outset of the program in 2002.[1391]

Short of significantly raising pay for uniformed service (a not-unheard-of proposition, with SDF servicemembers receiving ¥20,000 *a day* in Iraq), the forces will surely continue to struggle in attracting new recruits to fill their uniformed ranks. Perhaps because Japanese youth (as youth in other developed countries) remain disinterested in service that involves the "3 Ks", problems in recruiting also stem from increased competition with the private sector and other public entities. In fact, while over 91% of respondents had a positive impression of the SDF in the 2012 Cabinet-sponsored "Survey on the SDF and Defense Issues," only 6.6% of respondents said they would volunteer to serve in the SDF if Japan were "invaded by a foreign country." (Another 2.2% said they would undertake "guerilla-like resistance.")[1392] An invasion by a foreign force is perhaps the gravest immediate threat to a nation's sovereignty and indeed survival, such that it is surprising that only one in fifteen respondents would consider actually defending the country even in the direst of circumstances. While the survey question is academic—a true invasion would certainly elicit stronger feelings—it points to the difficulty Japanese recruiters face in gaining the interest of young Japanese men and women.

Post-war Japan has not attempted what other militaries have implemented when faced with recruiting difficulties. The U.S. Army, for example, allows non-U.S. citizens to serve in positions that do not require a security clearance, from band member to cavalry scout, helicopter mechanic to infantryman. Other U.S. services similarly allow non-U.S. citizens to serve. In return, non-U.S. citizens are granted expedited citizenship: while civilian applicants for US citizenship have to wait five years to become U.S. citizens, military service personnel wait only three years. The process was further expedited in July 2002 when President Bush signed Executive Order 329, granting expedited citizenship to noncitizen uniformed personnel who were serving in the Global War on Terror. The Department of Defense partnered with the Immigration and Naturalization Service to assist with the processing of uniformed members' citizenship applications, and the INS even created a dedicated office in Lincoln, Nebraska to handle the military applications. These efforts reduced the processing time from two years to six months. As many speak a language besides English, once naturalized, they are then eligible to apply for a security clearance and, if granted one, to employ their linguistic skills in more sensitive positions as well.[1393]

A Japanese version could conceivably focus on those non-Japanese citizens who already reside in Japan, and secondarily on descendents of the Japanese diaspora throughout Asia as was increasingly done in the 1990s by Japanese industry. Military service is one means to verify civic loyalties over time while also filling hard-to-recruit positions. (In fact, there is nothing to prevent a similar service-based immigration and naturalization system to help provide elder care in Japan.)

Ultimately, as the late-1990s UN study indicated, immigration is the only way to maintain or slow the decrease in population in those countries where the birthrate remains stubbornly below replacement levels.

EPILOGUE

Pyongyang on December 1, 2012, announced preparations for a launch of the *Kwangmyongsong-3*, a polar-orbiting earth observation satellite, by the middle of the month. While North Korean media did not expressly say so, the announcement was widely regarded as a way to mark the first year anniversary of the death of Kim Chong-il, who died on December 17, 2011. The launch attempt would be North Korea's second that year, having failed spectacularly with its previous launch in April.

Tokyo, Seoul, and Washington all asserted that any launch would be in violation of multiple Security Council resolutions calling for a halt to all missile tests. As a precaution, Tokyo deployed Aegis destroyers to monitor the launch and ordered PAC-3s to be deployed in Okinawa, since the launch was expected to be "southward." Invoking its now-operational missile defense capabilities, Tokyo issued standing orders to shoot down any missile that might target the archipelago.[1394] It also canceled bilateral talks scheduled to be held in Beijing in protest.

Japan also moved up a test of its new "J-Alert" nationwide warning system for disaster preparedness or armed attack. During the December 5 drill—originally scheduled to take place a week later—the central government sent two separate alerts to provincial and local authorities, which in turn broadcast alerts and sent e-mails to local residents. During an earlier September drill, 30 local governments experienced equipment problems that delayed or prevented the alert from being issued.[1395] The December 5 test was to verify that those deficiencies were fixed.

At just past noon on December 12, a proud yet stern female announcer appeared on Korean Central Television wearing a traditional pink Korean tunic. Her facial expression and festive outfit suggested a buoyant mood. "The launch of the satellite was a success!" she intoned.

Any operational satellite launched by North Korea—whether a broadcast satellite or an "earth observation satellite" that it failed to launch the previous April—would be very rudimentary and used purely for propaganda purposes. The missile, however, was a different story. If North Korea could launch an object into orbit, it could use the same missile technology to launch a warhead at intercontinental ranges.

The North's new leader, Kim Jong Un, was Kim Chong-il's youngest son. He was almost completely unknown both outside and inside North Korea, as not even a picture of the boy had been carried in any North Korean media until he began to appear at his father's side in 2010 to commemorate the 65th anniversary of the ruling WPK. Only a month earlier, the millennial Kim had been promoted to general and named vice-chairman of the Central Military Commission.[1396] He subsequently appeared with his father during high-level military delegation visits and inspection tours in the country.[1397]

While his age was not known, Kim Jong Un was widely thought to have been in his late 20s when he took over the reins of power after the older Kim died in late 2011. Throughout Asia, which venerates the wisdom that comes with age and experience, the younger Kim was a largely unknown figure in charge of an increasingly inscrutable system.

Kim Chong-il passed over his other sons for what were considered by North Korea watchers to be obvious reasons. His oldest son, Kim Jong Nam, had been caught ten years earlier entering Japan using a fake passport, apparently attempting to take his family to Tokyo Disneyland. His detention and subsequent deportation caused a major loss of face for the Kim family. Japanese media thereafter speculated that he was virtually unwelcome in North Korea, since he spent much of his time in China and Europe.

Kim's next son, Kim Jong-chol, who like his older brother had been educated at posh boarding schools in Europe, was thought to be considered too soft to succeed Kim Chong-il. In just one example, Japanese reporters for Fuji TV tracked him down in Europe in June 2006 attending Eric Clapton concerts with a young woman who was presumed to be his girlfriend. Demonstrating the length to which the Japanese politico-paparazzi went in trying to dig up details on the Kim family, the reporters speculated that a ring she wore indicated the two were engaged or even married. The two didn't respond to any questions, and their North Korean handlers quickly whisked them away. Japanese viewers could not help but note, however, the stark contrast between the doe-eyed middle son and his autocratic father.

The youngest son Kim Jong Un, however, spared little time in consolidating his power. Within a year, he appeared to be fully in control and confident in his new role. Unlike his father, who never spoke publicly, the younger Kim gave his first public speech mere months after Kim Chong-il's passing. To mark the "100th birth anniversary of great leader Comrade Kim Il-sung"—his grandfather—Kim Chong-un gave a lengthy address to thousands gathered in Kim Il Sung Square in Pyongyang on April 15, 2012. "By more fiercely raising the hot wind of Paektu training in the entire army, we should strongly prepare all people's army officers and men as full-blooded fighters who have mastered the ever-victorious strategies and tactics of Kim Il-sung and Kim Chong-il..." he declared in one of his more memorable phrases.[1398]

While North Korea had attempted to launch a satellite into orbit to mark the occasion, the launch failed. The mid-December 2012 launch, however, succeeded. In reaction to yet another denunciation by the UNSC, North Korea tested a third nuclear device just two months later, on February 12, 2013.

In response, South Korea announced that it had deployed sophisticated ship-to-shore cruise missiles on its Aegis destroyers that could reach any military site in North Korea. It also announced that it was planning to launch its own reconnaissance satellites to monitor the situation. Japan, for its part, had just launched two more reconnaissance satellites—one optical, one radar. Asia, it seemed, had entered into a missile and space race.

Meanwhile, China continued to increase its military budgets by double-digit percentages each year. The annual rate of growth was faster even than the rate of growth of China's economy. While Beijing announced a 10.7% increase in its defense budget to $115 billion, the U.S. DoD estimates of China's total actual military-related expenditures ranged between $135 billion and $215 billion—at least twice and up to four times Japan's $58 billion defense budget. China's defense policies remain opaque, even as Chinese commentators continue to discuss the "first island chain" and "second island chain" strategies. Moreover, China claims large areas of the South China and East China Seas, to include the Senkaku islands—which China calls the "Diaoyu Dao." China added the "nine-dash line" demarking most of the South China Sea as Chinese in maps and in all new PRC passports. China also published a White Paper calling the Senkaku/Diaoyu islands "inherent territory of China," and later it extended its air defense zone over much of the East China Sea.[1399] The claims have spurred a number of nationalist groups from both countries to attempt landings on the islands, even as both governments dispatch maritime law enforcement ships to patrol the area, increasing tensions there.

Domestically, Japan has continued to struggle. Even with the implementation of the "three arrows" of "Abe-nomics"—massive monetary and fiscal stimulus and structural reforms—at the start of Prime Minister Abe's second term in December 2012, the economy has experienced relatively tepid growth. Japan continues to run large budget deficits—some 43% in its proposed 2014 budget—while mandatory social welfare payments increase year after year in support of the country's rapidly aging demographic. While Tokyo hoped that a new round of tax increases in 2014 and 2015 will bring down deficits, a recession in Japan after a similar round of tax increases in the mid-1990s suggest similar results are just as likely in the mid-2010s. Japan looks as ever mired in low- to no-growth economic stagnation and long-term structural debt as its tax base continues to shrink.

Politically, Japanese leaders certainly do not help Japan's modern-era national security by visiting Yasukuni Shrine or announcing measures that seem to deny the full impact of Japanese policies in the run-up to and during World War II. The prime minister—whose grandfather Nobusuke Kishi served in the wartime cabinet—visited Yasukuni Shrine on December 26, 2013, and while he claimed to have visited "in a personal capacity," the visit caused an outcry among Asian countries. China denounced the visit as "beautifying aggression"—a phrase it has used for over a decade related to Yasukuni visits—while South Korea expressed "rage." More confoundingly to neighboring countries, the Abe administration in February 2014 announced its intention to "review" the Japanese government's 1993 acknowledgement of its World War II coerced use of local women as sex slaves—euphemistically called "comfort women"—for members of the Japanese Imperial Army. While government spokesman Yoshihide Suga did not provide any specifics about the future "review," it was widely suspected that the move was meant to appease conservatives in Japan who denied a government role in the coercion. The continued Yasukuni visits, coupled with periodic quasi-denials of Japan's role in the run-up to and during World War II, cause international headlines to focus on a supposed return of nationalism in Japan. However, while there is a degree of nationalism in Japan to be sure, the real story lies in the series of national security crises that have impacted Japan since the end of the Cold War, and Tokyo's attempts to deal with real defects in its national security and defense capabilities as a result.

Japan has successfully shifted from *hoppō jūshi* to an emphasis on the southwest and island defense—*nansei hōmen jūshi* and *ritō bōei* respectively. As part of this shift, Japan continues to increase the mobility of its military by developing lighter units capable of deploying jointly with air and maritime assets. It has also implemented a tiered missile defense system, a key strategic defense in an era of increasingly sophisticated missile systems that are potentially tipped with nuclear warheads. And Japan has strived to improve its intelligence structure and collection capabilities to better understand where and how threats evolve. In sum, Japan has developed the basic national security and defense capabilities to deal with the myriad of asymmetric threats in the near- and medium-term. Japan faces its greatest long-term threat, however, in its demographic decline. Left unresolved, in the very long term there will be few Japanese left to defend.

• • •

ACKNOWLEDGEMENTS

I would like to thank Steve M. for his mentorship over the years on all things related to Japanese media. I would also like to thank Michael M. for his help in editing and focusing my writing on a variety of topics related to Japan. I'd like to thank James Rexford and Peter Kachmar for their extensive reviews and feedback of this manuscript. Lastly, I'd like to thank my wife Alison for both her patience and support over the many, many early mornings and late evenings it took to complete this book. I can truly say that without her, this project would not have come to fruition.

ABOUT THE AUTHOR

Lee attended the Monterey Institute of International Studies, where he earned his Master's in International Policy Studies and a graduate certificate in Non-Proliferation Studies. Lee also attended Stanford University's Inter-University Center for Japanese Language Studies in Yokohama, Japan. Lee has lived, traveled, and worked throughout Asia, and currently lives and works in northern Virginia.

ENDNOTES

A note on endnotes – while I reference many articles found in Japanese dailies, I have elected to include only the English-language headlines for most of the Japanese dailies for the sake of brevity and because an English-language version is available for many of the articles below. I attempted to both transliterate and provide a translation for the titles of Japanese-language magazines, journal articles, and books cited below, although I did not include the macron over long (double) vowels as I have attempted in the main text.

1 "Two Japanese Hurt in Shootout With Crew of Pursued Ship," Kyodo, December 22, 2001, and "Suspected North Korean Ship Sinks, 15 Crew Members Missing," Kyodo, December 22, 2002.

2 "Cabinet's Crisis Management Center Left in Dark Over Spy Ship Incident," *Yomiuri Shimbun*, December 30, 2001.

3 "Cabinet's Crisis Management Center Left in Dark Over Spy Ship Incident," *Yomiuri Shimbun*, December 30, 2001.

4 "MSDF May be Mobilized To Capture Suspicious Ship: Nakatani," Kyodo, December 22, 2001.

5 "Discussions Underway on Strengthening Patrol of Waters Around Japan," *Asahi Shimbun*, December 28, 2001.

6 "Cabinet's Crisis Management Center Left in Dark Over Spy Ship Incident," *Yomiuri Shimbun*, December 30, 2001.

7 "Unidentified Ship Pretended To Be Chinese Fishing Boat," Kyodo, December 26, 2001.

8 Brooke, James, "Japan Says North Korea Boat In Sea Battle Was a Spy Ship," *New York Times*, October 5, 2002, www.nytimes.com/2002/10/05/world/japan-says-north-korea-boat-in-sea-battle-was-a-spy-ship.html.

9 "After Review of Late Response to 'Suspicious Vessel,' JCG To Equip With Helicopters for Special Security Teams," *Yomiuri Shimbun,* April 12, 2002, evening edition, p 23.

10 "Two Japanese Hurt in Shootout With Crew of Pursued Ship," Kyodo, December 22, 2001, and "Suspected North Korean Ship Sinks, 15 Crew Members Missing," Kyodo, December 22, 2002.

11 "Japanese Defense Experts Discuss Activity of Suspected Spy Ship," *Yomiuri Shimbun,* December 26, 2001.

12 "Officials Say Ship Fired Rocket-Propelled Grenades at Coast Guard Vessels," *Yomiuri Shimbun,* December 25, 2001.

13 "Unidentified Ship Used Soviet-Made Rockets," Kyodo, December 25, 2001.

14 "Officials Say Ship Fired Rocket-Propelled Grenades at Coast Guard Vessels," *Yomiuri Shimbun,* December 25, 2001.

15 "Suspected North Korean Ship Sinks, 15 Crew Members Missing," Kyodo, December 22, 2002.

16 "Two Bodies Believed To Be of Ship's Crew Recovered," Kyodo, December 23, 2001.

17 "Sunken Ship Resembles N. Korean Ship in 1998 Drug Case," Kyodo, December 23, 2001.

18 "Salvaged DPRK Spy Ship Found Disguised as Japanese-Chinese Fishing Boat," *Sankei Shimbun,* September 24, 2002.

19 "Electronic Marine Chart Made by Coast Guard Found in DPRK Spy Ship," *Asahi Shimbun,* October 22, 2002.

20 Brooke, James, "Japan Says North Korea Boat In Sea Battle Was a Spy Ship," *New York Times,* October 5, 2002, www.nytimes.com/2002/10/05/world/japan-says-north-korea-boat-in-sea-battle-was-a-spy-ship.html.

21 Joint Publication 1-02, *Dictionary of Military and Associated Terms,* November 8, 2010, p 21, www.dtic.mil/doctrine/new_pubs/jp1_02.pdf.

22 Joint Publication 3-04, *Combating Weapons of Mass Destruction,* June 10, 2009, p II-1, www.dtic.mil/doctrine/new_pubs/jp3_40.pdf.

23 Ina, Hisayoshi, "Post-Defense Guidelines: Nine Issues Japan Will Face," *Gaiko Forum,* December 1999, pp 80-91.

24 "*Tokushu: Anata no Jukyochi Erabi ha...,*" ("Special Feature: Your Choice for Residence is..."), *Mainichi Economisuto,* June 17, 2003, pp 95-99.

25 "*Kijun Chika, Tokyo-to Kubu de 15-nen buri Josho—Zenkoku Heikin 4.2% Geraku,*" ("Land Prices in Tokyo Wards Rise for First Time in 15 Years—Country Averages Drop of 4.2%"), *Nikkan Kogyo Shinbun,* September 21, 2005, p 1.

26 Armacost, Michael, "The Gulf War: Impact on Japan and US-Japan Relations," U.S. State Department Cable, Tokyo 04532, March 14, 1991, www.gwu.edu/~nsarchiv/NSAEBB/NSAEBB175/japan2-13.pdf.

27 Mansourov, Alexandre Y., "The Origins, Evolution, and Current Politics of the North Korean Nuclear Program," *The Nonproliferation Review,* Vol 2, No 3 (1995), pp 25-26, cns.miis.edu/pubs/npr/vol02/23/mansou23.pdf.

28 Wit, Joel S., Daniel B. Poneman, and Robert L. Gallucci, *Going Critical: The First North Korean Nuclear Crisis* (Washington DC: Brookings Institution Press, 2004), p 3.

29 IAEA, "Fact Sheet on DPRK Nuclear Safeguards," Media Advisory 2002/52, December 16, 2002.

30 Wit, Joel S., Daniel B. Poneman, and Robert L. Gallucci, *Going Critical: The First North Korean Nuclear Crisis* (Washington DC: Brookings Institution Press, 2004), pp 1-6, and Center for Nonproliferation Studies "North Korean Nuclear Developments: An Updated Chronology," cns.miis.edu/research/korea/nuc/chr4789.htm.

31 Poneman, Daniel B, "The History of the 1994 Agreed Framework," *Information Brief,* March 7, 2003, ffip.com/infobriefs030703.htm.

[32] "*Kitachosen he no Kaifu Sosai Shinsho,*" ("LDP President Kaifu's Signed Letter to North Korea"), *Nihon Keizai Shimbun,* October 5, 1990, p 2.

[33] Baker, James, "Dealing With the North Korean Problem: Impressions From My Asia Trip," November 18, 1991, www.gwu.edu/~nsarchiv/NSAEBB/NSAEBB175/japan2-14.pdf.

[34] Fialka, John, "CIA Says North Korea Appears Active in Biological, Nuclear Arms," *Wall Street Journal,* February 25, 1993, p A10.

[35] Center for Nonproliferation Studies, "North Korean Nuclear Developments: An Updated Chronology, 1993," cns.miis.edu/archive/country_north_korea/nuc/chr93.htm.

[36] "*Chosen Hanto Kincho de Yuji Jigen Rippo Kento, Ishihara Nobuo Mae Kanbofukuchokan in Kiku,*" ("Examination of Time-Limited Emergency Legislation During Korean Peninsula Crisis, Interview with Former Deputy Chief Cabinet Secretary Nobuo Ishihara"), *Asahi Shimbun,* September 17, 1996, p 2.

[37] S/Res/825 (1993), http://daccessdds.un.org/doc/UNDOC/GEN/N93/280/49/IMG/N9328049.pdf.

[38] Center for Nonproliferation Studies, "Chronology of North Korea's Missile Trade and Developments: 1980-1989," cns.miis.edu/research/korea/chr8089.htm, and Son Tae-kyu, "Uneasiness Over North Korean Scuds," *Hanguk Ilbo,* 4 October 1995, p 5.

[39] "Maritime Self-Defense Force Photographed North Koreans Ships Related to Missile Tests in Waters Near Noto on 29th Last Month," *Yomiuri Shimbun,* June 12, 1993, p 2.

[40] "*Kitachosen no Shisha Misairu, Higashi Engan Kara Hassha–Boeicho, Bunseki Kekka Happyo,*" ("North Korean Test Launch from Eastern Coast–Defense Agency Publishes Results of Analysis"), *Nihon Keizai Shimbun,* June 15, 1993, p 2.

[41] Ebata, Kensuke, *Joho to Kokka: Shushu, Bunseki, Hyoka no Otoshiana,* (Intelligence and the State: Pitfalls of Collection, Analysis, and Evaluation), (Tokyo: Kodansha, 2004), p 182.

42 "Defense Source Doubts U.S. Reports on Nodong Missiles," Kyodo, May 7, 1997.

43 Center for Defense Information, "Missile Defense," November 20, 2003, www.cdi.org; Taoka, Shunji, "Is The TMD System Useless Despite Japan's Contribution of Money and Technology?" *Aera*, October 11, 1993, pp 58-60.

44 "*Kakusareta Kitachosen Misairu Shito,*" ("Information on North Korea's Missile Test Firing Kept Secret"), *Mainichi Shimbun*, August 14, 1994, p 1.

45 "*Kitachosen Kaihatsu no Misairu 'Nodon-1go' Nihon ni Taisho Noryoku Nai,*" ("Japan Has no Ability To Respond to 'Nodong-1' Under Development by North Korea"), *Yomiuri Shimbun*, June 11, 1993, p 3.

46 "*Ishihara Nobuo Fukuchokan,*" ("Deputy Chief Cabinet Secretary Nobuo Ishihara, 'Shadow Prime Minister'"), *Tokyo Shimbun*, July 22, 1994, p 10.

47 "Administrative Deputy Chief Cabinet Secretary: 'Stage Managing' the Center of Power," *Ryukyu Shimpo*, November 23, 2002, p 6.

48 "Miyazawa, Others Comment on Reports of DPRK Missile Test," Kyodo, June 11, 1993.

49 "*Kitachosen no Shisha Misairu, Higashi Engan Kara Hassha--Boeicho, Bunseki Kekka Happyo,*" ("North Korean Test Launch from Eastern Coast–Defense Agency Publishes Results of Analysis"), *Nihon Keizai Shimbun*, June 15, 1993, p 2.

50 Uemura, Takeshi, "Pyongyang's Nuclear Threat Too Serious to Joke About," *Yomiuri Shimbun*, February 5, 2003.

51 Hughes, Christopher, "Sino-Japanese Relations and Ballistic Missile Defense," CSGR Working Paper No. 64/01, January 2001, p 30, www2.warwick.ac.uk/fac/soc/csgr/research/workingpapers/2001/wp6401.pdf/.

52 *ibid*, p 30.

53 "Intensifying Controversy Concerning TMD Inspired by the Launching of the Taepodong Missile," *Sentaku*, October 1998, pp 120-123.

54 LDP, "Period of President Kono's Leadership," www.jimin.jp/jimin/english/history/chap16.html.

55 "Government Carried Out Emergency Study for Korean Peninsula in 1993-1994," *Asahi Shimbun*, December 24, 1996.

56 "Government Carried Out Emergency Study for Korean Peninsula in 1993-1994," *Asahi Shimbun*, December 24, 1996.

57 "*Kitachosen no Kakukaihatsu Giwaku ni Taio, Gaimusho, Boeicho, Keisatsu de Joho Kaigi Shuinin de Seifu*," ("MOFA, DA, NPA Hold Intelligence Meetings as on North Korean Nuclear Suspicion Issue According to Lower House Diet Member"), *Mainichi Shimbun*, May 24, 1994, p 1.

58 "Government Carried Out Emergency Study for Korean Peninsula in 1993-1994," *Asahi Shimbun*, December 24, 1996.

59 Wit, Poneman, and Gallucci, *Going Critical*, p 118.

60 Yamagiwa, Sumio, "*Nichibei Shuno Kaidan Kanren, Kitachosen Keizai Seisai Kyocho Hyomei, Shusho, Beikoku no 'Koe' ni Ojiru*," ("At Summit Talks, Cooperation on North Korean Economic Sanctions, Prime Minister Complies With U.S. 'Voice'"), *Sankei Shimbun*, February 12, 1994, evening edition, p 2.

61 Omori, Yoshio, *Nihon no Interijensu Kikan*, ("Japan's Intelligence Structure"), Tokyo: Bungei Shinsho, 2005, pp 149-150.

62 Hashizume, Kunihiro, "Kyodo 'Focus': Third Crisis in Making on Korean Peninsula," Kyodo News Agency, June 9, 2003.

63 "Takemura Says Halting Remittances to DPRK 'Difficult'," Kyodo, February 13, 1994.

64 Wit, Poneman, and Gallucci, *Going Critical*, p 144.

65 "TV Airs Delegates' Remarks," KBS-1 Television Network, March 19, 1994, quoted in Wit et al, p 149.

66 Gordon, Michael R., "U.S. Will Urge UN To Plan Sanctions For North Korea, Diplomacy Near Collapse," *New York Times*, March 20, 1994, p 1.

67 Wit, Poneman, and Gallucci, *Going Critical*, pp 411-412.

68 Wit, Poneman, and Gallucci, *Going Critical*, pp 169-170.

69 Sanger, David E., "Tokyo Reluctant To Levy Sanctions on North Koreans," *New York Times*, June 9, 1994, p A1.

70 "*Seifu, 'Seisai' Meguri Yakimoki, Kitachosen 'Kaku' Mondai*," ("Government Anxious Concerning Sanctions, North Korea Nuclear Problem"), *Asahi Shimbun*, June 7, 1994, p 3.

71 Wit, Poneman, and Gallucci, *Going Critical*, p 209.

72 "Hodgepodge Emergency Legislation A Risk," *Asahi Shimbun*, May 16, 2003.

73 "*Chosen Hanto Kincho de Yuji Jigen Rippo Kento, Ishihara Nobuo Mae Kanbofukuchokan in Kiku*," ("Examination of Time-Limited Emergency Legislation During Korean Peninsula Crisis, Interview with Former Deputy Chief Cabinet Secretary Nobuo Ishihara"), *Asahi Shimbun*, September 17, 1996, p 2.

74 Wit, Poneman, and Gallucci, *Going Critical*, pp 201-202.

75 Wit, Poneman, and Gallucci, *Going Critical*, p 239.

76 "*Seifu, 'Seisai' Meguri Yakimoki, Kitachosen 'Kaku' Mondai*," ("Government Anxious Concerning Sanctions, North Korea Nuclear Problem"), *Asahi Shimbun*, June 7, 1994, p 3.

77 "*Jieitai Goken, Murayama Shusho ga Hyomei*," ("Prime Minister Says SDF Constitutional"), *Yomiuri Shimbun*, July 21, 1994, p 1.

78 Interview with Soichi Tahara, "JSP's Kubo Explains Shift in Policies, Disarmament Goal," Asahi Newstar TV, September 4, 1994.

79 "*Beigun ga Kuji Kichi Chosa, Chosen Hanto Yuji Sotei, Koho Shien mo Yosei ka*," ("U.S. Military Surveys ASDF Bases in Case of Emergency on Korean Peninsula, Might Request Rear Area Support"), *Chunichi Shimbun*, June 17, 1994, p 1.

[80] Wit, Poneman, and Gallucci, *Going Critical*, p 107.

[81] Wit, Poneman, and Gallucci, *Going Critical*, p 177.

[82] "Japan-US Security Arrangements and Studies on Emergencies: The Joint Staff Council Compiles Report on Japan's Support for US Forces," *Asahi Shimbun*, September 15, 1996, p 1.

[83] Wit, Poneman, and Gallucci, *Going Critical*, p 178.

[84] "Japan-US Security Arrangements and Studies on Emergencies: The Joint Staff Council Compiles Report on Japan's Support for U.S. Forces," *Asahi Shimbun*, September 15, 1996, p 1.

[85] "Government Carried Out Emergency Study for Korean Peninsula in 1993-1994," *Asahi Shimbun*, December 24, 1996.

[86] "*Kakubuso no Kanosei Hitei—Eishi Hodo de Boeicho Jimujikan*," ("DA Administrative Vice Minister Denies UK Paper's Report of Nuclear Arming Possibility"), *Mainichi Shimbun*, February 1, 1994, p 3.

[87] "Report Concludes Having Nuclear Weapons Not in Nation's 'Best' Interests," *Yomiuri Shimbun*, February 20, 2003; "Defense Agency Sees No Merit in Japan Going Nuclear," Kyodo, February 20, 2003; and Kamiya, Matake, "A Blow to Soft Power," in "Arguments of 42 Opinion Leaders Concerning Japan's Possible Nuclear Armament," *Shokun*, August 2003.

[88] "Government Considered Accepting Influx of Korean Refugees in 1994," *Yomiuri Shimbun*, January 4, 2003.

[89] Wit, Poneman, and Gallucci, *Going Critical*, pp 255-256.

[90] "*Kakusareta Kitachosen Misairu Shito*," ("Information on North Korea's Missile Test Firing Kept Secret"), *Mainichi Shimbun*, August 14, 1994, p 1.

[91] Omori, Yoshio, *Nihon no Interijensu Kikan*, ("Japan's Intelligence Structure"), (Tokyo: Bungei Shinsho, 2005), pp 153-154.

[92] Wit, Poneman, and Gallucci, *Going Critical*, pp 414-415.

93 Center for Nonproliferation Studies, "Korean Peninsula Energy Development Organization (KEDO)," *Inventory of International Nonproliferation Organizations and Regimes*, 2005.

94 "'*Naikaku Godo Joho Kaigi wo Josetsu ni,' Ishihara Fukuchokan, Kantei Kino wo Minaosu*," ("Deputy Chief Cabinet Secretary Ishihara Establishing 'Permanent Cabinet Joint Intelligence Council,' Reviewing PMOR Capabilities"), *Sankei Shimbun*, September 23, 1994, p 5.

95 "North Reportedly Deploying Nodong-1 Missiles," Kyodo, September 12, 1995.

96 Richardson, Bennett, "Severe Test of Japan's Readiness," *Christian Science Monitor*, October 26, 2004, www.csmonitor.com/2004/1026/p06s02-woap.html.

97 Figures according to the Japan Meteorological Agency, www.jma.go.jp/jma/index.html.

98 U.S. Geological Survey, "Large Historical Earthquakes: Kobe, Japan," USGS Web site, neic.usgs.gov/neis/eq_depot/world/1995_01_16.html.

99 "Kyodo Features Kobe's Recovery From Killer Quake," Kyodo, October 12, 1997.

100 Ogawa, Kazuhisa, "Why Didn't Helicopters Fly?" *Bungei Shunju*, February 1997; Aso, Iku, *Joho Kantei Ni Tassezu*, ("Intelligence that Does Not Arrive to the Prime Minister's Official Residence"), (Tokyo: Shinchosha, August 2001), pp 90-93.

101 U.S. Geological Survey, "Historic Earthquakes: Kobe, Japan," USGS Web site, earthquake.usgs.gov/regional/world/events/1995_01_16.php.

102 Aso, *Joho Kantei Ni Tassezu*, pp 85-87.

103 Ogawa, Kazuhisa, "Why Didn't Helicopters Fly?" *Bungei Shunju*, February 1997; Shikata, Toshiyuki, *Kyokuto Yuji: Kakute Nihon ha Senso ni Hikikomare*, ("Far-East Emergencies: The Day Japan Will Be Caught Up in a War"), (Tokyo: Crest, May 1996).

104 Ogawa, Kazuhisa, "Why Didn't Helicopters Fly?" *Bungei Shunju*, February 1997.

105 "*Haken Okureta Hyogo Nanbu Jishin, Jieitai to Jichitai, Renkei ni Kyokun*," ("Late Dispatch of SDF and Local Authorities to the Hyogo Southern Area Earthquake, A Lesson in Cooperation"), *Yomiuri Shimbun*, January 19, 1995, p 15.

106 Ogawa, Kazuhisa, "Why Didn't Helicopters Fly?" *Bungei Shunju*, February 1997.

107 Aso, Iku, *Joho Kantei Ni Tassezu*, ("Intelligence that Does Not Arrive to the Prime Minister's Official Residence"), (Tokyo: Shinchosha, August 2001), pp 72-76; 81-82.

108 "Ruling Party Leaders May Consider Cabinet Reshuffle," *Yomiuri Shimbun*, January 12, 1995, p 1.

109 "Great Hanshin Earthquake and Politics: Nagata-cho in Silence; Delayed Response, Attention Turns to 'Political Situation'," *Asahi Shimbun*, January 26, 1995, p 2.

110 "*Hyogo Nanbu Jishin Dokyumento*," ("Hyogo Southern Area Earthquake Document"), *Yomiuri Shimbun*, January 21, 1995; "*Murayama Nisshi, 17-nichi*," ("Murayama's Schedule, 17th"), *Sankei Shimbun*, January 18, 1995, p 1.

111 Aso, Iku, *Joho Kantei Ni Tassezu*, pp 76-79.

112 "Living on an Isolated Island—Quake Information Not Given To Prime Minister," *Asahi Shimbun*, January 24, 1995, p 2.

113 "Outmoded Methods, Cost-Cutting Blamed for Highway Damage," Kyodo, January 21, 1995.

114 "Quake Damage to Railways Estimated at 412 Billion Yen," Kyodo, January 23, 1995.

115 "Kobe Port Official Reports Quake Damage, Repair Work," Kyodo, January 31, 1995.

116 "*Hyogoken Nanbu Jishin, Keisatsu, Shobo, Kyuen Taisei Panku—Denwa Tsujizu, Hitodee Tarizu*," ("Hyogo Prefecture Southern Area Earthquake, Police, Fire, Rescue System Punctured—Telephone Lines Dead, A Shortage of Rescuers"), *Nihon Keizai Shimbun*, January 18, 1995, p 17.

117 Adamson, Sharlene, "First Aid Response to the Kobe Earthquake, January 17, 1995," *Quick Response Report #102*, 1997, www.colorado.edu/hazards/qr/qr102.html.

118 "*Hyogoken Nanbu Jishin, Umekigoetayori ni Kyushutsu, Hokai Byoin kara 46nin*," ("Hyogo Prefecture Southern Area Earthquake, Relying on Groaning Voices for Rescue, 46 People Pulled from Collapsed Hospital"), *Sankei Shimbun*, January 18, 1995, p 23.

119 "*Hanshin Daishinsai Dokyumento 1995-nen 1-gatsu 17-nichi*," ("Great Hanshin Earthquake, January 17, 1995"), *Mainichi Shimbun*, January 18, 1995, p 3.

120 "*Hanshin Daishinsai Dokyumento 1995-nen 1-gatsu 18-nichi*," ("Great Hanshin Earthquake, January 18, 1995"), *Mainichi Shimbun*, January 18, 1995, evening edition, p 3.

121 "*Hyogo Nanbu Jishin Dokyumento*," ("Southern Hyogo Earthquake Document"), *Yomiuri Shimbun*, January 21, 1995, p 2; Shikata, Toshiyuki, *Kyokuto Yuji: Kakute Nihon ha Senso ni Hikikomare*, ("Far-East Emergencies: The Day Japan Will Be Caught Up in a War"), (Tokyo: Crest, May 1996).

122 "*Rikujo Jieitai 1,000nin, Kyuen Shutsudo, Hyogo-ken Nanbu Jishin*," ("GSDF Dispatches 1,000 for Relief Operations to Hyogo Prefecture Southern Area Earthquake"), *Asahi Shimbun*, January 18, 1995, p 3.

123 "*Hyogo-ken Nanbu Jishin, Jieitai San-mannnin Haken he, Saigai Kyujo de ha Saidai Kibo*," ("SDF Plans to Dispatch 30,000 Personnel to the Hyogo Prefecture Southern Area Earthquake, Largest for Natural Disaster Relief"), *Yomiuri Shimbun*, January 18, 1995, evening edition, p 3.

124 "Behind the scenes of crises–Hanshin quake catastrophe and after (Part 1): US aircraft carrier dispatch ends up as an illusion; Nonnuclear principles blocked relief supplies?" *Mainichi Shimbun*, December 21, 2005, p 25.

125 NHK News 7, January 26, 1995.

126 Shelly, Christine, U.S. Department of State Daily Press Briefing, January 23, 1995.

127 "More Than 60 Nations Pledge Quake Aid, 23 Offers Accepted," Kyodo, January 30, 1995.

128 "Murayama Thanks For US Military Help in Quake-Hit Area," Kyodo, February 1, 1995.

129 "*Hyogo Nanbu Jishin Dokyumento,*" ("Southern Hyogo Earthquake Document"), *Yomiuri Shimbun,* January 21, 1995, p 2.

130 "*Hyogo Ken Nanbu Jishin: Yamaguchi-Gumi ga Busshi Haikyu, Honbu-Mae ni Cho-Retsu,*" ("Earthquake in Southern Hyogo Prefecture: Yamaguchi-Gumi Provides Food-Stuff, Long Line in Front of Main HQ"), *Hokkaido Shimbun,* January 20, 1995, p 31; "*'Boryokudan ga Saigai Enjo' to Eishi ga Issei ni Tosai, Hyogo-ken Nanbu Jishin de Yamaguchi-Gumi,*" ("All English Papers Carry Story 'Criminal Organizations Assist Following Natural Disaster,' Yamaguchi-Gumi in Southern Hyogo Prefecture's Earthquake"), *Asahi Shimbun,* January 21, 1995, evening edition, p 14; "*Hanshin Daishinsai Tanomi no Mo ha Boryokudan!? 'Taio Osoi Seifu, Yakusho' Beishi, Tsuretsu ni Hihan,*" ("Hanshin Natural Disaster: Request Network by Organized Crime!? US Paper Severely Criticizes 'Government's Late Response, Bureaucracy'"), *Sankei Shimbun,* January 23, 1995, evening edition, p 10.

131 "*Tokai Kaoku Kaitai no Fudosangyosha wo Kyohaku, Boryokudan Kanbura Taiho,*" ("Criminal Organization Leaders Detained, Threatened Realtor Dismantling Collapsed Houses"), *Yomiuri Shimbun,* February 9, 1995, p 27.

132 "Murayama Thanks North Korean Premier for Condolence Message," Kyodo, February 3, 1995.

133 "The Great Hanshin-Awaji Earthquake: Statistics and Restoration Progress," Kobe City, April 1, 2002, www.city.kobe.jp/cityoffice/06/013/report/january.2006.pdf.

134 "*Nomimizu, Shokuryo Buzoku Shinkoku,*" ("Pottable Water, Food Shortages Increasing"), *Asahi Shimbun,* January 19, 1995, p 1.

135 "Akihito Visits Quake-Hit Area," Kyodo, January 31, 1995.

136 "News Focus: Imported Prefab Houses Gain Attention in Quake-Hit Kobe," Kyodo, January 16, 1996.

137 "Support for Murayama Cabinet Falls After Quake," *Nihon Keizai Shimbun,* January 31, 1995, p 1.

138 "Support for Murayama Cabinet Falls After Quake," *Nihon Keizai Shimbun,* January 31, 1995, p 1.

139 "Former Premier Nakasone Discusses Disaster-Relief Measures," *Aera,* February 6, 1995, p 22.

140 Furukawa, Teijiro, *Kasumigaseki Hanseiki,* ("Writings of Half a Life in Government"), Saga: Saga Shinbunsha, 2005, p 192.

141 Omori, Yoshio, *Nihon no Interijensu Kikan* ("Japan's Intelligence Structure"), (Tokyo: Bungei Shinsho, 2005), p 47.

142 "Government To Set Up Disaster Information System," Kyodo, January 31, 1995.

143 Shikata, Toshiyuki, *Kyokuto Yuji: Kakute Nihon ha Senso ni Hikikomare,* ("Far-East Emergencies: The Day Japan Will Be Caught Up in a War"), (Tokyo: Crest, May 1996).

144 Murakami, Haruki, *Underground* (New York: First Vintage International, 2000), p 60.

145 "Former Doctor Admits To Producing Sarin Gas for Aum Sect," Kyodo, October 24, 1995.

146 "*'Chikatetsu Sarin' Zenyo Kaimei, Asahara Yogisha 'Sosa Kakuran no Tame Maku',*" ("'Subway Sarin' Plans Revealed, Asahara Says 'Spread [Gas] To Disturb Search'"), *Yomiuri Shimbun,* June 4, 1995, p 27.

147 Murakami, *Underground,* p 10.

148 Murakami, *Underground,* p 48.

149 Murakami, *Underground,* pp 108-110.

150 Murakami, *Underground,* p 120.

151 Murakami, *Underground,* pp 166-167.

152 "*'Hadaka no Kyoso...10-nenme no Shinjitsu' (4) 'Ue ni Tatsu'... Bogakko ni Genten (Rensai),*" ("'The Naked Guru...The Truth at 10 Years,' pt 4, 'I Will Rise Upward'...Origins in the School for the Blind (Series)"), *Yomiuri Shimbun,* February 4, 2004, p 38.

153 "'*Hadaka no Kyoso…10-nenme no Shinjitsu' (6) 'Nihon Chinbotsu' Mo Jisaku Jien (Rensai),*" ("'The Naked Guru…The Truth at 10 Years,' pt 6, Making 'Japan is Sinking' His Own (Series)"), *Yomiuri Shimbun*, February 6, 2004, p 38.

154 Lifton, Robert, *Destroying the World to Save It*, (New York: Henry Holt, 2000), p 36.

155 Lifton, *Destroying the World to Save It*, p 59.

156 Lifton, *Destroying the World to Save It*, p 27.

157 Watanabe, Manabu, "Religion and Violence in Japan Today: A Chronological and Doctrinal Analysis of Aum Shinrikyo," *Terrorism and Political Violence*, Vol 10, No 4, (Winter 1998), p 85.

158 Egawa, Shoko, "From The Other Witness Stand: Following the Aum Case," *Yomiuri Shimbun*, December 13, 1998, p 50.

159 Lifton, *Destroying the World to Save It*, p 48.

160 Watanabe, Manabu, "Religion and Violence in Japan Today: A Chronological and Doctrinal Analysis of Aum Shinrikyo," *Terrorism and Political Violence*, Vol 10, No 4, (Winter 1998), p 87.

161 "A Case Study on the Aum Shinrikyo," Senate Government Affairs Permanent Subcommittee on Investigations, October 31, 1995, www.fas.org/irp/congress/1995_rpt/aum/part03.htm.

162 "*Mura ga Nottorareru! 'Oumu Okoku' Zoshoku no 6-nen wo Kensho/Yamanashi, Kamikuishiki,*" ("The Village Has Been Hijacked! Examining the Six Years That Bred The 'Aum Empire'/Yamanashi, Kaikuishiki"), *Yomiuri Shimbun*, April 4, 1995, p 35.

163 Egawa, Shoko, "From Another Witness Stand: Following the Aum Case – Key Man Talks About Dark Side of Aum," *Shukan Yomiuri*, September 27, 1998, pp 122-123.

164 "*Bogofuku de Saikin Jikken, Moto Kanbu, 'Himitsu Ninmu' wo Shogen, Asahara Daihyo ni 'Inochi Kakerareru ka',*" ("Germ Experiments Wearing Protection Suits, a Former Leader Testifies of

'Secret Duty,' Asked by Asahara 'Will You Give Your Life?'"), *Yomiuri Shimbun*, April 15, 1995, p 35.

165 Lifton, *Destroying the World to Save It*, p 39.

166 Lifton, *Destroying the World to Save It*, pp 28-31; Senate Government Affairs Permanent Subcommittee on Investigations, "Operation of the Aum, Membership and Recruitment: Large and Highly Technical," *Global Proliferation of Weapons of Mass Destruction: A Case Study on the Aum Shinrikyo*, October 31, www.fas.org/irp/congress/1995_rpt/aum/part08.htm.

167 "*Oumu Shinrikyo, Kaigai Mo Shinshoku, Roshia Seikai ni mo Jinmyaku, Hofu na Shikin de Kyoten Tsugitsugi*," ("Aum Shinrikyo Expanded Abroad, Contacts in Russia, Used Abundant Resources to Build Footholds One After Another"), *Yomiuri Shimbun*, May 16, 1995, evening edition, p 3.

168 Krutakov, Leonid and Ivan Kadulin, "The Japanese God of Oleg Lobov. The Contribution of the First Deputy Prime Minister (Former) and the Russian Military to the Organization of the Gas Attack on the Tokyo Metro," *Izvestiya*, May 21, 1997, pp 1-2.

169 Kato, Akira, Sergey Pluzhnikov and Vladimir Zaynetdinov, "Russian Special Services Trained 'Aum-Shinrikyo' Gunmen. The Kremlin Was Well Aware of This Fact – This Is the Conclusion of *Komsomolskaya Pravda*'s Investigation," *Komsomolskaya Pravda*, October 19, 1995, pp 1-2.

170 Krutakov, Leonid and Ivan Kadulin, "The Japanese God of Oleg Lobov. The Contribution of the First Deputy Prime Minister (Former) and the Russian Military to the Organization of the Gas Attack on the Tokyo Metro," *Izvestiya*, May 21, 1997, pp 1-2.

171 Ichihashi, Fumiya, *Oumu Teikoku no Shotai*, ("The True Colors of the Aum Empire"), (Tokyo: Shinchosha, 2000), pp 60-62.

172 Krutakov, Leonid and Ivan Kadulin, "The Japanese God of Oleg Lobov. The Contribution of the First Deputy Prime Minister (Former) and the Russian Military to the Organiza-

tion of the Gas Attack on the Tokyo Metro," *Izvestiya,* May 21, 1997, pp 1-2.

173 "*Roseiken ni Arata na Gyakufu,*" ("The Russian Government Takes New Contradictory Stance"), *Sankei Shimbun,* March 30, 1995, p 5.

174 Agafonov, Sergey, "`Kremlin Dreamers' Strange Ties with Japanese 'Aum Shinrikyo' Sect," *Izvestiya,* March 28, 1995, pp 1-2.

175 "Russian Sleuths Follow Up Aum Cash Gift Allegations," Kyodo, May 31, 1995.

176 Ichihashi, *Oumu Teikoku no Shotai,* p 60-61.

177 *Global Proliferation of Weapons of Mass Destruction: A Case Study on the Aum Shinrikyo,* "Overseas Operations – The Aum Shinrikyo in Russia," October 31, 1995, www.fas.org/irp/congress/1995_rpt/aum/part06.htm.

178 "Asahara Reportedly Visited Russian Military Base," Kyodo, May 19, 1995.

179 "Aum Affiliate Accused of Copyright Infringement," Kyodo, June 14, 1995.

180 Ichihashi, *Oumu Teikoku no Shotai,* pp 48-50.

181 "Global Proliferation of Weapons of Mass Destruction: A Case Study on the Aum Shinrikyo," Senate Government Affairs Permanent Subcommittee on Investigations, October 31, 1995, www.fas.org/irp/congress/1995_rpt/aum/part03.htm.

182 "*Oumu, Doku Gasu, Saikin, Juki, Kakuseizai no Yon Bumon de Busoka Hakaru, 93nenki ni Issei,*" ("Aum in 1993 Planned Four Areas for Weaponization Including Poison Gas, Bacteria, Guns, and Amphetamines"), *Yomiuri Shimbun,* May 28, 1995, p 31.

183 Egawa, Shoko, "From Another Witness Stand: Following the Aum Case – Key Man Talks About Dark Side of Aum," *Shukan Yomiuri,* September 27, 1998, pp 122-123.

184 Senate Government Affairs Permanent Subcommittee on Investigations, "Chronology of Major Events: The Aum

Shinrikyo 'Doomsday Cult'," *Global Proliferation of Weapons of Mass Destruction: A Case Study on the Aum Shinrikyo*, Appendix D, October 31, www.fas.org/irp/congress/1995_rpt/aum/part08.htm.

185 Lifton, *Destroying the World To Save It*, p 32.

186 "*Oumu Shinrikyo, Kaigai Mo Shinshoku, Roshia Seikai ni mo Jinmyaku, Hofu na Shikin de Kyoten Tsugitsugi*," ("Aum Shinrikyo Expanded Abroad, Contacts in Russia, Used Abundant Resources to Build Footholds One After Another"), *Yomiuri Shimbun*, May 16, 1995, evening edition, p 3.

187 "The House That Aum Built," *Izvestiya*, February 25, 2000, p 1.

188 Ichihashi, *Oumu Teikoku no Shotai*, p 68.

189 Ichihashi, *Oumu Teikoku no Shotai*, p 63.

190 Egawa, Shoko, "From Another Witness Stand: Following the Aum Case – Key Man Talks About Dark Side of Aum," *Shukan Yomiuri*, September 27, 1998, pp 122-123.

191 "Aum Biologist: Asahara Ordered 1994 Sarin Attack," Kyodo, January 14, 1999.

192 "Aum Sarin Truck Sprayed Matsumoto Residents," Kyodo, July 17, 1995.

193 "Aum Sarin Truck Sprayed Matsumoto Residents," Kyodo, July 27, 1995.

194 Kaplan, David E., "Aum Shinrikyo," pp 207-226 (p 221), in *Toxic Terror*, ed Jonathan B. Tucker, (Cambridge: MIT Press, 2000).

195 Only three reports noted the Ebola story in 1995, one of which was a less-than-credible sports tabloid: "*Ebola Netsu Chosa Mo! 3-nen Mae Zairu he, AP Den ga Tsutaeru*," *Chunichi Shimbun*, May 24, 1995, evening edition, p 13; "*Oumu Shinrikyo, Asahara Yogisha, 92-nen ni Zairu Homon, Ichibayaku Ebora ni Kyomi?*" *Nikkan Supotsu*, May 24, 1995, p 23; and "*Beijoin Hokokusho de Akiraka ni, Oumu, Ebora Uirusu ni mo Kanshin*," *Nihon Keizai Shimbun*, November 1, 1995, evening edition, p 17.

196 Senate Government Affairs Permanent Subcommittee on Investigations, "The Operation of the Aum," *Global Proliferation of Weapons of Mass Destruction: A Case Study on the Aum Shinrikyo,* Part IV, October 31, www.fas.org/irp/congress/1995_rpt/aum/part04.htm.

197 "*Waidosho Arita Yoshifu-san ni Kiku,*" ("Interview with Yoshifu Arita"), *Sankei Shimbun,* December 27, 1995, p 16.

198 "Aum Doctor Admits Treating Members Made Ill by Sarin," Kyodo, May 20, 1995.

199 "*Yamanashi no Sanroku de Sarin Zanryubutsu Kenshutsu, 'Matsumoto Jiken' Chokugo, Kanren Kaimei Isogu,*" ("Sarin Detected at Base of Mountain in Yamanashi, Rush To Clarify Connection to 'Matsumoto Incident'"), *Yomiuri Shimbun,* January 1, 1995, p 1.

200 Watanabe, Manabu, "Religion and Violence in Japan Today: A Chronological and Doctrinal Analysis of Aum Shinrikyo," *Terrorism and Political Violence,* Vol 10, No 4, (Winter 1998), p 92.

201 Lifton, *Destroying the World To Save It,* p 40.

202 "*Chikatetsu Sarin Jiken, Kantei, Jitai Shoaku ni Yakki, 'Shireito' Buri Kyocho, Jieitai mo Shutsudo,*" ("Subway Sarin Incident, PMOR Eager To Take Command of Situation, Strengthens 'Command Tower,' SDF Also Dispatched"), *Yomiuri Shimbun,* March 21, 1995, p 2; "*Tonai Chikatetsu ni Modoku Gasu, Sarin Zanryubutsu? Kenshutsu, Shibo 6, Fusho 900-nin,*" ("Was Deadly Gas Left Behind in Metropolitan Subway Sarin? Six Killed, 900 People Injured"), *Yomiuri Shimbun,* March 20, 1995, evening edition, p 1.

203 "*Oumu 'Dai-7 Satian' Kagaku Puranto no Kozo Kaimei,*" ("Construction of Aum 'Satian No. 7' Chemical Plant Discovered"), *Yomiuri Shimbun,* April 17, 1995, evening edition, p 15.

204 "*30 Shurui no Kagaku Busshitsu wo Oshu—Oumu Shinrikyo Kyosei Sosa,*" ("30 Chemical Agents Seized—Forced Search of Aum Shinrikyo"), *Mainichi Shimbun,* April 1, 1995, p 30.

205 "*Oumu ga Saikin Baiyo Kenkyu, Sosa Honbu Handan, Yamanashi no Shisetsu de Kizai, Shiryo wo Oshu,*" ("Aum Was Researching Germ Cultivation Investigation Finds, Machinery and Materials Seized at Yamanashi Facilities"), *Yomiuri Shimbun,* April 2, 1995, p 1.

206 "Police Say Aum Atomizers Corroborate Germ-Warfare Testimony," Kyodo, June 22, 1995.

207 "Article Views Cult Biological Weapons Activities," *Shukan Yomiuri,* April 30, 1995.

208 "*Seibutsu Saikin Kenkyu no Puranto ka, Oshu no Sekkeizu to Hobo Itchi—Gunma no Oumu Shinrikyo Shisetsu,*" ("A Biological Germ Research Plant? Seized Plans Resemble Aum Shinrikyo Facility in Gunma"), *Mainichi Shimbun,* April 6, 1995, p 11.

209 "'*Shoju Kansei Mada ka': Asahara Hikoku, Shisakuhin ni 'Karusugiru,' Kibishii Kucho de Shiji,*" ("'Small Arms Haven't Been Completed Yet?' Suspect Asahara Says Trial Products are 'Too Light,' Issues Orders in Stern Tones"), *Yomiuri Shimbun,* July 15, 1995, p 11.

210 "*Jido Shoju no Seisaku Koteizu wo Oshu, Murai Hideo-shi ga Tanto ka,*" ("Plans for Production of Automatic Riffles Seized, Perhaps Headed by Hideo Murai"), *Mainichi Shimbun,* May 18, 1995, p 26.

211 "*Nankinjyotsuki Koshitsu Tasu, Oumu Shisetsu no Dai-ni Satian Ni-kai, Kankin Shisetsu ka,*" ("Majority of Individual Rooms on Second Floor of Satian No. 2 Have Locks Attached, Possibly Used for Confinement"), *Yomiuri Shimbun,* April 19, 1995, evening edition, p 15.

212 Shirakawa, Tadashi, "'Hayakawa Notebook' Describes Full Contents of Plans for Aum Shinrikyo's Armed Coup d'Etat," *Bungei Shunju,* June 1995, pp 104-110.

213 "*Oumu no Kenkin no Uketori wo Hitei, Robofu Roshia Moto Kokan,*" ("Former Russian Official Lobov Denies Receiving Contribution from Aum"), *Asahi Shimbun,* May 7, 1997, p 33.

214 "Lobov Denies Giving Sarin Information to Aum Shinrikyo," Interfax, May 6, 1997.

215 "GSDF Officer Gave Poison Gas Textbook to Aum," Kyodo, May 18, 1995.

216 "Aum Members Stole Tanks, Laser Equipment Data," Kyodo, May 25, 1995.

217 Ichihashi, *Oumu Teikoku no Shotai*, p 70.

218 Senate Government Affairs Permanent Subcommittee on Investigations, "Chronology of Major Events: The Aum Shinrikyo 'Doomsday Cult'," *Global Proliferation of Weapons of Mass Destruction: A Case Study on the Aum Shinrikyo*, Appendix D, October 31, www.fas.org/irp/congress/1995_rpt/aum/part08.htm.

219 "Aum's Sarin Attack Fouled Raid Plan," *Yomiuri Shimbun*, February 18, 2004.

220 "*Zen-Nikku Kinottori: Kyoki no Doraibu, Koatsu Denryu no Kendenyou*," ("ANA Flight Hijacking: Screwdriver for High Voltage Use Employed as Weapon"), *Hokkaido Shimbun*, June 24, 1995, p 31.

221 "*Haijakku Join Kaiken*," ("Interviews with Hijacked Crew"), *Hokkaido Shimbun*, June 27, 1995, p 25.

222 "Police Storm Hijacked ANA Plane, No Explosives Found," Kyodo, June 21, 1995.

223 "*Zen-Nikku Ki-haijakku Jikken, Keitai Denwa de Kokkoku 'Hannin Joho', Toire Kara 110ban*," ("ANA Flight Hijacking Incident: Cell Phones Used to Provide Information about Perpetrator Minute by Minute, Dialing 110 From the Toilet"), *Yomiuri Shimbun*, June 22, 1995, evening edition, p 18.

224 "*Sosetsu 18nen, Beru Nuida Keishicho 'Tai-Tero Tokushu Butai,' Zen-Nikku Kinottori Kyushutsugeki*," ("Eighteen Years After its Founding, Lifting the Veil from the National Police Agency's 'Counter-Terrorism Special Forces, Hijacked ANA Flight Rescue Drama"), *Sankei Shimbun*, July 4, 1995, evening edition, p 1; "Interviews with Hijacked Crew," *Hokkaido Shimbun*, June 27, 1995, p 25.

225 "Police Say Hijacker Planned To Kill Aum Leader, Self," Kyodo, July 3, 1995.

226 Sekisato, Okadate and Hidekazu Aoki, "*Tero wo Keikaku Shite Ita!*" ("They Were Planning Terror!"), *Sunde Mainichi*, December 2001, pp 40-43.

227 "Russian AUM Cultists Own Up To Planned Japan Terror," *Mainichi Shimbun*, December 5, 2001.

228 "Russian Court Sentences AUM Cultists Who Plotted Terror Strike," Kyodo, January 23, 2002.

229 "*Roshiajin Motoshinja no Tero Keikaku Kanyo Hitei: Oumu Joyu Kanbu*," ("Aum Leader Joyu Denies Relation to Terror Plot by Russian Former Adherent"), *Yomiuri Shimbun*, December 16, 2001.

230 Asamizu, Tomonori, "How Aum Infiltrated Software Industry," *Yomiuri Weekly*, April 30, 2000.

231 "DA To Impose Obligation on Computer Software Firms," *Mainichi Shimbun*, May 15, 2000, p 9.

232 "Asahara Found Guilty on All Charges, Sentenced To Death," Kyodo, February 27, 2004.

233 "Media Report on Lop Nor Nuclear Test," AFP, May 15, 1995.

234 Chin-hung, Lai, "China Conducted Another Underground Nuclear Test Yesterday Morning, Will Conduct More Tests Before the Nuclear Test Ban," *Lien Ho Pao*, August 18, 1995, p 2.

235 "Kono Urges Permanent NPT Extension," Kyodo, April 18, 1995.

236 "Protest Against PRC for Nuclear Test Reported," Kyodo, May 15, 1995.

237 "'Next' PRC Nuclear Test 'Agonizing' MOFA," *Ekonomisuto*, September 26, 1995, pp 14-15.

238 "Murayama Deplores China's Nuclear Test," Kyodo, August 18, 1995.

239 Hiramatsu, Shigeo, "China Aims at Modernization of Its Conventional Military Forces and Development of Next-Generation Nuclear Weapons," *Ekonomisuto*, October 10, 1995, pp 58-61.

240 "DA Obtains Chinese ICBM Test Launch Report," *Sankei Shimbun*, May 31, 1995, p 1.

241 "Murayama, Takemura Deplore French Nuclear Test," Kyodo, December 28, 1995.

242 Desaubliaux, Patrice-Henry, "France Is Ready for Simulation," *Le Figaro*, February 13, 1996.

243 "Military Official Discusses Mururoa Nuclear Site," AFP, October 13, 1996.

244 "Beijing's New Strategy Aims at Attacking Li Teng-hui and Suppressing Pro-Taiwan Independence Forces: Many Military Regions Move Troops in Expected Follow-Up Actions," *Lien Ho Pao*, July 20, 1995, p 1.

245 Fujii, Hisashi, "Facts Concerning China's Nuclear Forces, 2d Artillery Corps and 09 Submarine Fleet," *Gunji Kenkyu*, pp 115-126.

246 Yu Zhanchi, "A Statement Which Goes Against People's Desires – Fallacies of Li Denghui's Speech Made at Cornell University as Viewed From the Facts," *Renmin Ribao Overseas Edition*, August 29, 1995, p 5, and Li Jiaquan, "Li Teng-hui and Peng Ming-min," *Guangming Ribao*, August 28, 1995, p 7, are two of many examples.

247 Wo-Lap Lam, Willy and Vivien Pik-kwan Chan, "Further 'Pressure' Reportedly Planned for Taipei," *South China Morning Post*, December 4, 1995, p 1.

248 Virant, Christaan, "Kinmen Invasion Simulation Reportedly Scheduled," *Eastern Express*, December 4, 1995, p 1.

249 Lam, Willy Wo-Lap, "PLA Circulars Urge 'Quasi-War Preparations'," *South China Morning Post*, January 16, 1996, p 6.

250 "Editorial Blaming Li Teng-hui for Tension Viewed," Xinhua, March 8, 1996.

251 "PRC Military Exercises Concern Fishermen," *Okinawa Times*, March 6, 1996, p 19.

252 "Airlines Rerouting Flights To Miss Missile Exercises," Hong Kong AFP, March 7, 1996.

253 For one of many examples of disputes involving Yonaguni, see Lu, Ella, "Taiwan Navy Frigate Sails Near Waters Disputed With Japan," Kyodo, June 21, 2005.

254 "Government Urged To Act Against PRC Missile Test," Kyodo, March 8, 1996.

255 "Tokyo 'Greatly Concerned' Over PRC Missile Tests," *Yomiuri Shimbun*, March 9, 1996, p 3.

256 Handa, Shigeru, "No Answer to Concern of Islanders-Government Losing Public Trust in Border Town," *Tokyo Shimbun*, April 10, 1996.

257 Caihong, Huang and Sun Maoqing, "Xinhua Details Live-Fire Exercises," Xinhua, March 20, 1996.

258 "'Confidential' DA Documents Show GSDF To Defend Islands in PRC-Taiwan Conflict," Kyodo, May 14, 2004.

259 Shigeo Hiramatsu, a professor at Kyorin University and former researcher for the DA-affiliated National Institute of Defense Studies, highlighted these concerns in a 2005 article in the conservative daily *Sankei Shimbun*: "Those who control Taiwan would be able to exercise their influence over the South China Sea and Southeast Asian countries that surround it. The South China Sea is connected to the Pacific Ocean through the Bashi Channel, and is connected to the Indian Ocean through the Strait of Malacca. The sea lane that links the Middle East and East Asian countries runs through this area." Moreover, "as Taiwan faces the Pacific Ocean, if China brought Taiwan under its control, it would be able to sail out into the Pacific Ocean directly from Taiwan without having to go through the sea area between the main island of Okinawa and Miyakojima and the Bashi Channel between Taiwan and the Philippines as it had in the past." Hiramatsu, Shigeo, "Taiwan is Situated at the Key Spot

for Sea Lane Defense—China's Strategy Motives Must Be Understood," *Sankei Shimbun*, December 23, 2005.

260 Katsumata, Hidemichi, "Land Disputes Expose Weaknesses," *Yomiuri Shimbun*, April 21, 1998, p 3.

261 "Tokyo 'Greatly Concerned' Over PRC Missile Tests," *Yomiuri Shimbun*, March 9, 1996, p 3.

262 "Intensifying Controversy Concerning TMD Inspired by the Launching of the Taepodong Missile," *Sentaku*, October 1998, pp 120-123.

263 Yuasa, Hiroshi, "Source: Nodong-1 Missile Can Reach Anywhere in Japan," *Sankei Shimbun*, May 13, 1997, p 1.

264 "Defense Chief Casts Doubt on Report on DPRK Missile Range," Kyodo, May 13, 1997.

265 "North Korean Missiles Allegedly Installed on Launchers," Kyodo, September 22, 1997.

266 "MSDF To Deploy 2d Aegis Destroyer at Sasebo," Kyodo, September 5, 1997.

267 "Fujimori Convenes Council; Brother Among Hostages," Panamericana Television Network, December 18, 1996.

268 "Hostages Asked Rebel Leader for Autograph," Kyodo, December 23, 1996.

269 "Government Reports No Dead or Injured Among Hostages," Notimex, December 18, 1996.

270 Schemo, Diana J., "How Peruvian Hostage Crisis Became Trip Into the Surreal: Special Report," *New York Times*, April 26, 1997, p 1.

271 "Interview With Escaped Miraflores Mayor," Panamerican TV, December 18, 1996.

272 "Kyodo Cites 'Well-Placed' Sources on Details of Hostages," Kyodo, December 18, 1996.

273 "Hostages Asked Leader for Autograph," Kyodo, December 23, 1996.

274 "Army Report, Captured Documents Describe MRTA Goals," NOTIMEX News Agency, December 21, 1996.

275 "Military Commando Reportedly Preparing for Assault," AFP, January 9, 1997.

276 "President Fujimori Grants News Conference," America Television Network, April 10, 1995.

277 "Peruvian Police Knew of MRTA's Attack Plan in Advance," *Mainichi Shimbun*, February 20, 1997, p 1; "Fujimori Holds Police Liable for Assault on Envoy's Home," America Television Network, February 25, 1997.

278 "*Peru Taishi Kotei Senkyo, Shusho Mizukara Jinto Shiki–Kiki Kanri he no Hihan Fusshoku Nerau*," ("Prime Minister Takes Personal Command Following Occupation of Ambassador's Residence in Peru–Aims to Avoid Criticism of Crisis Management"), *Nihon Keizai Shimbun*, December 19, 1996, p 2.

279 "*12-gatsu 18-nichi (Shusho Kantei)*," ("December 18 (Prime Minister's Official Residence))," *Nihon Keizai Shimbun*, December 19, 1996, p 2.

280 "Spokesman Says Hashimoto To Head Peru Hostage Crisis Team," Kyodo, December 19, 1996.

281 "*Meakaku, Kuma Tsukuri...Hashimoto Shusho 'Yoru mo Nerenu'- -Peru Nihon Taishi Kotei Senkyo Jiken*," ("Red Eyes, Dark Circles...PM Hashimoto 'Can't Sleep at Night'– Occupation of Japanese Ambassador's Residence in Peru"), *Mainichi Shimbun*, December 24, 1996, p 2.

282 "*Peru Nihon Taishi Kotei Senkyo Jiken, Nihon Seifu 'Kikikanri Shokoku' Matamo*," ("Occupation of Japanese Ambassador's Residence in Peru, Japanese Government Still Exhibits 'Crisis Management of a Minor Country"), *Sankei Shimbun*, December 23, 1996, p 3.

283 Hisamoto, Yukio, "The Cabinet Secretariat and Crisis Management," *Voice*, August 1997, pp 134-145.

284 "*Peru Hitojichi Jiken, Tokushu Butai no 'Haken Giron Mada Hayai,' Keisatsucho to Jieitai ga Konwaku*," ("Peru Hostage

Situation, Special Operations 'Discussion of Dispatch is Still Early,' NPA and DA Perplexed"), *Yomiuri Shimbun*, December 20, 1996, p 30.

285 "*Towareru Kiki Kanri Noryoku*," ("Questionable Crisis Management Capabilities"), *Tokyo Shimbun*, December 20, 1996, p 2.

286 "*Daitoryo mo Shinrai, Peru Hoshojinin Obuzaba no Terada-shi*," ("President also Trusts Terada, Guarantor Observer in Peru"), *Asahi Shimbun*, February 5, 1997, p 3.

287 "*Kaiketsu he Fukusu Shinario, Nihon Seifu, "Kyoko' Fukume Taiosaku, Rima Hitojichi Jiken*," ("Several Scenarios for Resolution of Lima Hostage Situation Including 'Firm' Response Policy"), *Asahi Shimbun*, December 27, 1996, p 3.

288 "Government Reportedly Has Plan Ready To Free Hostages," La Republica, December 20, 1996.

289 "Hashimoto Denial About Ransom for Hostages," Kyodo, January 5, 1997.

290 "No Casualties, Damage Reported From Explosion," Kyodo, December 26, 1996.

291 "Communiqué No. 3," Radio Programas Del Peru, December 28, 1996.

292 "Hashimoto 'Not Optimistic' About Progress in Peru Siege," Kyodo, January 15, 1997.

293 "Government Allocates Funds To Enhance Embassy Security," Kyodo, December 24, 1996.

294 "Government To Tighten Security For Japanese Diplomats," Kyodo, January 17, 1997.

295 "*Keisatsucho no Tero Taisakuhi, Tokushu Butai no Shisetsu Nado Zero Satei Kara 10-oku Uwazumi*," ("NPA Counter-Terrorism Funds Increased to One Billion from Zero for Special Teams Facilities"), *Yomiuri Shimbun*, December 23, 1996, p 26.

296 "Hashimoto 'Not Optimistic' About Progress in Peru Siege," Kyodo, January 15, 1997.

297 "Government, MRTA Clash on Mediation Body Membership," Kyodo, January 17, 1997.

298 "Additional Hostage Released in Peru," Kyodo, January 26, 1997.

299 "Report Claims Specialized Troop Mock Exercises," AFP, January 21, 1997; "Government Protests Peruvian Police Actions in Lima," Kyodo, January 23, 1997.

300 "Police Board Up One Entrance To Japanese Residence," Panamericana Television, January 23, 1997.

301 "Assault Troops Station Next to Japanese Envoy's Residence," Kyodo, January 23, 1997.

302 "Police Repeat 'Mock Attack' Against Ambassador's Residence," EFE, January 25, 1997.

303 "Tokyo Included in New Five-Member Hostage Crisis Commission," Kyodo, January 30, 1997.

304 "Fujimori, Hashimoto Issue 9-Point Joint Declaration," Radio Programas Del Peru, February 1, 1997.

305 "Japan Asks Fujimori To 'Accelerate' End To Hostage Crisis," EFE, March 19, 1997.

306 "'Source Says Talks To Be Held At Private Residence," Kyodo, February 8, 1997.

307 "Further on Japanese TV Network Leaving Device in Embassy," Kyodo, February 15, 1997.

308 "MRTA Carries Out Defense Exercise In Japanese Residence," Notimex, April 8, 1997.

309 Nelan, Bruce, "How They Did It," *Time*, May 5, 1997, pp 56-60.

310 Nelan, Bruce, "How They Did It," *Time*, May 5, 1997, pp 56-60.

311 WItkin, Gordon, Peter Cary, Linda Robinson, "Peru Takes No Prisoners," *US News & World Report*, May 5, 1997, pp 32-38; News conference by Alberto Fujimori, Lima Radio and Television Networks, April 23, 1997.

312 Schemo, Diana J., "How Peruvian Hostage Crisis Became Trip Into the Surreal: Special Report," *New York Times*, April 26, 1997, p 1.

[313] "President Fujimori's Popularity Drops 10 Points," *Expresso*, April 21, 1997, p 4a.

[314] "Further on Monsignor Cipriani's Letter to Hashimoto," NOTIMEX News Agency, April 22, 1997.

[315] News conference by Alberto Fujimori, Lima Radio and Television Networks, April 23, 1997; Witkin, Gordon, Peter Cary, and Linda Robinson, "Peru Takes No Prisoners: Stunning Rescue Mission by the Book," *Us News and World Report*, May 5, 1997, p 32; Sims, Calvin, "A Signal, and Peru Hostages Opened Door to Raid," *New York Times*, April 24, 1997, p 1.

[316] News conference by Alberto Fujimori, Lima Radio and Television Networks, April 23, 1997; Witkin, Gordon, Peter Cary, and Linda Robinson, "Peru Takes No Prisoners: Stunning Rescue Mission by the Book," *Us News and World Report*, May 5, 1997, p 32; Nelan, Bruce, "How They Did It," *Time*, May 5, 1997, pp 56-60.

[317] Sims, Calvin, "A Signal, and Peru Hostages Open Door to Raid," *New York Times*, April 24, 1997, p 1.

[318] "Police Source: There Were Orders To Kill Rebels," Notimex, April 23, 1997.

[319] "Tupac Amaru Leader: Peruvian Government Must Publish Report on Exhumations," *AFP*, March 13, 2001.

[320] "Peruvian Government Supports Military Who Freed Japanese Embassy Hostages," Radio Programas del Peru, May 13, 2002.

[321] "Hashimoto on End of Lima Hostage Crisis," Web site of Prime Minister's Official Residence, April 23, 1997.

[322] "*Konshu no 'Hodo 2001' Chosa Kara, Peru Butai no Totsunyu Ha Tekisetsu, 85%*," ("From This Week's 'Hodo 2001' Survey, 85% Say Peruvian Forces' Assault Appropriate"), *Sankei Shimbun*, April 28, 1997, p 3.

[323] "Hashimoto Comments on Peru Ties, Terrorism," Kyodo, May 9, 1997.

324 “Japanese Prime Minister Visits Recovered Residence,” Kyodo News Agency, May 10, 1997.

325 “Hashimoto Pleased With Former Envoy’s Award From Peru,” Kyodo, May 22, 1997.

326 “Fujimori Returns Residence to Japanese Officials,” Panamericana Television, April 25, 1997.

327 “Japan Embassy in Peru Ends Self-Restraint on Parties,” Kyodo News Agency, May 30, 1999.

328 “Hashimoto Vows To Fight Terrorism,” Kyodo News Agency, April 23, 1998.

329 “Tokyo Intensifies Antiterrorism Efforts,” Kyodo News Agency, April 21, 1998.

330 “Kasumigaseki Confidential,” *Bungei Shunju*, February 1998, pp 234-236.

331 O Yong-chin, “Questions Piled Up About Modus Operandi of North Korean Infiltrators,” *Korea Times*, September 22, 1996; “Impenetrable Defense?” *The Digital Chosun Ilbo*, September 19, 1996.

332 “Captured Agent From N. Hamgyong; Details of Capture Noted,” Yonhap, September 18, 1996.

333 “DPRK Intruder Captured Alive; Total of ‘About 20’ Intruders,” Yonhap, September 18, 1996.

334 “Intruders Belonged to DPRK ‘Reconnaissance Bureau’,” Yonhap, September 18, 1996.

335 “‘Inconsistent Statements’ by Captured Infiltrator Noted,” *The Korea Herald*, September 21, 1996.

336 “Captured DPRK Guerrilla ‘Sneaked Into’ ROK July 1995,” Yonhap, September 20, 1996.

337 “Six N. Koreans Still at Large; 40,000 in Manhunt,” Yonhap, September 20, 1996.

338 “Two ROK Soldiers Die in Gun Battle With DPRK Infiltrators,” KBS-1 Radio Network, September 22, 1996.

339 "Army Ambushes 3 DPRK Infiltrators, Kills 1 on 28 Sep," KBS-1 Radio Network, September 28, 1996.

340 "ROK Soldier Shot After Being Mistaken for DPRK Infiltrator," Yonhap, September 30, 1996.

341 "Dead DPRK Infiltrator's Diary Reveals Escape Route," Yonhap, November 7, 1996.

342 "Search for Last DPRK Agent Reduced to Routine Operation," Yonhap, November 7, 1996.

343 "Government Rewards Those Who Helped During Sub Incident," Yonhap, December 30, 1996.

344 "Agency Releases Videotaped Testimony by DPRK Infiltrator," Yonhap, October 29, 1996.

345 Ham Yong-chun and Kim Ki-hun, "Captured Infiltrator Exposes DPRK Submarine Bases," *Choson Ilbo,* September 30, 1996.

346 Taoka, Shunji, "North Korean Submarine Incident Caused by Failure in 'Recovering Reconnaissance Agents," *AERA,* September 30, 1996.

347 "JCS Claims Submarine Was on Infiltration Mission," Yonhap, June 24, 1998.

348 Statement carried by KBS-1 Television Network, June 23, 1998.

349 "ROK Resumes Work To Salvage Sunken DPRK Submarine," Yonhap, June 24, 1998; "Navy Successfully Tows, Raises Submerged DPRK Sub," Yonhap, June 25, 1998.

350 "DPRK's Small Submarine Seems To Be Wrecked on East Sea," KCNA, June 23, 1998; "Yonhap Relays DPRK Report on Sub Going Astray," Yonhap, June 23, 1998.

351 "JCS Claims Submarine Was on Infiltration Mission," Yonhap, June 24, 1998.

352 "More on Crew, Equipment Found on DPRK Sub," Yonhap, June 26, 1998.

353 "More on ROK's Continuing Search for DPRK Infiltrators," Yonhap, July 13, 1998.

354 "June 20 Departure Date Found in DPRK Sub's Logbook," Yonhap, June 27, 1998.

355 Yi Chong-hun, "Workers Party Manages To Infiltrate the ROK," *Chugan Tong-A*, December 8, 1999.

356 Statement carried by KBS-1 Television Network, June 26, 1998.

357 Chang Yong-un, "Yi Un-hye, Who Taught Japanese to Kim Hyon-hui, Has Already Been Executed," *Bungei Shunju*, January 1998, pp 170-178.

358 Yi Yong-chong, "DPRK Reportedly Revamps Anti-ROK Organizations," *Chungang Ilbo*, November 10, 1997, p 2.

359 Lee Sung-Yul, "Agents Suspected of Committing Suicide Before Vessel Sank," *The Korea Herald*, December 21, 1998, p 3.

360 Oh Yong-chin, "JCS Says Agents Probably Not Dropped Off From DPRK Boat," *The Korea Times*, December 21, 1998, p 3.

361 "Bodies of Presumed DPRK Sailors Found Near Takahama," Yonhap, December 25, 1998.

362 "JCS Says Bodies Not Likely From DPRK Sub Crew," Yonhap, December 25, 1998.

363 Eya, Osamu, *Tainichi Boryaku Hakusho*, November 1999, pp 26-28.

364 "ROK, Japan Discuss Issue of DPRK Subs in Their Waters," *The Korea Herald*, July 10, 1998.

365 Yamamoto Ichita and Keiichiro Asao, "A List of Japanese Companies Related to 'North Korea Arms'," *Bungei Shunju*, August 1999, pp 94-107.

366 In just one example, Brigadier Feroz Hassan Khan, former director of the Arms Control and Disarmament Affairs office in Pakistan's Strategic Plans Division, noted that Japanese and U.S. officials "had conveyed their suspicions" to him directly "about the nature of cooperation and possible presence of North Korean nuclear scientists in KRL [Khan

Research Laboratories]." A. Q. Khan in turn claimed "that missile experts from Korea were training Pakistani engineers to be self-sufficient." Khan, Feroz Hassan, *Eating Grass: The Making of the Pakistani Bomb.* (Palo Alto: Stanford University Press, 2012), p 483.

367 "Video Shows Taepo Dong Engine Resembles Ghauri, Shahab-3," *Mainichi Shimbun,* September 11, 1999, p 7.

368 Sarin, Ritu, "Experts: Detained Korean Ship Carried Missile Material," *The Indian Express,* September 5, 1999.

369 Joshi, Manoj, "New Delhi Refuses To Release North Korean Cargo Ship," *The Times of India,* July 31, 1999.

370 Yuasa, Hiroshi, "Source: Nodong-1 Missile Can Reach Anywhere in Japan," *Sankei Shimbun,* May 13, 1997, p 1.

371 "Joint Staff Council Chairman on Alleged DPRK Missile Test," *Nihon Keizai Shimbun,* October 18, 1996.

372 "Do Not Poke Your Nose and Make a Fuss," Korean Central Broadcasting Network, November 5, 1996.

373 "DPRK Official Reportedly Expresses Regret Over Sub Incident," KBS-1 Radio Network, November 12, 1996.

374 "DPRK Ready To Test-Fire Missile in Sea of Japan," *Sankei Shimbun,* August 21, 1998, p 1.

375 "Japan's First Intelligence Satellites Will Be Able to Capture Images of 'North Korea' Only," *Shukan Bunshun,* December 19, 2002, pp 152-155.

376 In fact, the *Myoko* was Japan's only operational Aegis destroyer available for duty in the Sea of Japan: the *Kongo* was undergoing maintenance work in Sasebo, and the *Kirishima* was cruising to Hawaii to participate in joint US-Japan military exercises. The MSDF's newest Aegis destroyer, the *Chokai,* had been newly deployed to Sasebo in April and was engaged in a shake-down voyage. "Japan: State Incapable of Waging War," *Bungei Shunju,* November 1998, pp 151-2.

377 "Impact of the Missile," *Nihon Keizai Shimbun,* September 2, 1998, p 2.

378 "North Korea Fires Missile Into Pacific Over Japan," Kyodo, August 31, 1998.

379 "Japan: State Incapable of Waging War," *Bungei Shunju*, November 1998, pp 150-157.

380 "Japan: State Incapable of Waging War," *Bungei Shunju*, November 1998, pp 150-157.

381 Interview with Yuko Kuniya, "Nonaka on North Korean Missile Launching," Close-up Gendai, NHK TV, September 7, 1998.

382 "Is Japan Safe—Impact of the Taepodong: Firm Crisis Management System Needed," *Yomiuri Shimbun*, December 15, 1998, pp 1-2.

383 "Impact of the Missile," *Nihon Keizai Shimbun*, September 2, 1998, p 2.

384 "Japan Freezes Offer To Resume Normalization Talks," Kyodo, September 1, 1998.

385 Sato, Shigemi, "Japan Gives Symbolic Response to North Korean Missile," AFP, September 1, 1998.

386 "Radio Announces Successful 'Satellite' Launch," Pyongyang Korean Central Broadcasting Network, September 4, 1998.

387 "Successful Launch of First Satellite in DPRK," KCNA, September 4, 1998.

388 "Kim Yong-nam Speech at SPA" Korean Central Broadcasting Network, September 5, 1998.

389 Sim, Kyu-son, "North Korea's Taepo Dong Missile Officially Named 'Paektusan No. 1'," *Tong-a Ilbo*, September 7, 2001.

390 "LDP Says DPRK Risked War by Firing Missile," Kyodo, August 31, 1998.

391 "Obuchi Criticizes DPRK on Missile Firing," Kyodo, September 3, 1998.

392 "Nonaka Responds to KCNA Statement on Missile Launch," Kyodo, September 2, 1998.

393 "Diet Resolutions Condemn DPRK Missile Firing," Kyodo, September 3, 1998.

394 "Japan Urges Security Council To Discuss DPRK Missile Test," Kyodo, September 9, 1998.

395 "LDP Mission Seeks UNSC Statement on DPRK Rocket," Kyodo, September 12, 1998.

396 "Missile Group To Discuss Curbing DPRK Missile Exports," Kyodo, September 3, 1998.

397 MTCR Press Release, "Chairman's Statement on North Korean Missile Proliferation Activities, 1998," October 9, 1998, www.mtcr.info/english/public/1998.html.

398 MTCR Press Release, "Plenary Meeting of the Missile Technology Control Regime, Budapest, Hungary, 5-9 October 1998," October 9, 1998, www.mtcr.info/english/press/budapest.html.

399 "Japan Asks ICAO To Censure North Korea on Missile," Kyodo, September 4, 1998.

400 "Federation of Airline Unions Condemns Missile Tests," Kyodo, September 7, 1998.

401 "ICAO Criticizes North Korea's Rocket Launch," Kyodo, October 2, 1998.

402 "LDP To Set Up Reconnaissance Satellite Project Team," *Yomiuri Shimbun*, September 5, 1998, p 5.

403 "LDP Leader Pushes for U.S.-Proposed Missile Defense System," Kyodo, September 6, 1998.

404 "DA Report: BMD Concept Technologically Possible," *Nihon Keizai Shimbun*, September 7, 1998, p 2.

405 "DA To Decide on Acquiring Refueling Aircraft by August," Kyodo, December 30, 1998.

406 Tsuboi, Yuzuru, "Mr. Nonaka 'Grinds His Teeth' Over the North Korean Missile Issue," *Aera*, September 21, 1998, p 25.

407 "Nonaka: Japan To Halt All Charter Flights to DPRK," Kyodo, September 2, 1998.

408 Interview with Yuko Kuniya, "Nonaka on North Korean Missile Launching," Close-up Gendai, NHK TV, September 7, 1998.

409 Aso, Iku, "Self Defense Force Troops Came Close to Dying 'a Hero's Death' in Hot Drama of Chasing Spy Operation Ships," *Bungei Shunju,* May 1999, pp 146-152.

410 Suzuki, Toichi, "Self-Defense Forces' First 'Maritime Defense Activity'–Unfortunately Allowed Suspicious Vessels to Escape," *Shukan Daiyamondo,* April 10, 1999, pp 156-158.

411 Kotaki, Kunio, "Japanese Maritime Defense Industry: 3) Weapons," *Sekai no Kansen,* March 1997, pp 90-97.

412 Taoka, Shunji, "The Grand Sea Chase: Why the Spy Boats Could Not Be Captured," *Sekai no Kansen,* June, 1999, pp 110-113.

413 Taoka, Shunji, "The Grand Sea Chase: Why the Spy Boats Could Not Be Captured," *Sekai no Kansen,* June, 1999, pp 110-113.

414 Aso, Iku, "Self Defense Force Troops Came Close to Dying 'a Hero's Death' in Hot Drama of Chasing Spy Operation Ships," *Bungei Shunju,* May 1999, pp 146-152.

415 Taoka, Shunji, "The Grand Sea Chase: Why the Spy Boats Could Not Be Captured," *Sekai no Kansen,* June, 1999, pp 110-113.

416 "Ship Captain Regrets Failure To Stop Intruder Ships," Kyodo News Agency, March 28, 1999.

417 Taoka, Shunji, "The Grand Sea Chase: Why the Spy Boats Could Not Be Captured," *Sekai no Kansen,* June, 1999, pp 110-113.

418 Aso, Iku, "Self Defense Force Troops Came Close to Dying 'a Hero's Death' in Hot Drama of Chasing Spy Operation Ships," *Bungei Shunju,* May 1999, pp 146-152.

419 "Destroyers Fire at Ships; Obuchi To Summon Cabinet," Kyodo News Agency, March 23, 1999.

420 Aso, Iku, "Self Defense Force Troops Came Close to Dying 'a Hero's Death' in Hot Drama of Chasing Spy Operation Ships," *Bungei Shunju,* May 1999, pp 146-152.

421 Statement by Defense Agency Director Hosei Norota, NHK TV, March 23, 1999.

422 "Government Sources Say Mystery Ships Entered DPRK Waters," Kyodo, March 24, 1999.

423 "Further on Intruder Ships Entering DPRK Port," Kyodo, March 25, 1999.

424 "Source: SDF Detected Seven Suspicious Ships," *Tokyo Shimbun,* April 4, 1999, p 1.

425 Intelligence Issue Research Group, "The Threat of North Korea-Built Ships," *Chian Foramu,* April 2002, pp 2-9.

426 "Drug Trafficking as Foreign Policy?" *Bangkok Post,* June 13, 1999.

427 Hwang Chang-yop, "North Korean Economy," National Intelligence Service website, March 6, 2003.

428 "North's 'Tobacco Road' Leads to Opium," *Dong-a Ilbo,* February 1, 2006.

429 Kojima, Shinichi and An Myong-chin, "Are You Again Feigning Ignorance, Kim Chong-il!: Photos Proving North Korea's Cultivation of Opium Poppies as a 'National Scheme'," *Seiron,* February 2004, pp 148-155.

430 ROK National Intelligence Service, "Production of Drugs in North Korea," April 20, 2004.

431 Kang Ch'o'l-hwan, "China 'Ailing' From North Korean-Made Drugs – 'Drugs Now Bigger Problem Than North Korean Escapees'," *Choson Ilbo,* October 9, 2004.

432 Ch'oe Yong-chae, "Reporter Ch'oe Yong-chae, Disguised as a Drug Dealer, Witnessed the Secret Dealing of North Korea-manufactured Drugs – 'Life? We Cannot Guarantee You Life. Merchandise? We Can Guarantee You That'," *Sindong-a,* September 2002, pp 82-99.

433 "Japanese TV Reports North Korean Drug Trade on China-DPRK Border Area," TBS Television, October 23, 2005.

434 ROK National Intelligence Service, "Production of Drugs in North Korea," April 20, 2004.

435 "North Korea Said Flooding Asia With Illegal Narcotics," *Bangkok Post*, May 13, 1999.

436 "DPRK Ship Captain Nabbed on Suspicion of Drug Smuggling," Kyodo, April 19, 1997.

437 "Stimulants Found Off Kochi Allegedly From North Korea," Kyodo, January 7, 1999.

438 "ROK, Japan Seize DPRK Drugs Bound for Japan," *Choson Ilbo*, Ma 10, 1999.

439 "North Korea And Drugs," *Asahi Shimbun*, May 17, 2006.

440 "*Kyonen, Tairyo Sekishu Sareta Kakuseizai, Kitachosen Kara 33%*," ("33% of Large Seizures of Amphetamines From North Korea Last Year"), *Nihon Keizai Shimbun*, evening edition, February 17, 2000, p 19.

441 "Australia To Destroy DPRK Ship Reportedly Used To Smuggle Narcotics," Yonhap, March 22, 2006.

442 "North Korea And Drugs," *Asahi Shimbun*, May 17, 2006.

443 Mayama, Kenji, "Exposure of North Korean 'Suspected Stimulant-Carrier Vessel' Network – Smuggler-Broker Makes Shocking Confession on Clandestine Smuggling Routes," *Gendai*, June 2002, pp 40-47.

444 U.S. Department of State, *2002 International Narcotics Control Strategy Report*, p. VIII-43, www.state.gov/documents/organization/18168.pdf.

445 "Japan Coast Guard To Equip More Patrol Boats With 20-Millimeter Machine Guns," Kyodo, December 27, 2001.

446 "Mystery vessel likely multipurpose N. Korean spy ship: agency," Kyodo, December 28, 2001.

447 "Japanese Defense Experts Discuss Activity of Suspected Spy Ship," *Yomiuri Shimbun*, December 26, 2001.

448 "Coast guard confirms it has found missing sunken ship," Kyodo, February 26, 2002.

449 "Japan may consider compensation to China over salvaging ship," Kyodo, February 27, 2002.

450 PRC Vessel Keeps Monitoring Japan's Probe of Sunken Suspicious Ship," *Sankei Shimbun,* evening edition, p 11, February 27, 2002.

451 Handa, Shigeru, "What Will Come Out of the DPRK's 'Suspicious Ship'?" *Bungei Shunju,* September 2002, pp 322-328.

452 "*Amami Oki no Chinbotsu Fushinsen to Dogatasen, Chugoku Gunko ni Kiko, Beisatsuei, Nihon ni Teikyo,*" ("US Photographs Ship Similar to Suspicious Vessel Sunk in Waters Near Amami Stops at Chinese Naval Port, Provided to Japan"), Asahi Shimbun, March 1, 2002, p 1.

453 "U.S. Photos Show Sunken Ship May Have Docked in China," Kyodo, March 1, 2002.

454 "'Kita' Fushinsen, Shanhai Oki de Kyuyu, Yojo, Kosaku Bosen Kara, Jiken Chokuzen ni Tsushin Boju Nikai, Kei-sanseki Katsudo ka," ("Suspicious Vessel from 'North' Refueled in Waters Near Shanghai from Operations Mother Ship, Communications Intercepted Twice Immediately Before Incident, Three Ships Possibly Active"), Tokyo Shimbun, July 3, 2002, p 1.

455 PRC Foreign Minister Tang Jiaxuan News Conference, CCTV-1, March 6, 2002.

456 Hiramatsu, Shigeo, "Speculation Regarding the Appearance of Chinese Ships in Japanese Waters – Petroleum Resources Surveys or Military Strategy?" *Ekonomisuto,* March 19, 2002, pp 80-82.

457 "Japan Counters China's 'Rash' Remarks Over Suspicious Ships," Kyodo, March 8, 2002.

458 "*Unazukenu Tang Gaisho no Hatsugen,*" ("FM Tang's Statement of Disapproval,") *Nihon Keizai Shimbun,* March 8, 2002.

459 "Salvage of 'Spy Ship' Important," *Yomiuri Shimbun*, March 14, 2002.

460 "Li Understands Japan's Concern Over Ship Issue," Kyodo, April 3, 2002.

461 "Koizumi, Li To Seek Mutually Acceptable Solution Over Ship," Kyodo, April 4, 2002.

462 "*Higashi Shinakai-Fushinsen Jiken, Itai, Fune ni Kotei, Ropu de Fukusu*," *Yomiuri Shimbun*, May 5, 2002, p 1.

463 "Coast Guard Probe Team Leaves Sunken Ship Site," Kyodo, May 8, 2002.

464 "Five North Korean Defectors Fail To Enter Japan Consulate," Kyodo, May 9, 2002.

465 In the summer of 2000, two retired Ministry of Foreign Affairs diplomats attempted to rationalize in a Japanese conversation with this author how U.S. policy in the 1930s was an "act of war" that led to Tokyo's decision to bomb Pearl Harbor. Their arguments adhered closely to the historical narrative as espoused at the Yushukan, indicating that at least some officials in Tokyo continue to espouse that erroneous narrative.

466 "Foreign Ministry Spokesman's Press Conference on 25 June 2002," Ministry of Foreign Affairs of the People's Republic of China, June 25, 2002.

467 "Salvaged DPRK Spy Ship Found Disguised as Japanese-Chinese Fishing Boat," *Sankei Shimbun*, September 24, 2002.

468 "Sunken Ship Resembles N. Korean Ship in 1998 Drug Case," Kyodo, December 23, 2001.

469 "Geo-Positioning Systems on North Korean Spy Ship Were Japanese," Kyodo, October 20, 2002.

470 "Electronic Marine Chart Made by Coast Guard Found in DPRK Spy Ship," *Asahi Shimbun*, October 22, 2002.

471 "Interview with An Myong-chin, Former DPRK Agent," *Sankei Shimbun*, March 13, 1997.

472 "Updated List of Abducted, Missing Japanese Nationals," Kyodo, September 17, 2002.

473 "Governor Urges Diplomatic Response To Alleged Abduction," Kyodo, April 3, 1997.

474 "*Yokota Megumi-san Rachi Giwaku Nintei, Seifu, Tai-Kitachosen Seisaku wo Tenkan,*" ("With Recognition of Megumi Yokota's Suspected Abduction, Government Changes North Korea Policy"), *Sankei Shimbun*, May 2, 1997, p 2.

475 "Senior Police Official: DPRK Involved in 10 Kidnappings," Kyodo, May 1, 1997.

476 "Outline and Background of Abduction Cases of Japanese Nationals by North Korea," Ministry of Foreign Affairs website, April 19, 2002.

477 "Stop Foolish Acts," Korean Central Broadcast Network, June 13, 1998.

478 "Red Cross Official Decries Japan's Remarks on Kidnappings," Kyodo, June 25, 1998.

479 "Arimoto Disappeared While Studying in Britain in 1983," Kyodo, September 17, 2002.

480 "Updated List of Abducted, Missing Japanese Nationals," Kyodo, September 17, 2002.

481 "*'25nen Gaman Shita,' Rachi Jiken no Higaisha Kazoku, Koizumi Shusho to Menkai,*" ("'I've Waited 25 Years,' Families of Abduction Victims Meet Prime Minister Koizumi"), *Yomiuri Shimbun*, evening edition March 19, 2002, p 1.

482 "*Rachi Jiken 'Ichi-Nichi Mo Hayaku Kyushutsu wo,*" ("Abduction Incidents: "Please Rescue Them Quickly'"), *Yomiuri Shimbun*, March 20, 2002, p 30.

483 "Japan Red Army Community 'Live in Luxury' in DPRK," *Asahi Shimbun*, March 14, 2002.

484 "Japan Red Army Member Tanaka Gets 12 Years In Hijacking Case," Jiji Press, February 14, 2002.

485 "Former Japanese Red Army Hijackers Deny Role in Abductions, 'Ready To Come Home'," *Asahi Shimbun*, July 11, 2002.

486 "Spokesman for DPRK Foreign Ministry on Those Concerned With Plane Yodo," KCNA, July 26, 2002.

487 "Small Entourage To Accompany Koizumi To Pyongyang," Jiji, September 11, 2002.

488 NHK Television, September 17, 2002.

489 "Pyongyang Summit Talks Evolved Quickly," *Yomiuri Shimbun*, September 20, 2002.

490 "Abductee Yokota's Husband Might Be South Korean Named Kim Yong Nam," Kyodo, February 2, 2006.

491 NHK Television, September 17, 2002.

492 "Pyongyang Summit Talks Evolved Quickly," *Yomiuri Shimbun*, September 20, 2002.

493 "Japanese Official Meets Four Survivors of 11 Abductees," Kyodo, September 17, 2002.

494 "Yokota's daughter now 15, living in Pyongyang," Kyodo, September 18, 2002.

495 "Pyongyang Summit Talks Evolved Quickly," *Yomiuri Shimbun*, September 20, 2002.

496 "Koizumi, Kim Sign Joint Declaration – VIDEO," NHK Television, September 17, 2002.

497 "Full text of Japan-N. Korea Pyongyang Declaration," Kyodo, September 17, 2002.

498 "Poll Shows Large Majority Think Abduction Issue Must Be Resolved," *Yomiuri Shimbun*, September 20, 2002, p 2.

499 "Poll Shows Cabinet Rating Rising to 61 Percent After Summit Talks," *Asahi Shimbun*, September 20, 2002.

500 "Hardly 'Natural' Causes," *Asahi Shimbun*, September 20, 2002.

501 "Government To Seek North Korean Compensation for Abductions, Ship Battle," *Nihon Keizai Shimbun*, September 22, 2002.

502 "Support Group Asks Gov't To Search for '60 Other Abductees'," Kyodo, September 27, 2002.

503 "Police Add Soga, Mother, Two Men to Abduction List," Kyodo, October 8, 2002.

504 "*Jenkinsu-shi, Beijohokan Daho ni Kyoryoku ka, 68-nen, Kita de Choshuji Tsuyaku Nado,*" ("Jenkins Suspected in Cooperating With Seizure of US Intelligence Ship in 1968, Translating During Interrogations in North"), *Sankei Shimbun,* July 30, 2004, p 1; "Jenkins May Have Aided Seizure of U.S. Spy Ship, Paper Says," Kyodo, July 30, 2004.

505 "Relatives Describe Video of Abductees as Unnatural," Kyodo, October 3, 2002.

506 "Couple Abducted by North Korea Register Marriage in Hometown," Kyodo, October 23, 2002.

507 "Soga's Family Trying To Restore Her Name in Registry," Kyodo, October 22, 2002.

508 "Three More Abductees From North Korea Receive Japanese Passports," Kyodo, October 19, 2002.

509 "Japan Asks US To Grant Amnesty to Abductee's Husband," Kyodo, October 23, 2002.

510 "Japan Says Five Abductees Will Not Return to North Korea," Kyodo, October 24, 2002.

511 "Niigata Woman Tells Japanese Mission Story of Abduction to DPRK," Kyodo, October 3, 2002.

512 "Hasuikes tell how they were abducted to N. Korea 25 years ago," Kyodo, July 30, 2003.

513 "Two 'Top-Secret' North Korean Agencies Involved in Abductions," Kyodo, October 12, 2002.

514 "North Korea Engaged in Nuclear Development Since 1997," Kyodo, October 20, 2002.

515 "North Korea Carried on Nuke Program Due to Reactor Delays," Kyodo, October 18, 2002.

516 "DPRK Offers To Abandon Nuclear Program if U.S. Accepts 3 Conditions," Kyodo, October 18, 2002.

517 "Japan Told Of N. Korea Nuke Plan Before Summit," Jiji, October 17, 2002.

518 "Ex-Japanese PM Hashimoto Told DPRK Admitted Nuclear Arms Development at US Talks," Kyodo, October 17, 2002.

519 "Abduction Rows Cloud Japan-North Korea Talks Resumption," November 12, 2002.

520 "Baker Says Statute of Limitations for Jenkins Not Yet Begun, December 2, 2002.

521 "Japan, ROK Said Urging US To Continue Heavy Oil Shipments to DPRK," AFP, November 9, 2002.

522 "North Korea's Nuclear Complex Shut Off From Outside Monitoring," AFP, December 31, 2002.

523 "[DPRK] Will Not Return to NPT Even If Heavy Fuel Oil Supply Resumes," *Tong-a Ilbo*, January 13, 2003.

524 "Statement of DPRK Government," KCNA, January 10, 2003.

525 "[DPRK] Will Not Return to NPT Even If Heavy Fuel Oil Supply Resumes," *Tong-a Ilbo*, January 13, 2003.

526 "FM Spokesman Says DPRK 'Successfully Reprocessing' Fuel Rods in 'Final Stage'," KCNA and KCBS, April 18, 2003; "U.S. Sources Say Pyongyang Mistranslated Statement on Fuel Reprocessing," Kyodo, April 20, 2003.

527 "Editorial Calls For Diplomatic Solution to DPRK Nuclear Crisis," *Asahi Shimbun*, April 26, 2003.

528 "Further on US Source Confirms North Korea Reprocessing Nuclear Fuel," Kyodo, July 11, 2003.

529 Ota, Horoyuki, "What Should We Do If No Dong Missiles Are Fired?" *Aera*, April 7, 2003, pp 83-85.

530 "Editorial Calls For Diplomatic Solution to DPRK Nuclear Crisis," *Asahi Shimbun*, April 26, 2003.

531 "Crossing A Thin Line," *Asahi Shimbun*, July 15, 2003.

532 "Pressure Needed On North Korea," *Yomiuri Shimbun*, July 14, 2003.

533 "Kidnap victim receives reply from family in North Korea," Kyodo, May 12, 2003.

534 "North Korea refuses to accept abductees' letters to children," Kyodo, May 10, 2003.

535 "Soga, Chimuras Cast Ballots for First Time in Japan Since Return," Kyodo, April 13, 2003.

536 "Emperor, Empress Welcome Hasuikes Home from North Korea," Kyodo, June 13, 2003.

537 "North Korea Sounds Japan Out Trip by Abductees' Kin to Japan," Kyodo, July 31, 2003.

538 "No Talks Before Abductees' Kin Sent to Japan: Ministers," Kyodo, August 5, 2003.

539 "Daily Says DPRK To 'Conditionally' Allow Abductees' Families To Visit Japan," Kyodo, August 19, 2003.

540 An Yong-chol, "Former Ranking KPA Official Discloses the Whole Truth About Japanese Abductions, Tells of Megumi Yokota's Husband and the Korean Central News Agency," *Gendai*, July 2003.

541 "Kyodo: Pyongyang Sets up New Organization To Deal With Japan," Kyodo, January 7, 2004.

542 Toru Hasuike, Tsutomu Nishioka, Katsuei Hirasawa, "Mr. X Came to Beijing To Attend an 'Extremely Secret Contact': The True Identity of Kim Chong-il's Emissary," *Bungei Shunju*, March 2004, pp 138-146.

543 "Yamasaki, Hirasawa Make Secret Trip To China for N. Korea Talks," Kyodo, April 1, 2004.

544 Toichi Suzuki, "Effects of Visit to China by Prime Minister Koizumi's Secret Envoys, Yamasaki and Hirasawa," *Shukan Daiyamondo*, April 17, 2004, pp 116-118.

545 "Koizumi Brings Five Abductees' Kin But Greeted by Criticism," Kyodo, May 22, 2004.

546 "Koizumi's DPRK Visit Seen as Ceremonial, Serving Interests of Both Sides," Kyodo, May 22, 2004.

547 "Families of Missing Abductees Angry at Outcome of Summit," Kyodo, May 22, 2004.

548 "No Real Results From Koizumi's Pyongyang Trip," *Yomiuri Shimbun,* May 22, 2004.

549 "Japanese TV Airs Poll Results: 66 Percent Approve of PM Koizumi's 2nd DPRK Visit," TBS Television News 23, May 24, 2004.

550 "Koizumi Answers Questions on Meeting With Kim, Abduction, Nuclear Issues," NHK Television, May 22, 2004.

551 "Koizumi Makes Statement on Results of Talks With Kim Chong-il," NHK Television, May 22, 2004.

552 "US Army Loses Letters Proving Jenkins' Desertion to North Korea," *Yomiuri Shimbun,* April 22, 2003.

553 "Soga Rejects Beijing as Venue for Family Reunion," Kyodo, May 31, 2004.

554 "Reunion of Soga Family Planned on 9 July," Kyodo Clue II, July 5, 2004.

555 "Ex-LDP Vice President Yamasaki Says US Not Opposed to Soga-Jenkins Reunion," Kyodo, July 8, 2004.

556 "Indonesia Police To Provide Tight Security for Soga, Family," Kyodo, July 7, 2004.

557 "TV Asahi Shows Inside of Pyongyang Airport, DPRK Officials," Asahi Television, July 9, 2004.

558 Tatsuyoshi Tsutsumi and Atsuko Kinoshita, "Soga, Family Have Dinner With Envoy," *Yomiuri Shimbun,* July 12, 2004.

559 "Japan Rejects DPRK Request on Jenkins Meeting: Cabinet Secretariat Official," Agence France-Presse, July 12, 2004.

560 "Soga, Jenkins, Daughters Stay at Jakarta Hotel Saturday," Kyodo, July 10, 2004.

561 "US Amb. Urges Jenkins To Enter Plea Bargain With US," Jiji, July 16, 2004.

562 "Jenkins Not in Serious Condition But To Stay in Hospital," Kyodo, July 23, 2004.

563 "Jenkins Found Not To Have Cancer, Japanese Gov't Says," Kyodo, August 3, 2004.

564 "Alleged US Deserter Jenkins Begins Full-Time Duty at Camp Zama," Kyodo, September 17, 2004.

565 "Alleged US Deserter Jenkins Begins Full-Time Duty at Camp Zama," Kyodo, September 17, 2006.

566 "Jenkins Video Footage Released," *Yomiuri Shimbun*, September 16, 2004.

567 Kobayashi, Kakumi, "Jenkins Found Guilty of Desertion, Aiding Enemy," Kyodo, November 3, 2004.

568 "Prosecutors Seek 9-Month Jail for Jenkins, Dishonorable Discharge," Kyodo, November 3, 2004.

569 "Jenkins Given 30 Days in Jail, Dishonorable Discharge," Kyodo, November 3, 2004.

570 "Jenkins Released From U.S. Military Detention Facility," Kyodo, November 27, 2004.

571 McNeill, David, "Charles Jenkins: Prisoner of Pyongyang," *The Independent*, March 7, 2006. Jenkins offered some insights about the country in which he had lived most of his adult life, telling Kyodo in an interview, for example, that Pyongyang's foreigner-only department store stopped taking dollars because Pyongyang's counterfeiting efforts were beginning to backfire: counterfeiters were using the fake dollars at the department store in Pyongyang!

572 "Foreign Kin Join Call To Pressure North," *Asahi Shimbun*, January 1, 2006.

573 "Soga Talks To Thai Abductee's Kin, Group Meets Foreign Minister Aso," Kyodo, December 22, 2005.

574 Taoka, Shunji, "'*Itoteki' ka 'Koho Misu' ka, Chugoku Gensen no Ryokai Shinhan Jiken wo Kensho Suru*," ("'Intentional' or 'Navigational Error'? – Examining Chinese Nuclear Submarine's Violation of Japan's Territorial Waters") *Sekai no Kansen*, February 2005, pp 141-145.

575 Furumoto, Yoso, "Suspicious Submarine: Intrusion of Territorial Waters; DA Sends AWACS to Surrounding Ocean; Watch Out for Chinese Fighter Jets," *Mainichi Shimbun*, November 13, 2004.

576 Taoka, Shunji, "'*Itoteki' ka 'Koho Misu' ka, Chugoku Gensen no Ryokai Shinhan Jiken wo Kensho Suru*," ("'Intentional' or 'Navigational Error'? – Examining Chinese Nuclear Submarine's Violation of Japan's Territorial Waters") *Sekai no Kansen*, February 2005, pp 141-145.

577 580 "China Expresses Regret Over Submarine Incursion Due To 'Technical Glitch'; Rules Out Deliberation," *Sankei Shimbun*, November 17, 2004, p 1.

578 Photos of Chinese Ships Spotted Near Japan, NHK Television, November 10, 2004.

579 "Senior Officer Not Convinced of Technical Glitch," *Nihon Keizai Shimbun*, November 17, 2004, p 2.

580 Taoka, Shunji, "'*Itoteki' ka 'Koho Misu' ka, Chugoku Gensen no Ryokai Shinhan Jiken wo Kensho Suru*," ("'Intentional' or 'Navigational Error'? – Examining Chinese Nuclear Submarine's Violation of Japan's Territorial Waters") *Sekai no Kansen*, February 2005, pp 141-145.

581 "China Expresses Regret Over Submarine Incursion Due to 'Technical Glitch;' Rules Out Deliberation," *Sankei Shimbun*, November 17, 2004.

582 585 "China Admits Sub Entered Japan Waters, Expresses Regret," Kyodo, November 16, 2004.

583 Hiramatsu, Shigeo, "Speculation Regarding the Appearance of Chinese Ships in Japanese Waters – Petroleum Resources Surveys or Military Strategy?" *Ekonomisuto*, March 19, 2002, pp 80-82.

584 "PRC Ship Activities Near Japan," *Sankei Shimbun*, May 21, 1999.

585 Hiramatsu, Shigeo, "Speculation Regarding the Appearance of Chinese Ships in Japanese Waters – Petroleum Resources

Surveys or Military Strategy?" *Ekonomisuto,* March 19, 2002, pp 80-82.

586 Kayahara, Ikuo, "Military Aims of China's Ocean Forays – Objective Not Just Resources," *Chuo Koron,* October 2004, pp 62-69.

587 Hiramatsu, Shigeo, "The Aim of the Chinese Submarine in Waters Near Japan – With Taiwan in Mind, Preparing To Block US Aircraft Carriers," *Sankei Shimbun,* November 17, 2004.

588 "Excerpt of 2004 Defense White Paper," *2004 Boei Hakusho,* July 2004.

589 Guo Longlong, "The Chinese Nation Certainly Can Achieve Its Great Reunification Cause–Marking the 90th Anniversary of the 1911 Revolution," *Ta Kung Pao,* October 10, 2001.

590 Lu Baosheng, Guo Hongjun, "Okinawa: 'Hub' of the Pacific," *Jiefangjun Bao,* June 22, 2003, p 4.

591 "Four Vessels Start Serving PLA Navy," *Sing Tao Jih Pao,* July 21, 2004.

592 Lou Douzi, "Looking at Navy and Air Force Dispositions Following Establishment Restructuring (1)," *Jiefangjun Bao,* July 14, 2004

593 Hiramatsu, Shigeo, "The Aim of the Chinese Submarine in Waters Near Japan – With Taiwan in Mind, Preparing To Block US Aircraft Carriers," *Sankei Shimbun,* November 17, 2004.

594 "Key Question is Whether Japan's MSDF Can Mobilize its Sailors," *Jeitai vs. Chugoku Gun; Jieitai Wa Kakutatakaeri!* September 2005.

595 "Japan Scrambled Jets 107 Times Against Chinese Planes in FY '05," Jiji, April 20, 2006.

596 Hanzawa, Naohisa, "Surge Seen in PRC Intrusion Into Japanese Air Defense Identification Zone; Seen as Attempt To Make It Established Fact," *Sankei Shimbun,* February 21, 2006.

597 Singh, K. Gajendra, "Strategic Chess Moves Across Eurasia," *South Asia Analysis Group*, August 15, 2005.

598 "Russia, China May Repeat Military Exercise With Other Countries Next Year," ITAR-TASS, August 26, 2005. It could be argued that the title of that organization, "Shanghai Co-operation Organization," points to the intended fulcrum of power for the group.

599 US DoD, "Annual Report to Congress: Military Power of the People's Republic of China 2006," p i, www.defenselink.mil/pubs/pdfs/China%20Report%202006.pdf.

600 See "Chronology of U.S.-North Korean Nuclear and Missile Diplomacy," 2002, Arms Control Association, www.armscontrol.org/factsheets/dprkchron.

601 "Statement of DPRK Government on its withdrawal from NPT," KCNA, January 10, 2003.

602 "Situation of Human Rights in the DPRK," A/60/306, UNGA, August 29, 2005, daccess-dds-ny.un.org/doc/UNDOC/GEN/N05/474/77/PDF/N0547477.pdf.

603 "Resolution Adopted by the General Assembly on 16 December 2005: Situation of Human Rights in the DPRK," A/60/173, UNGA, December 16, 2005, www.un.org/en/ga/search/view_doc.asp?symbol=A/RES/60/173.

604 "Treasury Designates Banco Delta Asia as Primary Money Laundering Concern under USA PATRIOT Act," Press Center, U.S. Department of the Treasury, September 15, 2005, www.treasury.gov/press-center/press-releases/Pages/js2720.aspx.

605 Lague, David and Donald Greenlees, "Squeeze on Banco Delta Asia hit North Korea where it hurt," *New York Times*, January 18, 2007, www.nytimes.com/2007/01/18/world/asia/18iht-north.4255039.html.

606 Hanzawa, Naohisa and Taro Saito, "Response to Possible Launching of Taepo Dong," *Sankei Shimbun*, July 1, 2006.

607 "DPRK Foreign Ministry Spokesman on Its Missile Launches," KCNA, July 6, 2006, www.kcna.co.jp/item/2006/200607/news07/07.htm.

608 Sassa, Atsuyuki, "Speed Up Missile Defense Deployment to Counter North Korea's Missile Launches," *Sankei Shimbun*, July 6, 2006.

609 According to the Ministry of Defense's "Fundamental Concepts of National Defense," "Under international law, there is recognition that a state has the right of collective self-defense, that is, the right to use armed strength to stop armed attack on a foreign country with which it has close relations, although the state is not under direct attack. It is beyond doubt that as a sovereign state, Japan has the right of collective self-defense under international law. It is, however, not permissible to use the right, that is, to stop armed attack on another country with armed strength, although Japan is not under direct attack, since it exceeds the limit of use of armed strength as permitted under Article 9 of the Constitution." See the Ministry of Defense Web site, www.mod.go.jp/e/d_act/d_policy/dp01.html.

610 "Security Council Condemns DPRK's Missile Launches, Unanimously Adopting Resolution 1965 (2006)," United Nations Security Council SC/8778, July 15, 2006, www.un.org/News/Press/docs/2006/sc8778.doc.htm.

611 "Security Council Condemns DPRK's Missile Launches, Unanimously Adopting Resolution 1965 (2006)," United Nations Security Council SC/8778, July 15, 2006, www.un.org/News/Press/docs/2006/sc8778.doc.htm.

612 "DPRK Foreign Ministry Clarifies Stand on New Measure to Bolster War Deterrent," KCNA, October 3, 2006, www.kcna.co.jp/item/2006/200610/news10/04.htm.

613 Matsukawa, Takashi, "DPRK's Statement on Test Found Similar to that of PRC's Statement in 1964," *Tokyo Shimbun*, Evening Edition, October 5, 2006.

614 "Statement by the President of the Security Council," United Nations Security Council S/PRST/2006/41, October 6, 2006, www.un.org/en/ga/search/view_doc.asp?symbol=S/PRST/2006/41.

615 Miyano, Hiroyuki, "Japan Boosts Surveillance of North Korean Nuclear Bomb Tests in Coordination with Other Countries," *Sankei Shimbun*, October 7, 2006.

616 "Defense Agency Reinforces Surveillance on North Korea," *Nihon Keizai Shimbun*, October 8, 2006.

617 "Special Feature 2: The Even of 9 October 2006: A Test Case for the CTBT Verification Regime," *CTBTO Preparatory Commission Annual Report 2006*, pp 41-2, www.ctbto.org/fileadmin/content/reference/annualreport/2006/english/Complete_AR_2007_E.pdf.

618 Chanlett-Avery, Emma and Sharon Squassoni, "North Korea's Nuclear Test: Motivations, Implications, and U.S. Options," *CRS Report for Congress*, October 24, 2006, p 1, www.fas.org/sgp/crs/nuke/RL33709.pdf.

619 "Security Council Condemns Nuclear Test by DPRK, Unanimously Adopting Resolution 1718 (2006)," United Nations Security Council SC/8853, October 14, 2006, www.un.org/News/Press/docs/2006/sc8853.doc.htm.

620 "DPRK Foreign Ministry Vehemently Refutes UNSC's 'Presidential Statement'," KCNA, April 14, 2009, www.kcna.co.jp/item/2009/200904/news14/20090414-23ee.html.

621 "Efforts To Reorganize Government Ministries," *Nihon Keizai Shimbun*, November 20, 1998.

622 "Murayama's Resignation News Conference Reported," Kyodo, January 5, 1996.

623 *Morino Gunji Kenkyujo, Jiseidai no Rikujo Jieitai*, ("Next-Generation Ground Self-Defense Force: Fighting Future Wars"), (Tokyo: Kaya Shobo, 1996).

624 Kuwada, Etsu, "Former General Views Defense Issues," *Gekkan JADI*, May 1995, pp 13-19.

625 Kamei, Kotaro, "Japan-US Security Redefinition and Asian Arms Buildup Era," *Gunji Kenkyu*, July 1996, pp 198-209.

626 "Hashimoto Elected Prime Minister; Style Noted," Kyodo News Agency, January 11, 1996.

627 "Full Text of Prime Minister Ryutaro Hashimoto's Policy Speech to the Diet," Kyodo News Agency, January 22, 1996.

628 Given this lack of authority and rank, the October 1993 government reform recommendations included a proposal to raise the cabinet secretariat office director positions to the vice minister level and to extend the term of office in order to improve the authority of the cabinet secretariat in relation to the ministries. It was hoped that these reforms would enhance the prestige of the position and attract higher caliber personnel to the *Kantei*. "*San Shitcho wo Jikankyu ni*," ("Three Office Director Posts To Become Administrative Vice Minister-Level Ones"), *Sankei Shimbun*, August 13, 1994, p 2.

629 Hisamoto, Yukio, "The Cabinet Secretariat and Crisis Management," *Voice*, August 1997, pp 134-145.

630 Aso, *Joho Kantei ni Tassezu*, p 186.

631 Omori, *Nihon no Interijensu Kikan*, pp 37-38.

632 Hisamoto, Yukio, "The Cabinet Secretariat and Crisis Management," *Voice*, August 1997, pp 134-145.

633 "The Application of the Antisubversive Activities Law Is Obvious: The Dangerous Aum Remnant 'UP Team'," *Bungei Shunju*, November 1995, pp 148-155.

634 Aso, Iku, "Prime Minister's Office in Nervous Breakdown Over Crisis Management Problems," *Bungei Shunju*, July 1996.

635 Aso, *Joho Kantei ni Tassezu*, pp 176-182.

636 Sasajima, Masahiko and Takashi Nishida, "Poor Information Strategy Stands Out," *Yomiuri Shimbun*, April 17, 1998, p 2.

637 "Sectionalism Hampering Nation's Espionage," *Yomiuri Shimbun*, June 5, 2004.

638 Kajiyama, Seiroku, "Defense of Our Motherland; We Should Reject Contrivances Reflected in Security Debate; Why Have Japanese Neglected Common-Sense Approaches to Defending Their Own Country?" *Bungei Shunju*, June 1999, pp 160-173.

639 "Fukuda Would Take Over if Koizumi Incapacitated," Kyodo, September 22, 2003.

640 "*Inamori, Moroi, Ogura-shira... Gyokaku Honbu no Komon ni 'Arakuchi' Keizainin*," ("Administrative Reform Headquarters To Include Sharp-Tongued Businessmen as Advisors Such as Inamori, Moroi, Ogura"), *Mainichi Shimbun*, December 13, 1995, p 2.

641 "Cabinet Endorses Study To Move Capital Out of Tokyo," Kyodo, May 28, 1996.

642 "Hashimoto Directs CSAO Chief To Submit Monthly Report," *Asahi Shimbun*, August 17, 1996.

643 "Framework To Enhance Defense Guidelines Worked Out," *Mainichi Shimbun*, February 28, 1998, p 1.

644 "Toyoda Reportedly Hesitated Joining Reform Council," *Nihon Keizai Shimbun*, November 20, 1996.

645 "Hashimoto Urges New Panel To Push Administrative Reform," Kyodo, November 28, 1996.

646 "LDP Forms Subcommittee To Deal With International Terrorism," *Sankei Shimbun*, December 22, 1996.

647 "Anti-Terrorism Subcommittee Chairman on Crisis Management," *Sankei Shimbun*, December 30, 1996.

648 "LDP Subpanel Submits Proposals To Counter Terrorism," *Asahi Shimbun*, May 10, 1997, p 2.

649 "Government To Establish 'Intelligence Bureau' in Cabinet," *Yomiuri Shimbun*, March 31, 1997, p 1.

650 Hisamoto, Yukio, "The Cabinet Secretariat and Crisis Management," *Voice*, August 1997, pp 134-145.

651 The 20th meeting of the reform council, titled *gyosei kaikaku kaigi dai20kaigi jigaiyo* is available at: www.kantei.go.jp/jp/gyokaku/0707dai20.html

652 "Ex-Tokyo Police Chief Takes Crisis Management Post," Kyodo, April 1, 1998.

653 Sasajima, Masahiko and Takashi Nishida, "Poor Information Strategy Stands Out," *Yomiuri Shimbun,* April 17, 1998, p 2.

654 "Ando Named to New Cabinet Post for Crisis Management," Kyodo, April 7, 1998.

655 "Crisis Management Council Holds 1st Meeting," *Mainichi Shimbun,* May 12, 1998.

656 Sasajima, Masahiko and Takashi Nishida, "Poor Information Strategy Stands Out," *Yomiuri Shimbun,* April 17, 1998, p 2.

657 "*Kiki Kanri no Taiosaku Shiji, Kankei Shocho Renraku Kaigi ga Shokaigo,*" ("First Meeting of Government Agencies Involved in Crisis Management"), *Sankei Shimbun,* May 12, 1998, p 2.

658 "*Indoneshia Bodo, Zairyu Hojin Kyushutsu, Seifu, Jieitaiki Haken mo Junbi,*" ("Government Prepares Dispatch of SDF To Evacuate Japanese Nationals From Indonesia As Violence Errupts"), *Sankei Shimbun,* May 16, 1998, p 3.

659 "Japan Recommends Families To Leave Indonesia," Kyodo, May 17, 1998.

660 "Japan Steps Up Indonesia Rescue, Sends Planes, Ships," Kyodo, May 18, 1998.

661 "Tokyo Urges Restraint From Indonesia on Possible Rally," Kyodo, May 20, 1998.

662 "ASDF Evacuation Planes Depart Singapore for Home," Kyodo, May 27, 1998.

663 "*Kiki Kanrishitsu, Shokunren, Kokuki Fumei,*" ("Crisis Management Office Holds First Exercise Involving Missing Plane"), *Sankei Shimbun,* June 30, 1998, p 3; "First Drill Under New Crisis Management Chief Held," Kyodo News Service, June 29, 1998.

664 "Officials To Discuss Series of Poisoning Cases," Kyodo, September 18, 1998.

665 "*Shusho Kantei mo Kinpaku, Kanbochokanra Tsugi-tsugi Kaketsuke*," ("Prime Minister's Official Residence Was Also Tense as Chief Cabinet Secretary and Others Rushed In"), *Sankei Shimbun*, December 17, 1998, evening edition, p 11.

666 "*Joho Sakuso, Yureta Seifu, Kensho, Tepodon no Shogeki*," ("Intelligence Collection, a Shaken Government, the Shock of the Taepodong"), *Asahi Shimbun*, September 22, 1998, p 12.

667 "New Intelligence Committee Discusses DPRK at 1st Meeting," Kyodo, January 11, 1999.

668 "*Shikichigai no 5-nin mo Hibaku, Shain Arata ni 18-nin, Tokaimura no Kakunen Kojo Jiko*," ("Five Others Outside the Site Were Irradiated Bringing Number of Employees Irradiated to 18 in the Tokaimura Nuclear Fuel Plant Accident"), *Asahi Shimbun*, October 1, 1999, p 1.

669 "Tokyo Subway Trains Collide, 4 Killed, 33 Hurt," Kyodo, March 8, 2000; "Obuchi Went for Haircut After Setting Up Train Crash Team," Kyodo, March 8, 1999.

670 "Obuchi Instructs Cabinet To Cooperate Handling of Eruption," Kyodo, March 31, 2000.

671 "Gunman Hijacks Bus Carrying 3 Japanese in Greece," Kyodo News Agency, November 4, 2000.

672 "Greek Hijacker Kills Self After Freeing Japanese," Kyodo, November 5, 2000.

673 "Japan To Lay Out Unified Guideline for Crisis Situations," *Yomiuri Shimbun*, November 4, 2003.

674 Furukawa, Teijiro, *Kasumigaseki Hanseiki*, ("Writings of Half a Life in Government"), Saga: Saga Shinbunsha, 2005, p 192.

675 Sugita's replacement, Takeshi Noda—who took office in April 2004—was like Tadao Ando a former head of the Tokyo Metropolitan Police Department, and his appointment thus established a trend of appointing career police officials to the position. His appointment following Sugita's three years

of service also essentially established a three-year tenure for the position.

676 "Government Adopts Bills for Streamlining," Kyodo, April 27, 1999; and "List of New Ministries Under Administrative Reform Law," Kyodo, July 8, 1999.

677 "Government To Drop Plan To Upgrade Defense Agency," Kyodo, October 28, 1997.

678 "Prime Minister Koizumi Makes Last-Minute Cancellation of 26-September Japan-US Summit," *Shukan Bunshun*, September 8, 2005, pp 157-161.

679 "Foreign Ministry," *Kankai*, March 1998, pp 90-103.

680 "Increasing Centralization of Security Policy—Focusing of Functions on the Cabinet Secretariat," *Nihon Keizai Shimbun*, April 30, 2004.

681 See, for example, Kuroi, Buntaro, "*Tokubetsu Kikaku: Nihon ni ha Ima, Dorehodo no Taigai Joho Noryoku ga are no ka?*" in *Gunji Kenkyu*, September 2005, pp 232-241.

682 Aso, *Joho Kantei ni Tassezu*, p 184. See also, "*Naikaku Joho Chosashitsu to Nihon no Joho Komyunite*," ("The Cabinet Intelligence and Research Office and Japan's Intelligence Community"), in *Gunji Kenkyu: Nihon no Taigai Joho Kikan* (*Military Studies: Japan's Foreign Intelligence Organs*), September 2006, pp 24-31.

683 "*Naikaku Joho Chosashitsu to Nihon no Joho Komyunite*," ("The Cabinet Intelligence and Research Office and Japan's Intelligence Community"), in *Gunji Kenkyu: Nihon no Taigai Joho Kikan* (*Military Studies: Japan's Foreign Intelligence Organs*), September 2006, pp 24-31.

684 Kuroi, Buntaro, "*Tokubetsu Kikaku: Nihon ni ha Ima, Dorehodo no Taigai Joho Noryoku ga are no ka?*" in *Gunji Kenkyu*, Sept 2005, pp 232-241; pp 232-233.

685 Aso, *Joho Kantei ni Tassezu*, p 184. See also, "*Naikaku Joho Chosashitsu to Nihon no Joho Komyunite*," ("The Cabinet Intelligence and Research Office and Japan's Intelligence Commu-

nity"), in *Gunji Kenkyu: Nihon no Taigai Joho Kikan* (*Military Studies: Japan's Foreign Intelligence Organs*), September 2006, pp 24-31.

686 "Reform Council Wants To Give More Power to Cabinet," *Nihon Keizai Shimbun,* June 26, 1997, p 2.

687 "Security Information Council To Start Mid-January," *Nihon Keizai Shimbun,* December 30, 1998, p 2.

688 "Defense Plan Omits Okinawa Bases, Arms Exports," Kyodo News Agency, November 24, 1995.

689 "*'Nihon ha Anzen ka' Dainibu: Tepodon no Hamon*" ("'Is Japan Safe?' Part 2: The Ripple From the Taepodong") *Yomiuri Shimbun,* December 15, 1998, p 2.

690 "Government To Set Up New Panel To Enhance Role of Security Council," Kyodo News Agency, August 12, 2003.

691 "Government To Set up New Panel To Enhance Role of Security Council," Kyodo, August 12, 2003.

692 The Council on Security and Defense Capabilities, "*Anzen Hosho to Boeirkyoku ni Kan suru Kandankai Hoshokoku - Mirai he no Anzen Hosho-Boeiryoku Bijyon*" (The Council on Security and Defense Capabilities Report - Japan's Visions for Future Security and Defense Capabilities), October 2004, p 17;

The Japanese and English language versions of the Araki report can be accessed on the Kantei website at www.kantei.go.jp/jp/singi/ampobouei/dai13/13siryou.pdf.

693 "Increasing Centralization of Security Policy—Focusing of Functions on the Cabinet Secretariat," *Nihon Keizai Shimbun,* April 30, 2004.

694 "*Shin Kantei, Ogata Renkyu Ake Kado—Seisaku Kettei Kiki Kanri, Shusho Shudo no 'Utsuwa' Totonau,*" ("New PM Residence Operational Following Long Holiday, to Enhance Political Crisis Management Policymaking, Act as 'Recepticle' Under PM Leadership"), *Nihon Keizai Shimbun,* April 18, 2002, p 2.

695 "New Premier's Office Has Tight Security, Limits Press Access," *Sankei Shimbun,* May 12, 2002.

696 "Construction Starts on 'Secret Passage' to Koizumi's Official Residence," Kyodo, June 19, 2003.

697 "Premier's New Residence Due for Completion in 2002," Kyodo, January 1, 2001.

698 "Premier's New Residence Due for Completion in 2002," Kyodo, January 1, 2001.

699 Aso, Iku, "Prime Minister's Office in Nervous Breakdown Over Crisis Management Problems," *Bungei Shunju,* July 1996.

700 Aso, Iku, "Prime Minister's Office in Nervous Breakdown Over Crisis Management Problems," *Bungei Shunju,* July 1996.

701 "*Naikaku ni Okeru Bosai Joho no Katsuyo,*" ("Use of Information on Disasters in the Cabinet"), *Naikakukanbo Anzen Hosho/Kiki Kanri Tanto,* October 2002, p 3.

702 "FOCUS: Is Premier's New Office Ideal Emergency Headquarters?" Kyodo News Agency, May 8, 2002.

703 "*Naikaku,*" *ibid,* p 4.

704 Aso, Iku, *Joho Kantei ni Tassezu,* ("Intelligence That Does Not Reach The Prime Minister's Official Residence"), Shincho Bunko: Tokyo, 2001, pp 189.

705 Aso, Iku, "Prime Minister's Office in Nervous Breakdown Over Crisis Management Problems," *Bungei Shunju,* July 1996; see also "*Naikaku,*" *ibid,* p 7.

706 "*Nyusu Torendo: Ugokidashita Kasumigaseki WAN, Naru ka, Nihon Seifu no Denshi Johoka,*" ("News Trend: Kasumigaseki WAN Began Operations, Will Japanese Government's Electronic Informatization Come About?"), *Nikkei Pasokon,* March 10, 1997, p 222; "*Chuo Shocho, Kasumigaseki Net ga Yoyaku Honkakuka, Chiho he Kakuju 'Madoguchika' Kento,*" ("Central Government's Kasumigaseki Network Finally Operational, Examining 'Portalization' For Local Governments"), *Yomiuri Shimbun,* January 11, 1999, p 2.

707 Aso, Iku, "Prime Minister's Office in Nervous Breakdown Over Crisis Management Problems," *Bungei Shunju*, July 1996; see also "*Naikaku*," *ibid*, p 7.

708 "Central, Local Government To Form Council for E-Government Project," *Nihon Keizai Shimbun*, August 19, 2003.

709 "DA Elements Moving to Ichigaya," *Asagumo*, January 8, 1998, p 6.

710 "*Heiwaboke Retto Genkaimo ha Anadarake*," ("Alert Network in Pacifist-Obsessed Japan is Full of Deficiencies") *Yomiuri Weekly*, October 28, 2001, p 26.

711 "DA Elements Moving to Ichigaya," *Asagumo*, January 8, 1998, p 6.

712 "The Defense Agency Intelligence Headquarters," *Sentaku*, May 1997, pp 126-129.

713 Yamamura, Akiyoshi, "Behind-the-Scenes Struggle Between the Defense Agency and Prime Minister's Official Residence--Counterattack by 'Abused' Shigeru Ishiba," *Bungei Shunju*, May 2004, pp 210-218.

714 "Nakatani, Former SDF Officer, Heads DA," Kyodo News Agency, April 26, 2001.

715 "New Defense Chief May Not Mean Boost for Emergency Legislation," *Asahi Shimbun*, October 1, 2002.

716 For the Japanese Government's "tentative unofficial translation," see "National Defense Program Outline in and after FY 1996," December 1995, www.mofa.go.jp/policy/security/defense96/.

717 "Soviets Conduct More Exercises Around Japan," *Sankei Shimbun*, April 22, 1989, p 2.

718 "ASDF Moves To Warn Intruding Soviet Bomber," NHK Television, December 9, 1987.

719 "Scrambles by ASDF Fighters Decline in Fiscal 1992," Kyodo, April 9, 1992.

720 "Fighter Scrambles Fall By 48 to 263 in FY94," Kyodo, April 14, 1994.

[721] "Vice Defense Minister Says Troop Cut Unlikely Until 1995," *Asahi Shimbun,* January 31, 1992.

[722] "*Miyazawa Shusho Hasshin no Hamon Okiku, Boei Keikaku no Taiko Minaoshi,*" ("Powerful Ripples From PM Miyazawa's Declaration, A Review of the NDPO Defense Plan"), *Asahi Shimbun,* February 19, 1992, p 4.

[723] Interview with Sohei Miyashita, "New Defense Chief Interviewed on International Contributions," *Sankei Shimbun,* November 8, 1991, p 2.

[724] "Defense Agency Solidifies Plan To Reorganize Bureaus," *Sankei Shimbun,* December 3, 1991, p 3.

[725] "Miyazawa Says Government May Review Defense Strength," Kyodo, January 28, 1992.

[726] "Vice Defense Minister Says Troop Cut Unlikely Until 1995," *Asahi Shimbun,* January 31, 1992.

[727] "Debate Over Calling Witnesses May Delay Diet Panel," Kyodo, February 4, 1992.

[728] "Change in Defense Policy Urged," *Mainichi Shimbun,* August 8, 1992, p 5.

[729] "What is Necessary is Qualitative Rather Than Quantitative Buildup," *Yomiuri Shimbun,* August 16, 1992, p 5.

[730] "Defense Chief Wants More Peacekeeping Missions Considered," Kyodo, January 21, 1993.

[731] "Defense Agency To Start Drastic Review of Defense Outline," *Yomiuri Shimbun,* January 8, 1993, p 1.

[732] "New Defense Policy Revision Panel Members Selected," *Mainichi Shimbun,* February 2, 1994, p 1.

[733] A full translation of the report is available in Appendix A of Cronin, Patrick and Michael Green, "Redefining the US-Japan Alliance: Tokyo's National Defense Program," McNair Paper 31 (National Defense University: Washington, DC, November 1994), online at www.dtic.mil/dtic/tr/fulltext/u2/a421885.pdf.

734 Defense Department Briefing by Assistant Secretary of Defense for International Security Affairs, "On the 'Nye Report' Arguing for a Continued US Military Presence in East Asia," Federal News Service, February 27, 1995, link.lanic.utexas.edu/~bennett/__338/us_nye.htm.

735 "National Defense Program Outline in and After FY1996," *Defense of Japan 1996*, Defense Agency: Tokyo, 1996, pp 276-284.

736 "Statement by the Chief Cabinet Secretary on the National Defense Program Outline in and After FY1996," *Defense of Japan 1996*, Defense Agency: Tokyo, 1996, pp 276-284.

737 Ushiba, Akihiko, in an interview with Hiromi Kurisu, "The New National Defense Program Outline Lacks Determination," *Sankei Shimbun*, December 23, 1995.

738 Shikata, Toshiyuki, Atsuyuki Sassa, and Yukio Okamoto, "US Forces in Japan Can No Longer Act as a 'Guard Dog' and Defend Japan," *Shokun*, December 1998, pp 96-108.

739 "LDP Defense Panel To Set Up Subcommittee on Self-Defense Right," *Nihon Keizai Shimbun*, May 23, 2001.

740 "Government Mulls SDF Troop Redeployment to Southern Regions," *Nihon Keizai Shimbun*, August 5, 2001.

741 "Defense Agency Shifts Policy to Smaller Scale," *Asahi Shimbun*, September 4, 2001.

742 "National Defense Program Outline To Be Revised; Defense Agency to Review Its Concept of 'How Our Defense Capabilities Should Be Structured'," *Asagumo*, August 23, 2001, p 1.

743 "Japan's Defense Agency May Start Reviewing Capacity Next Week," Kyodo, September 11, 2001.

744 "Defense Panel To Discuss Counter-Terrorism, Troop Deployment," *Mainichi Shimbun*, September 22, 2001, p 5.

745 "Yamasaki Says Defense Outline Should Be Reviewed," Kyodo, October 4, 2001.

746 Funabashi, Yoichi, "*Anporigi ni Arata na Ibuki*," ("A New Breath With UNSC Decision"), *Asahi Shimbun*, November 29, 2001, p 14.

747 "Japan Revises Defeense Plan To Focus on Terrorism Attacks," *Yomiuri Shimbun*, January 9, 2002, p 1.

748 "Defense Agency Panel Begins Talk on Reviewing Defense Program Outline," *Yomiuri Shimbun*, January 19, 2002.

749 Imazu, Hiroshi, in an interview with an unnamed journalist, "'*Boei Daijin' to shite Jinji to Yosan no Kengen wo*," ("Provide 'Defense Minister' with Personnel and Budget Power"), *Kankai*, June 2004, p 69.

750 "Kyodo Obtains Advance Copy of Japanese Defense Agency 'White Paper'," Kyodo, May 5, 2002.

751 "Japan Eyes Unification of Regional Defense Bodies," Kyodo, May 25, 2002.

752 "Bring Up Review of the National Defense Program Outline," *Nihon Keizai Shimbun*, August 4, 2002.

753 "Ishiba Tells Rumsfeld Wish To Push Missile Defense," Kyodo, December 17, 2002.

754 "Defense Boss Ishiba Scrambles To Clarify Japan-US Missile Program Remarks," *Asahi Shimbun*, December 23, 2002.

755 "DA To Accelerate Study for Practical Use of Missile Defense System," Kyodo, December 29, 2002.

756 "Japan Reportedly Considers Deploying Parts of New US Missile Defense System," *Yomiuri Shimbun*, January 31, 2003.

757 "Missile Defense Next 'Crucial' Security Issue After Emergency Bills," Kyodo, May 19, 2003.

758 "U.S. Tells Japan North Korea Says it has Nuke Weapons," Kyodo, April 25, 2003.

759 "Japan Plans To Deploy Missile Defense From 2006," Kyodo, May 30, 2003.

760 "Japan To Upgrade Its Aegis-Equipped Destroyers for Missile Defense," Kyodo, August 24, 2003.

761 "Japan Defense Agency To Revise Concept of Basic Defense Capability," JijiWeb, April 5, 2003; "Agency Eyes New Defense Scheme With Missile Defense," Kyodo, May 4, 2003.

762 See the Defense Agency website, www.mod.go.jp/j/library/archives/yosan/2004/gaiyou.pdf.

763 "National Defense Policies at Historic Turning Point Need More Debate," *Nihon Keizai Shimbun*, December 22, 2003.

764 "Missile Shield Needed Against North Korea Threat," *Yomiuri Shimbun*, December 20, 2003.

765 "Inappropriate Procedures To Decide on Introduction of Missile Defense System," *Mainichi Shimbun*, December 19, 2003.

766 LDP Defense Policy Studies Subcommittee, "Recommendations on Japan's New Defense Policy—Toward a Safer and More Secure Japan and the world," LDP Web site, March 30, 2004.

767 The Council on Security and Defense Capabilities, "*Anzen Hosho to Boeirkyoku ni Kan suru Kandankai Hoshokoku - Mirai he no Anzen Hosho-Boeiryoku Bijyon*" (The Council on Security and Defense Capabilities Report - Japan's Visions for Future Security and Defense Capabilities), October 2004, pp 3-4, www.kantei.go.jp/jp/singi/ampobouei/dai13/13siryou.pdf.

768 *Ibid*, p 13.

769 *Ibid*, p 24.

770 "GSDF Secretly Pushes Plan to Establish a Permanent 'International Contribution Office'," *Foresight*, August 20, 2004, p 74.

771 Nakagawa, Kazuhiko, "*Boei Keikaku Daimo: Kanketsuteki Noryoku Kojo to Chugoku he no Taio ga Hitsuyo*," ("National Defense Program Outline: We Need To Enhance Our Self-Sufficient Capabilities and To Respond to China"), *Shukan Toyo Keizai*, June 12, 2004, pp 114-115.

772 Defense Agency, "National Defense Program Guideline, FY2005-," Defense Agency Website, www.mod.go.jp/e/policy/f_work/taikou05/fy200501.pdf, pp 2-3.

773 Defense Agency, "National Defense Program Guideline, FY2005-," Defense Agency Website, www.mod.go.jp/e/policy/f_work/taikou05/fy200501.pdf, pp 8-10.

774 Defense Agency, "National Defense Program Guideline, FY2005-," Defense Agency Website, www.mod.go.jp/e/policy/f_work/taikou05/fy200501.pdf, pp 4-7.

775 Yoshiyama, Kazuteru, "Protecting Japan Part V/ New Outline Promises Flexible Policy," *Yomiuri Shimbun*, December 12, 2004.

776 Defense Agency, "National Defense Program Guideline, FY2005-," Defense Agency Website, http://www.mod.go.jp/e/policy/f_work/taikou05/fy200501.pdf, p 12.

777 Katayama, Satsuki, "Japan's Self-Defense Forces Also Need Structural Reform," *Chuo Koron*, January 2005, pp 156-163.

778 "Ministries and Agencies – Winners and Losers," *Ekonomisuto*, October 7, 1997, pp 44-50.

779 "Ruling Camp To Study Upgrading Defense Agency at Ordinary Diet," *Nihon Keizai Shimbun*, December 14, 2002.

780 "A New Special Bill on Iraq Reconstruction Comes Before Bill To Establish Defense Ministry," *Asagumo*, June 26, 2003, p 1.

781 "A New Special Bill on Iraq Reconstruction Comes Before Bill To Establish Defense Ministry," *Asagumo*, June 26, 2003, p 1.

782 "Draft of Japanese Defense Agency's FY02 White Paper on Upgrading DA Into Ministry," *Asahi Shimbun*, May 5, 2002.

783 *Gekkan JADI*, September 2003, p 59; October 2003, p 59.

784 "LDP's Abe To Submit Bill To Set Up Defense Ministry, Notes Pending Contingency Bills," Jiji News Agency, March 5, 2004.

785 "Japan Enacts Education Reform, 'Defense Ministry' Laws," Kyodo, December 15, 2006.

786 "*Kankyocho no 2000-nendo Yosan, 1000-okuen Toppa no Kosan,*" ("Environment Agency's JFY2000 Budget To Break Y100 billion"), *Kagaku Kogyo Nippo,* August 9, 1999, p 8.

787 "Ministry of Agriculture, Forestry and Fisheries, Environment Ministry Preliminary FY2007 Budget Requests," *Nikkan Kogyo Shimbun,* September 6, 2006.

788 "*Aitsugu Chugokujin no Mikko, Shimokoshikijima, Osumi Hanto de kei 26-nin ga Taiho,*" ("Twenty-Six Chinese Stowaways Detained on Shimokoshiki Island and on Osumi Peninsula"), *Nishi Nihon Shimbun,* February 5, 1997, p 22.

789 "ASDF May Have Violated Law," Kyodo, February 6, 1997.

790 "*Mikko Sosaku 'Kuji Sanka ha Seito,*" ("'ASDF Participation Was Lawful' During Search for Stowaways"), *Nihon Keizai Shimbun,* February 8, 1997, p 2.

791 "Government Eyeing Marine Corps Unit for GSDF," *Yomiuri Shimbun,* January 6, 2004.

792 *Boei Hakusho Heisei 15nendo,* "*Dai 6sho: Kongo no Boeicho/Jieitai no Arikata: Dai 1setsu: Boeiryoku no Arikata Kento,*" p 302; the fact that the possibility of an invasion had lessened was also highlighted in "GSDF Secretly Pushes Plan to Establish a Permanent 'International Contribution Office'," *Foresight,* July 17, 2004, p 74.

793 *2004 Defense of Japan,* "Part 2: Our Country's Defense Policy," www.mod.go.jp/j/library/wp/2004/2004/index.html.

794 Tamura, Naoya, "*2004nendo Rikujo Jieitai no Shinsobi,*" ("New Equipment of the GSDF in JFY2004"), *Gunji Kenkyu,* December 2003, p 96).

795 "*Rito Boei ni 'Tokushu Butai', Minami Kyushu ni 10-nengo medo, Rikujo Jieitai ga Koso,*" ("GSDF Planning To Establish 'Special Forces' for Remote Island Defense of Southern Kyushu in 10 Years"), *Asahi Shimbun,* September 21, 1996, p 3.

796 Takai, Saburo, "Self-Defense Forces 'Senkaku Islands Defense Plan': Is It Possible To Counter the Chinese Military?" *Gunji Kenkyu,* November 1997, pp 110-117.

797 "Defense Institute Makes Long-Term Security Forecast," *Sankei Shimbun*, January 6, 1997.

798 "Five-Year Defense Buildup Plan Approved by the National Security Council and Cabinet," Prime Minister's Official Residence Web site, December 15, 2000.

799 Katsumata, Hidemichi, "*Boeicho no Gaisan Yokyu, Shuto to Engan Keibi ni Juten, Tero Taisaku nado Ninmu Tayoka*," ("Security of Capital and Shoreline Major Points in DA's Rough Budget Request, Duties Expanding to Counter-Terrorism"), *Yomiuri Shimbun*, September 6, 2000, p 23.

800 Nakamura, Atsushi, "*Gerira Taisaku de Jieitaiho Kaisei, Honshitsu Rongi Nuki ni, Yosanka Chakuchaku Susumu*," ("Revision of the SDF Law for Counter-Guerilla Policy, Budgets Proceed Without Essential Discussions"), *Mainichi Shimbun*, December 31, 2000, p 2.

801 "*Kenkyu Honbu (Asagumo) ga Shido: 'Chikamirai no Rikuji' ga Tsuikyu*," ("R&D Institute Goes Into Operation in Asagumo; Goal is To Prepare GSDF For Near Future"), *Asagumo*, April 12, 2001, p 3.

802 Fujii, Hisao, "*Rikujojieitai Futsukarentai*," ("The GSDF's Infantry Regiment"), *Gunji Kenkyu*, June 2004, pp 86-88.

803 Fujii, Hisao, "*Rikujojieitai Futsukarentai*," ("The GSDF's Infantry Regiment"), *Gunji Kenkyu*, pp 88-89.

804 Kazama, Minoru, "Little-Known Aspects of the Self Defense Forces: Changing Urban Defense Posture," *Sekai Shuho*, November 4, 2003, pp 38-39.

805 "*Kunren Shisetsu Tsukaezu Kitakyushu-shi ni Shinsetsu he, Rikujo Jieitai Gerira Taisaku*," ("New Training Facility in Kita Kyushu City, GSDF Guerrilla Countermeasures"), *Asahi Shimbun*, October 13, 1999, evening edition, p 6.

806 Fukuda, Masanori, "Aiming for the Defense Personnel of the New Century—Changing the Ground Self-Defense Force and Looking at Two Training Scenarios," *Sekai Shuho*, August 17-24, 2002, pp 46-49.

807 "*Rikuji, Bei de Shigaisen Enshu, Tai-gerira Sotei, 2002nendo, Higashi Fuji ni Shinshisetsu mo,*" ("GSDF To Train in Counter-Guerrilla Urban Combat Operations in US in FY2002, New Facilities Planned for Higashi Fuji"), *Hokkaido Shinbun*, August 27, 2000, p 3.

808 "*Shigaichisen wo Sotei, Nichibei ga Kyodo Kunren, Aibano Enshuba,*" ("Japan-US Joint Urban Combat Training at Aibano Training Area"), *Kyoto Shimbun*, February 24, 2006, p 30.

809 "Urban Warfare Training Center In Higashi-Fuji Shown For First Time; Supermarket, Family Restaurant In 30,000sq-meter Site; Full-Scale Facility For Anti-Guerilla Training, Completed By End of Fiscal Year," *Asagumo*, June 30, 2005, p 3.

810 "Urban Warfare Training Center In Higashi-Fuji Shown For First Time; Supermarket, Family Restaurant In 30,000sq-meter Site; Full-Scale Facility For Anti-Guerilla Training, Completed By End of Fiscal Year," *Asagumo*, June 30, 2005, p 3.

811 Tamura, Naoya, "*2004nendo Rikujo Jieitai no Shinsobi,*" ("The GSDF's New Equipment for JFY2004"), *Gunji Kenkyu*, December 2003, p 97.

812 "*Seibu Homen Futsukarentai no Shinpen,*" ("The Western Army Infantry Regiment New Organization"), *Heisei 14nendo Boei Hakusho*, (JDA: August 2002), p 161.

813 Sonoda, Yoshihiro, "Recent Status of Western Army Infantry Regiment Referred to as Second Airborne Brigade – Provides Rapid Response in Defense of Isolated Islands," *Asagumo*, November 6, 2003, p 3.

814 Kazama, Makoto, "Little Known SDF; SDF for Fiscal 2006," *Sekai Shuho*, October 4, 2005, pp 44-45.

815 Tamura, Naoya, "*2004nendo Rikujo Jieitai no Shinsobi,*" ("The GSDF's New Equipment for JFY2004"), *Gunji Kenkyu*, December 2003, p 97.

816 "*Boeicho, Taichu Keikai wo Kyoka: Rikuji, Beigun to Rito Boei Kunren,*" ("Defense Agency Strengthens Alert Regarding China: GSDF Trains Remote Island Defense With U.S. Forces"), *Nihon Keizai Shimbun*, December 31, 2005, p 2.

817 Walker, Mark, "Japanese Army To Train in Coronado," *NC Times*, January 4, 2006, www.nctimes.com/articles/2006/01/05/news/top_stories/21_39_591_4_06.txt.

818 "GSDF, US Marines To Stage Island Infiltration Exercise," *Yomiuri Shimbun*, January 1, 2006.

819 "Japan-US Alliance at Crossroads," *Mainichi Shimbun*, June 28, 2006, p 20.

820 "Full Details of Ground Self-Defense Force Central Rapid Response Regiment Specializing in Terrorism, Guerillas; Assault Teams to be Formed With Urban Warfare in Mind," JijiWeb, January 8, 2007.

821 "The Defense Ministry Will Drastically Review the Organization and Reorganize Units of the Self-Defense Forces," Kyodo, January 9, 2007.

822 "*Rikujiyo no 'Senshin Sogu Shisutemu': Saiba Senshi Kaihatsu he*," ("The 'Advanced Outfit System' for GSDF Use: Toward the Development of Cyber Warriors"), *Asagumo*, October 31, 2002, p 1.

823 "*Gihon ga 'Shoraikei Sorinsentosharyo' Kenkyu Shisaku*," ("TRDI Researches 'Future Wheeled Combat Vehicle"), *Asagumo*, March 25, 2004, p 6.

824 The GSDF requested ¥13.7 billion for 17 T-90 tanks in the JFY 2004 budget, for example, which comes to just over ¥8 billion per tank; see Tamura, Naoya, "*2004nendo Rikujo Jieitai no Shinsobi*," ("The GSDF's New Equipment for JFY2004"), *Gunji Kenkyu*, December 2003, p 95.

825 Federation of American Scientist Web site, www.fas.org/man/dod-101/sys/land/m1.htm

826 "Shift in the Number of Major Equipment Units," *Defense of Japan 2003*, p 429.

827 "SDF 50th Anniversary (2): Defense Strategies Overshadowed by Budget Concerns," *Nihon Keizai Shimbun*, July 1, 2004.

828 "*Juyo Shisaku: 15nendo no Boeihi wo Miru,*" ("Main Projects: A Look at the JFY2003 Defense Budget"), *Asagumo,* March 20, 2003, p 3.

829 "*Kuko no Gunji Riyoan ga Fujo,*" ("Proposal for Military Use of Airport Surfaces"), *Tokyo Shimbun,* November 4, 2004, pp 24-25.

830 "*Okinawa he no Chugoku Shinko Sotei, Rikuji 'Taiwan Yuji' de Himitsu Bunsho,*" ("GSDF 'Taiwan Emergency' Classified Document Hypothesizes Chinese Invasion of Okinawa"), *Chugoku Shimbun,* May 14, 2004, p 3.

831 "DA Stresses Importance of Shimoji Airoport for National Security," *Okinawa Times,* May 27, 2001, p 2.

832 Kuba, Yasushi, "Temporal Transfer of MCAS Futenma to Miyako Islands; Would Have Impact on Region, Mayors Share Sense of Crisis," *Ryukyu Shimpo,* October 22, 2004, p 2.

833 Yamazaki, Makoto, "*Kaijo Jieitai no Sakusen Noryoku: Posuto Reisengata Kaiyosen,*" ("MSDF Operational Capabilities: Post-Cold War Type Sea Battles"), *Sekai no Kansen,* June 2003, pp 80-83.

834 Nagata, Hiroshi, "21st Century Self-Defense Ships Will Look Like This," *Sekai no Kansen,* December 1995, pp 88-93.

835 The United States at the article's writing was concluding operations over Kosovo and was finalizing a 1990s reduction in forces, and President Bill Clinton had the year before famously skipped over Japan to visit China and Hong Kong, giving rise to the term "Japan passing," which also happened to rhyme with the popular fear in the 1980s of "Japan bashing."

836 Nagata, Hiroshi, "Martime SDF's Escort Flotilla One in 2010," *Sekai no Kansen,* October 1999, pp 112-115.

837 Yamazaki, Makoto, "*Kaijo Jieitai no Sakusen Noryoku: Posuto Reisengata Kaiyosen,*" ("Operational Capabilities of the MSDF: Post-Cold War-Type Sea Battles"), *Sekai no Kansen,* June 2003, pp 80-83.

[838] "*Kaijo Jieitai Heisei 16nendo Gyomu Keikaku no Gaiyo,*" ("Summary of MSDF Fiscal Year 2004 Operational Planning"), *Sekai no Kansen,* June 2004, p 142.

[839] Yamazaki, Makoto, "*Kaijo Jieitai no Sakusen Noryoku: Posuto Reisengata Kaiyosen,*" ("Operational Capabilities of the MSDF: Post-Cold War-Type Sea Battles"), *Sekai no Kansen,* June 2003, pp 80-83.

[840] *Jane's Fighting Ships 1998-1999,* editor Captain Richard Sharpe (Jane's Information Group: 1998), "Japan Maritime Self Defense Force Kaijoh Jiei-Tai," p 377.

[841] "Details of MSDF Transport 'Osumi'," *Asagumo,* November 21, 1996, p 2.

[842] *Jane's Fighting Ships 1998-1999,* p 377.

[843] Nagata, Hiroshi, "Operation of MSDF's *Osumi,*" *Sekai no Kansen,* August 1998, pp 78-81.

[844] *Gunji Joho Kenkyukai,* "'*98 Jieikantai no Seiryoku,*" ("Self-Defense Fleet Power in '98") *Gunji Kenkyu,* February 1998.

[845] "'*Mashu' wo Miru,*" ("View of Mashu"), *Sekai no Kansen,* August 2004, p 3.

[846] Nagata, Hiroshi, "Maritime SDF's Escora Flotilla One in 2010," *Sekai no Kansen,* October 1999, pp 112-115.

[847] *Sekai no Kansen* editorial board, "*7,700tonkei Goeikan,*" ("The 7,700-ton-type Escort"), *Sekai no Kansen,* January 2004, p 134.

[848] "New Missile Interceptors Slated for FY07 in Response to DPRK 'Threat'," *Yomiuri Shimbun,* June 21, 2003.

[849] "Japan Revises Law To Expedite Missile-Intercept Order," Kyodo, July 22, 2005.

[850] Tada, Satoshi, "*Suterusu Sakusenkan no Saishin Dezain to Kozo,*" ("Newest Designs and Construction of Stealth Warships"), *Gunji Kenkyu,* March 2006, p 63.

[851] *Sekai no Kansen* editorial board, "*Jisedai Junyo Goeikan (Nihon),*" ("Future Surface Escorts [Japan]"), *Sekai no Kansen,* December 2003, pp 82-83.

852 *Sekai no Kansen* editorial board, "*7,700tonkei Goeikan,*" ("The 7,700-ton-type Escort"), *Sekai no Kansen,* January 2004, p 134.

853 United Defense Web site, "Naval Gun, Mk 45 Mod 4," www.uniteddefense.com/prod/ngun_mk45.htm.

854 "*Shorai Kaki/Danyaku no Kenkyu Kaihatsu ni Kan Suru Teian (Sono 2),*" ("Proposal Regarding Research and Development of Future Fire Arms/Ammunition [Part 2]"), *Gekkan JADI,* January 2003, pp 30-46.

855 Okabe, Isaku, "*Kan-tai-Chi Kogeki: Kaijo Jieitai no Tai-chi Kogeki Noryoku,*" ("Ship-to-Shore Attack: the MSDF's Shore-Attack Capability"), *Sekai no Kansen,* April 2004, pp 92-95.

856 "Japan: Maritime Self-Defence Force," *Jane's Fighting Ships 1998-1999,* pp 367-368.

857 "Japan: Maritime Self-Defence Force," *Jane's Fighting Ships 1998-1999,* p 367.

858 Editorial Board, "*2,900-ton-gata Sensuikan,*" ("2,900-ton-type Submarine"), *Sekai no Kansen,* January 2004, pp 142-143.

859 "*2,900-ton-gata Sensuikan,*" ("2,900-ton-type Submarine"), *Sekai no Kansen,* January 2004, pp 142-143.

860 "*Kaiji Shinkei Missairutei no Kai,*" ("Mystery of the MSDF New Guided Missile Boats"), *Gunji Kenkyu,* p 78.

861 "Despite Upper House Rejection, Budget To Pass Diet on 17 March," Kyodo, March 17, 1999.

862 "*Kaiji Shinkei Missairutei no Kai,*" ("Mystery of MSDF New Guided Missile Boats"), *Gunji Kenkyu,* 78.

863 "*Fushinsen Ha Minogasanai,*" ("Spy Vessels Will Not Be Overlooked"), *Asagumo,* January 2, 2003, p 1.

864 "MSDF To Deploy 2 Patrol Boats With Guided Missiles in March," Kyodo, January 26, 2002.

865 "MSDF Ships Commissioned in March 2004," *Sekai no Kansen,* May 2004, pp 1-7.

866 Watanabe, Atsushi, "New Class Patrol Ship (1,000-ton Class)," *Sekai no Kansen,* July 2006.

867 *2002 Defense of Japan*, Reference 18, "Shift in the Number of Major Equipment Units," pp 429-433.

868 "*F-15 Sentoki Okinawa Haiten, Heisei 20nendo, Taichu Yokushiryoku wo Kyoka*," ("F-15 Fighters To Be Redeployed to Okinawa by FY2009, Increased Deterrence Against China"), *Sankei Shimbun*, May 28, 2005, p 1.

869 U.S. Navy News Release, "Data Link Solutions Awarded MIDS Terminal Contract," 18 June 2001, enterprise.spawar.navy.mil/UploadedFiles/ca-2001-029.pdf.

870 Kaga, Hitoshi, "*F-15 Kindaika Kaishu to Kyukeiki Mondai*," ("F-15 Modernization Improvement and the Problem of Aging Aircraft"), *Gunji Kenkyu*, January 2004, p 76.

871 The JDA purchased 8 F-2 airframes and engines in JFY2002 for a total cost of ¥76.5 billion, or just over ¥9.5 billion–$87 million–per unit, though the price tag did not include the avionics suite or other equipment; "*14nendo Chuo Chotatsu Sokuhochi*," ("JFY2002 Central Procurement Figures"), *Asagumo*, April 17, 2003, p 2.

872 Handa, Shigeru, "The F-2 Fighter Flying in an Incomplete Shape: The FSX Developed Jointly Even at the Cost of Japan-US Friction Is Found a 'Clunker' When Finally Produced," *Foresight*, March 2001, pp 106-107.

873 Handa, *ibid.*; "*Jiki Shien Sentoki 'F-2', Mata Mo Shuyoku Ni Ijo; Boeicho, Haibi Keikaku ni Eikyo mo*," ("Another Defect in the F-2 Main Wing; Will Effect Deployment According to JDA"), *Nikkan Kogyo Shimbun*, June 8, 1999, p 16.

874 Handa, *ibid.*

875 "Japan Defense Agency To Defer F-2 Fighter Deployment," Jiji Press Agency, April 5, 2002.

876 "F-2 Fighter's Radar System Has Technical Glitches," Kyodo, March 2, 2002.

877 "DA Plans To Purchase Russian Fighter for Research," *Sankei Shimbun*, March 14, 1997, p 1.

878 Sakai, Akari, "*Roshia Saikyo Sentoki 'Su-27', Kuji Pairotto Kunren Hiko–Minkan no Keiyaku de Jitsugen,*" ("ASDF Pilots Train To Fly Russia's Most Powerful Jet Fighter, the 'Su-27', Realized Through Contract with Private Company"), *Nihon Keizai Shimbun,* February 9, 1998, evening edition, p 2.

879 "*Suhoi-27 to Nihon no 'Gijutsu Rikkokuron',*" ("Sukhoi-27 and Japan's 'Technology Independence Argument'"), *Mainichi Shimbun,* May 23, 1998, p 3.

880 "*Kondo ha Buso Suhoi-27 ni Tojo, Kuji Sojushi Futari, Roshia Haken he,*" ("Two Pilots To Be Sent to Russia, This Time To Train in Armed Sukhoi-27"), *Tokyo Shimbun,* March 10, 1999, evening edition, p 1.

881 "Study on 'Future Fighter Jet' That Theft Exposed," *Foresight,* March 15, 2002, p 38.

882 "*Mata Mitsubishi Juko Shorai Sentoki Shiryo Nakusu*" ("MHI Again Misplaces Future Fighter Documents"), *Tokyo Shimbun,* December 3, 2002, p 27.

883 Mitsubishi Heavy Industries ad, *Gekkan JADI,* January 2003.

884 "Advanced Technology Demonstrator *Shinshin* Unveiled," *Koku Fan,* February 2007, pp 8-10.

885 Miyamoto, Isamu, "The Air Self-Defense Force in 2010: Predictions," *Gunji Kenkyu,* September 2001, pp 92-107.

886 "*F-4 Kokei ni 1-ki 300-okuen, F-22 Yuryoku*" ("Three-Hundred Million for One F-4 Successor, Powerful F-22"), *Tokyo Shimbun,* April 14, 2006, p 27.

887 *Boei Hakusho 13nendo,* "*Shinchu Kibo ni Morikomareta Shinki Sobi,*" ("New Equipment in the New MTDP"), p 99.

888 "Boeing 767 TT," *Air World,* May 2003, p 77.

889 Aoki, Yoshitomo, "Possibilities of the KC-767J and the C-X: The Dispatching of Troops Overseas by Tactical Airlift Divisions of Japan's Air Self-Defense Force," *Gunji Kenkyu,* April 2006, pp 40-49.

[890] "Rabbits' Ears and Doves' Dreams: Informtion on North Korea's Missile Test-Firing Kept Secret," *Mainichi Shimbun,* August 14, 1994, p 1.

[891] Sasajima, Masahiko and Takashi Nishida, "Poor Information Strategy Stands Out," *Yomiuri Shimbun,* April 17, 1998, p 2.

[892] "Death Knoll for Japan's Dwindling YS-11 Fleet Nearing," Kyodo News Service, June 28, 2002.

[893] "Our Nation's Signals Technology: Its Present State and Future Prospects," *Boei Gijutsu Janaru,* January 1998.

[894] "North Korean Airplanes Preparing To Attack Maritime Self Defense Force Airplane in March 2003," *Sankei Shimbun,* June 24, 2004.

[895] *Jane's Aircraft Upgrades 1997-1998,* "Kawasaki" and *Jane's Aircraft Upgrades 2005-2006,* "Lockheed Martin Aeronautics Company."

[896] "North Korean Airplanes Preparing To Attack Maritime Self Defense Force Airplane in March 2003," *Sankei Shimbun,* June 24, 2004.

[897] "The Hijacking of the 'Yodo-go' and the Movements of the 'Yodo-go' Group," *Focus,* Vol 271, National Police Agency, http://www.npa.go.jp/keibi/kokutero1/english/0302.html.

[898] Compiled from "Chronology of Overseas Hostage Crises Involving Japanese," Kyodo, April 15, 2004; Shigenobu, Fusako, "Commentary by Kyoko Otani," *I Decided To Give Birth to You Under An Apple Tree,* April 2001, pp 1-13.

[899] Ito, Koichi, *Keishicho-Tokushu Butai no Shinjutsu: Tokushu Kyushu Butai SAT,* ("The Truth of the Metropolitan Police Department's Special Forces: Special Assault Team"), (Tokyo: Dai-Nippon Kaiga, November 2004), p 195.

[900] "*Zumu Appu, SAT, Kohyo Sareta Keisatsu Tokushu Butai,*" ("Zoom Up, Police Special Team SAT is Revealed"), *Kahoku Shimbun,* June 3, 1996, p 5.

[901] "*Kokunai no Anzen Taisaku wo Sotenken, Tero Kikikanri, Nihon ha?*" ("General Questions Regarding Domestic Security Mea-

sures: What About Japan's Crisis Management in the Event of Terrorism?"), *Yomiuri Shimbun*, October 17, 2001, p 13.

902 Ito, *Keishicho-Tokushu Butai no Shinjutsu: Tokushu Kyushu Butai SAT*, p 195.

903 Ito, *Keishicho-Tokushu Butai no Shinjutsu: Tokushu Kyushu Butai SAT*, p 197.

904 "*Bakuon, Kemuri, Nifun no Kyushutsu*," ("An Explosion, Smoke, And A Two-Minute Rescue"), *Asahi Shimbun*, May 5, 2000, p 3; "*Basu Nottori, 15-Jikanhan no 'Kobo' Saigen*," ("Recreation of the Fifteen and One-Half Hour 'Fierce Battle' Bus Hijacking"), *Asahi Shimbun*, May 11, 2000, p 25; "Chronology of Bus Hijacking," Kyodo, May 3, 2000.

905 "*Bakuon, Kemuri, Nifun no Kyushutsu*," ("An Explosion, Smoke, And A Two-Minute Rescue"), *Asahi Shimbun*, May 5, 2000, p 3; "*Basu Nottori, 15-Jikanhan no 'Kobo' Saigen*," ("Recreation of the Fifteen and One-Half Hour 'Fierce Battle' Bus Hijacking"), *Asahi Shimbun*, May 11, 2000, p 25; "Chronology of Bus Hijacking," Kyodo, May 3, 2000.

906 "Bus Hijacker Sent Incoherent Message to NPA," Kyodo, May 13, 2000.

907 "Anti-Terrorism Measures: National Police Agency Considering Placing Sky Marshals on International Flights," *Sankei Shimbun*, May 13, 2004, p 31.

908 Komine, Takao and Shinichi Sakamoto, *Kaijo Hoancho Tokushu Butai SST*, ("The Japan Coast Guard's Special Forces SST"), (Tokyo: Namiki Shobo, November 2005), pp 46-51.

909 "Mutiny Reported on Freighter Off Okinawa Coast," Kyodo, August 14, 1989.

910 "Maritime Agency Warns Against South China Sea Pirates," Kyodo, August 13, 1989.

911 Komine and Sakamoto, *Kaijo Hoancho Tokushu Butai SST*, pp 92-106.

912 "Plutonium-Bearing Freighter Arrives From France," AFP, November 14, 1984.

913 "*Purutoniumu Genkai Yuso, Tokaimura ni Tochaku,*" ("Heavily Guarded Plutonium Shipment Arrives in Tokaimura"), *Nihon Keizai Shimbun,* evening edition, November 15, 1984, p 1.

914 Komine and Sakamoto, *Kaijo Hoancho Tokushu Butai SST,* p 107.

915 Komine and Sakamoto, *Kaijo Hoancho Tokushu Butai SST,* pp 112-116.

916 "*Kaijo ni Taitero Tokushu Butai, 92-93nen no Purutoniumu Yuso, 13nin 'Akatsukimaru' Keigo,*" ("Counter-Terrorism Special Teams Established in MSA, 13 Personnel From the 1992-1993 Plutonium Transport Escort 'Akatsukimaru'"), *Tokyo Shimbun,* January 5, 1998, p 23; "*Kaijo Hoancho Sho no Osaka Kaijo Tokushu Keibi Kichi, Izumisanoshi no Rinku Taun de Kaijoshiki,*" ("Maritime Safety Agency's Special Security Station's Opening Ceremony in Izumisano city's Rinku Town"), *Yomiuri Shimbun,* evening edition, May 30, 1996, p 2; "Maritime Safety Agency Has 'Secret Antiterrorism Team," Kyodo, January 4, 1997.

917 "*Kaijosho 'Umi no Keibitai' ga Hassoku, Kanku Taigan kara Zenkoku ni Shutsudo,*" ("MSA's First 'Sea Security Unit' is Inaugurated, Can Be Dispatched From Its Base Across from Kansai Airport to Anywhere in the Country"), *Kotsu Shimbun,* June 3, 1996, p 3.

918 Ugaki, Taisei, "*Tsuini Hassoku: Rikujo Jieitai no Tokushu Sakusengun,*" ("GSDF Special Operations Group is Finally Launched"), *Gunji Kenkyu,* June 2004, p 67.

919 "Maritime SDF Launches Secret Special Patrol Unit to Deal With Spy Ships," *Yomiuri Shimbun,* April 3, 2001.

920 Ugaki, Taisei, "*Tsuini Hassoku: Rikujo Jieitai no Tokushu Sakusengun,*" ("GSDF Special Operations Group is Finally Launched"), *Gunji Kenkyu,* June 2004, p 67.

921 Yoshiyama, Kazuteru, "Protecting Japan Part V/ New Outline Promises Flexible Policy," *Yomiuri Shimbun,* December 12, 2004.

922 "Defense Command Structure Reform Said Not To Streamline SDF," *Asahi Shimbun*, December 23, 2002.

923 "SDF Joint Staff Council To Exercise More Peacetime Power," *Yomiuri Shimbun*, July 29, 1997, p 1.

924 "Defense Command Structure Reform Said Not To Streamline SDF," *Asahi Shimbun*, December 23, 2002; "SDF Staff Council Chairman's Power To Be Expanded," Kyodo, December 19, 2002.

925 "Japan: Defense Agency Drafts Bill To Form Independent Joint Force," *Tokyo Shimbun*, February 8, 2004.

926 Yamanaka, Tsuyu, "Development of Infrastructure for Joint Operations–Behind-the-scenes activities of the Joint Operations Planning Office," *Securitarian*, May 2006, pp 15-17.

927 "Two Defense Bills Headed Toward Passage," *Asagumo*, July 21, 2005, p 1.

928 "Revised Self-Defense Forces Law Stipulates Procedure for Interception by Ballistic Missile Defense System; DA Director General To Issue Interception Order in Emergency," *Asagumo*, July 21, 2005, p 1.

929 Furumoto, Yoso, "SDF Law Revision in 2005: Integration With US in Responding to Emergencies," *Mainichi Shimbun*, July 23, 2005.

930 *Shiki Ichimotoka, Beigun wo Moderu, Shintobaku Soshiki 650nin Taisei*, Kyodo, February 15, 2004.

931 Yamanaka, Tsuyu, "Development of Infrastructure for Joint Operations–Behind-the-scenes activities of the Joint Operations Planning Office," *Securitarian*, May 2006, pp 15-17.

932 "*Boeicho Keikaku, Jieitai Tsushin wo Dijitaru ni–Saigai, Tocho ni Taisho*," ("JDA Plan: Digital SDF Communications to Go Digital–Response to Natural Disasters, Tapping"), *Nihon Keizai Shimbun*, December 24, 1984, p 2.

933 "*Boei Maikuro Kaisen wo Jichitai to Chokusetsu he, Antenna Setchi Dake de Tsuwa OK ni*," ("Local Authorities to Have Direct

Connection to DEMICS by Simply Putting Up Antenna"), *Yomiuri Shimbun,* February 4, 1995, p 2.

934 "*Boei Tsushin Shinsenryaku Keikaku/Gunma,*" ("New Strategic Plan for Defense Communications/Gunma"), *Mainichi Shimbun,* December 6, 1995, p 10.

935 Sagara, Yuta, "FOCUS: 'Peaceful Use Principle' in Japan's Policy Crumbling," Kyodo News Service, March 6, 2003.

936 Tamama, Tetsuo, "*Nihon no Uchu Seisaku to Anzen Hosho no Setten,*" ("Points in Common Between Japan's Space Policy and National Security"), *Defense Research Center,* June 2002, p 23.

937 Tamama, *ibid.*

938 "Japan's Maritime Defense Industry Viewed," *Sekai no Kansen,* March 1997, p 90-97.

939 Space Communications Corporation website, www.superbird.co.jp/english/aboutus/history.html.

940 "*Jieitai no Eisei Riyo, Honkakuka; Supabado-B Tosai no Chukeiki 7gatsu Kado,*" ("SDF Use of Satellites Taking Shape; Transponder on Superbird-B Operational from July"), *Asahi Shimbun,* May 31, 1992, p 3.

941 "DirecTV Satellite Launched Successfully," Kyodo News Service, July 28, 1997.

942 "*Riku, Kuji Ga Eisei Tsushin Honkaku Donyu, Daikibo Saigai nado Kinkyuji Kino no Anteisei Tsuyomi,*" ("Ground, Air SDF Incorporate Satellite Communications Capability, Strengthening Capability During Crises Such as Large-Scale Disaster"), *Yomiuri Shimbun,* April 19, 1998, p 13.

943 SCC company website, www.superbird.co.jp/english/superbird/d.html.

944 "*Kaijo Jieitai Heisei 15nendo Gyomu Keikakuan no Gaiyo,*" ("Draft on the Programming of Maritime Self Defense Force for JFY2003"), *Sekai no Kansen,* December 2002, pp 148-151.

945 "*Uchu Tsushin, Tsushin Eisei Uchiage Seiko, 7gatsu kara Sabisu,*" ("SCC Successfully Launches Communications Satellite, in

Service from July"), *Nikkei Sangyo Shimbun,* April 19, 2004, p 3.

946 "Daddy, You Look Good – Long-Awaited Video Phone Service Opens Between Al-Samawah and Japan," *Asagumo,* April 8, 2004, p 1; "Examining the Major Policy Measures in the FY05 Defense Budget," *Asagumo,* March 10, 2005, p 1.

947 For construction, see "Unit Training Reduced; Improvement of Intelligence Function Pushed," *Asagumo,* April 2, 1998, p 1; for JFY2002 budget, see "JDA Central Contract Office Releases Preliminary FY02 Procurement Figures," *Asagumo,* April 17, 2003, p 2; for operational status see Ishii, Koyu, "*Chumoku no 13,500tonkei DDH ha Konaru,*" ("This is What the 13,500-ton DDH Will Be Like"), *Sekai no Kansen,* July 2001, p 90.

948 *Heisei 11nendo Boei Hakusho* "*3: Heisei 11nendo no Boeiryoku Seibi,*" p 126.

949 Ishii, *ibid,* p 90; See also MOD website, www.mod.go.jp/j/info/hyouka/2002/sogo/san05.pdf.

950 As LTC Scott Stephenson observed in the May-June 2010 *Military Affairs,* "with the beginning of a full-blown insurgency in Iraq in late 2003, the use of 'RMA' as a Pentagon mantra came to an abrupt end" ("The Revolution in Military Affairs: 12 Observations on an Out-of-Fashion Idea," *Military Affairs,* May-June 2010, p 38). For a concise discussion of the RMA concept in the mid-1990s, see CRS/Theodor Galdi's "Revolution in Military Affairs? Competing Concepts, Organizational Responses, Outstanding Issues," December 11, 1995, http://www.fas.org/man/crs/95-1170.htm.

951 "Nation Exposed to Cyberterrorism Risk," *Yomiuri Shimbun,* June 14, 2004.

952 For the Japanese Government's "tentative unofficial translation" of the original document, see "Info-RMA: Study on Info-RMA and the Future of the Self-Defense Forces," September 2000, www.mod.go.jp/e/publ/w_paper/pdf/2006/rma_e.pdf.

953 "*FOCUS: Higashi Shinakai Fushinsen, Tsuho ni 9jikan, Boeicho mada Reisen Shifuto,*" ("FOCUS: Communication of Suspicious Vessels in the East China Sea Takes 9 Hours, JDA Yet to Shift From Cold War"), *Nishi Nihon Shimbun,* February 7, 2002, p 3.

954 Ishiba, Shigeru, in interview by Yutaka Nishizawa. "Special Report: Security Policy at a Turning Point," *Sekai Shuho,* August 19, 2003, pp 14-17.

955 Kazama, Minoru, "Unknown Facets of Self-Defense Forces--Ground, Maritime, and Air Self Defense Forces To Convert to Joint Operational System," *Sekai Shuho,* January 2003, pp 38-39.

956 "Outrageous Anachronistic 'New Defense Program' – 'Military Intelligence Revolution' Faces Vested Interest Barrier," *Sentaku,* October 2002, pp 60-61.

957 "*Arata na Kyoi he Taisho Jushi*" ("Emphasizing Response to 'New Threats'"), *Asagumo,* September 2, 2004, p 1.

958 "*Gihon 16nendo Gyomu Keikaku,*" ("TRDI's FY2004 Operational Plans"), *Asagumo,* November 13, 2004, p 1.

959 Tamura, Naoya, "*Joho Yuetsu Kakuho no Mitsu no Ki Pointo,*" ("Three Key Points for the Maintenance of Information Supremacy"), *Gunji Kenkyu,* June 2001, p 206.

960 "DA Chief Kyuma, Top Brass Attend DIH Opening Ceremony," *Asagumo,* January 23, 1997, p 1.

961 "Draft on the Programming of Maritime Self Defense Force For FY2003," *Sekai no Kansen,* December 2002, pp 148-151.

962 "Operational Concepts of JMSDF's New Flattop-Type DDH," *Sekai no Kansen,* November 2007, pp 92-95.

963 Togo, Yukinori, "Network System of New SS Soryu," *Sekai no Kansen,* November 2009, pp 100-102.

964 "MSDF JFY2003 Budget Proposals," *Sekai no Kansen,* December 2002, pp 148-151.

965 "*18-nendo Boeihi, Juyo Shisaku wo Miru: Kaijo Jieitai*" ("Examining Major Points of the FY2006 Defense Budget: MSDF"), *Asagumo*, March 2, 2006, p 1.

966 "New MSDF Helicopter-Carrying Escort Profiled," *Sekai no Kansen*, July 2001, pp 84-90.

967 "*Bajji Shisutemu no Kindaika*," ("Modernization of the BADGE System"), *Boei Hakusho*, 2002, p 165.

968 "Operations for Air Defense," www.mod.go.jp/e/pab/8aramasi/def412.htm.

969 "Air Defense System Powerless Against DPRK Missiles," *Yomiuri Weekly*, June 22, 2003.

970 See www.harpoonhq.com/encyclopedia/HTML_Files/facilites_files/facilities_db/664.htm.

971 *Gunji Kenkyu Johokai*, "*Saishin Sekai no Guntai: '98 Kuji no Seiryoku to Kino*," ("Latest Military Forces of the World: ASDF's Strength and Functions in '98"), *Gunji Kenkyu*, March 1998, p 134.

972 "DA Requests Funds for Anti-Taepodong Missile System," *Tokyo Shimbun*, December 21, 1998, p 9.

973 "NEC, *Jiki Boku Shisutemu Juchu, Sojigyohi 700 okuencho–2008nendo ni Unyo Kaishi*," ("NEC, Next-Generation Air Defense System, General Cost Over ¥70 Billion–Operational by JFY2008"), *Nihon Keizai Shimbun*, January 10, 2002, p 13.

974 "Agency to Test Radar for Missile System," *Daily Yomiuri*, February 18, 2004.

975 See www.harpoonhq.com/encyclopedia/HTML_Files/facilites_files/facilities_db/664.htm.

976 "Air Defense System Powerless Against DPRK Missiles," *Yomiuri Weekly*, June 22, 2003.

977 Miyamoto, Isao, "Air Self Defense Force Military Power in 2010; Introduction of F-2 and AWACS a Big Job," *Gunji Kenkyu*, June 1996.

978 "ASDF To Deploy Two AWACS Planes in Central Japan in March," Kyodo News Agency, February 26, 1998.

979 "*Nihon no Sora wo Mamoru Tame Ni,*" ("In Order to Defend Japan's Airspace"), *Securitarian,* April 2002, p 9.

980 "*Kitachosen nirami 'Nichibei Kyodo Sensen' Nashikuzushi, Kujidenshi Deta, Beigun he Teikyo Kento,*" *Yomiuri Shimbun,* April 7, 2003, p 26.

981 "Air Defense System Powerless Against DPRK Missiles," *Yomiuri Weekly,* June 22, 2003.

982 Hideaki, Kaneda, "How to Intercept a No Dong Launch in 'Ten Minutes'–How Do We Defend Against 100 Ballistic Missiles Traveling at Mach 7?" *Bungei Shunju,* June 2003, pp 184-190.

983 Hideaki, Kaneda, "How to Intercept a No Dong Launch in 'Ten Minutes'–How Do We Defend Against 100 Ballistic Missiles Traveling at Mach 7?" *Bungei Shunju,* June 2003, pp 184-190.

984 "Defense Technology Command Control Communications Intelligence," *Nikkei Sangyo Shimbun,* May 10, 1995, p 11.

985 "*NEC nado 7sha, Kyodo de Rikujo Jieitai no Yagai Tsushin wo Kodoka; Sogaku 1500 Okuen Kibo,*" ("7 Companies Including NEC To Jointly Improve GSDF's Field Communications; Will Cost Around ¥150 Billion"), *Nikkan Kogyo Shimbun,* March 30, 1996, p 1.

986 Tamura, Naoya, "*Joho Yuetsu Kakuho no Mitsu no Ki Pointo,*" ("Three Key Points for the Maintenance of Information Supremacy"), *Gunji Kenkyu,* June 2001, p 205.

987 Ugaki, Taisei, "Tank Prototype Unveiled: Compact Body, Technological Advantages, Rationale of New Development," *Gunji Kenkyu,* April 2008, pp 28-35.

988 "*Senkyo Riaru-Taimu de Haaku,*" ("Grasping the Battle Situation in Real Time"), *Asagumo,* October 23, 2003, p 5 and "*IT Katsuyo, Tekizenshin wo Soshi,*" ("Preventing Enemy Advancement Utilizing IT"), *Asagumo,* December 4, 2003, p 5.

989 "GSDF Commander in Sammawah Reports to Ishiba Via Satellite Phone," Kyodo News Agency, March 4, 2004, and

"*Taibo no TV-Denwa Kaitsu,*" ("Long-Awaited TV-Phoneline Opens"), *Asagumo,* April 8, 2004, p 1.

990 Tamura, Naoya, "*Joho Yuetsu Kakuho no Mitsu no Ki Pointo,*" ("Three Key Points for the Maintenance of Information Supremacy"), *Gunji Kenkyu,* June 2001, p 204.

991 "SDF Data Leak Reveals Defense Agency Laxity," *Yomiuri Shimbun,* August 8, 2002.

992 "DII's Strategic 'Closed Network' Becomes Operational," *Asagumo,* May 27, 2004, p 6.

993 "Nation Exposed to Cyberterrorism Risk," *Yomiuri Shimbun,* June 13, 2004; "Dozens of Unauthorized Access Attempts in Several Days," *Asagumo,* September 9, 2004, p 1.

994 Tamura, Naoya, "*2004nendo Rikujo Jieitai no Shinsobi,*" ("The GSDF's New Equipment for JFY2004"), *Guniji Kenkyu,* December 2003, p 98.

995 Ministry of Defense, *Defense Programs and Budget of Japan: Overview of FY2011 Budget Request,* August 2010, p 20.

996 "Interview with Deputy Director Takemasa Moriya, Defense Intelligence Headquarters," *Gunji Kenkyu,* October 1997, p 162.

997 Ebata, Kensuke, *Joho to Kokka: Shushu, Bunseki, Hyoka no Otoshiana,* ("Intelligence and the State: Pitfalls of Collection, Analysis, and Evaluation"), Kodansha: Tokyo, October 2004, pp 3-7.

998 Sassa, Atsuyuki et al, "National Strategy for an Age of Terrorism – Motojiro Akashi! Please Make an Appearance!" *Voice,* May 2004, pp 48-57; Suganuma, Mitushiro, "Second Investigation Department of the PSIA: 'What Has the PSIA Been Doing?'" *Bungei Shunju,* Nov 1995, pp 136-147; Okamoto, Yukio, Atsuyuki Sassa, and Toshiyuki Shikata, "Do-Nothing Policy at 'MOF on Monetary Affairs and MOFA on Information': Lack of Intelligence Capability Will Ruin Japan" *Shokun,* Jul 2000, pp 243-251.

999 "*Tsushin Boju, Bei ga Shudo (Interijensu Johoryoku, Jieitai 50nen),*" ("In Interception of Communications, US Leads Way—Intelligence Capabilities, 50th Anniversary of Foundation of SDF"), *Asahi Shimbun,* Sep 21, 2004, pp 12-13.

1000 Suganuma, Mitushiro, "Second Investigation Department of the PSIA: 'What Has the PSIA Been Doing?'" *Bungei Shunju,* Nov 1995, pp 136-147.

1001 "Intelligence Headquarters in E Tower of New Complex; Sectionalism Eliminated? Intelligence Unification," *Gunji Kenkyu,* January 1996.

1002 Sakamoto, Taiko, "*Boeicho no 'Joho Honbu' Shinsetsu, Sofuto Jushi he Shitsu Tenkan,*" ("The Establishment of the Defense Agency's 'Intelligence Headquarters," A Qualitative Shift Emphasizing the Soft"), *Yomiuri Shimbun,* January 11, 1989, p 13.

1003 "*Boeicho no Soshiki Kaikaku Koso wo Takeshita Shusho ni Hokoku/Nishihiro Boei Jikan,*" ("Defense Agency Organizational Reform Plan Reported to PM Takeshita/Administrative Vice Minister Nishihiro"), *Yomiuri Shimbun,* April 8, 1989, p 2.

1004 "*Boeicho no 'Joho Honbu' Setchi Koso ha Sakiokuri/Seifu,*" ("Plan To Establish Defense Agency 'Intelligence Headquarters" Postponed/Government"), *Yomiuri Shimbun,* December 20, 1990, p 2.

1005 "*Boeicho ga Honkakuteki Joho Kikan wo Setchi, Shushu, Bunseki wo Ichigenka, Soren Taio no Gote de Hansei,*" ("Defense Agency Will Establish an Intelligence Organization, Consolidate Collection and Analysis Following Review of Late Reaction To Events in Soviet Union"), *Yomiuri Shimbun,* August 26, 1991, p 9.

1006 "DA To Set Up `Information Headquarters'," *Tokyo Shimbun,* June 12, 1995, p 3.

1007 "Intelligence Headquarters Slated To Open in January," *Asagumo,* May 30, 1996, p 1.

1008 "Intelligence Headquarters Slated To Open in January," *Asagumo,* May 30, 1996.

1009 "New Defense Intelligence HQ Opens in Tokyo," Kyodo, January 20, 1997.

1010 Makino, Keijiro, "Internal Bureaus of Japan's Defense Agency and Profiles of Their Key Personnel," *Gunji Kenkyu*, February 2006, pp 204-223.

1011 "DA Chief Kyuma, Top Brass Attend DIH Opening Ceremony," *Asagumo*, January 23, 1997, p 1.

1012 Handa, Shigeru, "DIH Turf Battle Between Officers, Civilians Reported," *Tokyo Shimbun*, January 20, 1997.

1013 "Birth of Our Nation's Largest Intelligence Organization," *Asagumo*, January 9, 1997, p 1.

1014 "Defense Agency: Law Amendment Proposed To Build Intelligence Headquarters," *Wing*, February 14, 1996.

1015 "*Kaigai Joho Senmontai wo Setchi he, Taiki, Arata ni 2600nin, Jieitai Haken, Boeicho Hoshin*," ("Defense Agency To Establish International Intelligence Specialist Unit, 2,600 Personnel To Be on Alert for Self-Defense Force Dispatches"), *Asahi Shimbun*, August 25, 2005, p 1.

1016 "GSDF To Create Central Intelligence Unit, To Boost Info-Gathering for International Missions," *Yomiuri Shimbun*, December 30, 2006.

1017 Makino, Kentaro, "Interview with Intelligence Director Kunimi," *Gunji Kenkyu*, April 1997, p 162.

1018 Kuroi, Buntaro, "Special Project: What Are Japan's Foreign Intelligence Capabilities Now? (Part 2)," *Gunji Kenkyu*, November 2005, pp 232-241.

1019 "DA Chief Kyuma, Top Brass Attend DIH Opening Ceremony," *Asagumo*, January 23, 1997, p 1.

1020 "New Japan Central Intelligence Agency: A Total Survey of Operations, Activities of the Defense Agency's Defense Intelligence Headquarters," *Maru*, May 1997, pp 63-68.

1021 "'Intelligence Headquarters' in E Tower of New Complex; Sectionalism Eliminated? Intelligence Unification," *Gunji*

Kenkyu, January 1996; "The Defense Agency Intelligence Headquarters," *Sentaku*, May 1997, pp 126-129.

1022 "New Defense Intelligence HQ Background Viewed," *Gunji Kenkyu*, January 1996.

1023 Aso, Iku, "*Jieitaiin Ha 'Gyokusai' Sunzen Datta – Futatabi 'Sento Funo Kokka' Nippon*," ("Self Defense Force Troops Almost Died a 'Hero's Deatch' – Japan Again a Nation Unable to Fight"), *Bungei Shunju*, May 1999, p 147.

1024 *Sentaku, ibid.*

1025 *Sentaku, ibid.*

1026 Fujii, Hisashi, "Let Me Expose Japan's Intelligence Collection Capabilities Against North Korea: Build Up Japan's Independent Intelligence Network," *Gunji Kenkyu*, January 2005, pp 90-101.

1027 "Zero Growth for FY1998 Defense Budget Proposal," *Nikkan Kogyo Shimbun*, August 30, 1997, pp 3, 9.

1028 "DA Plans to Collect More Information on Asia," *Yomiuri Shimbun*, August 25, 1998, p 2.

1029 "*'Nihon no Mamori' Dai-3bu Johosen (6): Hito wo Sodatete Hito wo Shiru*," ("'Protecting Japan' Part III Information Warfare: Human Factor Key to Intelligence"), *Yomiuri Shimbun*, June 10, 2004, p 1.

1030 "*Riku-kai-ku Butai de Nendomatsu Shinkaihen*," ("Reorganization of Ground-Maritime-Air Units at End of Fiscal Year"), *Asagumo*, March 29, 2001, p 1.

1031 Fujii, Hisashi, "Let Me Expose Japan's Intelligence Collection Capabilities Against North Korea: Build Up Japan's Independent Intelligence Network," *Gunji Kenkyu*, January 2005, pp 90-101.

1032 "*'Nihon no Mamori' Dai-3bu Johosen (6): Hito wo Sodatete Hito wo Shiru*," ("'Protecting Japan' Part III Information Warfare: Human Factor Key to Intelligence"), *Yomiuri Shimbun*, June 10, 2004, p 1.

1033 A version of this section was published as Radcliffe, William, "Origins and Current State of Japan's Reconnaissance Satellite Program," *Studies in Intelligence*, Vol. 54, No. 3, September 2010, www.cia.gov/library/center-for-the-study-of-intelligence/csi-publications/csi-studies/studies/vol.-54-no.-3/index.html.

1034 *Kokkai Kaigiroku, "Shugiin: Gaimu Iinkai,"* No. 5, March 6, 1991, kokkai.ndl.go.jp/.

1035 Sunohara, Tsuyoshi, *Tanjo Kokusan Supai Eisei: Dokuji Johomo to Nichibei Domei*, (*The Birth of an Indigenous Spy Satellite: Independent Intelligence Network and the Japan-US Alliance*), Nihon Keizai Shimbunsha, 2005, pp 7-8.

1036 "*Teisatsu Eisei, Hoyu Fukume Kento; 'Kaihatsuhi Ha Icchoencho'-Boeicho Ga Himitsu Kenkyu Ripoto*," ("JDA Secretly Studied Reconnaissance Satellites Including Possession; 'Development to Cost Over ¥1 Trillion'"), *Mainichi Shimbun*, August 16, 1994, p 1.

1037 Science and Technology Agency, "Roles and Activities 1994," February 21, 1995, pp 1-38.

1038 "*Chugoku ga Seisashoto ni Wan mo Kensetsu, Nansashoto de no Sakusen Yoi ni, Yomiuri Shimbunsha ga Eisei Shashin wo Nyushu*," ("China Constructs Port on Paracel Islands, Allows For Easy Operations in Spratly Islands; Yomiuri Receives Satellite Photos"), *Yomiuri Shimbun*, August 21, 1993, p 4.

1039 Taoka, Shunji, "Japan's Turning Point Toward Spy Satellites and Information Independence; Decision Made To Launch Satellites in Four Years," *Aera*, January 11, 1999, pp 46-50.

1040 "*Jieitai no Eisei Riyo, Honkakuka; Supabado-B Tosai no Chukeiki 7gatsu Kado*," ("SDF Use of Satellites Taking Shape; Transponder on Superbird-B Operational from July"), *Asahi Shimbun*, May 31, 1992, p 3.

1041 Aikawa, Haruyuki, "LDP Researches Domestic Spy Satellite Development," *Mainichi Shimbun*, May 16, 1996.

1042 "US Opposes Japan's Plan for Spy Satellites," Kyodo News Agency, January 7, 1998.

1043 "*Joho Honbu Kongetsu-matsu ni Hassoku, Eisei Gazo no Busho mo,*" ("Defense Intelligence HQ To Commence Operations at the End of This Month, Will Have Satellite Imagery Posts As Well"), *Sankei Shimbun*, January 4, 1997, p 3.

1044 Ninagawa, Yoshihiko, "STA, NASDA Study Improved Satellite Monitoring Resolution," *Sankei Shimbun*, September 20, 1998, p 1.

1045 Taoka, Shunji, "Japan's Turning Point Toward Spy Satellites and Information Independence; Decision Made To Launch Satellites in Four Years," *Aera*, January 11, 1999, pp 46-50.

1046 Sunohara, Tsuyoshi, *Tanjo Kokusan Supai Eisei: Dokuji Johomo to Nichibei Domei*, (*The Birth of an Indigenous Spy Satellite: Independent Intelligence Network and the Japan-US Alliance*), (Tokyo: Nihon Keizai Shimbunsha, 2005), p 88.

1047 "Obuchi Supports Launching 'Multipurpose' Satellite," Kyodo News Agency, September 10, 1998.

1048 "NEC Executive Indicted in Procurement Scandal," Kyodo, October 28, 1998.

1049 Taoka, *ibid.*

1050 "Cabinet Approves Plan To Launch Spy Satellites," Kyodo News Agency, December 22, 1998.

1051 "Space Activities Commission Decides on FY2000 Space Budget Plans," *Nikkan Kogyo Shimbun*, August 5, 1999, p 6.

1052 "Cabinet Information Research Office To Launch Reconnaissance Satellites in FY03," *Sankei Shimbun*, January 26, 2002.

1053 "LDP Proposal on Intelligence Satellites," LDP Web site.

1054 "*NASDA, Joho Shushu Eisei de Junbishitsu wo Kaisetsu,*" ("NASDA Establishes Preparatory Office for Intelligence-Gathering Satellite"), *Nikkan Kogyo Shimbun*, December 15, 1998, p 5.

1055 "*Seifu, Joho Shushu Eisei no Kokusan wo Kettei,*" ("Government Decides On Domestic Development of Intelligence-Gathering Satellites"), *Nikkan Kogyo Shimbun*, April 2, 1999, p 2.

1056 Nogi, Keiichi. "Summing Up the Pluses and Minuses of Japan's Reconnaissance Satellite Development," *Gunji Kenkyu*, December 1998, pp 60-74.

1057 "*Joho Shushu Eisei, Uchiage 15-nen ni Enki, Seifu Kettei, Buhin Chotatsu ga Okureru*," ("Government Decides To Postpone Launch of Intelligence-Gathering Satellites Until 2003, Supply of Parts Late"), *Sankei Shimbun*, June 14, 2001, p 2.

1058 Sagara, Yuta, "'Peaceful Use Principle in Japan's Policy Crumbling," Kyodo, March 6, 2003.

1059 Sunohara, Tsuyoshi, *Tanjo Kokusan Supai Eisei: Dokuji Johomo to Nichibei Domei*, (*The Birth of an Indigenous Spy Satellite: Independent Intelligence Network and the Japan-US Alliance*), Nihon Keizai Shimbunsha, 2005, pp 208-209, 226.

1060 Sunohara, Tsuyoshi, *Tanjo Kokusan Supai Eisei: Dokuji Johomo to Nichibei Domei*, (*The Birth of an Indigenous Spy Satellite: Independent Intelligence Network and the Japan-US Alliance*), Nihon Keizai Shimbunsha, 2005, p 179.

1061 "Japan To Launch Two 'Spy' Satellites in Mar, Start Full-Fledged Operations in July," *Yomiuri Shimbun*, January 6, 2003.

1062 "Japan's 'Spy' Satellites Start 'Full-Fledged' Photo Surveillance Over DPRK," *Asahi Shimbun*, September 21, 2003.

1063 "Koizumi's Grave and Kim Chong-il's Betrayal; Interview With North Korea's Diplomatic Source in Beijing; Pressure From Hu Jintao, which materialized Japan-North Korea Summit," *Gendai*, July 2004, pp 28-36.

1064 "Protecting Japan Part III: Eyes in the Sky Vital for Security," *Yomiuri Shimbun*, June 8, 2004.

1065 "Rocket Failure a Double Setback," *Asahi Shimbun*, December 1, 2003.

1066 "*Eiseikan Tsushin Jikken ni Seiko*," ("Inter-Satellite Communications Experiment Successful"), *Air World*, May 2003, p 124.

1067 A photo of the northern site was available in the November 27, 2001 edition of *Tomamin*, a local news service provider in Hokkaido, www.tomamin.co.jp/2001/tp011127.htm.

1068 "*Joho Shushu Eisei Uchiage Junbi Tchakutchaku: 15nen Natsu ni Mazu 2ki,*" ("Preparation for Intelligence Satellite Launch Proceeds Apace: First 2 Devices Set for Summer 2003"), *Asagumo,* August 2, 2001, p 1, and *Nihon Keizai Shimbun,* 29 July 2002.

1069 *Yomiuri Shimbun,* 31 December 2001.

1070 Interview with Masahiro Kunimi, "*Joho Shushu Eisei, Uchiage 15-nen ni Enki, Seifu Kettei, Buhin Chotatsu ga Okureru,*" ("Government Decides To Postpone Launch of Intelligence-Gathering Satellites Until 2003, Supply of Parts Late"), *Sankei Shimbun,* June 14, 2001, p 2.

1071 "Government To Launch Monitoring Satellites in 2003 To Bolster Crisis Management," *Nihon Keizai Shimbun,* July 29, 2002.

1072 "*Naikaku (Jinji),*" ("PMOR (Personnel)"), *Nihon Keizai Shimbun,* August 5, 2003, p 4.

1073 "*Joho Shushu Eisei Uchiage Junbi Tchakutchaku: 15nen Natsu ni Mazu 2ki,*" ("Preparation for Intelligence Satellite Launch Proceeds Apace: First 2 Devices Set for Summer 2003"), *Asagumo,* August 2, 2001, p 1; Some Japanese mapping services available on the internet helpfully label the building, too: Mapion.co.jp labels the building directly to the north of the MOD Headquarters as "*Naikakufu Joho Senta*" ("Cabinet Satellite Center").

1074 "Defense Agency Intelligence Headquarters," *Sentaku,* May 1997, pp 126-129.

1075 "Larger Staff Set for Analyzing Information Satellite Data," *Yomiuri Shimbun,* July 16, 1999, p 1.

1076 Kuroi, Buntaro, "Special Project: What Are Japan's Foreign Intelligence Capabilities Now? (Part 2)," *Gunji Kenkyu,* November 2005, pp 232-241.

1077 http://jda-clearing.jda.go.jp/hakusho_data/2003/2003/html/15311300.html

1078 Ishizuka, Isao, "*Joho Shushu Eisei Seiko no Joken,*" ("Requirements for Successful Information-Collection Satellites"), in *DRC Nenpo 1999,* available at www.drc-jpn.org/AR3-J/mokuji-j.htm.

1079 Kuroi, Buntaro, "Special Project: What Are Japan's Foreign Intelligence Capabilities Now? (Part 2)," *Gunji Kenkyu,* November 2005, pp 232-241.

1080 See comprehensive list of satellites used by Japanese ministries and agencies on Cabinet Web site, www8.cao.go.jp/cstp/tyousakai/cosmo/haihu03/siryou3-5.pdf.

1081 "*Seifu, Rainendo Kara Joho Shushu Eisei no Kokeiki Keikaku ni Chakushu,*" ("Government Begins Planning Successor Intelligence-Gathering Satellites From Next Fiscal Year"), *Nikkan Kogyo Shimbun,* July 28, 2000, p 2.

1082 Sunohara, *Tanjo Kokusan Supai Eisei: Dokuji Johomo to Nichibei Domei,* p 225.

1083 "*Seifu, Jisedai Joho Eisei, Noryoku wo Ohava Kojo,*" ("Government To Improve Capability of Next-Generation Intelligence-Gathering Satellite"), *Nihon Keizai Shimbun,* June 13, 2000, evening edition, p 3.

1084 Sunohara, pp 226-227.

1085 Tamama, Tetsuo, "*Nihon no Uchu Seisaku to Anzen Hosho no Setten,*" ("Points in Common Between Japan's Space Policy and National Security"), *Defense Research Center,* June 2002, p 26.

1086 Tamama, *ibid.,* p 27.

1087 Hidaka, Tetsuo and Koichi Yasuda, "Better Spy Satellite System Needed: Reliance On US Intelligence On Missile Launch Shows Need For Improvement," *Yomiuri Shimbun,* July 31, 2006.

1088 Shikata, Toshiyuki, "*Shinsorikantei ni Kitai Suru Mono: Taisetsu na Joho Kozo no Kakuritsu to Kunren,*" ("Expectations for the New PMOR: Ensurance and Practice for an Important Information Structure"), *Securitarian,* April 2002, pp 50-51.

1089 Quoted in "Japan's First Intelligence Satellites Will Be Able to Capture Images of 'North Korea' Only," *Shukan Bunshun,* December 19, 2002, pp 152-155.

1090 Ebata, Kensuke, "The ASDF of the Future," *Securitarian,* April 2002, p 28.

1091 "Panel Drafts Outline of Bill To OK Military Use of Space," June 2, 2006.

1092 Yasuaki Hashimoto, "Enactment of the Basic Space Law: Japan's Space Security Policy," *Briefing Memo,* National Institute of Defense Studies, 27 June 2008.

1093 Shiro, Namekata, "Space Plan to Double Satellite Launches," *Asahi Shimbun,* 3 June 2009.

1094 Aso, Iku, "*Jieitaiin Ha 'Gyokusai' Sunzen Datta – Futatabi 'Sento Funo Kokka' Nippon,*" ("Self Defense Force Troops Almost Died a 'Hero's Deatch' – Japan Again a Nation Unable to Fight"), *Bungei Shunju,* May 1999, p 147.

1095 Kuroi, Buntaro, "Special Topic: How Capable Is Japan Of Gathering Foreign Intelligence? Extra Installment No. 2," *Gunji Kenkyu,* January 2006, pp 234-238.

1096 "*Kokusai Tero ni Taio, Gaiji Johobu wo Shinsetsu, Keisatsucho ga Soshiki Kaihen,*" ("Foreign Affairs and Intelligence Department To Be Newly Established To Respond to International Terrorism in NPA Reorganization"), *Sankei Shimbun,* April 1, 2004, p 29.

1097 "Relatives Pray for Hostages' Safety In Iraq," *Yomiuri Shimbun,* April 8, 2004.

1098 Kanazawa, Minoru, "Japan's Current Terrorism Measures Provide for Unprecedentedly High Level of Long-term Alert," *Sekai Shuho,* May 25, 2004, pp 10-11.

1099 "Japan Gaining Information on Hostage-Takers in Iraq," Kyodo, April 10, 2004.

1100 "The Weekly Post Special: Part 3: How Were Japanese Kidnapped?" *Shukan Posuto,* April 19, 2004.

1101 "Aisawa Denies Gov't Paid Ransom To End Hostage Crisis," Kyodo, April 20, 2004.

1102 "Three Ex-Hostages Were Snatched by Seven Or Eight Captors," Kyodo, April 27, 2004.

1103 "Revised Law Reinforces Police Authority," Kyodo, April 27, 2004.

1104 "Japan To Bolster Anti-Terrorism Measures," *Nihon Keizai Shimbun*, September 9, 2004.

1105 Kiyotake, Hidetoshi and Hiromi Yamamoto, "NPA Probes N. Korean Spies," *Yomiuri Shimbun*, February 8, 2003.

1106 "Focus: Murky Status of Government Discretionary Funds Highlighted," Kyodo, January 24, 2001.

1107 "*Gaimusho Kanbu 'Kimitsuhi' Ryuyo Giwaku, Mae Shitcho, Kado Kessai 1000-Man En Cho*," ("MOFA Executive Diversion of 'Secret Funds,' Former Office Head Used Credit Cards To Settle Over ¥10 Million"), *Mainichi Shimbun*, January 18, 2001, p 30; "Foreign Ministry Bans Credit Card Payment of Expenses," Kyodo, February 2, 2001; "Matsuo Gave No Official Receipts for 500 Mil. Yen Hotel Bills," Kyodo, February 8, 2001.

1108 "Ex-Foreign Ministry Officials Get Suspended Term," Kyodo, May 28, 2002.

1109 "Ex-Foreign Ministry Officials Get Suspended Term," Kyodo, May 28, 2002.

1110 "Foreign Ministry Begins Internal Investigation of Secret Diplomatic Funds," *Sankei Shimbun*, February 1, 2001.

1111 "Government Papers Show Illegal Fund Transfers: Sources," Kyodo, February 1, 2001.

1112 Toshikawa, Takao, "Allegation of Secret Fund; Impact of 'Furukawa Paper'," *Foresight*, March 2001, pp 108-109.

1113 "Foreign Ministry money scandals resurface in ex-diplomat's book," Kyodo, October 7, 2003.

1114 "PM Residence Officials To Be Quizzed in MOFA Official Embezzlement Case," *Mainichi Shimbun*, January 18, 2001.

1115 "Funds Used for 'Bonus' to Embassies During Premier's Trips," Kyodo, February 5, 2001.

1116 "Japan's Chief Cabinet Secretary Uses About 80 Percent of 'Secret Funds'," *Yomiuri Shimbun,* November 17, 2003.

1117 "Japanese Government Likely To Face Difficulties Over MOFA Embezzlement Scandal," *Yomiuri Shimbun,* February 3, 2001.

1118 Omori, Yoshio, *Nihon no Interijensu Kikan,* ("Japan's Intelligence Organization"), Bunshunshinsho: Tokyo, 2005, pp 58-60.

1119 Toshikawa, Takao, "Allegation of Secret Fund; Impact of 'Furukawa Paper'," *Foresight,* March 2001, pp 108-109.

1120 "Japanese Diplomats Having Ball at Taxpayers' Expense," *Asahi Shimbun,* January 30, 2001.

1121 Sassa, Atsuyuki and Shinzo Abe, "National Strategy for Age of Terrorism – Motojiro Akashi! Please Make an Appearance! – An Intelligence Agency That Competes with MOFA Would Reinforce Diplomacy and Security," *Voice,* May 2004, pp 48-57.

1122 Ehara, Naoki, "*Misairu Shisutemu no Chijo Sochi no Hanashi,*" ("Discussion of Missile Systems' Ground-Based Equipment"), *Securitarian,* July 2006, pp 52-53.

1123 Sasajima, Masahiko and Takashi Nishida, "Poor Information Strategy Stands Out," *Yomiuri Shimbun,* April 17, 1998, p 2.

1124 Aso, Iku and Raisuke Miyawake, "Japan is Still in First Year of Counterterrorism Preparations – Can the Terrorists Provoked by the SDF Dispatch to Iraq be Contained?" *Voice,* March 2004, p 92-101.

1125 "Defense Agency To Post More Military Attaches to China," Kyodo, August 12, 1997.

1126 Shikata, Toshiyuki, *Omoshiroi Hodo Yoku Wakaru Jieitai,* ("The Interesting and Easily Understandable Self Defense Forces"), (Tokyo: Nippon Bungeisha, 2004), pp 118-119.

1127 "'*Heiwa Rikkoku no Shiren' Dai 4bu: Tadayou Anzen Hoshou Yuragu Bei-Chu-Tai no Heikin*" ("'Japan and its Ordeal as a Pacifist Nation' Part Four: Security Adrift, Shaken Balance Between US, China, Taiwan"), *Mainichi Shimbun*, March 30, 2004, p 3.

1128 Sasajima, Masahiko and Takashi Nishida, "Poor Information Strategy Stands Out," *Yomiuri Shimbun*, April 17, 1998, p 2.

1129 Tu Po, "Japan Will Become an Intelligence Power," *Yazhou Zhoukan*, November 25, 1996.

1130 "Detained Military Attache Returns Home," Kyodo News Service, January 19, 1996.

1131 "AFP: Japanese Embassy Says Diplomat Not Expelled, But Recalled From Beijing," Hong Kong AFP, November 14, 2002, and "China Expels Japanese Defense Attache From Beijing," Kyodo News Agency, November 14, 2002.

1132 "The Subcommittee of the LDP's National Defense Division Points to the Improper Transmission of Information," *Asagumo*, November 7, 2002, p 1.

1133 Onami, Aya, "Four LDP Diet Members Emerge as Prominent Players in Defense Issues Debate," *Shukan Asahi*, October 19, 2001, p 32.

1134 "*Gaimusho Keiyu no Boei Joho, Boeicho ni mo Doji Soshin he*," ("Defense Information That Passes Through MOFA To Be Transmitted to JDA At Same Time"), *Yomiuri Shimbun*, April 20, 2004.

1135 "New Defense Intelligence HQ Background Viewed," *Gunji Kenkyu*, January 1996.

1136 Makino, Kentaro, "Intelligence Director Kunimi Interviewed," *Gunji Kenkyu*, April 1997, p 162.

1137 Sassa, Atsuyuki and Shinzo Abe, "National Security for the Age of Terrorism – Motojiro Akashi! Please Make an Appearance! – An Intelligence Agency That Competes With MOFA Would Reinforce Diplomacy and Security," *Voice*, May 2004, pp 48-57.

1138 Maeda, Tetsuo, *The Hidden Army: The Untold Story of Japan's Military Forces*, trans. Steven Karpa (Chicago: Edition Q, 1995), pp 239-240.

1139 "US Concerned Over Info Leak To Russia Through Japan Diplomat," Kyodo, May 18, 2002.

1140 "Dead Consular Official 'pushed To Leak Govt Info'," *Yomiuri Shimbun*, December 27, 2005; "Man Who Contacted Japanese Consular Official Who Committed Suicide Suspected To Be Chinese Intelligence Agent," *Yomiuri Shimbun*, December 29, 2005; "Shocking Scoop, National Secret Leak Scandal That Neither Prime Minister Koizumi Nor Foreign Minister Aso Know About; Staff member at Japanese Consulate General in Shanghai Hanged Himself After Being Threatened by Chinese Intelligence, Saying 'I Cannot Sell Out My Country'," *Shukan Bunshun*, December 28, 2005, pp 234-239.

1141 "Shocking Scoop, National Secret Leak Scandal That Neither Prime Minister Koizumi Nor Foreign Minister Aso Know About; Staff member at Japanese Consulate General in Shanghai Hanged Himself After Being Threatened by Chinese Intelligence, Saying 'I Cannot Sell Out My Country'," *Shukan Bunshun*, December 28, 2005, pp 234-239.

1142 "Dead Consular Official 'pushed To Leak Govt Info'," *Yomiuri Shimbun*, December 27, 2005.

1143 "MSDF Officer Quizzed Over China Trips: Petty Officer Had Classified Information On Foreign Military Vessels At His Home," *Yomiuri Shimbun*, August 2, 2006.

1144 "Shocking Scoop, National Secret Leak Scandal That Neither Prime Minister Koizumi Nor Foreign Minister Aso Know About; Staff member at Japanese Consulate General in Shanghai Hanged Himself After Being Threatened by Chinese Intelligence, Saying 'I Cannot Sell Out My Country'," *Shukan Bunshun*, December 28, 2005, pp 234-239.

1145 Ikeda, Toyoji, "*Gaimusho Kikou Kaikaku, 'Senryakuteki Gaiko' Zenmen ni (Kaisetsu)*," ("Commentary: MOFA Structural

Reforms At the Forefront of 'Strategic Diplomacy'), *Yomiuri Shimbun*, March 31, 1993, p 15.

1146 "*Gaimusho ga Kiko Kaikaku*," ("MOFA Undergoes Structural Reform"), *Asahi Shimbun*, July 27, 1993, evening edition, p 2.

1147 "*Kaigai de no Joho Shushu Kyoka, Zaigai Kokan ni Sennin Tanto-kan, Gaimusho*," ("MOFA To Establish Full-Time Managers At Embassies Abroad To Strengthen Intelligence Collection"), *Tokyo Shimbun*, November 4, 2005, p 3.

1148 "Ambassador to Israel Imai Shifted to Malaysia," Kyodo, April 16, 2004.

1149 "Togo Dismissed as Diplomat," Kyodo, April 26, 2002.

1150 "Japan Names 14 New Ambassadors," Jiji, July 30, 2004.

1151 "Japan Names Iimura as Ambassador To France," Jiji, April 25, 2006.

1152 Ogawa, Kazuhisa, "'Talkative Bureaucrats' and a 'Group of Boy Detectives': Japan's Intelligence and Security Capabilities Are Too Rough," *Sapio*, November 22, 1995, pp 23-25.

1153 "*Naikaku Joho Chosashitsu, 1000nin Taisei ni Kakudai, Bei-CIA Moderu ni*," ("CIRO to be Expanded to 1000-Person Structure, Modeled After US CIA"), *Sankei Shimbun*, March 29, 2004, p 3.

1154 Suganuma, Mitushiro, "Second Investigation Department of the PSIA: 'What Has the PSIA Been Doing?'" *Bungei Shunju*, Nov 1995, pp 136-147.

1155 Suganuma, Mitushiro, "Second Investigation Department of the PSIA: 'What Has the PSIA Been Doing?'" *Bungei Shunju*, Nov 1995, pp 136-147.

1156 Suganuma, Mitushiro, "Second Investigation Department of the PSIA: 'What Has the PSIA Been Doing?'" *Bungei Shunju*, Nov 1995, pp 136-147.

1157 Terashima, Jitsuro, "How Should We Construct an International Intelligence Strategy?" *Foresight*, Apr 2002, pp 9-11.

1158 Terashima, Jitsuro, "How Should We Construct an International Intelligence Strategy?" *Foresight*, Apr 2002, pp 9-11.

1159 Nakasone, Yasuhiro, Kiichi Miyazawa, Kinichi Matsumoto, "What's Wrong With Deploying the 'Self-Defense Forces' in Response to Barbarous Terrorism," *Shokun*, Nov 2001, pp 42-55.

1160 "Intelligence Capability: Need for the Modern Version of Motojiro Akashi," *Sankei Shimbun*, Dec 5, 2003.

1161 Abe, Shinzo and Atsuyuki Sassa, "National Strategy for an Age of Terrorism – Motojiro Akashi! Please Make an Appearance!" *Voice*, May 2004, pp 48-57.

1162 Sassa, Atsuyuki and Shinzo Abe, ""National Strategy for Age of Terrorism – Motojiro Akashi! Please Make an Appearance! – An Intelligence Agency That Competes with MOFA Would Reinforce Diplomacy and Security," *Voice*, May 2004, pp 48-57.

1163 "Focus: Japan Readying for Launch of 1st Spy Satellites," Kyodo News Agency, August 11, 2002.

1164 Matsumura, Masahiro, "Redsigning Japan's Command and Control System for Theater Missile Defense," *Defense Analysis*, Vol 16, No 2, 2000, pp 151-164 (158-160).

1165 Shikata, Toshiyuki, "*Kaku Yokushiryoku Igai no Anzen Hoshosaku wo*," ("[Develop] National Security Policies Beyond Nuclear Deterrence"), *Shokun!* August 2003, p 101.

1166 LDP Defense Policy Studies Subcommittee, "Recommendations on Japan's New Defense Policy—Toward a Safer and More Secure Japan and the world," LDP Website, March 30, 2004.

1167 Council on Security and Defense Capabilities, "Japan's Visions for Future Security and Defense Capabilities," *Prime Minister's Official Residence* Website, October 4, 2004, www.kantei.go.jp/jp/singi/ampobouei/dai13/13siryou.pdf, pp 15-16.

1168 Advisory Panel on the Strengthening of Foreign Intelligence-Gathering Capabilities, "Toward the Strengthening of Japan's Foreign Intelligence-Gathering Capabilities," Ministry of Foreign Affairs Web site, September 13, 2005.

1169 "Harpoon Missile," US Navy Factfile, August 7, 2003, www.chinfo.navy.mil/navpalib/factfile/missiles/wep-harp.html.

1170 Mori, Seiyu, "Retired GSDF General on Intelligence, Tactics," *Rikusen Kenkyu*, October 1996, pp 17-28.

1171 Statement by Ichiro Hatoyama, Read by Minister of State for Defense Naka Funada, February 29, 1956, *Kokkai Kaigiroku*, http://kokkai.ndl.go.jp.

1172 Statement by Shigejiro Ino, March 19, 1956, *Kokkai Kaigiroku*, http://kokkai.ndl.go.jp.

1173 Takama, Shoichi, Hidemitsu Satake, Saburo Takada, Yoshihisa Nakamura, "Military Officers on Revolution in Military Theory," *Rikusen Kenkyu*, January 1996.

1174 *Morino Gunji Kenkyujo*, "*Gunji Kakumei*," ("The Revolution in Military Affairs"), *Gunji Kenkyu*, February 1998, pp 163-167.

1175 Shigemura, Masahiro, "Meeting the Information Age; The Information Age Seen in U.S. Army's Force-21 Concept for the Future," *Rikusen Kenkyu*, July 1996.

1176 Funabashi, Yoichi, "US/UK Air Strikes and the Future of the Alliance," *Asahi Shimbun*, December 24, 1998, p 4.

1177 Yoneda, Kenzo, "Immediate Need for Upgrade in Offensive Capability for Self-Defense, and Shortcomings of Dependency on US," *Seiron*, April 2005, pp 278-287.

1178 "*Jimin, Taikita Misairu no Rongi wo Honkakuka*," ("LDP Debate Concerning North Korea's Missiles Deepens"), *Sankei Shimbun*, February 24, 1999, p 1.

1179 "LDP Team Discusses Countermeasures Against North Korea," Kyodo, February 24, 1999.

1180 "Liberal Democratic Party Crisis Management Team Interim Report," LDP Web site, www.jimin.jp, June 3, 1999.

1181 "On Information RMA," *ibid.*

1182 Debate by Yoshinori Suematsu, Yoriko Kawaguchi, and Shigeru Ishiba, House of Representatives Budget Committee, January 24, 2003, *Kokkai Kaigiroku*, http://kokkai.ndl.go.jp.

1183 "Japan DA Director General Ishiba Says Danger of DPRK Missile Launch 'Not Imminent'," Kyodo, February 14, 2003.

1184 Parry, Richard Lloyd and Robert Thomson, Interview with Shigeru Ishiba: "Japan Seeks Parasol in Shade of US Umbrella," *The Times*, February 26, 2003.

1185 Takashima, Hatsuhisa, "MOFA Spokesman on Military Aid to France, Germany, Other Issues," Ministry of Foreign Affairs Web site, February 28, 2003.

1186 "DA Starts Study on Possession of Capabilities to Attack Enemy," *Tokyo Shimbun*, March 27, 2003.

1187 "Peace Constitution Marks Birthday Amid Volatile International Scene," *Nihon Keizai Shimbun*, May 3, 2003.

1188 "Japan Not Mulling Cruise Missiles for Actual Use," Kyodo News Agency, March 28, 2003.

1189 Kyodo, *ibid.*

1190 Group of Junior Lawmakers To Establish the Security System for the New Century, "Urgent National Security Statement Adopted on 23 June," *Sekai Shuho*, August 19, 2003, pp 46-47.

1191 Interview with Shigeru Ishiba by Yutaka Nishizawa, "Special Report: Security Policy at a Turning Point – I Would Like to Implement a Missile Defense System as Soon as Possible. The Capability to Attack Enemy Territory Will be Left to the United States" *Sekai Shuho*, August 19, 2003, pp 14-17.

1192 Interview with Shigeru Ishiba by Yutaka Nishizawa, "Special Report: Security Policy at a Turning Point – I Would Like to Implement a Missile Defense System as Soon as Possible. The Capability to Attack Enemy Territory Will be Left to the United States" *Sekai Shuho*, August 19, 2003, pp 14-17.

1193 Okabe, Isaku, "Present and Future of MSDF's Land Attack Capabilities," *Sekai no Kansen*, April 2004, pp 92-95.

1194 "Legal Interpretation of the Relationship Between an Attack by Missiles and Self-Defense Right," Chapter 2: Japan's

Defense Policy, *2003 Defense of Japan*, (Tokyo: Japan Defense Agency, December 2003), p 117.

1195 Kaneda, Hideaki, "The Missile Defense Plan and Japan," *Sekai Shuho*, February 2003, pp 6-9; see also: Kaneda, Hideaki, "Is It Possible for the SDF To Attack Enemy Missile Bases?" *Sekai no Kansen*, February 2007, pp 96-99.

1196 Kaneda, Hideaki, "Is It Possible for the SDF To Attack Enemy Missile Bases?" *Sekai no Kansen*, February 2007, pp 96-99.

1197 Ushio, Masato, "What Will Japan Do If a Taepo Dong Is Fired? Post-Iraq North Korea," *Sekai Shuho*, 13 May 2003, pp 30-33.

1198 Ushio, Masato, "North Korea is Next! When the Time Comes, Will the SDF Be Ready?" *Voice*, April 2003, pp 98-105.

1199 "Air Defense System Powerless Against DPRK Missiles," *Yomiuri Weekly*, June 22, 2003.

1200 Shikata, Toshiyuki, "*'Gunjiryoku wo Hikaku Suru Toki no Shakudo,' (Boeiryoku seibi no Genten wo Saikento Subeki Jiki ga Kita),*" ("Measures To Compare Military Strength,' (The Time Has Come To Review Basic Military Equipment"), *Gunji Kenkyu*, October 2005, p 27.

1201 "Air Defense System Powerless Against DPRK Missiles," *Yomiuri Weekly*, June 22, 2003.

1202 "Protecting Japan: Candid Discussion Needed on Defense Systems," *Yomiuri Shimbun*, March 6, 2004.

1203 National Institute for Defense Studies, "Japan–National Emergency Legislation, Reconstruction Assistance in Iraq, and Countering the Threat of WMD," *East Asian Strategic Review 2004*, (Tokyo: NIDS, February 2004), pp 245-246, http://www.nids.go.jp/.

1204 Taoka, Shunji, "North Korean Emergency – Preemptive Strike of Missile Bases Impossible – Ridicule Ideology of Hawks," *Shukan Asahi*, July 28, 2006, p 32.

1205 "DPJ's Ozawa Interviewed," News 2001, August 5, 2006.

1206 "Public Supports Japan's Capacity To Attack Enemy Bases," Jiji Press, August 12, 2006.

1207 *"Choshatei Yudodan no Kenkyu Chakushu Miokuri, Jikibo, Komeito no Rikai Erarezu,"* ("Unable To Gain Komeito's Understanding, Next Five-Year Plan Postpones Research of Long-Range Guided Weapons"), *Asahi Shimbun,* December 8, 2004, p 3.

1208 "Air Defense System Powerless Against DPRK Missiles," *Yomiuri Weekly,* June 22, 2003.

1209 Boeing, "Joint Direct Attack Munition," www.boeing.com/defense-space/missiles/jdam/jdam_back.htm.

1210 "ASDF Plans To Acquire JDAM Guidance Kits From FY04," *Yomiuri Shimbun,* September 17, 2003.

1211 "*Arasuka no Takokukan Enshu, Kuji Sentoki ga Shosanka, Beigunki Kara Kuchu Kyuyu,*" ("ASDF Fighters Will Participate for First Time in Multilateral Training in Alaska, Will Conduct Aerial Refueling from US Plane"), *Sankei Shimbun,* May 4, 2003, p 1; "*Sokudo Awase, Subun de Hokkaido Seihooki, Nichibei Kyodo de Kuchu Kyuyu Kunren,*" ("Regulating Speeds for Several Minutes Over Waters West of Hokkaido, Japan and US Conduct Joint Aerial Refueling Training"), *Asahi Shimbun,* May 15, 2003, p 27.

1212 "*Kodai na Kuiki de Boku Sento, Beikugun Shusai 'Kopusanda' (Arasuka) Owaru,*" ("Air Defense Warfare in Wide-Open Skies, US-Military Sponsored 'Cope Thunder' (Alaska) Ends"), *Asagumo,* June 26, 2003, p 3.

1213 "*Sora No Nichibei Kyodo Kunren,*" ("Japan-US Joint Training in the Air"), *Asagumo,* June 3, 2004, p 2.

1214 "*Beiki Kara Juyu Kuchu Kyuyu Kunren,*" ("Taking On Fuel From a US Plane During Aerial Refueling Training"), *Asagumo,* June 22, 2006, p 3.

1215 "'Electrical Glitch' Linked to ASDF Jet's Strafing," *Yomiuri Shimbun,* June 27, 2001.

1216 "Experts Say Population Increase in ASDF Drill Range Led to Firing Incident," *Yomiuri Shimbun,* June 27, 2004.

1217 "ASDF F-4s Resume Air-to-Ground Firing Practice at Shimamatsu Firing Range," *Asagumo*, April 22, 2004, p 2.

1218 "Experts Say Population Increase in ASDF Drill Range Led to Firing Incident," *Yomiuri Shimbun*, June 27, 2001.

1219 "Experts Say Population Increase in ASDF Drill Range Led to Firing Incident," *Yomiuri Shimbun*, June 27, 2001.

1220 "*Bei to Kyodo de Taichi Jissen Kunren*," ("Counter-Ground Live-Fire Training With the US"), *Asagumo*, June 15, 2006, p 1.

1221 A picture of the GCS-1 at the TRDI museum in Tachikawa is featured in "*Boeicho Gijutsu Kenkyu Honbu (Dai-3 Kenkyujo)*," ("DA Technical Research and Development Institute [3rd Research Center]"), *Boei Gijutsu Janaru*, July 2003, p 27.

1222 Federation of American Scientists, "AGM-154A Joint Stand-off Weapon [JSOW]," www.fas.org/man/dod-101/sys/smart/agm-154.htm.

1223 For the XGCS-2 funding, see www.jda.go.jp/j/info/hyouka/h16keikaku.pdf.

1224 See MOD Web site, www.mod.go.jp/j/info/hyouka/2002/jizen/you07.pdf.

1225 "New Air-to-Ship Missile Tested," *Koku Fan*, October 2006, p 104.

1226 Ishikawa, Junichi, "Domestic Production of Air-Self-Defense Force Air-to-Air and Air-to-Ship Missiles—Will Anti-Surface Missiles Come Next?" *Gunji Kenkyu*, December 2006, pp 76-87.

1227 According to a summary in *Sankei Shimbun*: "*tai-chi kogeki kano na seimitsu yudo heiki wo hoyu*"—"possessing precision guided weapons capable of striking ground [targets]"; *Sankei Shimbun*, "'*Boeiryoku no Arikata Kento' Anyoshi*," ("'Study of the Defense Structure' Summary"), July 24, 2004, p 5.

1228 "Agency Eyes Longer Reach," *Asahi Shimbun*, July 26, 2004.

1229 "Capability to Attack Enemy Bases Unnecessary: DA Vice Deputy Director General Moriya," Kyodo News Agency, July 27, 2004.

1230 Ueda, Naruhiko, "On GSDF, High Technology," *Securitarian*, October 1996, pp 16-19.

1231 TRDI references the missile program in passing on its Web site, www.jda-trdi.go.jp/Japanese/gmj.html; budgets also refer to a guided missile program "SSM-88kai".

1232 Tamura, Naoya, "Artillery Brigade Firepower of Strategic Maneuver Divisions/Brigades is This," *Gunji Kenkyu*, September 2000, pp 84-93.

1233 Ueda, Naruhiko, "On GSDF, High Technology," *Securitarian*, October 1996, pp 16-19.

1234 Outline available on the MOD Web site at www.mod.go.jp/j/info/hyouka/2001/jizen/ you23.pdf.

1235 "Sense-and-Destroy Armor (SADARM) Submunition," www.sec.army.mil/arat/ARAT/Target_sensing_systems/Fire_Support/sadarm.htm.

1236 Outline available on the MOD Web site at www.mod.go.jp/j/info/hyouka/2001/jizen/ you23.pdf.

1237 Available online at www.jda-cco.go.jp/syuyoukeki-yakuhinn/14-5-1.pdf.

1238 "*Shorai Kaki/Danyaku no Kenkyu Kaihatsu ni Kan Suru Teian (Sono 2)*," ("Proposal Regarding Research and Development of Future Fire Arms/Ammunition [Part 2]"), *Gekkan JADI*, January 2003, pp 30-46.

1239 Okabe, Isaku, "Present and Future of MSDF's Land Attack Capabilities," *Sekai no Kansen*, April 2004, pp 92-95.

1240 Yamazaki, Makoto, "*Kaijo Jieitai no Sakusen Noryoku: Posuto Reisen-gata Kaiyosen*," ("Operational Capabilities of the Maritime Self-Defense Force: Post-Cold War Sea Warfare"), *Sekai no Kansen*, June 2003, pp 80-83.

1241 "Global Positioning System Fully Operational," Air Force Space Command Public Affairs, July 17, 1995, www.colorado.edu/geography/gcraft/notes/gps/foc.txt.

1242 For an informative guide to development of the Global Positioning System in the 1990s, see Peter H. Dana, "Global Positioning System Overview," The Geographer's Craft Project, Department of Geography, University of Colorado at Boulder, www.colorado.edu/geography/ gcraft/notes/gps/gps_f.html.

1243 The White House, "Presidential Decision Directive NSTC-6," March 28, 1996, Federation of American Scientists Web site, www.fas.org/spp/military/docops/national/gps.htm.

1244 Hirako, Yoshinori, "Japan Eyes Its Own GPS System To End Reliance on US Satellites," *Asahi Shimbun*, February 22, 2003.

1245 The White House, "Joint Statement by the Government of the United States of America and the Government of Japan on Cooperation in the Use of the Global Positioning System," Office of the Press Secretary, September 22, 1998, www.navcen.uscg.gov/pubs/gps/whsjapan.htm.

1246 "Defense Research Center Sends GPS Research Mission to United States," *Nikkan Kogyo Shimbun*, November 29, 1996, p 13.

1247 Yoshida, Akiji, "DRC Researcher on GPS, Warfare," *DRC*, May 1997, pp 12-13.

1248 "*Uchu Kaihatsu Iinkai, GPS Kaihatsu Keikakuan Matomeru*," ("Space Activities Commission Compiles GPS Development Proposals"), *Nikkan Kogyo Shimbun*, March 27, 1997, p 7.

1249 "*Tsusoken, Uchu Kukan Koseido Jiku Sekkei Shisutemu wo Kaihatsu he*," ("CRL To Commence Development of Space-Based Interval High Precision Space-Time Measurement System"), *Nikkan Kogyo Shimbun*, August 23, 1999, p 1.

1250 "*Jisedai GPS he Jiminto ga Suishin Giren*," ("LDP Promotes Next-Generation GPS"), *Asahi Shimbun*, July 7, 2002, p 2; "*Eisei Tsukau Ichi Sokutei Shisutemu, Nihonhan GPS Jitsugen he*

Ugoku–Jimin Giren, Yosan Yokyu," ("LDP To Request Funding For Realization of Japanese Satellite GPS,") *Nihon Keizai Shimbun*, August 5, 2002, p 2.

1251 Sagara, Yuta, "Japan Spy Satellites Spark Hopes for Space Industry," Kyodo, March 6, 2003.

1252 "*Jisedai GPS he Jiminto ga Suishin Giren*," ("LDP Promotes Next-Generation GPS"), *Asahi Shimbun*, July 7, 2002, p 2.

1253 Hirako, Yoshinori, "High Stakes: Space Race," *Asahi Shimbun*, February 22, 2003; Communications Research Laboratory, www2.crl.go.jp/ka/control/efsat/index-e.html.

1254 Kemase, Yoshiro, "*Kyosorkyoku Fukkatsu Mezashi 'Fokasu 21' Shido*," ("Focus 21 Begins, Goal is Reviving Japan's Competitive Power"), *Sankei Shimbun*, January 6, 2003.

1255 "Space Venture To Begin Business Operations Next Year," *Nihon Keizai Shimbun*, December 29, 2003.

1256 "*Nihon no Shinjo Tobu 'Juntencho Eisei'*," ("'Quasi-Zenith Satellites' Flying Directly Over Japan"), *Yomiuri Shimbun*, September 12, 2002, p 10.

1257 Advanced Space Business Corporation provides a range of services that will be available once the system is up and running, available on its Web site at www.asbc.jp/business/serviceE.html.

1258 "*Nihon no Shinjo Tobu 'Juntencho Eisei'*," ("'Quasi-Zenith Satellites' Flying Directly Over Japan"), *Yomiuri Shimbun*, September 12, 2002, p 10.

1259 Sasao, Akira, "Utilizing Quasi-Zenith Satellites in Defense (Part Two of Two)," *Gekkan JADI*, February 2004, pp 27-40.

1260 See "Mapping of Ground Stations," p 10, in "Quasi-Zenith Satellite System Navigation Service: Interface Specification for QZSS, V1.5," March 27, 2013, http://qz-vision.jaxa.jp/USE/is-qzss/DOCS/IS-QZSS_15_E.pdf.

1261 Taken from "*Kenkei, Soki Rikken ni Zenrkyoku, Kesshoso no Busshitsu, Bunseki Isogu*," *Chugoku Shinbun*, November 27,

1996, and "*Motojoinra Shorui Soken, Chugoku Kayaku Etajima Kojo Bakuhatsu Jiko,*" *Asahi Shimbun,* September 5, 1997.

1262 "Firm Imports South Korean TNT For Supply to SDF," Kyodo News Agency, April 7, 1997.

1263 "*Kyozai Kyoei (Heiwa Toshi No Kage De, Dai Yonbu Heiki Sangyo)*" *Asahi Shimbun,* June 7, 1998.

1264 "*Danyaku Meka (Heiwa Toshi no Kage de Dai Yonbu Heiki Sangyo)*", *Asahi Shimbun,* June 6, 1998.

1265 "*Taiho Meka (Heiwa Toshi no Kage de, Dai Yonbu Heiki Sangyo: 1)*", *Asahi Shimbun,* June 3, 1998.

1266 "Association Events," *Gekkan JADI,* January 1997, pp 57-58.

1267 "*Sagyo Teishi Tsuzuku Chugoku Kayaku Kojo, Kesseki Chiryo ni Eikyo,*" *Chugoku Shinbun,* April 24, 1997, p 26.

1268 "Munitions and Explosives Branch," *Gekkan JADI,* April 2002, pp 32-34.

1269 "*Chugoku Kayaku TNT Setsubi, Kensetsu he, Kuni Ga Kyoka,*" *Chugoku Shinbun,* May 16, 2001, p 26.

1270 "*Chugoku Kayaku Etajima Kojo de TNT Seisan Saikai he, Bakuhatsu Jikogo 5-nen 8-kagetsu Buri,*" ("Chugoku Chemical's Etajima Facility To Resume Production of TNT, 5 Years and 8 Months After Accident"), *Mainichi Shimbun,* June 7, 2002, p 23.

1271 Evening News, NHK Television, August 2, 2000.

1272 "Guided Weapons Branch," *Gekkan JADI,* February 2004, pp 32-38.

1273 "*Kayaku Kojo Bakuhatsu, Kega 56nin ni, Minda Higai 300ken Kosu,*" *Chunichi Shinbun,* August 2, 2000, p 1.

1274 "'*Nihon ha Kakuheiki Motsu Noryoku Aru,' Hata Shusho, Zenrei Nai Hatsugen,*" ("Saying 'Japan Has the Capability To Possess Nuclear Weapons,' PM Hata Makes Unprecedented Statement"), *Asahi Shimbun,* June 18, 1994, p 2.

1275 "Hata 'Acknowledged' Tokyo Can Produce Nuclear Weapons," Kyodo, June 17, 1994.

1276 "Hata Sees 'No Problems' With Remark on Nuclear Capability," Kyodo, June 19, 1994.

1277 "Tokyo 'Obviously' Can Produce Nuclear Weapons," Kyodo, June 20, 1994.

1278 Okawa, Yutaka, interview with Shingo Nishimura, "Nishimura Creates Stir in Interview," *Weekly Playboy*, November 2, 1999, pp 230-233.

1279 "Policy speech by Prime Minister Keizo Obuchi to the 146th extraordinary Diet session at the main chamber of the House of Representatives in Tokyo," NHK Television, October 29, 1999.

1280 "Opposition Leader Ozawa Says Japan Could Produce Nuclear Weapons, Surpass China," April 6, 2002.

1281 "Ozawa Defends Remarks on Japan as Nuclear Power," April 7, 2002.

1282 "Transcript of PRC FM Spokesman News Conference 9 April," Ministry of Foreign Affairs of the People's Republic of China website, April 9, 2002.

1283 "Japan Reiterates No Nuclear Arms Policy After Lawmaker's Comment," AFP, April 8, 2002.

1284 "Political World Bombshell: Deputy Chief Cabinet Secretary Shinzo Abe's Seminar Contents—Use of Nuclear Weapons Do Not Violate Constitution," *Sande Mainichi*, June 2, 2002, pp 24-27.

1285 "Japan Could Reconsider Three Nonnuclear Principles," Kyodo, May 31, 2002.

1286 "Nuclear Policy Remarks Send Ripples Through Japan Diet," Kyodo, June 3, 2002.

1287 "Foreign Ministry Spokesman Liu Jianchao Answers Reporters' Questions at Routine News Conference on 4 June 2002," Ministry of Foreign Affairs of the People's Republic of China website, June 4, 2002.

1288 Kobayashi, Kakumi, "Japan's Top Spokesman Admits Nuke Remarks Were His," Kyodo, June 3, 2002.

1289 "Koizumi Says His Cabinet Will Keep Nonnuclear Principles," Kyodo, May 31, 2002.

1290 Ito, Kan, ""Are We Prepared To Deal With Kim-Chong-il's 'Evil Bombs?: Some in the United States Voice for Japan's Nuclear Armament," April 2003, pp 86-94.

1291 "Agreement for Cooperation Between the Government of the United States of America and the Government of Japan Concerning Peaceful Uses of Nuclear Energy," November 1987, Article 2.1.b, www.nnsa.doe.gov/na-20/docs/Japan_Agam.pdf.

1292 International Atomic Energy Agency, "Model Protocol Additional To The Agreement(s) Between State(s) And The International Atomic Energy Agency For The Application of Safeguards," INFCIRC/540, IAEA Web site, www.iaea.org/Publications/Documents/Infcircs/1998/infcirc540corrected.pdf.

1293 "Japan's Nuclear Policy: Fukuda's 'Background' Remarks Were Out of Line," *Asahi Shimbun*, June 4, 2002.

1294 Statistics Bureau, "Population and Households – Total Populations 1920-2012," *Japan Statistical Yearbook 2014*, http://www.stat.go.jp/english/data/nenkan/index.htm..

1295 National Institute of Population and Social Security Research, "Reproduction Rate for Females," available online at http://www.ipss.go.jp/index-e.html.

1296 Rohlfs, Chris, Alexander Reed, and Hiroyuki Yamada, "Missing Women and the Year of the Fire Horse: Changes in the Value of Girls and Child Avoidance Mechanisms in Japan, 1846, 1906, and 1966," University of Chicago, September 2006, home.uchicago.edu/~car/firehorse.pdf.

1297 Foreign Press Center Japan, "Facts and Figures of Japan 2006, Population and Growth Trends," pp 13-14, http://fpcj.jp/old/e/mres/publication/ff/pdf/02_population.pdf.

1298 Furukawa, Teijiro, *Kasumigaseki Hanseiki*, ("Writings of Half a Life in Government"), (Saga: Saga Shinbunsha, 2005), pp 172-173.

1299 Furukawa, *Kasumigaseki Hanseiki*, pp 172-173.

1300 For the words to this song, see the Ministry of Health, Labor, and Welfare's 1992 *Hakusho*, on line at www.hakusyo.mhlw.go.jp/wpdocs/hpaz199201/b0050.html.

1301 Rates depended on family income: for a fuller description of the system, see the Ministry of Health, Labor, and Welfare website's *Jido Fuyo Teate Seido ga Kaisei Saremasu*, www.mhlw.go.jp/topics/2002/06/tp0626-2.html, the 2004 revisions to the law at www.mhlw.go.jp/topics/2004/02/tp0210-4.html, and a history of the subsidy program on Wikipedia at ja.wikipedia.org/wiki/児童手当.

1302 Doteuchi, Akio, "Toward a Prosperous Society With a Declining Birthrate–Enhancing the Social Environment for Childcare Support," *Nissei Kiso Kenkyujo*, 21 April 2004, pp 6-7.

1303 Cabinet website, "*Shoshika Shakai Taisaku wa Dono Yo ni Shinten Shite Kita ka*" ("Progress of Policies for a Low Birthrate Society"), www8.cao.go.jp/shoushi/whitepaper/w-2004/html-h/html/g1523030.html.

1304 Suzuki, Toru, "Fertility Decline and Policy Development in Japan," *The Japanese Journal of Population*, Vol 4, No 1, March 2006, pp 1-32 (1); www.ipss.go.jp/webj-ad/WebJournal.files/population/2006_3/suzuki.pdf.

1305 "Koizumi Wants To Follow Example of Dogs' Fertility in 2006," Kyodo, January 4, 2006.

1306 "Health Minister Hit for Calling Women Baby Machines," *Asahi Shimbun*, January 29, 2007.

1307 "Five-country survey on child-rearing: Only 40% of Japanese respondents – lowest rate among five countries – say they want to have more children," *Mainichi Shimbun*, April 28, 2006, p 1.

1308 Kobe University's Takashi Oshio highlighted the positive correlation between the birth of children to unwed mothers and higher fertility rates in OECD countries. Japan, where children born to unwed mothers make up only 2% of the total birthrate, is at the bottom of the fertility scale. See

Oshio, Takashi, "The Declining Birthrate in Japan," *Japan Economic Currents*, March 2008, p 3, www.kkc.or.jp/english/activities/publications/economic-currents69.pdf.

1309 Statistics Bureau, "Population and Households – Total Populations 1920-2012," *Japan Statistical Yearbook 2014*, www.stat.go.jp/english/data/nenkan/index.htm.

1310 Statistics Bureau, "Population and Households – Future Population," *Japan Statistical Yearbook 2014*, www.stat.go.jp/english/data/nenkan/index.htm.

1311 Ministry of Health, Labor, and Welfare, *Kani Seimeihyo* ("Latest Vital Statistics"), 2004, in Foreign Press Center Japan, "Facts and Figures of Japan 2006, Population and Growth Trends," pp 13-14, fpcj.jp/old/e/mres/publication/ff/pdf/02_population.pdf.

1312 "People Over 65 Top 20% of Japan's Population," Kyodo, June 2, 2006; see also Statistics Bureau, "Population and Households – Population by Age Group and Indices of Age Structure," *Japan Statistical Yearbook 2014*, www.stat.go.jp/english/data/nenkan/index.htm

1313 "Health Ministry: Population Aging Faster Than Expected," Kyodo, January 21, 1997.

1314 There are projected to be 37.4 million people over 65 in 2035, compared to a total population that is projected to number 112.1 million that year; see Statistics Bureau, "Population and Households – Population by Age Group and Indices of Age Structure," *Japan Statistical Yearbook 2014*, www.stat.go.jp/english/data/nenkan/index.htm.

1315 Takakura, Masaki, "Rural Communities Disappearing," *Yomiuri Shimbun*, October 5, 2007.

1316 "Nineteen of 47 Prefectures To See Over 20% Population Decline in 3 Decades," Kyodo, May 29, 2007.

1317 Dean, Meryll, "Japan: Refugees and Asylum Seekers," a Writenet analysis commissioned by the United Nations High Commissioner for Refugees, Protection Information Section (DIP), February 2006, available at www.unhcr.

org/cgi-bin/texis/vtx/refworld/rwmain/opendocpdf.pdf?docid=43f4a4b94.

1318 Statistics Bureau, "Population and Households – Total Populations 1920-2012," *Japan Statistical Yearbook 2014*, http://www.stat.go.jp/english/data/nenkan/index.htm.

1319 United Nations Secretariat, Department of Economic and Social Affairs, Population Division, "Japan," *Replacement Migration: Is It A Solution To Declining and Ageing Populations?* pp 49-54; www.un.org/esa/population/publications/migration/japan.pdf.

1320 Foreign Press Center Japan, "Facts and Figures of Japan 2006, Population and Growth Trends," pp 13-14, fpcj.jp/old/e/mres/publication/ff/pdf/02_population.pdf.

1321 "Pension System Needs More Drastic Reforms," *Yomiuri Shimbun,* June 11, 2004.

1322 Statistics Bureau, "Social Security – Social Security Benefits (Ratio to National Income)," *Japan Statistical Yearbook 2014*, www.stat.go.jp/english/data/nenkan/1431-20.htm.

1323 "Unpaid Pension Premiums Nears 1.9 Trillion Yen," Kyodo, July 25, 2003.

1324 "Before Pension Debate," *Asahi Shimbun,* May 14, 2004.

1325 Japan Institute for Social and Economic Affairs, "*Shakai Hosho Seido ni Kan Suru Anketo,*" ("Survey Regarding the Social Security System"), p 13; www.kkc.or.jp/society/survey/enq_050929.pdf.

1326 Jackson, Richard and Keisuke Nakashima, "Meeting Japan's Aging Challenge," *Japan Economic Currents,* March 2008, p 8, www.kkc.or.jp/english/activities/publications/economic-currents69.pdf.

1327 Statistics Bureau, "Public Finances – National Government Debt Outstanding," *Japan Statistical Yearbook 2014,* www.stat.go.jp/english/data/nenkan/1431-05.htm.

1328 Ujikane, Keiko, "Japan Unveils Record 2014 Budget Draft as Debt Burden Mounts," Bloomberg, December 21, 2013, www.bloomberg.com/news/2013-12-21/japan-unveils-record-budget-even-as-abe-trims-new-bond-sales.html.

1329 "METI: Japan's Work Force To Decline 30.3 Percent in 2050," *Nihon Keizai Shimbun,* March 2, 2002.

1330 "Leaders Must Be Fostered in An Age of Decline," *Yomiuri Shimbun,* January 4, 2006.

1331 "*Kyaria-kanryo ha Keien? Kokka Komuin 1-shu Moshikomisha ga Kako Saitei,*" *Asahi Shimbun,* April 24, 2006, www.asahi.com/national/update/0424/TKY200604240351.html.

1332 Shikata, Toshiyuki, "*Watashi no 'Sanchome no Yuhi'*" ("My '*Sanchome no Yuhi*'"), *Asagumo,* November 29, 2007, p 1.

1333 "Peacekeeping Role Inspires Graduate Rush to Join SDF" *The Daily Yomiuri,* January 8, 2004.

1334 Fujinawa, Yuji, interview by Haruyuki Suzuki, "GSO Chief Fujinawa on GSDF Changes," *Gunji Kenkyu,* December 1997, pp 186-199.

1335 Kano, Tadao, Interview with Fumio Kyuma, Director General of the Defense Agency, *Mainichi Shimbun,* June 1, 1998, pp 4-5.

1336 "*Dai 5sho: Kokumin to Boei,*" *Boei Hakusho 15nen* ("Section 5: The People and Defense," Defense White Paper 2003).

1337 "*Junsho, Jokyu Socho Nado Shinsetu he,*" ("Brigadier General, Sergeant Major Ranks To Be Established"), *Asagumo,* July 5, 2007, p 1.

1338 "*Boshu Kankyo no Akka ni Taisho,*" ("Responding to the Worsening Recruitment Environment"), *Asagumo,* July 26, 2007, p 1.

1339 "*Osaka Boshu Monogatari,*" ("Tales of Recruiting in Osaka"), *Securitarian,* p 16.

1340 Fujinawa, Yuji, interview by Haruyuki Suzuki, "GSO Chief Fujinawa on GSDF Changes," *Gunji Kenkyu,* December 1997, pp 186-199.

1341 "*'Chiho Kyoryoku Honbu' ga Stato,*" ("Prefectural Cooperation Office Starts Operations"), *Asagumo,* August 3, 2006, p 8.

1342 "*Chiren Monogatari*," ("Stories of the PLO"), *Securitarian*, September 2003, pp 12-14.

1343 "*Dai 5sho: Kokumin to Boei*," *Boei Hakusho 15nen* ("Section 5: The People and Defense," Defense White Paper 2003).

1344 "*Dai 5sho: Kokumin to Boei*," *Boei Hakusho 15nen* ("Section 5: The People and Defense," Defense White Paper 2003).

1345 *Asagumo*, December 12, 2002, p 6.

1346 "*Fukuokashi Chuoku, Tenjin no Ogata Gaito Sukuriin 'Soraria Bijon' Ni*," ("Large Urban Screens To Be Used in Central Fukuoka City, Tenjin"), *Nishi Nihon Shimbun*, May 1, 2003, p 31.

1347 "*Boshu Koho mo IT de, Rikubaku Boshuka ga 3-jimoto CG wo Sakusei*," ("Recruiters Also Using Information Technology, GSDF Recruitment Office Develops 3-D Computer Graphics"), *Asagumo*, August 16, 2001, p 1; "*DVD ni Yoru Purezenteshon, Gakko Setsumeikai ni 'Shinheiki'*" ("Using DVDs for Presentations, 'New Weapons' During School Visits"), *Asagumo*, August 16, 2001, p 6; "*Mamoru-kun to Mirai-chan, Kyarakuta no Aisho Kimaru*," ("Characters' Nicknames Have Been Decided: 'Mr. Defense' and 'Miss Future'"), *Asagumo*, March 28, 2002, p 2.

1348 "*Jieitai Kyarakuta Sutorappu, Airashii Hyojo PR ni Hitoyaku*," ("SDF Character Strap Will Play a PR Role"), *Hokkaido Shimbun*, August 28, 1999, evening edition, p 8.

1349 See www.mod.go.jp/j/kids/index.html.

1350 Mr. Takuma's Twitter feed is twitter.com/JGSDF_takuma, and Miss Yu's Twitter feed is Twitter.com/JGSDF_yu.

1351 "*Monbusho Nado 19 Shocho, Shochugakusei Taisho ni Kasumigaseki Kengaku Dei wo Jisshi he*," ("Nineteen Ministries and Agencies Including MOFA and Others To Sponsor a *Kasumigaseki* Tour Day For Primary and Middle School Students"), *Kagaku Kogyo Nippo*, August 13, 1999, p 8.

1352 "'*21-Seikikei Chiren' Mezasu*," ("Aiming for a 21st Century Setup"), *Asagumo*, June 19, 2003, p 6.

1353 "*Posuta, TVCM de Boshu Koho,*" ("Recruitment PR Uses Posters, Television Commercials"), *Asagumo*, June 20, 2000, p 6.

1354 "SDF Uses Pop Idols for Recruitment Poster in Image Revamp," Kyodo News Service, August 8, 2003.

1355 "DA Head Ishiba Said 'Very Unpopular' Among Staffers," *Shukan Shincho*, August 28, 2003, p 36.

1356 "*Daigaku, Jieitai, Jiwari Koryu, Chiren ga PR, Hihan mo,*" ("Universities and the SDF Conducting Exchanges, Recruiters Engage in PR, Some Criticism"), *Asahi Shimbun*, November 12, 2002, p 1.

1357 "*Anzen Hosho Mondai ni Tai sureu Igi no Mesadame: Daigaku to Kaijo Jieitai to no Koryu 2005,*" ("Waking Up to the Significance of National Security Issues: University and MSDF Exchange 2005"), *Securitarian*, September 2005, pp 56-57.

1358 "*'Kyodo Kenkyu, Daigaku to Jieitai', Kaigaku 100nen de Hatsu,*" ("'Joint Research Between University and SDF,' First Since the University's Founding 100 Years Ago"), *Kobe Shimbun*, December 7, 2002, p 27.

1359 "*Heisei 17nendo 'Daigakusei Supringu Tsua' wo Oete, Ima Made Yaku 600mei no Daigaku (in) sei ni Sanka Shite Itadakimashita,*" ("As the FY2005 'University Spring Tour' Finishes, Approximately 600 University (Graduate) Students Have Participated"), *Securitarian*, April 2006, p 56.

1360 "*Hajimete Boshu Koho Jitsugen,*" ("Recruitment Information Session Held for First Time"), *Asagumo*, August 16, 2001, p 6.

1361 "*Shizuoka no Koritsuchu, Zenkoku de mo Hajimete Seifukusugata de Seiki Jugyo,*" ("The First Regular Class Instruction in the Country Given in Uniform at Shizuoka Public Middle School"), *Asagumo*, December 20, 2001, p 8.

1362 "*Kakukikan to no Kyoryoku wo Kyoka, Annaijo ya Jimujo no Iten (Saga Chiren),*" ("Strengthening Cooperations with Organizations, Relocating Recruitment and Administrative Offices (Saga PLO)"), *Asagumo*, December 20, 2001, p 8.

1363 "*Soshiki Boshu Taisei wo Kyoka: Gakkokei wo Saihensei,*" ("Organizational Recruitment System Being Strengthened: Academic Sub-Program Being Restructured"), *Asagumo,* November 20, 2003, p 6.

1364 "322 Municipalities Gave Data to SDF Inappropriately," Kyodo, April 23, 2003; "Defense Agency Uses Resident Registries To Recruit," Kyodo, April 22, 2003.

1365 "Privacy Debate Erupts After DA's Access to Personal Data Revealed," *Asahi Shimbun,* April 24, 2003.

1366 "*Soshiki Boshu Taisei wo Kyoka: Gakkokei wo Saihensei,*" ("Organizational Recruitment System Being Strengthened: Academic Sub-Program Being Restructured"), *Asagumo,* November 20, 2003, p 6.

1367 "*Iraku Haken Taiin to Kokosei ga Terebi Kaigi wo Jisshi,*" ("Dispatched Units in Iraq and Middle School Students Conduct Televised Meeting"), *Securitarian,* April 2006, p 54.

1368 "*UNDOF Haken Taiin to Chugakusei ga Terebi Kaigi wo Jisshi,*" ("UNDOF Dispatched Units and Middle School Students Conduct Televised Meeting"), *Securitarian,* June 2006, p 57.

1369 "Peacekeeping Role Inspires Graduate Rush To Join SDF," *The Daily Yomiuri,* January 8, 2004.

1370 "*Jieikan no Shitsuteki Kojo to Jinzai Kakuho – Shorai no Katsuyo ni Kan Suru Teigen,*" ("Proposals for Future Activities To Improve the Quality of and Retain SDF Personnel"), *Asagumo,* June 14, 2007, p 3.

1371 "*Josei Jieikan Chumoku no Mato, Rikuji no Shigaisha 7-bai Kosu,*" ("Female Officers Target of Attention, Volunteers for the GSDF Grow Over 7 Times"), *Yomiuri Shimbun,* April 30, 2002, p 18.

1372 *Asagumo,* June 21, 2001, p 7.

1373 "MSDF Chief Yamamoto on 1998 Plans," *Wing,* January 14, 1998, pp 8-9.

1374 "ASDF Chief Hiraoka on 1998 Plans," *Wing,* January 7, 1998, p 2.

1375 "First Female ASDF Pilot Instructor Assumes Her Post," Kyodo News Agency, May 9, 2003.

1376 "Female Officer To Be Promoted to Admiral for 1st Time," Kyodo News Agency, March 16, 2001.

1377 *Bodai Sotsugyoshiki de no Shusho Junji* (The Prime Minister's Address to the NDA Graduation Ceremony), *Asagumo,* March 28, 2002.

1378 "*Higashi Chimoru PKO Haken: Jishi keikaku wo kettei*" ("PKO Forces Sent to East Timor: Implementing Plan Decided"), *Asagumo,* February 21, 2002, p 1.

1379 "Japan To Increase Number of Women in Self-Defense Forces," *Yomiuri Shimbun,* July 29, 2002.

1380 "*Jieikan Boshu wo PR, Ken ga Matsuyama Ekimae ni Maruchibi-jyon,*" ("Prefecture Begins SDF Recruitment PR Campaign on Multivision Video Billboard in Front of Matsuyama Station"), *Asagumo,* December 20, 2001, p 8.

1381 "*Heisei 14-nenpan Boshu Koho Posuta, Joyu Suenaga-san wo Kiyo,*" ("Actress Ms. Suenaga Employed in 2002 Recruitment PR Posters"), *Asagumo,* December 6, 2001, p 6.

1382 "*Tochigi Chiren, Samazama na Katsudo,*" ("Tochigi PLO's Various Activities"), *Securitarian,* September 6, 2007, p 8.

1383 "'*Dai 7kai Sora wo Ai Suru Joseitachi wo Hagemasu Sho' Hyoshoshiki,*" *Securitarian,* February 2004, p 40.

1384 *Asagumo,* August 1, 2002, p 1.

1385 "*Josei Jieikan no Genin,*" ("Women SDF Personnel"), *Boei Handobukku Heisei 19nen,* June 2007, p 238.

1386 "*Chiren,*" *ibid.,* p 14.

1387 "*Yobi Jiekanho,*" ("Reserve Cadet"), *Boei Hakusho,* 2002, p 251.

1388 "*Yobi Jiekanho,*" ("Reserve Cadet"), *Boei Hakusho,* 2002, p 250.

1389 "*Yobi Jiekanho,*" ("Reserve Cadet"), *Boei Hakusho,* 2002, p 250.

1390 "Japan To Recruit Candidates for Military Reserve," *Tokyo Shimbun,* January 10, 2002.

1391 "*Yobi Jiekanho,*" ("Reserve Cadet"), *Boei Hakusho,* 2002, p 250.

1392 "Outline of 'Public Opinion Survey on the Self-Defense Forces (SDF) and Defense Issues'," Public Relations Office, Cabinet Office, March 2012, www.mod.go.jp/e/d_act/others/pdf/public_opinion.pdf.

1393 Sample, Doug, "DoD Helps Noncitizen Service Members Become Full-Fledged Americans," American Forces Press Service, January 16, 2003, http://www.defenselink.mil/news/newsarticle.aspx?id=29569.

1394 "Order to Intercept North Korean Rocket to be Issued," Kyodo, December 2, 2012.

1395 "Fire, Disaster Officials Move Up Drill Following DPRK Launch Announcement," Kyodo, December 5, 2012.

1396 "Kim Jong Il Issues Order on Promoting Military Ranks," KCNA, September 27, 2010, www.kcna.co.jp/item/2010/201009/news27/20100927-17ee.html.

1397 See for example, "Kim Jong Il Meets High-level Military Delegation," KCNA, October 25, 2010, www.kcna.co.jp/item/2010/201010/news25/20101025-21ee.html, and "Kim Jong Il Inspects Newly Built Soy Sauce Shop at Ryongsong," KCNA, November 23, 2010, www.kcna.co.jp/item/2010/201011/news23/20101123-21ee.html.

1398 "Kim Jong Un's speech at the Kim Il Sung Centennial Celebration," April 15, 2012, translated by northkoreatech.org and available at www.ncnk.org.

1399 For a wide-ranging discussion on each of these topics, see "U.S. DoD Annual Report to Congress: Military and Security Developments Involving the People's Republic of China 2013," Office of the Secretary of Defense, 2013, www.defense.gov/pubs/2013_china_report_final.pdf

Made in the USA
Middletown, DE
26 February 2018